TRADITION AND RE-INTERPRETATION IN JEWISH AND EARLY CHRISTIAN LITERATURE

STUDIA POST-BIBLICA

INSTITUTA A P.A.H. DE BOER

ADIUVANTIBUS

L.R.A. VAN ROMPAY ET J. SMIT SIBINGA

EDIDIT

J.C.H. LEBRAM

VOLUMEN TRICESIMUM SEXTUM

LEIDEN
E. J. BRILL
1986

Jürgen - Christian Lebram

TRADITION AND RE-INTERPRETATION IN JEWISH AND EARLY CHRISTIAN LITERATURE

ESSAYS IN HONOUR OF JÜRGEN C. H. LEBRAM

EDITED BY

J. W. VAN HENTEN · H. J. DE JONGE
P. T. VAN ROODEN · J. W. WESSELIUS

LEIDEN
E. J. BRILL
1986

Given the special character of this volume, its publication in this series has been the exclusive decision of the two assistant editors

ISBN 90 04 07752 9

TABLE OF CONTENTS

VORWORT

Der Gelehrte, der mit dieser Festschrift geehrt wird, ist ein vielseitiger Forscher und eine lebhafte Persönlichkeit. Die Vielseitigkeit seiner wissenschaftlichen Arbeit kommt durch die Verschiedenartigkeit der folgenden Beiträge nicht genügend zum Ausdruck. Er ist jedoch nie ganz in der Wissenschaft aufgegangen und hat nur einen Teil seines Lebens der Universität gewidmet. Jürgen Lebram misst auch der Tatsache, dass er kürzlich, im Mai 1985, einen halben Marathon in einer Zeit von weniger als zwei Stunden zurückgelegt hat, grossen Wert bei! Er war bis in das mittlere Alter als Pastor tätig und wurde an eine Universität in einem Land berufen, das nicht sein eigenes war. In diesem Land hat er der Wissenschaft mehr als achtzehn Jahre gedient. Hier hat er, wie auch die Beiträge in diesem Band bezeugen, ausser Kollegen auch Freunde gewonnen. Der Universität Leiden hat er zur Ehre gereicht. Er hat dort Schüler ausgebildet und sie unter Anwendung seiner gesamten Erfahrung zu Historikern gemacht. Auf diese Weise stellt er auch seine Untersuchungen an. Er studiert Texte um zu zeigen, wie Menschen ihre Geschichte interpretierten, wie sie sich in der historischen Realität orientierten und ihr Leben erfassten und gestalteten. Dabei blieben intellektuelle Unabhängigkeit und geistige Freiheit ein Teil seines Wesens. Er hat noch immer etwas von einem Vagabunden! Als Kennzeichnung seiner Person zitierte er einmal die folgenden Zeilen aus Goethes *West-östlicher Divan*:

> Lasst mich nur auf meinem Sattel gelten!
> Bleibt in euren Hütten, euren Zelten!
> Und ich reite froh in alle Ferne,
> Über meiner Mütze nur die Sterne.

Dieser Band wurde nach einem neuen Verfahren hergestellt. Die Beiträge der Autoren wurden in der Form, in der die Redaktion sie erhielt, mit Hilfe eines Bildschirmgerätes verarbeitet. Die Redaktion dankt Frau A. Fuhrmann, die nicht nur diese Arbeit sorgfältig verrichtete, sondern auch zahlreiche kleine Inkonsistenzen beseitigte und andere Verbesserungen anbrachte. Die nicht ohne weiteres lesbaren *print-outs* wurden anhand der Manuskripte der Autoren von der Redaktion korrigiert. Der auf diese Weise auf sogenannte 'Disketten' gespeicherte Text wurde für den Computersatz verwendet. Für die Vereinfachungen und Unvollkommenheiten, die als Folge dieses Verfahrens entstanden sind, übernimmt die Redaktion die Verantwortung. Mehrere anderen Autoren wollten gern auch einen Beitrag liefern oder haben sogar tatsächlich einen geliefert. Leider musste die Redaktion aus technischen Gründen

Herrn Prof. dr. T. Baarda, Herrn dr. H.J. de Jonge, Herrn drs. H.A. Krop und Herrn Prof. dr. G.H.M. Posthumus Meyjes bitten ihren Artikel zurückzuziehen.

Der Leidener theologischen Fakultät sei für einen finanziellen Beitrag gedankt. Dank gebührt besonders dem Verlag N.V. Boekhandel en Drukkerij v/h E.J. Brill, Leiden, der die Herausgabe dieses Bandes ermöglicht hat.

Leiden, den 6. Juni 1985.

J.W. van Henten
H.J. de Jonge
P.T. van Rooden
J.W. Wesselius

A GRAMMATICAL NOTE ON THE YAVNE-YAM OSTRACON

by

J. Hoftijzer

In ll. 2f. of the Yavne-Yam ostracon (KAI 200) the following words occur: *ʿbdk qṣr hyh ʿbdk bḥṣr ʾsm*. In his original edition of the text, Naveh takes these words as belonging together, the first one being a *casus pendens*: 'thy servant (behold) thy servant was reaping in Ḥaṣar-Asam'[1]. Many interpreters followed him, giving the same or a comparable syntactic interpretation[2]. Amusin and Heltzer, however, thought the syntactic construction nevertheless to be 'apparently due to the lively speech of the man who dictated the complaint'[3]. Yeivin considered either the first or the second *ʿbdk* 'superfluous (logically and grammatically)'[4]. Röllig described 'die Stilisierung der Bittschrift' as 'recht primitiv', especially the numerous repetitions, of which the repeated *ʿbdk* in our formula was one[5].

Therefore Vinnikov and others preferred to consider the above-mentioned group of words as consisting of two clauses instead of one: a) *ʿbdk qṣr* and b) *hyh ʿbdk bḥṣr ʾsm*[6].

---

[1] J. Naveh, 'A Hebrew letter from the seventh century B.C.', *IEJ* x (1960), 129-139, on p. 134.

[2] Cf. e.g. F.M. Cross, 'Epigraphic notes on Hebrew documents of the eighth-sixth centuries B.C.: II the Murabaʿat papyrus and the letter found near Yavneh-Yam', *BASOR* clxv (1962), 34-46, on p. 44; S. Yeivin, 'The judicial petition from Meẕad Ḫashavyahu', *BiOr* xix (1962), 3-10, on p. 5; J.D. Amusin and M.L. Heltzer, 'The inscription from Meṣad Ḥashavyahu, complaint of a reaper of the seventh century B.C.', *IEJ* xiv (1964), 148-157 on p. 150; K.R. Veenhof, 'Nieuwe Palestijnse inscripties', *Phoenix* xi (1965), 243-260, on p. 250; J.C.L. Gibson, *Textbook of Syrian Semitic Inscriptions*, Volume I, *Hebrew and Moabite Inscriptions*, Oxford, 1971, 28; cf. also W.F. Albright, 'A letter from the time of Josiah', in *Ancient Near Eastern Texts relating to the Old Testament*[3] (with Supplement), ed. J.B. Pritchard, Princeton, 1969, 568.

[3] Amusin and Heltzer, art. cit., 151.

[4] Yeivin, art. cit., 5 n. 35.

[5] Röllig in KAI sub 200.

[6] I.N. Vinnikov, 'O vnov otkritoy nadpisi k yugu ot yaffi', *Archiv Orientální* xxxiii (1965), 546-552, on p. 547. Cf. also L. Delekat, 'Ein Bittschriftentwurf eines Sabbatsschänders (KAI 200)', *Biblica* li (1970), 453-470, on pp. 459f.; A. Lemaire, 'L'ostracon de Meṣad Ḥashavyahu (Yavne-Yam) replacé dans son contexte', *Semitica* xxi (1971), 57-79, on pp. 61, 63; idem, *Inscriptions hébraïques*, Tome 1, *Les ostraca*, Paris, 1977, 260, 262; D. Pardee, 'The judicial plea from Meṣad-Ḥashavyahu (Yavneh-Yam), a new philological study', *Maarav* i/1 (1978), 33-66, on pp. 36, 40f.; idem (with collaboration of S.D. Sperling, J.D. Whitehead and P.E. Dion), *Handbook of ancient Hebrew letters* (= Society of Biblical Literature, Sources for Biblical Study no 15, ed. B.O. Long), Chico, 1982, 20f.; Y. Suzuki, 'A Hebrew ostracon from Meṣad Ḥashavyahu, a form-critical reinvestigation', *Annual of the Japanese Biblical Institute* viii (1982), 3-49, on pp. 5, 6ff. Earlier, S. Talmon ('The new Hebrew letter from the seventh century B.C. in historical perspective', *BASOR* clxxvi (1964), 29-38, on p. 30), proposed — to avoid this problem — to interpret the first *ʿbdk* as an

In this article I want to tackle the problem anew. Our first question is, whether it is impossible to interpret the first *ʿbdk* as *casus pendens* to a clause *qṣr hyh ʿbdk bḥṣr ʾsm*. Naveh defended this interpretation with a reference to Gen. 37:30 (*ʾny ʾnh ʾny-bʾ*)[7]. Undoubtedly the first *ʾny* functions as *casus pendens* and its correspondant in the clause as such (the second *ʾny*) is completely identical with it. Still this is, as such, no sufficient justification for Naveh's interpretation of the relevant words in the ostracon: *ʾny* being a personal pronoun and *ʿbdk* a nominal form (with pronominal suffix). For, when the *casus pendens* is a nominal form or a name (or a constituent with a nominal form or a name as core/first element), its correspondant in the clause as such is often either an independent personal pronoun or a pronominal suffix. E.g. *hʾrṣ ʾšr ʾth škb ʿlyh lk ʾtnnh* (Gen. 28:13); *hʾnšym hʾlh šlmym hm ʾtnw* (Gen. 34:21); *hyld ʾynnw* (Gen. 37:30); *gd gdwd ygwdnw* (Gen. 49:19); etc., etc.[8] The same principle is used for those instances where the *casus pendens* is a prepositional phrase: the correspondant in the clause normally consists of the same preposition followed by a pronominal suffix, cf. e.g. *wmʿṣ hdʿt ṭwb wrʿ lʾ tʾkl mmnw* (Gen. 2:17); *wlṣlpḥd .... lʾ-hyw lw bnym* (Josh. 17:3), etc.[9] This pronominalization of the noun occurring as (element of the) *casus pendens* (or its adverbialization, cf. n. 9), however, is not inevitable, where the correspondant in the clause as such is concerned[10].

There are instances in which the correspondant in question consists of a noun (identical with the first element of the *casus pendens*) followed by a demonstrative pronoun. Cf. e.g. Lev. 20:6, where the *casus pendens* is *hnpš ʾšr tpnh ʾl-hʾbt whydʿnym bznt ʾḥryhm* and its correspondant *(b)npš hhwʾ*; for comparable instances, cf. Lev. 7:27; 17:3f.,8f; Jer. 27:8. There are also instances in which the correspondant in question consists of a noun (more or less synonymous with one used in the *casus pendens*) followed by a demonstrative pronoun. Cf. e.g. Gen.17:14 where the *casus pendens* is *ʿrl zkr ʾšr lʾ-ymwl ʾt-bśr ʿrltw* and its correspondant *hnpš hhwʾ* (for a comparable instance, cf. Ex. 12:15).

---

apposition to the preceding *ʿbdh*, an unlikely solution. Talmon's reference to 2 Sam. 9:11 does not fit, because in this text *ʿbdh* and *ʿbdk* cannot be grammatically combined.

[7] Cf. Naveh, art. cit., 131f. and the same, 'Ketovot kenaʿaniyot weʿivriyot 1960-1964', *Leshonenu* xxx (1965), 65-80, on p. 70.

[8] Cf. e.g. S.R. Driver, *A treatise on the use of the tenses in Hebrew* ...[3], Oxford, 1892. 265; F.E. König, *Historisch-comparative Syntax der hebräischen Sprache*, Leipzig, 1897, 441f.; *Gesenius' Hebrew Grammar as edited and enlarged by the late E. Kautzsch*[2], edited by A.E. Cowley, Oxford, 1910, § 143a, b; R.A. Davidson, *Hebrew Syntax*[3], Edinburgh, 1901, § 106; P. Joüon, *Grammaire de l'Hébreu Biblique*[2], Rome, 1947, § 156a.

[9] Cf. also Driver, *op. cit.*, 266f.; König, *op. cit.*, 438; Gesenius-Kautzsch-Cowley, § 143c; Joüon, *op. cit.*, § 156d. There are also instances where the correspondant of such a *casus pendens* is an adverb. Cf. e.g. *hśdh ʾšr-qnh ʾbrhm mʾt bny-ḥt šmh qbr ʾbrhm* ... (Gen. 25:10), *bqbry ʾšr kryty ly bʾrṣ knʿn šmh tqbrny* (Gen. 50:5), *wbmqwm ʾšr yškn-šm hʿnn šm yḥnw bny yśrʾl* (Numb. 9:17), *ʾl-hmqwm ʾšr-ybḥr YHWH ... šm tzbḥ* (Dt. 16:6), *wyhy bšmʿk ʾt-qwl ṣʿdh... ʾz tḥrṣ* (2 Sam. 5:24).

[10] Cf. Driver, *op. cit.*, 267.

However, there are comparable instances in which an (appositional demonstrative) pronoun is not (an element of) the correspondant. Cf. e.g. Numb. 14:7, where the *casus pendens* is *h'rṣ 'šr ʿbrnw bh ltwr 'th* and its correspondant *h'rṣ* (the correspondant being here identical with the first element of the *casus pendens*).

One may compare Numb. 35:30, where the *casus pendens* is *kl-mkh-npš* and its correspondant is a 'synonym' *('t-)hrṣḥ* and also Lev. 27:32, where the *casus pendens* is *kl-mʿśr bqr wṣ'n...* and its correspondant is a 'synonym' *hʿśyry*. Compare also Lev. 7:19 where the *casus pendens* is *hbśr* ... and its correspondant *bśr* and Lev. 25:44 where the *casus pendens* is *ʿbdk w'mtk 'šr* ... and its correspondant *ʿbd w'mh*.

In other words, although some form of pronominalization normally occurs in instances like these, there are indications that the correspondant in question could be realized without using a pronoun/pronominal suffix[11].

Against this background, an interpretation of the relevant words in KAI 200 according to which the first *ʿbdk* is *casus pendens* and the second one its correspondant in the clause as such, is possible, since the use of a pronoun is not inevitable for the correspondant[12].

Naveh has already pointed out that a clause ((*ʿbdk*) (*qṣr hyh ʿbdk bḥṣr 'sm*)) could be compared with 1 Sam. 17:34 *rʿh hyh ʿbdk l'byw bṣ'n* (here only the *casus pendens* is lacking)[13]. This last-mentioned clause contains the first words of a direct discourse spoken by David. In this clause, the basic information is given which is necessary to be able to understand what is told next. David's struggle with lion and bear and the fact that he was experienced on this point, become understandable when seen against the background of his once having

---

[11] I have not quoted here Lev. 18:9, where the *casus pendens* is *ʿrwt 'ḥwtk bt-'byk 'w bt-'mk mwldt byt 'w mwldt ḥwṣ* and its correspondant *ʿrwtn* (although the pronominalization of the first element of the *casus pendens* (*ʿrwt...*) has not taken place), because another element of the *casus pendens* is already pronominalized in the clause as such (*'ḥwtk bt-'byk 'w bt-'mk*). According to the massoretic interpretation, one also finds an example where the *casus pendens* is identical with its correspondant in 1 Kings 10:28 (cf. also Driver, *op. cit.*, 267): *mqwh* ... *mqwh*. It seems better, however, to combine the first mentioned *mqwh* with the preceding clause as is mostly done. Still it remains noteworthy that the Massoretes thought such a construction possible.

[12] Lemaire, art. cit., *Semitica* xxi, 63 considers the periphrastic construction used in a clause like this less probable for the time in which this ostracon was written (last part of the seventh century B.C.). Such a construction would rather be expected for a later period. His reference however to Joüon, *op. cit.*, § 121g is not convincing, because here only the use of the periphrastic construction for past events is discussed without any feature of continuation or frequency; cf. also Joüon, *op. cit.*, § 121f.

The examples quoted above where the pronominalization is absent prove that such a type of clause construction is not necessarily confined to contexts with a feature of high emotionality. This is against Suzuki, who considers the clause from Gen. 37:30 (*'ny 'nh 'ny-b'*) as 'a kind of a cry of horror' (art. cit., 6) and therefore considers clauses of this type as 'colloquial language' (art. cit., 6) and speaks of the 'colloquial habit of repetition such as stammering' (art. cit., 7) which cannot be expected in a document like KAI 200.

[13] Cf. Naveh, art. cit., *IEJ* x, 132. Cf. also Röllig KAI a.l.

been a herdsman. So in Judg. 12:2 the comparable formula *'yš ryb hyyty 'ny w'my wbny-'mwn m'd* (introducing a direct discourse spoken by Jephta) provides the background for Jephta's plea that he had to fight the Ammonites, even without the Ephraimites[14].

This would fit the situation we find in KAI 200: the words (*'bdk*) *qṣr hyh 'bdk bḥṣr 'sm* with which the plea of the unnamed plaintiff to the *śar* starts, then provide the general background necessary to understand this plea. Consequently, the interpretation of these words as *one* clause (preceded by *casus pendens*) is quite possible and fits the context.

We will now turn our attention to the interpretation of these words as *two* clauses: *'bdk qṣr* and *hyh 'bdk bḥṣr 'sm*.

It is undeniably possible to use a clause of the type *'bdk qṣr* (a nominal clause with as core elements[15] respectively a determinate and an indeterminate element) as the opening words used for addressing oneself to another person. Cf. Numb. 9:7 (*'nḥnw ṭm'ym lnpš 'dm*); 1 Kings 2:2 (*'ny hlk bdrk kl-h'rṣ*); 3:17 ((*by 'dny*) *'ny wh'šh hz't yšbt bbyt 'ḥd*); Hagg. 2:21 (*'ny mr'yš 't-hšmym w't-h'rṣ*). There are also comparable instances in which the indeterminate element precedes the determinate one: Gen. 23:4 (*gr-wtwšb 'nky 'mkm*); 31:5 (*r'h 'nky 't-pny 'bykn ky....*); Dt. 31:2 (*bn-m'h w'śrym šnh 'nky hywm*); Numb. 10:29 (*ns'ym 'nḥnw 'l-hmqwm 'šr...*), cf. also 2 Sam. 3:28; Ez. 2:3; Job 32:6[16].

In these instances also, basic information is given which is necessary to be able to understand what is told next[17]. This information concerns either the

---

[14] Cf. also Dt. 6:21, where the clause *'bdym hyynw lpr'h bmṣrym* provides the background to the exposition given by an Israelite of later times to his son.

[15] For the use of this terminology, cf. the author, 'The nominal clause reconsidered', *VT* xxiii (1973), 446-510, on pp. 487f., where it is argued that it is better to avoid the use of the terms subject and predicate, also because the identification of what is subject and predicate is very difficult, cf. art. cit., 466ff., 470f. On this point the author differs from the general approach, cf. also the recent study of R. Contini, *Tipologia della frase nominale nel semitico nordoccidentale del I millennio A.C.*, Pisa, 1982. The author is quite aware that one cannot study syntax without having recourse to functional and semantic ideas (cf. also the remarks of Contini, *op. cit.*, 30, n. 138). For purely practical reasons he wants (for this type of study: the study of languages not spoken for a long time) to use as its basis the formal phenomena ordered according to formal rules. He is aware that in the long run one cannot avoid the use of terms like subject and predicate (or at least comparable terms), but this does not necessarily mean that one has to use them (with all the uncertainties involved) for the basic ordering and description of the material.

[16] I do not quote here a text like Gen. 47:3: *r'h ṣ'n 'bdyk* (quoted by Lemaire, *Semitica* xxi, 63) because this clause functions in the context as an answer to a question and not as the opening words used to address oneself to another person.

[17] In my opinion the order determinate core element followed by indeterminate core element or *vice versa* is not of interest for the point in question, which is the function of nominal clauses with a determinate and an indeterminate core element when used as opening words to address oneself to another person (this obviously does not mean that this order has no function).

The remarks of P.E. Dion (with Pardee, art. cit., *Maarav* i, 60, n. 40), basing himself on F.I. Andersen, *The verbless clause in the Pentateuch* (Journal of Biblical Literature Monograph Series xiv, ed. R.A. Kraft), Nashville/New York, 1970, are less convincing. Andersen does not oppose a clause, with the order S (= definite noun, etc.) — P (= indefinite participle) having a declarative

present state or (in most of the instances in which a participle is the indeterminate element) the immediate future. For this reason an interpretation of the words *'bdk qṣr* in this context, presupposing that they refer to the past, seems less probable[18].

A clause *hyh 'bdk b* ... indicating that someone has found himself in the past in a certain place (/town/country) is, in itself, quite possible, cf. the following instances: a) with perfect-forms of *hyh*: Ex. 1:5; Is. 30:4; Neh. 1:1; 1 Chron. 11:13; b) with narrative form of *hyh*: Ex. 24:18; Judg. 17:12; 1 Kings 11:40; Jer. 37:13. For clauses with a comparable word order, cf. 2 Sam. 15:13 (*hyh lb-'yš yśr'l 'ḥry 'bšlwm*), cf. also Is. 33:9; Jer. 32:6; Ps. 22:15; 89:42; 114:2; Lam. 1:17; 2:5.

The question now is, which of the two interpretations is the most probable contextually. In my opinion, the interpretation of the words *'bdk qṣr hyh 'bdk bḥṣr 'sm* as *one* clause (preceded by *casus pendens*) is preferable, for the following reasons.

In the case of the single clause interpretation, the basic information (v. supra) given in the first clause of the plea as such[19] is complete: it informs us about the occupation of the plaintiff *and* about the place where he did his work (or at least: *that* place relevant to the case in question). It also tells us that the relevant events took place in the past (most probably a recent past). This is in complete agreement with what is told in the rest of the plea (the plaintiff has finished his work in Ḥaṣar-Asam)[20].

If we accept the second solution, the first clause with the basic information is *'bdk qṣr*. These words inform us that the plaintiff is at the moment (still) busy with harvesting[21], nothing more. The information that this (also) took

function to one with reversed order having a classifying function, but to one with reversed order having a precative function (cf. Andersen, *op. cit.*, 47ff.). So Dion's conclusions about the translation cannot be based on this. For a criticism of Andersen's standpoint, cf. the author, art. cit., *VT* xxiii, 457ff. Cf. also art. cit., 501ff. for a discussion of the function of the word order in these types of nominal clauses. On this subject, cf. also the remarks of Contini, *op. cit.*, 88ff.

[18] Against Suzuki, art. cit., 5, 8. I am only speaking here about nominal clauses used as 'opening words'. Selfevidently I do not deny that a nominal clause can refer to the past.

[19] I make a difference here between the polite introductory formula *yšm' 'dny hśr 't dbr 'bdh* and the rest of the text which contains the plea of the plaintiff.

[20] Cf. the words *k'šr kl ['] bdk 't qṣr* (l. 6) and *klt ' qṣry* (ll. 8f.). For this interpretation of respectively *kl* and *klt*, cf. e.g. Pardee, art. cit., *Maarav* i, 41f., *Handbook* ..., 21. (I will not go here into the discussion on the derivation of these words). Also, if one does not derive the *wykl* of l. 5 and *kl* and *klt* from a root *kly* but from a root *kwl* (to measure), the context indicates that the plaintiff has finished his work, cf. e.g. Suzuki, art. cit., 8ff.

[21] Selfevidently an interpretation (in itself quite possible) 'your servant is about to start harvesting' does not fit the context. For the translation 'is at the moment (still) busy harvesting', cf. the following considerations. It goes without saying that the 'job' of *qoṣer* is not one for the whole year, it indicates a type of work which is done only within certain months of the year. Therefore I avoided the translation 'your servant is a reaper/harvester' (cf. e.g. Delekat, art. cit., 459; Lemaire, art. cit., *Semitica* xxi, 61, *Inscriptions hébraïques* ..., 260), although in itself the translation is not erroneous, in order to avoid the mistaken notion of permanency.

place in Ḥaṣar-Asam is, in this case, not included in the clause. Moreover, in the instances discussed above as parallels for a possible clause *ʿbdk qṣr*, it is (in as far as they describe a present situation, and not one in the near future) important for the argument as a whole that the situation is *now* as described in them. The question whether the plaintiff is still harvesting elsewhere, is of no interest as far as the problem presented in the plea is concerned. Of basic interest is that he *was* harvesting in Ḥaṣar-Asam in the recent past and that he finished his work.

For these reasons I prefer, be it partly on other grounds, the solution given for the words *ʿbdk qṣr hyh ʿbdk bḥṣr ʾsm* by the original editor of the ostracon, J. Naveh.

THE RESTORATION OF HERMOPOLIS LETTER 6 AND THE RANSOM OF PRISONERS

by

J.W. Wesselius

It has been noted a long time ago already that the small collection of Aramaic letters dating to the early fifth century B.C. which were found in Hermopolis in 1945 and published in Bresciani and Kamil 1966 exhibits a remarkable inner coherence. Seven of the eight papyri (nos 1-6 and 8) have been written by a single scribe. They contain messages from a small group of people residing in Memphis for two families living in Luxor and Syene which were interrelated by marriage and they often repeat the same information. This renders the restoration of the damaged letter 6 somewhat less arduous than one would expect of a text from which the middle third part of all the lines has disappeared. This letter has been discussed in most treatments of the entire group, and B. Porten and J.C. Greenfield have even devoted a separate article to its restoration (Porten and Greenfield 1974). Their erudite article will form the basis of the present re-examination of the papyrus, though I shall not infrequently disagree with their proposals. I shall in general comment only briefly upon those features of this letter which are not directly connected with the problem of its restoration and have been dealt with satisfactorily by others. A drawing of the text and the proposed restorations can be found on page 16. I shall attempt to show that the text of this letter can be restored with confidence, apart from one or two words for which alternatives could be proposed, and that the transaction described in this letter, which has never before been explained satisfactorily, is crucial to our understanding of at least part of the *raison d'être* of these letters. One of the most important reasons for sending them will be shown to have been the redemption of a member of one of the families by a member of the other family, and the consequences of that act.

One of the possible sources for information concerning possible restorations, the genealogy of the families involved, is of extremely limited value on account of at least three distinct factors:

a. The senders usually designate their next of kin by name only, and almost without exception omit every designation of kinship, unless it is to be especially stressed (e.g. 1,8 *'rh l' 'ḥy hw ḥrwṣ*, 'Is Ḥaruṣ not my brother?') or is meant for someone in an evidently superior position, such as father or mother. Exceptions to this rule are occasionally found, e.g. in 6,4, where the designation 'my son', unaccompanied by the boy's name, cannot be explained easily (but note that the nominal sender may not have been the actual sender of the letter, see below).

b. We cannot be sure whether the designations 'my father' and 'my mother' may not have been applied to the wife's father and mother as well. Nabushe son of Petekhnum addressed Makkibanit's parents as 'my father' and 'my mother' (4,13-14), but he was apparently married to Makkibanit's sister Nanayḥam, so his use of this designation may derive from his marriage only. Unless firm proof to the contrary would come forth theories such as those proposed by Porten and Greenfield 1974, 27-29, that Makkibanit and Nabushe had the same mother but a different father, can be speculative only.

c. In Aramaic epistolary style all persons of equal social rank seem to address one another as 'my brother/sister' and to designate themselves as 'your brother/sister' in the heading and address of a letter (though not, apparently, elsewhere). Such a designation, it must be added, certainly does not exclude that the correspondents were brothers/sisters indeed.

It must be said that the considerations about the genealogy in the Greenfield-Porten article are sometimes misleading. J.T. Milik gave in his article a basically correct family tree of the two families involved; for our limited purpose in this article it suffices to keep in mind that it is virtually certain that Tashi was Makkibanit's wife and Nanayḥam Nabushe's.

The contents of the papyrus which is discussed here are clearly related to a passage in Hermopolis letter 2,4-10, which I shall often adduce in the commentary. But for this parallel restoration of the papyrus would have been near to impossible, so I shall also devote some space to the correct interpretation of that passage.

Text and translation.

1. *'l 'ḥty tby mn ['ḥky bnts]r brktky lptḥ zy*
2. *yḥwny 'pyky bš[lm .... b]ry š'l šlmky*
3. *wk't yhb m[kbnt br psmy] ḥtnh zy nbšh ksp*
4. *š 6 wzwz [ksp zwz l'šrth] w'pqny 'nh wbry*
5. *wktbt lh '[l spr k't 'zly] wzbny 'mr kzy tmṭ*
6. *h ydky w'w[šry l'bhy bs]wn hlw ksph zy hwh*
7. *bydh yhb '[p nbwšh wmk]bnt š'ln šlmky*
8. *wšlm trw [wkn 'mrn lkn k]'t šlm bntsr tnh*
9. *wbrh 'l t[ṣpn lhn wk't] 'nḥn b'n 'lp*
10. *wytwnh lkn l[šlmky. šlḥt sp]rh znh*

11. *'l 'my [tby mn bnt]srh 'py ybl*

1. To my sister Tabi from [your brother Banitsa]r. I bless you by Ptaḥ that

2. he may show me your face in pe[ace. ...] my son asks after your well-being.

3. And now: Ma[kkibanit, the son of Pasmi,] the brother-in-law of Nabushe gave

4. six shekels and one zuz of silver [— silver of one zuz [impurity] to the ten [shekels] —] and liberated us, me and my son,

5. and I wrote [a document] about this for him. [Go now] and buy wool as (much as)

6. you are able and se[nd it to his father in Sye]ne, for he has given (all) the money which was

7. in his hand. [Nabushe and Ma]kkibanit are [also] asking after your well-being and

8. the well-being of Taru, [and speak thus to you:] 'Banitsar is all right here now,

9. as well as his son. Do not [worry about them. And now:] we are looking for a boat

10. so that he may be brought to you.' For [your well-being I sent] this letter.

11. To my mother [Tabi, from Banit]sara. Let it be brought to Luxor.

Commentary.

Lines 1 & 2:

mn ['ḥky bnts]r — 'from your brother Banitsar'.

Even when taking the above-mentioned caution concerning the use of words expressing kinship into account, when considering the unequivocal line 11 of this text we cannot escape the conclusion that the addressee is the mother of the sender. In Hermopolis 2,5, in a context which is crucial for the restoration of letter 6, we find a reference to a certain *bntsr br tby*, 'Banitsar the son of Tabi'. Especially in such a close-knitted group of texts the presence of a son of Tabi whose name ends in a *resh*, in a context which is clearly identical to the one in which Banitsar son of Tabi appears in letter 2, obliges us to try very hard to restore his name here. This was already recognized by Milik 1968, 548, who indeed restored this name, but subsequently rejected in Porten and Greenfield 1974, who refrained from restoring any name. They adduced two weighty objections against Milik's restoration, but I shall attempt to show that neither can stand a closer scrutiny. Firstly, they already restored Banitsar's name in the lacuna in line 3, and, secondly, they assumed that it is the writer of the letter who speaks about Banitsar in the third person in line 8. In the commentary to these lines I shall demonstrate that neither assumption is mandatory.

[... b]ry — 'my son ...'.

The lacuna probably contained his name. He is again mentioned in line 4 and in Nabushe's and Makkibanit's message in line 9.

Lines 3 & 4:

m[kbnt br psmy] — 'Makkibanit son of Pasmi'.

Thus to be restored with Milik 1968, 548. It is evident from these letters that the relatives in Luxor belong to Nabushe's family only, so that a rather full introduction of Makkibanit is in its place here. Porten and Greenfield restored *yhb m[kbnt lbntsr] ḥtnh zy nbšh*, 'Makkibanit gave to Banitsar son-in-law of Nabushe ...'. I agree that the parallel of *[ ] ḥtnh zy nbšh* in this line with *bntsr br tby 'ḥt nbwšh*, 'Banitsar the son of Tabi, Nabushe's sister' in 2,5-6 is rather attractive, but assuming that Nabushe's daughter married his nephew and that this nephew is to be introduced in this letter in such a cumbersome way to his own mother Tabi (!!) is asking too much of the reader. The parallel between the two designations should rather be attributed to the fact that Makkibanit, writing to members of his own family, has to introduce Nabushe's relative Banitsar, as well as Banitsar's mother Tabi, to them in letter 2, whereas Makkibanit was apparently not well known to Nabushe's family (who, after all, seem to have lived in Luxor, while Makkibanit apparently came from Syene), and for that reason is introduced here with his name, the name of his father and his relation to Banitsar's family.

[ksp zwz l'šrth] — 'silver of one zuz (impurity) to the 10 (shekels)'.

A half-shekel (= 1 zuz) in every ten shekels is the usual degree of impurity of silver in the Elephantine Aramaic documents. An almost identical formula *ksp zwz l'šrt'* is attested in K 3,15-16 and K 7,17. The parallel in 2,6 has an abbreviated formula *ksp zwz*, which has been interpreted in this way already by R. Yaron, *JSS* 13 (1968), 202-203.

w'pqny — 'and he liberated us'.

Following a suggestion in Hoftijzer 1983, 118, note (h) for the translation of the *af'el* of *npq* as found here, I assume that Banitsar had been thrown into prison or was in some other kind of custody. We need not be surprised that the exact circumstances have not been mentioned explicitly here, because they had probably already been discussed in earlier letters.

We may translate the first person singular suffix as a plural here on the basis of a rarely discerned rule in the grammar of Official Aramaic. As a general rule it can be stated that, when a number of elements connected by *w*ᵉ, 'and', serve as the grammatical subject in a sentence, the verb, pronoun or predicate agrees in gender and number with the first element when they precede it, whereas they are taken as referring to all the elements together when they follow. As the available space does not suffice to give a full discussion of this phenomenon, I shall merely quote a very characteristic instance in K 3,10: *'nh bgzšt w'wbl kl 2 'nḥn zbn wyhbn lk*, 'We, Bagazušta and Ubil, all 2, we sold and gave (it) to you'. It must be noted, however, that there are a small number of exceptions. I hope to return to this problem elsewhere.

As mentioned above the transaction described here is apparently the same as the one mentioned by Makkibanit to his wife Tashi in 2,4-6 *hlw mst ksp' zy hwh bydy ntnt* (text: *nttn*) *wpdt lbntsr br tby 'ḥt nbwšh ksp š 6 wzwz ksp zwz*, 'because I have given as much silver as was in my hand and redeemed Banitsar the son of Tabi, Nabushe's sister — 6 1/2 shekels of silver, silver of one zuz (impurity to 10 shekels) ...'. The differences between my rendering of this passage and, for example, Porten's and Greenfield's are:

a. *hlw* is assumed to be a conjunction, giving the reason why Tabi can claim a certain amount of wool in 2,6-10. See also the commentary to *hlw* in line 6.

b. *wpdt* was derived from the verb *pdy*, 'to redeem, to ransom', which is common in (among others) Hebrew and Ugaritic, already in Donner 1971, 84. His rather less felicitous interpretation of this form as a 3 fem.sg. form may account for the fact that this doubtlessly correct suggestion has gained no further acceptance, except for brief references in two short notes by P. Swiggers (Swiggers 1981 and 1981/2). The *lamed* before the name Banitsar indicates the direct object of the verb *pdy*. The non-representation of the medial vowel *ē* in the first person singular *p*ᵉ*dēt* is hardly surprising in the orthography of the Hermopolis letters. This would be the first instance of this verb in Aramaic, but this is not in itself an argument against recognizing it here. It may belong to the not inconsiderable number of legal terms current in Official Aramaic which are not found anywhere in the later Aramaic dialects.

From the Hermopolis correspondence it is evident that this act of redemption by Makkibanit caused a new obligation, this time of Banitsar to Makkibanit. He had to confirm it in writing and his family had to start repaying his debt in various ways (see below); it is interesting to see that the consequences of ransom in the context of this letter seem to conform to its connotation in a legal text from Ugarit. In *KTU* 3.4 a certain Iwrikalli redeems certain persons whose names are listed from 'Beiruthians', but this clearly does not imply that they are free now; henceforth they must work for Iwrikalli until they have paid him back the money which he spent on their redemption. For ease of reference I give the text and translation of *KTU* 3.4, the translation mainly based upon R. Yaron's study of this text in *VT* 10 (1960), 83-90. Compare also B. Kienast in *UF* 11 (1979), 448-450.

> (1) *l ym hnd* (2) *iwrkl pdy* (3) *agdn bn nwgn* (4) *w ynḥm aḫh* (5) *w b'ln aḫh* (6) *wḥṯṯn bnh* (7) *wbtšy bth* (8) *w ištrmy* (9) *bt 'bdmlk aṯt[h]* (10) *w snt* (11) *bt ugrt* (12) *w pdy hm* (13) *iwrkl mit* (14) *ksp b yd* (15) *birtym* (16) *[w un]ṯ inn* (17) *lhm 'd ṯṯbn* (18) *ksp iwrkl* (19) *w ṯb l unṯhm*

> On this day Iwrikalli redeemed AGDN son of NWGN and YNḤM his brother and B'LN his brother and ḤTṮN his son and BTŠY his daughter and IŠTRMY daughter of 'BDMLK, his wife, and SNT, a 'daughter' of Ugarit; and Iwrikalli redeemed them for 100 (shekels) of silver from the Beiruthians. And there will be no unuššu-obligation for them until they have returned Iwrikalli's money and (then) they will return to their unuššu-obligation.

In this Ugaritic document we meet with almost exactly the same elements as in the two Hermopolis letters relating to the redemption of Banitsar: the verb *pdy* is used, the exact amount paid is indicated and we find a statement implying that the silver is to be repaid as soon as possible.

By inference from the Ugaritic parallel we may also conclude that the passages concerning this ransom in the Hermopolis letters clearly derive from a legal context; this may account at least in part for certain unexpected features such as the use of the rare verb *pdy*, the rather formal indication of the impurity of the silver and perhaps also as an archaic trait (?) the use of the perfect tense of *ntn* (*yhb* being the ordinary form for the perfect of 'to give' in Official Aramaic).

In the Old Testament, where *pdy* can both be used in a wordly, i.e. legal or cultic, sense and for designating God's acts of liberation for his servants, this aspect of *pdy*, i.e. causing an obligation of the ransomed to the ransomer, is apparently never made explicit, but it could be defended that on the basis of contemporary legal usage not a few early readers must have felt that juridically speaking it was God's leading Israel out of their former slavery in Egypt which gave him authority over the people.

Note that *pādā* and *hōṣī* (*hif.* of *yāṣā*) are used together in Dt. 9:26 *'l tšḥt 'mk wnḥltk 'šr pdyt bgdlk 'šr hwṣ't mmṣrym byd ḥzqh*, 'destroy not thy people and thy heritage, whom thou hast redeemed through thy greatness, whom thou hast brought out of Egypt with a mighty hand'. It is interesting to see both the verb *pdy* and the verb *npq* (*af.*), 'to bring out', occurring in the Hermopolis correspondence, and to recognize the skillful way in which the scribe varied his words and used *ntn* + *pdy* in 2,5 and *yhb* + *npq* (*af.*) here, and that in letters which were to be sent to different destinations (H 2 to Syene and H 6 to Luxor). There are a number of instances of such 'distant parallelism' in the Hermopolis letters; they prove that, whatever one may say about the professional qualities of the scribe (see Naveh 1971), he had a remarkable sense of style and really composed the Hermopolis correspondence as a whole.

Lines 5 & 6:

wktbt lh ʿ[l spr] — 'and I wrote for him a document concerning it'.

A plausible restoration suggested by Porten and Greenfield, but note that their restoration of the det.st. *sprh* instead of the abs.st. *spr* is due to a somewhat too consistent copying of the expression employed in Cowley 13,9f., *wsprʾ ktbt lky ʿlʾ*, 'and I have written the document for you about it', where, unlike the situation in our text, the document had already been mentioned. For the adverb *ʿella*, 'about it', a defective spelling as assumed here seems to be preferable, but their suggestion *ʿ[lh]* is certainly possible.

The debt resulting from Banitsar's redemption by Makkibanit was thus apparently confirmed in writing by making out a debt-note, comparable in function to the Ugaritic document quoted above, namely to define the resulting obligation of ransomed to ransomer.

[kʿt ʾzly] — 'go now!'

Possible, but far from being certain.

hlw ksph zy hwh bydh yhb — 'for he has given (all) the silver which was in his hand'.

This word *hlw* is usually interpreted as an interjection 'behold!'. The fact that it is used in almost exactly the same way in the parallel in 2,4-6 (see the commentary to *wʾpqny* above) made me suspect that it serves as a conjunction here, and this explanation seems to be valid in most instances of this word in Official Aramaic. Note that such a syntactically determined use of interjections, which causes them to function as conjunctions, apparently also underlies the Targumic translation of Hebrew *kī* by *ʾᵃre* (Onqelos and Jonathan) or *ʾᵃrum* (Palestinian Targum). I hope to return to its discussion elsewhere.

wʾw[šry lʾbhy bs]wn — 'and send (it) to his father in Syene'.

In agreement with the restoration proposed by Porten and Greenfield except for the word *ʾbhy*, 'his father', where they restore the name of Makkibanit's wife Tashi. Note, however, that if Makkibanit needed to be introduced to Nabushe's family, his wife was not very likely known to them either. His father had, as we have seen, probably already been mentioned in line 3. A possible alternative restoration would be *[lbyth]*, 'to his house'.

This is, after the restoration of line 3 (see the commentary there), another instance where caution must be exercised not to press the parallels between the letters too far. Makkibanit's wife Tashi was indeed asked in letter 2 to write to Tabi that she was to send Tashi wool, but that was to be only one shekel's worth of it. As Tabi was asked to buy wool 'as much as you are able', the amount mentioned in letter 2 was probably only part of the total amount which was due to Makkibanit.

Some clarification may be necessary about the passage in which Makkibanit instructed his wife in 2,6-7 *šlḥy ʿl tby wtwšr lky ʾmr mn qṣth zy ksp š 1*, 'send (a letter) to Tabi that she must send you wool to a value of one shekel of silver'. The expression *mn qṣth* is usually interpreted as 'from her share' or the like, which would be rather puzzling as we are not told anything about this share. Both here and in the only other passage where *mn qṣt* appears, C 35,4 *mn qṣt ksp' wnksky' zy ʿl spr ʾntwtky*, '*mn qṣt* the silver and goods which are on your marriage contract', a meaning 'the value of' fits in the context much better. For the use of *qiṣṣa* in prepositional phrases one may compare Syriac *b^{e}qeṣṣat*, 'on account of'.

Lines 7, 8 & 9:

ʾ[p nbwšh wm]kbnt šʾln šlmky — '[Nabushe and Ma]kkibanit [also] greet you'.

It would seem that the right-hand corner of the *aleph* is still visible on the photograph; otherwise a restoration *[wkʿt]*, 'and now:', might have been preferable in view of the width of the lacuna.

This sentence is usually restored as *[ʾnh wm]kbnt šʾln šlmky*, 'I and Makkibanit greet you', in order to account for the pronoun *ʾnḥn*, 'we', in line 9. As I propose another explanation for the use of *ʾnḥn* (see the commentary to *[wkn ʾmrn lkn k]ʿt* below) we do not need this restoration any more, and it would besides be somewhat unexpected if the sender of this letter, who implicitly greeted the recipient already by its beginning, would again be introduced here for the same purpose. The present restoration, which is already partly found in Grelot 1972, 166 and Gibson 1975, 141, is also supported by the fact that in letter 5 Nabushe and Makkibanit figure as senders, and Taru and Tabi as recipients.

[wkn ʾmrn lkn k]ʿt šlm bntsr tnh wbrh — 'and speak thus to you: Banitsar, as well as his son, are all right here now'.

Nabushe and Makkibanit are apparently introduced as speaking here. This is not as improbable as it looks at first sight. Firstly, it should be noted that a letter addressed to one person can also contain a message which directly addresses another (e.g. 3,5ff. or 4,13), so that it is not really surprising that this letter would introduce a new sender in these lines, and, secondly, the four persons involved here are the senders and addressees of letter 5 (Nabushe and Makkibanit to Taru and Tabi), and are all involved in Banitsar's release from custody and the reimbursement of the money spent for that purpose. As I shall demonstrate below, it is quite probable that this letter was really written at the instigation of Nabushe and Makkibanit, for unlike all the other letters it really is a 'one-purpose' document, entirely lacking the passages expressing personal interest which abound in the other letters and only concerned with the theme of Banitsar's release and its consequences; Makkibanit and Nabushe were probably literally looking over his shoulder, may even have dictated the letter, and could easily have inserted the following sentences. Unlike the other instances of *kʿt* in these letters, where it seems to serve as a pause in the reading only, the word should be taken quite literally here as 'now, at this moment', namely after their intervention on his behalf.

The addition of a second subject at the end of a sentence is not without parallels in Egyptian Aramaic, for example K 5,8-9 *wʾnty šbyqh mn ṭlʾ lsmšʾ wyhyšmʿ brtky*, 'and you are released from the shade to the sun, as well as your daughter Jahishma'.

ʾl t[ṣpn lhn] — 'do not worry about them'.

With the typical form of the jussive 2 fem.pl., compare *tdʿn*, 'you (fem.pl.) should know', in 5,2.

Lines 10 & 11:

l[šlmky šlḥt sp]rh znh — 'For your welfare I have written this letter'.

The usual final formula in this correspondence.

ʾl ʾmy [tby mn bnt]srh — 'To my mother Tabi from Banitsara'.

Compare the way in which the outside address is written on Makkibanit's letter to his father 3,14 *ʾl ʾby psmy mn mkbnt br psmy*, 'to my father Pasmi from Makkibanit, son of Pasmi'. Note that the formulation of the outside address may sometimes be dictated by the limitation imposed by the fact that it was usually written after the document was rolled and tied and could thus, for example, never contain more than one line. This somewhat irregular fashion of writing the outside address may also account for the fact that there seems to be a small vacant space before the *samekh*. The form of the name *bntsrh*, which is of course identical with the usual *bntsr*, probably indicates the presence of a short vowel *a* after the *resh*.

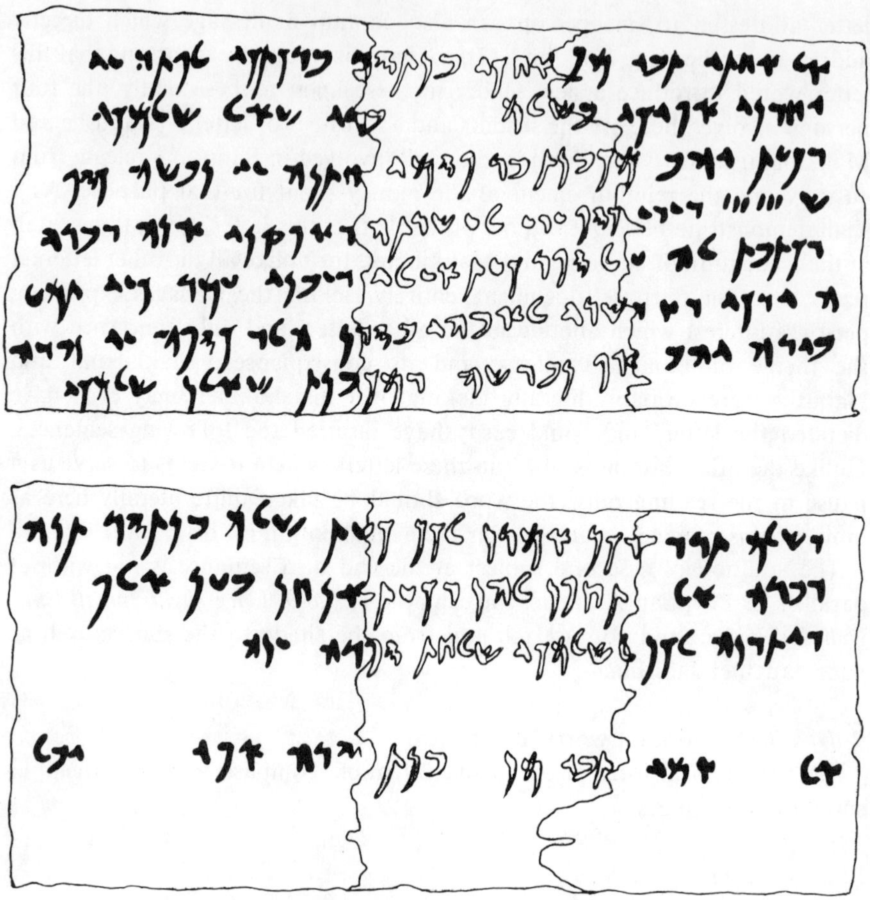

What happened prior to the writing of this letter and occasioned its being sent to Luxor can be summarized as follows. Banitsar, a nephew of Nabushe, was taken into some kind of custody, perhaps in a working-house or prison, together with his son, possibly as a consequence of incurring certain debts. Makkibanit, Nabushe's brother-in-law agreed to furnish the silver necessary for having Banitsar released, but wanted the silver returned in due time. In order to achieve this Makkibanit and Nabushe made Banitsar write a debt-note for the silver which Makkibanit had paid, and later they made him send a letter to his mother Tabi, in which he asked her to send a large amount of wool to Makkibȧnit's family in Syene, to which letter they appended a note stressing Banitsar's well-being and their willingness to send him home to Luxor (letter 6), apparently with the intention to support Banitsar's request in this way. Did they intend to let him go before the money was paid? We cannot be sure of that. At the same time Makkibanit sent a letter to his wife Tashi in which he asked her to exert some pressure on Tabi as well and to claim and receive part of the wool, equivalent to one shekel of silver (letter 2). Nabushe also wrote a rather high-handed letter to Tabi, who was his sister, requiring the shipment of certain goods (letter 5). The fact that Makkibanit was there also mentioned as a sender of the letter may indicate that the intention was the same, namely to reimburse Makkibanit for the silver he spent on Banitsar's release from custody. The fact that Tabi was asked to collect as much wool as she could (6,5-6) may indicate that it was not expected that she could meet the amount of 6 1/2 shekels of silver in this way, and that another way of payment would be necessary. It is not entirely clear if Nabushe was a willing or unwilling partner of Makkibanit in this entire procedure, but he probably had no choice anyway, as Makkibanit seems to have had some possibility of 'complaining' (2,10) in case his wishes were not fulfilled. Makkibanit had apparently gained power and authority over the people whom he had redeemed, as well as over their family, just as Iwrikalli did over the people whom he had redeemed from the Beiruthians in *KTU* 3.4.

Though we do not have any legal document concerning the ransom of prisoners in Official Aramaic, we now realize that we have for some time already possessed something which may be even more valuable: a series of documents which make it clear to us how such a legal transaction involving ransom worked out in practice and which provide informal information about the degree to which family relations could be affected by such a ransom.

Bibliography

E. Bresciani and M. Kamil, *Le lettere aramaiche di Hermopoli*, Rome, 1966.

H. Donner, 'Bemerkungen zum Verständnis zweier aramäischer Briefe aus Hermopolis', in: H. Goedicke (ed.), *Near Eastern Studies in Honor of W.F. Albright*, Baltimore/London, 1971.

J.C.L. Gibson, *Textbook of Syrian Semitic Inscriptions*, II, Aramaic Inscriptions, Oxford, 1975.

J.C. Greenfield, 'The 'Periphrastic Imperative' in Aramaic and Hebrew', *IEJ* 19 (1969), 199-210.

P. Grelot, *Documents araméens d'Egypte*, Paris, 1972.

E. Hammershaimb, 'Some Remarks on the Aramaic Letters from Hermopolis', *VT* 18 (1968), 265-267.

J.P. Hayes and J. Hoftijzer, 'Notae Hermopolitanae', *VT* 20 (1970), 98-106.

J. Hoftijzer, 'De Hermopolis-papyri', in: K.R. Veenhof (ed.), *Schrijvend Verleden*, Zutphen, 1983, 107-119.

E.Y. Kutscher, 'The Hermopolis Papyri', *Israel Oriental Studies* 1 (1971), 103-119.

J.T. Milik, 'Les papyrus araméens d'Hermoupolis et les cultes syrophéniciens en Egypte perse', *Biblica* 48 (1967), 546-622.

J. Naveh, 'The Palaeography of the Hermopolis Papyri', *Israel Oriental Studies* 1 (1971), 120-122.

B. Porten, *Archives from Elephantine*, Berkeley, 1968.
B. Porten, 'The Religion of the Jews of Elephantine in Light of the Hermopolis Papyri', *JNES* 28 (1969), 116-121.
B. Porten and J.C. Greenfield, 'The Aramaic Papyri from Hermopolis', *ZAW* 80 (1968), 216-231.
B. Porten and J.C. Greenfield, 'The Guarantor at Elephantine-Syene', *JAOS* 89 (1969), 153-158.
B. Porten and J.C. Greenfield, 'Hermopolis Letter 6', *Israel Oriental Studies* 4 (1974), 14-30.
P. Swiggers, 'Notes on the Hermopolis Papyri I and II', *AION* 41 (1981), 144-146.
P. Swiggers, 'Note sur le papyrus IV d'Hermoupolis', *Aegyptus* 61 (1981/2), 65-68.
P. Swiggers, 'The Hermopolis Papyri III and IV', *AION* 42 (1982), 135-140.
J.W. Wesselius, 'Reste einer Kasusflektion in einigen früharamäischen Dialekten', *AION* 40 (1980), 265-268.

Abbreviations employed in this article:
C — A.E. Cowley, *Aramaic Papyri of the Fifth Century B.C.*, Oxford, 1923.
DISO — Ch.-F. Jean & J. Hoftijzer, *Dictionnaire des inscriptions sémitiques de l'ouest*, Leiden, 1965.
H — E. Bresciani & M. Kamil, *Le lettere aramaiche di Hermopoli*, Rome, 1966.
K — E.G. Kraeling, *The Brooklyn Museum Aramaic Papyri*, New Haven, 1953.
KTU — M. Dietrich, O. Loretz & J. Sanmartín, *Die keilalphabetischen Texte aus Ugarit*, Neukirchen/Vluyn, 1976.

DIE BEDEUTUNG VON JACHIN UND BOAZ IN 1 KÖN. 7:21 (2 CHR. 3:17)

von

M.J. MULDER

Über die Bedeutung der Namen der zwei Säulen vor der Vorhalle des salomonischen Tempels in Jerusalem gibt es seit alters viele Meinungen. Bereits im Targum zu 2 Chr. 3:17 wird gesagt, dass Jachin *dᵉ'atqānat malkûtā dᵉbêt dāwid*, 'das Konigtum des Davidshauses ist befestigt', und Boaz *rab bêt 'abbā lᵉbêt yᵉhûdā dᵉminnêh nᵉpāqû kol malkayyā dᵉbêt yᵉhûdā*, 'Haupt der Sippe des Hauses von Juda, aus welcher alle Könige des Hauses von Juda hervorgegangen sind', bedeute. Deutlich bezieht Letztgenanntes sich auf den in Ruth 4:13-22 erwähnten Stammbaum Davids, von dem Boaz Stammvater war. In der langen Geschichte der Auslegung dieses Textes (1 Kön. 7:21 und/oder 2 Chr. 3:17) gibt es viele Ausleger und Gelehrte, die der Ansicht waren, die Namen der Säulen seien Namen bekannter oder unbekannter Personen. Wilhelm Gesenius z.B. meldet in seinem berühmten *Thesaurus* unter Boaz: '...una e duabus columnis ante Salomonis templum constitutis vel ab architecti, vel, si forte ἀνάθημα fuit, a datoris nomine ita appellata'[1]. Dass man hin und wieder die Namen als Personennamen gefasst hat, ist durchaus verständlich, weil auch Jachin an anderen Orten im Alten Testament gelegentlich auf Personen hinweist[2]. Andere Gelehrte suchten eine Lösung der sich hier findenden Probleme in abstrakten oder symbolischen Erklärungen, etwa Seb. Münster: 'Vocavit autem Solomo columnam unam *Jachin*, quod *Firmationem* significat; et alteram *Boaz*, i. *Fortitudo in eo*; quòd re ipsa optabat et precabatur ut Deus domum illam firmam et stabilem in perpetuum conservaret'[3].

Ziel dieses Artikels, mit dem ich meinen Kollegen und Freund J.C.H. Lebram zu seinem 65. Geburtstag ehren möchte, ist es nicht, eingehend alle

---

[1] G. Gesenius, *Thesaurus Philologicus Criticus Linguae Hebraeae et Chaldaeae Veteris Testamenti*, Lipsiae, 1829, 223.

[2] Gen. 46:10; Ex. 6:15; Num. 26:12; Neh. 11:10; 1 Chr. 9:10; 24:17; vgl. auch M. Noth, *Die israelitischen Personennamen im Rahmen der gemeinsemitischen Namengebung*, Stuttgart, 1928, 202; W. Kornfeld, 'Der Symbolismus der Tempelsäulen', *ZAW* 74 (1962), 51.

[3] S. Münster, in: *Criticorum Sacrorum sive Annotatorum ad Libros Historicos et Librum Job*, II, 1698, col.34 (*ad* 1 Kön. 7:18); vgl. hier auch Isid. Clarius und Fransc. Vatablus.

Meinungen, die seit alters über dieses Problem vorgetragen sind, zu behandeln. Dazu hätte ich hier auch zu wenig Zeilen zur Verfügung. Aufgrund meiner Untersuchungen zum Text von 1 Kön. 7 möchte ich eine (neue) Lösung vortragen, nachdem ich zuvor einige Ansichten neuerer Forscher erwähnt habe[4].

H. Ewald ist in seiner *Geschichte des Volkes Israel* der Meinung, dass die Säulen Jachin und Boaz 'gewiss nach damals beliebten Männern, vielleicht jungen Söhnen Salomo's' genannt waren, und in einer Anmerkung wundert er sich 'wie man noch immer auf gut Rabbinisch in diesen Namen der zwei Säulen einen bildlichen Sinn suchen kann, als bezögen sie sich auf Eigenschaften Gottes'[5]. Ganz anderer Meinung ist ein anderer Grossmeister der Geschichtsforschung Israels des vorigen Jahrhunderts, E. Renan in seiner *Histoire du peuple d'Israël*[6]. Er achtet es nicht unmöglich, dass 'ces deux mots eussent été écrits, comme des *graffiti* talismaniques, par les fondeurs phéniciens, sur les colonnes'. Die Bedeutung wäre: 'Que [Dieu la] fasse tenir droite par [sa] force'. Diese zwei Wörter würden nachher durch Leute 'peu au courant des choses phéniciennes' für Namen der Säulen gehalten.

Nirgends aber wird mitgeteilt, dass die Namen auf den Säulen *geschrieben* waren. Unser Text sagt nur: *wayyiqrā' 'et šᵉmô*, 'seinen Namen nennen', oder so etwas. Jedoch halten viele Forscher es für richtig, dass die Namen auf den Säulen graviert waren. So meint R.B.Y. Scott, dass die Namen von 'initial words of dynastic inscriptions like that of Gudea' abgeleitet waren[7]. Und, so fährt er einige Zeilen weiter fort, 'the first pillar may have borne an inscription like: 'He will establish [*yākîn*] the throne of David forever.' The second inscription may also have had dynastic significance — e.g., 'In the strength of [*bᵉʿōz*] of Yahweh shall the king rejoice' (cf. Ps. 21:1 - H 21:2) — or it may have had a mythological or cultic reference (cf. Ps. 74:13; 96:6)'[8].

Die Form *yākîn* — oder, nach einigen Manuskripten der LXX, *yākûn*[9] — ist als Imperf. *qal* des Verbs *kûn* zu fassen[10]. Die Form *boʿaz* hingegen wird

---

[4] Übersichten über die verschiedenen Meinungen gibt es, ausser bei Kornfeld (Anm. 2), 50-57, und den (Real-)Wörterbüchern (etwa G.B. Winer, *Biblisches Realwörterbuch*[3], Leipzig, 1847; oder E.C.A. Riehm, *Handwörterbuch des Biblischen Altertums*, Bielefeld und Leipzig, 1884; und den neueren Handwörterbüchern in verschiedenen Sprachen), auch bei H. Bergema, *De Boom des Levens in Schrift en Historie*, Hilversum, 1938, 452-458.

[5] H. Ewald, *Geschichte des Volkes Israel*, III[3], Göttingen, 1866, 323f.

[6] E. Renan, *Histoire du peuple d'Israel*, II, Paris, 1889, 143f.

[7] R.B.Y. Scott, 'Jachin and Boaz', *IDB*, II, 781; vgl. denselben, 'The Pillars Jachin and Boaz', *JBL* 58 (1939), 143-149.

[8] Vgl. auch L.H. Vincent, *Jérusalem de l'Ancien Testament*, II, Paris, 1956, 409; W.F. Albright, *Archaeology and the Religion of Israel*[3], Baltimore, 1953, 139; M. Noth, *Könige*, I, Neukirchen-Vluyn, 1968, 153ff.; Th.A. Busink, *Der Tempel von Jerusalem von Salomo bis Herodes*, Leiden, 1970, 299-321, spez. 311.

[9] LXX nach der Ausgabe von A.E. Brooke - N. McLean - H.St.J. Thackeray, Cambridge, 1930, *ad* 3 Reg. 7:7; vgl. auch die unterschiedliche Schreibung von Boaz in der LXX.

[10] K. Koch, '*kûn*', *TWAT*, IV, 96f.

manchmal in *bô* und *'az* zerlegt, aber H. Gressmann und andere waren der Ansicht, dass *ba'al* zu lesen wäre[11]. Es ist nicht verwunderlich, dass man immer wieder an eine Kombination beider Wörter, oder auch an zwei (kürzere oder längere) Sätze, von denen diese beiden Wörter den Anfang bildeten, gedacht hat. Ebensowenig ist es verwunderlich, dass man in den mit netzartigem Ornament und Granatäpfeln geschmückten Säulen (1 Kön. 7:41) entweder Symbole der kosmischen Säule, der mythologischen Berge, zwischen denen die Sonne aufsteigt, der Paradiesbäume, oder ägyptische Obeliske, Massebôth oder Djedpfeiler sah[12]. Der Weg zu Spekulationen ist offen, und die Feststellung *non liquet* liegt auf der Hand. Aber zum letztgenannten Verdikt, übrigens nicht immer fehl am Ort, ist es u.E. noch zu früh.

Der Wortlaut unseres Textes betont die Verben *qûm* und *qārā*. Letztgenanntes Wort bedeutet öfter 'anrufen', zu einer Gottheit 'rufen' (Ps. 99:6 usw.)[13]. Dies deutet auf eine kultische Begehung hin. Weiterhin fällt auf, dass die Säulen Jachin und Boaz nur am salomonischen Tempel vorkamen und offenbar als 'heidnische' Symbole galten[14]. Am meisten liegt es auf der Hand bei 'heidnisch' an kanaanäischen oder phönizischen Einfluss zu denken. In dieser Hinsicht war Renan schon auf der richtigen Spur[15]. Oder um es mit den Worten von Kornfeld zu sagen: 'Die Geschichte Israels rollte ... nicht im luftleeren Raum ab, sondern zeigt vielfältige Wechselbeziehungen zu den übrigen Völkern und Kulturen des alten Orients'[16].

Was aber war die (praktische) Funktion dieser Säulen? Auch auf diese Frage gibt es in der jüngsten Forschungsgeschichte verschiedene Antworten, von denen wir nur einige wenige vorführen wollen. So ist W.F. Albright der Meinung, dass Jachin und Boaz 'lofty cressets' zum Brennen von Weihrauch gewesen sind[17]. Schon vorher hat W. Robertson Smith die Vermutung geäussert, dass die Säulen gebaut waren 'on the model of those altar candlesticks which we find represented on Phoenician monuments'[18]. In diesem Zusammenhang weist er auf Mitteilungen und Figuren aus der Umwelt Israels hin, aber diese Ansicht von Smith hat schon früh Bestreitung gefunden[19].

---

[11] H. Gressmann, *Die Lade Jahves und das Allerheiligste des Salomonischen Tempels*, Berlin usw., 1920, 62 Anm. 72; vgl. J.A. Montgomery, 'Some Hebrew Etymologies', *JQR* 25 (1935), 265: *Ba'al-'az*, 'Baal is strong'.

[12] Vgl. für ein Verzeichnis sämtlicher Erklärungen: Kornfeld, a.a.O., 53f.

[13] Vgl. C.J. Labuschagne, '*qr'* rufen', *THAT*, II, 666-674, spez. 672f.

[14] Siehe auch Busink, a.a.O., 317f.

[15] Oben, Anm. 6.

[16] Kornfeld, a.a.O., 53.

[17] W.F. Albright, 'Two Cressets from Marisa and the Pillars of Jachin and Boaz', *BASOR* 85 (1942), 18-27; vgl. H.G. May, 'The Two Pillars before the Temple of Solomon', *BASOR* 88 (1942), 19-27, spez. 19.

[18] W. Robertson Smith, *The Religion of the Semites*, (Edinburgh, 1889,) New York, 1959, 488 (Note K).

[19] Wir nennen M.-J. Lagrange, *Etudes sur les Religions sémitiques*[2], Paris, 1905, 215: ' ... les

Th.A. Busink hält die Säulen für 'die Standarten des Tempels, welche besagten, dass der Tempel das Haus Jahwes, nicht des Ba'al, Moloch, usw. war'; und etwas weiter: 'Die Säulen Jachin und Boas waren u.E. als stilisierte Leuchter Symbole Jahwes'[20]. Seiner Meinung nach war das Kapitell der Säulen 'zweifellos das wichtigste Element der Säulen und bei der Frage nach dem symbolischen Sinn wird man demnach dieses Element in Rechnung zu stellen haben'[21]. Neben genannten Gelehrten gibt es auch Forscher, die nur an 'neutrale' Eingangsmassebôth denken, wie etwa J. de Groot: '...niets anders dan ingangsmasseben...; zij hadden allereerst architektonische beteekenis, doch golden den god van den hemel Jahve, gelijk ook bij Phoenicische en Egyptische tempels twee zuilen aan goden waren gewijd'[22]. Kornfeld ist jedoch zuzustimmen, dass die Säule 'zu den primären Symbolen der Menschheit' gehört, und deshalb nicht so 'unschuldig' ist, wie De Groot meint[23]. Steinverehrung war in Israel und bei seinen benachbarten Völkern bekannt[24]. Als Lucian von Samosata (± 120-185 n. Chr.) in seinem bekannten Büchlein von der 'Syrischen Göttin' (*De dea Syra*) Tempel und Verehrung dieser Göttin in Hierapolis (Mabbugh) in Syrien auf seine lebendige Weise schildert, dann meldet er auch: καὶ φαλλοὶ δὲ ἑστέασι ἐν τοῖσι προπυλαίοισι δύο κάρτα μεγάλοι, ἐπ' ὧν ἐπίγραμμα τοιόνδε ἐπιγέγραπται: 'Τούσδε φαλλοὺς Διόνυσος Ἥρῃ μητρυιῇ ἀνέθηκα' (Par. 16). Der Zusammenhang dieser Worte erwähnt, dass Bacchus der Stifter dieses Tempels sei, und dass viele Sachen im Tempelgebäude dies zeigen, u.a. die Inschrift: 'Diese Phallen habe ich, Dionysos, der Juno, meiner Stiefmutter aufgestellt'. Wie sehr man auch Argwohn hegen kann und darf gegen Lucians Erörterungen in seinem Buch, und wie sehr auch äusserste Vorsicht geboten ist, Daten aus späterer Zeit und anderem Ort auf den Jerusalemer Tempel zu beziehen, ist es doch beachtenswert, dass er die zwei Säulen vor dem Tempel in Hierapolis als phallische Kultsymbole deutet. In diesem Zusammenhang ist die Meinung von B.D. Eerdmans nicht so abstrus wie sie manchem Gelehrten vorkam: 'The phallic nature of both pillars is expressed in this case by the names, he establishes, and in him is force'[25].

---

raisons de W.R. Smith reposent en grande partie sur une confusion de ces objets avec les colonnes-pylônes'.

[20] Busink, a.a.O., 317; vgl. auch K. Galling, *BRL*¹, 518.

[21] Busink, a.a.O., 316; vgl. hierzu auch F.J. Hoogewoud, 'Moderne benaderingswijzen van Salomo's Tempel', in: *De Tempel van Salomo*, ed. J.F. van Agt, J.C.E. Belinfante usw., 's-Gravenhage, 1976, 96.

[22] Joh. de Groot, *Palestijnsche Masseben (Opgerichte Steenen)*, Groningen, 1913, 42; vgl. 93: Zusammenhang mit 'demonengeloof en demonenvrees'. S. Yeivin, 'Jachin and Boaz', *PEQ* 91 (1959), 6-22, meint, dass die freistehenden Säulen am Tempeleingang ein Nachklang beduinischen Brauchtums seien: ging der Mann in das Zelt seiner Frau, so steckte er seine Lanze am Eingang zum Zeichen seiner Anwesenheit in die Erde.

[23] Kornfeld, a.a.O., 52.

[24] Beispiele etwa bei B. Stade, *Geschichte des Volkes Israel*, I, Berlin, 1887, 456-460; Robertson Smith, a.a.O., 200-212; und in der Arbeit von De Groot (oben, Anm. 22).

[25] B.D. Eerdmans, *The Religion of Israel*, Leiden, 1947, 64.

Wohl bemerkt er dazu ergänzend: 'Yet there is no evidence that they had in Jerusalem any other meaning than of stylish ornaments'. Und er hat u.E. recht, wenn er, nachdem er einige andere Meinungen erwähnt hat, hinzufügt: 'But none of these theories seems probable in view of the statement of Lucian, which fully agrees with antique oriental customs and thought'.

K. Rupprecht hat u.a. in seinem Werk über den Tempel von Jerusalem darauf hingewiesen, dass seiner Ansicht nach dieser Tempel nicht ohnehin als Gründung Salomos angemerkt werden kann, sondern dass es sich um ein jebusitisches Erbe handelt[26]. Wie diese Hypothese auch in Einzelheiten zu beurteilen sei, sie kann allerdings erklären, warum es am Anfang der Übernahme des ursprünglich kanaanäischen Tempels durch Salomo noch verschiedene Kultgegenstände gegeben hat, welche später nicht mehr erwähnt wurden, unter denen die beiden Säulen. Schon J. Wellhausen hat richtig bemerkt, dass es Unstimmigkeiten gab zwischen etwa 1 Kön. 8:4, wo über das Hinaufbringen des heiligen Zeltes und aller heiligen Geräte gesprochen wird, und 1 Kön. 7, wo über die Neuanfertigung aller Kultgeräte berichtet wird[27]. Aufgrund aller dieser Beobachtungen ist anzunehmen, dass die Säulen aus einem jebusitisch-kanaanäischen Heiligtum in den durch Salomo erneuten Tempel mit hinübergenommen sind. In der vor-salomonischen Zeit hatten sie mehr als bloss stilistischen Wert: sie waren unbedingt Kultsymbole der kanaanäischen Religion[28].

Das dreimal wiederholte *wayyāqem* unseres Verses deutet nachdrücklich auf die Tätigkeit des priesterlichen Königs hin: 'er richtete auf'. Zweimal wird dazu wiederholt: 'und er hiess', 'und er nannte den Namen'. Meistens nimmt man an, dass der König (oder ein anderer) in diesem Augenblick den Säulen einen Namen gab, aber der hebräische Ausdruck gestattet auch zu übersetzen: 'den Namen nennen', im Sinne von 'den Namen aussprechen', den die Säulen in jenem Moment schon trugen, und den sie aus dem kanaanäischen Bereich übernommen hatten[29]. Allem Anschein nach hatten diese Namen eine kultische Bedeutung.

Im Ugaritischen gibt es einen Text (*KTU* 1.17, I, 25f.), — die Aqat-Legende — in dem der Gott Baʿal den Gott El um Nachkommenschaft für Danel bittet und um Kindersegen für ihn betet, wobei folgende Formel gebraucht wird: *ykn.bnh b bt. šrš. b qrb hklh*, '...dass er zeuge einen Sohn in seinem Haus, einen

---

[26] K. Rupprecht, *Der Tempel von Jerusalem. Gründung Salomos oder jebusitisches Erbe?*, Berlin usw., 1977 (*BZAW* 144).

[27] J. Wellhausen, *Prolegomena zur Geschichte Israels*[6], Berlin, 1905, 45f.

[28] Vgl. Johs. Pedersen, *Israel, its Life and Culture*, III-IV, London/Copenhagen, 1940, 243 und Anm. 2 (688f.).

[29] Hier sei noch die Ansicht von T.K. Cheyne, *Critica Biblica*, London, 1903/4 (=reprint Amsterdam, 1970), 324, erwähnt: 'The two pillars were, in fact, dedicated to the N.Arabian deity, sometimes called by the Israelites Jerahmeel and Ishmael'.

Spross in seinem Palast'[30]. Die Form *ykn* vom Verb *kn* oder *kwn* hält man öfter für eine Kurzform eines Wortes, das im Gemeinsemitischen im allgemeinen 'sein' bedeuten soll, aber das auch durch 'in das Sein rufen', 'zeugen', 'gründen' übersetzt werden kann[31]. Wie bekannt, ist Nachkommenschaft nicht nur für den König als individuelle Person, sondern vor allem auch für Land und Volk von grossem Nutzen. In der Erhaltung der Dynastie lebt auch die völkische Gemeinschaft weiter.

Wie oben bereits erwähnt, wird das Wort *boʿaz* oft in die Präposition b^e und das Wort *ʿz* zerlegt. *ʿz* braucht im Ugaritischen nicht nur Substantiv zu sein, sondern findet sich in dieser Sprache auch als Verb im Sinne von 'stark, kräftig sein'[32]. Öfter findet sich, etwa in *KTU* 1.6, VI, 17-20, der Ausdruck: *mt.ʿz.bʿl.ʿz*, 'Motu ist stark (potent), Baʿlu ist stark (potent)'[33]. In *KTU* 1.108, 21f. findet sich in einem lückenhaften Text, ...] *rpi.mlk ʿlm. b ʿz [rpi] m*lk.ʿlm. b ḏmrh*... M. Dietrich und O. Loretz übersetzen diese Worte: '[...]des Heilers, des ewigen Königs, durch die Kraft des Heilers, des ewigen Königs, durch seine Stärke...'[34]. In dem hymnenartigen Lied, in dem sich die angeführten Worte finden, haben wir es mit einer mit Gesang und Musik aufspielenden Gottheit zu tun, die Dietrich und Loretz als Baʿal *Rpu* bezeichnen, nachdem schon vorher viele Studien diesem 'ugaritischen Psalm' gewidmet waren[35]. Neuerdings hat J. Sapin sich mit diesem Text beschäftigt und ihn als ein 'rituel' bezeichnet, das 'vise à renforcer le pouvoir politique du roi d'Ugarit dans le cadre de son royaume en l'identifiant au pouvoir gouvernemental d'une divinité éminente laquelle est qualifiée de *rpu mlk ʿlm*'[36]. Er meint, dass das Ritual daraufhin ausgerichtet ist, 'où l'on place les statues de divinités, le roi...plaçant la statue de *Baal rpu*, puis une femme, la reine probablement ...plaçant celle d'Anat', und er fügt hier unmittelbar hinzu: 'En effet, la manipulation des statues cultuelles est toujours attribuée au roi dans les rituels qui l'évoquent'. Er ist wohl der Meinung, dass am Schluss der Tafel, auf der sich unsere Worte finden, 'un officiant confirme au roi d'Ugarit que ses voeux et souhaits seront accomplis 'grace au Guérisseur, le Roi éternel, par sa force

---

[30] Vgl. auch Z. 43f., und J.C.L. Gibson, *Canaanite Myths and Legends*, Edinburgh, 1978, 104f.

[31] Siehe J. Aistleitner, *Wörterbuch der ugaritischen Sprache*, Berlin, 1963, 151 (Nr. 1335); C.H. Gordon, *Ugaritic Textbook*, Rome, 1965, 410f., 418 (Nr. 1096 und 1213); vgl. weiter F.L. Benz, *Personal Names in the Phoenician and Punic Inscriptions*, Rome, 1972, 332; G. del Olmo Lete, *Mitos y Leyendas de Canaan segun la Tradicion de Ugarit*, Madrid, 1981, 566; und *HAL*, 443 (*pol*, 1^d).

[32] Aistleitner, a.a.O., 229f. (Nr. 2021); Gordon, a.a.O., 455 (Nr. 1835); Gibson, a.a.O., 154.

[33] Gibson, a.a.O., 80.

[34] M. Dietrich - O. Loretz, 'Baal *RPU* in KTU 1.108; 1.113 und nach 1.17 VI 25-33', *UF* 12 (1980), 174; vgl. J.C. de Moor, 'Studies in the New Alphabetic Texts from Ras Shamra I', *UF* 1 (1969), 175-179. Er fasst *ʿz* wie hebr. *ʿōz* im Sinne von 'protection'.

[35] Bibliographie bei Dietrich - Loretz, a.a.O., 171-179 in den Anmerkungen.

[36] J. Sapin, 'Quelques systèmes socio-politiques en Syrie au 2e millenaire avant J-C ... ', *UF* 15 (1983), 179.

(*'z*), sa vaillance (*dmr*) ...” usw. Der König jedoch beendet das Ritual mit dem Beten dieser Aufzählung der Regierungsqualitäten des ewigen Königs: ‘O Guérisseur de la Terre...que ta force, ta vaillance, ton pouvoir, ta décision, ton éclat, soient au milieu d’Ugarit pour la durée de Šapaš et de Yariḫ et les années favorables de El’[37]. Der Funktion, nicht der Natur nach ist der König fast mit Gottheiten identisch, meint Sapin: ‘la fonction sacralisante du sacerdoce sacrificiel’.

Auffallend ist es, dass in einem anderen Text, *KTU* 1.102, oft als ‘Götterliste’ bezeichnet[38], oder auch als Personenliste[39], einmal *'z b'l* (Z. 27) vorkommt. M. Dietrich - O. Loretz - J. Sanmartín sind der Meinung, dass die in Z. 15-28 sich findenden Worte Gebetsrufe sind, die als Götternamen verwendet wurden, ‘da sie wahrscheinlich zur Bezeichnung von Statuen der Gottheiten im Tempel während der Feiern gedient haben’[40]. Auf diese Weise würde sich auch erklären, warum sie im Onomastikon von Ugarit fehlen, und warum sie einer vorangehenden Götterliste zugefügt sind.

Betrachten wir diesen ugaritischen Gebrauch der Wörter *ykn* und *b'z*, so können wir uns des Eindrucks nicht erwehren, dass auch im vorisraelitischen Tempel in Jebus (Jerusalem) Rituale bei Säulen und Statuen stattgefunden haben, vom priesterlichen König begangen. Bei der einen Säule könnte er ein Gebet verrichtet haben für die Dynastie und Nachkommenschaft, bei der anderen ein Gebet für die göttliche Beschaffenheit seiner Regierung. Wie in Ugarit und anderen kanaanäisch-phönizischen Städten stehen solche Gebete auch in Jerusalem in Verbindung mit Fruchtbarkeit und Vegetation. Möglich wäre immerhin, dass die Säulen ursprünglich phallische Symbole waren, oder Repräsentanten der (agrikulturellen) Fruchtbarkeitsgötter. In 1 Kön. 7:40ff. wird erzählt, dass die Säulen nicht nur Kugelknäufe oben auf den Säulen hätten, und dazu zwei Geflechte zur Bekleidung der Knäufe, sondern dass auch 400 Granatäpfel an jedem Geflecht waren. Möglich ist, dass die Säulen als stilisierte Granatapfelbäume mehr auf israelitische Weise die Fruchtbarkeit symbolisierten[41], wobei die kanaanäischen Gebete dem israelitischen Kult angepasst wurden. Auffallend ist es, dass die Säulen, ebensowenig wie etwa ‘die eherne Schlange’, den ersten Tempel nicht überlebt haben. Zu deutlich war ihr kanaanäischer Ursprung. Dazu kommt, dass Salomo in der israelitischen Geschichte auch nicht als richtiger Jahweverehrer vermerkt wird. Auf jeden Fall ist beim Aufrichten der Säulen und der ‘Nennung’ der Namen durch

---

[37] Sapin, a.a.O., 180.

[38] M. Dietrich - O. Loretz - J. Sanmartín, ‘Die Götterliste RS 24.246 = UG.5, S. 594 Nr. 14’, *UF* 7 (1975), 545f.

[39] J.J. Stamm, ‘Erwägungen zu RS 24.246’, *UF* 11 (1979), 753-758.

[40] Dietrich - Loretz - Sanmartín, a.a.O., 546.

[41] F.J. Hoogewoud, a.a.O., 96 (s. oben, Anm. 21).

Salomo nicht an etwas ganz Neues zu denken. Salomo übernahm beim königlichen Tempel das Ritual seiner früheren kanaanäischen Kollegen: *ykn.bnh b bt. šrš. b qrb hklh* ..., und: *b ʿz yhwh mlk.ʿlm. b d̲mrh*... Seit alten Zeiten trugen diese Säulen darum diese Namen Jachin und Boaz, ohne dass die Namen auf sie geschrieben waren...

EXEGETISCHE UND RELIGIONSGESCHICHTLICHE STUDIE ZU PSALM 141:5d-7

von

BENEDIKT HARTMANN

J. Hausheer hat in seiner in der Zürcherbibel[1] erschienenen Übersetzung des Alten Testamentes für Ps. 141:5d-7 an Stelle einer Übersetzung folgende Fussnote vorgezogen: 'Der Schluss von Vers 5 und die Verse 6 und 7 sind unübersetzbar'. Ein Blick in die anderen Bibelübersetzungen, Psalmkommentare und Einzeluntersuchungen[2] zu unserer Stelle zeigen die Schwierigkeiten der Übersetzung und Interpretation des Übersetzten überdeutlich. Entweder kommt ein kaum zu verstehender Text heraus, oder man arbeitet mit Konjekturen, die vom ursprünglichen Text wenig übriglassen. Es ist also nicht besonders ermutigend, sich mit diesen drei Psalmversen zu beschäftigen, und doch möchte ich mein Glück auch versuchen, und zwar mit dem überlieferten Konsonantentext ohne jede Änderung. In einem ersten Teil wird mit allen zur Verfügung stehenden Mitteln eine sprachliche Erklärung versucht. Ein zweiter Teil soll die vorgeschlagene Übersetzung auf ihre inhaltliche Brauchbarkeit prüfen.

A. *Die sprachliche Durchleuchtung von Ps. 141:5d-7.*

1. Vers 5d:

kī ʿod ūtᵉfillāti bᵉrāʿōtēhäm.

Der Konsonantentext lautet: *ky ʿwd wtflty brʿwtyhm.* Vor allen Dingen haben die ersten drei Wörter Schwierigkeiten gemacht. Das *w* 'und' vor *tflty* ist schwer verständlich. Ich möchte den Worttrenner zwischen *w* und *tflty* machen und *w* mit *ʿwd* verbinden, also *ʿwdw* lesen und dies als Pi. eines Verbums *ʿwd* vokalisieren, also: *ʿiwwᵉdu.* Der normale Intensivstamm der Verba mediae *w/y* ist zwar das Polel; aber im AT kommen auch starke Formen dieser Verben vor, und zwar in jüngeren Texten unter Einfluss des Aramäischen[3]. Bislang

[1] Zwingli Verlag, Zürich, 1939 oder später.

[2] H. Junker, 'Einige Rätsel im Urtext der Psalmen', *Biblica* 30 (1949), 204-206; R. Tourney, 'Le Psaume 141', *VT* 9 (1959), 58-64.

[3] H. Bauer und P. Leander (= *BL*), *Historische Grammatik der hebräischen Sprache des Alten*

sind im Bhe. zwei Wurzeln *ʿwd* belegt: I *ʿwd* verwandt mit ar. *ʿwd* und II *wʿd* als Denominativ von *ʿēd* ‘Zeuge’[4]. *ʿwd* in Vers 5d verbinde ich mit ar. *ʿwḏ* ‘Zuflucht suchen’, das nach semitischen Lautgesetzen zu he. *ʿwz* in derselben Bedeutung wird und im AT häufig vorkommt[5], vergl. auch das dazu gehörige Nomen *ʿōz* ‘Zuflucht, Schutz’[6]. Im Aramäischen würden wir lautgesetzlich *ʿwd* erwarten, was ich allerdings nur in palmyrenischen Eigennamen finden kann: *ʿwdʾl*[7], *ʿwydlt*[8]. Ar. *ʿwḏ* heisst im I. ‘Schutz, Zuflucht suchen, bewahren, schützen’, II. ‘feien’. An Stelle von Sg. *tᵉfillātī* möchte ich Pl. *tᵉfillōtai* lesen. *Häm* bezieht sich wohl auf die *pōʿᵃlē ʾāwän* von Vers 4: ‘Menschen die Übles tun’ und präludiert auf Vers 9, wo der Beter um Schutz vor Übeltätern (*pōʿalē ʾāwän*) bittet: ‘Behüte mich vor der Schlinge, die sie mir gelegt, und vor den Fallstricken der Übeltäter’. Wir erhalten dann folgende Übersetzung von 5d:

Denn meine Gebete feien/schützen gegen ihre Bosheiten.

2. Vers 6:

nišmᵉṭu bīdē sälaʿ šōfᵉṭēhäm
wᵉšāmᵉʿū ʾamārai kī nāʿēmū.

Nišmᵉṭu ist ni. von *šmṭ* mit der Bedeutung ‘loslassen, freigeben, erlassen (Schuld, Darlehen)’. Ar. *smṭ* II und mhe. *šmṭ* pi. beziehen sich auf die Schuld (des Schuldners), also ‘Schuld erlassen, freisprechen’, evtl. ‘erlösen von der Schuld’.

Bīdē drückt wie sonst oft im AT das Mittel aus: ‘durch’[9], hier mit einer Sache, sonst mit Personen.

Šōfᵉṭēhäm: falls es ein Pl. ist, könnte es Subjekt zum Verbum sein. Die Stellung rät, es als Genetiv zu *sälaʿ* aufzufassen. Den Pl. möchte ich als pluralis majestatis verstehen[10]. Er wird hie und da verwendet, wenn sich das Wort auf Gott bezieht, z.B. *ʿōsai* ‘mein Schöpfer’ Hi. 35:10. In Vers 6 also: ‘ihr Richter’ = Gott.

Sälaʿ hat in diesem Vers die grössten Schwierigkeiten verursacht. Es wird oft getilgt oder nach Vers 7 verschoben. Die Bedeutung ‘Fels, Stein’ passt auch

---

Testamentes, Halle, 1922 (= Neudruck Hildesheim, 1962), 394: In späterer Zeit treten, wahrscheinlich unter dem Einfluss des Aramäischen, Neubildungen nach dem starken Verbum ein.

[4] L. Koehler-W. Baumgartner, *Hebräisches und aramäisches Lexikon zum Alten Testament* (= *HAL*), 3. Auflage neubearbeitet, Leiden, 1967ff, 751.

[5] *HAL*, 753.

[6] *HAL*, 762.

[7] J.K. Stark, *Personal Names in Palmyrene Inscriptions*, Oxford, 1971, 104; cf. bhe: *ʿUzziʾel.*

[8] *Id.*, 105.

[9] *HAL*, 101, nr. 16; cf. auch pun. (*DISO*, 104), ug. und kan. *ba-di-u* (*EA* 245,35).

[10] P. Joüon, *Grammaire de l'hébreu biblique*, Rome, 1947, 416f.

gar nicht in den Zusammenhang. Nun bieten aber, wohl von der Bedeutung 'Stein'[11] ausgehend, ja., nab.[12] und sy.[13] die sekundäre Bedeutung: 'Geld'. Im Mhe. wird eine tyrische Münze *säla'* genannt. ich möchte das Wort hier sogar als 'Lösegeld' auffassen.

'amārai: Das Suffix *y* der 1. Person sing. macht deutlich Schwierigkeiten. Jod als Possessivsuffix kann aber im Phönizisch-Punischen und zwar am Nomen im Sing. und im Pl. auch die 3. Person sg. masc. ausdrücken: z.B. *mb'y* 'sein Eingang'[14]. Also in Vers 6: 'seine Worte'. Diese Interpretation wäre auch für Sach. 12:10 möglich: 'Sie werden hinschauen auf ihn, (*'elai*), den sie durchbohrt haben'[15].

Kī fasse ich wie in Gen. 3:19 etc. als Relativum auf, also: 'die lieblich sind — die lieblichen'.

Zur Satzsyntax ist zu sagen, dass ich in Vers 6 eine konditionale Periode sehe. Die übliche Reihenfolge ist: Bedingung — Bedingtes. In einigen Fällen ist aber auch das Umgekehrte belegt, z.B. Gen. 18:28[16].

Die Übersetzung von Vers 6 lautet also:

Sie werden durch das (Löse-)Geld ihres Richters freigesprochen werden, wenn sie auf seine lieblichen Worte hören.

3. Vers 7:

k^{e}mō pōlēaḥ ūbōqēa' bā'āräṣ
nifz^{e}rū 'aṣāmēnu l^{e}fī š^{e}'ōl

K^{e}mō wird in Gen. 9:15 als temporale Konjunktion aufgefasst, und zwar im Gegensatz zum viel häufigeren *k^{e}* an dieser Stelle ohne Infinitiv: *ūk^{e}mō haššaḥḥar 'ālā wajjā'īsū hammal'ākīm b^{e}loṭ* 'Sobald die Morgenröte heraufkam, trieben die Engel Lot zur Eile an'. So muss *k^{e}mō* auch an unserer Stelle übersetzt werden.

Pōlēaḥ ūbōqēa' sind Synonyme. *Plḥ* ar. 'spalten', mhe. ja. sy. 'graben'[17]. *Bq'* 'spalten'[18]. Das Subjekt ist wohl eher der Richter/Gott als ein unbekannter Jemand.

B^{e} steht in jüngeren Texten manchmal als nota accusativi, um die Verbindung des Verbums mit dem Objekt deutlicher zu machen[19], z.B. *pā'ar b^{e}fä*,

---

[11] Cf. schweizerdeutsch: Stai (Stein) = Franken.
[12] *DISO*, 193.
[13] C. Brockelmann, *Lexicon Syriacum*, Halle a. S., 1928, 477f.
[14] J. Friedrich, *Phönizisch-punische Grammatik*, Roma, 1951, 102f.
[15] M.J. Mulder, *Kanaänitische Goden in het Oude Testament*, Den Haag, 1965, 82.
[16] Joüon, *op. cit.*, 517f.
[17] *HAL*, 878.
[18] *HAL*, 143.
[19] *HAL*, 101, nr. 20.

'den Mund aufsperren' Hi. 16:10. So auch in unserem Vers 7: 'die Erde spalten'.

'äräṣ hier wohl Erdkruste als Trenner zwischen der Erdoberfläche und dem Erdinnern, wo sich das Totenreich befindet.

Nifzᵉrū: Dieses Wort, der Form nach ein Ni. (aber siehe auch unten) von *pzr* hat die grössten Schwierigkeiten dieses Verses verursacht. Es wird durchgängig von *pzr*, ar. *baḏ/zara*, 'säen, ausstreuen, zerstreuen', so auch ja. mhe. *pzr* abgeleitet[20]. Zu dieser Wurzel gehören, wie ich sehe, alle ausser zwei Stellen. Daneben gibt es aber auch ein zweites ar. *bazara*, das 'keimen (Pflanze)' bedeutet und ein *fzr*, das im II. Stamm im syr. ar. 'ausweiden, ausnehmen (ein Tier)' bedeutet[21]. Als Grundbedeutung können wir für II. *pzr* 'herauskommen' sekundär evtl. 'auferstehen' ansetzen. In unserem Vers 7 wird wohl Ni. Synonym zu Qal sein[22]. Oder haben wir es mit einer Imperfektbildung wie im Ostaramäischen zu tun, wo die 3. m. sg. und pl. nicht mit *y* als Präfixkonsonant gebildet wird, sondern mit *n*[23]. In diesem Fall könnten wir auch Qal vokalisieren.

An der 2. Stelle kommt das Verb im Pi. vor, nämlich Ps. 53:6, und zwar in kausativer Bedeutung[24]. Die beiden Psalmen 14 und 53 sind bis auf die Verse 14:5f. und 53:6 identisch. Die *kī*-Sätze können kausativ oder adversativ aufgefasst werden. Sie sind meiner Meinung nach deutlich positiv.

Ps. 14:5f.:

šām pāḥadū pāḥad	*kī 'älōhīm bᵉdōr ṣaddīq*
'aṣat 'ānī tābīšū	*kī jhwh maḥsēhū*

Maḥsēhū wird meist mit dem Substantiv *maḥsä* erklärt. Besser wäre es, das Wort als Partizip Hi. zu erklären von *ḥāsā* mit der Bedeutung 'Zuflucht finden lassen/gewähren'. Wir können also wie folgt übersetzen: 'Da trifft sie gewaltiger Schrecken; aber Gott ist dagegen beim Geschlecht der Gerechten. Ihr wollt zu Schanden machen den Trost der Elenden; aber Jahwä dagegen gewährt ihm (dem Elenden als *ṣaddīq* gesehen) Zuflucht'.

---

[20] *HAL*, 870, und bhe. *bzr* mit derselben Bedeutung, *HAL*, 114, akk. *pazāru* 'sich verbergen', W. von Soden, *Akkadisches Handwörterbuch* (= *AHw*.), Wiesbaden, 1965ff., 852.

[21] A. Barthélemy-H. Fleisch, *Dictionnaire arabe-français, Dialectes de Syrie*, Paris, 1950ff., 606. Die Passage in den El-Amarna-Briefen 169,30: *i-pa-a(z)-ru-nim* bei J.A. Knudtzon (*Die El-Amarna-Tafeln*, Leipzig, 1915, I, 674f.) noch so ergänzt und übersetzt: 'hervorschleichen', wird jetzt zu *ipaṭṭarunim* ergänzt, cf. *AHw*, 850, und *The Assyrian Dictionary*, Chicago, 1980, N 6. Diese Stelle ist also für uns nicht mehr zu gebrauchen. Für den Hinweis danke ich meinem Schüler C. Koelewijn.

[22] G. Bergsträsser, *Hebräische Grammatik*, 2. Teil: Verbum, Leipzig, 1929, 90c.

[23] C. Brockelmann, *Grundriss der vergleichenden Grammatik der semitischen Sprachen*, I Laut- und Formenlehre, Berlin, 1908, 565.

[24] Zum Pi. als Kausativ zu Nif., cf. Bergsträsser, *o.c.*, 93f.

Ps. 53:6:

šām pāḥadū pāḥad	*ki 'ălōhīm pizzar 'aṣmōt ḥōnāk*
häbīšōtā	*kī 'ălōhīm m^{e}'āsām*

Pizzar ist Pi. von II. *pzr* 'herauskommen/auferstehen lassen'. Für *ḥōnāk* lese ich *ḥōnīm*, Part. Qal. von I. *ḥānā* 'sich beugen, demütig sein'. *K* und *m* sind in der phönizischen Schrift sehr ähnlich und können darum leicht verwechselt werden. *M^{e}'āsām* wird durchgängig von *m's*, 'verwerfen' abgeleitet. Ich schlage vor, die Form als Part. Pi. von der Wurzel *'s'/w/y* aufzufassen: Ja., sam., sy., md. *'s'* Pa. 'heilen', ar. *'sw/y* I. 'pflegen (Wunde)'. Dass das Suffix oft direkt an den 2. Radikal angefügt wird, ist bekannt[25]. Die Übersetzung kann dann wie folgt lauten: 'Da trifft sie gewaltiger Schrecken; aber dagegen lässt Gott die Gebeine der Demütigen (aus den Gräbern) hervorkommen/auferstehen. Sie werden zu Schanden; dagegen heilt sie (die Demütigen) Gott'.

'aṣāmēnū muss wohl gerade im Hinblick auf Ps. 53:6, wo *'äṣām* ebenfalls mit *pzr* verbunden wird, wörtlich übersetzt werden.

Le muss wohl als Synonym zu *min* 'aus' aufgefasst werden[26], wie auch oft im Ugaritischen: Gordon 68,12: *grš jm lkseh* 'vertreibe Jam von seinem Thron'.

Die vorgeschlagene Übersetzung von Vers 7 lautet also:

> Sobald er die Erd(kruste) aufbricht und spaltet,
> werden unsere Gebeine aus dem Mund des Totenreiches hervorkommen/auferstehen.

B. *Die sachliche Interpretation von Ps. 141:6 und 7.*

I. Wir müssen uns zunächst mit dem religionsgeschichtlichen Hintergrund der beiden Verse auseinandersetzen. Welche religionsgeschichtlichen Vorstellungen haben den Dichter von Ps. 141:6f. inspiriert?

1. a) In Vers 6 sind wir in einer Gerichtssituation. Es ist von Freisprechen die Rede. Ein Richter wird genannt, der zugleich Gott ist. Dadurch und im Hinblick auf die in Vers 7 erwähnte Auferstehung werden wir es wohl mit einem Totengericht, evtl. mit dem Gericht am jüngsten Tag, zu tun haben. Falls das zutrifft, müssen wir den religionsgeschichtlichen Hintergrund entweder in Ägypten oder in Persien suchen.

Ägypten liefert die älteste Erwähnung eines Totengerichtes, das in dem

---

[25] *BL*, 588.

[26] *HAL*, 483, nr. 5.

Augenblick notwendig wird, als im allgemeinen 'Demokratisierungsprozess' nach dem Ende des alten Reiches auch die Religion erfasst wurde und so jedem Ägypter, und nicht mehr nur wie bis anhin dem Gottkönig allein, ein Leben nach dem Tod mit Auferstehung und Himmelfahrt möglich machte. In diesem Augenblick ist die Notwendigkeit eines Totengerichtes unter Leitung von Osiris entstanden, das darüber zu wachen hat, dass nur Gerechte von der Möglichkeit eines ewigen Lebens Gebrauch machen können. Die abgewiesenen Ungerechten, die nicht nach den Normen von Maat gelebt haben, werden von einem krokodilköpfigen Mischwesen verschlungen und aufgefressen. Diejenigen aber, die nach dem Willen der Maat gelebt haben, leben entweder bei Osiris im Reich der Seligen, das im Westen gelegen ist, oder fahren mit Re in seinem Boot zum Himmel[27].

Die andere alttestamentliche Umweltreligion, die ein Totengericht kennt, ist die persische. Sie kennt zunächst direkt nach dem Tode und dann am Ende der Tage ein Gericht, das sich mit dem Problem 'gut und böse' befasst. In jenem kommen die Gerechten sicher über die breite Brücke in ein Paradies, die Ungerechten aber fallen von der schmalen Brücke in eine düstere Schlucht. Am Ende der Tage müssen alle zu einem Gottesurteil antreten und dabei einen Metallfluss überqueren. Die Gerechten, d.h. die nach Aša gelebt haben, passieren den Fluss ohne weiteres. Die Glaubensfeindlichen, Gottlosen werden in ihm geläutert und kommen aber auch an das jenseitige Ufer und werden als Geläuterte zusammen mit den Gerechten des ewigen Lebens teilhaftig. Dies ist ein schönes Beispiel für eine ἀποκατάστασις (τῶν) πάντων, wobei πάντων wirklich alle bedeutet, die Gläubigen und Gottlosen[28]. Sowohl im ägyptischen, als auch im persischen Totengericht sitzt ein Gott dem Gerichtsakt vor.

b) Wenn wir die ältesten Quellen für Lösegeld aufsuchen, müssen wir in den babylonischen Texten suchen. Im jüngeren, semitischen Text von der Unterweltsfahrt der Göttin von Uruk, Ištar[29], hören wir, dass Ištar die Unterwelt, d.h. das Totenreich, verlassen darf und von einem Begleiter nach der Oberwelt zurückgebracht wird. Dieser Begleiter bekommt folgenden Auftrag:

'Falls sie (Ištar) dir das Lösegeld nicht bezahlt, so bringe sie wieder zurück.'[30]

Im älteren, sumerischen Text wird von der Göttin ein Stellvertreter gefordert. Das Wort für Lösegeld: *napṭiru/ipṭiru*[31] ist gleich dem neutestamentli-

[27] S. Morenz, *Aegyptische Religion*, Stuttgart, 1960, 134ff., 138ff., 214, 220.

[28] G. Widengren, *Iranische Geisteswelt, von den Anfängen bis zum Islam*, Baden-Baden, 1961, 169-180, 215-221.

[29] Cf. J.B. Pritchard: *Ancient Near Eastern Texts relating to the Old Testament* (= *ANET*), Princeton, ²1955, 106f.

[30] *ANET*, 109.

[31] *AHw*, 385.

chen λύτρον von *paṭāru*, resp. λύω 'lösen' abgeleitet. In Ps. 141 dagegen ist die Bedeutung Lösegeld von Geld abgeleitet. Sachlich bedeutet dies aber keinen Unterschied.

2. a) In Ištars Unterweltsfahrt wird auch das Thema von Vers 7, die Auferstehung, erwähnt, allerdings mit einem anderen Bild geschildert:

Pförtner, öffne dein Tor, auf dass ich eintrete.
Wenn du das Tor nicht öffnest und ich nicht hineinkomme,
zerschlage ich die Tür, zerbreche ich die Riegel,
zerschlage ich die Schwelle, hebe aus die Türen,
bringe ich hinauf die Toten, dass sie die Lebenden fressen,
dass die Toten zahlreicher seien als die Lebenden.[32]

Dieses Bild vom Totenreich als Stadt mit Toren und Türen ist dem AT auch nicht unbekannt, z.B. Ps. 9:14 *mrmmy mšʿry mwt*, 'der du mich aus den Pforten des Todes erhebst'. Es ist auch das geläufige Bild, das wir in christlichen Auferstehungsbeschreibungen und Malereien finden. Ich möchte nur das grandiose Bild aus dem prächtigen Hymnus des Syrers Romanus aus dem 5. Jahrhundert erwähnen. Der gefesselte Hades gibt seinen Leuten folgenden Befehl:

Torwächter, eilt herbei und seht wie ich Gewalt leide.
Schnellt herbei, ihr, schliesst die ehernen Tore und bewacht sie,
schiebt die eisernen Riegel vor die Tore
und lasst keinen von denen, die er auferweckt hat,
aus seinem Grabmal heraus.[33]

Auf Auferstehungsikonen steht Christus auf den aufgebrochenen Toren des Totenreiches, Schlüssel, Angeln und Riegel liegen zerbrochen zu seinen Füssen.

b) Ps. 141 beschreibt das Bild anders, nämlich als Maul des Totenreiches. Diese Vorstellung geht letztlich wohl auf ugaritische Texte zurück. Im Streit zwischen Baal und Mot ist die Rede von der Einladung Mots an Baal. Dann wird in grandioser Weise der Riesenrachen Mots beschrieben:

Eine Lippe hat er an der Erde, die andere am Himmel,
die Zunge reicht ihm bis zu den Sternen.
Es möge Baal durch seinen Mund in sein Inneres niedersteigen.[34]

---

[32] *ANET*, 107.
[33] H. Hunger, *Reich der neuen Mitte*, Graz, 1965, 218, cf. 80.
[34] *ANET*, 138.

Dem Bild vom Höllenrachen, dem die Ungerechten ausgeliefert sind, sind wir oben beim ägyptischen Totengericht begegnet. In Ugarit ist Mot aber wertfrei, also nicht die Hölle. Die Unterscheidung zwischen Himmel und Hölle ist in Ugarit noch nicht bekannt. Das Bild vom Höllenrachen aber findet sich auch auf christlichen Darstellungen vom Jüngsten Gericht. Die Verdammten verschwinden im Höllenrachen.

c) Der Vorstellung, dass die Toten durch das Aufbrechen oder Spalten der Erdkruste befreit werden, begegnen wir entweder im Bild vom Aufbrechen der Gräber zur Auferstehung oder in Totenbeschwörungen. In der Beschwörung des Geistes Samuels durch die Hexe von Endor bittet Saul: 'Wahrsage mir doch durch den Totengeist und bringe mir den herauf, den ich dir nenne' (1 Sam. 28:8). Und in Vers 13 heisst es: 'Das Weib sprach zu Saul: Einen Geist sehe ich aus der Erde heraufsteigen'. Noch deutlicher wird bei zwei anderen Totenbeschwörungen gesagt, dass der Tote nur dem Totenreich entsteigen kann, wenn in der Erde ein Loch gemacht wird.

1) Gilgamesch will mit seinem Freund Enkidu reden, um zu hören, wie es in der Unterwelt aussieht. Er trägt den Wunsch Ea vor:

Sobald als Vater Ea dies vernommen,
hub an zu Nergal er, dem Kampfeshelden, zu reden:
O, Nergal, Held im Kampf, höre mich,
tu auf ein Loch nun in der Unterwelt
dass ihr entsteigen kann Enkidus Geist
und seinem Bruder künd' des Hades Ordnung ...
Es hörte Nergal, Held im Kampf, auf Ea
tat gleich ein Loch auf in der Unterwelt.
Alsbald entstieg Enkidus Totengeist
dem Hades einem Windhauch gleich
und sie umarmten sich und setzten sich zusammen.[35]

2) Der 11. Gesang der Odyssee ist der Totenbeschwörung gewidmet. Odysseus beschwört die Schatten der Toten und unterhält sich mit ihnen.

Ich aber zog indessen mein scharfes Schwert vom Schenkel,
warf eine Grube dann aus, eine Elle in Länge und Breite.
Schüttete rund um sie eine Spende für alle die Toten ...[36]
Dann rief ich die Völker der Toten mit Bitten und Beten,

---

[35] Gilgamesch-Epos XII, 78ff., *ANET*, 98; H. Schmökel, *Das Gilgamesch-Epos*, Stuttgart, 1966, 118f. Für unsere Frage ist es gleichgültig, ob Enkidu als Geist oder körperlich erschienen ist.

[36] 24-26.

packte die Tiere und schnitt ihnen über der Grube den Hals ab.
Dunkel dampfend rann da ihr Blut. Aus dem Düster indessen
Kamen in Scharen die Seelen der lang schon erstorbenen Toten.[37]

Beide Texte zeigen deutlich, dass, nachdem ein Loch in die Erde gegraben ist, die Toten aufsteigen können.

d) Man könnte sich noch fragen, ob die ausdrückliche Erwähnung der Knochen sowohl in Ps. 141:7 als auch in Ps. 53:6 im Zusammenhang mit der Auferstehung eine Rolle spiele. Wenn ja, dann sehe ich dazu nur in persischen Texten Parallelen. Am Anfang des eschatologischen Geschehens heisst es:

Zuerst wird Sošjans (der Erlöser) die Gebeine des Gayōmart aufrütteln, dann jene von Mišye und Mišyānē und dann wird er diejenigen der übrigen Menschen aufrütteln. Während 57 Jahren wird Sošjans die Toten aufrütteln, alle Menschen auferstehen lassen sowohl die Gerechten wie die Gottlosen.[38]

II. Nach diesen mehr detaillierten Fragen möchte ich noch einige allgemeine Bemerkungen zu den Versen 6 und 7 von Ps. 141 machen:

a) Das Lösegeld, das als Voraussetzung für die Rückkehr aus dem Totenreich im babylonischen Text von Seiten Ištars, das heisst der Göttin, die den Tod überwinden will, entrichtet werden muss[39] (wie übrigens im sumerischen Text der Stellvertreter[40], der von dem, der das Totenreich verlassen will, gestellt werden muss), wird im Psalm vom Richter selbst bezahlt, also als Gnadenakt Gottes von ihm aufgebracht. Wir haben im Psalm zum ersten Mal die später im Neuen Testament auftretende Verbindung von Gott — Richter — Lösegeld — freisprechen.

b) Der babylonische Text erzählt uns in grellen Farben von der schrecklichen, gefürchteten Möglichkeit, dass die Toten unter den Lebenden erscheinen, d.h. das Totenreich verlassen könnten.

Ich bringe hinauf die Toten, dass sie die Lebenden fressen,
dass die Toten zahlreicher seien als die Lebenden.[41]

---

[37] 34-37.
[38] G. Widengren (s. Anm. 28), 217f.
[39] *ANET*, 109.
[40] S.N. Kramer, *Proceedings of the American Philosophical Society*, vol. 107, 1963, 493, Linie 27.
[41] *ANET*, 107.

Ištar droht damit und kann die Drohung wahr machen. Dies passt ganz zum anastasiphoben Charakter der babylonischen Religion. Demgegenüber wird in unserem Psalm, die Auferstehung, d.h. das Verlassen des Totenreiches durch seine Bewohner als eine Wohltat Gottes gepriesen und erhofft. Es stehen sich also zwei diametral entgegengesetzte Vorstellungen von Auferstehung und Tod gegenüber. Der Psalmist gebraucht die alten Bilder, um etwas ganz Neues auszudrücken.

c) Ps. 141:7 und 53:6 liefern zwei neue Stellen zum Auferstehungsgedanken im AT, was besonders willkommen ist, da die Quellen des AT in dieser Hinsicht nur sehr spärlich fliessen.

d) Wer ist in Ps. 141:6 mit 'sie' gemeint, d.h. wer ist Subjekt von *nišmeṭū* ? Die einzige Handhabe im übrigen Psalm sind die *pōʿalē ʾāwän* in Vers 4 und 9. Die Übeltäter sind die einzigen Personen in der Mehrzahl, die als Subjekt in Frage kommen. Falls diese Verbindung und Interpretation richtig ist, bringt Vers 6 auch für Übeltäter eine Verheissung. Wir wissen so auch, wofür das Lösegeld gebraucht wird. Es soll ihre Schulden und Sünden tilgen und sie vor Gericht, das doch wohl als das Endgericht aufgefasst werden muss, von Schuld freisprechen und reinigen, allerdings unter der Bedingung, dass die Übeltäter das Wort Gottes hören. Dieses Hören muss dann wohl im Sinne von Gehorchen verstanden werden. Wenn dieser Vers so aufgefasst und interpretiert werden muss, haben wir in diesem Vers einen Beleg für eine ἀποκατάστασις (τῶν) πάντων[42], wobei allerdings (τῶν) πάντων nur alle Gläubigen betrifft. Also nur die Sünden der Gläubigen werden durch das Lösegeld getilgt. Im folgenden Vers muss das 'wir' den Psalmist, d.h. 'ich' in den Versen 1-5 und 8-10 und die Übeltäter (*pōʿalē ʾāwän*) meinen, die beide die Auferstehungsverheissung bekommen. Das passt gut zu den *rᵉšāʿīm* in Vers 10, die verloren sind. Sie sind eben, was mit *rāšāʿ* gemeint ist, Gottlose, die nicht auf Gottes Wort hören im Gegensatz zum *ṣaddīq*[43].

III. Damit sind wir bei der Frage nach Zeit und Ort angelangt, wann und wo unsere zwei Verse verfasst wurden. Zur Lösung dieser Fragen scheinen mir drei Beobachtungen wichtig zu sein.

1. Die Gedanken in Vers 6, besonders die Vorstellung von der Rettung aller, der Sündlosen und der Sünder, wohl mit der Einschränkung, dass sie nur für Gläubige gilt (dies Letztere im Gegensatz zur persischen Auffassung, wie wir

[42] Cf. persische Religion, oben B.I.1.a.

[43] Cf. L. Koehler, *Theologie des Alten Testamentes*, Tübingen, 1936, 153-160.

sie oben kennengelernt haben), scheinen mir gerade wegen des Läuterungsgedankens doch eher in das persische Schema als in das ägyptische zu passen.

2. Die Verarbeitung von typisch an Syrien haftenden Bildern, z.B. den Mund der Hölle, machen es doch wahrscheinlich, dass der Verfasser mit der altkanaanäischen Tradition wohl vertraut war und natürlich auch mit dem babylonischen Kulturkreis (vergl. das Lösegeld).

3. Das Sprachliche, nämlich die Aramaismen, weist auf eine späte Abfassung. Die Zeit kann darum leichter angegeben werden als der Ort. Die beiden Verse müssen doch wohl aus sprachlichen und inhaltlichen Gründen spät angesetzt werden, in der persischen oder gar hellenistischen Periode. Der Ort ist schwierig zu bestimmen. Es könnte Babylonien sein.

JAKOB UND MOSE: HOSEA 12:3-14 ALS EINHEITLICHER TEXT

von

Hartmut Gese

Der Text Hos. 12:3-14 ist besonders interessant durch die hier vorliegende Anspielung auf die Jakobtradition. Dass dabei Hosea in einem negativen Sinn auf Jakob Bezug nimmt, kann heute als *communis opinio* gelten[1]. Ausgehend von dem Gegensatz von V. 13 und V. 14, von Jakob, der aus Aram flieht, wo er um seines Weibes willen Knecht ist und hütet (*šamar*), und Mose, der Israel aus Ägypten heraufführt und bewahrt (*nišmar*), und unter dem Gesichtspunkt einer Anklage (*rib*) gemäss dem einleitenden Vers 3 werden die z.T. dunklen Anspielungen Hoseas auf Jakob in verurteilendem Sinn verstanden. Es sollte aber zunächst als methodisches Prinzip gelten, dass bei Anspielungen auf die Jakobtradition, die wegen ihrer Undeutlichkeit und der Kürze ihrer Formulierung schwer zu beurteilen sind, eher ein Verständnis vorauszusetzen ist, das mit der Tradition geht als umgekehrt, weil eine Entgegensetzung zu dem bei Hoseas Zeitgenossen üblichen Verständnis von ihm klar zum Ausdruck gebracht werden müsste, wenn er verstanden sein will.

---

[1] Sie findet sich seit J. Wellhausen, *Die kleinen Propheten*, Berlin, 1892, in immer stärkerem Masse in der protestantischen Forschung bis hin zum neueste Kommentar von J. Jeremias, *Hosea*, ATD 24,1, 1983, in katholischer Forschung erst in neuerer Zeit. Nach dem Versuch von P.R. Ackroyd, 'Hosea and Jacob', *VT* 13 (1963), 245-259, eine positive Rezeption der Jakobtradition bei Hosea vorauszusetzen, folgte wieder eine Gegenreaktion bei E. Jacob, 'Der Prophet Hosea und die Geschichte', *EvTh* 24 (1964), 281-290: 286, W. Rudolph, *Hosea*, KAT 13,1, 1966, 220-235, E.M. Good, 'Hosea and the Jacob Tradition', *VT* 6 (1966), 137-151, C. van Leeuwen, *Hosea*, Nijkerk, 1968, 237-251, J.L. Mays, *Hosea*, London, 1969, 161-171, R.B. Coote, 'Hosea XII', *VT* 21 (1971), 389-402: 392ff., L. Ruppert, 'Herkunft und Bedeutung der Jakob-Tradition bei Hosea', *Bibl* 52 (1971), 488-504, J. Vollmer, *Geschichtliche Rückblicke und Motive in der Prophetie des Amos, Hosea und Jesaja*, Berlin, 1971, 105-115, R. Kümpel, *Die Berufung Israels. Ein Beitrag zur Theologie des Hosea*, Diss. Bonn, 1973, 61-70, F. Diedrich, *Die Anspielungen auf die Jakob-Tradition in Hosea 12,1-13,3*, Würzburg, 1977, R. Vuilleumier, 'Les Traditions d'Israel et la Liberté du Prophète: Osée', *RHPR* 59 (1979), 491-498: 496, F.I. Andersen-D.N. Freedman, *Hosea*, Anchor Bible 24, 1980, 593-623, L.M. Eslinger, 'Hosea 12:5a and Genesis 32:29: A Study in Inner Biblical Exegesis', *JSOT* 18 (1980), 91-99, H. Utzschneider, *Hosea, Prophet vor dem Ende*, Freiburg-Göttingen, 1980, 186-211, A. Deissler, *Zwölf Propheten, Hosea, Joel, Amos*, Neue Echter-Bibel, 1981, 53-56. Auf meine Anregungen hin hat H.-D. Neef in seiner Tübinger Dissertation *Die Heilstraditionen Israels in der Verkündigung des Propheten Hosea*, 1984, 24-36 zu Hos. 12:4f.13 eine positive Aufnahme der Jakobtradition bei Hosea verteidigt.

Dass dieses zeitgenössische Verständnis Jakobs negativ gewesen sei, wird man grundsätzlich ausschliessen dürfen. Es wird sich nicht stark unterschieden haben von dem, was uns der vorpriesterschriftliche Bestand in Gen. 25:21-34; 27:1-45; 28:10-33:20; 35:1-7 und einigen weiteren, hier nicht interessierenden Stoffen bietet. Diese vorpriesterschriftliche Jakobtradition in Gen. 25-35 wird kompositionell zusammengehalten und inhaltlich bestimmt von der Zwillingsbrüderschaft zu Esau und der damit gegebenen Konkurrenz[2]. Die Geschichte von der Geburt Esaus und Jakobs 25:21-28 enthält kein negatives Jakobbild. Das JHWH-*Orakel* verheisst, dass der Ältere dem Jüngeren dienstbar sein wird, und dem entspricht das *Omen*, dass bei der Geburt Jakob die Ferse (*ʿaqeb*) Esaus festhält, worauf sich auch die Etymologie des Namens Jakob bezieht. V. 28 zeigt den Anschluss an c. 27, da dort die Liebe des Vaters für das Wildbret und die Mutterliebe für Jakob vorausgesetzt wird. Die nicht weiter explizierte Begründung für V. 28b, die Liebe Rebekkas zu Jakob, ist natürlich das ihr gegebene JHWH-Orakel. Ist 25:21-28 nur ein später Vorbau für c. 27? Wo immer der Inhalt von c. 27 erzählt worden ist, ist eine Geburtsgeschichte Voraussetzung. 25:29ff. steht unter dem Verdacht, ein späterer Zuwachs zu c. 27 zu sein; aber 27:36 setzt wenigstens für die jetzige Gestalt von c. 27 dieses Stück voraus, darüber hinaus wird die kulturtypologische Interpretation des Verhältnisses Esaus und Jakobs, die c. 27 zugrunde liegt, nur hier expliziert. In die Geschichte des Verkaufs der Erstgeburt werden gern negative Züge eingetragen (erpresserische Ausnützung der Notlage Esaus); dass der Erzähler anders denkt, lehrt V. 34b, und er macht es auch in der Zeichnung des unbeherrschten (V. 30) und unweisen (V. 32), eben eines der Verantwortung als Erstgeborenen nicht gerecht werdenden Esau deutlich. Bei der Beurteilung von c. 27 wird gern übersehen, dass List in bestimmter Weise eine antike Tugend darstellt und dass im übrigen die Initiative ganz bei Rebekka liegt, die das erste (V. 6ff.) und letzte Wort (V. 42ff.) führt, die Jakob befiehlt (V. 8 ist nicht Angebot, sondern dringender Befehl) und folgerichtig

[2] Die Anwendung des weitverbreiteten Erzählmotivs der feindlichen Brüder in den Erzvätergeschichten ist seltsam. Hier kommt es heilsgeschichtlich dermassen auf die legitime Erbfolge an, dass eine sekundäre Infragestellung aus erzählmotivischen Gründen unwahrscheinlich ist. Auf dem Hintergrund der allein durch Isaak im Gegensatz zu Ismael oder zum Hausknecht Elieser vertretenen heilgeschichtlichen Erbnachfolge Abrahams sollte eine nur spielerisch-erzählerische Problematisierung der heilsgeschichtlichen Erbnachfolge von Jakob durch einen eigentlich erstgeborenen Zwilling Esau nicht möglich sein. Hinzu kommt, dass überall in den Geschichten die Gleichung Esau-Edom vorausgesetzt ist (25:23, 25, 30; 27:16, 40 usw.), Esau also unbeschadet der kulturtypologischen Deutung Jäger-Hirt/Bauer geschichtlich reale Gestalt ist. Es ist sehr zu erwägen, ob nicht gerade ein historischer Zusammenhang voredomitischer Bevölkerungsgruppen mit vorisraelitischen den historischen Kern dieser Überlieferung von der Zwillingsbrüderschaft darstellt, die dann erzählmotivisch kulturtypologisch gedeutet worden ist. Nach der heute üblichen überlieferungsgeschichtlichen Auffassung verhält es sich gerade umgekehrt: Esau ist, da mit der Gesamtkomposition verhaftet und erzählmotivisch erklärbar, eine nur sekundäre Figur, die dann auch nur sekundär mit Edom (warum gerade mit ihm?) identifiziert worden ist; aber weder das eine, noch das andere ist, wie gesagt, wahrscheinlich zu machen.

auch alle Verantwortung auf sich nimmt (V. 13). Das JHWH-Orakel ist eben hier wie in 25:28b unausgesprochene Voraussetzung. Dass der Erzähler dagegen Esau negativ zeichnet, und zwar nicht nur als unweise (er bittet um denselben Segen, dann um den übrigen und schliesslich um einen anderen, V. 34-38), sondern auch als böse (V. 41), ist deutlich. Am Ende steht der trügerisch gesegnete Jakob als Flüchtling da, der bei dem betrügerischen Laban Knechtsdienste tun muss, doch steht er unter dem Schutze des sich bei Bethel offenbarenden verheissenden Gottes. Nach der Flucht und Trennung von Laban und vor der Begegnung mit Esau kommt es im Ringkampf mit dem Engel in Pnuel endlich zu der göttlichen wahren Segnung Jakobs, der nun Israel heisst. Dem freundlichen Esau sagt Jakob: 'Wenn ich Gnade in deinen Augen gefunden habe, dann nimm mein Geschenk aus meiner Hand an; denn dafür habe ich dein Angesicht gesehen, wie man das Angesicht Gottes (*p^ene ʾ^älohim*)[3] sieht, und du hattest Wohlgefallen an mir. Nimm doch mein Segensgeschenk (*berakā*) ...!' (33:10f.). Über Sichem und seiner Heiligtumsbegründung führt schliesslich der Weg nach Bethel zurück, den dieser Erzvater Israels zur Erlangung des wahren Erstgeburtssegens gegangen ist. Wir müssen annehmen, dass ungefähr dies oder doch ein Grundbestand dessen die für Hoseas Zeitgenossen vorauszusetzende Jakobtradition ist. Eine negative Zeichnung Jakobs wird darin ebensowenig wie in Gen. 25-35 zu finden sein. Gibt Hosea diesem Traditionsstoff eine ganz neue Deutung?

Wir wollen unentschieden lassen, ob die *rib*-Einleitung V. 3 zum ursprünglichen Hoseatext gehört oder redaktionell ist. Die Erwähnung von Juda in V. 3a spricht für die judäische aktualisierende Redaktion, und da V. 3b Wiederaufnahme der Formulierung von 4:9 ist, bleibt die Echtheit umstritten, und es ist nicht geraten, durch die Konjektur Israel für Juda einen unanstössigen Text herzustellen[4]. Wie dem auch sei, spricht *rib* durchaus nicht gegen eine positive Beurteilung Jakobs in den zunächst folgenden Versen; denn bei einer *historischen* Argumentation — und die liegt hier zweifellos vor — müsste vom Abfall Israels gesprochen werden unter der Voraussetzung der Erwählung und der göttlichen Heilsbegründung durch sie, d.h. von Jakob als dem Anfang der Erwählung müsste positiv gesprochen werden (vgl. z.B. Jer. 2:1-13 mit dem positiven Einsatz V. 1-3). Dass der Erwählte selbst schon von Mutterleib an eine fragwürdige negative Figur ist, müsste die *rib*-Argumentation geradezu *ad absurdum* führen. Abgesehen davon wird bei Hosea sonst der Abfall mit dem Übergang Israels in das Kulturland definiert (13:6) — wir werden unten sehen, dass das auch hier (V. 8f.) zutrifft. Von V. 3 her ist darum eher an eine positive Aufnahme der Jakobtradition zu denken.

---

[3] Vgl. auch das Wortspiel mit *panim* (*quinquies*) in 32:21f. unmittelbar vor der Pnuelgeschichte.

[4] Dazu zuletzt G.I. Emmerson, *Hosea, an Israelite Prophet in Judean Perspective*, Sheffield, 1984, 63ff.

Der erste Abschnitt V. 4f.7[5] (V. 4: 3+3, V. 5a: 3+3, V. 5b: 3+3, V. 7: 3+3+3) bezieht sich inhaltlich in V. 4a auf die Geburtsgeschichte Jakobs, in V. 4b.5a auf die Pnuelgeschichte, in V. 5b.7 auf die Bethelgeschichte in knappsten Formulierungen. Zunächst werden in V. 4 im Parallelismus nebeneinander und mit 'im Mutterleib' und 'und in seiner Manneskraft' gegeneinander gesetzt zwei zentrale Formulierungen der Geburts- und Pnuelüberlieferung, die zugleich die beiden Namen Jakob und Israel etymologisch begründen. Bei *sarā 'ät *ᵃ*lohim* (vgl. Gen. 32:29b) ist das unbestritten[6], in V. 4a kann man nicht bestreiten, dass es sich um die Geburtsgeschichte handeln muss. Dann aber kann *'aqăb* nur 'an die Ferse packen', nicht aber im übertragenen Sinn 'hintergehen, betrügen' bedeuten; denn 1. passt 'hintergehen' nicht. Jakob wird eben nicht als erster, sondern als zweiter geboren, kann also Esau nicht hintergangen haben. Wäre nur der Versuch des Hintergehens gemeint, wäre das Imperfekt gefordert. 2. sagt das eindeutig die Tradition, die in Gen. 25:26 vom Packen an die Ferse (*bă'ᵃqeb*) Esaus spricht. 3. wird zwar in Gen. 27:36 von Esau eine neue Namensdeutung gegeben, in der *'qb* als 'betrügen' verstanden wird, aber diese Etymologie ist deutlich spielerisch (man vergleiche das weitere Wortspiel *bᵉkorati laqăḥ / laqăḥ birkati*) und hat nichts mit der Geburt zu tun, auf die hier in Hos. 12:4a ausdrücklich Bezug genommen wird[7].

Der Vers 4 stellt also die beiden Situationen am Anfang und am Höhepunkt des Lebens Jakobs zusammen, die sich auf die Namengebung Jakob und Israel beziehen. Die zweite, bedeutendere der endgültigen göttlichen Segensverleihung beim Einzug in das Land wird in V. 5a weiter ausgeführt. Mit einer Anadiplose wird das Verbum *sr(h)* am Anfang aufgenommen[8] und präpositionell[9] statt des wegen der Israel-Etymologie in V. 4b notwendigen *'ᵃlohim*

---

[5] Dass am Ende von V. 5 mit LXX *'immo* (oder *'immännu*, vgl. J. Jeremias, a.a.O., 148 Anm. 6 und die dort angegebene Literatur) zu lesen und V. 6 Glosse ist, die die jerusalemische Gottesbezeichnung einfügt, ist mit Recht weithin anerkannt (z.B. H.W. Wolff, *Dodekapropheton 1 Hosea*, BK 14,1, 1961, 266, 276, K. Elliger in *BHS*, 1970, z.St.; J. Jeremias, a.a.O., 148, 154; anders W. Rudolph, a.a.O., 229 Anm. 19 ohne eigentliche Begründung).

[6] Deswegen ist auch hier notwendigerweise *'ᵃlohim* gebraucht, und erst in V. 5 ist dann konkret vom *măl'ak* die Rede.

[7] Dass in Jer. 9:3 auf Jakob mit ebenderselben Etymologie wie in Gen. 27:36 verwiesen wird, lässt sich durchaus nicht wahrscheinlich machen, da die nach dem Gesetz des Achtergewichts steigernde Parallele *rakil jähᵃlok* keine Anspielung enthält; sollte eine solche bei *'aqob jă'qob* beabsichtigt sein, müsste man zumindest die umgekehrte Stellung erwarten. Man darf nicht einfach bei einem normalen Gebrauch des Verbums *'qb* mitten im Satz eine Anspielung auf Jakob heraushören; vgl. P.R. Ackroyd, a.a.O., 254.

[8] Man sollte also ein *wăjjisăr* erwarten; die die Wurzel *swr* (das Hi. von *srr* kommt von der Bedeutung her nicht in Frage) voraussetzende Punktation *wăjjasăr* (*wajjasăr* in *BHS* ist fehlerhaft) könnte, wenn sie nicht einfach eine Nebenform zu *sr(h)* darstellt (so Kimchi z.St.), der Versuch sein, das Verbum *srr* mit dieser Nebenform einzuführen: 'Er zeigte sich als Fürst gegenüber dem Engel und hielt stand' (so Targum und dann Ibn Esra z.St.). Da aber an der Anadiplose nicht zu zweifeln ist, kann es sich bei *wjsr* nur um ein 'Er kämpfte' handeln.

[9] *sr(h)* muss mit einer Präposition konstruiert werden, wofür Gen. 32:29 *'im*, Hos. 12:4 *'et* ('mit') gebraucht wird. Das im Sinne von *'äl* gebrauchte *'äl* (Baumgartner, *HAL*³ s.v. *'äl* 3.) ist

jetzt konkret *măl'ak* angeschlossen, während das *wăjjukal* ganz Gen. 32:29b entspricht: 'Er kämpfte gegenüber einem Engel und hielt stand'. Und dieser reagierenden Handlung Jakobs in der ersten Vershälfte von V. 5a entspricht in der parallelen zweiten die agierende Handlung: 'Er weinte und flehte ihn an'[10]. Da bisher die Darstellung der Überlieferung in Gen. 32:23ff. entspricht, ist auch für das letztere von ihr auszugehen: Dem Ruf 'Ich lasse dich nicht, du segnest mich denn!' (Gen. 32:27), der von einem Flehen ja nicht weit entfernt ist, muss diese Aussage entsprechen. Hos. 12:5a beschreibt also die eigentliche Tat Jakobs in der Pnuelszene, dem Höhepunkt des Jakoblebens unmittelbar vor dem Eintritt in das gelobte Land als der gesegnete Erbe: er kämpft aufs standhafteste gegenüber der absoluten Macht, der Transzendenz[11], und er erfleht aufs intensivste den Segen. Bei der Interpretation von V. 5a ist also weder von einem konjizierten Text, noch von der Annahme einer Glossierung oder einer anderen Hypothese auszugehen[12], und ebensowenig ergibt sich, dass Hosea in seiner Darstellung Jakobs die Tradition auf den Kopf stellt. Eine solche Umkehrung ihrer Aussage in das Gegenteil müsste vielmehr von ihm deutlich formuliert sein.

Wenn nun in V. 5b.7 nach dem Anfang und Höhepunkt des Lebens Jakobs abschliessend der Zentralpunkt der Betheloffenbarung und -verheissung zur Sprache kommt[13], so bestätigt der kaum zu bestreitende positive Inhalt dieser Verse die bisherige positive Jakobdarstellung. Während V. 5b von dem Geschehen der 'Findung' Gottes in Bethel (vgl. neben dem J-Text Gen. 28:16 auch den E-Text Gen. 28:17) und der Redeoffenbarung spricht, zitiert V. 7 in einem Tristich V. 7a.bα.bβ die Gottesrede: 'Du wirst (darfst) mit deinem Gott

---

dabei durchaus passend, wie ein Vergleich mit *nilḥăm* 'kämpfen' zeigt, wo neben *bᵉ* sich wie bei *sr(h)* sowohl der Gebrauch von *'im* und *'et* ('mit') findet, als auch der von *'ăl* = *'ăl* (vgl. Jer. 21:2 *'ăl*, Jer. 1:19; 15:20 *'ăl*).

[10] Dass das *lo* wegen V. 4a sich auf Esau beziehe, wie W.L. Holladay, 'Chiasmus, the Key to Hosea 12:3-6', *VT* 16 (1966), 53-64: 56ff. will, heisst einem angenommenen Chiasmus zuviel zumuten. Noch weiter hergeholt ist die Vermutung von E.M. Good, a.a.O., 144, hier wäre auf eine Tradition von der Tränenеiche Gen. 35:8 angespielt.

[11] Der der Pnuelgeschichte zugrundeliegende religionsgeschichtliche Stoff wird zum Schaden des Verständnisses der Tradition im allgemeinen unrichtig bewertet. Die bekannte kanaanäische Hypostasenbildung 'Angesicht von ...' kann sich nur auf höchste Gotteserscheinungen beziehen. Die hier gemeinte Hypostase der El-Epiphanie meint nicht eine niedere Lokalgottheit, sondern El selbst. Über dessen Lokalisierung an den (Ur-)Wassern und seine Jenseitigkeit im Verhältnis zum kosmischen Tag, sein Wesen vor allem Sein vgl. *RM* 10,2, 96ff. Jakob begegnet in der Nacht und im Jabbokwasser von Pnuel an der Grenze vor dem Eintritt in das verheissene Land dem Absoluten, dem Jenseitsraum der 'heiligen Hinterwelt', dem er standhält und so als Erstgeburtssegensträger legitimiert werden kann. Das 'Angesicht Els', die El-Epiphanie, ist kein Nachtgespenst oder Flussdämon.

[12] Kein noch so gedrängter Überblick über diese so zahlreich vertretenen Konjekturen, die die Last des Beweises tragen müssen, kann hier gegeben werden, vgl. J. Jeremias, a.a.O., 154 Anm. 15.

[13] *bet'el* bzw. *(wᵉ)šam* werden betont vorangestellt; die Imperf. *jimsa'ännu* und *jᵉdăbber* werden daher präterital zu übersetzen sein.

zurückkehren[14], bewahre Huld und Recht und harre auf deinen Gott beständig!' Die mit der Bezeichnung des Vätergottes am Anfang und am Ende wohlkomponierte Rede umfasst einerseits die Verheissung der Rückkehr aus dem Laban-Exil in Haran und damit die Verwirklichung der Verheissungserbfolge, andererseits das im Parallelismus entfaltete Gebot treuen Lebens im Verhältnis zu Mensch und Gott. In dieser Verheissung und Lebensordnungsoffenbarung eine tadelnde Zurückweisung des Erzvaters sehen zu wollen — und das gegen die ältere Tradition dieses Stoffes —, sollte schon wegen der bei beidem, Rückkehr und Lebensordnung, betonten Verbindung mit dem Vätergott[15] unmöglich sein; vielmehr kommt der Jakobabschnitt V. 4f.7 mit der verheissenden und heilvolles Leben eröffnenden Rede von Bethel zu einem volltönenden Abschluss.

Allerdings bildet die Rede von der dem Vater Jakob zuteilgewordenen Erbverheissung mit dem Lebensgebot von *ḥäsäd-mišpaṭ* und Gottesverbundenheit auch die Voraussetzung für die kritische Behandlung der Verwirklichung dieser Erwählung im Lande Kanaans im nächsten Abschnitt V. 8f., und diese Voraussetzung ist auch der Anlass, das *ḥäsäd-mišpaṭ*-Gebot besonders hervorzuheben (V. 8f.: 3 Verse in Weiterführung des Sechsermetrums, aber in der Struktur 2+2+2 mit Parallelen zwischen den letzten Zweiern in V. 8 und 9a). Gegenübergestellt wird Kanaan, der Trug und Bedrückung liebende Händler, der Repräsentant des vor- (und ausser-)israelitischen Lebens im Land (V. 8) und Ephraim als Repräsentant Nordisraels (V. 9). Es sollte kein Zweifel daran bestehen, dass in V. 8 tatsächlich Kanaan gemeint ist gerade im Gegensatz zu Jakob und seiner Verheissung. Einer Verwechslung von beidem widersetzt sich nicht nur die ausdrückliche Bezeichnung Kanaan (im Gegensatz zu Jakob und Israel V. 4), sondern auch die Argumentation gegenüber Ephraim in V. 9[16]: Gegenüber Trug und Bedrückung des Kanaanäers behauptet Ephraim, der wie der Kanaanäer reich geworden ist (*ʿšr*), Vermögen (*ʾon*) erlangt hat, dass aller dieser von ihm erworbene Besitz (*jᵉgiʿim*) 'ihm keine Schuld einbringt, die Sünde wäre'[17]. In der aus der hebräischen Poesie genugsam bekannten Stilform der 'dekuvrierenden Rede' (vgl. in den Psalmen die Zitate der Feindesrede an den Höhepunkten der Feindesbeschreibung)

---

[14] Die Subjektsinversion *ʾättā* muss syntaktische Bedeutung haben. Man könnte zunächst an eine Subordination denken: 'Kehrst du nun zurück mit deinem Gott, so ...'; aber man beachte die Regel der Kenntlichmachung des Einsatzes direkter Rede durch eine solche Subjektsinversion, was hier sicherlich vorliegt.

[15] Zur Rückkehr aus dem Laban-Exil mit Hilfe des Gottes von Bethel vgl. besonders Gen. 31:3; 32:10 (J); 31:13 und auch 48:15f. (E).

[16] Auf die wenn auch nur scheinbare Unterscheidung von Kanaan und Ephraim in V. 8f. geht H.W. Wolff, a.a.O., 277f., nicht ein. J. Jeremias, a.a.O., 148, macht aus V. 8 von vornherein einen Vergleichssatz.

[17] Die Inversion *kol jᵉgiʿäj* bringt Subordination zum Ausdruck, wörtlich: '... ich habe Vermögen gefunden, wobei mein Erwerb mir nicht Schuld gefunden hat, die Sünde wäre.'

zeigt sich Israel im Besitz der Väterverheissung als ein nur vermeintlich sich von Kanaan unterscheidender Reicher. Im Gegensatz zu Kanaan meint Israel für seinen Reichtum heilsgeschichtliche Legitimität zu haben, so dass nicht *'awon*, was als *ḥeṭ'* zu rechnen wäre, an diesem Reichtum klebt. Im Grunde aber — und das will die Zusammenstellung von V. 8f. sagen — ist Ephraim nichts anderes als ein Kanaanäer geworden. Das stilistisch auffällig gedoppelte *mṣ'* in V. 9 bezogen auf materiellen Besitz steht im Gegensatz zu *mṣ'* mit dem Objekt Gott bei Jakob in V. 5b. Von der göttlichen Lebensordnung des *ḥäsäd-mišpaṭ* (V. 7) ist in dieser Prahlrede Ephraims nichts mehr zu spüren. V. 8f. schliesst, wenn auch unvermittelt-kontrastartig, so doch vortrefflich an V. 4f.7 an.

Die zweite Hälfte unseres Textes Hos. 12:3-14 kommt nach dem Rückbezug auf die Erzväterverheissung in der ersten Hälfte auf das heilsgeschichtliche Zentrum, die JHWH-Offenbarung im Zusammenhang mit dem Auszugsgeschehen, also auf die Exodus- und Sinaitradition in V. 10f. zu sprechen (in der zweiten Hälfte geht der Sechser der ersten Hälfte in den Fünfer 3+2 oder in seine erweiterte Form 3+3+2 über: V. 10a: 3+2, V. 10b: 3+2, V. 11: 3+3+2[?])[18]. Die berühmte JHWH-Selbstvorstellungsformel V. 10a, in 13:4a in bezeichnendem Kontext 13:4f. identisch wiederholt und in geringfügig erweiterter Form als Dekalogpräambel bekannt (Ex. 20:2, Dtn. 5:6), braucht in ihrer Bedeutung als Zusammenfassung der Sinai- (und Exodus-)Tradition nicht erläutert zu werden, das Auffällige von Hos. 12:10 ist, dass V. 10b nicht weiter auf das ursprüngliche Sinaigeschehen eingeht, sondern auf die für Hosea so bedeutende zukünftige Wiederholung des Geschehens, die Neubegründung Israels im Zusammenhang mit dem Gericht am jetzigen Israel. Dieses Gericht wird also vorausgesetzt, was vorzüglich zu der in V. 8f. enthaltenen Anklage der Kanaanisierung Israels passt und wieder die unvermittelt-kontrastartige Kompositionsart zeigt. Während V. 10b von dem zukünftigen Begegnungsgeschehen im heiligen Lager entsprechend dem Sinaivorgang spricht, geht V. 11 auf die prophetisch vermittelte Wortoffenbarung ein[19]. Im Anschluss an V. 10b ist es das einfachste, V. 11 auch auf dieses zukünftige Heil reichen und intensiven prophetischen Wortgeschehens zu beziehen, das dann die ewige Verbundenheit Israels mit seinem Gott sichert — man beachte die betonte Fülle der Gesichte. Die Perspektive könnte aber auch

[18] Das Metrum 3+3+2 findet sich zweifellos in V. 12aβb, V. 13 und V. 14, und wegen des unten erwiesenen Zusammenhangs von V. 10-14 wäre demnach dieses Metrum auch in V. 11 vorauszusetzen, wobei einem Zweier in V. 11b allerdings der Artikel vor *nᵉbi'im* entgegensteht (*ubᵉjäd nᵉbi'im* könnte einhebig gelesen werden); ist er wegen des *hännᵉbi'im* V. 11aα in V. 11b erst sekundär oder lässt sich V. 11b mit dem Artikel als hypermetrischer Zweier halten?

[19] In V. 11aα ist *'äl* = *'äl*, vgl. V. 5; in V. 11aβ zeigt die Inversion Subordination an: 'wobei ich die (prophetische) Schauung vielgemacht habe'; in V. 11b ist die Punktation von W. Rudolph (a.a.O., 223) *'äddämmä* 'ich stelle mich selbst dar' sehr erwägenswert, wenn auch nicht unbedingt nötig (*'ᵃdämmä* 'ich rede abbildhaft').

ins Grundsätzliche erweitert sein und, das endgültige Heilsgeschehen, die erneuerte Sinaioffenbarung V. 10b begründend, die kontinuierliche *successio Mosaica* (vgl. Dtn. 18:15ff.) im Auge haben; das lässt sich nicht scharf unterscheiden.

Wird in V. 10f. auf die mosaisch-prophetische Offenbarung verwiesen, so doch deutlich unter Voraussetzung des Gerichts, das der Verfallszustand, wie der in V. 8f. gezeichnete, forderte. V. 12 — der Vers darf auf keinen Fall, wie üblich aus dem Zusammenhang herausgerissen werden — weist diese Gerichtsnotwendigkeit nach:

Wenn Gilead Unheil ist,
sind *sie* nichts als Nichtigkeit geworden. (3+2)
In Gilgal haben sie Stiere geopfert,
aber auch *ihre* Altäre sind wie Steinhaufen
an den Feldackerfurchen. (3+3+2)

Gilead wird die Bezeichnung des Ostjordanlandes sein[20]; 'sie' im Gegensatz dazu also das Westjordanland, das in keiner Weise sich besser verhält. Der Beweis wird mit einem falschen Gilgalkult Gileads geführt. Wir erfahren darüber im Alten Testament nur etwas in der späten Gestalt der Überlieferung von Jos. 22:10ff., die deutlich der P-Tradition entstammt. Danach hatten die ostjordanischen Stämme in Gilgal einen besonderen Altar errichtet, der als kultischer Abfall von JHWH, bzw. als Abfall vom Kult Israels betrachtet wurde und den heiligen Krieg gegen diese Stämme auszulösen drohte. Die feierliche Erklärung der Ostjordanier, dieser Altar sei kein Altar *in actu*, sondern nur ein Zeichen (Zeuge) für ihre Zugehörigkeit zur JHWH-Religion, beschwichtigt die Westjordanier. Zweifellos ist die nur symbolische Funktion des Gileadaltars in Gilgal eine Umdeutung der traditionsgeschichtlichen Spätform von Jos. 22:10ff., die zur Zeit des Josua keinen Abfall Israels kennt. Dass dem ursprünglich nicht so war, zeigt in Jos. 22:10ff. noch die deutlich zu spürende kritische Situation einer drohenden innerisraelitischen Auseinandersetzung mit Gilead. Wir können also mit Sicherheit erschliessen, dass es einmal einen besonderen gileaditischen JHWH-Kult in Gilgal, konkret am gileaditischen Altar von Gilgal aufzuweisen, gegeben hat, der vom westlichen Hauptteil Israels mit grösstem Missfallen betrachtet wurde. Darauf bezieht sich Hos.

[20] Die hier vorliegende Paronomasie *gil'ad, gilgal, gallim* ist auffällig. Von da aus könnte sich nahelegen, dass mit Gilead jenes östliche Grenzheiligtum gemeint ist, von dem Gen. 31:45ff. die Rede ist (vgl. *găl* in V. 46-48, 51f.). Da aber dies in 5:1 unter dem Namen Mizpa erscheint (vgl. Gen. 31:49) — das Tertium von Tabor (Dtn. 33:19) und Sittim (Num. 25) und dem gileaditischen Mizpa ist, dass es sich um Grenzheiligtümer handelt, an denen Israeliten in Fremdkulte mit Ausländern hineingezogen werden, mit Mizpa wird also in 5:1 ebendies gileaditische Mizpa gemeint sein —, wäre hier der Name Gilead dafür nicht zu erwarten.

12:12aβb, das in derselben Struktur wie V. 12aα ('wenn [auch] Gilead ..., so nicht weniger / erst recht das westjordanische Israel...') besagt, dass das westjordanische Israel (Ephraim) mit der Masse seiner Altäre, die wie Steinhaufen an den Ackerrändern sind, die Landgabe nicht weniger entweiht haben als Gilead mit seinem Gilgalaltar. V. 12 ist Anklage und Gerichtswort in einem in der deutlich zu greifenden Situation nach Abtrennung der Provinz Gilead 732 v. Chr., dem Verlust der ostjordanischen Landgabe: Das westjordanische Kernland (Ephraim) ist nicht besser, d.h. ihm wird in Bälde das gleiche Gericht, der Verlust der Landgabe, drohen.

Wie in der ersten Hälfte in V. 8f. das *ethische* Fehlverhalten Ephraims im Lande des Jakoberbes angegriffen wird, so in der zweiten Hälfte in V. 12 das *kultische* Fehlverhalten Ephraims gegenüber der Landgabe, wodurch der Verlust unausweichlich wird. Aber im Gegensatz zur Landgabe der Verheissung an Jakob (V. 4f. und besonders V. 7) führt die mosaisch-prophetische Gottesoffenbarung weiter (V. 10f.), nach Verlust des Landes wird die Offenbarung im heiligen Lager der Gottesbegegnung empfangen. Die Moseoffenbarung als die Selbstoffenbarung Gottes ist mehr als die Landverheissung Jakobs; sie ist transzendent zu der verwirkten Geschichte Israels im Land.

Eben dies wird im letzten, dritten Teil der zweiten Hälfte, dem zusammenfassenden Abschluss des Ganzen, zum Ausdruck gebracht in der Gegenüberstellung von Jakob und Mose (Metrum 3+3+2 in V. 13 und V. 14[21]). Nichts Negatives wird über Jakob gesagt; denn dass er vor Esau in das Aramgefild floh (nichts anderes meint *wăjjibrăḥ*, vgl. Gen. 27:43) und dass er um Lea-Rahel diente (vgl. zu *wăjjăʿabod* Gen. 29:20, 30; 30:29), d.h. dass er Hütedienste tun musste (vgl. zu *šamar* Gen. 30:31) ist nur Beschreibung des Jakoblebens zwischen Bethel und Pnuel. Es ist nichts Verwerfliches, diese Zeit des knechtischen Hütedienstes eines nur verborgenen Erstgeborenen, diese Zeit der Begründung der israelitischen Stämme in der Ehe mit Lea und Rahel, sondern sie steht im Gegenteil unter der Führung des Bethelgottes (vgl. V. 7a). Die Eisegesen in den Text von V. 13, dass mit der Flucht eine Flucht vor Gott und mit dem Hütedienst ein kanaanäischer Sexualkult gemeint sei, sind das verzweifelte Ergebnis der vorgefassten Meinung, Hosea könne über Jakob nur verurteilend reden. Aber um wieviel grösser[22] ist das, was Mose, der Prophet (bis, vgl. V. 11), der Mittler der Selbstoffenbarung Gottes, oder vielmehr, wie der Text deutlich herauskehrt, JHWH selbst durch den Propheten tut: Israel wird aus der knechtischen Existenz geführt und selbst behütet. Und so hoch die Moseoffenbarung über der Jakobverheissung steht, so können wir fort-

[21] V. 13f. kann nicht, wie J. Vollmer, a.a.O., 110, will, weil prosaisch, für sekundär erklärt werden.

[22] Diese Perspektive von V. 14 gegenüber V. 13 — und sie ist wohl hauptsächlich der Anlass für die Annahme eines negativen Jakobverständnisses in V. 4-7 — kommt bei P.R. Ackroyd, a.a.O., zu kurz (ebenso bei H.-D. Neef, a.a.O., 39-42).

fahren, wird auch Israels Errettung aus dem Gericht im neuen Exodus über den Verlust der Gabe des Jakoblandes hinausführen.

V. 13f. bindet am Ende die beiden Hälften V. 4ff. und V. 10ff. zusammen. Uns tat sich eine klare mit Kontrasten arbeitende Komposition auf von jeweils zwei positiven Stücken V. 4f.7 (Jakob) und V. 10f. (Mose und seine prophetischen Nachfolger) und zwei negativen Stücken V. 8f. (die ethische Sünde des reich gewordenen Israel) und V. 12 (seine kultische Sünde, die zum Verlust des Jakoblandes führen muss), während V. 13f. die Summe zieht und die zwei heilsgeschichtlichen Ereignisse des Väterdienstes und der prophetischen Moseoffenbarung in ihrem Gegensatz nebeneinanderstellt[23]. Beide Hälften V. 4-9 und V. 10-14 umfassen jeweils sieben poetische Verse, die erste im Sechsermetrum (mit Erweiterung zum Neuner), die zweite im Fünfermetrum (mit Erweiterung zum 3+Fünfer). Es ist üblich, die Komposition von Hos. 12:3-14 in verschiedene Stücke zu zerreissen und bestenfalls einen komplizierten traditionsgeschichtlichen Prozess des Zusammenwachsens zu rekonstruieren. Auch diese Hypothesen erscheinen als unnötig. Es liegt vielmehr eine einheitliche Komposition vor, die unter dem Eindruck der katastrophalen Ereignisse von 732 v. Chr. stehend, eine umfassende Perspektive der Offenbarungsgeschichte enthält.

---

[23] Zu dem Versuch, V. 13f. Hosea abzusprechen, vgl. H.-D. Neef, a.a.O., 41f. Dazu ist auch die Annahme eines Midrasch (Midraschvorform) in Hos. 12:7, 13f. bei I. Willi-Plein, *Vorformen der Schriftexegese innerhalb des Alten Testaments*, Berlin, 1971, 215-217, (zu J. Vollmer s.o. Anm. 21) zu ziehen.

ISA. 56:9-57:13 — AN EXAMPLE OF THE ISAIANIC LEGACY OF TRITO-ISAIAH*

by

W.A.M. Beuken

On the question if it is right to assume a Third Isaiah (TI), and on questions connected therewith, such as what kind of character his authorship might possess, and with which chapter the prophecies of TI might begin, little light has been shed lately. And yet extensive and often excellent studies have been published about the whole of Isa. 56-66, especially about the composition and the *Überlieferungsgeschichte* of this collection of oracles[1]. Maybe the research must orientate itself more on the relation of Ch. 56-66 to the entire book of Isaiah. In any case the latest studies about the redactional history of the First Isaiah in connection with the book itself have proved to be productive for a renewed interpretation of Isa. 1-39[2].

In this article we endeavour to make a similar inquiry into TI. In the space allocated to us we can do no more than study one single text unit, i.e. 56:9-57:13. As we cannot isolate this passage from the first text unit of this 'prophet', to wit 56:1-8, we hope that this study will show something about the way in which TI links up with the heritage of his two predecessors in the book, the First Isaiah (FI) and the Second Isaiah (SI). When we speak of TI, we mean the final redaction of Isa. 56-66, so that questions of literary criticism are not dealt with. The results of this research remain upright, whichever redactional history one accepts. But neither do they plead against a long process of coming into being. We found the motive for this study in Hugo

* With thanks to Mrs. W. Quarles van Ufford (Amsterdam) for the translation of this article into English.

[1] C. Westermann, *Das Buch Jesaja. Kap. 40-66* (ATD 19), Göttingen, 1966. K. Pauritsch, *Die neue Gemeinde: Gott sammelt Ausgestossene und Arme (Jesaia 56-66)* (AnBib 47), Rome, 1971. P.-E. Bonnard, *Le Second Isaie, son disciple et leurs éditeurs. Isaie 40-66* (EtB), Paris, 1972. P.D. Hanson, *The Dawn of Apocalyptic*, Philadelphia, 1975. J. Vermeylen, *Du prophète Isaie à l'Apocalyptique*, Tome II, (EtB), Paris, 1978.

[2] P.R. Ackroyd, 'Isaiah I-XII: Presentation of a Prophet', in: *Congress Volume Göttingen* (VT.S XXIX), Leiden, 1978, 16-47. id., 'Isaiah 36-39: Structure and Function', in: *Von Kanaan bis Kerala* (Festschrift J.P.M. van der Ploeg), (AOAT 211), Neukirchen, 1982, 3-21. H. Wildberger, *Jesaja. 3. Teilband* (BK.AT X/3), Neukirchen, 1982, Kap. II: Die Entstehung von Jesaja I, 1529-1576. Cf. the studies which they deal with and on which they build further.

Odeberg's 'Trito-Isaiah', a book which is in danger of being forgotten, more is the pity[3]. For all the passages of TI the author gives a 'table of affinities', on which he also elaborates. Painstakenly verse after verse and word after word is indicated, where elsewhere a similar term or expression occurs, divided over the following rows: Trito-Isaiah, Deutero-Isaiah, Proto-Isaiah, Jeremiah, Ezekiel, Ezra, Nehemiah, Deuteronomium and *alia*. Odeberg sorts out the mass of material that he has collected, only in a literary-historical way (later than the supposed author of the bible-book in question) and according to contents (another or opposite meaning). For us these categories are hardly useful any more. What we miss is a sorting of the parallels as to character of relationship and function. Does TI quote, does he allude to other texts or does he simply use common idiom expressions which are proper to a certain *Sitz-im-Leben* or belong to a certain theme?

It is not our intention to give this classification ourselves, not even for the chosen fragment 56:9-57:13. We think that such an undertaking only succeeds when, beforehand, we get a better insight into the contextual background of the passage(s) in question. For, on closer examination, the number of parallels with Jeremiah and Ezekiel are no less important for our passage than the similarities with FI and SI[4]. Of course the exile is a traditio-historical frame which creates relationship between texts we find in different books of the Bible. And yet one may assume that the book of Isaiah forms the primary context for whichever passage in this book. The research of the latter years has proved the fruitfulness of this supposition. One has been able to indicate, within the book of Isaiah, connections between divergent texts and between texts far removed from one another. The surmise arises that a most ingenious fabrication binds together the prophecies of this book[5].

Thus this article will be a study of Isa. 56:9-57:13 against the background of the book of Isaiah. In recent literature it is no longer disputed that this passage is a unity. The question is rather: what kind of unity is this?[6] Terms

---

[3] H. Odeberg, *Trito-Isaiah (Isaiah 56-66). A Literary and Linguistic Analysis* (UUA 1931, Teologi 1), Uppsala, 1931.

[4] Odeberg, o.c., 62-67, 94.

[5] R. Lack, *La Symbolique du Livre d'Isaie. Essai sur l'image littéraire comme élément de structuration* (AnBib 59), Rome, 1973. W. Brueggemann, 'Unity and Dynamic in the Isaiah Tradition', *JSOT* 29 (1984), 89-107. R. Rendtorff, 'Zur Komposition des Buches Jesaja', *VT* 34 (1984), 295-320.

[6] Pauritsch (o.c., 51-66) has defended the unity of Isa. 56:9-57:13. Hanson (o.c., 186-202) has followed him therein. A. Schoors, *Jesaja* (BOT IX), Roermond, 1972, 339) speaks of a section consisting of originally loose units without a clear editorial connection, directed, however, against both the leaders and the people. Bonnard (o.c., 353) considers 56:9-57:21 as 'un assemblage ingénieux de trois morceaux (56:9-57:2; 57:3-13; 57:14-21), dont chacun se termine par une finale formant antithèse avec le développement précédent, et qui sont soudés de telle manière, que leur rapprochement fasse ressortir leurs contrastes'.

as 'a prophetic liturgy'[7], 'a kerygmatic unity'[8] and 'a unified composition, resulting from the organic growth from 56:9-57:2 to the larger unit'[9] lack the accuracy that characterizes the present-day research with its meticulous methods of prosody, structuralism and stylistics. The result of this study will give occasion to suppose that the unity of the passage is determined precisely by the fact that, as a whole, it is a commentary on Isa. 55, the conclusion of SI. As the preceding passage, 56:1-8, has the same intention, we cannot overlook this opening text of TI either.

I *The opening motif of the Third Isaiah: 'The Holy Mountain'.*

It causes astonishment that the commentaries do not attach any importance to, even do not notice the fact that the second passage of TI (56:9-57:13) is connected with the first (56:1-8) by the concept 'my holy mountain' (56:7; 57:13: *har qodšī*). The places where one meets this expression are similar also: at the end of the promises of salvation (56:8 is a rather independent maxim[10]). There is only a difference as far as the parallel word is concerned: respectively 'my house of prayer' and 'the land' (*bēt tᵉfillātī* and *'ereṣ*). The fact that one has not recognized this concept as connecting motif, may be the result of the circumstance that many people consider 56:1-8 as being of a later date[11] or see vs. 3-7 as secondary[12], while others reckon the passage as belonging, parly or completely, to SI[13]. As far as we know, Alonso Schökel was the first scholar who noticed this connection between 56:7 and 57:13; we see this in a chapter about the metaphor of the mountains in the book of Isaiah, in his fundamental study about Hebrew poetry[14]. In Isa. 1-39 'the mountain' appears to have various metaphorical values, but the mount Zion is an important theological idea, which combines the varied material of FI (2:2f.; 4:5; 8:18; 10:12, 32; 11:9; 16:1; 18:7; 24:23; 25:6; 27:13; 29:8; 30:29; 31:4; 37:32). It is amazing that in Isa. 40-55 mount Zion is missing completely. Here Zion plays the part of mother and city, especially in Ch. 49-54. (Only 40:9 rouses an association between Zion and a mountain. In general, in SI mountains do have an own meaning[15]). But in Isa. 56-66 mount Zion does

[7] G. Fohrer, *Das Buch Jesaja. 3. Band: Kapitel 40-66* (ZBK), Zürich, 1964, 190.

[8] Pauritsch, o.c., 53.

[9] Hanson, o.c., 193.

[10] Pauritsch, o.c., 40ff., 45, 48ff.

[11] E. Sehmsdorf, 'Studien zur Redaktionsgeschichte von Jesaja 56-66 (I)', *ZAW* 84 (1972), 542-557.

[12] Pauritsch, o.c., 31-38.

[13] W.A.M. Beuken, *Jesaja Deel II B* (De Prediking van het Oude Testament), Nijkerk, 1983, 277.

[14] L. Alonso Schökel, *Estudios de poética Hebrea*, Barcelona, 1963, 297-301. Cf. Pauritsch, 37, note 196.

[15] Beuken, o.c., 161f.

play an important part. Here God gathers the nations (56:7), while these bring back the children of Israel there (66:20). This mountain becomes the possession of those people who dwell in the shelter of YHWH (57:13). Those who forget it, shall die (65:11), while all evil finds an end there (65:25). Here TI links up with FI: 56:7 takes up 2:1-4; 11:9f.; 25:6 (the conversion of the peoples), 66:20 is an echo of 11:9-12; 27:13 (the return from exile) and 65:11 refers to 11:9 (peace on mount Zion). Briefly, the holy mount Zion is a nodal point in the artistic ordering of the book of Isaiah[16]. One can add to these observations that the conception occurs in TI in the chapters which form the beginning and the end of this prophetic collection[17].

Apparently TI felt the need to make clear, as from the beginning, that 'the holy mountain' will be the focus of all salvation. In general he may have missed this theme in SI, but probably especially in the latter's final chapters. That the name Zion or Jerusalem is missing in Isa. 54, remains, although easy to explain[18], very remarkable, especially because much attention is given to a city founded by God. In Isa. 55 the lack of an adjunct of place continues to be remarkable. Where can this abundance of wheat, wine and milk be found (vs.1-2)? Of course near YHWH (vs.3, 6), but where can *He* be found? The place to which one goes out (vs.12), is not mentioned either. At the most one might suppose that a place is involved in 'for a memorial, for an everlasting sign' (vs.13: *lᵉšēm lᵉʾōt ʿōlām*)'[19]. It goes with TI's care to be concrete that, in 56:1-8, he wants to make firm the aim of the going out, which was just mentioned, and also the place of the aforementioned abundance of salvation: 'I will give in my house and within my walls a monument and a name' (vs.5: *yād wāšēm*) ... 'These I will bring to my holy mountain' (vs.7). Thus he does not stop mentioning — following the fundamental condition put by SI: 'Let the wicked forsake his way' (55:7) — the concrete conditions for taking part in this salvation: a righteous way of living, the keeping of the sabbath and the respect for the covenant (vs.1f., 4, 6). In this way he also brings clarity concerning the idea 'justice', in which the human part after Ch. 54 (vs.14, 17: *ṣᵉdāqā*) was perhaps not clear. Finally he is concrete as far as those people are concerned who may participate in this salvation: the mortals, also the foreigner who joins YHWH, the eunuch, yes all nations (vs.2f., 7). They can all be YHWH's 'servants' (*ʿᵃbādīm*). 'Servants', too, is a notion that was introduced by SI at the end of his book (insofar as it is a plural: 54:17; before that the plural is missing). It had got a first filling-in there (55:1: 'every one who thirsts/who has no money'), but it did require a closer definition[20].

---

[16] Alonso Schökel, o.c., 301.

[17] Lack, o.c., 127f., 130.

[18] Beuken, o.c., 273-276.

[19] Beuken, o.c., 301, 305f.

[20] J. Blenkinsopp, 'The 'Servants of the Lord' in Third Isaiah', *Proceedings of the Irish Biblical Association* 7 (1983), 1-23.

Thus we get the impression that, in this first passage (56:1-8), TI elucidates further the place to which one goes, the categories of persons who are allowed in there, and the conditions on which they can enter. The perspective is: all the nations will come together in God's house on his holy mountain (vs.7). With this important conception from FI he clarifies the end of SI.

We suppose that, in the following passage, he continues his intent, namely in Isa. 56:9-57:13. The conception 'my holy mountain' also closes this passage: 'But he who takes refuge in me shall possess the land, and shall inherit my holy mountain' (57:13b). Sometimes this line was considered secondary, because here the prophet does not use the direct way of adressing[21]. Later on one had a better eye for the fact that forms of language and idiom from the psalms dominate 57:1-2 and 13. The typical prophetic accusation of 57:3-13a' stands in the framework of a topic from the literature of prayer: the godless do indeed oppress the righteous, but they will not escape their punishment, while he who expects all things from God will not be forsaken[22]. It is not always clear whether scholars consider the frame of vs.1-2 and vs.13 original. Upon closer inspection we must state that vs.13a" ('The wind will carry them all off, a breath will take them away') may not be separated from vs.13b ('But he who takes refuge in me shall possess the land, and shall inherit my holy mountain'). Both lines contain a general statement in the third person and together they are a current contrast: the different destiny of the godless and of those who rely on God. Because vs.13a" does not precisely mention the godless, but refers to those people who act according to the aforementioned accusation ('them all'), it is not an independent maxim. This goes for vs.13b too, in view of the close thematic connection between both lines. Also the contrast between vs.12b-13a' and vs.13a" (' ... and your doings, but they will not help you! When you cry out, let your collection of idols deliver you!' and 'The wind will carry them all off, a breath will take them away') pleads for the original connection between vs.13a"-b and the preceding. Nowadays this is admitted more often[23].

The first colon of the last verse line contains words which only here occur in TI ('to take refuge' and 'to possess'). But the conceptions of the second colon are frequent in TI: except 'my holy mountain' (see above) also 'to inherit' (*yrš*). Elsewhere this verb has 'the land' (60:21; 61:7), 'thy heritage' (63:18) and 'my mountains' (65:9) as object. The semantic collocation of the last verse

---

[21] K. Elliger, *Die Einheit des Tritojesaja (Jesaja 56-66)* (BWANT 45), Stuttgart, 1928, 13, 125. P. Volz, *Jesaja. Kapitel 40-66* (KAT IX), Leipzig, 1932, 211. A. Dillmann, R. Kittel (*Der Prophet Jesaja* (KEH 5), Leipzig, 1898, 484) add vs.13 to vs.14-21.

[22] Westermann, o.c., 241f., 255f., 259. Pauritsch, o.c. 53, 65.

[23] Pauritsch, o.c., 65. W. Kessler, *Gott geht es um das Ganze. Jesaja 56-66 und Jesaja 24-27* (BAT 19), Stuttgart, 1960, 52.

line is thus predominantly composed of words which are characteristic for TI, even though, at the same time, they form a motif from the psalms.

To whom do the two last verse lines refer with the words 'them all' (*kullām*) and 'he who takes refuge in me'? Viewed syntactically 'them all' refers back to 'your collection of idols' (*qibbūṣayik*) in vs.13a', but in this explanation a contrast arises in vs.13a''-b between the idols and 'he who takes refuge in me'. A contrast between the godless and the pious is more probable. In that case 'them all' refers back to 'you, ... sons of the sorceress' (vs.3), to whom the accusation of vs.3-5 is directed. In vs.6 this form of addressing changes, without a new vocative, to the person of a woman, a harlot, apparently the mother of the 'sons' who were spoken to earlier. She remains the one addressed in vs.6-13a'. We see a similar change of addressing in SI: first mother Zion (49:14-26), then her children (50:1). The close identification of those spoken to in the plural with their adultress-mother makes it possible, after the lengthy accusation addressed to this woman (57:6-13a'), to return to her children. In this way the end of the segment corresponds to the beginning. As in vs.1-3 'the sons of the sorceress' are set opposite 'the righteous', thus, opposite 'them all' in vs.13, we see 'he who takes refuge in me'. With these latter words 'the righteous' is meant, who suffers under the arrogance of the godless.

The preceding proves that vs. 13b is quite included in the model of the speech-direction of the context. Moreover the words ' ... shall inherit my holy mountain' belong to TI's own vocabulary. Therefore one may view this promise as a pithy summary of what the salvation contains for the prophet.

If one does not see vs.13b as an addition, but gives to the verse line its weight of a final statement, then one will not easily overvalue the contrast between this verse and vs.7: 'Upon a high and lofty mountain you have set your bed and thither you went up to offer sacrifice'. The expression *har gābōah wᵉniśśā'* does not occur any more in TI, neither the root *gbh* (*nś'* nif'al still in 57:15; 66:12). Here we definitely stand before an allusion to Isa. 40:9 (*'al har gābōah ʿᵃlī lāk*), especially if we see that 'to go up' (*'lh*), the second verb in 57:7, returns in 57:8 ('Deserting me, you have uncovered your bed, you have gone up to it'), while 'to go up to offer sacrifice' is prepared by 'you have brought a cereal offering' (*heʿᵉlīt*) in vs.6b. Precisely that single text in SI where 'mountain' does not mean mount Zion, but yet can be associated with it (40:9), moreover the only text in SI where the root *gbh* refers to mountains (*nś'* never designates mountains in SI), has been taken up by TI to create an antithesis with 'my holy mountain'. The woman addressed, the adulterous Zion, does not climb the mountain as a herald of good tidings to announce God's arrival (40:9), but she climbs the holy mountain of YHWH in order to bring there to her lovers, the gods, offerings in adultery (57:7).

But there is more. Elsewhere in the Bible *har* occurs linked up with *gābōah* (Isa. 30:25; Jer. 3:6; Ez. 17:22; plural: Gen. 7:19; Ps. 104:18)[24], but with *niśśā'* only in Isa. 2:2 (= Michah 4:1)[25]. (*niśśā'* does not occur linked up with *gib'ā*: Isa. 2:14; 30:25). So the combination *gābōah wᵉniśśā'* of 57:7 is not stereotype, although the book of Isaiah itself has the following pairs of words: *gbh/rwm* (2:11, 17; 10:33; 52:13) and *rwm/nś'* (2:12ff.; 6:1; 13:2; 33:10; 37:23; 49:22; 52:13; 57:15)[26]. Consequently, the combination *har gābōah wᵉniśśā'* is especially remarkable as concerns the element *niśśā'*, although the nif'al of *nś'* itself can be found often in the book of Isaiah[27]. Concerning these data in Isaiah 57:7, Odeberg remarks the following: 'The epithets *gābōah wᵉniśśā'* are probably due to the writer's repeated reading or meditation upon Isa'[28]. Perhaps we can go one step further. Insofar as *niśśā'* in 57:7 is applied to the mountain of idolatry, the prophet not only refers to SI (40:9), but also to FI (2:2). Thus a contrast originates between the harlot, who ascends to sacrifice, and the nations (*gōyīm/'ammīm*), who also ascend (2:3: *na'ᵃle*), but to learn the law. The broader contexts of 2:2 and of 57:7 strengthen this reference. In 2:2 'the mountain of the house of YHWH' is mentioned (cf. vs.3), in 56:7 'my holy mountain' is the place where God's house stands (cf. vs.5), where He gathers all the nations (*'ammīm*) so that they can bring Him offerings.

Further, as far as the unique combination *gābōah wᵉniśśā'* (57:7) is concerned, of the two current combinations *gbh/rwm* is not applied anywhere to YHWH himself, *rwm/nś'* is so (6:1; 33:10; 49:22). Once does this combination typify Sennacherib's arrogance regarding the Holy One of Israel: 'Against whom have you raised your voice and haughtily lifted your eyes?' (37:23). Briefly, while TI sets the mountain of the adultery (57:7) opposite to that of Zion's good tidings (40:9) and of the ascending of the nations (2:2), at the same time he alludes, by the element *niśśa'*, to the haughtiness which turns itself against YHWH. The remarkable contamination of the pairs of words *gbh/rwm* and *rwm/nś'* into *gābōah wᵉniśśā'* is very functional then. The fact that the woman has placed her bed 'upon a high and lofty mountain' characterizes her adultery as a behaviour that pits itself against YHWH. It goes against all his intentions with the holy mountain and thus refuses to acknowledge Him (cf. vs.8: 'deserting me'; vs.11: ' ... and did not remember me').

---

[24] A. Even-Shoshan, *A New Concordance of the Bible* I-IV, Jerusalem, 1977-1980, 404.

[25] Even-Shoshan, o.c., 1461.

[26] W.R. Watters, *Formula Criticism and the Poetry of the Old Testament* (BZAW 138), Berlin, 1976, 158, nr. 69 and 71.

[27] According to Odeberg (o.c., 78) 11 times in Isaiah, 14 times elsewhere in the Bible. According to *ThHAT*, II, 110 (F. Stolz) 14 times in Isaiah, 19 times elsewhere.

[28] Odeberg, o.c., 79.

In this connection we wish to remind of the explanation that the bed of the harlot (*miškāb*), which is spoken of here three times (vs.7f.), does not refer to the heights in the land, where sacrifices were brought to the gods, but alludes to the dwellingplace (*miškān*) of YHWH on mount Zion[29]. The harlot's behaviour is a counter-gesture against God's presence there (cf. 8:18: 'YHWH of hosts, who dwells (*haššōkēn*) on Mount Zion'). But because the roots *škb* and *škn* are not used pregnantly in FI and SI, there is no question here of an allusion to certain texts in the book of Isaiah.

In the preceding pages the harlot was already spoken of: the woman who brings sacrifices to the gods, her lovers, and practices sorceries to attach them to herself. She is announced as 'sorceress' and 'harlot' (57:3). It is to her alone that YHWH speaks in vs.6-13a'. This passage shows remarkable similarities with Isa. 47, where 'the daughter of Babylon' is depicted in her haughtiness and humiliation. One should compare the following groups of verses:

1) 57:10 With the length of your way you wearied yourself
bᵉrōb darkēk yāga'at
47:12 ... and in your many sorceries with which you wearied yourself
ūbᵉrōb kešāfayik ba'ᵃšer yāga'at
47:9 in spite of your many sorceries and the strength of your enchantments
bᵉrōb kᵉšāfayik bᵉ'oṣmat ḥᵃbārayik
47:15 Such to you are those with whom you wearied yourself
kēn hāyū lāk 'ᵃšer yāgā'at
47:13 You are worn out by your many counsels
nil'ēt bᵉrōb 'ᵃṣātāyik
2) 57:11 You did not take to heart
lō śamt 'al libbēk
47:7 You did not take these things to heart
lō śamt 'ēlle 'al libbēk
3) 57:12 But they will not help you
wᵉlō yō'īlūk
47:12 Perhaps you may be able to succeed
'ūlay tūklī hō'īl
4) 57:13 Let your collection of idols deliver you
yaṣṣīluk qibbūṣayik
47:13 Let those who divide the heavens save you
wᵉyōšī'uk hōbrē šāmayim

---

[29] Hanson, o.c., 199f. His historical-sociological interpretation of 57:7 must be left on the author.

47:14 They can not deliver themselves
lō yaṣīlū nafšām
47:15 There is no one to save you
'ēn mōšī'ēk

This summary does not give a complete inventory of the biblical parallels from which the picture of the harlot is built up. Isa. 57:6-13a contains other similarities, with FI and SI as well as with other books of the Old Testament[30]. But the relationship with Isa. 47 strikes the eye the most, especially as far as material from vs. 9-15 of that chapter is concerned. This is precisely the segment in which the magical practices of 'the daughter of Babylon' are described. This woman is not depicted as a harlot, but as wife and mother (vs.8f.) and 'mistress of kingdoms' (vs.5ff.). The woman in 57:6-13 is indeed also mother of children, but not out of a legal alliance (vs.3f.), and therefore her motherhood plays no part in the position that she has acquired for herself. No more is she described as a queen. On the contrary, out of fear, although for the wrong people, she has humiliated herself (vs. 9, 11). Thus it is only the sorcery which is shared by the female figures in Ch. 57 and Ch. 47. This explains why 57:6-13 only borrowed from Ch. 47 to a limited degree.

After our research of Isa. 56:7-13 we can state that TI continues to make a connection with the end of SI in the second passage of his prophecies. The preceding passage (56:1-8) has identified the place where Israel can find life (Ch. 55), with 'the holy mountain' of YHWH and declared it accessible to all the peoples (56:7). Here we are shown how the godless destroy this place by oppressing the righteous one. And yet the latter will acquire 'my holy mountain' (57:13). But the godless demonstrate herewith that they are children of the adulterous woman, who leaves YHWH to please her lovers (57:3-12). This is not a new picture, it is already known from Hosea and Jeremiah, while FI identifies the woman with the city of Zion (1:21). What is new is that here this woman, with the aid of allusions to Isa. 2:2-4 and 40:9, is localised on a mountain which is the contrast of mount Zion. Further, with allusions to Isa. 47 it is suggested that she is like 'the daughter of Babylon' on account of her sorceries. Thus TI sets the abuses which he berates in a theological frame that he takes from FI and SI.

II *Isa. 56:9-12: God's repast perverted.*

The passage begins with a summons that one likes to call a quotation from Jer. 12:9. The texts ought to be compared:

---

[30] Cf. Odeberg, o.c., 75-92, 96-99.

Isa. 56:9		Jer. 12:9b
	a^1	*lekū 'isfū*
kōl ḥaytō śādāy	b^1	*kol ḥayyat haśśāde*
'ētāyū le'ekōl	a^2	*hētāyū le'oklā*
kol ḥaytō bayyā'ar	b^2	

Actually the similarities are not so great. Opposite two cola with vocatives and one single imperative ($b^1a^2b^2$) in Isaiah, there are two cola with imperatives and one single object ($a^1b^1a^2$) in Jeremiah. This object consists of the same animals which form the first vocative in Isaiah's text. The cola which the texts have in common are slightly different in formulation (b^1a^2). The resemblance between both texts is strengthend by the fact that, in their context, the negative behaviour of shepherds is spoken of (Isa. 56:11a"; Jer. 7:10). On the other hand, the context of Jer. 12:7-17 speaks in detail about the destruction of God's *heritage* (*naḥalā*), while in Isa. 56:9-12 any allusion to cultivated land is lacking. Here the question is how the 'watchmen' (vs.10a': *ṣōfāw*), elaborated in the metaphorical language as 'dogs' (vs.10a") and 'shepherds' (vs.11), behave.

To the question: 'What is there to eat for 'the beasts of the field/the beasts in the forest' (Isa. 56:9)?' the commentators answer more or less emphatically: 'the flock of Israel'[31]. They like to appeal to the suffix in *ṣōfāw* (vs.10a) and let this refer to *yiśrā'ēl* (vs.8), which might therefore be the suppressed object of vs.9. The animals are summoned to come and devour Israel, because the dogs and the shepherds have abandoned their flock. This summons, then, is meant sarcastically. God denounces that, because of the outrageous negligence of Israel's leaders, the people have become an easy prey for the wild animals. A minority of the commentators see the animals as the nations that may attack Israel (cf. Lev. 26:22; Deut. 32:24; Ez. 34:5, 8; 39:17; Hos. 13:8)[32].

However, one can bring forward fundamental objections against the explanation that the animals are invited to devour Israel. It is true, these dogs and shepherds are said to be greedy for food (cf. vs.11a, 12) and one could imagine that especially the dogs prey on the flock which they ought to watch. But such a perversity would undoubtedly be strongly denounced if indeed it were meant like that (cf. Ez. 34:3, 10). Moreover, of the shepherds it is merely said that they have their own interest in view (vs.11b). From their words their passion for drinking-bouts appears, so that they clearly neglect their task (vs.12).

---

[31] J.A. Alexander, *Commentary on the Prophecies of Isaiah*, Vol.2, Grand Rapids, 1976 (reprint 1875^2), 337. Dillmann - Kittel, o.c., 478.

[32] W. Gesenius, *Philologisch-kritischer und historischer Commentar über den Jesaja*, Leipzig 1821, II, 229f. F. Feldmann, *Das Buch Isaias*, vol. II, (EHAT XIV/2), Munster i.W., 1926, 203.

Furthermore, there is a literal resemblance between the summons to the animals and the invitations of the negligent shepherds for each other to celebrate: 'Come (*'ētāyū*) to eat' (vs.9) and 'Come (*'ētāyū*), let me get wine, let us fill ourselves with strong drink' (vs.12a). Might not this remarkable parallel suggest that, if the shepherds do themselves well at the expense of Israel ('to get wine' (*lqḥ*) meaning 'to take it away from others, because one is stronger'; cf. Gen. 27:35f.; 31:34; 1 Sam. 2:16; 2 Kings 4:1; Jer. 20:5; Job 40:28; Prov. 27:13; Esther 2:7[33]), the animals can also over-indulge in the products of the earth? Besides, it is noticeable that the verb *'th* qal rarely means 'to approach threateningly' (Job 3:25; 30:14; Prov. 1:27), but it nearly always has a positive meaning (Deut. 33:2; Isa. 21:14; 41:23, 25; 44:7; 45:11; Jer. 3:22; Micah 4:8; Ps. 68:32; Job 37:22; neutral in Deut. 33:21; Isa. 21:12; Job 16:12). It is true that 'the beasts of the field' are said to devour flesh (Lev. 26:22; with *'kl*: Ez. 34:5, 8; 39:4, 17; with *bq'*: Hos. 13:8), but also that they eat vegetable food (with *'kl*: Ex. 23:11; Jer. 12:9; Hos. 2:14) or trample on it (2 Kings 14:9). 'The beasts of the forest' (*ḥayyat hayya'ar* or *bayya'ar*), more than 'the beasts of the field', present a threat (Ez. 34:25), but the dangerous animals of the forest are generally called by their names (lion: Jer. 5:6; 12:8; Amos 3:4; Micah 5:7; bear: 2 Kings 2:24; wild boars: Ps. 80:14) and 'the beasts of the forest' are also mentioned without the secondary sound of danger (Ps. 50:10; 104:20)[34]. Finally the word 'watchmen' (root *ṣph*) never evokes the situation of a flock, but of a watch-tower or a military look-out (Num. 23:14; 1 Sam. 14:16; 2 Sam. 13:34; 18:24-27; 2 Kings 9:17-20; Isa. 52:8; Jer. 6:17; 48:19; Ez. 33:2-7; Nah. 2:2; Hab. 2:1; Cant. 7:5; Lam. 4:7), if it is not used in a more general sense (Gen. 31:49; 1 Sam. 4:13; Isa. 21:5f.; Ez. 3:17; Hos. 9:8; Micah 7:4, 7; Ps. 5:4; 37:32; 66:7; Prov. 15:3). With the prophets the term is often used for the leaders of Israel because of their task to warn the people against danger. Against the background of this semantic field, given the resemblance between Isa. 56:9 and 12 and in the light of the context of Jer. 12:9, where 'the beasts of the field' come to eat of the vineyard and the field, it seems advisable to understand vs.9 as an invitation to the animals to come to eat of the fruit of the land that belongs to Israel. They can do as they like because the 'watchmen' are blind and do not watch over the heritage.

Briefly, the watchmen, the dogs as well as the shepherds, do not do themselves well on the flock, but they neglect it[35]. In the following verse lines this behaviour and its results are the subject of the accusation: 'The righteous man perishes, and no one lays it to heart; devout men are taken away, while no one understands' (57:1).

---

[33] *ThWAT*, IV, 592 (H. Seebass).
[34] *ThWAT*, III, 784 (M.J. Mulder).
[35] F. Delitzsch, *Commentar über das Buch Jesaja* (BC), Leipzig, 1889⁴, 548.

For the sake of completeness we mention that in Jewish tradition an explanation of vs.9 has developed which either sees 'all the beasts in the forest' or 'all the beasts of the field' as object of 'come to eat'. In some editions of the Masoretic text this can be read from the accentuation[36]. The first explanation is the favourite. The weaker animals of the field, the proselytes or Israel, are invited to devour the beasts of the forest, the mighty nations. In the other case the nations are invited to devour the sinful Israel[37].

With this explanation of vs.9 the surmise arises that the scene with which Isa. 56:9-57:13 opens elaborates the invitation for 'every one who thirsts/he who has no money' in Isa. 55:1-3. In a sarcastic manner our passage summons the beasts to do themselves well on the place where God gives his people an abundance of food, because the carelessness of Israel's leaders and their greed have already perverted the destiny of this site. Perhaps the number of words and notions which both passages have in common is not so big, but they set in strong relief the similarity of themes:

— 'come' (*'ētāyū, lᵉkū*): 56:9; 55:1, 3.
— 'to eat' (*'kl*): 56:9; 55:1f.
— 'to have a mighty appetite' (*'āzzē nefeš*), cf. 'delight yourselves' (*tit'annag nafšᵉkem*): 56:11; 55:2.
— 'they never have enough' (*lō yādᵉ'ū śōb'ā*), cf. 'that which does not satisfy' (*bᵉlō lᵉśob'ā*): 56:11; 55:2.
— 'wine' (*yayin*): 56:12; 55:1.

These terms function in opposite situations. The invitation of SI is emphatically directed to the needy: 'every one who thirsts/he who has no money ... without money and without price' (55:1f.). For SI the poor are the same as 'the poor and needy' and as 'the prisoners', who go forth (41:17; 49:9f.). God has prepared a place of abundance for them. When TI calls the victims of the bad situations 'the righteous man/devout men' (57:1), then he describes how the abundance which God meant to be for every one has been perverted by the greed of the watchmen. Where actually abundance, free and easily obtainable, is within reach for all, now the poor people die, while the greed of the responsible class knows no bounds. And thus the situation of salvation that YHWH wished to bring about has changed to the contrary. The powerful people undo God's salvation.

---

36 Delitzsch, o.c., 547.

37 E.F.C. Rosenmüller, *Scholia in Vetus Testamentum. Vol.II: Scholia in Jesajae Vaticinia*, Lipsiae, 1835, 716f. Dillmann - Kittel, o.c., 478. A.J. Rosenberg, *Miqra'ot Gedolot. Isaiah* II, New York, 1983, 444. Cf. C. Vitringa, *Commentarius in librum prophetiarum Jesaiae* II, Herbornae Nassaviorum, 1722, 337f.

The connection between 56:9-12 and 55:1-3 is strengthened by the fact that these powerful people are described with words derived from SI:

1. The watchmen are blind, dumb and lying down dreaming (56:10). Thus they are in contrast to the watchmen who raise their voice, because eye to eye they see how YHWH returns to Zion (52:7f.). The characteristic 'blind' links up with a certain use of the word, i.e. in a negative sense, by SI. He applies it to that Israel which is not open for God's plans (42:18f.; 43:8; next to 'blind' in the sense of having been hit by exile: 42:7, 16). Also the parallel expression 'without knowledge' (56:10f.: *lō yādᵉʿū [hābīn]*) is derived from SI and he, too, sometimes uses it as a parallel for 'not seeing' (44:9, 18; 45:20). In these watchmen and shepherds is continued that Israel which shows no understanding for what befalls it.

2. From 'the watchmen', a metaphor which suggests especially an observation-post for danger, the figurative language moves over to 'dogs' and 'shepherds' (56:10f.), a combination that evokes the idea of a flock. Although in SI 'dog' is missing and although he does not use the metaphor 'shepherd' and 'pasture' frequently (49:9), one may suppose that 'to gather', which is used very emphatically (three times) in 56:8, is the point of contact for the term 'shepherds' in 56:11. Then the association is aroused through the prologue of SI (40:11), where 'shepherd' and 'to graze' stand in one single collocation with 'to gather'. The shepherd who performs his task so conscientiously there, is the opposite of the shepherds in 56:11f.

3. The metaphor of the wicked shepherds is strengthened by a verse line which really links up closely with SI:

53:6	*kullānū kaṣṣ̈ōn tāʿīnū*	*ʾīš*	*lᵉdarkō*	*pānīnū*	
56:11	*kullām*		*lᵉdarkām*	*pannū*	
		ʾīš	*lebiṣʿō*		*miqqāṣēhū*

53:6 All we like sheep have gone astray;
we have turned every one to his own way.
56:11 They have all turned to their own way,
each to his own gain, one and all.

There is an important difference. In 53:6 the speakers compare themselves to sheep, in 56:11 the leaders of Israel are compared to shepherds. Therefore in 56:11 precisely those words are lacking which in 53:6 refer to sheep (*kaṣṣōn tāʿīnū*). Because for this reason the verse line of 56:11 threatened to be reduced to one single colon, there follows another colon having a different meaning. But the latter does begin with the same word as the second colon of 53:6 (*ʾīš*) and furthermore it is filled with the conception 'gain' (*beṣaʿ*), a term also occurring in the next passage and there too, connected with the theme of the self-chosen way: 'Because of the iniquity of his covetousness (*biṣʿō*) I was angry ... but he went on backsliding in the way of his own heart' (57:17)[38]. The metaphor does change from 53:6 to 56:11, but the fact that the leaders are characterized by words derived from the confession of those who consider themselves guilty of the suffering of the Servant, means a very special judgment. Even the vicissitudes of the Servant have not been able to bring them to repentance.

Our passage does not only show a relationship with SI, but also with FI, as a matter of fact in the quotation which must characterize the exclusive attention of the shepherds for their own happiness (56:12). From the translations and commentaries it appears that one generally interprets the verse as follows: some one from the circle of the leaders promises to see to the wine ('let me get wine') and invites others for a proper drinking-bout, lasting till the next day: 'Come ... let us fill ourselves with strong drink; and tomorrow will be like this day, great beyond measure'. The thing that is denounced here is simply the self-indulgence of the people who are responsible. But if the quotation characterizes the leaders as persons who enrich themselves at the expense of those for whom they must care, then one can better interpret 'to get wine' (*lqḥ*) as meaning 'to take away from others' or 'to appropriate at the expense of others'. The verb *lqḥ* occurs in that meaning[39] also in SI (49:24f.; 52:5). Already in Ibn Ezra one finds the explanation that this wine has been obtained in an unjust way[40]. The theme can be found in Amos 4:1; Prov. 31:4f. That the shepherds do themselves well at the expense of the flock, is a biblical theme, and nowhere is it so clearly exposed as in Ez. 34. If 56:9-12 links up with the invitation for the repast at the time of salvation (55:1-3) and if in 56:12 the prophet speaks of a drinking-bout at the expense of others, then this verse acquires an extremely bitter pointe. The leaders appropriate the goods — examplarily called 'wine' — which YHWH has prepared precisely for the poor. On the place where money and fortune no longer need to play a role, the mighty ones see their opportunity to exercise a material oppression. Such is the extent of their greed.

If this is the background of the quotation, then the surmise is not unfounded that Isa. 5, too, was a model for Isa. 56:9-12. In the first text YHWH is disappointed about his vineyard Israel, because instead of 'righteousness' there are merely 'cries of distress' (5:7) (NEB; pay attention to the play of rhyme in Hebrew). Next the abuses in the house of Israel are elaborated in a sixfold 'woe' (5:8-23). The second 'woe' goes thus: 'Woe to those who rise early in the

[38] The last word with which 56:11 is 'filled' to a bicolon, *miqqᵉṣēhū*, is explained in various ways (cf. the commentaries ad loc.) or erased (Elliger, o.c., 8). The word occurs once still in TI (62:11), in the same compound in which it occurs only in SI: *qᵉṣē*/*qᵉṣōt hā'āreṣ*.

[39] Cf. note 33.

[40] M. Friedlaender, *The Commentary of Ibn Ezra on Isaiah*, London, 1873 (reprint New York, 1964), 259.

morning, that they may run after strong drink, who tarry late into the evening till wine inflames them!' (vs.11f.). If we read 56:12 against the background of 55:1f., then we can determine a strong resemblance to Isa. 5. Also in TI the place where God sees to an abundance of good wine (parallel to the grapes in Isa. 5:2), is sullied by those who appropriate this harvest in limitless greed. The resemblances between 5:11 and 56:12 are first of all found in the pair of words 'strong drink/wine' (*šēkār/yayin*). The reversed sequence hereof can denote a deliberate quotation[41]. Another resemblance is the topos of the adjuncts of time: in 5:11 one drinks from 'early in the morning' till 'late into the evening' (*maškīmē babbōqer ... me'aḥarē bannešef*), in 56:12 from 'this day' till 'tomorrow' (*wehāyā kazze yōm māḥār*). These adjuncts of time are not exactly similar: in 5:11 one counts in parts of the day, in 56:12 in whole days. The last motif is characteristic for the drinking song. It expresses the recklessness of people who do not want to think about the fact that the day of tomorrow will put an end to a life of pleasure (Amos 4:1f.), or who, precisely because of that, want to make the most of to-day (cf. Isa. 22:13; Wisdom of Solomon 2:5-9)[42]. The cry of woe therefore establishes 'want of knowledge' (5:13: *mibbelī da'at*; cf. 56:10, 11b: *lō yāde'ū [hābīn]*), following 'they do not regard ... or see' (vs.12: *lō yabbīṭū ... lō rā'ū*).

The sixth and last cry of woe of Isa. 5 goes back to the theme of the drinking-bouts: 'Woe to those who are heroes at drinking wine, and valiant men in mixing strong drink, who acquit the guilty for a bribe, and deprive the innocent of his right!' (vs.22f.). The accusation, which is connected here to the cry of woe, suggests that the drinking-bout is paid for by unjust behaviour. Maybe that accusation is already contained in the way of addressing: 'heroes/valiant men' (*gibbōrīm/ 'anšē ḥayil*). These are men of power, who misuse their social position in the administration of justice to organise banquets for themselves[43].

The last colon of 56:12 (*gādōl yeter me'ōd*) has two different explanations, but perhaps a third is possible, which contains a typical word relationship with SI. From Vg, Tg[44], Martin Luther, AV and StV on, there is an explanation which gives to *yeter* a comparative function: 'Tomorrow shall be as this day, *and* much more abundant' (AV). Because it is not easy to see why the day of tomorrow will be better than the present day, others explain *yeter* and *me'ōd* as adverbs of grade (elatives): 'And tomorrow shall be like this day, great beyond

[41] P.C. Beentjes, 'Inverted Quotations in the Bible. A neglected Stylistic Pattern', *Bib.* 63 (1982), 506-523.

[42] *ThWAT*, IV, 816 (G. André).

[43] Delitzsch, o.c., 115.

[44] Isa. 56:12 is lacking in LXX.

measure' (RSV)[45]. A third explanation has been proposed by Bonnard[46] and has found its way into TOB: 'Le surplus est en abondance!'. Then *yeter* (residue) refers to 'strong drink' in the preceding verse line. This same use of *yeter* also occurs in SI: 'Half of it I burned in the fire, I also baked bread on its coals ... and shall I make *the residue* of it an abomination?' (44:19). We dare to make a connection between the meaning of the word *yeter* in 56:12 and 44:19. Both times the question is that the use of the residue, there of wood, here of wine, shows the wrong attitude of the user. In that way he takes a direct stand against God.

The remarkable similarities between the beginning of 56:9-57:13 and SI and FI end, until further, with 56:12. The following verses, 57:1-2, are firmly related to 56:9-12, because they pronounce the moral judgment over the situation that has just been described (vs.1a-b') and, next, adumbrate 'the eternal destiny' of the oppressed (vs.1b''-2)[47], but the terminology of these verses is largely derived from the psalms[48]. This can explain the fact that we cannot establish here any 'affinities' with SI or FI[49]. Neither do we note in 57:3-6 any parallels with the two predecessors of TI, although terms like *qrb* (vs.3) and *zera'* (vs.3f.) as well as the disputation style can be investigated further. Only in vs.7 does another segment begin, showing great affinity with FI and and SI, as we saw in section I.

Our research of Isa. 56:9-12 demonstrates that TI depicts the abuses around YHWH's holy mountain in contrast to God's intention with the place of salvation, described by SI in 55:1-2. In doing this he uses images and idiom from FI and SI, such as the watchman (52:7f.), the shepherd (40:11) and the drinking-bout (5:11f., 23f.). The predecessors of TI, within the book, once more offer the theological background against which he draws the sad situation in the postexilic community.

Conclusion

This study offers an example of the way in which TI uses the literary legacy of FI and SI. The aspect of representativity ought really to belong to the definition of an example. In that aspect the word 'example' is rather premature here. Only further investigation of TI can determine according to which pattern his predecessors have left their traces within his prophecies. Present-day exegesis does have an inkling of this fact itself. However, to determine the

---

[45] Alexander, o.c., 339f. T.K. Cheyne, *The Prophecies of Isaiah* II, London, 1882, 67. B. Duhm, *Das Buch Jesaia* (HK 3/1), Göttingen, 1892, (1968⁵), 425.

[46] Bonnard, o.c., 356. Thus already Gesenius (o.c., 212) referring to Ps. 31:4.

[47] B. Renaud, 'La mort du juste, entré dans la paix (Is.57:1-2)', *RevSR* 51 (1977), 3-21.

[48] Westermann, o.c., 255.

[49] Odeberg, o.c., 95.

extent and the character of the Isaianic legacy in TI, much study is still required.

The text unit which was investigated here, does not yet permit general conclusions concerning the influence of the first and the second Isaianic master upon the third. In any case, the parallels that were found do not deny the independence of TI in language, poetical form or way of thinking. We stand — at least in 56:9-57:13 — before a literary and theological personality in his own right. Selectively, purposefully and subtly, he has used the prophecies of FI and SI for his particular message, in a situation that was quite different. Therefore the term 'anthological style' does not seem apt to us. One thing, however, is certain. In this passage TI uses intensively the heritage of his two predecessors, not only their range of ideas but also their way of voicing. The question whether this prophecy must be called an early phenomenon of scribal activity, can only be answered after a similar research of the rest of TI. However, that question does begin to arise.

We therefore hope that this study is not misplaced in a volume dedicated to a scholar who has devoted his life to the study of apocalyptic. TI does not answer the criteria which this savant himself determined for that kind of writings[50] although others have wished to see the beginning of the apocalyptic literature in this last Isaianic prophet[51]. However, the continual care of Jürgen Lebram not to see apocalyptic from a point of view of *Ideengeschichte*, but to investigate it closely according to its literary character, is an example and an inspiration for the studying of biblical texts which, chronologically, are not far distant from the apocalyptic era.

---

[50] *TRE* III, 192, 196f. (J.C.H. Lebram).
[51] Hanson, o.c., 186-202.

MALACHI'S STRUGGLE FOR A PURE COMMUNITY

Reflections on Malachi 2:10-16

by

A.S. van der Woude

All commentators[1] hold that Malachi's third prophecy (2:10-16) in its present form deals with two abuses in the postexilic community of Jerusalem and

---

[1] The following commentaries and monographs have been consulted:
Commentaries:
J.G. Baldwin, *Haggai-Zechariah-Malachi* (Tyndale Old Testament Commentaries), London, 1972; C.T. Chary, *Aggée-Zacharie-Malachie* (Sources Bibliques), Paris, 1969; D. Deden, *De kleine profeten* (BOT), Roermond-Maaseik, 1953-1956; (M. Delcor -) A. Deissler, *Les petits prophètes* (La Sainte Bible, Pirit-Clamer VIII), II, Paris, 1964; R.C. Dentan, 'The Book of Malachi', *IB* VI, Nashville, 1956, 1115-1144; K. Elliger, *Das Buch der zwölf kleinen Propheten* II (ATD 25/II), Göttingen, 1964[5]; M. Haller, *Das Judentum* (SAT II/3), Göttingen, 1925[2]; F. Hitzig - H. Steiner, *Die zwölf kleinen Propheten* (KEH), Leipzig, 1881[4]; A. van Hoonacker, *Les douze petits prophètes* (Etudes Bibliques), Paris, 1908; (Th.H. Robinson -) F. Horst, *Die zwölf kleinen Propheten* (HAT I/14), Tübingen, 1964[3]; D.R. Jones, *Haggai, Zechariah and Malachi* (Torch Bible Commentaries), London, 1962; H. Junker, *Die zwölf kleinen Propheten* II (HSchAT VIII/3/II), Bonn, 1938; C.F. Keil, *Biblischer Commentar über die zwölf kleinen Propheten*, Leipzig, 1888[3]; K. Marti, *Das Dodekapropheton* (KHC XIII), Tübingen, 1904; R. Mason, *The Books of Haggai, Zechariah and Malachi* (Cambridge Bible Commentaries), Cambridge, 1977; H.G. Mitchell, *Haggai and Zechariah* (ICC), Edinburgh, 1912; J.C. de Moor, *De profeet Maleachi*, Amsterdam, 1903; F. Nötscher, *Zwölfprophetenbuch* (Echter-Bibel), Würzburg, 1957[2]; W. Nowack, *Die kleinen Propheten* (HK III/4), Göttingen, 1922[3]; C. von Orelli, *Die zwölf kleinen Propheten*, München, 1908; J. Ridderbos, *De kleine profeten* III (KV), Kampen, 1952[2]; W. Rudolph, *Haggai - Sacharia 1-8 - Sacharia 9-14 - Maleachi* (KAT XIII/4), Gütersloh 1976; E. Sellin, *Das Zwölfprophetenbuch* (KAT XII), Leipzig, 1929/1930[2-3]; G. Smit, *De kleine profeten* III (TU), Groningen-Den Haag-Batavia, 1934; G.A. Smith, *The Book of the Twelve Prophets*, London, 1928[2]; P. Verhoef, *Maleachi* (COT), Kampen, 1972; (S. Amsler - A. Lacocque -) R. Vuilleumier, *Aggée-Zacharie-Malachie* (Commentaire de l'Ancien Testament XIc), Neuchatel, 1981; J. Wellhausen, *Die kleinen Propheten übersetzt und erklärt*, Berlin, 1963[4]; A.S. van der Woude, *Haggai. Maleachi* (Prediking van het Oude Testament), Nijkerk, 1982.
Monographs:
M. Adinolfi, 'Il ripudio secondo Mal. 2, 14-16', *Bibbia e Oriente* 12 (1970), 247-256; R. Althann, 'Malachi 2, 13-14 and UT. 125,12-13', *Bibl* 58 (1977), 418-421; G.J. Botterweck, 'Schelt- und Mahnreden gegen Mischehen und Ehescheidungen', *Bibel und Leben* 1 (1960), 179-195; A. von Bulmerincq, *Einleitung in das Buch des Propheten Maleachi*, Dorpat, 1926; A. de Nicola, 'La moglie della tua giovinezza', *Bibbia e Oriente* 12 (1970), 153-183; A. Renker, *Die Tora bei Maleachi*, Freiburg, 1979, 86-90; S. Schreiner, 'Mischehen - Ehebruch - Ehescheidung. Betrachtungen zu Mal. 2,10-16', *ZAW* 91 (1979), 207-228; A. Tosato, 'Il ripudio: delitto e pena (Mal. 2,10-16)', *Bibl* 59 (1978), 548-553.
These commentaries and monographs are referred to in the following notes by their author's name.

Judah: intermarriage with foreign women and divorce. Many of them, however, subscribe to the view of G.A. Smith[2] that the passage originally treated only the theme of divorce[3]. In their opinion, vss. 11-12 (or 11b-12[4] or even 11b-13a[5]) are a later addition. It has been pointed out that in a community that permitted polygamy, contracting a new marriage with a foreign woman has in principle nothing to do with divorce[6], that, because of their descriptive character, vss. 11-12 do not tally with Malachi's style[7], and that criticism of mixed marriages contradicts the prophet's universalism attested by Mal. 1:11[8].

This text analysis must be called into question. The mutual faithlessness mentioned in vs. 10b does not refer to divorce. The very phrasing of the text contradicts this interpretation. That vs. 11 cannot derive from the prophet because of its descriptive character, is refuted by Mal. 3:16. It must be admitted that the denouncement of mixed marriages is at variance with the universalism of Mal. 1:11, but this fact does not prove the inauthenticity of 2:11, since Mal. 1:11-14 is a later addition to Malachi's prophecies[9]. *More decisive, however, is our conviction that Mal. 2:10-16 does not deal with divorce at all.* The opposite view, to this present day shared by all commentators, is based on a very disputable interpretation of vs. 16 which in our opinion does not speak about repudiation, but about the secondary status of a former Jewish wife. In point of fact, the main theme of Mal. 2:10-16 is the marriages contracted by members of the Yahweh community with foreign women. These relations jeopardized the national and religious unity of Israel and entailed a faithless treatment of the Judaean wife of one's youth. Accordingly, at least vs. 11 is vital to Malachi's argument.

The background of our pericope should be sought in the social and economic situation prevailing in Judah during Malachi's lifetime. By marrying foreign women Judaeans tried to share the privileges of their alien overlords. The common cause they made with them gave rise to severe tensions between a well-to-do class and the poor in one and the same religious community[10].

---

[2] *Op. cit.*, 340.

[3] Cf. Nowack, Marti, Sellin, Haller, Elliger, Rendtorff (*RGG*³ IV, col. 629), Vuilleumier, Mason and Renker (p. 90). Chary distinguishes three sermons linked by the theme of *bāgad* (vs. 10; vss. 11-12; vss. 13-16), cf. also Baldwin. Botterweck is of the opinion that vss. 11-12 are added as an elucidation. Verhoef and Rudolph strongly contest the view that Mal. 2,10-16 is not a literary unity. An analysis of the text which considers vss. 11-12 a later addition entails also the deletion of *šēnīt* in vs. 13a.

[4] So e.g. Vuilleumier.

[5] So e.g. Elliger.

[6] Cf. Smith, Marti, Sellin.

[7] Cf. Sellin.

[8] Cf. Sellin.

[9] Cf. Elliger, Horst, Rendtorff (*RGG*³ IV, col. 628) and van der Woude.

[10] Only well-to-do people could permit themselves polygamy. The rift caused in the Judaean community by marriages with foreign women is exemplified by Ezra 9:1ff. and Neh. 13:23ff.

Malachi, piously persuaded that the mixed marriages constituted a menace to the national and religious unity of Yahweh's people, was induced to raise his voice against these destructive developments that inevitably would lead to an estrangement from Israel's spiritual heritage, particularly with a new generation, and to an undermining of the covenant community.

In view of the imperiled brotherhood Malachi begins his protest by asking: 'Have we not all one Father? Did not one God create us? Why then are we faithless to one another by violating the covenant (community) of our forefathers?' (vs. 10). The 'one father' is neither Adam nor Abraham or Jacob[11], but, as indicated by the parallel line, Yahweh[12], not in the sense of the Father of all men but as the Father and Creator of Israel (cf. Is. 43:1, 15; 44:7; Ps. 102:19 etc.). Salvation history had united the Lord with his people and this connectedness is the very foundation of mutual loyalty in the bosom of Israel's community. The one God and Father makes faithlessness an anomaly, incompatible with his will and the covenant of the forefathers. *B^e rit* may have here already, as in vs. 14, the meaning of covenant community. What is clear, however, is that vs. 10 does not refer to divorce. The expression *'īš b^e'āḥīw* would not have been chosen by the prophet if he had had in mind the relation between a man and his wife. Furthermore, divorce as such could hardly violate the covenant community, cf. Deut. 24:1. Our text envisages the internal controversies in the Judaean community engendered by those who preferred social privileges and economic gains to religious and national loyalty and unity by marrying foreign women. Malachi does not shrink from calling this conduct *tō'ēbā*, an abhorrance to the Lord[13], because the holiness of his people is at stake, just like Ezra some decennia later denounced mixed marriages as an abomination (cf. Ezra 9:1, 11, 14). Because Judah loves and marries 'daughters of a foreign god', i.e. foreign women who do not worship the Lord[14], the *qōdeš yhwh* is violated. The repeated use of *ḥillēl*, 'to violate', not only corroborates the interpretation that the unity of the community is jeopardized by *intermarriage*, but also suggests that *qōdeš yhwh* is synonymous

---

[11] Some manuscripts of LXX transpose the first two clauses of vs. 10, due to the desire to give God the first place, because 'father' was understood as Abraham. The same interpretation of 'father' was proposed by Jerome, Luther, Calvin and in more recent times by von Bulmerincq and Jones. Abrabanel found an allusion to Adam, Aben Ezra, David Kimchi, Grotius and more recently de Moor and Horst to Jacob.

[12] So the majority of recent commentators.

[13] The term is not only used for the faithlessness towards the covenant, but also with a social connotation, cf. Judg. 9:23; Lament. 1:2.

[14] Mitchell's explanation that the alliance of Yahweh's people with other nations is meant, is utterly unconvincing. Many commentators consider *'^ašer* to be a relative particle ('the sanctuary that He loves') but it is improbable that the verbal forms *'āhēb* and *bā'al* have a different subject. In contradistinction to vs. 11a, 'Judah' in vs. 11b is masculine because individual members of the community are meant.

with 'covenant community'[15] in vs. 10. Ezra 9:2 points equally in this direction by saying that mixed marriages engender mixing of 'the holy seed' with 'the people of the land'.

Vs. 12 states the desire that anyone who does this abomination may be banished by the Lord from the dwellings of Judah, together with all his relatives[16], even though he is a worshipper of the Lord. The metre, the wording and the contents of the verse strongly suggest that it is a gloss[17]. But even if it is authentic[18], it need not be discussed here in detail, since the contents which harken back to the preceding verses, cannot but be taken as a confirmation of the point we are trying to make, i.e. that Mal. 2:10-16 speaks about mixed marriages and their consequences.

Marrying foreign brought about another evil[19]: disdainful treatment of the Jewish wife whom the man had married in his youth. But before stating explicitly what he wants to show up (the shameful treatment of the wife of the youth), the prophet exhibits the mental blindness which had taken possession of so many of his compatriots. While they violate the community by their conduct, they fail to understand why the Lord refuses to look at their offerings and to accept them graciously. Are they not drowning the altar of the Lord with their tears? Malachi answers that Yahweh bears witness against each of them on behalf of the wife of their youth to whom they are unfaithful, although she is their *ḥ^aberet* and *'ēšet b^erīt*. Usually, *ḥ^aberet* is interpreted as partner, but it must be doubted that Malachi only wanted to state that the wife was the man's companion in life, for this would hold true for the foreign wife as well. Therefore, it is more probable that the word designates the woman as belonging to the same national-religious community as that of her husband (cf. for the religious connotation of the term Is. 44:11). Similarly, *'ēšet b^erīt* does not seem to refer to a woman united to her husband by means of a connubial contract, but to a woman who was a member of the covenant community to which also her husband belonged[20]. That *b^erīt* means 'covenant

[15] Some interpret the expression of the sanctuary of Yahweh (Smith, Marti, Mitchell, Chary, Dentan), others of Judah as the holy people of Yahweh (Verhoef, cf. Von Orelli and Sellin), of the holy land (cf. Rudolph), or of the holiness of Yahweh (recently Schreiner, 'Mischehen - Ehebruch - Ehescheidung', *ZAW* 91 (1979), 210).

[16] The meaning of *'ēr w^e'one* is still unclear, cf. Verhoef and van der Woude for a list of proposed interpretations.

[17] The curse clashes with the call on the audience of the prophet to heed to their spirit and not to be unfaithful, cf. vs. 16.

[18] So Verhoef and Rudolph.

[19] Perhaps *zō't* is a substantive in the sense of 'shame', 'shameful act', cf. Ps. 7:4; 44:18; 74:18; Job 17:8 and M. Dahood, *Psalms* I (Anchor Bible), Garden City, NY, 1966, 42; H.J. van Dijk, *Ezekiel's Prophecy on Tyre* (Biblica et Orientalia, 20), Rome, 1968, 19f.; L. Sabottka, *Zephanja* (Biblica et Orientalia, 25), Rome, 1972, 88f. Deletion of *šēnīt* is unwarranted (despite LXX) and only based on the false thesis that the prophecy of Malachi originally spoke of divorce only.

[20] Correctly so Rudolph.

community' is intimated by Mal. 2:10; 3:1c and Ps. 74:20a[21] (cf. also Dan. 11:28, 30, 32 and the use of *b^erīt* in the Dead Sea Scrolls)[22].

In vs. 14, the use of *bāgad* does not necessarily imply divorce. The prophet denounces the disgraceful treatment of the Jewish partner by her husband who had married a foreign woman upon whom he bestows all his attention, attachment and love. As indicated by the use of *ḥ^aberet* and *'ēšet b^erīt*, the essential faithlessnes, however, concerns the neglect of the Jewish wife as a member of Israel's religious community. The predilection for the foreign wife means the subordination of the Jewish wife who is humilated and disdained. Meanwhile, the new family will drift away from Israel's religious and cultural heritage, cf. Neh. 13:23-27.

Mal. 2:15 is one of the most difficult passages of the whole Old Testament. It would be a hopeless task to record all the attempts that have been made to explain this verse[23]. Exegetes who find in it a reference to Genesis 2[24] take *'eḥād* as 'one single person' and interpret that the Lord did not create man as a single individual (cf. Rudolph: 'Er hat ja nicht ein Einzelwesen erschaffen'). A similar interpretation is proposed by those commentators who alter *w^elō'* into *h^alō'*[25] and translate: 'Did He not create (them) as one?' These interpretations have the drawback that they entail a number of text emendations in the rest of vs. 15a[26] which detract from the reliability of the proposed translations on the background of Genesis 2. Apart from this, it does not sound plausible that vs. 15 alludes to this chapter since a Jewish man and a foreign woman constitute no less a conjugal unity than a Jewish man and a Jewish woman.

Equally improbable is the interpretation already propounded by Jerome, that connects Abraham with the 'one' (cf. Is. 51:2; Ez. 33:24) who did not repudiate Sarah, although he had only a 'rest of life' (because of his age) and desired to have progeny[27]. In that case *rūaḥ* would have a different meaning in vs. 15a and vs. 15b.

Others render *lō' 'eḥād* by 'no one', 'nobody'[28], but it is unlikely that the author of the verse could refer to 'no one' by 'that one' (*hā'eḥād*).

With things as they are, the text of the Septuagint which twice reads ἄλλος (Hebrew *'aḥēr*), would seem to deserve special notice. If we change *'eḥād* into *'aḥēr* and if we interpret the latter word in the sense of 'foreigner', 'non-Jew', a

[21] Psalm 74 dates to exilic times.

[22] Cf. A.S. Kapelrud, 'Der Bund in den Qumranschriften', *Bibel und Qumran*, Hans Bardtke zum 22.9.1966, Berlin, 1968, 137-149.

[23] Cf. de Moor, von Bulmerincq and Verhoef for lists of interpretations.

[24] Cf. Deissler ('le verset fait manifestement allusion à Gén., ii, 24') and Rudolph.

[25] Cf. Wellhausen, van Hoonacker, Sellin, Nötscher, Deden, Deissler.

[26] Cf. Rudolph who changes *š^e'ār*, 'remnant', into *š^e'ēr*, 'flesh', and *rūaḥ*, 'spirit', into *rewaḥ*, 'room'. He further adds *mišš^e'ēro* to *š^e'ēr*.

[27] Keil and Hitzig-Steiner interpret *lō 'eḥād* as 'nobody', *hā'eḥād* however as referring to Abraham. But Abraham did not seek the promised progeny only (Hagar!).

[28] Cf. Vuilleumier and Horst.

meaning that is widely attested in later Hebrew[29], we can render vs. 15 as follows:

A foreigner does not do this,
  as long as he has a remnant of spirit.
What is such a foreigner?
  One who wants godly children!
Then take heed to your spirit
  and let no one be unfaithful to the wife of his youth[30].

In accordance with Mal. 1:11, the glossator to whom we owe our verse holds up worshippers of other gods as an example for the people of the Lord. A foreigner, he claims, would not undermine the religious and national unity of his community the way Malachi's compatriots do. He would wish for a new generation attached to the spiritual heritage of his religion. The strange expression *zeraʿ ʾᵉlōhīm*, rendered above by 'godly children' for want of a better translation, seems to refer to descendants who worship the same gods as their fathers revere, and who do not invalidate their community, cf. the use of *zeraʿ haqqōdeš*, 'holy seed', 'holy community', in Ezra 9:2. Vs. 15 comments on the preceding verse and makes an attack on marriages with foreign women.

According to all commentators whose works we have consulted, vs. 16 speaks about divorce. Some of them regard *śānēʾ* (if they do not change the text) as a verbal adjective in the sense of a participle and assume that the subject of the first person singular is suppressed: 'for I hate sending away', i.e. 'for I hate divorce'[31]. The Lord would be the subject of *śānēʾ* and *šallaḥ* would mean the repudiation of the woman[32], cf. Deut. 24:2; Is. 50:1. Others wish to read *šillaḥ* (perf. piʿel) instead of *šallaḥ* (inf. piʿel) and render: 'if a hater repudiates', i.e. 'if one repudiates because of hatred'[33], hatred being interpreted in the sense of aversion or neglect[34]. The disadvantage of the first proposal is that vs. 16ab cannot be retained in its present form[35]. The second interpretation avoids emendation of vs. 16b, if vs. 16ab is rendered by: 'If a

---

[29] Cf. M. Jastrow, *A Dictionary of the Targumim, the Talmud Bavli and Yerushalmi, and the Midrashic Literature*, New York, 1950, I, 41.

[30] The change-over from the 3rd pers. sing. of the verbal form to the 2nd pers. sing. of the suffix of the noun is stylistically possible in Biblical Hebrew, cf. Is. 1:29; Ps. 49:20, and Keil, Verhoef, and Schreiner, 213.

[31] So Rudolph. Horst reads: 'Yahweh hates divorce'. Others change *śānēʾ* into *śānēʾtī*, 'I (= Yahweh) hate', cf. Elliger and Botterweck.

[32] The verb *śānēʾ* in the sense of divorce is attested in the Aramaic of the Elephantine papyri, not however in Biblical Hebrew. 'Hating' could of course lead to divorce, cf. Deut. 24:1ff.

[33] E.g. van Hoonacker, Junker, Nötscher, Chary.

[34] Cf. the dictionaries.

man divorces (his wife) because of aversion, ... he covers his garment with violence', but it must sincerely be doubted whether in Old Testament times even a prophet would have denounced divorce as a crime. Deuteronomy 24 tells against this interpretation.

We hold the opinion that *šallaḥ* does not mean 'send away', 'repudiate' or 'divorce' in vs. 16. It is much more probable that the verbal form[36] is an abbreviation of the idiomatic expression *šālaḥ yād* (the same abbreviation can be found in 2 Sam. 6:6 and Obadiah 13) that designates a morally detestable hostile act[37]. We can render as follows:

> ... for he who neglects (his Jewish wife)
> puts forth his hand (in hostility) ...

This interpretation tallies perfectly with 'and covers his garment with violence', likewise an idiomatic expression for (the result of) a violent act. It turns out that vs. 16 constitutes the direct continuation of vs. 14.

Malachi does not propound a general statement (as suggested by commentators) that contradicts Deuteronomy 24, but he makes a vigorous attack on the prevailing practices of his time: the subordination and maltreatment of married Jewish women because of foreign heathen wives. It should not surprise us that Yahweh is expressly designated in this connection as 'the God of Israel', thus accentuating that He is concerned about the community of his chosen people.

If the foregoing short interpretation of Mal. 2:10-16 stands up to scrutiny, the inference may be drawn that the text does not deal with divorce and cannot be looked upon as a prelude of what Jesus had to say about it (Matt. 19:6, 9)[38]. Accordingly, the pericope does not contradict Deut. 24:1, but rather paved the way for Ezra's struggle for a pure community and his call on the assembly of Judah to separate themselves from alien contacts[39].

---

[35] Many change *w^ekissā* into *k^ekassē*.
[36] Reading *šālaḥ* (qal).
[37] Cf. P. Humbert, 'Etendre la main', *VT* 12 (1962), 383-395.
[38] As asserted by nearly all commentators.
[39] Cf. Ezra 9-10.

A CASE OF REINTERPRETATION IN THE OLD GREEK OF DANIEL 11

by

ARIE VAN DER KOOIJ

Our jubilee has made an important contribution to the study of the Book of Daniel, paying in particular attention to the phenomenon of apocalyptic interpretation of history ('apokalyptische Geschichtsdeutung'). The present article will deal with the Old Greek version of Dan. 11, a chapter which, in its Hebrew form, offers such an interpretation of history.

I

The text of the Old Greek of Daniel (LXX Dan.) is attested by a very small group of manuscripts: ms 88, the Syro-Hexaplar, and the Chester Beatty Papyrus 967. Because of its date (round 200 A.D.) and its type (pre-hexaplaric) the last witness is most important. For his Göttingen edition J. Ziegler, however, had only access to a part of the Daniel-text of this papyrus[1]. In recent times the Daniel-text of 967 has been edited by A. Geissen, W. Hamm and R. Roca-Puig[2].

LXX Dan. belongs together with LXX Isaiah, Job, Proverbs, and 1 Esdras to the freely translated books of the Septuagint[3]. In terms of classical

---

[1] See J. Ziegler, *Susanna, Daniel, Bel et Draco* (Septuaginta, Vol. XVI,2), Göttingen, 1954, 7: he had only access to the text of Dan. 3:72-8:27 of 967 (order in 967: ch. 7-8, ch. 5-6) in the publication of F.G. Kenyon, *The Chester Beatty Biblical Papyri*, Fasc. vii, London, 1937.

[2] A. Geissen, *Der Septuaginta-Text des Buches Daniel Kap. 5-12, zusammen mit Susanna, Bel et Draco, sowie Esther Kap. 1,1a-2,15, nach dem Kölner Teil des Papyrus 967* (PTA 5), Bonn, 1968; W. Hamm, *Der Septuaginta-Text des Buches Daniel Kap. 1-2 nach dem Kölner Teil des Papyrus 967* (PTA 10), Bonn, 1969; W. Hamm, *Der Septuaginta-Text des Buches Daniel Kap. 3-4 nach dem Kölner Teil des Papyrus 967* (PTA 21), Bonn, 1977; R. Roca-Puig, *Daniel. Dos semifolis del còdex 967, Papir de Barcelona, Inv. no 42 i 43*, Barcelona, 1974 (published as article in *Aegyptus* 56 (1976), 3-18).

[3] Comp. R.A. Kraft, 'Septuagint', in *IDBS*, Abingdon, 1976, 814: he classifies LXX Dan., Isaiah, and 1 Esdras as 'nonparaphrastic free renderings'. See also R. Sollamo, *Renderings of Hebrew Semiprepositions in the Septuagint* (AASF 19), Helsinki, 1979, 284 (LXX Dan. as one of the most freely rendered books of the Septuagint). On the question of 'literal' and 'free'

antiquity itself LXX Dan. is to be classified as a *sensus de sensu* translation[4].

As to date and place of origin it is quite probable that LXX Dan. has been written in the second half of the second century B.C. in Egypt (Alexandria). Arguments for this dating are *inter alia* specific relations between LXX Dan. and 1 Macc., and between LXX Dan. and LXX 1 Esdras[5]. An interesting piece of evidence which points to Ptolemaic Alexandria as place of origin, is the expression γραμματικὴ τέχνη in 1:17[6]. To this the use of γραμματικός in 1:4 may be added. In LXX Dan. 11 the expression 'the king of the South' has been rendered by 'the king of Egypt', whereas the other one, 'the king of the North', has not been interpreted in such a way. This element, too, is in favour of an Egyptian locale, because the expression 'the king of the South' (i.e. the king of Egypt) would have been misunderstood by Egyptian readers.

II

Chapter 11 of the Book of Daniel presents in the form of prophecies 'a survey of history from the age of 'the four Persian kings' down through the Hellenistic age culminating in the reign of Antiochus Epiphanes'[7]. These prophecies are of the type of the so-called *vaticinia ex eventu*, attesting a literary genre which is also known from ancient Babylonia, Egypt and Egyptian Judaism[8].

As to LXX Dan. 11 the important question is: how has its author dealt with the prophecies in this chapter? Did he produce a Greek text in which the

---

translations see J. Barr, *The Typology of Literalism in Ancient Biblical Translations* (MSU XV), Göttingen, 1979. For characterizations of LXX Dan. see especially A. Bludau, *Die alexandrinische Übersetzung des Buches Daniel und ihr Verhältnis zum massorethischen Text* (Bst. II, 2-3), Freiburg im Breisgau, 1897; J. A. Montgomery, *The Book of Daniel* (ICC), Edinburgh, 1927 (^{3}1959), 35-39. The unpublished thesis of A.P.J. McCrystall, *Studies in the Old Greek Translation of Daniel* (Oxford, 1980) was not available to me.

[4] For this expression see S. Brock, 'Aspects of Translation Technique in Antiquity', *GRBS* 20 (1979), 69-87; G.J.M. Bartelink, *Hieronymus, Liber de optimo genere interpretandi (Ep. 57)*, Leiden, 1980, 46ff.

[5] See Bludau, *Übersetzung*, 7-9, 143; Montgomery, *Daniel*, 38; R.H. Charles, *A Critical and Exegetical Commentary on the Book of Daniel*, Oxford, 1929, LI. On the close relationship between LXX Dan. and 1 Esdras see Hamm, *Septuaginta-Text* (1969), 79 (note 1 (lit.)). On the date of 1 Esdras see Z. Talshir, 'The Milieu of 1 Esdras in the Light of its Vocabulary', in: *The Septuaginta. Studies in honour of John William Wevers on his sixty-fifth birthday*, ed. by A. Pietersma and C. Cox, Mississauga, Ontario, 1984, 141.

[6] Comp. P.M. Fraser, *Ptolemaic Alexandria*. Vol. I. Oxford, 1972, 470; id., Vol. II, 680.

[7] Montgomery, *Daniel*, 420.

[8] For Mesopotamia see e.g. H. Unger and S.A. Kaufman, 'A New Akkadian Prophecy Text', *JAOS* 95 (1975), 371-375; A.K. Grayson, 'Assyria and Babylonia', *Or.* 49 (1980), 183f.. For Egypt see e.g. J. Gwyn Griffiths, 'Apocalyptic in the Hellenistic Era', in *Apocalypticism in the Mediterranean World and the Near East*, ed. D. Hellholm, Tübingen, 1983, 273-293. For Egyptian Judaism see J.J. Collins, *The Sibylline Oracles of Egyptian Judaism* (SBL Diss. Ser. 13), Missoula, 1972.

prophecies as *vaticinia ex eventu* make sense? Did he know to which events the Hebrew text alludes? A. Bludau is quite pessimistic about this last question. In his view the author of LXX Dan. knew next to nothing of the political events Dan. 11:5-39 refers to. ' ... die Ereignisse aus jüngerer Zeit, die Kriege, Bündnisse, Verschwägerungen der späteren Ptolemäer und Seleuciden, sind ihm unbekannte Dinge'[9].

Some elements in LXX Dan. 11, however, do not support this view. An interesting one for instance is the rendering of Ῥωμαῖοι in vs 30 (Hebrew: *ktym*). Here the translator offers a correct interpretation, for Dan. 11:30 refers to the Romans who in 168 B.C. forced Antiochus IV to leave Egypt[10].

Further, one has also to take into account the possibility, that LXX Dan. alludes to other events than the Hebrew text does, or that LXX Dan. presents a different view on some event.

All this requires a full analysis of LXX Dan. 11 in comparison with MT Dan. 11. Such an analysis should be carried out on several levels, not only on the level of word-word relations between Hebrew and Greek (which dominates too much in the method of analysis of Bludau), but also on the level of syntax, style, and semantics of the Greek text, both in comparison with the Hebrew and on its own, on the level of the context of LXX Dan. as a whole, and on the level of interpretation or reinterpretation of the prophecies[11]. Within the limits of this article we confine ourselves to one of the verses of Dan. 11: vs 14.

III

The Hebrew (Masoretic) text of Dan. 11:14 reads in translation as follows:

> And in those times many shall stand up against the king of the South, and violent men among your own people shall lift themselves up in order to fulfil a vision, and they shall stumble.

This verse forms part of the prophecies (vs 10-19) about the exploits of Antiochus III (223-187 B.C.). Vs 14a refers to political actions against the king of Egypt, in the last years of the third century B.C.. Vs 14b knows of 'violent men' among the Jewish people in Judaea, who try by means of violent actions

---

[9] Bludau, *Übersetzung*, 88.

[10] For exegetical elements in LXX Dan. 11 see F.F. Bruce, 'The Earliest Old Testament Interpretation', in: *The Witness of Tradition* (OTS 17), Leiden, 1972, 42f.; R. Hanhart, 'Die Übersetzungstechnik der Septuaginta als Interpretation (Daniel 11,29 und die Aegyptenzüge des Antiochus Epiphanes)', in: *Mélanges Dominique Barthélemy* (OBO 38), Fribourg/Göttingen, 1981, 136-157.

[11] I have dealt with these 'levels' in my forthcoming article 'The Septuagint and the Exegesis of the Bible'.

to fulfil a vision. These men are characterized in a very negative way. It is not very likely that the choice of the word *pryṣ* ('violent one') has been made in order to express the idea of 'breaching (*prṣ*) the Law'[12]. It is more probable that the author of Dan. 11 uses the plural of *bn pryṣ* (comp. Ez. 18:10) in order to condemn their violent way of fulfilling a vision, because this conflicts with the view of the Book of Daniel[13].

It is not clear which Jewish group is meant[14], but from vs 14a one may assume that it was an anti-ptolemaic group or party. They apparently believed that the time of fulfilment of a vision (or: visions, i.e. prophecies, in a general sense[15]) had come[16]. One is tempted to think of the time of 202 or 201 B.C., when Antiochus III occupied Palestine, including Judaea and Jerusalem[17]. Ptolemaic Egypt seemed to be the loosing party. In that case the 'stumbling' of the violent men (end of vs 14) refers to the successful counterattack of the Ptolemaic army in the winter of 201-200 B.C., resulting in the reoccupation of Palestine[18].

IV

Daniel 11:14:

MT Dan. (Ketib)- LXX Dan. (ed. Ziegler)

wb'tym hhm- καὶ ἐν τοῖς καίροις ἐκείνοις
rbym y'mdw- διάνοιαι ἀναστήσονται
'l mlk hngb- ἐπὶ τὸν βασιλέα Αἰγύπτου
wbny pryṣy 'mk- καὶ ἀνοικοδομήσει τὰ πεπτωκότα τοῦ ἔθνους σου

---

[12] E. Meyer, *Ursprung und Anfänge des Christentums*, II, Stuttgart und Berlin, 1921, 127f.

[13] See J.C.H. Lebram, 'The Piety of the Jewish Apocalyptists', in: *Apocalypticism*, ed. Hellholm, 184. With this use of the word (*bn*) *pryṣ* one may compare the use of λῃστής by Josephus, denoting members of the Zealot party; see M. Hengel, *Die Zeloten* (AGAJU, 1), Leiden/Köln, ²1976, 42-47 (on the word λῃστής). For the equivalence: *pryṣ* — λῃστής, see LXX Jer. 7:11.

[14] For various suggestions see A. Schlatter, 'Die *Bᵉne pariṣim* bei Daniel: 11,14', *ZAW* 14 (1894), 145-151 (the Tobiads); E. Täubler, 'Jerusalem 201 to 199 B.C.E.. On the History of a Messianic Movement', *JQR* 37 (1946-47), 1-30; B.Z. Wacholder, *The Dawn of Qumran. The Sectarian Torah and the Teacher of Righteousness* (MHUC 8), Cincinnati, 1983, 200-202 ('Is Daniel's Reference to the Unfulfilled Vision an Allusion to Qumran?'). For a critical discussion see V. Tcherikover, *Hellenistic Civilization and the Jews*, New York, 1975 (= 1959), 77-80.

[15] As is the case with the similar expression *hqm ḥzwn* in Sirach 36:15!

[16] Cf. J.C.H. Lebram, *Das Buch Daniel* (Zürcher Bibelkomm. AT 23), Zürich, 1984, 127.

[17] See H.H. Schmitt, *Untersuchungen zur Geschichte Antiochos' des Grossen und seiner Zeit* (Historia, Einzelschriften 6), Wiesbaden, 1964, 235f. (on the chronological aspects of this event).

[18] Cf. N.W. Porteous, *Das Danielbuch* (ATD), 137; M. Hengel, *Judentum und Hellenismus* (WUNT 10), Tübingen, ²1973, 14. On the Ptolemaic military action itself see below.

yns'w- καὶ ἀναστήσεται
lh'myd ḥzwn- εἰς τὸ ἀναστῆσαι τὴν προφητείαν
wnkšlw- καὶ προσκόψουσι

> As for the Greek text Pap. 967 has the reading διανοιαν[19] (instead of διανοιαι), but this reading does not make sense as object of the verb in this part of the sentence; it may be due to a mechanical error (comp. the beginning of the next word in the Greek text).

There are some striking differences between the MT and the LXX of Dan. 11:14[20]. We will deal with them on several levels in order to find out which may be the reasons for them.

On the level of word-word relations the following observations can be made:

— *rbym* - διάνοιαι: according to Bludau the Greek here reflects a different Hebrew *Vorlage* (*r'ym*)[21]; another possibility is the reading of *rb* as *lb* ('heart').

— 'the king of the South' - 'the king of Egypt' : see above.

— *wbny* - καὶ ἀνοικοδομήσει: a rendering via *bny/bnh* ('to build').

— *pryṣy* - τὰ πεπτωκότα: a rendering via *prṣ* ('breach'); for this equivalent see Amos 9:11 (MT and LXX)! For *bnh* + *prṣ* compare Eccles. 3:3.

— *yns'w* - καὶ ἀναστήσεται: the singular in the Greek text is in line with the sing. of the preceding verb.

— *ḥzwn* - τὴν προφητείαν: for this rendering see also 2 Chron. 32:32, and Sirach 36:15 (14). In LXX Dan. this rendering of *ḥzwn* is not the usual one; in all other instances this Hebrew word is translated as ὅρασις or ὅραμα.

The differences between MT and LXX are, however, not only a matter of some word-word relations; they affect also the syntax of the whole sentence. Whereas MT consists of three parts, containing a verb in each of them, LXX is a sentence composed of four parts, with a verb in each of them. In MT all verbal forms are in the plural; in LXX the situation is as follows: one verb in the plural (subject: 'thoughts'), two verbs in the sing. ('he'), and one in the plural ('they'). It stands to reason that 'he' in LXX is the king of Egypt.

The next question concerns semantics and lexical aspects. What does the Greek text of the LXX mean semantically? Does this text make sense on its own, or not? In translation the text reads as follows:

---

[19] See Geissen, *Septuaginta-Text*, 252.

[20] The so-called Theodotion-text, on the other hand, is in agreement with MT: καὶ ἐν τοῖς καιροῖς ἐκείνοις πολλοὶ ἐπαναστήσονται ἐπὶ βασιλέα τοῦ νότου καὶ οἱ υἱοὶ τῶν λοιμῶν τοῦ λαοῦ σου ἐπαρθήσονται τοῦ στῆσαι ὅρασιν καὶ ἀσθενήσουσι.

[21] Bludau, *Übersetzung*, 73.

And in those times thoughts shall stand up against the king of Egypt, and he shall rebuild the ruins of your people, and he shall stand up in order to realize the prophecy, and they shall stumble.

The word διάνοια in our text has the meaning of 'thought' in the sense of (political) intention or plan. Comp. also LXX Dan. 11:25 (διανοίᾳ , MT *mḥšbwt*). For its plural see for instance LXX Jos. 5:1 (MT *lb*); comp. further plurals like βουλαί (Dan. 7:8), λογισμοί (11:24), and μέριμναι (11:26).

The expression ἀνοικοδομεῖν τὰ πεπτωκότα is also found in LXX Amos 9:11: καὶ ἀνοικοδομήσω τὰ πεπτωκότα αὐτῆς. For πεπτωκότα in the sense of ruins see also LXX Isaiah 49:19 (the ruins of Sion)[22].

As to the phrase ἀναστῆσαι τὴν προφητείαν LXX Ez. 13:6 is to be mentioned: τοῦ ἀναστῆσαι λόγον (MT *lqym dbr,* in connection with false prophets). A similar expression is used in LXX Sirach 36:14: καὶ ἔγειρον προφητείας ... (Hebrew *hqm ḥzwn*). Its meaning is 'to fulfil prophecies'. (For *hq(y)m* in this sense comp. 1 Sam. 3:12 (MT *'qym* — LXX ἐπεγερῶ)). The last verb of our text (προσκόπτειν) occurs also in 11:19, 33.

Semantically, the text of LXX Dan. 11:14 can be considered as making sense. But at the same time it will be clear that with all this the full meaning of the Greek text is not yet established. The text, presenting itself as a prophecy, requires further examination, mainly as to the question to which events it refers.

As for the wider context LXX Dan. 11:14 forms part of the prophetic passage of LXX Dan. 11:2-12:3. This part of the Old Greek of Daniel is called ὅραμα and πρόσταγμα (10:1). It contains what will happen to the people of Daniel in the last period of days (see 10:14), being revealed to him by a divine messenger. The things which will happen are called προστάγματα (10:11, 15; 12:4, 9) (MT *dbr*), i.e. events which are seen as decisions of God. One of these προστάγματα is LXX Dan. 11:14. From this it follows that this text can be treated as a prophecy about certain events 'in the last period of days'.

The question then is to which events our text possibly alludes. According to the middle part of it 'he', the king of Egypt, 'will rebuild the ruins of your people'. Describing some event before 168 B.C. (see LXX Dan. 11:30), the quoted part of 11:14 has probably to be connected with the reoccupation of Judaea by the Ptolemaic army in the winter of 201-200 B.C. As Polybius puts it, 'Scopas, the general of Ptolemy, set out for the upper country and during the winter subdued the Jewish nation' (... τὸ 'Ιουδαίων ἔθνος)[23]. The fact

---

[22] Comp. also LXX Sirach 49:13: τείχη πεπτωκότα (c. ἐγείρειν), and 4 Macc. 2:14: καὶ τὰ πεπτωκότα συνεγείρων. On the verb ἀνοικοδομεῖν see P.D.M. Turner, 'ἀνοικοδομεῖν and intra-Septuagintal borrowing', *VT* 27 (1977), 492f. The Hebrew *prṣ* often refers to breaches in *walls* (2 Ki. 14:13; Neh. 1:3; 2:13; 2 Chron. 25:23; 26:6; 32:5).

[23] See M. Stern (ed.), *Greek and Latin Authors on Jews and Judaism.* Vol. I. Jerusalem, 1974,

that Polybius describes this event rather negatively constitutes no argument against our interpretation. It is very well possible that the same event is looked upon by others more positively.

LXX Dan. 11:14 speaks of the rebuilding of the ruins of the people (ἔθνος) of Daniel. This probably refers to the restoration of what has been destroyed, during war(s), in Judaea, and particularly in the most important place of the Jewish ἔθνος, Jerusalem. From some texts we know that the matter of restoration of this city was a very important one in the first years of the second century B.C.. It is one of the main points of the famous letter which Antiochus III wrote to Ptolemy, the governor of Coele-Syria and Phoenicia: 'we have seen fit on our part to require them (sc. the Jews) for these acts and to restore their city which has been destroyed by the hazards of war' (... καὶ τὴν πόλιν αὐτῶν ἀναλαβεῖν κατεφθαρμένην ὑπὸ τῶν περὶ τοὺς πολέμους συμπεσόντων)[24].

The next part of LXX Dan. 11:14 says that 'he', the king of Egypt, 'will stand up in order to fulfil the prophecy'. One may safely assume that this 'prophecy' relates to the restoration motif. Restoration and rebuilding, particularly of Jerusalem, is a well-known theme in the prophecies of the Old Testament.

Thus one gets the impression that 'the prophecy' in LXX Dan. 11:14 is meant in a general sense. But the question arises if this is the case indeed. The interesting and striking correspondence between LXX Dan. 11:14 and LXX Amos 9:11 suggests that Amos 9:11 is 'the' prophecy. It seems very likely that the author of LXX Dan. 11:14 has read his Hebrew *Vorlage* in the light of Amos 9:11, especially as far as the word *prṣ* is concerned[25]. But, because of the fact that the theme of rebuilding and restoration of Jerusalem and Judaea is a common one in the prophecies, it seems more probable that the author of LXX Dan. 11:14 made use of Amos 9:11 only as a means to introduce this common theme into Dan. 11:14. Therefore, 'the' prophecy in this text is best understood in the sense of the (written) prophecies in general[26].

The first part of LXX Dan. 11:14 speaks of political intentions or plans against the king of Egypt. As for the last years of the third century B.C. this is

---

113 (with comments on p. 113f.). Comp. also Jerome (in his commentary on Daniel, ad 11:14b): Cumque Antiochus teneret Iudaeam, missus Scopas, Aetholi filius, dux Ptolemaei partium, adversum Antiochum fortiter dimicavit cepitque Iudaeam.

[24] Josephus, Ant. 12:138, in the translation of R. Marcus (see LCL 365, 71). For a positive view on the authenticity of the letter of Antiochus III see esp. E. Bickerman, *Studies in Jewish and Christian History* (AGAJU 9), Vol. 2, Leiden, 1980, 44-85 ('La charte séleucide de Jérusalem'); Th. Fischer, *Seleukiden und Makkabäer*, Bochum, 1980, 3-7 (lit.). On the restoration of Jerusalem see also Sirach 50:1-4.

[25] Turner is of the opinion that the expression ἀνοικοδομεῖν τὰ πεπτωκότα in LXX Dan. 11:14 has been borrowed from LXX Amos 9:11 (see *VT* 27 (1977), 492f.).

[26] Comp. Tobit 14:3-8: about the splendid rebuilding of Jerusalem and its temple, καθὼς ἐλάλησαν περὶ αὐτῆς οἱ προφῆται (vs 5, mss BA).

to be related, first of all, to the treaty between Philip of Macedonia and Antiochus III on the partition of Ptolemaic dominions. According to this treaty Antiochus III should take possession of Coele-Syria and Phoenicia[27]. Further the anti-ptolemaic intentions in Judaea may be meant, as we know them from MT Dan. 11:14 (see above).

The end of LXX Dan. 11:14 reads 'and they will stumble'. The problem is to whom or to what 'they' refers. In vs 19 and vs 33 the same verb is used for persons, but this does not fit very well in vs 14. Here 'they' is best related with the plural in the first part of the verse: διάνοιαι. The meaning then is: the plans will fail. (Comp. for a similar expression LXX Jos. 5:1: καὶ ἐτάκησαν αὐτῶν αἱ διάνοιαι.) 'The plans will fail', because Scopas reoccupied the Ptolemaic dominion, including Judaea. And in LXX Dan. 11:14 this action of the king of Egypt is described in terms of 'eschatological' salvation.

V

As may be clear from the above the Old Greek of Daniel 11:14, as a prophecy, makes good sense. Just as its Hebrew counterpart this Greek text can very well be related to certain events in the period about 200 B.C. This outcome does not support the opinion of Bludau that the author of LXX Dan. 11 should have known next to nothing of political events in the third and second century B.C.[28].

We will now return to the question of the differences between the MT and LXX of Dan. 11:14. What does our interpretation of LXX Dan. 11:14 mean for the question of the reasons for these differences? Because of the fact that the Hebrew text of Dan. 11:14 makes good sense on its own, the assumption of a different *Vorlage* is an unlikely one, and because of the fact that the Hebrew text does not contain difficult words, LXX Dan. 11:14 needs not to be considered as resulting from guesswork. On the contrary, if our interpretation of LXX Dan. 11:14 is correct, the differences between MT and LXX are to be seen as intentional ones, necessary for a particular reinterpretation of Dan. 11:14, and arrived at by means of certain exegetical devices of that time[29].

Whereas MT Dan. 11:14 speaks of anti-ptolemaic actions of violent men in Judaea, condemning these actions because of the 'violence' involved, the Old

---

[27] On this treaty see H.H. Schmitt, *Untersuchungen zur Geschichte Antiochos' des Grossen*, 237-261.

[28] Our treatment of vs 14 alone is, of course, a very limited one. A broader analysis of LXX Dan. 11 has to be carried out in order to see if the other verses also make sense as *vaticinia ex eventu*.

[29] Such as different vocalizations, the interchange of similar letters (be it graphic or phonetic similarity), etymological exegesis. See E. Tov, *The Text-Critical Use of the Septuagint in Biblical Research* (Jerusalem Biblical Studies 3), Jerusalem, 1981, 239ff.

Greek version of this text very likely refers to the military action of the Ptolemaic army under the command of Scopas, describing this action in very positive terms. Instead of mentioning the Jewish rebels, the author of the Greek text apparently wished to stress the positive way in which, in his view, the Ptolemaic king had dealt with Judaea and Jerusalem in the winter of 201-200 B.C. One gets the impression that he belonged to a pro-ptolemaic party[30]. Be that as it may, LXX Dan. 11:14 presents an interesting case of reinterpretation (or reactualization) of the prophecy of Dan. 11:14, attesting a very positive view on king Ptolemy V Epiphanes[31].

---

[30] Lebram is of the opinion that the author-redactor of the Hebrew-Aramaic Book of Daniel belonged to a pro-ptolemaic group. See his article on 'Daniel/Danielbuch' in *TRE* VIII, Berlin/New York, 1981, 339.

[31] One is remembered here of the decree on the Rosetta stone, written by Egyptian priests, assembled at Memphis in the year 197-196 B.C.; in this decree Ptolemy V Epiphanes is honoured because of his benefactions to the temples of Egypt, his restoration of peace and security in Egypt, and his punishment of rebels. See E.A. Walter Budge, *The Rosetta Stone*, London, 1929 (= New York, 1976), 51ff.

DIE ANTIKE ELEMENTARLEHRE UND DER AUFBAU VON SAPIENTIA SALOMONIS 11-19

von

PETER T. VAN ROODEN

Sapientia Salomonis wird gewöhnlich in drei Abschnitte untergebracht. Dabei ist man sich über die Abgrenzung nicht einig. Der erste Teil (Kap. 1 - Anfang oder Ende Kap. 6) handelt vom Schicksal des weisen Gerechten. Der zweite Teil (Anfang/Ende Kap. 6 bis einschliesslich Kap. 9 oder 10) beschreibt das Wesen der Weisheit. Thema des Schlussteils (Kap. 10/11 - 19) ist das Handeln der Weisheit in der Geschichte. Darin werden ab Kap. 11 die einzelnen Plagen der Ägypter mit den Mühsalen der Israeliten auf ihrem Zug durch die Wüste verglichen. In der Nachfolge von F. Focke wird dieser letzte Teil meistens als Synkrisis zur Illustration des Hauptteils des Buches, Kap. 6/7 - 9/10 bezeichnet[1]. Nun ist eine Synkrisis eine formale Stilfigur, die durch Vergleiche zwischen Sachen oder Personen zeigen will, dass die aufgeführten Objekte besser, schlechter, oder gleich gut sind. Nach der Feststellung, dass in Sap. 11-19 eine Serie Synkrisen vorkommt, bleiben noch zahlreiche Fragen offen. So wird die Reihe der Vergleiche durch zwei Exkurse unterbrochen (Kap. 12 - 15). Zudem scheint der Schluss dieses Teils (Kap. 19) mit den vorangegangenen Vergleichen nicht direkt in Verbindung zu stehen. Es besteht darum Anlass, Intention, Form und Aufbau dieses letzten, grossen Teils von Sapientia genauer zu untersuchen.

1.

Nach Kap. 10, ein in sich geschlossener Teil über die Wirkung der Weisheit in der Geschichte, der sieben Beispiele ihres rettenden Handelns an grossen Figuren aus der biblischen Geschichte schildert, fängt Kap. 11 an mit einer Beschreibung des Zuges der Israeliten durch die Wüste (11:1-3)[2]. Einerseits ist diese eine allgemeine Einleitung zu den folgenden Kapiteln, andererseits ein für einen guten Anschluss an Kap. 10 notwendiger Übergang. Denn Kap. 10

---

[1] F. Focke, *Die Entstehung der Weisheit Salomos*, Göttingen, 1913, 12-15. Für einen allgemeineren Überblick und viele Beispiele aus der klassischen Literatur, s. seinen Artikel 'Synkrisis', *Hermes* 58 (1923), 327-368.

[2] In 11:1 muss nicht σοφία als Subjekt gelesen werden. Εὐόδωσεν ist intransitiv. Kap. 10 schliesst mit einer Klimax. 11:1 ist ein neuer Einsatz. S. J.M. Reese, 'Plan and Structure in the Book of Wisdom', *CBQ* 27 (1965), 329.

endet mit der Rettung der Israeliten aus Ägypten und dem Untergang der Ägypter im Roten Meer. Die Synkrisen behandeln danach die Plagen, die die Ägypter schon vorher erlitten haben. Um die chronologische Reihenfolge beizubehalten, ist es notwendig, nach dem Schluss von Kap. 10 den Fortgang der Darstellung am Schicksal der Israeliten zu orientieren. Darum beginnt in 11:4 der erste Vergleich mit einer Beschreibung des Wunders vom Wasser aus dem Felsen, das den dürstenden Israeliten geschenkt wird[3]. In Vers 5 wird eins der formalen Prinzipien, die den Aufbau der Vergleiche bestimmen, ausgedrückt.

> Denn durch eben das, wodurch ihre Feinde gezüchtigt wurden,
> empfingen sie, wenn sie in Not waren, Wohltat.

In diesem und den folgenden Vergleichen wird aufgezeigt, dass den Israeliten bei ihrem Zug durch die Wüste mit denselben Mitteln geholfen wurde, mit denen die Ägypter während der Plagen gestraft wurden. Daher wird in 11:6-7 eine diesem Prinzip entsprechende Plage der Ägypter beschrieben. Sie litten Durst, nachdem das Wasser des Nils durch Vermischung mit 'Mordblut' untrinkbar geworden war. In einem Nachsatz wird der Leser auf ein zweites Prinzip verwiesen, nach dem Sapientia bei der Konstruktion der Vergleiche vorgeht. Das Wasser hatte sich in Blut verwandelt, weil die Ägypter die israelitischen Kinder getötet hatten. Es ist (11:16) das *principium talionis*,

> dass, wodurch jemand sündigt, er eben dadurch gestraft wird.

11:8-10 kehrt zu den Israeliten zurück, die in der Wüste ebenfalls, wenn auch in geringerem Masse, Durst litten, bevor sie das Wasser aus dem Fels empfingen. Auf diese Art und Weise verstanden sie, wie schwer Gott ihren Feind gestraft hatte. Dies ist das dritte Konstruktionsprinzip der Vergleiche.

> Denn es sollte über jene, die Unterdrücker, ein unabwendbarer
> Mangel kommen;
> diesen aber sollte nur gezeigt werden, wie ihre Feinde gequält
> wurden (16:4).

Wir finden also in dieser ersten Synkrisis (11:3-14) drei Prinzipien, die Sapientia bei seiner besonderen Paraphrase von Exodus benutzt. Die Plagen der Ägypter werden mit den Wohltaten, die den Israeliten während des Durchzu-

---

[3] Der erste Vergleich wird von zwei Stichworten eingerahmt: εδίψησαν / διψήσαντες. Die Benutzung dieser sogenannten 'inclusions' ist in Sapientia relativ häufig. Vgl. Reese, 'Plan and Structure'.

ges zukommen, verbunden, weil entweder Strafe und Wohltat mit demselben Mittel vollzogen werden, oder die Israeliten dasselbe erlitten wie die Ägypter, nur in geringerem Ausmass. Ferner werden die Plagen der Ägypter so beschrieben, dass der Zusammenhang zwischen Sünde und Strafe deutlich wird. Alle Vergleiche sind gemäss diesen Prinzipien aufgebaut, jedoch werden diese nicht alle in jedem Vergleich angewendet[4].

Wir wollen zunächst das Vorkommen dieser Prinzipien in den Vergleichen analysieren. In 11:15 scheint Sapientia gleich mit der Beschreibung einer zweiten Plage anzufangen. Weil die Ägypter ekelhafte Tiere verehren, werden sie durch solche Tiere am Essen gehindert. Es stellt sich jedoch heraus, dass es sich um den Beginn zweier Exkurse handelt. Der erste (11:15-12:27) hat Gottes Barmherzigkeit zum Thema. Diese Barmherzigkeit wird aus dem in 11:16 genannten *principium talionis* entwickelt, mit dem Gott dem Menschen seine Sünde in Erinnerung zu rufen versucht, sodass er sich rechtzeitig bekehren kann. Der Exkurs endet mit demselben Prinzip, nun jedoch verbunden mit dem anderen, nach dem die Israeliten in geringerem Masse dasselbe erleiden wie die Ägypter (12:19-22). Dieser Schluss nimmt gleichzeitig die zweite Plage wieder auf[5]. Die Ägypter werden als Strafe für ihren Götzendienst von ekelhaften Tieren gequält. So geht der erste Exkurs fliessend in den zweiten (Kap. 13 - 15) über, der die Greuel des Götzendienstes behandelt. Dieser zweite Exkurs arbeitet auf eine Klimax hin. Er beschreibt zunächst relativ milde Formen des Götzendienstes, so wie der Verehrung von Sternen, behandelt dann ernstere, die Verehrung von Götzenbildern, und endet mit dem verwerflichsten Beispiel dieses Irrtums: der Verehrung ekelhafter Tiere durch die Ägypter. In Kap. 16 kann dann mühelos mit der zweiten Synkrisis begonnen werden (16:1-4)[6].

Hier bilden die Ägypter, die Hunger litten, weil sie von Tieren (Fröschen) vom Essen abgehalten wurden, einen starken Kontrast zu den Israeliten, die von anderen Tieren (Wachteln) gespeist wurden. In dieser Synkrisis werden alle Prinzipien aus dem ersten Vergleich angewendet. Die Ägypter werden durch Frösche bestraft, weil sie ekelhafte Tiere verehrten, und die Israeliten werden von anderen Tieren gerettet, nachdem sie kurze Zeit Hunger gelitten hatten (16:3).

Im dritten Vergleich (16:5-14) wird die Heuschrecken- und Stechfliegenplage

---

[4] Dass diese *drei* Prinzipien die Vergleiche konstituieren hat nur C.L.W. Grimm, *Das Buch der Weisheit*, Leipzig, 1837, 331 bemerkt. Nahezu alle anderen Kommentatoren nehmen nur ein Prinzip an.

[5] Für den Zusammenhang der zwei Exkurse und den zweiten Vergleich, s. Focke, *Weisheit Salomos*, 10-14; J. Fichtner, *Weisheit Salomos*, Tübingen, 1938; A.G. Wright, 'The Structure of the Book of Wisdom', *Biblica* 48 (1967), 178 (Wright lässt zu Unrecht den zweiten Exkurs bereits in 15:17 aufhören und entzieht ihm so die Klimax); D. Winston, *The Wisdom of Solomon*, New York, 1979, 145.

[6] Die 'inclusions' sind (16:1,4): ἐβασανίσθησαν / ἐβασανίζοντο.

(durch deren Stich bei Sapientia die Ägypter sterben) dem Anfall der Schlangen auf die Israeliten in der Wüste gegenübergestellt. Allerdings herrscht über diesen Vergleich in der Forschung Uneinigkeit. Einige zählen ihn zu 16:1-4, andere wollen ihn nicht als selbständigen Vergleich ansehen[7]. Es kommt jedenfalls in diesem Vergleich keine wirkliche Wohltat an den Israeliten vor. Es wird nur erwähnt, dass diese beinahe, nur dank der Hilfe Gottes nicht, an Schlangenbissen sterben, im Gegensatz zu den Ägyptern, die an dem Anschein nach viel ungefährlicheren, kleineren Tieren sterben. Das Prinzip von 11:5, dass womit den Israeliten wohlgetan wird, die Ägypter gestraft werden, wird hier also nicht angewendet. Ein zweiter Grund, diesen Teil als eine eigene Synkrisis zu eliminieren[8], ist, dass er nicht den von Focke konstatierten Regeln dieser Stilform entspricht[9]. Er beginnt nicht mit dem schwachen Teil des Vergleichs, den Ägyptern, sondern mit dem starken, den Israeliten. Nun kann gegen das Letztgenannte der Einwand erhoben werden, dass auch die erste Synkrisis mit den Israeliten (11:4) beginnt, und dass die meistgenannte biblische Parallele für eine Synkrisis (Jes. 65:13ff) der Regel von Focke ebenfalls nicht entspricht. Dem ersten Einwand kann man entgegnen, dass hier zwar in der genauen Bedeutung des Wortes von einer Wohltat keine Rede ist, dass jedoch die Rolle des Prinzips von 11:5 übernommen worden ist von dem Prinzip von 11:9-10 und 16:4: Die Israeliten erleiden in geringerem Masse dasselbe wie die Ägypter. 16:5-14 ist deutlich eine formale Einheit[10], und ihr Inhalt wird am Ende von Sapientia in einer Art Rückblick als gesonderte Plage genannt (19:10). Das Stück muss also als eine gesonderte Synkrisis betrachtet werden.

Der vierte Vergleich, 16:15-29, hat den kämpfenden Kosmos zum Thema. Bei den Ägyptern ist seine Waffe der Blitz, das Feuer, das inmitten des Hagels seine Kraft verändert, bisweilen heftiger brennend um die Nahrung der Ägypter zu verzehren, dann wieder ruhiger, um die Tiere der vorangegangenen Plage zu schonen. Die Israeliten empfingen durch das Manna, das sich ebenso verändert und anpasst an den jeweiligen Geschmack, Wohltaten. Dieser Vergleich hat auf Grund seiner ausgearbeiteten theoretischen Aussagen über den Kosmos, der seine Macht ausübt um den Gottlosen zu strafen und dem Frommen zu helfen (16:24), am meisten Beachtung gefunden. Das 'kosmologische Prinzip' ist der eigentliche Vergleichspunkt in dieser vierten Synkrisis. Die Ägypter werden nicht durch etwas gestraft, womit sie gesündigt haben,

[7] Ersteres tun z.B. Grimm und A. Drubbel, *Wijsheid*, Roermond-Maaseik, 1957. A.G. Wright, 'The Structure of Wisdom 11-19', *CBQ* 27 (1965), 28-34 elimiert es als Vergleich.

[8] Wright, 'Book of Wisdom', 182.

[9] Focke, *Weisheit Salomos*, 10. Er betrachtet 16:5-14 zwar als eine echte Synkrisis, die jedoch seiner Meinung nach erst in 16:9 beginnt. Vers 5-8 lässt er weg.

[10] Zwei parallel laufende Teile über Israel (16:5-7, 10-12) umschliessen einen Teil über die Ägypter. Im gesamten Stück wird siebenmal γάρ benutzt.

und die Israeliten erleben nicht, was die Ägypter erlitten. Nur das Prinzip von 11:5 ist mit einiger Mühe wiederzuerkennen: Das Feuer zerstört die Nahrung der Ägypter, während den Israeliten durch Nahrung Wohltat zu Teil wird.

Im fünften Vergleich, 17:1-18:4, werden die Plage der Finsternis und die leuchtende Wolke, die die Israeliten durch die Wüste führt, einander gegenübergestellt. Die Strafe findet die weitaus meiste Beachtung. Nur ein Vers ist der Wohltat gewidmet. Bei der Plage liegt die Betonung auf der Beschreibung der Angst, die die Ägypter mit ihrem slechten Gewissen überfiel als es finster wurde. Es wird ausführlich erklärt, wie sehr die Ägypter, die im Finstern ihre Pläne schmiedeten um Israel, das Licht der Welt, zu unterdrücken, zu Recht mit Finsternis gestraft werden. Es fehlt nur das Prinzip, nach welchem die Israeliten in geringerem Masse ebenfalls unter Dunkelheit hätten leiden müssen.

Von hier ab wird der Gedankengang in Sapientia Salomonis so undurchsichtig, dass es bisher niemandem gelungen ist, einen befriedigenden Vorschlag für die Einteilung der letzten beiden Kapitel zu machen[11]. Es ist nicht einmal deutlich, wieviele Synkrisen noch darin vorkommen. Das Problem ist das Folgende.

In 18:5-8 werden die beiden folgenden Episoden angekündigt: der Tod der Erstgeborenen der Ägypter und ihr Untergang im Roten Meer. Für beide Strafen wird in diesen Versen derselbe Grund angegeben: der Mord, den die Ägypter gegen die israelitischen Kinder begingen. Ferner wird in diesen Einleitungsversen erwähnt, dass Gott hier die Ägypter mit demselben Mittel (ᾧ / τούτῳ) strafte und den Israeliten wohltat, und nicht, wie bei den anderen Vergleichen, dass es mit ähnlichen Mitteln passierte (ὧν / τούτων; 11:16). Sowohl der Tod der Erstgeborenen der Ägypter, als auch ihr Untergang im Roten Meer sind also Plage und Wohltat zugleich, was ein Hinweis sein könnte, dass hier die echten Synkrisen aufhören. Dann folgt in 18:9-20 die Beschreibung der sechsten Plage, des Todes der Erstgeborenen. 18:20-25 folgt ein paralleles Ereignis, das den Israeliten widerfuhr: die Epidemie in der Wüste, die von Aaron zum Stillstand gebracht wurde[12]. Viele lehnen es ab, in diesen zwei Episoden eine echte Synkrisis zu sehen, hauptsächlich auf Grund

---

[11] Für zehn vorgeschlagene Einteilungen, s. Wright, 'Wisdom 11-19', 30.

[12] Die Spekulation über das Gewand des Hohenpriesters in dieser Passage, das den Kosmos repräsentiert, ist nicht nur im griechisch sprechenden Judentum weit verbreitet (Vgl. Philo, *De Vita Mosis* II, 117, 133; *De Spec. Leg.* I, 95; Josephus, *Antiq.* III, 182), sondern hat eine Parallele in der allegorischen Homer-Exegese des Schildes von Achilles und in Plutarchs Interpretation der Kleider von Isis und Osiris (U. Früchtel, *Die kosmologischen Vorstellungen bei Philo von Alexandrien*, Leiden, 1968, 84, 93.)

[13] Die Passage als 'Digression' zu betiteln, wie Winston, *Wisdom*, 12, in Nachfolge von Reese, 'Plan and Structure', 399, gibt dem Kind nur einen anderen Namen. Mann sollte überhaupt gegenüber Versuchen, Teile von Sapientia 11-19 als reine Parenthesen zu erklären, äusserst misstrauisch sein.

des Fehlens einer wirklichen Wohltat an den Israeliten[13]. Hier könnte allerdings dasselbe gelten wie bei dem dritten Vergleich (16:5-14), nämlich, dass die Synkrisis nur auf dem Prinzip beruht, dass die Israeliten in geringerem Masse dasselbe erleiden wie die Ägypter.

In 19:1-5 werden schliesslich die Ereignisse beschrieben, die zum Untergang der Ägypter im Roten Meer führten. Das Ereignis selber wird nur in 19:5 angedeutet: Die Ägypter fanden einen seltsamen Tod. Bei dieser Episode fehlt sogar ein paralleles Ereignis für die Israeliten.

19:6-8 beschreibt den Durchzug der Israeliten als die neue Schöpfung[14]. In Vers 9 beginnt eine Rekapitulation, in der erzählt wird, wie die Israeliten sich an die Wunder erinnern, die in den vorigen Kapiteln beschrieben sind: zunächst die Insekte des dritten Vergleichs (Vs. 10) und die Frösche und Wachteln des zweiten (Vs. 10-12), dann, nach einem kurzen Verweis auf den Blitz des vierten (Vs. 13), eine ausgearbeitetere Wiederholung des Vergleichs der (fünften) Plage von der Finsternis (Vs. 13-17), worin das Schicksal der Ägypter und der Sodomiter vor Lots Tür verglichen wird. Nach der wichtigen Aussage, dass die Elemente diese Wunder dadurch zustandebrachten, dass sie ihr Verhältnis untereinander veränderten (Vs. 18), wird in den Versen 19-21 nochmals auf den zweiten und vierten Vergleich verwiesen. Mit der Doxologie von 19:22 schliesst das Buch.

Über diese Einteilung in kleinere Stücke ist man sich nahezu einig[15]. Das Problem ist, ob man von 18:5 an grössere Einheiten konstruieren und ihre Bedeutung bestimmen kann. Das ist allerdings nur dann möglich, wenn Deutlichkeit über den gesamten Aufbau von Sapientia 11-19 und die Art des dort Erzählten besteht.

2.

Nun, Sapientia 11-19 ist ein pädagogisches Drama. Es erzählt, wie die Ägypter durch ihr Unvermögen, aus dem Gelernten die Konsequenzen zu ziehen,

---

[14] Mit diesem Vers wird meist — neben der Übereinstimmung der Plagen aus Offenbarung mit denen aus Exodus — der Gedanke des apokalyptischen Characters von Sapientia verbunden (G. Kühn, 'Beiträge zur Erklärung des Buches der Weisheit', *ZNW* 28 (1929), 334-41; P. Beauchamp, 'Le salut corporel des justes et la conclusion du livre de la Sagesse', *Biblica* 45 (1964), 491-526; etwas vorsichtiger, 'apokalyptisierend', J. Fichtner, 'Die Stellung der Sapientia Salomonis in der Literatur- und Geistesgeschichte ihrer Zeit', *ZNW* 36 (1937), 113-132). Dies ist nicht richtig. Mit J.J. Collins, 'Cosmos and Salvation: Jewish Wisdom and Apocalyptic in the Hellenistic Age', *History of Religions* 17 (1977) muss gesagt werden, dass diese neue Schöpfung in der Vergangenheit stattgefunden hat, und ein 'natürliches' Ereignis war. Die Rettung der Welt unterstellt nach Sapientia keine völlig neue Ordnung, sondern gerade Werke des natürlichen Prozesses. Vgl. 6:24. In Sapientia ist auch nicht die Rede von einer Depravation der Geschichte. Für eine parallele Benutzung des Ausdrucks 'neue Schöpfung' ist eher an Philo zu denken, der ihn für die Welt nach der Sintflut benutzt (*De Vita Mosis* II, 64).

[15] Für die in Kap. 18 und 19 benutzten 'inclusions', s. Wright, 'Book of Wisdom', 183.

zugrunde gingen. Das wichtigste Erzählprinzip ist die wiederholte Erteilung von fühlbaren Belehrungen. Der Hintergrund zum Drama wird im ersten Exkurs (11:15-12:22) geschildert. Die Erzählung von den Ägyptern ist eine Darstellung der dort beschriebenen Prinzipien des Handelns eines barmherzigen, allmächtigen Gottes.

Gott straft die Ägypter zunächst leicht und gibt ihnen auf diese Weise Zeit zur Reue (12:10), da sie noch an seiner Macht zweifeln. Diese Strafen führen tatsächlich zu einem Resultat. Die Ägypter erkennen den wahren Gott an (12:27: der zweite Vergleich). Sie sehen ein, dass sie durch Gottes Urteil gezüchtigt wurden (16:18: der vierte Vergleich) und dass das Volk Gottes Sohn ist (18:19: der sechste Vergleich). Wenn sie dann alle Lektionen gelernt haben und das Volk trotzdem noch verfolgen (19:2-4), kommt das Urteil in seiner ganzen Strenge über sie, und sie finden (dem Prinzip von 12:17 zufolge) einen seltsamen Tod: Gott lässt diejenigen seine Kraft spüren, die daran zweifeln, aber die, die ihn kennen und trotzdem sündigen, straft er in aller Strenge[16]. So handelte er auch bei den Kanaanitern (12:3-11). Dass Gott vorher wusste, dass die Ägypter sich nicht bekehren würden, sowie er es auch von den Kanaanitern wusste (12:10), tut der Gerechtigkeit der Strafe keinen Abbruch. Es ist eine ἀξία ἀνάγκη[17]. Diese Gottesvorstellung erklärt ausser der grossen Anzahl der Plagen auch das Prinzip, demzufolge Gott mit demselben Mittel straft, womit gesündigt wurde. Damit wird beabsichtigt, den Menschen dadurch zu rechter Einsicht zu bringen, dass man ihm seine Sünde in Erinnerung ruft (12:2). Die Regel, dass die Israeliten in geringerem Masse dasselbe erleiden mussten wie die Ägypter, wird auf diese Weise ebenfalls erklärt. Israel lernte, wie barmherzig und gerecht Gott ist (12:20-21).

Sapientia hat eine äusserst intellektualistische Ethik. Was gut und slecht ist, wird bestimmt durch die richtige Erkenntnis. Die letzte Sünde der Ägypter ist ein Vergessen (19:4), aber sie waren schon vorher schuldig. Der Gipfel falscher Erkenntnis, also von Sünde, ist der Götzendienst:

> Denn der Dienst der namenlosen Götzen ist
> der Anfang alles Übels, sowie dessen Ursache und Vollendung (14:27).

Es waren gerade die Ägypter, die die schrecklichste Form von Götzendienst hatten. Der zweite Exkurs will das beweisen (15:14-19).

---

[16] Diese Vorstellung der pädagogischen Bestrafung durch Gott kommt ebenfalls, allerdings selten, in der klassischen Literatur vor. Gott ist φιλάνθρωπος und straft den Menschen darum langsam, sodass er sich bekehren kann. Dieser Gedanke ist auch in der Homer-Exegese zu finden, s. R. Pfeiffer, *History of Classical Scholarship*, Oxford, 1968, Exkurs 4.

[17] Das Problem von Freiheit und Determinismus wird in Sapientia ohne allzu grosse Widersprüche gelöst: Der Mensch hat eine freie, moralische Wahl (Sapientia verschweigt konsequent die Verhärtung des Herzens von Pharao durch Gott), das Ergebnis dieser Wahl wird jedoch durch die ursprüngliche Zusammenstellung der Seele bestimmt (12:10-11). Vgl. Winston, *Wisdom*, 46-58.

So wird der Gang und die Einheit der Erzählung von Sapientia 11-19 durch das Schicksal der Ägypter bestimmt. Beide Exkurse zeigen den Hintergrund der Erzählung und die Rechtfertigung des Dramas, das ihnen widerfährt. Nur die Ägypter können den Stoff für eine Erzählung liefern. Sie können nämlich etwas lernen und es wieder vergessen. Was sie vergessen, ist Gott, und das zeigt sich in ihrer Verfolgung von Israel. Obwohl die letzte Plage sie einsehen lässt, dass Israel Gottes Sohn ist (18:13), verfolgen sie das Volk erneut. Diese Sünde ist darum so schwer, weil Israel die richtige Erkenntnis auf beispielhafte Weise besitzt. Israel ist in Sapientia nicht mehr das menschliche Volk wie in Exodus, sondern eine sündlose Gemeinschaft von Heiligen[18]. In den verschiedenen Episoden über die Israeliten in den Synkrisen findet man darum keinen Fortschritt und keine Entwicklung[19]. Ein Heiliger kann sich nicht entwickeln. Die Episoden über die Israeliten sind, was die Erzählung betrifft, irrelevant. Sie dienen nur der Illustration, um die Sünde der Ägypter besser hervorzuheben. Welche Wohltat mit welcher Plage verbunden wird, wird bestimmt durch die zwei, einander einigermassen widersprechenden Prinzipien, dass die Israeliten in geringerem Masse dasselbe erlitten wie die Ägypter, und dass den Israeliten mit demselben Mittel wohltgetan wurde, mit dem die Ägypter bestraft wurden. Obwohl dieses letzte Prinzip mit dem Hauptzug der Erzählung, Gott als Pädagoge (11:13), in Zusammenhang gebracht wird, ist es enger mit dem kosmologischen Prinzip des vierten Vergleichs verbunden. Der Kosmos passt sich seinem Ziel an, um dem Gerechten wohlzutun und den Sünder zu strafen.

> Denn die Schöpfung ist dir, dem Schöpfer, untertan;
> sie steigert sich zur Züchtigung gegen die Ungerechten und
> sie beruhigt sich wiederum zum Wohlthun an denen, die sich auf dich verlassen. (16:24)

Nun spielt das kosmologische Prinzip eine sehr wichtige Rolle im Schluss von Sapientia 11-19. Die Rekapitulation 19:6-21 ist durch zwei kosmologische Aussagen (19:6, 18) eingeklammert. Dort wird eine naturwissenschaftliche Erklärung für die Veränderung des Kosmos gegeben. Die Elemente haben durch gegenseitige Kombinationen die Wunder zustande gebracht. Der Schluss scheint damit in keiner Weise mit der vorhergehenden Erzählung in Zusammenhang zu stehen, da doch das kosmologische Prinzip nur im vierten Vergleich angewendet wird. Im folgenden Paragraphen soll jedoch dargelegt

[18] Alle Sünden Israels, bei den Wachtelnerzählung (Num. 11:33-34), und in den Erzählungen der Wüste (Num. 17:6-15) und der Plage der Schlangen (Num. 21:4-9), werden ausgelassen.

[19] Während die Plagen der Ägypter, mit einigen Auslassungen und Zusammenziehungen, der Reihenfolge von Exodus folgen, ist das nicht der Fall bei den Episoden bezüglich des Zuges der Israeliten durch die Wüste.

werden, dass dies dennoch der Fall ist, und dass der Schluss auf ein Elementenschema innerhalb der sieben Episoden der Erzählung über die Ägypter zurückverweist.

3.

Die allgemeineren kosmologischen Aussagen von Sapientia über den Kampf des Kosmos für den Gerechten (5:17-20; 16:17, 24; 19:6, 18) haben in der Forschung viel Beachtung gefunden[20]. Man hat jedoch nicht bemerkt, dass die Kosmologie auch den Aufbau der Erzählung Sapientia 11-19 bestimmt hat. In der Schlussbetrachtung, der Rekapitulation (19:6-21), werden nicht nur ausdrücklich die Wunder durch die Elemente erklärt, sondern es werden auch verschiedene Strafen und Wohltaten mit einzelnen Elementen verbunden. Beim *Feuer* im vierten Vergleich ist das ohne Weiteres deutlich (19:13, 20-21), aber auch vom zweiten Vergleich wird gesagt, dass das *Wasser* die Frösche und Wachteln hervorbringt[21] (19:10-12). Auf die gleiche Weise werden die Mücken des dritten Vergleichs von der *Erde* hervorgebracht (19:10).

Nun ist die Vorstellung, dass jedem Element lebende Wesen zugeteilt werden, schon sehr alt[22]. Es geht dabei um eine Einteilung der Elemente nach Lebensräumen der verschiedenen Tiere. Eine solche Zuordnung finden wir auch bei Philo[23]. Ausserdem gibt es bei ihm im Rahmen der Vorstellung vom kosmischen Baum[24] leichte Hinweise, dass die verschiedenen Lebewesen von den verschiedenen Elementen hervorgebracht worden sind[25]. Die Verbindung von Elementenlehre und Zoogonie ist stoisch, wahrscheinlich posidonisch. Sie ist deutlich bei Cicero in einer von Reinhardt dem Posidonius zugeschriebenen Passage[26] ausgedrückt. Die Elemente konnten diesen Theorien zufolge nur bei einer bestimmten Konstellation, im *magnus annus*, dem Beginn eines neuen kosmischen Zyklus[27], Lebewesen hervorbringen. In Sapientia sind die Plagen eine zweite Schöpfung, in der die Elemente Erde und Wasser die Tiere

---

[20] J.P.M. Sweet, 'The Theory of Miracles in the Wisdom of Solomon', *Miracles*, C.F.D. Moule, (ed.), London, 1965, gründet sich z.B. nur auf diese Verse.

[21] Die Frösche kommen aus dem Fluss, die Wachteln aus (ἐκ) dem Meer. Ziegler hat in seiner kritischen Ausgabe von Sapientia Salomonis (Göttingen, 1962) die *lectio facilior* ἀπό des Vaticanus, die vermutlich durch Num. 11:31 beeinflusst ist, zu Unrecht dem ἐκ des Sinaiticus, einer Lesung, die auch Origenes hat, und die ebenfalls von Minuskeln unterstützt wird, vorgezogen.

[22] z.B. *Timaeus* 39E.

[23] z.B. Philo, *De Gig*. 53-68.

[24] Vgl. Früchtel, *ibid*., 53-68.

[25] *De Plantat*. 11ff; *De Somniis* I, 135.

[26] Cicero, *De Natura Deorum* II, 42: *Cum enim aliorum animantium ortus in terra sit, aliorum in aqua, in aere aliorum....*; s. K. Reinhardt, *Kosmos und Sympathie*, München, 1926, 70-86. Dort mehrere Parallelen zu dieser Vorstellung. S. auch K. Reinhardt, *Posidonius*, München, 1921, 152, 238.

[27] Reinhardt, *Posidonius*, 368-369.

hervorbringen, mit denen die Ägypter gestraft werden. Sapientia konnte diese Wiederholung der Urzeugung, die die stoische Philosophie lehrt, in der LXX-Version der ersten Schöpfungsgeschichte in Genesis[28] zurückfinden. Auch dort bringen Erde und Wasser die Tiere und Vögel hervor (Gen. 1:20-24).

Diese Interpretation der Verse 19:10-12 ergibt ausser einer Textverbesserung (s. Anm. 21) eine Erklärung für die *crux interpretum* in 19:19. Da werden neben Wassertieren, die zu Landtieren werden (den Fröschen), auch Landtiere genannt, die zu Wassertieren werden. Wenn man hierin nicht einen überzogenen und undurchdachten Vergleich sah (Grimm), bezog man es auf den Zug durch das Rote Meer. Alle Lebewesen, die das Meer durchzogen haben, sind hier als 'Landtiere' angesehen worden: von den Israeliten (z.B. Winston, Gregg, Drubble) über die Ägypter (Fichtner) bis zu den Pferden der Letzten (Grotius, Feldmann). Nun sind die in 19:19 verwendeten Worte (χερσαῖα / ἔνυδρα) die Standardausdrücke für die Zuteilung von Lebewesen zu den Elementen[29]. Am einfachsten ist es darum, bei der Einheit von 19:19a zu bleiben, und auch die erste Hälfte davon auf den zweiten Vergleich zu beziehen. Die Landtiere, die zu Wassertieren werden, sind die Wachteln, die im Wasser entstanden sind, während sie von Natur aus auf dem Land erzeugt werden (die Luft bringt - auch in der Urzeugung - nicht so etwas Massives wie ein Tier hervor, sondern nur Seelen und Geister[30])[31].

Wie wir gesehen haben, wird in der Rekapitulation auch auf die Plage der Finsternis zurückgegriffen (19:14-17). Die Beschreibung dieser Plage im fünften Vergleich (17:1-18:4) ist die rhetorisch am meisten ausgearbeitete Passage von Sapientia. Grimm bemerkte 1837 bereits, dass die Dunkelheit, die die Ägypter überfällt, mit der Unterwelt in Zusammenhang gebracht wird (17:14, 21). Dies kann verschärft werden. Das Stück weist deutliche Parallelen mit dem literarischen Genre der *Nekyia*, des Abstiegs zur Unterwelt[32] auf. Gerade in den ersten Jahrhunderten vor Christus wurde, teils unter dem Einfluss der Naturwissenschaften, teils durch eine neue Theorie über das

---

[28] Vgl. Beauchamp, 'Salut corporel'. Seine Hypothese, dass der gesamte Teil 19:6-21 mit der Schöpfungsgeschichte parallel läuft, ist, wie er selber zugibt (S. 504) von Vers 10 ab äusserst spekulativ.

[29] S. Anm. 22, 23 und 25. Vgl. auch Passagen wie die von Aetius: *Doxographi Graeci*, H. Diels, ed., Berlin, 1965⁴, 432.

[30] Reinhardt, *Kosmos und Sympathie*, 73; Vgl. auch Philo, *De Somniis* I, 135: Auf der Erde sind die χερσαῖα, in den θαλάτταις δὲ καὶ ποταμοῖς (vgl. Sap. 19:10-12) die ἔνυδρα, in der Luft befinden sich ebenfalls Wesen, μὴ αἰσθήσει καταληπτά.

[31] Dass der zweite und der dritte Vergleich, beides Tierplagen, die dem Exkurs über den Götzendienst folgen, an die Elemente Wasser und Erde gekoppelt sind, ist möglicherweise mit Philo, *Decal.* 78 in Zusammenhang zu bringen: Die Ägypter haben aus den beiden Elementen, die dem Menschen dienen, Erde und Wasser, die wildesten Tiere ausgewählt um sie als Götzen zu verehren. Zu ergänzen wäre dann 'und darum werden sie durch Tiere dieser beiden Elemente bestraft'.

[32] E. Osty, *Le Livre de la Sagesse*, Paris, 1950, 101.

Schicksal der Seele nach dem Tod, aber vor allen Dingen durch die allegorische Homerexegese, besonders der Ilias XV, 193ff, der Ort des Hades neu interpretiert. Dort wird die Welt unter Zeus, Poseidon und Hades verteilt, wobei Hades die Luft erhält[33]. So wurde die Unterwelt fortan zwischen Erde und Mond, in der *Luft* lokalisiert. Diese Luft des Hades ist die ἀφώτιστος ἀήρ[34]. Dies führt zur Interpretation von 17:10, wo von den von der Dunkelheit überfallenen Ägyptern gesagt wird, dass sie nicht einmal mehr wagten, zu τὸν μηδαμόθεν φευκτὸν ἀέρα hinzusehen. Winston hat plausibel gemacht, dass ἀήρ hier mit 'dark gaze' übersetzt werden muss[35]. Dann schliesst das Wort bei der Bedeutung an, die es bei Homer und den Naturphilosophen hat, 'Mist, Nebel', im Gegensatz zum hellen Äther. 'Αήρ wird bei Homer meistens mit νέφος, ζόφος, νύξ usw. verbunden[36]. Diese Bedeutung von ἀήρ behauptet sich neben der neuen, nach der ἀήρ eins der Elemente ist[37]. Für Philo ist, in Nachfolge der Stoa, die Bemerkung, dass die Luft von Natur aus dunkel ist, eine Selbstverständlichkeit[38]. Wir können hieraus folgern, dass sowohl die Verbindung Finsternis — Luft als Finsternis — Hades — Luft allgemein üblich war. Diese Erwägungen werden dadurch verstärkt, dass sowohl in Nachfolge der Theorien der Stoa als auch der Epikureer die Luft ein unentbehrliches Medium beim Sehen war[39]. Für Posidonius ist die Luft sogar eine Kraft, die aktiv beim Sehen mitwirkt: *Aer nobiscum videt*[40]. Die Plage von der Finsternis im fünften Vergleich kann also mit dem Element *Luft* in Zusammenhang gebracht werden.

Andererseits ist dieser Zusammenhang dadurch in den Hintergrund getreten, dass der Autor allmählich von dem physischen Kontrast hell — dunkel übergeht auf den spirituellen zwischen den Ägyptern, gequält von Gewissensbissen, und den israelitischen ethischen Helden, unterstützt vom gesamten

---

[33] Vgl. F. Buffière, *Les mythes d'Homère et la Pensée Grecque*, Paris, 1956, 117-122, 401, 495; F. Cumont, *Afterlife in Roman Paganism*, New Haven, 1922, 82. Die Lehre wurde von der Stoa angenommen, sicherlich seit Posidonius. Für eine schöne Beschreibung, Plutarchus, *De facie lunae* 943.

[34] Heraclitus, *Alleg. Hom.* 43.

[35] Winston, *Wisdom*, 308. Vor allen Dingen aufgrund der angeführten Parallele über die Dunkelheit, die die Argonauten auf ihrer Rückreise überfällt, von Callimachus (Pfeiffer, *Frag.*, 17-18) mit der Luft und von Apollonius Rhodius (*Argonautica* IV, 1694-1700) auch mit dem Hades verbunden.

[36] C.H. Kahn, *Anaximander and the Origins of Greek Cosmology*, New York, 1961, 141.

[37] z.B. *Timaeus* 58D.

[38] *Stoicorum Veterum Fragmenta*, I. ab Arnim, ed., Leipzig, 1919, 429-430. Philo, *De Vita Mosis* II, 118; *De Spec. Leg.* I, 94-96. Sehr überzeugend in *Opific.* 29: Gott schuf die Luft zuerst, und er nannte sie σκότος, ἐπειδὴ μέλας ὁ ἀὴρ τῇ φύσει. Auch für Hieronymus repräsentiert das Lila des Hohepriestergewandes noch die Luft, *propter coloris similitudinem.* (*Saint Jérome, Lettres*, J. Labourt, ed., Paris, 1949-1963, III, 132).

[39] Vgl. M. Pohlenz, *Die Stoa*, Göttingen, 1964^2 I, 88; *Stoicorum Veterum Fragmenta*, 863-871. Für die Epikureer, Lucretius, *De Rer. Nat.* IV, 216-251, vor allen Dingen 246-249; Macrobius, *Sat.* 7, 14, 2-4.

[40] Cicero, *De Nat. Deor.* II, 83. Von Reinhardt Posidonius zugeschrieben (*Posidonius*, 238).

Kosmos, die die Welt mit ihrem Gesetz erleuchten werden. Das grösste Interesse des Autors liegt in der psychologischen Beschreibung der Ägypter, die sich selber mehr zu Last sind, als dass sie unter der Dunkelheit leiden (17:21). Aus dem gesamten Vergleich spricht die Neigung von Sapientia, die auch den vierten Vergleich bestimmt, physische Ereignisse zu spiritualisieren[41].

Sapientia Salomonis 11-19 liegt also ein Schema zugrunde, das vier der sieben Episoden mit einem Element verbindet. Wir können uns nun fragen, ob dieses Schema aus der Beschreibung der Plagen von Ägypten von Sapientia entwickelt wurde, oder aus einer anderen exegetischen Tradition übernommen wurde, und, sollte das Letzte der Fall sein, mit welchen Vorstellungen dieses Schema in Zusammenhang steht.

4.

Das Auslegen von Wundern mit Hilfe einer Veränderung der Elemente ist im griechisch sprechenden Judentum gebräuchlich[42]. Es gibt allerdings auch Hinweise auf die Existenz einer exegetischen Tradition, die die Elemente als Verursacher der Plagen in Ägypten beschrieb. Bei Josephus sind davon Spuren zu finden (er beschreibt die Plage der Finsternis als eine Veränderung der Luft[43]) und Philo beginnt seine Beschreibung der Plagen sogar mit der Bemerkung, dass die vier Elemente, die der Welt bei der Schöpfung zum Heil gereichten, die Ägypter ins Verderben führten (*De Vita Mosis* I, 96). In der Fortsetzung dieser Einleitung seiner Plagenerzählung erwähnt er, wie die ersten drei Plagen, die von Erde und Wasser, von Aaron ausgeführt wurden. Moses bewirkte die folgenden Drei, die von Luft und Feuer, während die Siebente, wobei kein Element genannt wird, von beiden gemeinsam zustande gebracht wurde. Die letzten drei Plagen werden Gott selbst zugeschrieben. Wenn wir nun der eigentlichen Beschreibung der Plagen folgen, dann stellt sich heraus, dass dieses Programm nicht vollständig ausgeführt wird. Die ersten zwei Plagen (die Veränderung des Wassers und die Frösche) werden tatsächlich mit Wasser (*DVM* I, 103) verbunden, sowie die Dritte, die von der σκνίπες mit der Erde (*DVM* I, 107). Bei den Plagen von Moses fehlt jedoch das Feuer. Die Plage von Blitz und Hagel (die einander auch bei Philo erstaunlicherweise nicht berühren) und die der Heuschrecken (*DVM* I, 118 120) werden noch mit der Luft verbunden. Bei der Plage der Finsternis wird jedoch nicht ausdrücklich ein Element genannt, sodass das angekündigte Schema eigentlich abbricht.

---

[41] Winston, *Wisdom*, 301.

[42] Philo erklärt z. B. das Manna-Wunder durch ein μεταβάλλειν τὰ στοιχεῖα (*De Vita Mosis* II, 266-267).

[43] *Antiq.* II, 14,5. Wegen der dichten Finsternis können die Ägypter nicht mehr sehen. Sie ersticken selbst beinahe im σκότος βαθύ.

Obwohl die Dunkelheit bei Philo unstreitig physikalisch gedacht ist, zu erklären durch ein Zusammenziehen der Wolken oder eine besonders lange Sonnenfinsternis, liegt auch bei ihm der Nachdruck auf dem psychischen Leiden der Ägypter. Er erwähnt selbst, dass die Israeliten von der Dunkelheit nicht belästigt wurden, obwohl sie inmitten der Ägypter wohnten[44]. Diese Anpassung des Kosmos an die Forderung des Augenblicks, je nachdem ob er einem Gerechten oder einem Sünder gegenübersteht, kennen wir aus Sapientia 16:24. Sie wird von Philo in seiner Schlussbetrachtung sehr deutlich formuliert. Er bemerkt, dass die vier Elemente, denen man nicht entrinnen kann, die Israeliten schonten. Das Merkwürdige war, dass 'durch dieselben Dinge, zur selben Zeit am selben Ort, die Einen zugrunde gingen, die Anderen gerettet wurden«[45].

Bei Philo ist nur noch ein Hinweis auf eine Verbindung von der Plage der Finsternis mit dem Element Luft zu finden. In einem Exkurs darüber, dass die Ägypter die Dunkelheit nicht durch Anzünden von Feuer vertreiben konnten (Sapientia 17:5!), gibt er als Grund hierfür den starken Wind an oder βάθος τοῦ σκοτοῦς[46].

Für die Bestimmung dieses Elementenschemas ist die folgende Parallele sehr wichtig. In dem von Eusebius überlieferten Fragment des Mosesromans von Artapanos, das von den Plagen handelt, finden wir eine ähnliche Einteilung[47]. Die eigentliche Beschreibung der Plagen zerfällt hier, in Abweichung von Philo und Sapientia, in vier Episoden. Die Erste beginnt, wenn Moses mit seinem Stab auf das Wasser des Nils schlägt, der dann über seine Ufer tritt. Das Wasser bleibt in Pfützen stehen und verfärbt sich rot, sodass die Wassertiere (τὰ ποταμία ζῷα) sterben, während die Menschen verdursten. Nach dem Ende dieser Plage und einer kurzen Beschreibung einiger Proben der Zauberkunst der ägyptischen Priester folgt die zweite Episode. Moses schlägt mit seinem Stab die Erde und lässt so fliegende Tiere (ζῶον τι πτηνόν) entstehen, die den Ägyptern unheilbare Geschwüre zufügen. Nochmals (παλίν) schlägt Moses die Erde mit seinem Stab, und es entstehen βάτραχον, ἀκρίδες und σκνίφες. In einem dieser Episode zugefügten Exkurs, der die Anwesenheit von Stäben in den ägyptischen Isis-Tempeln versucht zu erklären, wird die gesamte Passage nochmals ausdrücklich mit der Erde verbunden.

Hiernach lässt Moses nachts Hagel und Erdbeben entstehen, sodass Pharao die Israeliten gehen lässt. Der Untergang der Ägypter im Roten Meer wird

---

[44] Auch nach Exodus werden die Israeliten nicht von der — physischen — Dunkelheit belästigt, und zwar weil sie an einem anderen Ort wohnen (Ex. 10:23).

[45] *De Vita Mosis* I, 143; dasselbe bei Josephus. Obwohl der Nil wirklich zu Blut wird, ist das Wasser, das die Israeliten daraus schöpfen, gut zu trinken (*Antiq.* II, 14,1; Vgl. auch *De Vita Mosis* I, 144).

[46] *De Vita Mosis* I, 124. S. Anm. 43.

[47] Eusebius, *Praep. Ev.* IX, 27,1-37; *Fragmenta Pseudepigraphorum quae supersunt graeca*, A.-M. Denis, ed., Leiden, 1970, 187-195.

rationalisierend (Moses benutzt seine Kenntnis von Ebbe und Flut) und viel ausführlicher, mit Betonung des Wünders, erzählt. Moses bekommt von einer göttlichen Stimme den Befehl, mit seinem Stab auf das Wasser des Meeres zu schlagen. Dieses teilt sich, und die Israeliten ziehen hindurch, während die verfolgenden Ägypter von einem Feuer aufgehalten werden, das sie verzehrt, während zur gleichen Zeit das Wasser zurückströmt. So gehen sie alle zugrunde.

Die Beschreibung der Plagen trifft hier mit dem Elementenschema zusammen. Die Episode wird in vier Ereignisse erzählt, die jedes mit einem Element verbunden sind: die Plage vom Nil mit dem Wasser, die Tierplage mit der Erde, der Hagel (und das Erdbeben) mit der Luft, und, schliesslich, das Feuer, das die Ägypter beim Roten Meer verzehrt. Die Elemente treten, wie bei Philo, in ihrer natürlichen Reihenfolge, von unten nach oben auf. Die Zuteilung der Plagen zu den Elementen ist jedoch anders als bei Philo oder bei Sapientia.

Diese Parallele gibt ein Hinweis auf die Absicht des Schemas. Bei Artapanos ist Moses der θεῖος ἀνήρ, der auf Grund seiner ἀρετή von Gott erfüllte Mensch, der über übermenschliche, göttliche Kräfte verfügt[48]. In der jüdisch-hellenistischen Tradition hat diese Vorstellung, angewandt auf Figuren der eigenen Vergangenheit, ihren Platz in der Apologetik gefunden, eng verbunden mit kosmologischen Spekulationen. Der Kosmos wird als die Manifestation des Willens und der Macht von Gott betrachtet. Seine Wirkungen treffen mit denen Gottes zusammen. Natürlich geht diese Gleichstellung nicht in eine Identifikation über: Gott bleibt absolut transzendent. Daher die zweideutigen Äusserungen über den Kosmos, der einerseits wie ein Automat den Sünder straft (Sapientia 16:15-25; 19:18), andererseits nur ein Instrument in der Hand Gottes ist (Sapientia 5:17-23; 19:6). Die wichtigste jüdisch-hellenistische theoretische Ausarbeitung über die Macht des θεῖος ἀνήρ über den Kosmos finden wir — wie könnte es anders sein — bei Philo. In *De Vita Mosis* I, 155ff[49] beschreibt er, wie eng Mose[50] mit Gott verbunden war. Da Gott ihn für würdig hielt, Teilnehmer (κοινωνός) an seinem eigenen Besitz zu sein, überei-

---

[48] S. für den Begriff θεῖος ἀνήρ |H. Windisch, *Paulus und Christus*, ein biblisch-religionsgeschichtlicher Vergleich, Leipzig, 1934, 24-115; L. Bieler, ΘΕΙΟϚ ΑΝΗΡ, Wien, 1935-1936; D. Georgi, *Die Gegner des Paulus im 2. Korintherbrief*. Studien zur religiösen Propaganda in der Spätantike, Neukirchen, 1964, 145-168.

[49] Für eine ausführliche Analyse dieses Textes, Georgi, *ibid.*, 153-157.

[50] Bieler zählt zwar am Moses Philos die Charakterzüge des θεῖος ἀνήρ auf (*ibid.* II, 33-36), schliesslich meint er jedoch, dass dieser eher der πνευματικός der späteren Gnosis ist. Das Argument von W.A. Meeks (*The Prophet King*, Moses Traditions and the Johannine Christology, Leiden, 1967, 104-106) hiergegen, und seine Schlussfolgerung, dass das Schwancken von Moses bei Philo zwischen Gott und Mensch 'remains within the compass of the θεῖος ἀνήρ', ist überzeugend. Es muss allerdings bemerkt werden, dass Moses bei Philo eher den Aspekt des gesetzgebenden, des herrschenden θεῖος ἀνήρ hat, im Gegensatz zu Sapientia und Artapanos, wo er der Wundertäter ist.

gnete er ihm die ganze Welt als Eigentum. Darum gehorchte ihm als Herrn[51] jedes der Elemente und veränderte sich auf seinen Befehl:

> τοιγαροῦν ὑπήκουεν ὡς δεσπότῃ τῶν στοιχείων ἕκαστον ἀλλάττον ἣν εἶχε δύναμιν καὶ ταῖς προστάξεσιν ὑπεῖκον.

Diese Herrschaft über die Elemente bedeutet, dass der θεῖος ἀνήρ Wunder verrichten kann.

Moses, im jüdisch-hellenistischen Denken der θεῖος ἀνήρ slechthin[52], kommt auch in Sapientia 11-19 vor. Er wird, wie jede historische Figur des Buches, nie beim Namen genannt. Die erste Erwähnung, wo er sofort als wundertätiger Menschenretter eingeführt wird, befindet sich in Kap. 10. Dieses Kapitel, dass das Wirken der Weisheit in der Geschichte beschreibt, besteht aus sieben Episoden. In der Letzten, der Klimax, wird beschrieben, wie die Weisheit das Volk aus Ägypten rettete. Das geschah durch Mose:

> Sie zog ein in die Seele des Dieners des Herrn und widerstand furchtbaren Königen unter Wundern und Zeichen (10:16).

Hier ist Moses der typische θεῖος ἀνήρ, der, erfüllt von einer göttlichen Macht, Wunder verrichtet. Die zweite Erwähnung von Moses befindet sich in 11:1, sozusagen der Überschrift von Sapientia 11-19:

> Alle ihre (der Weisheit) Werke gelangen durch einen heiligen Propheten.

Die anderen beiden Erwähnungen von Moses in Kap. 11-19 handeln von seinen Abenteuern als Kind und junger Mann (11:14; 18:5). Diese Stellen sind bedeutungsvoll. Sie geben den Schlüssel zum Aufbau von Sapientia 11-19. Der zweite, dritte, vierte und fünfte Vergleich (16:1-18:4) bilden einen Block. Es sind die vier Plagen, die mit einem Element (resp. Wasser, Erde, Feuer und Luft) verbunden sind, und worauf in der Rekapitulation in Kap. 19 verwiesen wird. Davor, getrennt durch die zwei Exkurse und eingerahmt von zwei Erwähnungen von Moses (11:1, 14), steht der erste Vergleich, die Plage vom Blut, womit der Nil verunreinigt wird[53], die Strafe für den Kindermord.

---

[51] Dies ist ein festes Motiv der Vorstellungen vom θεῖος ἀνήρ; s. Bieler, *ibid.* I, 103.

[52] Auch bei Josephus ist Moses der θεῖος ἀνήρ (etwas weniger ausgeprägt als bei Philo oder Artapanos, s. Bieler, *ibid.* I, 18f; II, 30-34; Meeks, *ibid.*, 139). Bei Josephus wird die Vorstellung auch mit dem Hohepriestergewand verbunden; dem Vorwurf des Atheismus, der den Juden gemacht wird, stellt er gegenüber, dass aus der kosmologischen Symbolik des Hohepriestergewandes und des Tabernakels verstanden werden kann, dass Moses ein θεῖος ἀνήρ war (*Antiq.* III, 180). Eine ähnliche Vorstellung bei Philo. Auf Grund seines Gewandes ist der Hohepriester οὐκ ἄνθρωπος ἀλλὰ λόγος θεῖος (*De Fuga* 108). S. auch Windisch, *ibid.*, 107-108.

[53] Auffallend und bezeichnend ist die Veränderung in der Beschreibung dieses Wunders gegenüber der LXX: ταραχθέντος (Sap. 11:6) statt μεταβάλλει (Ex. 7:18-20). Diese Veränderung

Nach dem Block der vier Elementenplagen folgt die Einleitung zu den zwei letzten Episoden (18:5-8), wo wieder als Grund der Kindermord gegeben wird, und wo, zum dritten und letzten Mal in Sapientia 11-19, Moses erwähnt wird. Wie eng die letzten zwei Episoden untereinander verbunden sind, ist oben bereits erwähnt. Durch die Motive des Kindermordes und von Moses sind diese letzten zwei Episoden auch mit der ersten Synkrisis verbunden. Wir bekommen so das folgende Schema der sieben Vergleiche:

I//	II	III	IV	V//	(VI + VII)
	Wasser	Erde	Feuer	Luft	

Hier sehen wir deutlich, warum der Aufbau von Sapientia 11-19 so viele Probleme aufwirft. Sapientia hat auf gewandte Weise eine Erzählung, die sieben Episoden umfasst, aus einem traditionellen vierfachen Elementenschema entwickelt. Das Elementenschema wurde ins Zentrum gestellt, während die Episoden, die die Siebenzahl vollmachen, um das Schema herum angeordnet wurden. Um diese Struktur verwirklichen zu können, mussten die letzten zwei Episoden untereinander enger verbunden werden (durch eine gemeinsame Einleitung) und gegenüber den vorangegangenen Vergleichen eine abweichende Position bekommen. Daher treffen bei diesen letzten beiden Episoden Plage und Wohltat zusammen, sodass die Synkrisis eigentlich aufgegeben wird.

Auch diese Analyse des Aufbaus von Sapientia 11-19, die von zwei eng verbundenen Einteilungsprinzipien bestimmt wird, zeigt die schon öfter konstatierte grosse, rhetorische Kraft von Sapientia und seine sehr sorgfältige Komposition, die Überliefertes kunstvoll in eine neue Form einfügt.

---

ist nur als zielbewusster Versuch zu werten, die erste Plage aus dem Elementenschema zu halten. Philo verbindet die Plage mit einer Veränderung (τρέπεται / μεταβάλλει) des Elementes Wasser (*De Vita Mosis* I, 99 101). Auch andere Veränderungen des LXX-Textes (mit dem Sapientia sehr vertraut war: C. Larcher, *Etudes sur le Livre de la Sagesse*, Paris, 1969, 101ff), sind sehr aufschlussreich. So folgt Sapientia bei der Froschplage fast wörtlich Ex. 7:28: ἐξερεύξεται ὁ ποταμὸς βατράχους (Vgl. Sap. 19:10), ersetzt jedoch bei der Mückenplage die einfache Mitteilung von Ex. 8:13: καὶ ἐγένοντο οἱ σκνῖφες durch ἐξήγαγεν ἡ γῆ σκνῖπα (Sap. 19:10).

ZUR KOMPOSITIONSTECHNIK DES LUKAS IN LK. 15:11-32

von

JOOST SMIT SIBINGA

'Eines der vollkommensten Gemälde aus Rembrandts letzter Periode ist in der Kasseler Gemäldegalerie aufbewahrt'. Diesem Gemälde, 'Jakob segnet Josephs Söhne' (1656), und der exegetischen Tradition, der es zugehört, hat Jürgen Lebram einen schönen, gehaltvollen und seine Betrachtungsweise kennzeichnenden Aufsatz gewidmet[1].

Ein noch späteres, vielleicht aus dem letzten Lebensjahr, 1669, stammendes Bild Rembrandts, das in Leningrad bewundert werden kann, stellt die Rückkehr des verlorenen Sohnes dar (Lk. 15:11-32). Es bildet unter den verschiedenen Darstellungen des Themas durch Rembrandt den Höhepunkt und die letzte Vervollkommung[2]. Aber auch die aus früherer Zeit stammenden Zeichnungen — in Haarlem gibt es ein besonders schönes Beispiel — haben die Aufmerksamkeit der Exegeten auf sich gezogen. Diesen ist Rembrandt einmal geradezu als 'echter Interpret' des Gleichnisses vom verlorenen Sohn zum Vorbild gemacht worden. Im Leningrader Ölbild sind nämlich dem Beschauer nur noch Gestalt und Antlitz des Vaters zugewandt. Vor ihm sieht man den knieenden Sohn, der, dem Beschauer abgewandt, sein Gesicht im Schosse des Vaters birgt, von den Händen des Vaters gehalten[3]. In der Auffassung vieler ist das, auch im Sinne des Evangelisten, richtig: die Hauptgestalt der Erzählung ist weniger der 'verlorene Sohn' als der liebevoll vergebende Vater. Nach Jeremias wäre es angebracht, vom 'Gleichnis von der Liebe des Vaters' zu reden[4].

Wenn auch, unter mehreren, G. Bornkamm ihm zustimmt, so ist doch in der heutigen Forschung die Tendenz zu anderen Bezeichnungen unverkennbar.

---

[1] J.C.H. Lebram, 'Jakob segnet Josephs Söhne...', in P.A.H. de Boer (ed.), *Oudtestamentische studiën* 15 (1969), 145-169.

[2] Hanna Jursch, 'Der verlorene Sohn in der Kunst Rembrandts', *Wissenschaftliche Zeitschrift ... Jena*, 8 (1958-59), Gesellschafts- und Sprachwissenschaftliche Reihe, 59-69; s. Abbildung 10. Zur Ikonographie s. L. Réau, *Iconographie de l'art chrétien*, II, ii, Paris, 1957, 333-38. Die vier Abbildungen bei Pieter H. Schut, *Toneel ofte Vertooch der Bybelsche Historien* ..., Amsterdam, 1659, n. 41-44, (= Réau, (2), (3), (5) und (6)), stimmen merkwürdigerweise überein mit der Beschreibung in A.S. Puschkins Novelle *Der Postmeister* (1831), die eine Variation zum Thema des verlorenen Sohnes bietet. Es handelt sich also um eine langjährige und weitverbreitete ikonographische Tradition. Nur dem Titel nach ist mir bekannt: Ewald Vetter, *Der verlorene Sohn. Lukas-Bücherei zur christlichen Ikonographie*, 7, Düsseldorf, 1955.

[3] So G. Bornkamm, *Jesus von Nazareth*, Stuttgart, 1956, 116-17.

[4] J. Jeremias, *Die Gleichnisse Jesu*, Göttingen, ⁴1956, 113.

Der älteste Name ist bekanntlich 'das Gleichnis von den zwei Söhnen' [5], und es mutet wie ein wohlüberdachter Kompromiss an, wenn z.B. neuerdings Grelot von 'Le père et les deux fils' [6] spricht, oder K.E. Bailey von 'The Father and the two lost sons' [7].

Die traditionelle Benennung, das Gleichnis vom verlorenen Sohn, zur Zeit Rembrandts etwa in der holländischen Statenvertaling [8] verwendet, wurde kräftig und noch immer eindrucksvoll von Jülicher verteidigt — wie öfters im Anschluss an die Ausführungen Van Koetsvelds [9].

Nun schliessen die verschiedenen Bezeichnungen für eine wohlbekannte Erzählung einander natürlich nur dann aus, wenn z.B. eine Überschrift gewählt werden muss. Der Ausleger könnte unter Umständen legitimerweise etwa von komplementären Aspekten der verschiedenen Teile der Erzählung sprechen.

Jedoch sind Umfang und Einteilung des Gleichnisses alles andere als klar und gesichert. Zum Ersten: die Auffassung, dass am Ende der Erzählung etwas fehlt, ist weit verbreitet. Heisst dies, dass der Text unvollständig [10], vielleicht beschädigt ist? Oder hat der Evangelist eine Geschichte mit einem 'offenen Ende' schreiben wollen? In der literarischen Theorie des Altertums ist ja die Überzeugungskraft derjenigen Worte die ungesagt bleiben anerkannt [11]. Wie steht es also um die Vollständigkeit der Form des Gleichnisses?

Zur Einteilung folgendes. Zu Rembrandts Zeit vertritt die schon genannte Statenvertaling eine Zweiteilung. Nach V. 11-24 werden V. 25-32 als eine Verteidigung des Verhaltens des Vaters gegenüber den Protesten des älteren Bruders aufgefasst. Die gleiche Zweiteilung findet sich heutzutage bei zahllosen Autoren, in Textausgaben, Übersetzungen, Kommentaren und Spezialuntersuchungen. Den Anfang des zweiten Teils bildet, in V. 25, der Satz in dem der ältere Sohn auftritt: 'Sein älterer Sohn aber war auf dem Felde ...'. Nun schliesst aber der vorangehende, also der erste Teil bereits mit den Worten V. 24b 'er — der jüngere Sohn — war verloren und wurde gefunden' ab. Die

---

[5] Irenaeus, *Adv. Haer.* 4.36.7 (Harvey 2, S. 283; Rousseau, SC 100/2, S. 910): *parabola duorum filiorum.* Vgl. Y. Tissot, 'Allégories patristiques de la parabole lucanienne des deux fils (Luc 15, 11-32)', in: F. Bovon, G. Rouiller, *Exegesis* ..., Neuchâtel-Paris, 1975, S. 250, Anm. 2.

[6] P. Grelot in *RB* 84 (1977) 321-48, 538-65.

[7] K.E. Bailey, *Poet and Peasant*, Grand Rapids, 1976, 158. Vgl. R. Bultmann, *Geschichte der synoptischen Tradition*, Göttingen, ^{4}1958 (= ^{2}1931), 212.

[8] S. die Überschrift zu Lk. 15.

[9] A. Jülicher, *Die Gleichnisreden Jesu*, Tübingen, ^{2}1910, 2, 335: '... mit Recht hat man ... die Parabel immer als die vom verlorenen Sohn oder vom filius prodigus, nicht 'von den zwei Söhnen' überschrieben'. C.E. van Koetsveld, *De gelijkenissen van den Zaligmaker*, Schoonhoven, 1869, 2, 113-57, s. z. B. 115.

[10] K.E. Bailey, 191, versucht das fehlende zu rekonstruieren. Vgl. A. Resch bei Jülicher, 2, 358f. In der Kathedrale zu Bourges (Cher, Frankreich) stellt ein Glasfenster (13. Jh.) die Szene dar, die man vermisst hat: die Versöhnung der beiden Söhne mit dem Vater.

[11] Demetrius, *Eloc.* IV. 222 (W. Rhys Roberts, LCL 199 (1932), 438).

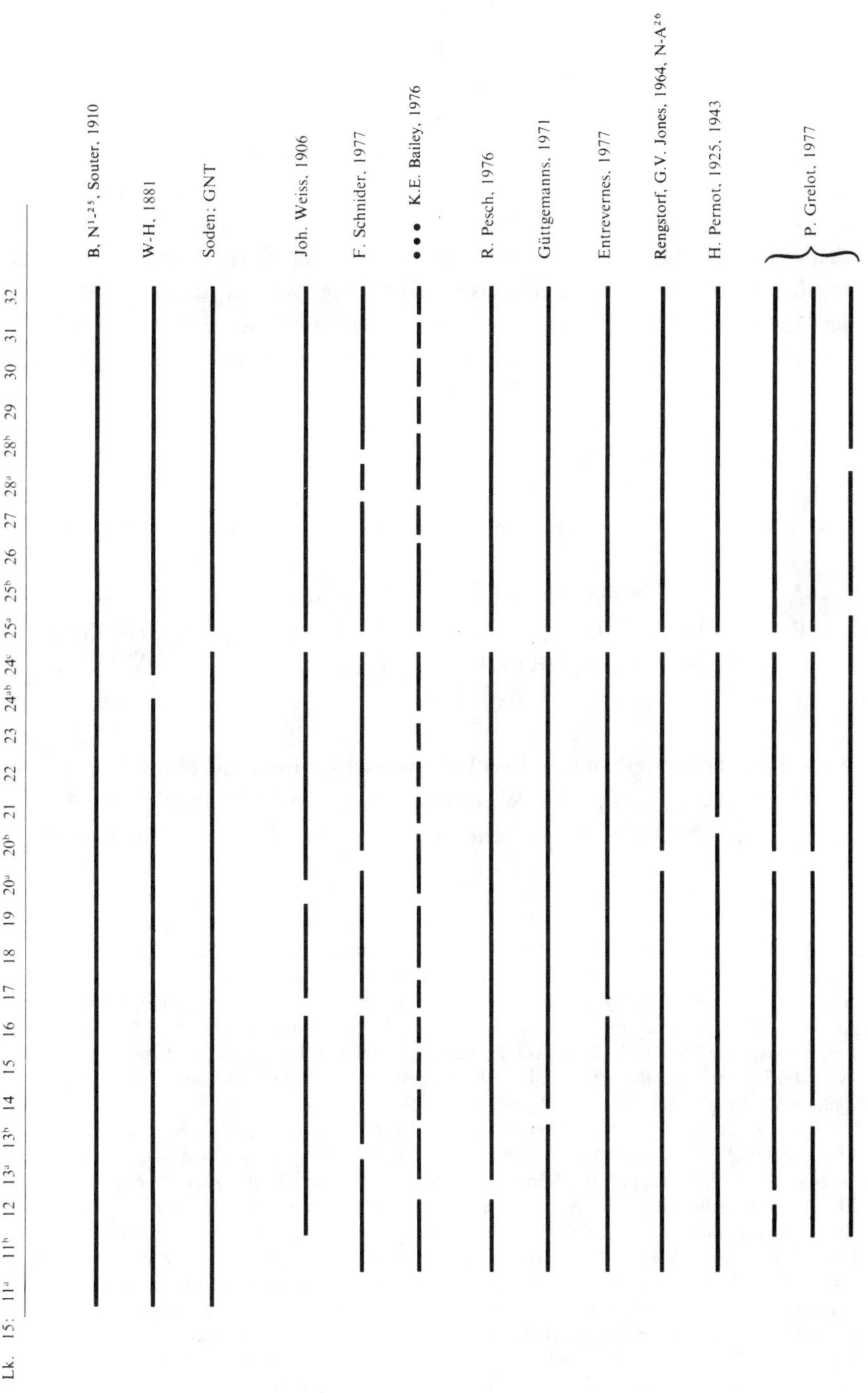
Lk. 15: 11a 11b 12 13a 13b 14 15 16 17 18 19 20a 20b 21 22 23 24ab 24c 25a 25b 26 27 28a 28b 29 30 31 32
B, N1-25, Souter, 1910
W-H, 1881
Soden; GNT
Joh. Weiss, 1906
F. Schnider, 1977
K.E. Bailey, 1976
R. Pesch, 1976
Güttgemanns, 1971
Entrevernes, 1977
Rengstorf, G.V. Jones, 1964, N-A26
H. Pernot, 1925, 1943
P. Grelot, 1977

eindrucksvolle Parallelie zu V. 32, wo am Ende das Gleiche nochmals ausgesagt wird, ist dafür ein schwerwiegendes Argument. So versteht es sich, dass in der Textausgabe von Westcott und Hort (1881), und weiter bei Jülicher und manchen späteren Auslegern, V. 24c schon den Anfang des zweiten Teils bildet[12]. Neben diesen Zweiteilungen gibt es aber in Textausgaben, Übersetzungen sowie in der Sekundärliteratur sehr verschiedene Dreiteilungen; ebenso Vierteilungen und manche anderen Versuche, das Ganze sinnvoll zu gliedern, ohne dass immer deutlich ist, warum der Text so und nicht anders geteilt und aufgefasst werden müsse[13]. Die Frage scheint unausweichlich: hat der Autor selber an so etwas wie eine Gliederung dieser Erzählung gedacht? Wir möchten in dieser Festgabe für einen teuren Freund versuchen, diese Frage einen Schritt näher zur Lösung zu bringen.

Zuerst eine kurze Bemerkung zum Text. Nach meiner Meinung hat man für Lk. 15:11-32 in Nestle-Aland[26] den richtigen Text vor sich, wenn man nur in V. 16 statt χορτασθῆναι liest: γεμίσαι τὴν κοιλίαν αὐτοῦ.[14]. In diesem Text lässt sich der genaue Umfang der Erzählung V. 11b-32 wie folgt festlegen:

A	V. 11^b	ἄνθρωπός τις	—	V. 16 αὐτῷ	:	205 Silben
B	V. 17	εἰς ἑαυτὸν δέ	—	V. 24^b εὑρέθη	:	297 Silben
C	V. 24^c	καὶ ἤρξαντο	—	V. 32 εὑρέθη	:	295 Silben

A wäre zu überschreiben mit: Das Lebensgeschick des jüngeren Sohnes bis zur Wende; B mit: Wende und Wiederaufnahme, und C handelt vom älteren Bruder. Um die Parallelie zwischen den äusseren Teilen A und C und die

[12] Jülicher, 2, 353: '... ein zweiter Teil, der nicht zufällig ebenso wie der erste endet 24c-32'.

[13] Einen Eindruck der vielen Möglichkeiten vermittelt die Übersichtstabelle. Ein Teil der Angaben ist dem Aufsatz von P. Grelot (s. Anm. 6) entnommen. N = Nestle(-Aland); GNT = *The Greek New Testament* (UBS, 1966); B = *codex vaticanus graecus* 1209; G.V. Jones = G.V. Jones, *The Art and Truth of the Parables*, London, 1964, 120-22. Wir konnten nicht zu Rate ziehen: R. Meynet, 'Deux paraboles parallèles. Analyse 'rhétorique' de Luc 15,1-32', in *Annales de Linguistique* de la Faculté des Lettres et des Sciences humaines, Université Saint-Joseph, Beyrouth, 1980, 1-17 [+8], s. *NRT* 103 (1981) 698. [Nachtrag: die Arbeit erschien in den *Annales de Philosophie* der gleichen Fakultät, 2 (1981), 89-105].

[14] Die kurze Notiz bei B.M. Metzger, *A Textual Commentary on the Greek New Testament*, London-New York, 1971, 164 ist ungenügend. Besser B.F. Westcott, F.J.A. Hort, *The N.T. in the Original Greek*, 2, London, 1907, Appendix, 62. Richtig Jülicher, 2, 344: χορτασθῆναι stammt aus Lk. 16:21, γεμίσαι τὴν κοιλίαν ... 'erschien einem Korrektor wohl zu derb'. S. auch J.M.S. Baljon, *Commentaar op ... Lukas*, Utrecht, 1908, 381-82; Th. Zahn, *Das Evangelium des Lucas*, Leipzig, 1913, 562; A. Pott, *Der Text des NTs*, Leipzig-Berlin, [2]1919, 77; J.Jeremias, *Gleichnisse*, 114, Anm. 9; F. Bovon in *Exegesis, problèmes de méthode et exercices de lecture*, Neuchâtel-Paris, 1975, 42, *etc.* Auch in V. 29 τῷ πατρὶ αὐτοῦ hat N-A[26] gegen N-A[25] denselben Text wie Westcott-Hort. Diesmal mit Recht; vgl. z.B. M. Zerwick, *Graecitas biblica*, Romae, 1955, Par. 148; N. Turner in J.H. Moulton, *A Grammar of N.T. Greek*, 3, Syntax, 1963, 38; G.D. Kilpatrick, 'The Greek N.T. Text of Today and the *Textus Receptus*', in H. Anderson, W. Barclay (ed.), *The N.T. in Historical and Contemporary Perspective*, Fs. G.H.C. Macgregor, Oxford, 1965, 204.

Mittelstellung von B zum Ausdruck zu bringen, und auch V. 11a mit aufzunehmen, stelle ich die Ausmasse wie folgt dar:

	V. 11^a Einführungsformel		3
A	11^b-16	205	
B	17-24^b		297
C	24^c-32	295	

Wenn man die verschiedenen Teile einander in dieser Weise zuordnet[15], beläuft sich hier demnach das Ganze auf 300 + 500 = 800 Silben. Eine zahlenmässig bestimmte Vollendung der äusseren Form der Erzählung und eine klare Disposition wurde also in sorgfältigster Weise realisiert. Dies hat sich auch in der Überlieferung bzw. in der kritischen Rekonstruktion des Textes, wie sie die modernen Ausgaben darbieten, weitgehend bewahrt[16].

Auch eine zweite zahlenmässig bedingte literarische Technik kann in diesem Aufsatz nur flüchtig angedeutet werden: wie andere frühchristliche Texte ist auch dieser Teil des Lukasevangeliums nicht nur nach Silben, sondern auch nach Worten zahlenmässig organisiert. Das zeigt schon der Anfang des Gleichnisses, V. 11b-16 (Teil A). Es lässt sich leicht feststellen, dass der Text in diesem Abschnitt folgenden Zahlen entspricht:

	V. 11^a		V. 11^b-13		V. 14-16
	3		97		100 Silben
	2		48		50 Worte
oder:	V. 11-13		V. 14-16		V. 11-16
	100	+	100	=	200 Silben
	50	+	50	=	100 Worte

Diese Aspekte der literarischen Technik des Evangelisten[17] werden wir hier nicht *en détail* untersuchen. Auch wenn wir die These einer silben- und wortmässig bestimmten Kompositionstechnik des Lukas zur richtigen Beschreibung und zum sachgemässen Verständnis des Textes für unentbehrlich

[15] Wer dazu veranlasst wird, 297 (= 3 x 99) und 3 zusammenzuzählen, muss sich, auch im Sinne des Autors, vielleicht vergegenwärtigen, dass er das Fehlende gesucht und gefunden hat. Vgl. Lk. 15:3-7 und die Auslegung der Parabel vom verlorenen Schaf bei Irenaeus, *Adv. Haer.* 1.16.1-2 (Harvey 1, 157-61) und im *Evangelium der Wahrheit*, 31-32.

[16] Im *Textus receptus* ist der Umfang 803 *S.*, in N-A[25] 798 *S.*, in N-A[26] 797 *S.* Vgl. J. Smit Sibinga, *Literair handwerk in Handelingen*, Leiden, 1970, 18, 25, zu Apg. 2 und 12. In Lk. 20:27-40 ist N-A[25] = N-A[26], und der Totalumfang ist 400 *S.* — also genau die Hälfte von Lk. 15:11-32.

[17] Zur Frage der mathematischen Wahrscheinlichkeit, s. M.J.J. Menken, *Numerical Literary Techniques in John* (SNT, 55), Leiden, 1985, 275-77.

halten, wollen wir hierauf nicht näher eingehen, sondern anderes betrachten. Dabei sind wir des verehrten Jubilars strenger Auffassung eingedenk, dass 'lebendige Gedanken, die schriftlich konserviert sind, missbraucht werden, wenn man mit ihnen nur Thesen beweisen will'[18]. Die These, die wir im Folgenden zu begründen und illustrieren versuchen, beabsichtigt nämlich, die Organisation und Gliederung des Textes nicht nur zu analysieren, sondern auch nachzuempfinden und auf diese Weise, soweit möglich, einigermassen wieder zum Leben zu bringen.

Ein Kriterium, das man verglichen mit dem Kriterium der Silben- und Wortzahlen vielleicht als makrosyntaktisch bezeichnen kann, wird auf eine grössere Textpartie, d.h. Lk. 14:1-17:10, global angewendet; für Lk. 15:11-32 wird die Untersuchung ins Einzelne gehen. Es handelt sich um ein überaus wichtiges Element des Satzes, als solches gesondert betrachtet und rein zahlenmässig erfasst: die Verbalformen[19].

Lk. 14 vereinigt in einer Gastmahl-Szene eine Sabbathheilung samt Streitgespräch (V. 1-6) mit weiteren Konversationsstücken für Gäste und Gastgeber und mit dem Gleichnis vom grossen Abendmahl (V. 15-24). Dazu fügen sich V. 25-27 ('von der Schwere der Jüngerschaft') und, in V. 28-30 und 31-32, zwei weitere Gleichnisse. Für die Zahl der Verbalformen in diesen Abschnitten gelten die nachfolgenden Angaben:

V. 1-6:	5 + 10 + 5 =			20	
7-11:			28		
12-14:			12/	40/	60
15-24:		51			
25-35:		48/			99/159 *V.*[20]

Nachdem Lk. im 14. Kapitel vier Gleichnisse verarbeitet hat, fügt er in Kap. 15 und 16 noch fünf hinzu, und Lk. 17:7-10 ('Vom Knechtslohn') dürfte eine Reihe von zehn Gleichnissen schliessen. Das Haupt- oder Nebenthema der Mahlzeit ist den meisten dieser Gleichnisse gemeinsam. In Kap. 15 und 16 (siehe zuerst 15:7) ist die Bekehrung des Sünders ein weiteres Hauptmotiv.

[18] J.C.H. Lebram in *Vetus Testamentum* 20 (1970), 127.

[19] Die These wurde zuerst kurz skizziert in E.J. Epp, G.D. Fee (edd.), *New Testament Textual Criticism* ..., Fs. B.M. Metzger, Oxford, 1981, 19-21, für Mt. 14:22-33. In der modernen Sprachwissenschaft ist, wie ich nachträglich sehe, das Verfahren nicht unbekannt. S. z.B. L. Tesnière, *Eléments de syntaxe structurale*, Paris, 1959, und H. Weinrich, 'Die Textpartitur als heuristische Methode' (1972), in W. Dressler (ed.), *Textlinguistik* (WdF 427), Darmstadt, 1978, 391-412.

[20] Ein beliebiges Beispiel für die Verwendung der Primzahl 53 in der Silbentechnik des Lukas: in Lk. 24:13-19b sind die Ausmasse: N 159, D 53, S 212 *S.* Vgl. *Literair handwerk*, 21-24 über Apg. 26.

Und zwar gibt es Gleichnisse, in denen es zur Bekehrung kommt — zur rechten Zeit: der verlorene Sohn; oder erst im letzten Augenblick: der ungerechte Verwalter (16:1-9) — und daneben andere, in denen die Bekehrung weniger eine Rolle spielt — 15:7 und 10 nur im Epimythion, nicht im eigentlichen Gleichnis — bzw. zu spät kommt: der reiche Mann (16:19-31). So erscheint es sachgemäss, in Kap. 15 und 16 die Gleichnisse einander in zwei Gruppen zuzuordnen: dem Gleichnis von der rechtzeitigen Bekehrung (15:11b-32) schliesst sich 16:1-18, ein Gleichnis über Bekehrung in letzter Stunde *cum annexis* an (Spalte B). Diese Abschnitte verwenden 5 x 19 + 4 x 19 = 9 x 19 oder 171 Verbalformen[21]. Spalte A zeigt, dass der übrige Teil von Kap. 15 und 16, also 15:1-10 und 16:19-32, fast den Umfang — immer nach dem Massstab der Zahl der Verbalformen — von 15:11b-32 erreicht. Dessen Einführungsformel, V. 11a Εἶπεν δέ, könnte den Ausgleich machen[22]. Die Totalsumme der Verbalformen ist jedenfalls, ebenso wie der Totalwert für die Abschnitte 15:11b-32 und 16:1-18, ein Vielfaches von 19, nämlich 266 oder 14 x 19.

Kap. 17 verfolgt zuerst noch das Thema der Bekehrung, μετάνοια, (s. V. 3f.), und bringt ausserdem noch ein Gleichnis, das von einer Mahlzeit handelt (17:7-10)[23]. Die Ausmasse sind, mit dem erwähnten Massstab: V. 1-6 = 26 *V.*, V. 7-10 = 26 *V.*[24]

Übersicht der Verbalformen in Lk. 15:1 - 17:10

		(A)		(B)		
15:1-10		43				
11ᵃ			1			
11ᵇ-32				95		
16:1-18				76		
19-32		51				
		94 +	1 +	171 =	266	
17:1-10	(C)				52/	318 *V.* (TIH)

[21] 171 ist die Dreieckszahl von 18; vgl. I. Thomas, *Selections illustrating the History of Greek Mathematics*, London-Cambridge (Mass.), 1951, 1, 90-95; D.E. Smith, *History of Mathematics*, New York, 1958, 2, 24; W. Burkert, *Weisheit und Wissenschaft*, Nürnberg, 1962, 404. In Lk. 16 ist die Totalsumme der Zahlwörter 342 = 2. 171; vgl. Fs. Metzger, S. 31, Anm. 43.

[22] Lukas überrascht manchmal den modernen Leser durch mehr oder weniger mangelhafte (z.B. 5:14; 7:31), überflüssige (4:24; 6:5; 11:4) oder unklare (16:8; 19:26) Angaben hinsichtlich eines Überganges zur direkten Rede oder des Auftretens eines anderen Sprechers.

[23] Auch zeitlich gehört 17:1-10 noch zum szenischen Zusammenhang der vorgehenden Stücke, s. F. Hauck, *Das Evangelium des Lukas*, Leipzig, 1934, 211.

[24] Das Gleichnis im eigentlichen Sinn, 17:7-9, wird mit 19 Verbalformen erzählt. Dem Gleichnis vom verlorenen Schaf mit seiner Anwendung entsprechen die Zahlen 15 (für 15:4-6) und 4 (für V. 7), zusammen 19 *V.*

Für den Stoff, den er in Lk. 14, 15-16 und 17:1-10 darbietet, verwendet Lukas also 159 (= 3.53), 266 (= 5.53 + 1) und 52 (= 53 - 1) Verben. Das heisst, für Lk. 15:1 - 17:10 wird die Zahl 318 erreicht, welcher der Barnabasbrief eine besondere Bedeutung beimisst: TIH — das ist Jesus und das Kreuz[25]. Kap. 14, dessen Organisation der Zahl 888 entspricht [26] und das in V. 27 *expressis verbis* das Kreuz erwähnt, schickt diesen 318 Verbalformen die Hälfte, nämlich 159 Formen voraus[27].

In diesem Kontext hat nun Kap. 15 eine eigene Thematik, die mit den zwei Begriffen 'suchen' und 'finden' angedeutet wird, s. V. 8. Das Objekt des Suchens und Findens ist das Verlorene, s. V. 4, 8, 24, 32. Schaf und Groschen werden verloren, gesucht und dann wiedergefunden. Der Sohn aber — und nur im Gleichnis vom Sohn handelt es sich um eine Bekehrung — wird nach V. 24 und V. 32 'gefunden', ohne dass er gesucht wurde[28]. Etwas künstliches hat die Zusammenfügung der drei Gleichnisse wohl an sich. Um so deutlicher dürfte aber so die Absicht zutage treten, das Ganze zu einer Einheit zu verbinden.

Dieses Ganze, Lk. 15, hat auch eine eigene Mitte. In der von Lukas verwendeten Technik der gezählten Verbalformen kommt der Verbalform, die in Mittelstellung steht, öfters eine besondere Bedeutung zu[29]. Das scheint auch in Lk. 15 der Fall zu sein. Ohne Zweifel wird in V. 24 und 32, in den feierlichen Worten des Vaters über den Sohn 'er war tot und wurde wieder lebendig', Wesentliches ausgesagt. Man kann kaum sagen, dass es sich hier um ein 'understatement' handelt. Vielmehr wird der Lebensgang des Sohnes in höchst dramatischer Steigerung zusammengefasst[30]. Seine Umkehr und Rückkehr ist, wie das neue Leben des getauften Christen nach Rm. 6:3-4, 13 oder Eph. 5:14, eine Auferstehung von den Toten[31]. Wenn dem so ist, sollte man in Lk. 15:18 das Partizipium ἀναστάς in der Exegese nicht verharmlosen.

---

[25] S. Barn. 9:8-9. Die Summe der in Lk. 15 gebrauchten Zahlwörter ist 100 + 1 + 99 + 1 + 99 + 10 + 1 + 1 + 2 + 1 + 1 + 1. + 1= 318 (s. die VV. 4, 7, 8, 10, 11, 15, 19, 22, 26).

[26] Die Ausmasse von Lk. 14 sind: V. 1-10 = 350 *S*., V. 11-14 = 159 *S*., V. 15-24 = 38 + 341 *S*. Also: V. 1-24 = 888 *S*. Weiter: V. 25-27 = 112 *S*. (d.h. V. 1-27 = 1000 *S*.); V. 28-33 = 230 *S*., V. 34-35 = 58 *S*. (d.h. V. 25-35 = 400 *S*.). Das Ganze: 1288 *S*. Für die Zahl 888, s. Irenaeus, *Adv. Haer*. 2.24.1 (Harvey 1, S. 334). Ι + η + σ + ο + υ + ς = 10 + 8 + 200 + 70 + 400 + 200 = 888. Man beachte die Abrundung auf 1000 *S*. in V. 27, wo das Kreuz erwähnt wird.

[27] Damit sind nur die Proportionen innerhalb des Komplexes angedeutet. So wird nicht etwa gesagt, dass mit 17:11 nach einer Zäsur ein neuer Abschnitt des Evangeliums anfänge.

[28] Vgl. Jülicher 2, 352.

[29] Z.B.: Lk. 20:9-19 (das Gleichnis von den bösen Winzern) zählt 53 Verbalformen. Die Nummer 27 ist, in V. 14, ἀποκτείνωμεν in der verhängnisvollen βουλὴ πονηρά (s. Is. 3:9 LXX) der derzeitigen Inhaber des Weinbergs. Auf eine Formel gebracht: 26 + (V. 14) ἀποκτείνωμεν + 26 = 53 *V*.

[30] In der Stoa werden Menschen, die nicht zum philosophischen Leben erwacht sind, als tot, νεκρός, bezeichnet, s. R. Bultmann in G.Kittel (ed.), *ThWbzNT* 3, 1938, 12, mit Belegstellen.

[31] G. Braumann, 'Tot — lebendig, verloren — gefunden (Lk. 15,24 und 32)', in W. Haubeck, M. Bachmann (edd.), *Wort in der Zeit*, Fs. K.H. Rengstorf, Leiden, 1980, 156-64.

Joachim Jeremias z.B. übersetzte ἀναστὰς πορεύσομαι mit 'ich will mich sofort aufmachen'[32]. Auch von seinen Voraussetzungen her scheint mir das, wenn auch möglich, doch keineswegs selbstverständlich[33]. Dieses 'aufstehen' — oder muss man sagen: 'auferstehen'? — nach dem 'zugrundegehen' (V. 17) ist das Moment, woran V. 24 und V. 32 anknüpfen. Ἀναστάς in V. 18 ist auch die Verbalform, die im ganzen Kapitel genau in der Mitte steht. Für die Verbalformen in Lk. 15:1-32 gilt die Formel: 69 + (V. 18) ἀναστάς + 69 *V*. Diese Verbalform wird von ἀπόλλυμαι (V. 17) und πορεύσομαι (V. 18) in sinnvoller Weise flankiert.

Die Gesamtzahl der Verbalformen für Lk. 15:11b-32, 95, teilt sich in 57 Formen für V. 11b-24b und weitere 38 Formen für V. 24c-32. Einem analogen Formschema von 38 + 57 Silben entsprechen einige Zeilen aus der Pascha-Homilie des Meliton von Sardes, in denen er dem 'älteren' Gesetz den 'neuen' Logos gegenüberstellt[34].

---

[32] J. Jeremias, *Die Gleichnisse Jesu*, Göttingen, ^{4}1956, 114: Ἀναστὰς πορεύσομαι = aram. *ʾ^{a}qum w^{e}ʾezel* ...; in seinem Aufsatz 'Zum Gleichnis vom verlorenen Sohn, Luk. 15,11-32', *ThZ* (Basel) 5 (1949) 228-231 nahm er diesen Ausdruck nicht in der Liste der Semitismen in Lk. 15 auf. Weizsäcker und Menge übersetzen: 'Ich will mich aufmachen'. In der *New English Bible* liest man: 'I will set off ...'. Vgl. G.B. Winer-G. Lünemann, *Grammatik des ntl. Sprachidioms*, Leipzig, 1867, 565: '*unverzüglich will ich* u.s.w.'; Blass-Debrunner, Par. 419: 2A. Richtig W.F. Howard in J.H. Moulton, *A Grammar of N.T. Greek*, 2, Edinburgh, 1929, 452: 'It is hard to say when the participle is really pleonastic ...'. S. auch Lagrange in seinem Kommentar zur Stelle (S. 425); Ch. E. Carlston in *JBL* 94 (1975) 371: ' ... in some of these cases 'arise' is by no means redundant'. Der Gedanke, dass es sich um einen Semitismus handelt, findet sich schon bei Joh. Menochius (1575-1655). Er bemerkt zu Lk. 15:18 *surgam*: *Hebraismus est quo utuntur Hebraei cum alicuius operis exordium significant, quia cum nihil agimus sedere solemus, cum aliquid agere aggredimur, surgimus* (s. *Biblia maxima versionum*, tom. xiv, Lutetiae Parisiorum, 1660, S. 195).

[33] S. z.B. C.C. Torrey, *The Four Gospels*, London, ^{2}1947, 156: 'I will arise and go to my father ...'. In Apg. 22:10, wo es heisst ἀναστὰς πορεύου, liegt Saulus zu Boden (s. V. 7); für Lk. 17:19 ἀναστὰς πορεύου trifft ähnliches zu (s. V. 16). Im Lied von der Perle der syrischen Thomasakten kommt dem analogen Motiv (V. 42) 'erhebe dich und steh auf von deinem Schlafe' selbständige Bedeutung zu. Für den Text s. z.B. T. Jansma, *A Selection from the Acts of Judas Thomas*, Leiden, 1952, S. [37^{8}], und vgl. A. Adam, *Die Psalmen des Thomas* ... (BZNW 24), Berlin, 1959, S. 51, 59, 86. Für Lk. 15:18 und 24 liesse sich vergleichen Gen. 43:8 ... ἀναστάντες πορευσόμεθα, ἵνα ζῶμεν καὶ μὴ ἀποθάνωμεν ... Auch diese Auffassung hat eine alte Tradition, vgl. die Katene bei J.A. Cramer, *Catenae in evangelia S. Lucae et S. Joannis*..., Oxford, 1841, 119^{4-6}, die Glossa interlinearis zu Lk. 15:18 *surgam*: *quia me iacere cognovi*, und Joh. Pricaeus in: *Criticorum sacrorum ... annotata in quatuor evangelia*, (= tomus 6), Amsterdam, 1698, [Lucas] 597.

[34] S. O. Perler (ed.), Méliton de Sardes, *Sur la Pâque, et fragments* (SC 123), Paris, 1966, 62-64:

5	Ἀντὶ γὰρ τοῦ [ἀμνοῦ θε]ὸς ἐγένετο	12	
	καὶ ἀντὶ τοῦ προβάτου ἄν[θρωπ]ος,	10	
	[ἐ]ν δὲ τῷ ἀνθρώπῳ Χριστός,	8	
	ὃς κεχώρηκεν [τὰ] πάντα.	8/	38
6	Ἡ γοῦν τοῦ προβάτου σφαγὴ	8	
	καὶ ἡ τοῦ πάσχα πομπὴ	7	
	καὶ ἡ τοῦ νόμου γραφὴ	7	
	εἰς Χριστὸν Ἰησοῦν κεχώρηκεν,	9	
	δι' ὃν τὰ πάντα ἐν τῷ πρεσβυτέρῳ νόμῳ ἐγένετο,	17	
	μᾶλλον δὲ ἐν τῷ νέῳ λόγῳ.	9/	57/ 95 *S.*

Die Verbalformen in Lk. 15:11b-32

	D_N		D_D	S		
V. 11^{b}-12	3		(*1*) 2	5		
13-16	16		–	16/	21	
17-19	2		(*2*) 9	11		
20	8		–	8		
21	1		(*3*) 3	4		
22-24^{b}	1		(*4*) 12	13/	36/	57
24^{c}	2		–	2/	2	
25-27	8		(*5*) 4	12		
28-30	7		(*6*) 7	14		
31-32	1		(*7*) 9	10/	36/	38
V. 11^{b}-32	49	+	46			= 95 *V.*

Zur Übersichtstabelle sei Folgendes bemerkt. Der in der modernen Literaturwissenschaft gängige Unterschied zwischen 'Narrative' (hier: N) und 'Discourse' (D)[35] war in der Antike wohlbekannt und wurde zweifellos auch von Lukas angewendet[36]. Wir unterscheiden im Gleichnis, das als Ganzes von einer Person, die der Verfasser als redend einführt, erzählt wird, und das also D, discourse, ist, die gesprochenen Partien von den erzählten Vorgängen als D_D von D_N. Die Selbstüberlegung des Sohnes enthält in V. 18-19 mit '... ich werde ihm sagen: ...' von neuem einen Übergang zur direkten Rede; diese ist in der Tabelle nicht notiert[37]. Ebenso wie im Gleichnis vom grossen Abendmahl (Lk. 14:16-24) kommt in der Erzählung Lk. 15:11-32 siebenmal ein Sprecher zu Wort; die gesprochenen Partien sind in einen erzählenden Kontext eingefügt, der 49 Verbalformen verwendet. Darunter gibt es 7 Imperfecta (s. die VV. 11, 16, 25f., 28: εἶχεν, ἐπεθύμει, ἤσθιον, ἐδίδου, ἦν, ἐπυνθάνετο, παρεκάλει). Unter den Verbalformen der direkten Rede gibt es 7 *indicativi praesentis* (s. die VV. 17, 19, 21, 29, 31: περισσεύονται, ἀπόλλυμαι, εἰμι, εἰμι,[38] δουλεύω, εἶ, ἐστιν), 7 *imperativi* (s. die VV. 12, 19, 22f.: δός, ποίησον,[39] ἐξενέγκατε, ἐνδύσατε, δότε, φέρετε, θύσατε), und 7 Partizipien (s. die

[35] S. z.B. Mabel Lang, *Herodotean Narrative and Discourse*, 1984; vgl. P. Wendland, *Die urchristlichen Literaturformen* (Handbuch zum NT, I/ii-iii), Tübingen, $^{2-3}$1912, 270-71, 275, 278, 285-86, 291, 301-02.

[36] Thucydides 1.22 ...ὅσα μὲν λόγῳ εἶπον ... τὰ δ'ἔργα τῶν πραχθέντων ...; Aristoteles, *Poetica* 15.2 (1454a) ὁ λόγος ἢ ἡ πρᾶξις; Apg. 1:1 ...ποιεῖν τε και διδάσκειν...; Papias, Frgm. II bei Eusebius, *Kirchengeschichte* III. 39.15: ... ἢ λεχθέντα ἢ πραχθέντα...

[37] Nennt man diese direkte Rede $D_{D'}$, dann gilt: $D_D = 42$, $D_{D'} = 4$.

[38] In V. 21 wiederholt aus V. 19.

[39] In V. 19, aber nicht wiederholt in V. 21; vgl. die *varia lectio*.

VV. 12, 18, 23f., 27, 30, 32: ἐπιβάλλον, ἀναστάς, φαγόντες, ἀπολωλώς, ὑγιαίνοντα, καταφαγών, ἀπολωλώς).

Vielleicht muss auch hervorgehoben werden, dass die Erzählstücke 24mal den Indikativ des Aorists verwenden. Darunter stehen (V. 20bc) εἶδεν, ἐσπλαγχνίσθη, ἐπέπεσεν, κατεφίλησεν in der Mitte (also: 24 = 10 + 4 + 10). Es scheint mir nicht abwegig, hier einen oder vielleicht den Gipfel der dramatischen Handlung zu erblicken. Es muss auffallen, dass der Vater hier die handelnde Person ist[40]. Zu den 7 Partizipien der direkten Rede gesellen sich 12 im Erzählstoff. Auf insgesamt 95 Verbalformen gibt es also 19 Partizipien. Ein einziges Mal ist der Vater Subjekt: V. 20c δραμών[41] und dieses Mittelwort steht an der zehnten Stelle — Formel also: 19 = 9 + 1 + 9.

Neben den 24 Indikativen des Aorists in der Erzählung stehen in der direkten Rede (d.h. in D_D) 12 Formen dieser Art. Und wir werden der Zahl zwölf auch in anderer Weise noch als Ordnungsprinzip begegnen[42].

Gibt es nun auch für das Gleichnis als Ganzes eine Mitte, die mit diesem Aspekt der literarischen Technik als solche aufzuweisen wäre? Der Auftrag des Vaters V. 22bc-23 erfüllt annähernd die Bedingung, dass er von ebensovielen Einheiten vorbereitet wird, als es nachher noch geben wird. Für die in diesem Auftrag verwendeten sieben Verbalformen gilt: V. 11b-22a + V. 22bc-23 + V. 24-32 = 45 + 7 + 43 = 95 *V*. Genau in der Mitte steht jedoch V. 22c δότε: 'gebet (oder: tut) ihm einen Ring an den Finger'. Für dieses Moment im Gleichnis kann man den Platz folgenderweise formulieren: 47 + 1 + 47. Dass es sich hier um ein Moment höchster Wichtigkeit handelt, hat man schon öfters dargelegt[43].

In der direkten Rede treten vier Personen als Sprecher auf: der Vater, die beiden Söhne und, in V. 27, einer der Knechte. Dabei ergeben sich für die Rede des Vaters die Werte 12 (V. 22-24) und 9 (V. 31-32), d.h. insgesamt 21 Verbalformen; für den jüngsten Sohn 2 (V. 12), 9 (V. 17-19) und 3 (V. 21), also beieinander 14 Verbalformen, und für den älteren Sohn 7 (in v. 29f.). Wiederum ist ein Gleichgewicht realisiert worden: der Vater verwendet ebensoviele Verbalformen wie die beiden Söhne zusammen, und wiederum stützt sich ein mit eindeutigem Kriterium arbeitendes Schema auf die Zahl sieben.

---

[40] Vgl. die oben angedeutete Frage nach dem richtigen Namen des Gleichnisses, und s. Calvins Bemerkung zu V. 20: *Hoc est caput parabolae: si homines, qui .., paternus ... amor inflectit, ut clementer filiis ignoscant et misere perditos ultro requirant, Deum, cuius immensa bonitas omnes patrum amores superat, nihilo fore nobis duriorem* (A. Tholuck, ed., *Ioannis Calvini in N.T. commentarii*, 2, Berolini, 1833, 138).

[41] K.E. Bailey, *Poet and Peasant*, 181-82, hebt mit Recht das Ungewöhnliche und Auffällige in dieser Handlung hervor — wie schon Bengel: *parentes alias non facile occurrunt filiis.* Man vgl. im *Test. Abr.* A c. 2 (James, 78[16-29]) mit c.3 (79[27-29]). Nur von Isaak heisst es: ἔδραμεν.

[42] Man beachte auch, dass das Wort *Vater* zwölfmal vorkommt.

[43] S. die Angaben bei Bailey, *Poet and Peasant*, 185, Anm. 198, besonders K.H. Rengstorf, *Die Re-Investitur des verlorenen Sohnes..*, Köln/Opladen, 1967, 29-39, vgl. 68.

der Vater: - (*4*), (*7*) -	12 + 9 =	21
der jüngere Sohn: - (*1*), (*2*), (*3*) -	2 + 9 + 3 = 14	
der ältere: - (*6*) -	7/	21/ 42 *V*.

Für das entscheidende Gespräch zwischen Vater und jüngerem Sohn und das vorbereitende Selbstgespräch des letzteren, d.h. für (*2*), (*3*) und (*4*), werden resp. 9 + 3 und 12 Formen benutzt.

Man darf wohl sagen, dass die Faktoren 7 und 12 auf mancherlei Weise in der so analysierten inneren Organisation des Gleichnisses zu Tage treten[44].

Dies alles gilt für verschiedene Aspekte der Kompositiòn des Gleichnisses in seinem ganzen Umfang. Nun wollen wir versuchen, dem Gedankengang und dem Aufbau der Erzählung schrittweise nachzugehen. Das Kriterium ist nach wie vor die Zahl der Verbalformen.

Nach dem Ausgangspunkt, 'Jemand hatte zwei Söhne', mit einer einzelnen Verbalform, εἶχεν, V. 11b, zerteilt sich der erste Akt der Erzählung natürlicherweise in fünf Teile[45]. Jeder Teil verwendet vier Verbalformen, und in der erzählten Geschichte entsprechen einander die Entwicklungsstufen von Aufstieg — wenn man so sagen darf — und Niedergang:

(a)	V. 12:	der Sohn fragt und bekommt was er wünscht
(b)	V. 13:	er lebt in Luxus und Verschwendung
(c)	V. 14:	sein Los wendet sich
(b')	V. 15:	er lebt in Abhängigkeit und Entbehrung
(a')	V. 16:	und bekommt nicht was er verlangt.

Die Wende tritt ein, wenn in V. 14 Hungersnot über das Land kommt, ἐγένετο λιμὸς ἰσχυρά ...; mit diesem ἐγένετο als elfte Verbalform entsprechen V. 11b-16 der Formel: 10 + 1 + 10 = 21 *V*. Unter diesen 21 Verbalformen gibt es

[44] Vergleichbares ergibt sich bei der Analyse von Lk. 9:10b-17. Hier genügen fünf Brote und zwei Fische, also sieben Dinge, zur Ernährung einer Menge, und es bleiben noch zwölf Korbe. Der Text entspricht folgenden Zahlen:

		N		D	S
(vor dem Wunder)	V. 10ᵇ-11:	76		—	76
(die Speisung)	V. 12-17ᵃ:		133	+ 117	250
(nachher)	V. 17ᵇ:	19		—	19
	V. 10ᵇ-17:	95 +	133	+ 117 oder	
		(5.19) +	(7.19)	+ 117 oder	
			12.(12+7)	+ 117 =	345 *S*.

[45] Man spürt die Logik eines schulgerechten Dramas in Miniatur. Zur Fünfteiligkeit, vgl. Horatius, *De arte poetica*, 189-190; zur Nachwirkung etwa W. Kayser, *Das sprachliche Kunstwerk*, Bern, [15]1971, 172. Nach Philon von Alexandrien ist fünf, die Zahl der Sinne, ein Symbol des Menschen, der sich dem Leib und der Aussenwelt ergibt, s. *De migratione Abr*., Par. 203. Vgl. W. Burkert, *Weisheit und Wissenschaft*, S. 230, Anm. 48.

zwei in der direkten Rede (V. 12 δός und ἐπιβάλλον) und 19 weitere im Erzähltext.

Wer sich vergegenwärtigt, dass das Gleichnis als ganzes von 95 Verbalformen getragen wird und sich, wie die Tabelle zeigt, sinnvoll gliedert in Teile, die 57, bzw. 38 Verbalformen verwenden, wird in den 19 Verbalformen der Erzählung in V. 11b-16 eine Grundlage der inneren Organisation der Parabel erblicken: die Recheneinheit wird zu Anfang der Komposition dargeboten. Dass es, wenn man bei V. 14 δαπανήσαντος δέ anfängt, bis zum nächsten von δέ markierten Neuansatz dreimal eine Sequenz von vier Verbalformen gibt, kann auch der moderne Leser wohl ohne Mühe nachempfinden. Für die 19 erzählenden Verbalformen in V. 11b-16 empfiehlt sich also eine Disposition in 7 + 12 Formen.

Auch für die nächste, in sich geschlossene Episode, V. 17-24b, ist — und zwar in verschiedener Weise — eine innere Organisation aufgrund von je zwölf Verbalformen anzunehmen. Die Totalsumme der Verba, von V. 17 ἐλθών bis V. 24b εὑρέθη beläuft sich auf 36. Was der Sohn in V. 17-19 überdacht und geplant hat, vollführt er — oder sagen wir: wird ihm möglich — in V. 20-21, und zwar in zwölf Verben. Der Vater erteilt in V. 22b-24 seine Aufträge in 5 Verbalformen (ἐξενέγκατε bis θύσατε), erwähnt das Ziel mit zwei (φαγόντες εὐφρανθῶμεν) und fügt zur Begründung seines Vorhabens weitere 5 Verba zu (V. 24 ἦν¹ bis εὑρέθη); er verwendet also zwölf Formen. Für den erzählenden, bzw. den gesprochenen Teil des Textes ergeben sich als Totalwerte 12, bzw. 24 Verbalformen:

	D_N		D_D		S
V. 17-19	2		9		11
20-21	9		3		12
$22\text{-}24^b$	1		12		13
V. $17\text{-}24^b$	12	+	24	=	36

Es ist leicht ersichtlich, dass das erste Verbum in V. 22, εἶπεν, mit dem der Vater das Wort nimmt, gemäss dem Gewicht dieses Erzählmoments, in einer Mittelstellung steht: V. 20-24b = 12 + 1 + 12[46].

Unsere Analyse hat nun einen Punkt erreicht, den man nach der gängigen Auffassung als Grenze des ersten Teils oder Übergang zum zweiten bezeichnen kann. Die kleine, aber nicht so leichte Frage, ob V. 24c, καὶ ἤρξαντο εὐφραίνεσθαι, zur ersten oder zur zweiten Hälfte gehört, muss hier des Näheren untersucht werden. Nach Klostermann eröffnen diese Worte den zweiten Teil der Parabel[47]. Andere jedoch sprechen diese Funktion dem V. 25

[46] Dem entspricht, z.B. die Stellung von εἶπεν in Lk. 9:13 oder 22:67. Lk. 9:10-17: 21 + 1 + 21 *V.*; 22:66-69: 6 + 1 + 6 *V.*; und s. unten zu εἶπεν in 15:31.

[47] E. Klostermann in *HzNT*, 2, 1919, S. 522, vgl. 518. Vgl. A. Plummer in *ICC* (1896), S. 377; Lagrange (1921), S. 426; T.W. Manson, *The Sayings of Jesus* (1937), London, 1949, S. 285; F.

zu: Ἦν ..., mit grossem Anfangsbuchstabe; so wird der griechische Text tatsächlich in mancher modernen Textausgabe dargeboten, wie z.B. bei Von Soden, Merk und Nestle-Aland 26.

Für Wellhausen bildet V. 24c den Übergang, und er sagt von diesem kleinen Satz, dass er 'überhängt'[48]. Für Andere scheint er sogar überflüssig, wenn sie ihn in einem Überblick über die Parabel ganz fortlassen[49]. Vielleicht kann die bescheidene Häresie, die in diesem Aufsatz vorgetragen wird, zur Lösung dieser Frage etwas beisteuern.

Schon mehrmals ergab die Analyse der gezählten Verbalformen für einen bestimmten Abschnitt ein symmetrisches Ordnungsprinzip nach der Formel a + b + a. Oft ist b viel kleiner als a, bisweilen ist b gleich eins. Und das Moment dieser einen Verbalform, oder dieser wenigen Formen, scheint manchmal von besonderer Bedeutung zu sein. Dieses *Gesetz der Mittelstellung* trifft auch für V. 24c zu.

Denn für V. 17-24b, V. 24c, V. 25-32 ergeben sich die Zahlen 36 + 2 + 36 *V*. Diese Formel wird nicht nur der refrainartigen Gleichheit von V. 24ab und V. 32bc gerecht, sondern enthält auch die Anerkennung einer eigenen und wichtigen Funktion von V. 24c. Die mit καὶ ἤρξαντο εὐφραίνεσθαι angedeutete Festfreude ist — was nach V. 6f. und V. 9f. für die zwei ersten Parabeln in Lk. 15 auch für die dritte nicht unerwartet kommt — ein wesentliches Element, das seine zentrale Stellung verdient[50].

Bovon in *Exegesis* (s. oben, Anm. 14), 48: 'Il faut rattacher les mots 'Et ils se mirent à festoyer' (v. 24c) à la suite du récit ...'. Und s. die Textausgabe von Westcott-Hort, 1881. Das Argument ist die abschliessende Wirkung des Refrains V. 24ab, und diese muss man wohl, mit z.B. Jülicher, 2, 353 und Jeremias, 115, anerkennen.

48 J. Wellhausen, *Das Evangelium Lucae*, Berlin, 1904, 83. Vgl. Jülicher 2, 353: 'nur ... Überleitung'; F. Hauck (oben, Anm. 23), 199, und viele andere.

49 Z.B. A. Edersheim, *The Life and Times of Jesus the Messiah* (1883, ²-³1886), Grand Rapids, 1936, 2, 262-63; Joh. Weiss in *Die Schriften des NTs*, Göttingen, 1906, 446; ³1917, 467-68; J.D. Crossan (1973), s. W. Harnisch, *Die neutestamentliche Gleichnisforschung* ... (WdF 575), Darmstadt, 1982, 153f. C.E. van Koetsveld, und vielleicht nicht nur er, empfindet in V. 24c eine Schwierigkeit: ' ... *En zij*, de dienaren, *begonnen vrolijk te zijn*. Dit staat er niet van den vader, die zijnen kinderen een feest bereidt, maar zelf te diep en ernstig gevoelt op dit oogenblik, om zoo kinderlijk vrolijk te wezen. En het staat er even min van den zoon ...', 2, 131. Dagegen z.B. P. Dausch, *Die drei älteren Evangelien*, Bonn, 1918, 485f.: 'An dem zu seiner Ehre veranstalteten Festmahl ... nehmen alle Hausgenossen teil'. Besonders klar ist die Verlegenheit bei A. Loisy, *Les évangiles synoptiques*, 2, Ceffonds, 1908. Auf S. 150 fängt der zweite Teil der Parabel an mit V. 25; aber S. 151, Anm. 1, heisst es: 'V. 24 καὶ ἤρξαντο εὐφραίνεσθαι n'est pas la conclusion de la première partie, mais le commencement de la seconde ...'.

50 Die Analyse der vom Evangelisten benutzten Technik der Wortzahlen kann hier nicht ausführlich erörtert werden. Über Stellung und Funktion von V. 24c gibt aber auch folgendes Modell Aufschluss:

	D_N		D_D		S
V. 22-24b	8		43		51
24ᶜ	3		—		3
25-27	34		17		51
V. 22-27	45	+	60	=	105 *W*.

Aus der Symmetrie, womit der Passus V. 17-32 aufgebaut ist, muss man auch folgern, dass V. 25-32 nicht, wie zu Anfang des Jahrhunderts Wellhausen und Johannes Weiss meinten, von fremder Hand zugefügt wurde[51]. V. 24c ist nicht, meinen wir, ein Indiz irgendeiner kompositorischen Unordnung oder eines Vorfalls in der Entstehungsgeschichte der Parabel. Er ist ein Höhepunkt in der Erzählung, der bei der Analyse zu Rück- und Vorausblicken Anlass und Gelegenheit bietet.

Für die zwei folgenden Episoden, V. 25-27 und V. 28-32, zeigt das Erzählgerüst der Verbalformen ebenso wie für V. 17-24b den Faktor zwölf auf. In V. 25-27 fasst V. 27 das Ergebnis der bisherigen Vorfälle kurz zusammen. Mit der direkten Rede kommt hier, wie schon früher, nur einer der beiden Sprecher zu Wort. Er verwendet vier Verbalformen. Für die Situationsschilderung V. 25 gilt dasselbe (ἦν, ἐρχόμενος, ἤγγισεν, ἤκουσεν). Für Erzähltes und Gesprochenes, im Sinne von D_N und D_D, entsprechen die Zahlen der Verbalformen wiederum einfachster Arithmetik: 8 + 4 = 12 *V*.

	D_N		D_D		S
V. 25	4		-		4
26	3		-		3
27	1		4		5
V. 25-27	8	+	4	=	12 *V*.

Ähnliches zeigt sich am Ende der Parabel bei der Begegnung zwischen dem Vater und dem älteren Sohn, V. 28-32. V. 28 kann zu dieser abschliessenden Partie gestellt werden: der ältere Sohn wurde zornig, aber warum, das ergibt eben gerade die Fortsetzung. Entsprechendes lässt sich vom Vater sagen: er ladet ein, und zwar insistiert er[52], wie V. 31-32 deutlich macht. Eine leichte

---

Klar sind unter anderm 1. der Gebrauch des Faktors 17 (s. auch die Sinnabschnitte V. 23b-24b θύσατε καὶ φαγόντες ... εὑρέθη = 17 *W*.; V. 27 ὁ ἀδελφός σου ... ἀπέλαβεν = 17 *W*.), 2. die Verteilung von 105 = 7. 15 *W*. auf D_N und D_d im Verhältnis 3:4, und 3. die Mittelstellung von V. 24c — Zum Thema der Festfreude in Lk. 15 vgl. P. Bonnard, 'Approche historico-critique de Luc 15', in *Anamnesis, recherches sur le Nouveau Testament,* Genève, Lausanne, Neuchâtel, 1980, S. 95f., 99, 101.

[51] J. Wellhausen, *Evangelium Lucae*, 83: 'Dieser zweite Teil ist eine spätere Fortsetzung des ersten'; Joh. Weiss, in *Die Schriften des NTs*, 1906, 447; vgl. R. Bultmann, *Geschichte der synoptischen Tradition*, Göttingen, 1921, 109, 117, 123 ('wahrscheinlich'); [2]1933, 212: 'Man könnte ... fragen ... '. Vgl. J.T. Sanders, 'Tradition and Redaction in Luke XV. 11-32', *NTS* 15 (1968-69) 433-38: '... a later addition, perhaps by the author of the Third Gospel himself' (433). S. zur Sache auch R.W. Funk, 'Structure in the Narrative Parables of Jesus', *Semeia* 2 (1974), 51-81, bes. 62f., = 'Die Struktur der erzählenden Gleichnisse Jesu', in W. Harnisch (ed.), *Die neutestamentliche Gleichnisforschung* ... (WdF 575), Darmstadt, 1982, 224-47, bes. 235-37. Auch die Formulierung, dass man in Lk. 15:11-32 eigentlich zwei Gleichnisse vor sich hat trifft nicht zu. So z.B. J. de Zwaan, *Het evangelie van Lucas* (Tekst en uitleg), 1917, 114 und K.E. Bailey, *Poet and Peasant*, 159 ('a double parable').

[52] Vgl. M. Zerwick, *Graecitas biblica*, Par. 202; Moulton-Turner, 65.

Zäsur am Anfang des Dialogs, also zwischen V. 28 und V. 29, wie sie die Ausgabe von Nestle bis Nestle-Aland 25 (1963) zu empfehlen scheint, ist indessen, von unserer These her gesehen, angebracht. Wie folgende Tabelle zeigt, wird dieses Zwiegespräch mit 19 Verbalformen dargestellt. D.h.: für den als einheitlich erkennbaren Abschluss der Parabel verwendet Lukas eben die Zahl, die dem Plan der ganzen Erzählung zugrunde liegt. Der abschliessende Dialog wird mit genau ein Fünftel aller 95 Verbalformen dargestellt.

	D_N		D_D	S
V. 28	5		-	5/ 5
29-30	2		7	9
31-32	1		9	10/19
V. 28-32	8	+	16	= 24 *V.*

Auch diesmal verhalten sich die Zahlen für erzählende und in direkter Rede gesprochene Partien wie Teiler und Vielfaches. Nur ist hier die Zahl für D_N nicht, wie in V. 25-27, das Doppelte, sondern die Hälfte der Zahl für D_D — wie in V. 17-24b. Und für den kleinen Dialog, V. 29-32, muss man, wie in der Begegnung des Vaters mit dem jüngeren der beiden Brüder, V. 20-24b, feststellen, dass das Verbum εἶπεν, mit dem der Vater V. 31 redend eingeführt wird, in Mittelstellung steht. Für V. 29-32 gilt: 9 + 1 + 9 = 19 *V.*

Was nun die lebendigen Gedanken in V. 31-32 betrifft, ist es vielleicht angebracht, die Aufmerksamkeit auf das — verglichen mit der Parallelstelle V. 24ab — in V. 32 Zugefügte zu lenken. Man 'musste', ἔδει, sich der Feier und der Freude widmen; das war einfach eine Notwendigkeit[53]. Dieses ἔδει ist wiederum im Kontext die mittlere Verbalform: für V. 31b-32 zählt man 9 = 4 + 1 + 4 Verbalformen.

Fassen wir zusammen. Im allgemeinen kommt in der modernen Exegese einer möglichst adäquaten Textbeschreibung hohe Bedeutung zu. Daher muss die literarische Technik eines Autors — vorausgesetzt, dass es eine gibt — aufs eingehendste untersucht werden. Hinsichtlich Lk. 15:11-32 war es immer schon manchem klar, dass sich in der Parabel ein sinnvoller und planmässiger Aufbau zeigt[54]. Man sprach auch von grosser Sorgfalt in der Komposition und von höchster künstlerischer Vollendung. Eine solche Bewertung haben wir

[53] Vgl. Ch.H. Cosgrove, 'The Divine δεῖ in Luke-Acts', *NT* 26 (1984), 168-90, bes. 172f. Seine Terminologie ('ordinary', 'patently ordinary') ist methodisch fragwürdig und führt wenigstens hinsichtlich Lk. 15:32 zu einem Fehlschluss. Man vgl. Mk. 2:18-20 und Joh. 2:1-10; s. H. Palmer, 'Just married, cannot come', *NT* 18 (1976) 241-57, bes. 249.

[54] So z.B. M. Dibelius, *Die Formgeschichte des Evangeliums*, Tübingen, ²1933, 251; Grelot (s. oben Anm. 6) spricht von 'une composition très étudiée' (563), 'une composition très soignée qui fait honneur au génie artistique de l'évangéliste' (541); F. Bovon, *Exegesis*, 50 von 'la composition ... impeccable du récit'; vgl. 294 'une allure classique'; G. Bonaccorsi, *Primi saggi di filologia neotestamentaria*, 1, Torino, 1933, 225, etc.

bestätigt gefunden, und zwar in ganz spezifischer und konkreter Weise. Der Evangelist hat hier bei der Textgestaltung verschiedene zahlenmässig bedingte Kompositionsprinzipien angewendet. Nicht nur sind Umfang und Organisation des Ganzen und der verschiedenen Teile nach Silben- und Wortzahlen rationell, d.h. arithmetisch, bestimmt — so dass z.B. V. 11-13 und V. 14-16a einen Umfang von genau 100 Silben aufweisen, das ist ein Achtel der ganzen Komposition, V. 11-32 (= 800 *S.*). Es hat sich ausserdem gezeigt, dass die Verwendung, Auswahl und Disposition der Verbalformen sorgfältigst zahlenmässig bestimmt ist. In dieser Hinsicht sind für Lk. 15:11-32 die Zahlen sieben, zwölf und neunzehn von grundlegender Bedeutung.

Einige unserer Ergebnisse sind für die Förderung traditioneller Probleme nicht ganz ohne Bedeutung. Die Funktion von V. 24c konnte klar herausgestellt werden. Wichtig ist vielleicht auch, dass das ganze Gleichnis nicht nur einheitlich organisiert, sondern auch vollständig überliefert ist. V. 25-32 gehören mit dazu, und V. 32 muss wirklich als Schluss gelten. Eine Haupteinteilung V. 11b-16, V. 17-24b, V. 24c-32, also eine Dreiteilung, ist exakt nachweisbar. Daneben muss man für V. 17-32 eine sinnvolle Gliederung anerkennen, in der V. 24c ein Moment von einzigartiger Bedeutung darstellt. V. 20-24b (Vater und jüngerer Sohn begegnen sich) und V. 28-32 (Gespräch des älteren Bruders mit dem Vater) sind in analoger Weise aufgebaut. Eine leichte Zäsur empfiehlt sich vor V. 29. Das Ganze zeigt nicht nur Sorgfalt, sondern auch erstaunliche Raffinesse und feinsinnige Artikulation.

Auch hat sich ein symmetrischer Ordnungstypus nach der Formel *a* - *b* - *a* abgezeichnet, der geeignet ist, die spezielle Bedeutung des Mittelgliedes herauszustellen — ein Prinzip, das für die Exegese in mehr allgemeinem Sinn fruchtbar sein dürfte[55]. Dass unsere These auch eine grosse Anzahl neuer Fragestellungen hervorruft, wird der verehrte Jubilar uns gewiss nicht übelnehmen. Er selber hat in vorbildlicher Weise den Mut gezeigt, neue Aufgaben zu übernehmen, und daher grüssen wir ihn recht dankbar.

---

[55] Für die gesprochenen Teile von V. 29-32 trifft auch *a-b-c-b-a* zu: für V. 29bc, 30, 31cd, 32a, 32bc sind die Zahlen: 4, 3, 2, 3, 4 *V*. Dieser Komposition zufolge kommt den Aussagen von V. 31cd ('du bist immer bei mir, und dir gehört alles ...') vielleicht erhöhte Bedeutung zu. Die Isolierung der direkten Rede ist aber einstweilen fraglich. — Wir danken Herrn Prof. Dr. H. Daiber für seine Hilfe bei der Überprüfung des Deutschen dieses Aufsatzes.

PSEUDO-CYPRIAN, JUDE AND ENOCH

Some Notes on 1 Enoch 1:9

by

B. Dehandschutter

The reading of the Epistle of Jude confronts us with Jude's use of the Pseudepigrapha. This is obvious in the quotation from 1 Enoch 1:9 in Jude 14-15. In other verses the use of Enoch can also be assumed, but the text of vv. 14-15 is particularly significant: here Enoch is quoted directly and the text quoted parallels that of other witnesses of the Enoch-text. This cannot be said of most of the other early Christian quotations of 1 Enoch. For our knowledge of the early transmission of 1 Enoch, the testimony of Jude is therefore an important one, beside the Greek, Aramaic, Ethiopic and (possibly) Latin texts. Though there is much agreement about the fact that Jude quotes 1 Enoch, New Testament commentaries differ widely about the form of the quotation. This question is complicated, moreover, by the possibility of a quotation from memory. As a rule, commentaries only mention the Greek and Ethiopic texts. But with the publication of the Aramaic fragments of 4Q new possibilities emerge: C.D. Osburn has considered the hypothesis that Jude himself was translating from an Aramaic text. On the other hand, the Latin text also received fresh attention in more recent contributions. In the following pages I shall examine the form of the quotation in Jude[1] as a contribution to the study of an early stage in the history of the Christian transmission of the book of Enoch.

Jude 14-15 as a quotation.

The *Ethiopic* text of 1 Enoch 1:9[2] is shorter than that of the other witnesses; the phrase 'the harsh words which have been spoken' is omitted at the end. In

[1] I maintain the text of Nestle[25] against Nestle[26] in reading in v.15 καὶ ἐλέγξαι πάντας τοὺς ἀσεβεῖς. The alternative reading πᾶσαν ψυχήν is not commented by B.M. Metzger, *A Textual Commentary on the Greek New Testament*, London-New York, 1971. See our commentary *De Brief van Judas* (Het Nieuwe Testament vertaald en toegelicht), Boxtel, 1983, 139 n.85. Other readings, no longer acceptable, do exist, some of them nearer to the text of Enoch: ἦλθεν has an alternative reading ἔρχεται in versional and patristic tradition, see C.A. Albin, *Judasbrevet*, Lund, 1962. The addition of ἀγγέλων to μυριάσιν; comp. pseudo-Cyprian; the addition of λόγων to σκληρῶν is the most important case: it brings Jude nearer to the Greek Enoch (and was accepted in the text of Jude by Tischendorf and Bover, also with hesitation by von Soden).

[2] See M.A. Knibb, *The Ethiopic Book of Enoch*, Oxford, 1978, vol. I, 4-5.

the previous phrase too there is some abridgement: 'concerning everything which ...' instead of 'concerning all the works of their *impiety*'. These omissions have been regarded as an abridgement of the original text[3]. It is more difficult to follow J.T. Milik in presuming that the Ethiopic version has also been adapted to the text of Jude. Milik gives only one instance of this possibility: the ἰδού, 'behold'[4]. M. Black also considered this possibility but he wonders why the Ethiopic text did not take over κύριος as well[5]. I think that Milik's supposition derives from his hypothesis about the original text *k*ᵉ*dī**. Another instance, which he does not mention, could be the tense of the verb ἐλέγχω in v.15, but the Ethiopic tradition is divided at this point.

The *Aramaic* text of 1 Enoch 1:9. A fragment of 4Q probably containing 1:9 was published by Milik in 1976. Already in the early seventies both Black and Milik referred to this fragment, and Black published an English translation in the Moule-Festschrift[6]. According to Milik the fragment dates from the end of the first century B.C. Though his reconstruction of the fragment is very impressive, only a few words can be read for certain. These do not contain any reading which deviates from the text of the early versions, apart from the addition at the end of '*proud* and harsh words'. But we may wonder why this double expression should be original and the σκληροὶ λόγοι an abridgement (so Milik). We can only say that the Aramaic fragment testifies against the Ethiopic to the existence of a phrase on 'the harsh words *or* things'. Above all the Aramaic confirms the reading πᾶσαν σάρκα; the text of Jude 15 stands alone in leaving these words out.

The *Greek* text of 1 Enoch 1:9 has only been transmitted by the Achmim-codex (6th century)[7]. The text of this manuscript has a rather striking introduction: ὅτι; the present ἔρχεται and the twofold σὺν ταῖς μυριάσιν αὐτοῦ καὶ τοῖς ἁγίοις αὐτοῦ. Recently R.J. Bauckham has provided a satisfactory interpretation of the last reading. The separation of μυριάσιν from ἁγίοις seems to reflect the combination of two early Christian interpretations of Zach. 14:5[8]. At the end of our passage, the Achmim-text adds after ὧν ἐλάλησαν λόγων: καὶ περὶ πάντων ὧν κατελάλησαν. On the one hand

---

[3] So M. Lods, *Le Livre d'Hénoch*, Paris, 1892, 99; R.H. Charles, *The Ethiopic Version of the Book of Enoch* ..., Oxford, 1906; J.T. Milik, *The Books of Enoch. Aramaic Fragments of Qumran Cave 4*, Oxford, 1976, 185.

[4] J.T. Milik, *o.c.*, 186.

[5] M. Black, 'The Maranatha Invocation and Jude 14, 15 (1 Enoch 1:9)', in *Christ and the Spirit in the New Testament. Studies in Honour of C.F.D. Moule*, Cambridge, 1973, 189-196, see p. 194-195.

[6] See notes 3 and 5.

[7] See the edition of M. Black, *Apocalypsis Henochi Graece*, Leiden, 1970. On the Greek text and its editions, see M.A. Knibb, *o.c.* II, 15-20.

[8] R.J. Bauckham, 'A Note on a Problem in the Greek Version of 1 Enoch 1:9', *JTS* 32 (1981), 136-138; see now his commentary *Jude, 2 Peter*, Waco, 1983, 93-98.

this has been considered a dittography[9], on the other hand an element of the original text because of a possible parallel in pseudo-Cyprian[10]. However, the Greek text in the Achmim-codex is not an early one. Unfortunately, Clement of Alexandria does not quote the passage in his *Adumbrationes.* Only Jude provides us with an early Greek version.

The *Latin* text of 1 Enoch 1:9. Did there exist a Latin version of the book of Enoch? T. Zahn was convinced that he had found a proof in the case of our text. According to him, two quotations from Church Fathers, pseudo-Cyprian *ad Novatianum* 16,5 and pseudo-Vigilius *contra Varimadum* I,13, offer *not* a quotation from Jude, but from a Latin version of 1 Enoch[11]. Zahn's conception was soon approved by A. Harnack, R.H. Charles, M.R. James, J. Leipoldt and others[12]. Among New Testament commentators only G. Wohlenberg[13] seems to be aware of the solution. In more recent times the *possibility* is accepted by C. Albin, M.A. Knibb, A.M. Denis[14]. Milik, on the other hand, is very sceptical, not only about this text but also about the existence of a Latin version at all[15]. Zahn based his conviction on the agreements of pseudo-Cyprian with 1 Enoch against Jude. The most important are:

the omission of κύριος;
multis milibus nuntiorum *suorum*; this is a construction taken from Enoch with the change of ἁγιων into ἀγγέλων
the presence of *et perdere omnes impios*;
the reading *omnem carnem*.

---

[9] See R.H. Charles, *o.c.*, 5; M. Black, *Apocalypsis Henochi*, 19; M.A. Knibb, *o.c.*, 60.

[10] J.T. Milik, *o.c.*, 186.

[11] T. Zahn, *Geschichte des neutestamentlichen Kanons II*, Erlangen-Leipzig, 1892, 797-801; comp. *Forschungen zur Geschichte des neutestamentlichen Kanons V*, Erlangen-Leipzig, 1893, 158. Both *ad Novatianum* and *contra Varimadum* are available now in modern editions, see *Corpus Christianorum. Series latina IV, Novatiani opera*, ed. G.F. Diercks, Turnhout, 1972, and *Corpus Christianorum. Series latina XC. Florilegia biblica africana saec. V*, ed. B. Schwank (e.a.), Turnhout, 1961. For *ad Novatianum* see also H. Koch, *Cyprianische Studien*, Bonn, 1926, 358-420.

[12] R.H. Charles, *o.c.*, 7; A. Harnack, *Eine bisher nicht erkannte Schrift des Papstes Sixtus II vom Jahre 257/8*, Leipzig, 1895, 57; M.R. James, *Apocrypha anecdota*, Cambridge, 1893, 146-150; J. Leipoldt, *Geschichte des neutestamentlichen Kanons I*, Leipzig, 1906, 16.

[13] G. Wohlenberg, *Der erste und zweite Petrusbrief und der Judasbrief*, Leipzig, 1915, 316-318.

[14] C. Albin, *o.c.*; M.A. Knibb, *o.c.*; A.M. Denis, *Introduction aux pseudépigraphes grecs de l'Ancien Testament*, Leiden, 1970, 26. Also in the recent edition of *The Old Testament Pseudepigrapha I* (ed. J.H. Charlesworth), London, 1983, 14; pseudo-Cyprian and ps. Vigilius are taken as testimony to the text of Enoch.

[15] It has to be noted that J. Daniélou, *Les origines du christianisme latin*, Paris, 1978, 139-144, does not reckon with a Latin version of Enoch, not even in the case of Tertullian whose 'defence' of Enoch is well-known. See on the whole problem also H.J. Lawlor, 'Early Citations from the Book of Enoch', in *The Journal of Philology* 25 (1897) 164-225.

Zahn and Harnack stress the fact that the quotation is introduced by *sicut scriptum est*. This is an exception in *ad Novatianum* and points to pseudo-Cyprian being aware of quoting a pseudepigraphon, not Jude. Pseudo-Vigilius is less important but Zahn maintains that the text cannot be derived from Jude. The whole theory was upset by W. Thiele in his edition of the Catholic Epistles in the Vetus Latina of Beuron[16]. M.J. Lagrange already referred to the particular Latin text in *ad Novatianum*, surprisingly without mentioning Zahn's solution[17]. Thiele, however, does not speak about a quotation from 1 Enoch, but according to him pseudo-Cyprian supports the so-called 'Karthago-Text', which is very near to its source 1 Enoch 1:9 and which we know from Cyprian. Otherwise, pseudo-Cyprian proves the use of an archaic form of the text of Jude in early Latin textual tradition[18]. The only problem seems to be that there is no other manuscript evidence available for the K-text in Jude 14-15. But to what extent is a peculiar *Latin* form of Jude 14-15 to be accepted? It is quite clear that in the second part of the quotation, from *de omnibus factis* on, pseudo-Cyprian is independent both of Enoch and of Jude. There is no overall adaptation of the text of Enoch[19]. Such a situation also leaves the possibility of a partial adaptation to a Greek text of Enoch in the case of pseudo-Cyprian.

After this survey of the different texts of 1 Enoch 1:9, what can be said about the value of Jude's quotation? This depends of course on the question of whether Jude is quoting a Greek text *or* translating an Aramaic text. The latter possibility has been defended by C.D. Osburn[20] but his argument is not convincing because it is based on excessive faith in the value of Pap. 72. In the end we come up against a problem of method: are the differences between the existing witnesses to be explained by the stress of an *hypothetical* Aramaic *Vorlage*, or is it preferable to explain the form of our witnesses by verifiable manuscript evidence? Another problem also remains. At least in the case of the Achmim-text and of the Ethiopic version we have to do with the text of the book of Enoch, while in the case of Jude there is a *quotation*. Quotations are often adapted to their context. Thus in the case of Jude 15 it is possible that the omission of καὶ ἀπολέσει πάντας τοὺς ἀσεβεῖς may have resulted from the omission of ἀπολέσει and πᾶσαν σάρκα in the Enoch text. (This was seen by Osburn, but he used this phenomenon only to prove that Jude did not

---

[16] *Vetus latina. Die Reste der altlateinischen Bibel ...26/1. Epistulae catholicae*, Freiburg, 1956-1969, 92; text pp. 426-428.

[17] M.J. Lagrange, *Critique textuelle II. La critique rationelle*, Paris, 1935, 563.

[18] J.T. Milik, *o.c.*, 185-186, agrees with Thiele.

[19] W. Thiele, 'Probleme der Versio latina in den Katholischen Briefen', in K. Aland (ed.), *Die alten Übersetzungen des Neuen Testaments, die Kirchenväterzitate und Lektionare*, Berlin-New York, 1972, 93-119, see p. 105.

[20] C.D. Osburn, 'The Christological Use of I Enoch i.9 in Jude 14,15', in *NTS* 23 (1976-77), 334-341.

quote from memory[21]). In this way Jude does not only avoid some repetitions but also stresses the fact that the divine judgement is directed against the wicked, the ἀσεβεῖς, the people of whom he is speaking in his epistle.

Jude 14-15 as a testimony for the original text of 1 Enoch 1:9.

This question can be discussed word by word. One should bear in mind that Jude is the earliest of our witnesses with the exception of the 4Q fragments.

ἰδού: Jude agrees here with the Ethiopic and Latin versions. Already Lods supposed that the Achmim-text had introduced ὅτι in order to make a better connection with the preceding phrase[22]. According to Charles ὅτι is a misreading of ἰδού[23]. On the other hand Milik suspects ὅτι to be a slightly corrupted ὅτε, Aram. *k^e dī*, and translates: 'when he comes'[24]. But is the οτει of the codex sufficient for such a supposition? An Aramaic Vorlage has been suggested by others (see Osburn, Knibb, Bauckham[25]), but I do not think it necessary in order to explain the difference between Jude and the Achmim-text: in 1:8 this text differs considerably from the Ethiopic. It is quite possible that ὅτι is part of this adaptation.

ἦλθεν: already Lods noted: 'l'aoriste de Jude a une couleur plus hébraique et doit etre plus ancien'[26]. It is commonly accepted that Jude imitated a prophetic perfect. This is connected with the Old Testament background of the phrase, Deut. 33:2. According to Charles, dependence on this text demonstrates that the passage must have a Hebrew Vorlage[27]. Black argued that a prophetic perfect was also possible in Aramaic[28]. But as for the preceding word, there is no clear evidence in the Aramaic fragment, and nothing in favour of Milik's hypothesis of a future tense. But it is not necessary to see in ἦλθεν the proof of an Aramaic Vorlage of Jude: ἦλθεν could also be present in the case of a Greek Vorlage.

κύριος: the absence of κύριος in every witness except Jude supports the generally accepted conclusion that Jude added this subject to the clause. This is possible, but we must remember that Enoch often speaks explicitly about the coming of the Lord, e.g. in 91:7 and 100:4. Jude could have had such texts in mind. There seems to be no reason to think immediately of a christological adaptation. Jude himself uses the complete formula 'our Lord Jesus Christ' (4; 17; 21; 25) while in the judgement-contexts of v.5 and 9 the anarthrous κύριος

---

[21] Id., *ibid.*, 338.
[22] M. Lods, *o.c.*, 99.
[23] R.H. Charles, *o.c.*, 5.
[24] J.T. Milik, *o.c.*, 186.
[25] C.D. Osburn, *art.cit.*, 335-336; M.A. Knibb, *o.c.*, 59; R.J. Bauckham, *art.cit.*, 136-137.
[26] M. Lods, *o.c.*, 99.
[27] R.H. Charles, *o.c.*, 5.
[28] M. Black, *art.cit.*, 194-195.

is used. The question is: was κύριος an element of the original text? In view of the secondary character of the *Greek* Enoch we cannot suppose that a text like the Achmim-text was the Vorlage of Jude. The absence of κύριος in the Ethiopic version may be due to an omission in the common ancestor of the manuscripts. On the other hand, one could wonder whether Jude would have chosen this quotation if it was not saying explicitly that *the Lord is coming*. What has been argued in favour of the view that κύριος in Jude is a secondary addition, due to the style of theophany in comparison with Zach. 14:5, for example, can equally well be argued in favour of the originality of κύριος in 1 Enoch.

ἐν ἁγίαις μυριάσιν αὐτοῦ: Osburn again sees in the more extensive Greek text an indication of the 'reliance upon the Aramaic by Jude', accepting at the same time the Pap. 72-reading ἐν ἁγίων ἀγγέλων μυριάσιν which could be a good rendering of 4Q[29]. But the value of Pap. 72 is not to be overestimated. This text shows only, as other witnesses do, the necessity of an explanation of the 'Jewish' οἱ ἅγιοι in Christian tradition. The Aramaic fragment on its own gives no reason for accepting the reading ἀγγέλων. The expression illustrates very clearly the difficulty of arguing for a Hebrew or Aramaic Vorlage of a Greek text. In this connection it is interesting to look at Jude's use of ἐν which is peculiar among the witnesses (with the exception of pseudo-Vigilius). This ἐν should be the equivalent of Hebrew *b*ᵉ as used to describe accompanying circumstances. But it cannot be explained on the basis of the Hebrew text of Deut. 33:2, the interpretation of which raises a problem.

ποιῆσαι κρίσιν κατὰ πάντων: here the text edited by Knibb does not agree with the other witnesses: 'to execute judgement upon them'. In this case it is difficult to argue from the hypothetical Aramaic or from Jude. The text of the latter may have been influenced by the whole context of stressing the judgement against *all* the wicked. In any case I cannot accept Osburn's observation that Jude translated the Aramaic text almost literally[30].

περὶ πάντων τῶν ἔργων: Lods suggests that the abridgement of the Ethiopic version is the result of homoioteleuton[31]. As may appear from Pap. 72, this can be correct. Jude, however, is an important witness here and his text has been followed by Charles in detail. Also according to Milik Jude is very close to the original, but has nevertheless abbreviated it, omitting the only distinctive element in the Aramaic fragment *rabrᵉbīn* (Knibb)[32]. Admittedly Enoch speaks about μεγάλους καὶ σκληροὺς λόγους (see 5:4; 101:3), but in 27:2 only σκληρά is used. It is difficult to judge whether Jude is here following a

[29] C.D. Osburn, *art.cit.*, 337-338.
[30] Id., *ibid.*, 338.
[31] M. Lods, *o.c.*, XL.
[32] J.T. Milik, *o.c.*, 186; M.A. Knibb, *o.c.*, 60: see now also K. Beyer, *Die aramäischen Texte vom Toten Meer*, Göttingen, 1984, 232.

Vorlage or whether he is adapting the quotation in view of v.16, where the element καὶ τὸ στόμα αὐτῶν λαλεῖ ὑπέρογκα reminds us of 27:2: οἵτινες ἐροῦσιν τῷ στόματι αὐτῶν κατὰ κυρίου φωνὴν ἀπρεπῆ, καὶ περὶ τῆς δόξης αὐτοῦ σκληρὰ λαλήσουσιν.

Some remarks must be added about the additions in both the Achmim-text and pseudo-Cyprian. As for the Greek Enoch I mentioned the addition of καὶ περὶ πάντων ὧν κατελάλησαν. At least according to one manuscript, the codex Vossianus, Pseudo-Cyprian adds after '*quae fecerunt impie*' '*et de re* (?) *locuti sunt*'. According to Milik this coincidence points to an element of the original text, and he restores 'works of wickedness which they have committed in deed and word'. Thiele too maintains the reading of codex Vossianus in his text of the old Latin version, though admitting that there is some corruption in 'de re'[33]. However, the fact that the addition in both cases is not found at the same place in the text does not make this supposition very convincing. It is also significant that Diercks should have come to the same conclusion as Hartel by relegating the words to the apparatus[34]. In the third place, Jude as an early witness does not show any trace of such an addition.

What then is the role of Jude 14-15 in the reconstruction of the original text? Charles has paid much attention to Jude in his reconstruction as has recently Milik. But in the case of Charles one could suspect a tendency to arrive at a perfect parallelism[35], and in the case of Milik his belief in the value of pseudo-Cyprian is not justified[36].

Nevertheless we can conclude that Jude as an early witness to the text of Enoch still stands his ground. Even if it is unlikely that it should be read as the direct rendering of an Aramaic text, the possibility of a third form of the Greek text of Enoch has to be taken into account[37]. The author of Jude has been quoting that text consciously[38].

[33] J.T. Milik, *o.c.*, 186; W. Thiele, *o.c.*, 427.

[34] See the edition which is mentioned in n. 11.

[35] See his reconstruction, *o.c.*, 7.

[36] It should be noted that the fact that ps.Cyprian introduces the quotation by 'sicut scriptum est', does not involve the citation of a pseudepigraphon. In the early Church the canonical status of Jude itself was not taken for granted for a long time (see e.g. K.H. Ohlig, *Die theologische Begründung des neutestamentlichen Kanons in der alten Kirche*, Düsseldorf, 1972, 79.). In this way the introduction of the quotation in ps.Cyprian could be due to the circumspection of its author about the canonicity of *Jude*.

[37] See e.g. H. Windisch, *Die katholischen Briefe*, Tübingen, 1951³, 45.

[38] Recently, three new translations of 1 Enoch appeared: *The Apocryphal Old Testament*, edited by H.F.D. Sparks, Oxford, 1984 (the translation of 1 Enoch is M. Knibb's, cf. p. 185 for our text); S. Uhlig, 'Das Äthiopische Henochbuch (*JSHRZ* V,6), Gütersloh, 1984, 509-510; M. Black, *The Book of Enoch or 1 Enoch. A New English Edition*, Leiden, 1985, 108-109. Both Uhlig and Black refer to the testimony of the Ethiopic *Liber Nativitatis* (ed. K. Wendt, CSCO, 221-222), where twice a parallel to our text is quoted. The problem is, however, that the quotations differ from the Ethiopic Enoch; they rather show the possibility of expansion and abridgement of a quotation; moreover they seem to refer to *Jude*. But as long as we don't have a reliable text of Jude in Ethiopic, it is not possible to decide upon the value of those quotations for the text of Enoch.

STREIT UM GOTTES VORSEHUNG

Zur Position der Gegner im 2. Petrusbrief

von

Klaus Berger

Eigenart und Position der Gegner im 2. Petrusbrief werden fast immer ebenso stiefmütterlich und oberflächlich abgehandelt wie dieser Brief selbst. Trotz einer ganzen Reihe von Angaben, die der Brief zu Gegnern macht (s. unter Par. 1), begnügt man sich entweder damit, dass eine genaue, nähere Bestimmung unmöglich sei[1], oder man rückt den Brief in mehr oder weniger grosse Nähe zur Gnosis, da er wesentliche Merkmale der Gnosis des 2. nachchristlichen Jahrhunderts trage[2]. Als solche Merkmale werden vor allem genannt: Libertinismus (die Freiheitsparole in 2:19), gnostische Umdeutung alttestamentlicher Prophetie (1:20), gnostische 'Mythen' (1:16), vor allem aber die Leugnung der Parusie (Entsprechung der Vorwürfe von 2:10, 18 mit 3:3 und besonders 3:4 mit der Antwort in 3:5-10). Die Schnelle, mit der hier auf die fast schon üblichen 'gnostischen Gegner' geschlossen wird, wenn man Genaueres nicht weiss, erscheint verdächtig, wenn man bedenkt, dass es sich um ein Forschungs-Stereotyp handelt[3], und wenn man um die Wackeligkeit der These vorchristlicher Gnosis überhaupt weiss[4]. Einen wirklichen Fortschritt bedeutet demgegenüber die Dissertation von J.H. Neyrey von 1978[5]. Neyrey hat

[1] So W.G. Kümmel, *Einleitung in das Neue Testament*, Heidelberg, [19]1978, 381 ('Eine nähere Bestimmung ist jedoch unmöglich'); ähnlich: A. Lindemann, *Paulus im ältesten Christentum* (Beitr.z.Hist.Theol.58), Tübingen, 1979, 262.

[2] So ausser W.G. Kümmel, a.a.O., 381 auch Ph. Vielhauer, *Geschichte der urchristlichen Literatur*, Berlin, 1975, 597, und W. Schrage, *Der Zweite Petrusbrief*, in H. Balz, W. Schrage (Hrsg.), *Die Katholischen Briefe* (NTD 10), Göttingen, 1973, 120f. Die Einleitung zum Kommentar Schrages ist gespickt mit Werturteilen, so als wolle sich der Kommentator dafür entschuldigen, dass er sich mit der Materie überhaupt abgegeben hat.

[3] Dazu: K. Berger, 'Die impliziten Gegner. Zur Methode des Erschliessens von 'Gegnern' in neutestamentlichen Texten', in D. Lührmann, G. Strecker (Hrsg.), *Kirche* (FS G. Bornkamm), Tübingen, 1980, 373-400.

[4] Kritisch dazu: E.M. Yamauchi, *Pre-Christian Gnosticism. A Survey of the Proposed Evidences*, London, 1973; K. Berger, 'Gnosis' I, *TRE* XIII (1984), 519-535.

[5] J.H. Neyrey, *The Form and Background of the Polemic in 2 Peter: The Debate over Prophecy and Parousia*, Diss. Yale, 1978. Vgl. auch den zusammenfassenden Aufsatz 'The Form and Background of the Polemic in 2 Peter', *JBL* 99 (1980), 407-431.

aufmerksam gemacht auf eine Position, die den Gegnern des 2. Petr. ganz offensichtlich sehr viel näher steht als 'Gnostiker' irgendwelcher Spielart, nämlich die Gegner des Plutarch in seiner Schrift *De Sera Numinis Vindicta*. Es handelt sich dort um vulgären Epikureismus. Es käme nun freilich darauf an, diese These so fortzuführen, dass die Gegner des 2. Petr. auch historisch verständlich werden. Denn es nützt ja nichts, eine verwandte philosophische Position in der hellenistischen Antike aufzuspüren, wenn es nicht gleichzeitig gelingt, zu zeigen, wie Christen (Judenchristen oder Heidenchristen) dazu gelangen konnten, eine solche Position oder ihr Verwandtes einnehmen zu wollen. Und ausserdem bleibt bei J.H. Neyrey ungeklärt, was eine epikureische Position mit dem Lästern von Engelwesen zu tun haben soll, wie es ja in 2. Petr. von den Gegnern gleichfalls behauptet wird. Indem wir diesen Fragen nachgehen, meinen wir, den Intentionen des verehrten Jubilars treu zu bleiben, der stets sowohl den typisch 'griechischen' Horizont frühjüdischer und frühchristlicher Überlieferung betont hat wie auch die Lebenserfahrung konkreter Gruppen als Voraussetzung für theologische Aussagen zu ermitteln versuchte. Wir werden, um das Material straff zu organisieren, nach der Darbietung der wichtigsten Voraussetzungen unsere Position in Thesenform entfalten.

1. *Angaben des 2. Petr. über Gegner.*

a) *Übliche Gegnerpolemik* (z.T. aus antisophistischer Tradition), die keine besonderen Schlüsse zulässt: 1:16 ('erklügelte Fabeln'); 2:1 ('Falschlehrer', 'verderbliche Sonderlehren'); 2:2 (wie 2:7, 18: 'Ausschweifungen'); 2:2 ('der Weg der Wahrheit wird geschmäht'); 2:3 ('Habsucht', 'erdichtete Worte' und Androhung des Verderbens); 2:12 ('wie die unvernünftigen Tiere', Androhung des Untergangs); 2:13 ('Betrügereien'); 2:14 (wie in 2:3: 'Habsucht'); 2:15 ('sie haben den rechten Weg verlassen und sind in die Irre geraten'); 2:17 ('Brunnen ohne Wasser und Wolken, vom Wirbelwind umgetrieben', Androhung des Verderbens); 2:22 (Vergleich mit Hund und Schwein).

b) *Kennzeichnung des verbalen Verhaltens der Gegner*: Vor allem fällt auf, dass die Gegner 'leugnen' und 'lästern'. Nach 2:1 leugnen sie den 'Herrn, der sie erkauft hat' (in Jud. 4 hiess es: 'sie leugnen den einzigen Herrscher und unseren Herrn Jesus Christus'), nach 2:2 wird der Weg der Wahrheit 'gelästert', nach 2:10 verachten sie 'Herrschaft' (κυριότης) und 'zittern nicht vor Herrlichkeiten (δόξαι), indem sie lästern'. Nach 2:18 äussern sie Übermütiges mit nichtigem Charakter. Offensichtlich auf die Gegner bezogen ist auch 1:20: Demnach treiben sie selbständig 'eigenwillige' Erklärung der Schrift. Schriftauslegung wird in diesem Milieu ganz offenkundig noch als 'prophetische' Leistung aufgefasst (1:21) — den Gegnern wird aber eben unterstellt, dass sie aufgrund nur menschlicher Voraussetzungen Prophetie treiben wollen, und das ist ein Selbstwiderspruch —, und entsprechend heissen die Gegner in 2:1 auch

Falschpropheten. Nach 3:16 gehören zu diesen falsch ausgelegten 'Schriften' auch Paulusbriefe.

c) Die Gegner sind besonders durch alle Arten von *Unreinheit* gekennzeichnet: Nach 2:10 wandeln sie 'nach dem Fleisch in der Begierde der Befleckung' (dann folgen die Aussagen über das Verhalten zu 'Herrschaften' und 'Herrlichkeiten'), nach 2:13 veranstalten sie Schlemmereien am Tage und schwelgen dabei 'beschmutzt und befleckt', nach 2:18 reizen sie 'durch Begierden des Fleisches zu Schwelgereien' die erst kürzlich Bekehrten, die nach 2:20 den 'Befleckungen' der Welt entflohen sind. Auch die Verbindung von Sau und Kot in 2:22 ist deutlich so zu verstehen, dass frühere Unreinheit erneuert wird. Im Gegenzug dazu war das Gebot, das ihnen gegeben wurde, 'heilig' (2:21)[6]. Auch Ehebruch und Fluch nach 2:14 sind Prädikate der Unreinheit. Die Konsequenz ist nach 2:13b indirekt angegeben: Der Verf. wünscht offensichtlich, dass die gemeinsamen Mahlzeiten aufgegeben werden (συνευωχούμενοι). Und die Gemeinde versteht ihrerseits ihre Qualität vor Gott als kultische Heiligkeit (3:14 'unbeschmutzt und unbefleckt', dieselben Begriffe wie in 2:13), auch noch in der Gerichtssituation.

d) Die Gegner vergehen sich an Sitten, wie sie im *Aposteldekret* und in verwandten Texten (Apk. 2:14, 20f.) geboten werden (vgl. auch 1. Kor. 5f., 8, 10); wie in Apk. 2 und in 1. Kor. geht es vor allem um Essen (2:13: Schlemmen am hellen Tag in Verbindung mit Unreinheit; 2:2, 18 Ausschweifungen; nach 2:22 frisst der Hund das Ausgespieene) und Unzucht/Ehebruch (2:7 Unzucht; 2:14 Ehebruch; 2:18 Unzucht und fleischliche Lust). Bedeutsam ist vor allem das Stichwort 'Freiheit' in 2:19 (nach der Rede von Unzucht in 2:18). Wichtig ist auch, dass das Bileam-Beispiel offenbar in derartiger Diskussion traditionell ist (Apk. 2:14 und 2. Petr. 2:15f.).

Grundsätzlich auf Affinität zu dem, was traditionell als *heidnisch* gilt, weist die Rede von 'Begierden' (2:10, 18; 3:3 vgl. mit 1:4!).

e) Zur *eschatologischen Position* der Gegner: nach 3:3f. werden sie als 'Spötter' gekennzeichnet, die sagen: 'Wo ist die Verheissung seiner Parusie? Denn nachdem die Väter entschlafen sind, bleibt alles so (wie) von Anbeginn der Schöpfung'. Aus 3:9 geht hervor, dass sie sagen: 'Der Herr verzögert die Verheissungen' (βραδύνει κύριος τῆς ἐπαγγελίας). Denn es gebe Leute, die dieses für Verzögerung (βραδύτης) halten.

Es wird zu fragen sein, ob es möglich ist, diese verschiedenen Elemente zu koordinieren. Andernfalls müsste man mit mehreren und voneinander unab-

---

[6] Die Wiedergabe von Mt. 7:6 in Clem *Recogn* III, 1, 5f ist ganz in dem antihäretischen Sinn zu lesen, den auch 1. Petr. 2:22 dem Bild gab: '(Petrus) ne mittat verborum eius margaritas ante porcos et canes, qui adversum eas argumentis ac sofismatibus reluctantes, ipsas quidem caeno intellegentiae carnalis involvant, latratibus autem suis et responsionibus sordidis rumpant et fatigent praedicatores verbi dei'. Man beachte besonders die ausgeführte Beziehung zur Unreinheit.

hängigen Gruppen von Gegnern rechnen. Dafür freilich gibt es keine Hinweise.

2. *Vergleichbares aus Plutarchs Schrift* De Sera Numinis Vindicta.

Plutarch (45 n.Chr.-125 n.Chr.) greift in seiner Schrift epikureische Polemik gegen die göttliche Vorsehung an, nach der Gott nicht richtet, urteilt und vergilt. Bei den Epikureern wurde dieses zu Schmähsucht (vgl. 2. Petr. 3:3 'Spötter' und die oben unter Par. 1b genannten Texte über Lästern etc.) gegen die Vorsehung (Kap. 1). Im Einzelnen:

a) Beim nicht rechtzeitigen Vollzug der göttlichen Strafe spricht Plutarch von '*Zögern*' als der Art des Göttlichen (βραδύτης καὶ μέλλησις) und vom Aufschub, der freilich die Hoffnung niederdrücke und Frechheit und Kühnheit des Bösen mehre (θρασύτης) (alles Kap. 2). In Kap. 3 fällt das Stichwort 'Langsamkeit' (διατριβαὶ καὶ μελλήσεις), die allen Glauben an die Vorsehung nehme. Dieses entspricht 2. Petr. 3:9 (βραδύτης). Vom Zögern Gottes (σχολαίως) spricht auch Kap. 5.

b) Für Plutarch hängen dagegen zusammen ein postmortales Leben, d.h. der Glaube an die Unsterblichkeit der Seele, und die göttliche Vorsehung (Kap. 17-18). Dem entspricht, dass in 2. Petr. 3 Argumente für das kommende Gerichtshandeln Gottes genannt werden. Nach 3:13 wird es dann 'Gerechtigkeit' geben, so wie nach Plutarchs Schrift (Kap. 4) Gott der Verwalter der Gerechtigkeit ist. Die Stelle der postmortalen Unsterblichkeit nimmt in 2. Petr. die apokalyptische Eschatologie ein.

G. Vermes hat freilich darauf aufmerksam gemacht, dass eine Position, die mit Nachdruck das Kommen des künftigen Gerichtes behauptet, auch 'pharisäisch' im Gegenüber zu Sadduzäern genannt werden kann[7], wie sie sich häufiger in Gegenüberstellungen von Kain und Abel artikuliert[8]. Die sadduzäische Position kann also auch die epikureische sein, ja diese Übereinstimmung geht noch weiter darin, dass die Sadduzäer nach Josephus auch die εἱμαρμένη leugnen und damit etwas, das der von den Epikureern geleugneten Pronoia direkt vergleichbar ist[9]. In 2. Petr. haben wir es wohl kaum mit einer sadduzäischen Position zu tun, auch kaum mit einer ausgeprägt epikureischen. Vielmehr wird Material, das im Kampf gegen beide entwickelt wurde, hier einer skeptischen und die Identität aufgebenden Position entgegengestellt, wie zu zeigen sein wird (Par. 5).

---

[7] G. Vermes, 'The Targumic Versions of Genesis 4:3-16', in G. Vermes, *Post-Biblical Jewish Studies* (Studies in Judaism in Late Antiquity 8), Leiden, 1975, 92-138, 114-116.

[8] Vgl. dazu besonders die targumischen Versionen zu Gen. 4:8 nach G. Vermes, 'ibid.', 115f. Kain leugnet jeweils gerechtes Gericht, göttliche Gerechtigkeit, Belohnung und Bestrafung und überhaupt die kommende Welt.

[9] Vgl. dazu: Josephus, *Bell* II, 164-165.

c) Nach Plutarch dient die verzögerte Strafe der Sinnesänderung und gibt *Zeit für Besserung* (Kap. 5 und 6: ἐπανορθεῖν, νουθετεῖν). Gott gibt Zeit, sich zu ändern (πρὸς μετάνοιαν ἐνδίδωσι, καὶ χρόνον ... προσορίζειν). Dem entspricht genau 2. Petr. 3:9 ('er hat Geduld mit euch und will nicht, dass jemand verloren werde, sondern dass sich jedermann zur Busse kehre')[10].

d) Nach Plutarch, Kap. 9 ist den Göttern 'der ganze Zeitraum eines menschlichen Lebens ein Nichts', *dreissig Jahre sind wie ein Tag* (διάστημα τὸ μηδέν ἐστι). Dieses entspricht überraschend dem Argument in 2. Petr. 3:8, wonach tausend Jahre vor dem Herrn wie ein Tag sind. Beachtenswert ist, dass die alttestamentlichen und jüdischen Parallelen zu dieser Stelle sich alle nicht auf den Zeitraum bis zum Gericht beziehen[11]. Das bedeutet: Der Ausdruck in 2. Petr. 3:8 ist zwar jüdisch, der Verwendungszweck jedoch durch die anti-epikureische Tradition vorgegeben.

e) Nach Plutarch, Kap. 10 sind Traumvisionen, Erscheinungen und Ähnliches Beispiele dafür, *dass die Gottheit unmittelbar und direkt in die Welt einwirkt* und daher Erweise für die Pronoia. In diesem Sinne ist der Rekurs auf die Verklärung Jesu in 2. Petr. 1:16-21 ein Argument für die Möglichkeit, dass der Herr auch 'kommen' wird (1:16 παρουσία; 1:19). Wenn Gott so einwirkt, kann es auch überhaupt ein Ende geben.

f) Immer wieder nimmt Plutarch in seiner Schrift auf *Orakel* Bezug. Es könnte sie nicht geben, wenn es keine Pronoia gäbe, und die noch unerfüllten Orakel weisen auf künftige Strafe. In diesem Sinne geht es 2. Petr. um Prophetie, prophetisches Wort (1:19-21) und Erfüllung der Verheissungen (3:4).

Für jetzt bleibt vorläufig festzuhalten: Trotz des Fehlens apokalyptischer Eschatologie bei Plutarch (daher der Unterschied von 30 Jahren, bezogen auf ein individuelles Leben, und 1000 Jahren, bezogen auf apokalyptische Eschatologie nach Element d)) finden sich wichtige Entsprechungen zum 2. Petr., die wohl am leichtesten verständlich werden, wenn man eine gemeinsame Basis von anti-epikureischen Traditionen annimmt[12].

---

[10] Es handelt sich um ein weiter verbreitetes Argument: Vgl. Plutarch, *De Coh Ira* 459E; Sap Sal 12:10; *Targum Gen* 6:3; Philo, *All* III, 106 und *Prov* II, 6.

[11] Der Vergleich wird sonst nicht auf Verzögerung bezogen, vgl. *Jub* 4:29f.; *SlavHen* 33:1-2; Gen r 8:2 und *Barn* 15:4 als älteste weitere Belege neben einer Fülle von ähnlichen rabbinischen Texten.

[12] Zu den Kategorien wissenschaftlichen Vergleichens im Rahmen religionsgeschichtlicher Forschung vgl. C. Colpe und K. Berger in der Einleitung zu dem im Druck befindlichen NTD-Ergänzungsband 'Religionsgeschichtliches Textbuch zum Neuen Testament', Göttingen, 1986 ('Zur Einführung', Par. 2).

3. *Vergleichbares aus Philos Schrift* De Providentia.

Ähnlich wie Plutarch widmet auch Philo eine ganze Schrift Leugnern der göttlichen Vorsehung. Die Relevanz dieser Schrift für 2. Petr. ist, soweit ich sehe, noch nicht wahrgenommen worden. Wir kommen hier jedoch in bestimmten Einzelheiten noch erheblich näher an 2. Petr. heran, als es mit Plutarchs Schrift möglich war. Zur Ergänzung werden auch andere Schriften Philos herangezogen.

a) *'Schmähen', 'Lästern', und 'Anklagen'* sind bei Philo Weisen, in denen Menschen ihren Unmut über die göttliche Weltregierung äussern, und zwar besonders gegenüber Himmelswesen und der göttlichen Vorsehung.

Nach Philos Schrift *De Somniis* II, 131f. schmähen Menschen Himmelswesen, wenn nicht eintrifft, was sie von ihnen erhoffen, mit verleumderischer Zunge, und sie klagen sie an[13]. — Um Lästern und Beschuldigen geht es auch in Philos Schrift *De Confusione Linguarum*, 154. Das Lästern schade freilich nur den ungerechten Anklägern selber[14]. In *Prov.* I, 57, fragt Philo schliesslich ausdrücklich: 'Ist jemand weiser als die Vorsehung selbst, so dass er das von ihr Geschehende tadelt?' Schon in I, 60, wird das Thema wiederaufgegriffen: Da die Vorsehung alles weiss, gilt: 'Da dem so ist, soll sich niemand anmassen, die Vorsehung zu tadeln, dass sie ohne umfassendes Urteil jeden seinem Ende zugeführt habe, als ob sie die einzelnen ohne Auswahl unklug dahinraffe'. Nach I, 69, gilt vom Tugendhaften: 'Er klagt die Vorsehung nicht an, sondern sagt den Anklägern Lebewohl', und das gilt in der Situation ungerechten Leidens. Nach II, 66, gibt es 'lästerhafte Zungen', die 'zügellos sich anmassen, Teile der Natur zu verleumden'. Ursache ihrer Gottlosigkeit sei die Lust. Nach II, 72, sehen Menschen, die Widerspruch lieben, in den himmlischen Erscheinungen Anlässe zur Anklage; vgl. auch II, 98. I, 2, spricht davon, dass man die 'Vorsehung mit Anschuldigungen' überhäuft.

Es ergibt sich in den Schriften Philos ein Wortfeld mit den Elementen Anklage, Tadel, Lästern und Leugnen, das sich gegen Gottes Vorsehung

---

[13] Philo, *De Somniis* II, 131f.: 'Würde ein solcher (sc.Mensch) sich es überlegen, Sonne und Mond und die anderen Sterne zu schmähen, wenn etwas von dem, was man sich im Verlaufe der Jahreszeiten erhoffte, entweder überhaupt nicht oder nicht mühelos eintrifft ...? Alle Segel eines zügellosen Mundwerks und seiner verleumderischen Zunge zieht er auf, um die Sterne anzuklagen, als hätten sie den gewohnten Tribut nicht dargebracht, weil er es für richtig hält, dass von den himmlischen Wesen den irdischen und vor allem ihm selbst um so mehr Ehre und Anbetung erwiesen werde, als er in seiner Eigenschaft als Mensch von den anderen Lebewesen verschieden zu sein glaubt' (133: 'So werden die Chorführer des leeren Wahnes von uns geschildert ...').

[14] Philo, *Conf.*, 154: '... wurden sie (sc. die Menschen) der Laster gegen das, was auf der Erde, im Meere und in der Luft sich befindet, ... überdrüssig und hatten die Absicht, sich gegen die göttlichen Wesen im Himmel umzustellen; diesen aber ist kein Geschaffenes imstande, ausser der Lästerung, auf irgendwelche Weise Schlimmes zuzufügen; ja, selbst das Lästern bringt keinen einzigen Schaden den Gelästerten, die die eigene Natur nie einbüssen, vielmehr (bringt es) unheilbare Leiden denen, die mit Anklagen (gegen jene) auftreten'.

richtet — oder auch gegen die 'olympischen Wesen' (*Conf.*, 114) oder 'göttliche Naturen' (*Conf.*, 154). Bei der Schilderung der zukünftigen Eschatologie in I, 90 ist dann plötzlich davon die Rede, dass 'die über die Welt gestellten Wächter' sie verlassen werden. Damit sind zweifellos nach jüdischem Verständnis Engel gemeint. Neben der Rede von der Vorsehung steht daher unvermittelt auch der traditionell jüdische Sprachgebrauch von 'Wächtern', und ausserdem kann Philo von den 'olympischen Wesen' oder 'göttlichen Naturen' in diesen Zusammenhängen sprechen. Auch wenn man sich nicht dazu entscheiden kann, strikte Deckungsgleichheit anzunehmen ('Engel' sind eher die Exekutoren der Vorsehung), so ist doch an einer engen Zuordnung festzuhalten (vgl. im übrigen unten Par. 4,1).

b) Bei Philo ist die Vorsehung regelmässig mit dem *Richten Gottes über die Welt* verbunden (I, 23; 30 als kontinuierliches Weltgericht; I, 34 Endgericht, 'wenn Himmel und Erde vergangen sein werden', vgl. 2. Petr. 3:10; I, 35 'Untergang der Welt und ihr Hinschwinden'; I, 60 Gericht, das zwischen Gerechten und Ungerechten unterscheidet). Damit wird 'Vorsehung' hier mit einer universalen Dimension verknüpft, dic bei Plutarch fehlt, die aber Philo mit 2. Petr. 3 verbindet (vgl. auch unter e).

c) Nach I, 70 hängen eng zusammen die Verwerfung der Vorsehung, die *Freiheit* des Menschen und das Verletzen der Gerechtigkeit[15]. Dieses ist de facto auch mit der Leugnung Gottes verbunden. Wichtig ist hierbei der negative Bezug auf das Gesetz. Er wurde ja auch durch das Kain-Beispiel (vgl. Anm. 8) nahegelegt.

d) Dass Leugnen der Vorsehung mit der Leugnung Gottes zusammenhängt, geht aus Philo, *Conf.* 114 hervor: ' ... vielmehr wagt sie (sc. die Untugend) auch an die olympischen Wesen, Worte der Unfrommheit und der Gottlosigkeit schleudernd, indem sie behauptet, dass die Gottheit nicht existiere (οὐκ ἔστι), oder dass sie zwar existiere, jedoch sich nicht (um die Welt) kümmere (οὐ προνοεῖ), oder dass die Welt keinen Anfang ihres Entstehens habe, oder dass sie zwar entstanden sei, aber nicht nach bestimmten Gesetzen, sondern wie es der Zufall mit sich bringt, sich bewege ...'. Die Formulierungen mit 'es gibt ihn nicht', 'er kümmert sich nicht' sind so apodiktisch formuliert wie die epikureischen Reden Kains (vgl. Anm. 8 'Es gibt kein Gericht ...', vgl. dazu auch 1. Kor. 15:13![16]).

---

[15] Philo, *Prov* I, 70: 'Einzig und allein der mit Freiheit beschenkte Bürger der Welt, der Mensch ... hat ... die Vorsehung verworfen und das Gesetz der Gerechtigkeit missachtet. Erscheint es da nicht ungerecht, nach Verwerfung der Vorsehung sich selbst für den eigenen Fürsorger zu erklären und zu behaupten, als kluger Mann alles selbst geistreich in Bewegung zu setzen?' Ähnlich wird übrigens nach Clemens v.A., *Strom* I, 50, 6 den Epikureern vorgeworfen ἀναιρεῖν τὴν πρόνοιαν.

[16] Auch in 1. Kor. 15:13 zeigt sich eine bemerkenswerte Konvergenz von sadduzäischer und vulgär-epikureischer Position eines allgemeinen Skeptizismus. Zur Formulierung vgl. den Tosefta-Text bei G. Vermes (Anm.7), S. 116: 'Es gibt kein Gericht, es gibt keinen Richter, es gibt keine andere Welt. Es gibt nicht das Geschenk guter Vergeltung für die Guten und keine Bestrafung für

e) Philos Schrift weist sehr enge Beziehungen zur *apokalyptischen Eschatologie* des 2. Petr. auf, insbesondere zu dem sonst nicht belegten Motiv der 'Auflösung der Elemente' in 2. Petr. 3:10[17]; in diesem Kontext ist auch von Langmut die Rede (vgl. 2. Petr. 3:9, 15).

Aufgrund des Befundes bei Philo, insbesondere in seiner Schrift *De Providentia*, ergibt sich die Möglichkeit, die Elemente 'Lästern', 'Gericht', apokalyptische Eschatologie nach Art von 2. Petr. und Gesetzlosigkeit bei den Lästerern zusammenzubringen. Sie hätten einen gemeinsamen Ursprung in der Diskussion um die Frage, ob Gott die Welt überhaupt im Stich gelassen habe und sich noch um sie kümmere.

4. *Weitere wichtige Texte aus dem Judentum und dem Christentum des 1. und 2. Jh. n. Chr.*

1) Justin *II Apol.* 5,2f.: 'Gott hat die ganze Welt gemacht ... und die Vorsehung (πρόνοιαν) für die Menschen und die Dinge unter dem Himmel Engeln anvertraut (ἀγγέλοις παρέδωκεν), die er über diese setzte (οὓς ἐπὶ τούτοις ἔταξε). Die Engel aber haben ... diese Ordnung übertreten ...'. Wichtig ist dieser Text, weil hier die für Philo bereits vermutete (vgl. Par. 3a) *Verbindung von Pronoia und Engeln* begegnet. Die Engel führen Gottes Vorsehung aus, sie sind deren verantwortliche Vollstrecker.

2) In der Syrischen *Baruch-Apokalypse* 21, 23f. wird Gott von Baruch gebeten, seine Herrlichkeit erscheinen zu lassen. Baruch fährt fort mit der Bitte um die Auferstehung und begründet sie: 'Denn viele Jahre sind verstrichen gleich denen, die seit den Tagen Abrahams, Isaaks und Jakobs vergangen sind und aller, die ihnen ähnlich sind, die schlafen in der Erde — um ihretwillen, sagtest du, dass du die Welt erschaffen hast. (25) Alsbald zeige deine Herrlichkeit und schiebe nicht hinaus, was du verheissen hast'. — Dieser Gebetsschluss ist wichtig für den Vergleich mit 2. Petr., da 1. das Motiv der entschlafenen Väter begegnet wie in 2. Petr. 3:4, und da 2. die Verzögerung, bzw. das

---

die Bösen'. Paulus geht demnach mit dem sadduzäischen (oder die sadduzäische Position markant auf einen Nenner bringenden) Schlagwort vor gegen Skeptiker in Korinth. Dass in Korinth Sadduzäer sassen, wird man kaum glauben können.

[17] Philo, *Prov* I, 89: 'Da aber die menschliche Natur von der Vorsehung abgewichen ist ... und ein ruchloses Leben angenommen hat, ... so wird die gerechte Strafe die künftige völlige Auflösung der Elemente sein ... Es mögen also die Elemente fliehen ... und was Werkzeug für die Mannigfaltigkeit der überaus schönen Welt war, möge die Auflösung des Verderbens bekommen ... (90). Da dem so ist, wie gesagt ist, mit welchem Recht kann da die Welt eine weitere Dauer zu besitzen wünschen, da die Vorsehung ihre Langmut schon durch viele Zeiten gezeigt hat? Wider ihren Willen wird die Welt dann aufgeschreckt werden, und die Herrlichkeit der Elemente wird erzittern, wenn sie den Zorn der Vorsehung erblicken, und die über die Welt gestellten Wächter werden sie verlassen, wenn sie vom verdienten Richter gepackt wird. Nicht mehr ist dann in ihr die herrliche Schönheit der Elemente; weggenommen ist ihre Pracht ... die Materie beeilt sich, ihre Form abzulegen ...'.

Hinausschieben direkt zur Sprache gebracht wird. Gott soll nach dem Gebet Baruchs nicht weiter verzögern. Schliesslich ist 3. von den Verheissungen die Rede wie in 2. Petr. 3:4, 9.

3) In der Syrischen *Baruch-Apokalypse* 25,4 werden Menschen geschildert, die aufgrund der grossen Drangsal, die über sie kommt, die Hoffnung aufgeben, bzw. nicht mehr damit rechnen, dass Gott sich um die Welt kümmert: 'Und wenn es geschehen wird, dass sie in ihrem Denken sagen werden um ihrer grossen Drangsal willen: 'Der Mächtige gedenkt nimmermehr der Erde!' — dann also wird's geschehen, wenn sie die Hoffnung aufgegeben haben: dass dann die neue Zeit erwachen wird'. Der Text bezeugt ausdrücklich, dass es *nach der Zerstörung Jerusalems* im Jahre 70 die Position von Skeptikern gab, die zu der Überzeugung gelangt waren: 'Der Mächtige gedenkt nimmermehr der Erde', und damit der Sache nach das vertraten, was ohne entsprechende Erfahrungen die Ansicht des Epikureismus war. Hinzukommt, dass in dem folgenden Abschnitt Baruch auch die *Verzögerungsthematik* anspricht: 'Die Drangsal, die dann sein soll, wird doch nicht lange währen, und jene Not wird doch nicht viele Jahre dauern!?' (26,1).

4) Nach 1. Kor. 6:3 werden die Christen 'Engel richten'. Fraglich ist, ob es sich dabei um das Gericht über die abgefallenen Engel nach Gen. 6 handelt, denn diese sind doch schon gerichtet. Wahrscheinlicher ist, dass es sich dabei um eine Funktion handelt, die das Tun der Engel in der Welt im allgemeinen beurteilen soll, wie sie in den unter Par. 3a genannten Texten und auch in Jud. 9, besonders aber in Philo, *Som* II, 130-133 ausdrücklich abgelehnt wird ('dass nämlich der ganz unglückselige Mensch sich mit dem ganz seligen Wesen zu vergleichen wagte'). Für unseren Zusammenhang ist hier nur wichtig, dass nach Paulus die Gemeinde künftig jene richterliche Hoheit haben wird, die ihr im Judasbrief ganz abgesprochen werden soll (Alles weist darauf, dass es sich im Jud. um eine Opposition gegen bestimmte Ausprägungen urchristlichen Pneumatikertums handelt[18]), während in 2. Petr. das 'Lästern' möglicherweise

---

[18] Begründung: 1) ἐπιτιμᾶν wie Jud. 9 wird in den Evgl. auf das Schelten der Dämonen etc. bezogen. Lästerndes Urteilen wird als Steigerung verstanden (Jud. 9), setzt also jedenfalls das Bewusstsein noch grösserer pneumatischer Vollmacht voraus. 2) Das Ablehnen des Herrschers und Herrn nach Jud. 4 steht in Kontrast zum Selbstverständnis des Verf. in Jud. 1 (Sklave). Die Gegner hätten dann eine Position, wie sie in Joh. 15:15 zum Ausdruck kommt: Nicht Sklaven, sondern Freunde. 3) Der Missbrauch der Gnade zu Ausschweifung (Jud. 4) zeugt von Pneumatikern, die sich über das Gesetz erhaben fühlen. 4) Jud. 19f. setzt Diskussion über den Gegensatz 'psychisch'/'pneumatisch' voraus. 5) Lästern gegenüber Engeln (gr.: pneumata) ist nach Analogie des Lästerns des Geistes in Mk. 3:29parr zu verstehen. Nach Jud. 9 geht es vielleicht darum, dass dem Satan als 'pneuma' die Verbindung mit Gott abgesprochen wird (das war Lästern des Pneumas jedenfalls in Mk. 3:29). Dazu passt auch, dass Michael eben nicht so weit gegangen ist, sondern nur Schelte aussprach. In der Praxis geht es dann um ein Scheiden zwischen Geistern (vgl. 1. Joh. 4:1-6). Im Sinne von 1. Joh. 4 handelt es sich vielleicht darum, ein Pneuma als das des Antichrist zu bezeichnen. Geht es um eine Warnung davor, die Praxis der Unterscheidung der Geister bis zur Verketzerung durchzuführen? Oder handelt es sich um Formen des Exorzismus, in dem die bösen Geister mit Fluchworten o.Ä. bedacht werden? Oder geht es um Leute, die aufgrund des

im Zusammenhang steht mit der Leugnung von Gottes Weltregierung und Pronoia. Gegenüber Jud. wäre dann diese Tradition sehr viel anders verwendet worden.

5) Dass es in 2. Petr. 3:4, wie bereits oben unter 2) und 3) angedeutet, um ein Element handelt, das gegen Ende des 1.Jh. im Judentum geläufig war, geht auch aus zwei sehr ähnlichen Zitaten hervor, die in *1.* und *2. Clem.* bewahrt sind und mit einiger Wahrscheinlichkeit einer jüdischen Schrift entstammen. In *1. Clem.* 23:3 heisst es: 'Ferne sei von uns diese Schriftstelle (γραφή), wo es heisst: 'Unglückselig sind die Zweifler (δίψυχοι), die geteilten Herzens sind (διστάζοντες τῇ ψυχῇ), die sagen: Dies hörten wir auch zur Zeit unserer Väter, und siehe, wir sind alt geworden, und nichts davon ist uns widerfahren". 23:5 enthält dann eine Aussage über die Parusie: 'Wahrhaftig, schnell und plötzlich wird sein Wille in Erfüllung gehen ...'. Ähnlich ist in *2. Clem.* 11:1 vom Glauben an Gottes Verheissung die Rede. Wer nicht daran glaubt, wird unglückselig sein. In 11:2 folgt das Zitat: 'Denn es sagt auch das prophetische Wort: 'Unglückselig sind die Zweifler, die in ihrem Herzen zwiespältig sind, die da sprechen: Dies haben wir längst gehört auch schon zur Zeit unserer Väter, wir aber warteten von Tag zu Tag und haben nichts von dem geschaut". Die Anwendung im Kontext geht auf Standhalten in Unruhen und Drangsalen. Wie in 2. Petr. 3:4 und in *SyrBar.* 21:23f. ist von den Vätern im Zusammenhang mit der Verzögerung der Parusie die Rede. Den Spöttern von 2. Petr. 3:3 entsprechen hier die Zwiespältigen und Zweifler. In *SyrBar.* dagegen verbindet der Beter Baruch das Motiv mit der Bitte um baldiges Kommen. Der Ursprungsort dieses 'prophetischen Wortes' ist unbekannt. Ganz offensichtlich handelt es sich um eine Schrift aus der jüdischen Apokalyptik dieser Zeit mit pseudepigraphem Charakter.

6) *ÄthHen.* 46:7 (Schilderung der Ungerechten): 'Und diese sind es, die die Sterne des Himmels richten und die, die ihre Hand gegen den Höchsten emporrecken' (in Verbindung mit Reichtum und Götzendienst). Das Vergehen gegen die Sterne entspricht dem gegen Engel und Himmelswesen in der oben genannten Tradition. 'Richten' ist jedenfalls: sich ein Urteil anmassen. Zu fragen ist aber, wieweit ein Zusammenhang mit magischer Astrologie besteht (κρίνειν = beurteilen).

7) Im Rahmen der Paulusakten (*PHeid* nach Hennecke-Schneemelcher, *Neutestamentliche Apokryphen* II, 1964, 258f) werden die Gegner in Korinth wie folgt gekennzeichnet: Nach 1,15 wird von ihnen behauptet, 'die Welt sei nicht Gottes, sondern der Engel', nach 3,19 'stossen sie die Vorsehung zurück, indem sie (fern vom Glauben) behaupten, Himmel und Erde und alles, was in

---

Pneumabesitzes oder aus anderen Voraussetzungen keine andere Autorität über sich anerkennen, weder Jesus als Kyrios (V.4) noch Engelmächte (V.8-9)? Denn wer selber Pneuma hat, braucht kein Mittlerwesen zu respektieren, da die Nähe zu Gott unüberbietbar gegeben ist. Das wäre gleichzeitig eine Art von Aufgeklärtsein (Jud. 10).

ihnen ist, seien nicht Werke des Vaters'. Wie in den anderen Texten so wird auch hier die Diskussion über Vorsehung mit der Frage der Gottesferne der Welt und dem Regiment von Engeln in der Welt zusammengebracht. Die Wendung zu gnostisierenden Tendenzen ist hier freilich eindeutig vollzogen: Engel regieren in der Welt aber eben gerade nicht eine Vorsehung.

5. *Folgerungen und Thesen für 2. Petr.*

1) Die Verzögerung der Verheissung, die schon an die Väter erging, ist insbesondere ein *Problem des Judentums* des 1. Jh.n.Chr., wahrscheinlich im Zusammenhang mit der Zerstörung Jerusalems im Jahre 70 n.Chr. Die hinter 2. Petr. 3:4 liegende Tradition lässt erkennen, dass es einen Skeptizismus jüdischer Genese gegeben hat, der insbesondere wohl wegen dieses Ereignisses an den Verheissungen verzweifelte. In der Eigenperspektive des judenchristlichen Verfassers von 2. Petr. ist Jesus, insbesondere seine Verklärung und seine zu erwartende Wiederkunft, die Erfüllung aller jüdischen Hoffnungen, die fast schon aufgegeben waren. Das Jesusgeschehen ist für die jüdischen Erwartungen die Wende im Geschick Israels. Ob die heidenchristlichen Hörer des Verf. das auch so sahen, ist freilich zu fragen.

2) Das Problem der Parusieverzögerung ist mithin dem 2. Petr. sehr deutlich aus jüdischer Tradition vorgegeben. Aktuell wird es freilich hier im Rahmen eines *Skeptizismus*, der nicht nur aus dem Geschick des jüdischen Volkes herrührt, sondern der auch die ehemaligen Heiden und jetzigen Christen als Adressaten des Briefes kennzeichnet. Es geht dabei um Gottes Wirksamkeit in der Geschichte überhaupt. Dieses Problem behandelt der Verf. mit Hilfe traditionellen Materials aus der Diskussion über Gottes Vorsehung, bzw. 'Weltregiment'.

3) In der Sicht des Verf. des 2. Petr. gehören zu diesem Wirksamsein Gottes in der Geschichte: Verklärung und Wiederkunft Jesu als Eckpfeiler, damit zugleich aber das Gericht, in der Gegenwart 'gesetzliche' Vorschriften mit Affinität zum Aposteldekret (vgl. oben Par. 1d) und das Akzeptieren von vermittelnden Instanzen wie Gesetz und Engelmächten (Doxai und Kyriotetes). Wer dieses alles ablehnt, und das tun in seiner Sicht die Gegner, fällt ins Heidentum zurück und wird durch Unreinheit befleckt, die auch ein Bestehen im Gericht unmöglich macht. Mit 'Freiheit' (2:19) wird die Ablehnung dieser Reinheitsvorstellungen auf Seiten der Gegner beschrieben.

4) Konkret sind daher die 'Gegner' durch folgendes ausgezeichnet: Sie sind ehemalige Heiden und haben sich wohl zu dem einen Gott bekehrt, 'Teilhabe and der göttlichen Natur' könnte ihr soteriologisches Prinzip sein (1:4). Sie sind jedoch dabei, eine 'Zwischenschicht' judenchristlicher Vorstellungen abzulegen, zu der auch einige christologische Vorstellungen gehören (2:2: abgelehnt wird das Bild von Christen als Sklaven, die durch einen Herrn gekauft wären

— das widerstrebt der christlichen 'Freiheit'), vor allem aber apokalyptische Eschatologie und die Notwendigkeit, hier bestimmte Reinheitsvorstellungen zu bewahren, sowie der Glaube an Engelwesen. Die Ablehnung der Gegner betrifft mithin alles, was ein aufgeklärter Skeptizismus zu allen Zeiten als 'mythologisch' oder 'ritualistisch' verworfen hat oder zu umgehen suchte, oder anders formuliert: was sich als unphilosophischer Rest konkreter jüdischer Religiosität erhalten hatte.

5) Gegenüber dieser Position greift der Verf. des 2. Petr. nun auf Material zurück, das selbst paganer Philosophie entstammt, wenn auch einer antiskeptischen. *Er verteidigt sein genuin jüdisches 'Weltbild' mit Hilfe von Vorstellungen, die sich aus der anti-epikureischen Tradition anboten.* Diese sind oben in Par. 2-3 genannt. Der Effekt ist, dass die ehemaligen Heiden gewissermassen mit den eigenen Waffen oder doch jedenfalls mit Heidnischem geschlagen werden sollen, was freilich zum Teil nur spärliche Verkleidung jüdischer Grundzüge ist. So hat fortan die Argumentation des Verf. gewissermassen zwei Seiten: Im Rahmen hellenistischer Argumente für Gottes Pronoia verteidigt der Verf., dass Gott überhaupt in die Welt eingreift, und gleichzeitig wird damit eine ältere jüdisch-pharisäische Position bewahrt, wie im folgenden darzustellen ist.

6) Für die '*pharisäische*' *Ausgangsposition* sind folgende Elemente wichtig: a) die kultische Respektierung (2:10: τρέμειν, vgl. Jak. 2:19) von Engelwesen, nämlich κυριότητες und δόξαι[19]. Diese werden sonst auch als 'pneumata' zusammengefasst, und der Glaube an solche Engelwesen ist für Pharisäer typisch (Act. 23:8). b) In engem Zusammenhang mit solchen Engelwesen steht die pharisäische Konzeption von Reinheit. Das wird aus dem Gedankengang von 2. Petr. 2:10ff. deutlich erkennbar. Dieser Zusammenhang ist offenbar so zu begründen, dass diese Pneumata als solche höchste kultische Reinheit besitzen, denn sie sind die nächsten vor Gottes Thron, und dass die pharisäischen Gerechten (vgl. die Gemeinde in Qumran) eine kultische Gemeinschaft mit diesen Engeln zu sein beabsichtigten. Von daher ist auch die Vorstellung der Geisttaufe (= Reinigung) und der Gegenüberstellung von Jesu reinem Pneuma und den 'unreinen Geistern' nach Mk. 1 zu verstehen. Aus der Affinität von Kyrioswesen und Pneumata wird auch 2. Kor. 3:17 verständlich. Zwischen Gottes Pneuma und diesen Pneumata besteht eine gewisse Interferenz, so dass beide die Art und Weise sein können, in der Gott in die Welt eingreift und in ihr handelt. c) Frühchristliche Opposition gegen diese hohe Funktion von Engelwesen bietet vor allem Kol. 2:10-15, besonders in V.15.

---

[19] Belege über den Kyrios-Titel bei Engeln: K. Berger, 'Zum traditionsgeschichtlichen Hintergrund christologischer Hoheitstitel', *NTS* 17 (1970/71), 391-425, 415, 417 Anm. 3 und 5, 418 Anm. 1f. Doxa als Engelgruppe: Ex. 15:11 LXX; *Test Juda* 25:2; *1 QH* 10:8; *SlavHen* 21:1, 3. Auch der Kyrios-Titel Jesu ist von dem der hohen Engelwesen nicht strikt zu trennen.

Hier ist der Sühnetod Jesu entscheidend, und die auffällige, fast völlige Abstinenz des Kol. gegenüber der Grösse 'Pneuma' wird von hierher verständlich. Auch bei Paulus gibt es eine Konkurrenz zwischen der Funktion des Pneumas und des Sühnetodes. Nur ist bei Paulus das Pneuma eben kein Engelwesen, wie es in Kol. Position der Gegner ist. Doch weist die Verbindung von Pneuma, Auferstehung und Gottessohnschaft möglicherweise schon in diese Richtung (vgl. auch Lk. 20:36). d) Zur pharisäischen Grundposition von 2. Petr. gehört auch die Opposition gegen Unzucht und 'Fressgelage' (vgl. oben Par. 1c,d), eine eindeutige Abgrenzungsposition. Die gefährdeten Christen in der Gruppe der Adressaten dagegen sind offenbar reich (sie können am Tage Gelage feiern, nicht erst abends: 2:13) und in der Gefahr, hellenistisch angepasst zu sein. e) Gesetz und Engel gehören vor allem auch sachlich zusammen (vgl. Gal. 3:19; Act. 7:53), weil so Gott die Welt 'ordnet'. Diese pharisäische Grundposition des Verf. wird nun freilich überlagert durch Argumente für Gottes Pronoia. Gemeinsamkeiten zwischen beiden Positionen wurden ja offenbar schon von Josephus gesehen (vgl. oben zu Josephus Anm. 9).

7) In folgenden Punkten greift der Verf. des 2. Petr. *traditionelle Diskussion über Gottes Pronoia* auf: a) Die Verheissung ist nur verzögert, die Verzögerung dient der Umkehr, und die göttlichen und menschlichen Zeitmassstäbe sind verschieden. b) Das Lästern gegen Vorsehung oder das (negative) Urteilen über Himmelswesen werden gleichgesetzt. Der Verf. deutet den anti-mythologischen und anti-spekulativen Skeptizismus seiner Gegner, vielleicht auch ihre Hinweise auf den Zustand der Welt, im Sinne des traditionellen Lästerns gegen Himmelswesen. Demgegenüber will er zeigen: Gott kümmert sich sehr wohl um die Welt, wie man an Verklärung und künftigem Gericht sieht. Wer Engelwesen bei Gott leugnet, der bestreitet überhaupt eine Verbindung von Gott und Welt (vgl. dazu unter 6b). c) Wer eine Vorsehung leugnet, ist auch gesetzlos.

8) Theologiegeschichtlich gehört der Skeptizismus auf Seiten der Gegner ganz eindeutig auf die *Linie der paulinischen 'Starken'*, die schon in 1. Kor. 8:1f. durch eine aufgeklärte Position sich auszeichnen (vgl. dazu den Begriff 'Erkenntnis' in 2. Petr. 1:3-8; im Anfang seines Briefes holt der Verf. daher seine Leser bei ihrer eigenen Position ab). Freilich gehen diese Starken nun über Paulus hinaus, wenn sie ihn auch verwenden (2. Petr. 3:15f.). Sie entfernen von der paulinischen Freiheit gewissermassen alle Elemente des Pharisäers Paulus (vgl. zur Unzucht und zum Engelglauben) zugunsten einer Position, die in dem, was sie leugnet, einiges mit Sadduzäern gemeinsam hat, freilich nur darin. Der Verf. des 2. Petr. dagegen argumentiert von der Position der paulinischen Schwachen aus und nimmt pagane philosophische Elemente zur Hilfe.

9) Für das negative verbale Verhalten gegenüber Engeln, Sternen, Geistern, Himmelsmächten oder Vorsehung ergeben sich daher folgende Möglichkeiten aus der Tradition:

A. *Negativ* beurteiltes Verhalten solcher Menschen:
- Unzufriedenheit mit der Leistung für die Menschen (Philo),
- Leiden und Verzögerung der Parusie (jüd. Apokalypsen),
- Protest gegen das Geschick (äthHen.)
- Es wird bestritten, dass ein Geist von Gott ist (Legitimitätsfrage), (Mk. 3:29)
- Schelte bei Exorzismen (Synopt. Evv.)
- Ablehnung von pneumatischen Mittlerwesen (Judasbrief?, vgl. 'Unterscheidung von Geistern' wie 1. Joh. 4.)
- Skeptizismus gegen Gottes Wirken in der Welt (2. Petr.)

B. *Positiv* beurteiltes Verhalten:
1. Kor. 6:3 (im eschatologischen pneumatischen Zustand wird die Gemeinde über Engel erhoben sein und sie 'beurteilen' können). Es gab Hinweise dafür (vgl. Anm. 18), dass die Gegner im Judasbrief der Meinung waren, diese pneumatische Vollmacht schon zu besitzen.

In 2. Petr. geht es weder um die Legitimität des Pneumas noch um Exorzismus, gegenüber Jud. sind alle Hinweise auf Pneumatikertum in der Gemeinde getilgt. Daher wird es sich am ehesten, wie in den jüdischen Belegen (*äthHen.*, Philo, jüd. Apokalypsen) um eine Beurteilung des Wirkens Gottes in der Welt handeln.

6. *Zur theologischen Bedeutung des Streits um Gottes Vorsehung in 2. Petr.*

1) In 2. Petr. erweist sich, was auch sonst im Neuen Testament häufiger zu beobachten ist: Stark judenchristlicher Einfluss, wie ihn der Verf. des 2. Petr. verkörpert, ist regelmässig ein Bollwerk gegen nivellierende Angleichung des Christentums an pagane Allerweltsmeinung und -philosophie.

2) Christologie und apokalyptische Eschatologie sind als Eckpfeiler von Gottes Weltregiment eng aufeinander bezogen. Die Verklärung Christi macht das Ende gewiss.

3) Der göttlichen Natur als Qualität wird die Gerechtigkeit als Ordnung entsprechen (1:4 und 3:13). Das Vergehen der Welt im Feuer ist auch Folge und Zeichen dessen, dass sie vor ihm nicht bestehen kann (3:5f., 12), bzw. Symptom einer umfassenden Reinigung: Die *pharisäische Reinheitskonzeption wird ins Universale ausgeweitet* (vgl. auch 3:14).

4) Für die Wirkungsgeschichte bleibt wichtig, dass die Scheidung zwischen alter und neuer Schöpfung nirgends so krass ausgebildet ist wie in 2. Petr., und zwar aus den unter 3) erwähnten Gründen. Hier liegen wesentliche Voraussetzungen für die spätere Doktrin der Orthodoxie über die *annihilatio mundi.*

5) Wahrscheinlich stehen öfter als erwartet nicht bestimmte exotische Häresien im Hintergrund der neutestamentlichen Argumentationen gegen Gegner, sondern verbreiteter Skeptizismus, der entweder überhaupt vorhanden war oder sich zumindest doch bei der Berührung mit den jüdischen Elementen der christlichen Botschaft entzünden musste. Diesen Skeptizismus bemerkten wir für 2. Petr. wie für 1. Kor. 15. Da diese Haltung — im Unterschied zu speziellen Häresien der Antike — aber weit auch heute verbreitet ist, findet der hermeneutisch interessierte Theologe eine nicht unwillkommene Analogie.

DATIERUNG UND HERKUNFT DES VIERTEN MAKKABÄERBUCHES

von

JAN WILLEM VAN HENTEN

Die jüdische Schrift, die im Altertum als das Vierte Makkabäerbuch bekannt wurde und manchmal auch Josephus zugeschrieben wurde, ist ganz besonders ein Märtyrertext.[1] Sie hat die literarische Form der Diatribe, ist aber zugleich stark beeinflusst von der Form und Thematik der griechischen Grabrede über Kriegsgefallene.[2] Das Buch ist sehr stark rhetorisch stilisiert. Es beschreibt den Märtyrertod des neunzigjährigen Priesters Eleasar und der sieben jugendlichen Brüder zur Zeit der Verfolgung des Antiochos IV. Dieser Tod regte den Verfasser wie die Autoren der athenischen Grabrede (ἐπιτάφιος λόγος) an, die Gestorbenen vor dem Publikum eingehend zu loben. Dazu charakterisiert er die Märtyrer auf verschiedene Art und Weise. Er betont ihre gegenseitige Solidarität und ebenfalls ihre Treue zu den nationalen Überlieferungen. So bekommen die Märtyrer als zeitgenössische Juden eine ähnliche Bedeutung wie die nationalen Helden aus der Vergangenheit.[3] Die Märtyrer sind die musterhaften Repräsentanten der jüdischen Nation. Zweitens sind sie, und mit ihnen auch das ganze Volk, Philosophen, und sogar besondere Philosophen, weil sie ihre Philosophie im tatsächlichen Handeln bestätigten.[4] Drittens wird die

---

* Dieser Artikel ist eine Bearbeitung eines Teiles einer Vorlesung für die niederländische Arbeitsgemeinschaft für Judaistik (18. Dez. 1984). Jürgen Lebram war seit der Gründung 1979 der stimulierende Sekretär und später Vorsitzende dieser Gemeinschaft. Ich danke B.G.A.M. Dehandschutter, B. Hartmann, G. van der Kooij, S. Moors, H.W. Pleket und P.T. van Rooden für ihre Bemerkungen zum Konzept dieses Artikels.

[1] J.W. van Henten, 'Einige Prolegomena zum Studium der jüdischen Martyrologie', *Bijdragen* 46 (1985), 381-390. J.W. van Henten, *De martelaar als voorbeeld van de Joodse existentie in de oudheid*, Kapitel 6. Es sind nur wenige ausführliche Studien über 4 Makk publiziert, siehe die Kommentare von A. Dupont-Sommer, *Le quatrième livre des Macchabées. Introduction, traduction et notes*, Paris, 1939, und M. Hadas, *The Third and Fourth Book of Maccabees*, New York, 1953, und vor allem U. Breitenstein, *Beobachtungen zu Sprache, Stil und Gedankengut des Vierten Makkabäerbuchs*, Basel/Stuttgart, 1976.

[2] J.C.H. Lebram, 'Die literarische Form des Vierten Makkabäerbuches', *VigChr* 28 (1974), 81-96.

[3] J.W. van Henten, *De martelaar*. Vgl. van Henten, 'Die Charakterisierung der jüdischen Märtyrer', erscheint in J.W. van Henten; B.A.G.M. Dehandschutter; H.J.W. van der Klaauw, *Die Entstehung der jüdischen Martyrologie*, die Publikation des Leidener Workshops über die Entstehung der Vorstellung des jüdischen Märtyrers (6.-8. Sept. 1984).

[4] Siehe besonders 4 Makk 7:9 über den alten Eleasar: καὶ διὰ τῶν ἔργων ἐπιστοποίησας τοὺς τῆς θείας φιλοσοφιας σου λόγους. Dazu van Henten, *De martelaar*. Ein Überblick über Texte, in denen die Juden wie Philosophen dargestellt werden, gibt J.J. Collins, *Between Athens and Jerusalem. Jewish Identity in the Hellenistic Diaspora*, New York, 1983, 175-194.

Entscheidung zum Martyrium anhand agonistischer und militärischer Metaphern bildhaft beschrieben. Der Märtyrer ist der wahre Athlet und der mutigste Soldat.[5] Viertens überbieten die Märtyrer ihren Gegner, weil sie dem Tyrann nicht gehorchen und so über ihn siegen. Im Gegensatz zum Tyrann sind die Märtyrer gerecht, mutig und bescheiden, wie man es von einem guten König erwarten darf.[6]

Ein Werk solchen Inhalts weckt die Neugierde auf nach der Zeit der Entstehung und der Herkunft des 4 Makk, gerade weil 4 Makk das Martyrium des Eleasars und der sieben Brüder beschreibt, das uns schon aus 2 Makk bekannt ist (2 Makk 6:18-7:42). Zudem hat die Datierung von 4 Makk wichtige Konsequenzen für das Verhältnis zwischen jüdischen und christlichen Märtyrertexten. Man nimmt an, dass zwischen 4 Makk und christlichen Schriften Übereinstimmungen der Terminologie und der Vorstellung des Märtyrers bestehen.[7] Falls 4 Makk früh genug datiert wird, kann man noch einen Schritt weiter gehen, und annehmen, dass die Auffassung des Jesus von Nazareth von seinem bevorstehenden Sterben selbst oder die Interpretation dieses Sterbens durch die ersten Christen als Sühneopfer durch 4 Makk beeinflusst wurde. Solche Standpunkte sind tatsächlich formuliert worden, obwohl die konkrete historische Information in 4 Makk minimal ist. Deshalb ist eine neue kurze Untersuchung nach der Zeit der Entstehung dieser Schrift gerechtfertigt.

4 Makk ist von 2 Makk abhängig. Ausser der Geschichte des Märtyrertums Eleasars und der sieben Brüder entlehnte der Verfasser des 4 Makk auch den Stoff des historischen Rahmens des Martyriums (4 Makk 3:20-4:26) aus 2 Makk (3:1-6:11).[8] Das heisst, dass 4 Makk auf jeden Fall später als 125 v. Chr. geschrieben ist. Tatsächlich wird das Buch aber nicht vor dem Ende des 1. Jahrhunderts v. Chr. entstanden sein, wie schon Grimm meinte und Bickerman weiter plausibel macht.[9] Bei der Betrachtung der verschiedenen Äusserungen über das Datum zeigt sich, dass wir von einer frühen und einer späten Datierung sprechen können. Einige Gelehrte beziehen eine Mittelposition. Dupont-Sommer ist der wichtigste Protagonist der späten Datierung. Er setzt das zweite Jahrhundert n. Chr. voraus und meint, dass 4 Makk in den ersten Jahren Hadrians geschrieben wurde, kurz nach dem jüdischen Krieg von ungefähr 117 n. Chr.[10] Dieser Datierung hat niemand wirklich zugestimmt,

---

[5] Siehe zum Beispiel 17:11-16, weiter V.C. Pfitzner, *Paul and the Agon Motif. Traditional Athletic Imagery in the Pauline Literature*, NT S 16, Leiden, 1967, 57-65.

[6] Van Henten, *De martelaar,* Kapitel 6.

[7] Einflussreich war O. Perler, 'Das Vierte Makkabäerbuch, Ignatius von Antiochien und die ältesten Märtyrerberichte', *RivAc* 25 (1949), 47-72.

[8] Van Henten, *De martelaar,* Kapitel 2 und 6.

[9] C.L.W. Grimm, *Viertes Buch der Maccabäer*, KHAAT IV, Leipzig, 1856, 317; vgl. 293f. E.J. Bickerman, 'The Date of Fourth Maccabees', in *Louis Ginzberg Jubilee Volume*, English Section, New York, 1945, 108.

[10] Dupont-Sommer, *Le quatrième livre*, 75-85.

und sie wurde von Williams schwer kritisiert.[11] Dagegen hat Bickermans Vorschlag einer Datierung in die ersten Dezennien des ersten Jahrhunderts, zwischen 18 und 54,[12] viele Anhänger bekommen. Hadas folgt Bickerman und präzisiert sogar die Periode. Er verweist auf die Wirren rundum den Befehl zur Aufstellung einer Statue für Caligula im Jerusalemer Tempel und denkt an die Regierungszeit Caligulas.[13] Kürzlich hat Collins der Datierung Bickermans und Hadas noch zugestimmt.[14]

Die Folgen einer frühen Datierung zeigen sich zum Beispiel in der Studie von Williams über die Wurzeln und den Hintergrund der neutestamentlichen Idee des Sühnetodes Christi. Williams nimmt zu Recht an, dass die Idee und Terminologie des Todes als stellvertretendes Opfer in klassischen und hellenistisch-griechischen Texten schon anwesend ist.[15] Für seine These, dass 4 Makk die Brücke zu den vorpaulinischen Formeln in Röm 3:24-26 und 1. Kor 15:3-5 bilde, und dass die Christen aus Antiochien wegen ihrer Kenntnis des 4 Makk zu ihrer Interpretation und der Auffassung des Sühnetodes Christi kamen, ist die frühe Datierung des 4 Makk unentbehrlich.[16] Dasselbe gilt mehr oder weniger für O'Neill, der zeigen will, dass Jesus selber seinen Tod als ein Exemplum für den kleinen Kreis der Jünger auffasste und dass dieser Märtyrertod von ihm und seinen Nachfolgern eine stellvertretende Bedeutung für alle Menschen habe. Er begründet diese Ansicht teilweise durch die Verweisung auf Passagen in 4 Makk über das reinigende und stellvertretende Sterben der Märtyrer und das Brandopfer Isaaks (6:29; 17:21 und 18:11).[17]

So hat die frühe Datierung des 4 Makk eine grosse Relevanz für die neutestamentlichen Sühnetexte. Die neueren Optionen für die frühe Entstehung stützen sich auf Bickerman, und darum wird die ingeniöse These Bickermans hier im einzelnen besprochen. Bickerman meint, dass der Tempel nach 4 Makk noch nicht vernichtet sei, weil 4 Makk den Tempel nennt, laut Bickerman in 4:20 und 14:9.[18] Schon deshalb ist ein Datum vor 70 vorausgesetzt. Weiterhin leitet er von der Erwähnung des Apollonios als Gouverneur von

[11] S.K. Williams, *Jesus' Death as Saving Event. The Background and Origin of a Concept*, Missoula, 1975, 197-200.

[12] Bickerman, 'Date', 105-112.

[13] Hadas, *Fourth Book*, 95f. Siehe Philo, *LegGai* 188.207ff; Josephus, *Bell* 2,184-203; *Ant* 18,261-309. Über eine Statue für den Tyrann erfahren wir in 4 Makk nichts.

[14] Collins, *Between*, 187.

[15] Williams, *Jesus*, 137-161.

[16] Vgl. den Schluss von Williams, *Jesus*, 253: *Thus did the author of IV Maccabees make available to early Christians, probably in Antioch, a concept in terms of which it was natural and meaningful for them to interpret the death of another man faithful unto death, Jesus of Nazareth.* Williams, 200-202, stimmt der Datierung von Bickerman und Hadas bei.

[17] J.C. O'Neill, 'Did Jesus teach that his death would be vicarious as well as typical?' in W. Horbury; B. McNeil, *Suffering and Martyrdom in the New Testament*, Cambridge, 1981, 19-27.

[18] Bickerman, 'Date', 108 Anm. 13, nennt 4:20 und 14:9. In 14:9 kommt der Tempel nicht zur Sprache; nur in 4:1-14, 16-18, 20 ist das der Fall.

Syrien, Phoenizien und Kilikien in 4:2 eine Präzisierung des Datums her.[19] Einer der Apollonioi in 2 Makk, der Sohn des Thraseas, war nach 2 Makk 3:5 nur Gouverneur von Syrien und Phoenizien. Aus dieser Verschiebung von 4 Makk gegenüber 2 Makk schliesst Bickerman, dass der Umfang des Bezirks die Situation zur Zeit der Entstehung des 4 Makk widerspiegele. Die drei Gebiete bildeten eine Provinz. Zum Beweis dessen führt er Gal 1:21 und Act 15:41, ein Zitat des Agrarhistorikers Columella (2,10,18) und eine Inschrift aus 86 oder später über den Ringkämpfer Flavius Artemidorus an, der zweimal den Pankrationwettkampf des κοινόν von Syrien, Phoenizien und Kilikien gewann.[20] Es ist fragwürdig ob diese Stellen die Verbindung von Kilikien mit der Provinz Syrien beweisen. In Gal 1:21 (..ἔπειτα ἦλθον εἰς τὰ κλίματα τῆς Συρίας καὶ τῆς Κιλικίας..) macht die Weglassung des zweiten τῆς mit u.a. Sin* und Min 33 wenig für den Beweis aus, dass beide Namen eine Provinz bezeichneten.[21] Die Stelle bei Columella bezieht sich auf die Sesampflanze. Columella sagt, dass er selbst in Syrien und Kilikien beobachtet hat (..*sed hoc idem semen Ciliciae Syriaeque regionibus ipse vidi*), dass diese Pflanze in den Monaten Juni und Juli gesät und im Herbst geerntet wurde. Schliesslich ist die Inschrift über Flavius Artemidorus jünger als 70 und sind die Siege in Antiochien nicht datiert. Diese Wettkämpfe wurden durch den Landtag von Syrien, Phoenizien und Kilikien organisiert. In einem solchen Landtag konnten noch längere Zeit Städte vertreten sein, die wegen einer Verwaltungsreform nicht mehr zum Gebiet der bezüglichen Provinz gehörten.[22] So verweist diese Inschrift höchstens auf eine unbestimmte Periode einer Union von Syrien und Kilikien. Man kann also darauf schliessen, dass die genannten Stellen nur von den Gegenden Syrien und Kilikien sprechen, ohne jeglichen Nachweis einer unierten Provinz von Syrien mit Kilikien.

Trotzdem hat Bickerman teilweise recht mit seiner Darstellung. Man muss jedoch das gebirgige und unwirtliche, westliche Kilikien, *Cilicia aspera*, auch

---

[19] Bickerman, 'Date', 109, nennt irrtümlicherweise 4:9. Diesen Fehler haben Hadas, *Fourth Book*, 95, und Collins, *Between*, 187, übernommen. In der zweiten und verbesserten Ausgabe in E.J. Bickerman, *Studies in Jewish and Christian History* I, AGSU 9, Leiden, 1976, 275-281, sind nicht alle Fehler korrigiert, auch dieser (siehe *Studies*, 278) und das Zitat von Columella nicht, das 2,10,18 sein muss und nicht 2,10,16, siehe 'Date', 110 Anm. 20 und *Studies*, 279 Anm. 21.

[20] Bickerman, 'Date', 109f. Siehe *CIG* 14 746 R. 15f: κοινὸν Συρίας Κιλικίας Φοινείκης ἐν Ἀντιοχείᾳ β ἀνδρῶν πανκράτιον. Diese Inschrift aus Neapel datiert von 86 oder später, weil R. 4-6 referiert wird an die ersten Wettkämpfe der grossen Kapitolinischen Spiele, die in 86 zum ersten Mal organisiert wurden, siehe G. Wissowa, art. 'Capitolia', *RE* III, 1527-1529.

[21] Dasselbe gilt für das Beibehalten des zweiten τὴν in Act 15:41.

[22] Vgl. schon Th. Mommsen, *Res gestae Divi Augusti*, Berlin, 1883, 173 Anm. 1, siehe weiter L. Moretti, *Iscrizione agonistiche greche*, Rom, 1953, 185. Anders J. Deininger, *Die Provinziallandtage der römischen Kaiserzeit von Augustus bis zum Ende des dritten Jahrhunderts n. Chr.*, Vestigia 6, München/Berlin, 1965, 87 (vgl. 83). J.-P. Rey-Coquais zeigt überzeugend, dass es eine vergleichbare Situation hinsichtlich der Städte östlich des Jordan wie Gerasa und Philadelphia gab, die seit Trajan zur Provinz Arabia gehörten, aber sich trotzdem am Kaiserkult des Landestages von Koilesyria in Damas beteiligten, siehe J.-P. Rey-Coquais, 'Syrie romaine, de Pompée à Dioclétien', *JRS* 68 (1978), 53f; idem, 'Philadelphie de Coelesyrie', *ADAJ* 25 (1981), 27-31.

Τραχεῖα oder Τραχειῶτις genannt (Strabo, 14,5,1), von dem wohlhabenden *Cilicia campestris* (Πεδιάς), an der östlichsten Südküste Kleinasiens, nordwestlich von Antiochien unterscheiden.[23] *Cilicia campestris* wurde 44 v. Chr., oder ein wenig später, mit der römischen Provinz *Syria* zusammengefügt.[24] Lokale Fürsten regierten *Cilicia aspera*, natürlich unter dem wachsamen Auge der Römer. Nach 38 n. Chr. regierte zum Beispiel Antiochos IV. von Kommagene über dieses Gebiet und ebenfalls über einen Teil von *Cilicia campestris.*[25] Vespasian beendete diese Situation ungefähr 72. Er zwang Antiochos IV. das Gebiet abzutreten und machte beide Kilikien zu einer Provinz, wie Suetonius, *Vesp* 8,4, entnommen werden kann.[26] Dieser Sachverlauf wird durch die Liste der uns bekannten Gouverneure von Kilikien bestätigt. Zwischen 44 und 72 n. Chr. sind keine Gouverneure einer Provinz Kilikien nachzuweisen.[27]

Die Datierung von Bickerman ist auf andere zeitliche Festlegungen der Union von *Syria* und *Cilicia campestris* gegründet, nämlich 18 und 54 n. Chr. Er schliesst das aus zwei Stellen bei Tacitus (*Ann* 2,58 und 13,8), und meint: *there is no evidence that in the reign of Augustus Cilicia did belong to Syria and, secondly, that it was already separated from Syria under Nero.*[28] Aber zeigen beide Stellen das wirklich? Tacitus erzählt *Ann* 2,58, dass Germanicus auf

---

[23] Siehe über die zwei Teile Kilikiens W. Ruge, art. 'Kilikia', *RE* XI, 385-389; G.A. Harrer, *Studies in the History of the Roman Province of Syria*, Princeton, 1915, 72-77; A.H.M. Jones, *The Cities of the Eastern Roman Provinces*, Oxford, 1971, 192-214, und T.B. Mitford, 'Roman Rough Cilicia', *ANRW* 7,2, 1230-1261.

[24] D. Magie, *Roman Rule in Asia Minor to the End of the Third Century after Christ*, I und II, Princeton, 1950, I, 418-433; II, 1271f.

[25] Jones, *Cities*, 205.208.210f.

[26] ..*item Trachiam Ciliciam et Commagenem dicionis regiae usque ad id tempus, in provinciarum formam redegit*, dazu Jones, *Cities*, 208; Magie, *Roman Rule*, I, 576; II, 1439f, der der Argumentation von Harrer, *Roman Province*, 74f, folgt, dass *Cilicia campestris* mit *Cilicia aspera* zusammengefügt sein muss, weil die Provinz sonst viel zu klein gewesen wäre.

[27] Siehe die Liste im Appendix 1D bei Magie, *Roman Rule*, II, 1594-1596. Die Liste soll wegen der Publikation einer neuen Inschrift erweitert werden mit P. Nonius Asprenas Caesius Cassianus, der ungefähr 72-74 Statthalter von Kilikien war und damit wahrscheinlich der erste kaiserliche *legatus* der Provinz *Cilicia*. Siehe für die Inschrift *AE* 1966 N. 486. Weiter B. Kreiler, *Die Statthalter Kleinasiens unter den Flaviern*, München, 1975, 120f; W. Eck, 'Prokonsuln von Asien in der Flavisch-Traianischen Zeit', *ZPE* 45 (1982), 149-151, und W. Eck, 'Jahres- und Provinzialfasten der senatorischen Statthalter von 69/70 bis 138/139, *Chiron* 12 (1982), 291 mit Anm. 38.

[28] Bickerman, 'Date', 111. Diese Argumentation erweitert er noch in E.J. Bickerman, 'Syria and Cilicia', *AJP* 68 (1947), 353-362. S. 358 nennt er eine Inschrift in der ein bestimmter Proculus *procurator* von Nero heisst: *proc(uratori) Nero[nis Cl]audi Ca[esaris] Aug(usti) Germa[nici pr]ovinciae [Capp]adociae et Ciliciae*, zie W.M. Calder, 'Colonia Caesarea Antiocheia', *JRS* 2 (1912), 99f. Diese Inschrift impliziert nach Bickerman nicht, dass Kappadozien und Kilikien eine Provinz formten, sondern, dass Kilikien nicht mehr zu Syrien gehörte, weil Syrien einen eigenen kaiserlichen Prokurator hatte. Diese Beweisführung ist nicht zwingend. Nach Calder hatte Proculus eine steuerliche Aufgabe. Ein finanzieller *procurator* wurde öfters über einen Bezirk ernannt, der nicht mit den provinziellen Grenzen zusammentraf, siehe z.B. C. Cassius Salamallas, der 98-102 *procurator* war von Lykien und Pamphylien (seit Vespasian eine Provinz) und Galatien, siehe R.K. Sherk, *The Legates of Galatia from Augustus to Diocletian*, Baltimore, 1952, 96. Vgl. Jones, *Cities*, 1937, 439 Anm. 30.

Wunsch des derzeitigen Königs der Parthen, Artabanos III., seinen Vetter und Konkurrenten, den in Rom aufgewachsenen und in 7/8 n. Chr. durch Augustus zum König der Parther gemachten Vonones, von Antiochien nach Pompeiopolis (d.h. Soli) brachte: *Vonones Pompeiopolim, Ciliciae maritimam urbem, amotus est.* Artabanos wollte lieber nicht, dass Vonones in Syrien in sicherem Gewahrsam gehalten würde (*..petere interim, ne Vonones in Syria haberetur*). Germanicus konnte das gegen den Willen des derzeitigen Gouverneurs Syriens, Cn. Calpurnius Piso tun, weil er in 18 das *imperium proconsulare maius* bekommen hatte und die Angelegenheiten im Osten in Ordnung bringen sollte. Das Verhältnis zwischen Germanicus und Piso war sehr schlecht.[29] Das Motiv von Artabanos ist deutlich. Er fürchtete die Einwirkung des Vonones auf die Klanhäupter der Parther, weil Vonones sich in Antiochien ziemlich nahe beim parthischen Gebiet befand. Denn Tacitus setzt die Bitte des Artabanos so fort: *..neu proceres gentium propinquis nuntiis ad discordias traheret.* Ausserdem hatte Vonones gute Beziehungen zu Piso, dessen Frau er sich zu Dank verpflichtet hatte. Germanicus konnte Artabanos bevorzugen und zugleich Piso einen bösen Streich spielen. So transportierte er Vonones von Antiochien in eine der westlichsten Städte Kilikiens, entlang der Küste mindestens 200 Km. von Antiochien entfernt. Das heisst, dass die Namen Syrien und Kilikien in dieser Passage nur eine geographische Bedeutung haben. Über eine Änderung der Provinzgrenze Syriens wird nichts gesagt.

Für die Datierung des 4 Makk ist vor allem die obere Grenze von Bickerman, 54 n. Chr., wichtig. In der Beweisstelle *Ann* 13,8 spielt wiederum ein Machtskonflikt zwischen dem Gouverneur Syriens und einem anderen hohen römischen Machthaber mit einem besonderen Kommando eine wichtige Rolle. Tacitus erzählt hier vom Verleihen einer speziellen Befügnis an Corbulo in 54, zum Behalten von Armenien. Wir kennen das Amt nicht genau, aber es betraf sicherlich eine militärische Aufgabe.[30] Der Legat Syriens, Ummidius Quadratus, musste die Hälfte seiner 'Bürger' und 'Bundesgenossen' Corbulo überlassen, d.h. zwei Legionen mit Hilfstruppen. Dazu marschierte Quadratus in die kilikische Stadt Aegae auf. Daraus schliesst Bickerman, dass Quadratus in Kilikien keine Gewalt besass und dass Kilikien deswegen von Syrien abgespaltet war. Die Pointe dieses Textes führt allerdings zu einer anderen Schlussfolgerung. Nach seiner Ernennung machte sich der kommunikativ begabte Corbulo unmittelbar in Richtung Armenien auf. Tacitus teilt mit, dass die Könige der Bundesgenossen und auch die Mehrzahl der Soldaten auf der Seite Corbulos waren. Quadratus fürchtete den Verlust seiner Autorität, wenn

---

[29] Tacitus, *Ann* 2,55-71.

[30] E. Stein, art. 'Domitius (Corbulo)', *RE* S III, 397, leitet von Tacitus, *Ann* 13,35 (*..et habiti per Galatiam Cappadociamque dilectus*) ab, dass Corbulo *legatus Augusti pro praetore* war. Siehe ebenfalls Sherk, *Legates*, 32-34. Vgl. das allgemeine *dux in Armeniam* bei Plinius, *Histnat* 2,47. Corbulo führte Krieg mit dem parthischen König Vologeses.

er Corbulo in Syrien einziehen lassen würde. Wegen seiner mächtigen äusseren Erscheinung und grossen Überredungskraft würden aller Augen auf Corbulo gerichtet sein. So kann man einen Teil von *Ann* 13,8 paraphrasieren.[31] Deshalb ist es verständlich, dass Quadratus Corbulo entgegenzog um ihn so schnell wie möglich zur Übertragung der Truppen zu treffen. Je weiter von Syrien entfernt, desto besser, so dass Quadratus nicht in Syrien durch Corbulo in den Schatten gestellt werden konnte. Aus dem Text geht nichts über eine grössere, geschweige definitive Trennung von Syrien und Kilikien hervor. Dass die Übergabe in Aegae stattfand, zeigt vielmehr, dass der Gouverneur Syriens ungeachtet der Präsenz Corbulos in Kilikien seine Verfügung über *Cilicia campestris* behielt. Die Gewalt Corbulos hatte auch keine spezifische Beziehung auf die 'Provinz' Kilikien.[32]

So entbehren die *termini post* und *ante quem* von Bickerman jeder Grundlage, und es gibt keinen Grund nicht am Jahr 72 als Zeitpunkt der Formation einer separaten Provinz Kilikien festzuhalten. Es ist jedoch auch hinsichtlich dieses Jahres fragwürdig, ob es als *terminus ante quem* fungieren darf. Auch die Art der Argumentation von Bickerman ist fragwürdig. Bickerman unternimmt nämlich zwei Schritte auf einmal, wenn er erstens voraussetzt, dass die Änderung einer faktischen Notiz, die auch irgendwo anders in einer verwandten Arbeit vorkommt, die Reminiszenz einer bestimmten historischen Situation bilde, und zweitens meint, dass dieser Text dann auch in dieser Periode geschrieben sein muss. Dieser zweite Schritt ist äusserst zweifelhaft und kann völlig falsche Interpretationen verursachen. Ein Beispiel aus 4 Makk zeigt das schon. Die Passage wird uns im weiteren noch von Nutzen sein. In 4 Makk 3:20 kommt der seleukidische König Seleukos Nikanor zur Sprache. Wir kennen verschiedene Seleukiden mit dem Namen Seleukos, und sogar einige mit dem Namen Seleukos Nikator.[33] In der betreffenden Passage von 2 Makk, welcher dieser Vers entlehnt sein wird, wird Seleukos IV. als 'Seleukos der König Asiens' angedeutet (3:3). Mit Bickerman könnte man argumentieren, dass es einen Seleukos Nikanor gegeben habe und dass 4 Makk zur Zeit seiner Regierung verfasst worden sei. Oder, wenn man annimmt, dass Nikanor eine Verschreibung von Nikator sei, dass 4 Makk zur Zeit von Seleukos I. Nikator († 281 v. Chr.) geschrieben sei, oder was vielleicht besser stimmen würde, zur Zeit von Seleukos VI. Epiphanes Nikator (96-95).[34] Es ist deutlich,

---

[31] *Ann* 13,8: *Qui (Corbulo) ut famae, quae in novis coeptis validissima est, consularet itinere propere confecto apud Aegeas civitatem Ciliciae obvium Quadratum habuit, illuc progressum, ne, si ad accipiendas copias Syriam intravisset Corbulo, omnium ora in se verteret, corpore ingens, verbis magnificis et super experientiam sapientiamque etiam specie inanium validus.*

[32] Tacitus, *Ann* 13,35 sagt z.B., dass Corbulo Rekruten in Galatien und Kappadozien aushebt, siehe Anm. 30.

[33] Siehe unten und Anm. 56.

[34] Unten S. 147.

dass ein solches Verfahren ungekannte aber auch einander widersprechende Möglichkeiten für eine Datierung bietet. Wenn man dem ersten Teil einer solchen Argumentation zustimmt, darf man nur die Schlussfolgerung ziehen: *in hoc tempore aut post hoc temporem*, das heisst, mit Bickerman, während 18-54 n. Chr. *oder* nach 54 n. Chr. Kehren wir zurück zum ersten Schritt. Derartige Änderungen können ein Hinweis auf das Datum sein, aber sie können ebensogut aus anderen Gründen in den Text gekommen sein.

Die frühe Datierung von Bickerman muss zurückgewiesen werden. 54 n. Chr. kann man nicht als *terminus ante quem* für die Entstehung des 4 Makk auffassen, und dasselbe gilt für den Zeitpunkt, an dem beide Kilikien wohl eine Provinz wurden, 72 n. Chr. Die Datierungen, die von Bickermans These abhängen, werden gleichfalls ungültig. Ein späteres Datum wäre gut möglich. Tatsächlich zeugt die Rede inhaltlich und formell für ein Datum nach 72. Laut Bickerman bestand der Tempel nach 4 Makk noch. Der Tempel kommt jedoch nur im 'historischen' Teil 3:20-4:26 zur Sprache, der nach Information und Tendenz aus 2 Makk 3-6 herrührt. 4 Makk kennt schon die Vorstellung des Vaterlandes; aber dieser Begriff hat in 4 Makk vielmehr eine ideelle oder spiritualisierte als reelle Bedeutung.[35] Gleichwie 4:2 sagt auch der Inhalt anderer Verse nur sehr wenig Konkretes über das Datum. Das gilt auch für den Ausdruck ζωγραφῆσαι in 17:7.[36] Uns bleiben nur generelle Anzeichen wie der Stil, das Vokabular oder vielleicht das Verhältnis zu den verwandten nichtjüdischen Märtyrertexten.

Norden hat den Stil des 4 Makk als asianistisch gekennzeichnet und Breitenstein hat das bestätigt.[37] Diese Feststellung nützt uns nur wenig zur Datierung, weil der Asianismus schon im 3. Jahrhundert v. Chr. bezeugt ist.[38] Dupont-Sommer setzt den Autor des 4 Makk in die sogenannte Zweite

---

[35] Van Henten, *De martelaar,* Kapitel 6.

[36] Dupont-Sommer, *Le quatrième livre*, 76, verwendet diesen Ausdruck auch als Argument für die Datierung ins 2. Jahrhundert. Er nennt das jüdische Verbot, Abbildungen von Göttern und lebenden Wesen zu schaffen (Josephus, *Ap* 2,75). Der Ausdruck ist wie die athletische Bildersprache in 17:11-16 metaphorisch gemeint und wird so schon 2 Makk 2:29 verwendet. Die Juden waren natürlich einigermassen bekannt mit der üblichen Sportpraxis wie mit der Malerei und den Verzierungen von Häusern usw. Die Wirkung der hellenistischen und römischen Dekoration auf die Juden war sogar ziemlich gross, wie schon die ältesten Synagogen in Israel aus dem dritten Jahrhundert zeigen und ebenfalls die Katakomben von Beth-Shearim, wo z.B. Gräber bekannter Rabbinen mit Bildern von Tieren und Menschen dekoriert wurden. Siehe z.B. N. Avigad, art. 'Chorazain', in M. Avi-Yonah, *Encyclopedia of Archaeological Excavations in the Holy Land* I, Oxford/Jerusalem, 1975, 302; N. Avigad; B. Mazar, art. 'Beth-She'arim', in Avi-Yonah, *Encyclopedia* I, 234-244.

[37] E. Norden, *Die antike Kunstprosa vom VI. Jahrhundert v. Chr. bis in die Zeit der Renaissance* I, Leipzig/Berlin, 1915, 419, Breitenstein, *Beobachtungen*, 130.178f. Siehe zum Asianismus U. Wilamowitz, 'Asianismus und Atticismus', *Hermes* 35 (1900), 1-52, und Norden, *Kunstprosa*, 131-149.

[38] In der Person von Hegesias von Magnesia a.d. Sipylos, siehe H. Hommel; K. Ziegler, art. 'Rhetorik', *KP* IV, 1402.

Sophistik.[39] Diese Bewegung wurde vor allem von Hadrian angeregt. Sie ist jedoch viel zu allgemein, um einige Gewissheit hinsichtlich der Datierung zu geben. Gerth weist daraufhin, dass die meisten griechisch schreibenden nachchristlichen heidnischen Schriftsteller zur Zweiten Sophistik gehörten.[40] Dasselbe gilt für die Meinung, dass 4 Makk zu den Früchten der Wiedergeburt der hellenistischen Philosophie gehöre. Ausserdem ist es gar nicht sicher, ob 4 Makk unmittelbar aus einer der Perioden der Judenverfolgung hervorgegangen ist. Der Autor beschreibt das Martyrium zur Zeit des Antiochos IV. Epiphanes, das für ihn Jahrhunderte her ist.

Abgesehen von der Spiritualisierung des Vaterlandes zeigt auch das Vokabular, dass 4 Makk wahrscheinlich nach 70 n. Chr. entstanden ist. Mit Hilfe der nützlichen Wortstatistik Breitensteins können wir den Wortschatz des 4 Makk mit anderen jüdischen und nicht-jüdischen Schriften vergleichen. Es ergibt sich, dass das Vokabular des 4 Makk weniger dicht bei der LXX als beim Neuen Testament steht.[41] Ein beträchtliches Teil der Worte, die 4 Makk nur mit den Apokryphen der LXX teilt, oder die sogar ganz in der LXX fehlen, kommen ebenfalls im Neuen Testament und bei den Apostolischen Vätern vor (165 der 569) und davon wieder 110 nur bei den Apostolischen Vätern.[42] Deshalb kann man feststellen, dass 4 Makk was das Vokabular betrifft den Schriften der Apostolischen Väter relativ nahe steht und wahrscheinlich rund 100 n. Chr. oder vielleicht noch später geschrieben wurde.

Diese Schlussfolgerung wird bestätigt, wenn man die heidnische und christliche Literatur über Märtyrertum oder verwandte Arten des Sterbens zum Vergleich heranzieht. Heidnische Genres und Traditionen wie der ἐπιτάφιος λόγος, der Tod des Philosophen, die Überlieferung über die *devotio* des römischen Feldherrn und die alexandrinischen Märtyrerakte, haben gewisse Aspekte mit 4 Makk gemeinsam, wie zum Beispiel die patriotische Tendenz der athenischen Grabrede und der alexandrinischen Akten.[43] Trotzdem ist 4 Makk am meisten mit den christlichen Texten verwandt, die ebenfalls religiös

---

[39] Dupont-Sommer, *Le quatrième livre*, 76-78.

[40] K. Gerth, art. 'Zweite Sophistik', *RE* S VIII, 722. Siehe die lange Liste der Autoren die zu dieser 'Bewegung' gehörten, Gerth, 731-772. Der Name ist Philostratus, *Vita soph* 2,27 entlehnt.

[41] Breitenstein, *Beobachtungen*, 16f, zählt die Eigennamen ausgenommen in 4 Makk 1582 verschiedene Worte. Davon sind 413 (26.2%) nicht belegt in allen sonstigen Büchern der LXX (a). Von den Worten die wohl in den andern Büchern der LXX belegt sind, begegnen wir 156 (9.9%) sonst nur noch in den apokryphen Büchern der LXX (b). Teilweise sind diese Worte direkt 2 Makk entlehnt, Breitenstein, 18. 174 der übrigen Worte sind weiter nur noch 1 oder 2 Mal in den Büchern der LXX belegt, die zum Hebräischen Kanon gehören. Zum Vergleich verwendet Breitenstein das Neue Testament. Von den 5436 verschiedenen Worten des Neuen Testamentes fehlen 1054 (19.4%) total in der LXX oder in den Büchern des Hebräischen Kanons in der LXX (a + b). Die Kategorie a + b ist bei 4 Makk 36.1%.

[42] Breitenstein, *Beobachtungen*, 21-24.

[43] Siehe z.B. N. Loraux, *L'invention d'Athènes. Histoire de l'oraison funèbre dans la 'cité classique'*, Paris, 1981, und H. Musurillo, *The Acts of the Pagan Martyrs*, Oxford, 1954, 253-258.

orientiert sind und viel mehr Reflektion über die Vorstellung des Märtyrertums bieten. Hier kann nur ein Beispiel dieser partiellen Verwandtschaft der Ideen und Mentalität gegeben werden. In 4 Makk zeigt die Figur des Märtyrers die wünschenswerte religiöse, politische und sozial-kulturelle Existenz der Juden. Der Märtyrer wählt in der Situation der Verfolgung zielbewusst den Märtyrertod und relativiert auf diese Weise die irdische Wirklichkeit. Der christliche Bischof Antiochiens, Ignatius, wurde ungefähr 110 verhaftet und zur Hinrichtung nach Rom transportiert. In seinem Römerbrief äussert er sich geringschätzig über 'diesen Aeon' und bezeichnet den Märtyrertod als die wahre Vollendung seines Lebens: 'Lasst mich reines Licht empfangen. Dort angekommen werde ich Mensch sein' (..ἐκεῖ παραγενόμενος ἄνθρωπος ἔσομαι, 6,2). Abgesehen von seiner spezifischen christlichen Theologie[44] hat Ignatius mit 4 Makk gemeinsam, dass nur der Märtyrer durch das Martyrium seine Existenz als Jude beziehungsweise als Christ bestätigt: 'Erfleht mir einzig Kraft, innerlich und äusserlich, damit ich nicht nur rede, sondern auch wolle, nicht damit ich nur ein Christ heisse, sondern auch (als solcher) erfunden werde! Denn wenn ich (als solcher) erfunden werde, kann ich auch so heissen und kann dann ein Gläubiger sein, wenn ich für die Welt nicht mehr zu sehen bin.' (3,2).[45] Man darf die Bedeutung dieser Gemeinsamkeiten nicht übertreiben. Die Briefe des Ignatius handeln bestimmt nicht nur vom Martyrium und auch das Vokabular des Ignatius ist nicht typisch verwandt mit 4 Makk. Aber diese und andere Ideen der christlichen Märtyrertexte kommen 4 Makk näher als heidnische Texte. Wenn wir das kombinieren mit dem über den Wortschatz gesagten, bedeutet das doch, dass ein Datum von ungefähr 100 oder etwas später wahrscheinlicher ist als eine Datierung in die erste Hälfte des 1. Jahrhunderts n. Chr. Ist das wirklich der Fall, dann muss das Verhältnis zwischen 4 Makk und den christlichen Märtyrertexten anders aufgefasst werden als in manchen Studien üblich ist. 4 Makk wird dann nicht mehr eine mögliche, oder sogar sehr wichtige Quelle für die christlichen Märtyrerschriften sein, sondern ein Werk, das ungefähr gleichzeitig mit diesen Texten entstanden ist.[46]

---

[44] Siehe für einen Überblick der Märtyrertheologie von Ignatius T. Baumeister, *Die Anfänge der Theologie des Martyriums*, Münsterische Beiträge zur Theologie 45, Münster, 1980, 270-289.

[45] μόνον μοι δύναμιν αἰτεῖσθε ἔσωθέν τε καὶ ἔξωθεν, ἵνα μὴ μόνον λέγω, ἀλλὰ καὶ θέλω, ἵνα μὴ μόνον λέγωμαι Χριστιανός, ἀλλὰ καὶ εὑρεθῶ. ἐὰν γὰρ εὑρεθῶ, καὶ λέγεσθαι δύναμαι καὶ τότε πιστὸς εἶναι, ὅταν κόσμῳ μὴ φαίνωμαι, Text und Übersetzung J.A. Fischer, *Die Apostolischen Väter*, München, 1956. J. Rius-Camps, *The Four Authentic Letters of Ignatius, The Martyr*, OrChrA 213, Rom, 1980, hält nicht sieben, sondern nur vier Briefe des Ignatius für authentisch, darunter den Römerbrief, siehe S. 134-136.

[46] Die These von Perler, 'Viertes Makkabäerbuch', 48-57, dass Ignatius von Antiochien 4 Makk gekannt habe, beruht vor allem auf der gemeinsamen Terminologie. Wie Perler selbst zugibt hat 4 Makk ebenfalls einige charakteristische Ausdrücke gemeinsam mit den anderen christlichen Märtyrertexten (z.B. *MLugd*, *MPol* und *1 Klem* 5-6). Die agonistische Metapher war jedoch Gemeingut in der ganzen antiken Welt, siehe Pfitzner, *Athletic Imagery*. Wir finden sie z.B. auch

Die Herkunft des 4 Makk ist wegen des nicht Vorhandenseins konkreter Information ebenfalls problematisch. Wir sind nochmals auf Einzelheiten angewiesen, die zufälligerweise den Schleier über der Stadt oder der Gegend kurz lüften. Weiterhin gibt der Inhalt natürlich eine globale Anweisung. Die historische Information beschränkt sich nahezu auf den kurzen Überblick über die Regierungszeit des Seleukos und Antiochos Epiphanes in 3:20-4:26, der 2 Makk 3:1-6:11 entlehnt ist. Nur in 18:5 zeigt sich nochmals, dass das Martyrium nach der Meinung des Schriftstellers in Jerusalem stattfand. Das Konzept des Vaterlandes ist sozial-ethisch geartet und ausserdem spiritualisiert. Das heisst, dass 4 Makk in der Diaspora geschrieben sein muss.[47] Die Zielsetzung der Arbeit ist in einer Diasporasituation auch viel verständlicher. Der stark rhetorische Charakter von 4 Makk setzt voraus, dass der Autor ziemlich gebildet war und zumindest die übliche Ausbildung als Ephebe genossen hat.[48] Einige Schriftsteller meinen, dass 4 Makk deshalb in einer der grossen Metropolen der Antike entstanden sei und nennen dabei Alexandrien.[49] Manche halten diese Bildung auch in der wichtigsten Stadt Syriens, Antiochien, für möglich, und laut ihrer Meinung hat diese Stadt wegen des Kultes der makkabäischen Märtyrer in Antiochien den Vorzug vor Alexandrien.[50] So hat Antiochien als Heimat des Verfassers viel für sich. Trotzdem geben zwei Verse in 4 Makk (3:20 und 4:2) eine etwas andere Richtung an.

Ein sorgfältiger Vergleich von 4 Makk 3:20-4:26 mit dessen Grundlage, 2 Makk 3:1-6:11, zeigt neben der von Bickerman aufgezeigten Verschiebung in 4:2 noch einige kleine Änderungen. Die oben absichtlich nicht ganz identifizierten seleukidischen Könige in 4 Makk 3:20ff sind im 2 Makk Seleukos IV. Philopator (187-175 v. Chr.) und Antiochos IV. Epiphanes (175-164 v. Chr.). Seleukos wird in 2 Makk 3:3 ὁ τῆς 'Ασίας βασιλεύς genannt.[51] Antiochos IV., nach 2 Makk 4:7 mit dem Beinamen Epiphanes, tritt als seleukidischer König ab 2 Makk 4:7 auf und wird weiter zum Beispiel 4:21 mit Namen genannt.[52] 4 Makk introduziert Seleukos als ὁ τῆς 'Ασίας βασιλεὺς Σέλευκος

---

bei Philo, Pfitzner, 38-48. Auch andere typische Worte sind nicht nur in 4 Makk, sondern auch bei Philo bezeugt, siehe Perler, 'Viertes Makkabäerbuch', 51.53f. So ist die These von Perler unbegründet. Vgl. auch die Kritik von Breitenstein, *Beobachtungen*, 22-24, und Baumeister, *Anfänge*, 287f.

[47] Siehe schon J. Freudenthal, *Die Flavius Josephus beigelegte Schrift Über die Herrschaft der Vernunft (IV Makkabäerbuch)*, Breslau, 1869, 107-112.

[48] Siehe H.I. Marrou, *Histoire de l'éducation dans l'antiquité*, Paris, 1948, 257-261; vgl. 268-282.

[49] Z.B. Grimm, *Viertes Buch*, 293; C.C. Torrey, 'Maccabees (Fourth Book)', *EB* III, 2283, und R.H. Pfeiffer, *A History of New Testament Times with an Introduction to the Apocrypha*, New York, 1949, 215.

[50] Dupont-Sommer, *Le quatrième livre*, 67-75; Hadas, *Fourth Book*, 98.109-113, und Williams, *Jesus*, 248-253. Zeichen eines (christlichen) Märtyrerkultes in Antiochien haben wir bei Augustinus, *Sermo* 300 (PL 38, 1379) und z.B. im Syrischen Martyrologium von Edessa aus 411, siehe F. Nau, *Un martyrologe et douze ménologes syriaques. Edités et traduits*, Patrologia Orientalis 10, Paris, 1912/1915, 19 R. 6f.

[51] Weiter erscheint seine Name noch 4:7; 5:18 und 14:1.

[52] Vgl. 2:20.

ὁ Νικάνωρ (3:20)[53] und Antiochos wird nach dem Tode dieses Seleukos als ὁ υἱὸς αὐτοῦ ᾿Αντίοχος ὁ ᾿Επιφανής vorgestellt (4:15).[54] Diese Namen und ihre Familienbeziehungen können sich kaum auf Seleukos IV. und Antiochos IV. beziehen. Antiochos IV. war der zweite Sohn des Antiochos III. und der Bruder des Seleukos IV.[55] Der Beiname Nikanor ist uns von Seleukos IV. nicht bekannt, und ebensowenig von einem anderen Seleukiden. Es ist äusserst unwahrscheinlich, dass der Namen ebenfalls 2 Makk entlehnt ist und dass Seleukos IV. in 4 Makk mit dem Feldherrn Nikanor von 2 Makk 8.14f identifiziert wurde. Der Beiname versteht sich aber leicht als Verschreibung für Nikator. Sowohl Seleukos I. wie Seleukos VI. hatte den Beiname Nikator.[56] Deshalb liest man in 3:20 am besten mit der alten syrischen Version Νικάτωρ.[57]

Diese Änderungen in bezug auf 2 Makk könnten reiner Zufall sein, weil der Autor von 4 Makk seine Abhängigkeit von 2 Makk verhüllen wollte oder keine Ahnung von der Geschichte hatte. Der äusserst rhetorische Stil und das komplizierte Vokabular setzen wiederum eine ausführliche Bildung voraus und das lässt eher das Gegenteil vermuten. Dann hat der Verfasser wirklich konkrete Seleukiden vor Augen gehabt. Seleukos I. liegt nicht auf der Hand, obwohl sein Nachfolger, Antiochos I. Soter, tatsächlich sein Sohn war. Wenn der Autor die Fürsten wirklich zielbewust änderte, wird er das mit Rücksicht auf seine spätere Zeit getan haben. Er wollte die Geschichte aktualisieren. Der zweite Seleukos mit dem Beinamen Nikator, Seleukos VI. Epiphanes Nikator, würde dann gut passen. Mit ihm kommen wir in die Zeit der letzten und wenig erhebenden Zuckungen der Seleukiden.[58] Diese vollzogen sich grösstenteils in Nordsyrien und auch in Kilikien. Seleukos VI. ergriff 96 v. Chr. das Szepter, indem er seinen Onkel, Antiochos IX. Kyzikenos, erschlug. Er konnte sich nur kurz an der Macht freuen. Wegen des Sohnes des Kyzikenos musste er bald nach Mopsuestia in Kilikien fliehen. Dort sammelte er wieder Geld, aber weitere Pläne wurden durch das Volk von Mopsuestia vereitelt, das seinen Palast in Brand setzte und ihn und seine Freunde tötete.[59] Sein Gegner und Nachfolger hiess wie in 4 Makk Antiochos, Antiochos X. Eusebes. Er war jedoch nicht der Sohn des Seleukos VI. und das stimmt nicht mit 4 Makk überein. Es fragt sich jedoch, ob der Verfasser alle Einzelheiten der äusserst komplizierten dynastischen Geschichte der Seleukiden zu seiner Zeit kannte.

---

[53] Vgl. weiter 4:3f,13,15.

[54] Weiter 4:21; 5:1,5 und 18:5.

[55] W. Sontheimer, art. 'Antiochos', *KP* I, 389.

[56] H. Volkmann, art. 'Seleukos', *KP* V, 86-89.

[57] Siehe R.L. Bensly, *The Fourth Book of Maccabees and Kindred Documents in Syriac. First edited on Manuscript Authority*, Cambridge, 1895, l.c. und xv.

[58] A. Bouché-Leclerq, *Histoire des Seleucides* I, Paris, 1913, 605-609, und A.R. Bellinger, 'The End of the Seleucids', *Transactions of the Connecticut Academy of Sciences* 38 (1949), 51-102, vor allem 72-75.

[59] Josephus, *Ant* 13,366-368. Vgl. Porphyrios von Tyros bei Eusebius, *Chron* (*FGrH* 260 F32,25f), und Appianos, *Syr* 69.

Antiochos X. war zum Beispiel mit Selene verheiratet, die auch die Frau seines Vaters, Antiochos IX., und seines Onkels, Antiochos VIII. Grypos, war.[60] Antiochos VIII. war wiederum der Vater des Seleukos VI. Dass der (wichtigste) Beiname des Antiochos X. Eusebes war und nicht Epiphanes, sagt wenig, weil zu dieser Zeit Epiphanes das Epitheton vieler Seleukiden war.[61] Vielleicht steckt hinter der Bemerkung über Antiochos in 4 Makk 18:5 wieder ein Hinweis auf Antiochos X.: 'da war er von Jerusalem abgerückt und wider die Perser (ἐπὶ Πέρσας) gezogen'. Mit den Persern waren damals die Parther gemeint und von Antiochos X. ist überliefert, dass er während eines Feldzuges gegen die Parther gestorben ist.[62] Es ist übrigens auch möglich, dass der Autor einen der noch späteren Fürsten mit dem Namen Antiochos meinte, der den Beinamen Epiphanes trug.[63]

Die letzten Beobachtungen sind natürlich einigermassen spekulativ. Verknüpfen wir sie jedoch mit der Hinzufügung Kilikiens in 4:2, dann erscheint es plausibel, dass die Verschiebungen bei den Königen Seleukos und Antiochos in 4 Makk 3:20ff gegenüber 2 Makk nicht zufällig sind, sondern durch Reminiszenzen der späteren Seleukiden als Seleukos IV. und Antiochos IV., auf jeden Fall Seleukos VI., und darum vielleicht Antiochos X. oder eines noch späteren Antiochos veranlasst sind. In beiden Änderungen in 3:20 und 4:2 schimmert die Gegend Kilikien hindurch. Ein schmählicher Tod wie der des Seleukos VI. in Mopsuestia wird bestimmt lange in der Erinnerung der Einwohner dieser Stadt weitergelebt haben. Aber neben Mopsuestia ist eine andere kilikische Stadt wie zum Beispiel Aegae, Seleucia oder Tarsos gut vorstellbar.[64] Philo nennt Kilikien im einzelnen als eines der Länder der Diaspora[65] und Josephus erzählt über Eheverbindungen zwischen Herodianern und Gliedern der örtlichen Adelsfamilien.[66] Weiterhin ist es gut möglich,

---

[60] Appianos, *Syr* 69.

[61] Neben Seleukos VI. Nikator Epiphanes kennen wir z.B. Antiochos VI. Epiphanes Dionysos (gestorben 142 v. Chr.), Antiochos VIII. Epiphanes Philometor Kallinikos Grypos (gestorben 96), Antiochos XII. Dionysos Epiphanes Philopator Kallinikos (gestorben 84). In dieser Gegend hatten im 1. Jahrhundert n. Chr. die Fürsten von Kommagene Antiochos I. und IV. den Beinamen Epiphanes. Siehe Sontheimer, 'Antiochos', 390-392.

[62] Siehe Josephus, *Ant* 13,369-371. Nach Porphyrios (*FGrH* 260 F32,27) flüchtete er zu den Parthern, nach Justinus 40,2,3 zog er sich zurück nach Kilikien, nach Appianos, *Syr* 49,70 wurde er durch den armenischen König Tigranes aus Syrien vertrieben. Siehe über Antiochos X. U. Wilcken, art. 'Antiochos', *RE* I, 2484f.

[63] Siehe Anm. 61. Besonders Antiochos IV. von Kommagene kommt in Betracht, weil er über einen Teil Kilikiens regierte, siehe oben. Anfänglich soll er gute Kontakte mit den Juden gehabt haben, er verlobte seinen Sohn mit Drusilla, der Tochter Agrippas. Die Heirat wurde nicht vollzogen, weil dieser Epiphanes sich weigerte die jüdischen Sitten (wahrscheinlich vor allem die Beschneidung) anzunehmen, Josephus, *Ant* 19,355; 20,139. Später sand Antiochos IV. Truppen zu Titus für den Krieg in Judea, Tacitus, *Hist* 2,81; 5,1; Josephus, *Bell* 5,460.

[64] Zur Zeit des Plinius gab es 3 freie Städte in Kilikien, Tarsos, Aegae und Mopsuestia, *Nathist* 5,91f.

[65] Philo, *LegGai* 281. Siehe ebenfalls Josephus, *Bell* 1,428.

[66] Die älteste Tochter Agrippas, Berenice, war eine Zeitlang verheiratet mit Polemon II.,

dass ein Rhetor wie der Verfasser des 4 Makk Bürger einer kilikischen Stadt war. Aus Tarsos kennen wir nicht nur den (später) christlichen Apostel Paulus, sondern auch den Sophisten und Redner Hermogenes, aus dem zweiten Jahrhundert n. Chr. Mehrere Inschriften bezeugen eine jüdische Bevölkerung in Kilikien.[67] Wer diese Änderungen in 4 Makk gegenüber 2 Makk ernst nimmt, kann zu keinem anderen Schluss kommen, als dass 4 Makk wahrscheinlich in einer kilikischen Stadt geschrieben wurde. Das reimt sich wie die Datierung um ungefähr 100 n. Chr. gut mit der Entstehung des späteren Märtyrerkultus für die Makkabäer in Antiochien.

Josephus, *Ant* 20,145f. Polemon II. war nicht nur König von Pontus (37-63), sondern hatte auch die Verwaltung über einen westlichen Teil von *Cilicia aspera*, siehe W. Hoffmann, art. 'Polemon', *RE* XXI,2, 1285-1287; Magie, *Roman Rule* II, 1407, und Jones, *Cities*, 208f. Vgl. Josephus, *Ant* 16,11.131.

[67] Aus *Cilicia campestris* oder *aspera* kommen her *CIJ* 783-4 (Seleucia a.d. Kalykadnos); 785-794 (Korykos) und 795 (Olba). Siehe ebenfalls 925, über einen Judas, den Sohn von Josè aus Tarsos. Vgl. Act 9:11; 21:39 und 22:3,28. Man soll den Inschriften des *CIJ* noch eine jüdische Grabinschrift aus Selinos zufügen, ausgegeben durch G.E. Bean; T.B. Mitford, 'Sites Old and New in Rough Cilicia', *Anatolian Studies* 12 (1962), 206f; Text *SEG* 20 N. 87. Siehe auch *BE*, 1965 N. 426.

TWO MESSIAHS IN THE TESTAMENTS OF THE TWELVE PATRIARCHS?

by

M. DE JONGE

1. *Introduction.*

1.1. Studies of Messianism in the Dead Sea Scrolls often include a discussion of the messianic expectations in the Testaments of the Twelve Patriarchs. Two early examples of this are A.S. van der Woude's important monograph *Die messianischen Vorstellungen der Gemeinde von Qumrân*[1] and J. Liver's 'The Doctrine of the Two Messiahs in Sectarian Literature in the Time of the Second Commonwealth'[2]. Van der Woude and Liver have been followed by many other scholars until the present day. Of recent authors I mention here M. Delcor[3], A. Caquot[4], A. Hultgård[5] and A.M. Laperroussaz[6]; we may also point to a number of publications of various nature aiming at a non-specialist

---

[1] Assen, 1957. See chapter II, 'Die messianischen Vorstellungen der Testamente der Zwölf Patriarchen', 190-216. The present author discussed Van der Woude's approach in great detail in the article 'Christian Influence in the Testaments of the Twelve Patriarchs', *Nov.Test.* 4 (1960), 182-235, now in M. de Jonge (ed.), *Studies on the Testaments of the Twelve Patriarchs. Text and Interpretation*, (S.V.T.Ps. 3), Leiden, 1975, 192-246 (see, especially, pp. 195-199 and 210-230).

[2] *H.Th.R.* 52 (1969), 149-185, now also in L. Landman, *Messianism in the Talmudic Era*, New York, 1979, 354-390, esp. 368-384.

[3] *D.B.S.* 51 (1979), V 'Doctrines des Esséniens', col. 960-980, esp. 'Le messianisme', 974-977. Delcor mentions the Testaments only in passing.

[4] 'Le messianisme qumrânien', in M. Delcor (ed.), *Qumrân. Sa piété, sa théologie et son milieu* (B.E.Th.L. 46), Paris-Gembloux-Leuven, 1978, 231-247 with only a short reference to the work of Van de Woude on p. 240.

[5] *L'eschatologie des Testaments des Douze Patriarches I. Interprétation des Textes*, Uppsala, 1977, see esp. Chapter I, 'Lévi et Juda' (pp. 15-81) and Chapter III, 'Le prêtre sauveur', pp. 268-381. For a convenient survey of his approach (concentrating on T.L. 18; T.Jud. 24 and T.D. 5:10-12) see his 'The ideal 'Levite', the Davidic Messiah and the Saviour Priest in the Testaments of the Twelve Patriarchs' in John J. Collins and George W.E. Nickelsburg (edd.), *Ideal Figures in Ancient Judaism. Profiles and Paradigms* (S.B.L. Septuagint and Cognate Studies 12), Chico Cal., 1980, 93-110.

[6] *L'attente du Messie en Palestine à la veille et au début de l'ère chrétienne*, Paris, 1982, 138-148. Regrettably, this author gives a very one-sided picture of scholarly opinion on the Testaments, following mainly A. Dupont-Sommer, M. Philonenko and A. Caquot, and a corresponding evaluation of the available evidence. (For his views on the Dead Sea Scrolls, see F. García Martínez's critical review of this book in *R.d.Q.* t. 11, no 43 (1983), 444-452).

audience, like P. Grelot, *L'Espérance juive à l'heure de Jésus*[7], G.W.E. Nickelsburg and Michael E. Stone, *Faith and Piety in Early Judaism*[8] and D. Dimant, 'Qumran Sectarian Literature' in M.E. Stone (ed.), *Jewish Writings of the Second Temple Period*[9].

In these publications particular attention is paid to the parallels in the Testaments to the doctrine of the two Messiahs, a priestly and a royal one, which is found in the Qumran documents. Scholars are well aware of the many problems in interpreting the relatively few texts in the Dead Sea Scrolls speaking about 'the agents of divine deliverance' (a felicitous phrase used by Nickelsburg and Stone) and they realize that the passages in the Testaments which deal with the future role of Levi and Judah and of 'agents' connected with these two tribes show a great variety, but a certain parallelism between the Scrolls and the Testaments is generally assumed.

1.2. This article will not deal with the question of the unity and variety of messianic expectations in the Dead Sea Scrolls and of developments in the views of the Qumran sect at this point[10]. It concentrates on the statements concerning the future in the Testaments of the Twelve Patriarchs and will defend a twofold thesis: (1) In delivering their testaments to their descendants the sons of Jacob predict a central role for the tribes of Levi and Judah in the history of Israel. (2) Wherever 'a human agent of divine deliverance' comes into the picture, there is only one: Jesus Christ. To prove this it will deal, first, with the passages speaking about Levi and Judah and, then, with two often quoted chapters,T. Levi 18 and T. Judah 24[11].

All along it will be necessary to emphasize that we have to try to explain the text of the Testaments *as it lies before us*. Long ago the present author discovered[12] that Charles's eclectic edition of the text which overestimates the importance of the Armenian translation (particularly in the passages dealing with the future) was not a reliable starting-point for critical study of this document. Preparation of a new critical edition was needed. After the

---

[7] (Collection 'Jésus et Jésus-Christ' 6), Paris, 1978, 77-86.

[8] Philadelphia, 1983. Pp. 168-177 in their Chapter 5 'The Agents of Divine Deliverance' are devoted to the Testaments and the Dead Sea Scrolls (in this order!).

[9] (Compendia Rerum Iudaicarum ad Novum Testamentum II,2), Assen-Philadelphia, 1984, Chapter 12 (pp. 483-550), see especially pp. 538-542.

[10] On this see M. de Jonge, 'The Role of Intermediaries in God's Final Intervention in the Future according to the Qumran Scrolls' in O. Michel *et al.*, *Studies on the Jewish Background of the New Testament*, Assen, 1969, 44-63.

[11] For a more detailed treatment of the passages concerned, see H.W. Hollander and M. de Jonge, *The Testaments of the Twelve Patriarchs. A Commentary* (S.V.T.Ps. 8), Leiden, 1985, *in loc.*; see also INTRODUCTION par. 7 'Expectations concerning the Future in the Testaments'.

[12] See *The Testaments of the Twelve Patriarchs. A Study of their Text, Composition and Origin*, Assen, 1953 (^{2}1975), Chapter I, pp. 13-36.

appearance of this edition in 1978[13] it is, unfortunately, still necessary to warn against *ad hoc* selection of readings in difficult places, using the evidence of the Armenian translation where it seems 'less Christian' and employing textual criticism to solve literary-critical problems[14]. Apart from these basic considerations, we shall have to ask whether it is at all possible to reconstruct the 'messianic' views of the Testaments in an earlier pre-christian form or even, as some scholars have attempted to do, to detect different stages in the development of the views of the group which produced the Testaments and handed them on[15]. In other words, the question is whether the available evidence allows us to reconstruct the complex process of interpolation or redaction which led to the great variety in the passages concerned, or to explain this as the result of a long process of transmission.

Finally, it should be stressed that there is no evidence whatever that the Testaments originated, or were read, in the Qumran sect. They are a document written in Greek which uses much Jewish traditional material; among other things it incorporates notions which are also found in the Dead Sea Scrolls, and shows acquaintance with Aramaic and Hebrew material found at Qumran[16]. For our present subject it is necessary to note that the present Testament of Levi shows numerous points of contact with fragments of an Aramaic Levi document found at Qumran (and known earlier from fragmentary texts found in the Cairo Genizah as well as Greek additions to Ms *e*). It is difficult, if not impossible, to define the exact literary and historical relationship between the Testaments and the Levi material preserved in Aramaic (and Greek). It is likely, that the present testament was modelled upon a Levi document. The Aramaic Levi document reconstructed from the various fragments gives us some idea as to how the author of the Testaments worked (in general he produced a shorter text leaving out the elements which did not suit his purpose), but many details remain obscure. But we should remember that similarity of ideas or literary relationship (of some sort) do not prove a common (or at least closely related) origin or a continuous development.

---

[13] M. de Jonge, H.W. Hollander, H.J. de Jonge and Th. Korteweg, *The Testaments of the Twelve Patriarchs* (Ps.V.T.G. I 2), Leiden, 1978.

[14] In this respect the current translations (with short notes) aiming at a non-specialist audience, J. Becker, *Die Testamente der Zwölf Patriarchen* (J.S.H.R.Z. III 1), Gütersloh, ²1980 and H.C. Kee, 'The Testaments of the Twelve Patriarchs', pp. 775-828 in J.H. Charlesworth, *The Old Testament Pseudepigrapha* vol I, Garden City-New York, 1983, have to be used with utmost caution. On dubious eclecticism and wrong use of the Armenian version in A. Hultgård's *L'eschatologie des Testaments des Douze Patriarches* II, Uppsala, 1982, see the present author's review in *J.S.J.* 14 (1982), 70-80. On the relationship between textual criticism and literary criticism see M. de Jonge, 'Textual criticism and the analysis of the composition of the Testament of Zebulun' in *Studies* (see note 1), 144-160.

[15] The most detailed analysis of this kind is found in A. Hultgård's studies mentioned in note 5.

[16] On this, and the following, see H.W. Hollander and M. de Jonge, *Commentary* (see note 11), INTRODUCTION, 3,1; 3,3; 3,4. On Greek as the original language of the Testaments see 3,8.

2. *The Levi-Judah passages.*

2.1. With the exception of Zebulun, Asher and Benjamin all patriarchs speak about the position of Levi and Judah in the history of Israel; the pseudepigraphical position chosen by the author enables him to include the period up to his own time as well as the future in the patriarchal predictions. The passages concerned show a clear similarity in form and structure and have, therefore, been grouped together as L(evi)-J(udah) passages[17].

Within this group there is considerable variety. In T.R. 6:5-7; T.S. 5:4-6; T.D. 5:4 (cf. T.N. 8:2) we find predictions of rebellion of the sons of the patriarch concerned against Levi and Judah. In these cases, as well as in a few other ones, we also find exhortations to obey these two sons of Jacob: T.R. 6:8, 10-12; T.S. 7:1-2; T.I. 5:7a-8; T.N. 8:2; T.G. 8:1; T.Jos. 19:6; cf. T.Jud. 21:1-6a; T.D. 5:9-10. More important for our purpose is that in a number of instances the predictions and the exhortations are followed by descriptions of the role assigned to the tribes (T.R. 6:5-7; 6:8, 10-12; T.S. 5:4-6; T.Jud. 21:1-6a; T.J. 5:7-8a; T.D. 5:4; cf. T.N. 5-6) and that in other cases the reason for obedience lies in the fact that salvation will come out (of one) of these tribes (T.S. 7:1f; T.N. 8:2; T.G. 8:1; T.Jos. 19:6; cf. T.L. 2:11; T.Jud. 22:2; T.D. 5:10).

2.2. The exhortation to obey Levi and Judah in T.J. 5:7-8a is very straightforward. These two tribes should be obeyed because the Lord glorified them; he 'gave an inheritance among them; and to the one he gave the priesthood and to the other the kingdom'. T.D. 5:4 explains that the predicted future rebellion of the sons of Dan against the two tribes will fail, 'for an angel of the Lord guides them both, because Israel will stand by them'.

In T.Jud. 21:1-6a we find a significant specification. Here the sons of Judah are exhorted to obey the sons of Levi and not to rebel against them because of the superiority of the priesthood (connected with heaven) to the kingship (which is concerned with earthly conditions)[18].

T.S. 5:4-6 focuses on Levi and mentions Judah only in passing. Here the rebellious sons of Simeon will be conquered by Levi 'because he will wage the war of the Lord'. This expression is reminiscent of 1 Sam. 18:17; 25:28 (cf. 17:47) where it is used in connection with David. In T.S. 5 *Levi* is the warrior

[17] See M. de Jonge, *The Testaments of the Twelve Patriarchs* (see note 12), 86-89.

[18] See in particular v. 4 which, however, mentions a significant restriction: 'As heaven is higher than the earth, so is the priesthood of God higher than the kingship on earth, unless it falls away from the Lord through sin and is dominated by the earthly kingship'. Remarkable is the transition to the second person singular in vv 5-6 (cf. a similar change in T.I. 5:4-5; do we find here (pseudo-) quotations from blessings directed to the patriarch?). We should also note the order of the sons of Jacob at the resurrection predicted in chapter 25. Levi is the first, Judah the second, Joseph the third etc. (v.1, see also v.2!).

of the Lord[19], as in the Shechem episode in T.L. 5-6, where the patriarch, in a heavenly vision, receives the blessings of the priesthood (5:2) and is given a sword and a shield by the angel who accompanies him, with the express command to execute vengeance on Shechem because of Dinah (5:3; cf. 6:1). The angel promises him 'I will be with you, because the Lord has sent me' (cf. 5:5-7).

T.R. 6 is complicated because it contains two consecutive L.J.-passages; Levi is, again, the central figure whereas Judah plays a very secondary role. Vv. 5-7 predict a rebellion which will be unsuccessful because God will avenge the sons of Levi, 'For to Levi did the Lord give sovereignty (ἀρχή) and to Judah, and with them also to me and to Dan and to Joseph to be for rulers'. There is a clear distinction between Levi and Judah, and the other tribes (cf. Num. 2:10, 18, 25); Levi is superior to Judah, for sovereignty belongs to him in the first place. In the second passage vv.8, 10-12 Levi is pictured as one who knows the law of the Lord, gives ordinances for judgment and sacrifices for all Israel. We also hear that 'he will bless Israel and Judah' (v.11). To this is, somewhat surprisingly, added 'the Lord has chosen him[20] to be king over all the nations'. His seed 'will die for us in visible and invisible wars and will be among you king for ever' (v.12).

Levi's task lies in the priesthood, as might be expected, and his priesthood is superior to Judah's kingship. It is this qualified juxtaposition of the two sons of Jacob that has attracted the attention of scholars studying the Dead Sea Scrolls. They have often pointed to a wider stream of tradition, represented by Jer. 33:17f; Ezek. 44-46; Zech. 4:14 (6:4-14); see also Sir. 45:6-26; 47; 49:11f; 51:12 (1-16) and, in particular, Jub. 31:9-23 (33:20). In the description of Levi's priesthood relatively little attention is paid to his sacrificial duties (T.R. 6:8; T.L. 2:10-12; 8:16-17; T.Jud. 21:5; T.L. 9:7-14)[21]. More emphasis is laid upon Levi as man of insight and teacher of Israel (T.R. 6:8, 10; T.L. 2:10; 4:2-6; 8:2, 17; 13 *passim*[22]). We notice that the distinction between priesthood and kingship is not upheld in those passages which describe Levi as a warrior (T.S. 5:4-6; T.L. 5-6) or as a ruler and a king (T.R. 6:5-7, 10-12).

This variety can at least partly be explained by the author's acquaintance with the Levi document. In the Ar. Levi document we find not only extensive instructions for sacrifices (compared to which T.L. 9:7-14 gives only scanty extracts) but also a 'Prayer of Levi' (already known in Greek, and recently

[19] Judah is only mentioned together with Levi in the adapted version of Jacob's prediction in Gen. 49:7 found in v.6.

[20] The most natural explanation is that the ἐν αὐτῷ refers to Levi and not to Judah who has just been mentioned beside Israel.

[21] Twice, in T.L. 14:5 and T.L. 16:1, we hear of gross neglect of the sons of Levi in carrying out their duties in this respect (cf. T.L. 9:9!).

[22] For T.L. 18:2-3; 7-9 see 3.1 below.

discovered in Aramaic) in which Levi asks for wisdom, knowledge and strength, and a long section parallel to T.L. 13 which speaks about the wisdom and the instruction of the sons of Levi[23]. The Shechem-episode in the Aramaic Levi fragments is, unfortunately, very mutilated but there is every reason to assume that the picture of Levi found in T.L. 5-6 corresponds to that of the Levi document, particularly, because Levi acts here as a new Phinehas (cf. Num. 25; 31:6) whose zeal was regarded as exemplary already in the time of the Maccabees[24]. Greenfield and Stone[25] remark that the Ar. Levi fragments consistently apply royal terminology to Levi. They point to 1Q 21 Levi fragm. 1 with the expression *mlkwt khnwt'* and Cambr. fragm. col c, 5-7 (corresponding to T.L. 11:4-6) where *qht* is explained in the same fashion as the verb *yqht* in Gen. 49:10[26]. We may add that Jub. 31 (more or less corresponding to T.L. 9[27]) records a blessing of Isaac for Levi and Judah (in this order), in which the sons of Levi are not only mentioned as priests but also as 'princes and judges and chiefs of all the seed of the sons of Jacob'[28] notwithstanding the fact that also Judah hears 'A prince shalt thou be, thou and one of thy sons, over the sons of Jacob' (vv 18-20).

2.3. The passages under discussion speak about the tribes Levi and Judah; in T.R. 6:12, however, there is reason to think that 'his seed' is not meant collectively, but refers to Jesus Christ as 'eternal king' who 'will die in visible and invisible wars'[29]. We note that in T.R. 6:8 Levi's teaching activity is limited to the period 'until the consummation of times (the times) of the anointed highpriest, of whom the Lord spoke'. This highpriest is announced by Levi himself in T.L. 18 but without mentioning that he will come from his tribe. His descendants are singled out as sinners against Jesus Christ in T.L. 4:4 and in T.L. 10; 14-15; 16. In fact, when Levi is appointed as priest in T.L. 5:2 we hear that he receives the blessings of the priesthood 'until I come and

---

23 See J.C. Greenfield and M.E. Stone, 'Remarks on the Aramaic Testament of Levi from the Geniza', *R.B.* 86 (1979), 214-230. On p. 226 they refer for this tradition to Deut. 33:10; Mal. 2:7; Sir. 45:17. We may also mention Deut. 17:8-13; 19:16-21; 2 Chron. 19:8-11; Ezek. 44:23-24.

24 See M. Hengel, *Die Zeloten*, Leiden-Köln, 1961, 154-188.

25 In the article cited in note 22, pp. 219 and 223.

26 The corresponding Greek text in Ms *e* has the expression αὐτὸς καὶ τὸ σπέρμα αὐτοῦ ἔσονται ἀρχὴ βασιλέων ἱεράτευμα τῷ Ἰσραήλ.

27 Which mentions a visit by Levi and Judah, but only instruction of Isaac to Levi. The corresponding part in the Ar. fragments does not mention Judah at all.

28 Vv. 14-15; cf. T.L. 8:17. See also the rest of v. 15 which emphasizes their teaching function: 'And they will speak the word of the Lord in righteousness, and they will judge all his judgments in righteousness, and they will declare my ways to Jacob and my paths to Israel. The blessing of the Lord will be given in their mouths to bless all the seed of the beloved' (cf. T.R. 6:8, 10-11a). See also the note on v. 15 in K. Berger, *Das Buch der Jubiläen* (J.S.H.R.Z. II,3), Gütersloh, 1981.

29 Cf. T.R. 4:10; T.D. 5:10, 13; T.Jos. 19:7 but also Justin, *Dial.* 34:2; 74:3; Eusebius, *In Pss.*, Ps. 90; *Ecl* I 14 and other early Christian parallels in H.W. Hollander - M. de Jonge, *Commentary*, *in loc.*

sojourn in the midst of Israel'. Finally, T.L. 8:14 announces 'a king' who 'will arise from Judah and will establish a new priesthood after the fashion of the Gentiles for all Gentiles'. In short: T. Levi glorifies Levi as the ideal priest-teacher, but predicts grave sins of his sons in the future, and a new priest of a different order, Jesus Christ[30].

The picture found in T. Judah is different. T.Jud. 21:1-6, quoted above, is followed by an announcement of the sins of the sons of Judah and divisions in Israel (21:7-22:1) leading to the end of Judah's kingship ἐν ἀλλοφύλοις 'until the salvation of Israel comes' (22:2). The clause which follows speaks about 'the appearing of the God of righteousness' who will bring peace to Israel and the Gentiles. Clearly Jesus Christ is meant who is regarded as a descendant of Judah. V. 3b states that the predictions about Judah's eternal kingship will be fulfilled in him. This is also said *expressis verbis* in T.Jud. 24 (the passage parallel to T.L. 18) which follows after another description, in T.Jud. 23, of the future sins of Judah's offspring and the punishment which is to follow until the Lord in his compassion will bring them back from exile.

The situation is no different in T.D. 5 where v. 4 (just mentioned) is followed by an announcement of the sins of the sons of Dan together with those of Levi and Judah (vv. 5-7) leading to exile and return after repentance (vv. 8-9). Then 'there will arise unto you from the tribe of Judah and Levi the salvation of the Lord' (v. 10a). The last sentence, again, introduces a long description of an eschatological saviour and the salvation effected by him (vv. 10b-13 plus most of ch. 6) which is, in many details, unmistakably Christian[31]. It should also be noticed that T.S. 5:4-6 is the beginning of a whole sequence of statements concerning the future, which ends, in 7:1-2, with another Levi-Judah passage connecting God's salvation with these two tribes; this passage, too, bears a Christian stamp (see v. 2b)[32].

2.4. Levi and Judah form the mainstay of Israel, but they envisage the future sins of their descendants. In the final stage of God's dealings with Israel and the world *one* 'agent of divine deliverance' will appear. In the Testaments, as they lie before us, this is Jesus Christ. In many of the passages already mentioned he is connected with Levi *and* Judah (T.S. 7:1-2; T.L. 2:11; T.D.

[30] For this view on T. Levi see also M. de Jonge, 'Levi, the sons of Levi and the Law, in *Testament of Levi* X, XIV-XV and XVI', in J. Doré, P. Grelot, M. Carrez (ed.), *De la Tôrah au Messie. Mélanges H. Cazelles*, Paris, 1981, 513-523. We should note that after 2:10 which speaks about Levi's proclaiming 'him who will redeem Israel' v. 11 explains: 'by you *and Judah* the Lord will appear among men, saving through them the whole race of men'.

[31] See my article, 'The Future of Israel in the Testaments of the Twelve Patriarchs' (to be published in *Journal for the Study of Judaism*), section 5.

[32] For the sake of completeness I mention here the role of Levi and Judah in the two visions in T.N. 5-6. In the versions found in the Testaments the unity between Levi and Judah is emphasized both in 5:5 and in 6:6. For further details (also on the relationship between this version and that found in Hebr. T. Naphtali) see H.W. Hollander - M. de Jonge, *Commentary*, *in loc.*

5:10). T.S. 7:1-2 specify that he will come from Levi 'as a highpriest' and from Judah 'as a king', but the (high)priest mentioned in T.R. 6:8; T.L. 8:14; 18:2 is not connected with Levi. The future king, however, will be a descendant of Judah (T.Jud. 22:3; 24) and not only in T.D. 5:10, but also in T.G. 8:1 and T.Jos. 19:6 which mention two tribes in connection with the future salvation, Judah is mentioned *before* Levi. T.N. 8:2 mentions Levi and Judah, but continues with the words 'for through Judah salvation will arise unto Israel and by him Jacob will be blessed'. Here we may compare T.S. 7:1 which connects redemption with Judah in particular (καὶ ἐν Ἰούδᾳ λυτρωθήσεσθε). In T.R. 6:12, however, the future 'eternal king' comes from Levi; in T.L. 18:3 the star of the new priest is said to 'arise in heaven, as a king'.

In short, we find that a number of different traditions concerning Levi and Levi *and* Judah were utilized, and that the Christian author/redactor incorporated this material in various ways, fitting it into his overall view on the place of Israel in God's history of salvation, and about Jesus Christ as saviour for the entire world[33]. It belongs to the task of the interpreter of the Testaments to acquire an idea about the traditions used by the author; the discovery of the Dead Sea Scrolls has increased the material which may be compared for that purpose. The finds at Qumran have not, however, put us in a better position to determine the contents of possible pre-Christian Testaments. Those who followed Charles's simplistic solution of bracketing only the unmistakably Christian expressions as interpolations[34] have never stopped at that. They, as well as others, have resorted to further literary critical operations, or to some theory of stages of redaction, to detect the supposedly less varied and more consistent messianic views in the reconstructed pre-Christian stage(s) of the present Testaments — which may, then, be compared with those in other documents. There is reason for considerable doubt, however, whether this approach will ever lead to more than hypothetical results. In any case our primary task is to look for consistent elements in the great variety in form and content in the text which lies before us. This point may be further illustrated by a short discussion of the important chapters T.L. 18 and T.Jud. 24 in the next section.

3. *The ideal priest and king in T.L. 18 and T.Jud. 24.*

3.1. The announcement of the coming of a new priest in T.L. 18:2 follows on the very complicated picture of a decline of the priesthood and a steady

---

[33] On this see again my article 'The Future of Israel in the Testaments of the Twelve Patriarchs', which deals with the passages on the resurrection of the patriarchs, the Sin-Exile-Return passages and the Levi-Judah passages dealing with God's salvation in the future.

[34] The brackets in his edition remain (too) suggestive until the present day, as many of the publications mentioned in section 1 show!

deterioration in the state of the people in the previous chapter. In 17:8-10 the Sin-Exile-Return pattern can be discerned. The return to the desolate country and the renewal of the house of the Lord is, however, followed by a new period of priestly sins (17:9) followed by vengeance from the Lord and a (definitive) failing of the priesthood (18:1). In a comparable way the announcement of the new king from Judah in T.Jud. 24:1 follows immediately after the Sin-Exile-Return passage in chapter 23; chapter 24 is appended to the phrase 'the Lord will both visit you with mercy and bring you up from captivity among your enemies' in 23:5.

There are many parallels between the two chapters, as is generally acknowledged. The new priest is 'both the recipient and the dispenser of revealed, saving knowledge of God'[35]. He 'will light a light of knowledge' and be as a sun on the earth (vv. 3-4), just as Levi himself would 'light up a bright light of knowledge in Jacob' and would 'be as the sun to all the seed of Israel' (4:2). We hear about the new priest's 'true judgement' (v. 2), the 'knowledge of the Lord' which is poured out (v. 5, cf. vv. 8-9 — the latter verse emphasizes the knowledge of the gentiles over against the ignorance of Israel). The parallel between T.L. 4:2-6 and the beginning verses of T.L. 18 (esp. vv. 3 and 7), the emphasis on knowledge and teaching (already found in Ar. Levi) and the fact that the chapter (see vv. 2, 5, 7) draws on the royal messianic oracle in Isaiah 11[36] (corresponding to royal elements connected with Levi's offspring in Ar. Levi) lead Nickelsburg and Stone to believe that chapter 18 corresponds to what must have been the climax of Ar. Levi. Unfortunately, however, the Genizah fragments break off somewhere in a passage which sings the praise of the wise man, corresponding to T.L. 13. There is a fragmentary text roughly corresponding to T.L. 14:3f — and that is all. We are, therefore, not in a position to know whether the author of T.L. 18 had any consistent picture of an eschatological priest before him or not, let alone, what it looked like[37]. Nickelsburg and Stone admit this when they write: 'Although we cannot be certain of the original shape of the Jewish form of this chapter, the Greek text is interesting as a bridge between Jewish speculations about the eschatological priest and early Christian views about Jesus as a priest'[38]. Even this cautious assessment of the situation, however, goes beyond the evidence.

One of the striking features of T.L. 18 is the clear reference to the story of the baptism of Jesus in vv. 6-7; it corresponds with a similar reference in

---

[35] So Nickelsburg and Stone, *Faith and Piety* (see note 8), p.70; they wrongly call him 'this latter-day descendant of Levi'.

[36] Compare v.3a 'And his star will arise in heaven, as a king'.

[37] J.T. Milik (who assumes some kind of treatment of weeks and jubilees in the document corresponding to T.L. 16-17) writes 'We shall never know how the author of the Aramaic Testament dealt with the final era, since chapter 18 has undergone very extensive Christian adaptation' (see his *The Books of Enoch*, Oxford, 1976, pp. 253f.)

[38] *Faith and Piety*, p. 168.

T.Jud. 24:2. The first verse of this chapter, corresponding to T.L. 18:3-4, reminds of Num. 24:17 LXX and Mal. 4:2 (3:20): 'and after these things a star will arise to you from Jacob in peace, and a man will arise from my seed like the sun of righteousness'[39]. The predicted son of Judah is called 'the branch of God Most High' (v. 4; cf. Gen. 49:9) 'the fountain unto life for all flesh' (*ibid.*.) and 'the sceptre of my kingdom' (v. 5; cf. Num. 24:17 M.T.). The patriarch announces 'from your root a stem will arise, and in it a rod of righteousness ...' (vv 5-6; cf. Isa. 11:1). This 'rod of righteousness' will judge the gentiles (Isa. 11:10) and save all who call upon the Lord (v. 6).

In both chapters we find a wealth of allusions to biblical prophecies; a detailed analysis shows that many of the texts referred to were also used as prophecies of Jesus Christ in the Early Church[40]. No matter how much Jewish traditional material went into the making of these two chapters, and in what way it reached the author of the present text, the patriarchal words in the form before us clearly made sense to an early Christian audience. The parallels between T.L. 18 and T.Jud. 24, and the emphasis on revelation, knowledge, righteous judgment and royal activity in both chapters are to be explained by the fact that they both spoke about the same saviour: Jesus Christ.

3.2. It may be useful to add a few remarks about A. Hultgård's exegesis of these two chapters in his 'The ideal 'Levite', the Davidic Messiah and the Saviour Priest in the Testaments of the Twelve Patriarchs' which gives a good idea of the traditio-historical analysis of the Testaments found in his two books on the eschatology of this document[41]. Hultgård posits three stages. First there was a non-Hellenizing Zadokite group (200-150 B.C.) which produced the 'Apocryphon of Levi' used in our T.Levi. At this stage there is already an idealization of the highpriest and the priesthood 'displaying them as models of purity, of zeal for the Torah and as bringers of divine wisdom' (p.95). The second stage is represented by the original Testaments produced by Levitic sages. They also dreamed of an ideal priesthood, assisted by the Davidic Kingdom, along the lines of Jer. 33:17-18. Hultgård admits that the Levi-Judah passages have been reworked, but in and behind them he still discovers this idea (see e.g. T.D. 5:4). Interestingly, he finds no expectation of a personal priest at this stage; there are, however, 'clear hints at the hope for the Davidic Messiah' (p.95) in T.Jud. 24:4-6, T.Jos. 19:8 and T.N. 8:2-3 (where v. 3 mentions Judah only!). Unfortunately the reconstruction of the

---

[39] For Mal. 4:2 see also T.Z. 9:8. As to Num. 24:17, a well-known proof-text in the Dead Sea Scrolls, we should note that our verse refers to the LXX-version and speaks about *one* person. The word 'sceptre' in v.5 may be a reminiscence of the Hebrew version of the verse — see also my discussion with Van der Woude and Philonenko in *Studies* (see note 1), 211-213.

[40] See H.W. Hollander - M. de Jonge, *Commentary* on these chapters.

[41] See note 5 above.

first two passages is very difficult and only possible with the help of the Armenian version which Hultgård (at least occasionally) values very highly. T.L. 18:2-14 and T.Jud. 24:1-3 (with T.D. 5:10-12) belong to a third stage at which the Testaments underwent a major redaction. On them Hultgård says: 'There are, however, other texts in the Testaments describing a coming ideal figure who is difficult to identify either with the ideal 'Levite' or with the Davidic Messiah. Nor is it reasonable to assume that the group which produced the Testaments could believe in all three figures simultaneously' (p.99). Although T.L. 18 no doubt incorporates elements belonging to stages one and two, it has been reworked so drastically as to form a new composition. And if T.L. 18 represents a different conception, then this must also be true of the parallel passage T.Jud. 24:1-3 which can easily be separated from 24:4-6. The same applies to T.D. 5:10-12. The (one) messianic figure found in these (and a few other) places may conveniently be called 'the saviour priest'. He combines priestly, royal and angelic elements; he overcomes the demons and evil powers, and is a universal saviour. Hultgård compares him to the idealized royal messiah in Pss. Sol. 17, the figure of Melchizedek in 11Q Melch and the Son of Man in the Similitudes of Enoch. A clear correspondance may be observed with the ruler cult and the expectations of coming saviour figures in the Hellenistic culture of the time.

Hultgård gives an interesting picture of a series of possible developments; he does not exclude, of course, final Christian additions. One may agree with him when he states: 'If we refrain from putting forward new hypotheses research will certainly not proceed' (p.94), but will immediately ask how a very complicated hypothesis like the one put forward by him can be verified. To make a comparison between what is left of the earlier Levi document and the Testaments is one thing. To distinguish two stages plus a Christian redaction in the admittedly heavily reworked Testaments must lead to a great number of assumptions which are only evident in the context of the overall hypothesis. Apart from that, Hultgård's textcritical methods and the use of textual criticism in his traditio-historical analysis are highly questionable[42].

4. *Final remarks.*

The interpretation of the passages concerning Levi and Judah and of those about the ideal priest and the true king of the future remains difficult — even if one restricts oneself to describing and interpreting the variety and the coherence, in and between the different passages.

The variety goes, at least partly, back to the use of different Jewish traditions concerning Levi and Judah and of the Levi document represented

[42] See note 14 above.

by the Qumran and Genizah fragments and the extra-passages in Ms *e*. The search for new parallel material and the study of traditions already known should continue. The more we get to know about the pre-history of the text and the activity of its author(s) the better. There are no clear traces of two 'agents of divine deliverance', one from Levi and one from Judah. Every time a 'messianic' figure appears, there is one, clearly Jesus Christ, who is connected with Judah, or with Judah and Levi. Once one takes seriously that the passages concerning the future intend to express a Christian point of view on Israel and the nations, and on Jesus as universal saviour, the consistency and coherence of the many different statements becomes clearer.

The passages under discussion should also be compared with (more or less) parallel interpretations of O.T. motifs in early Christian christology and eschatology. These, too, are by no means uniform: particularly as commentators of Scripture early Christian authors do not strive at a systematic presentation of beliefs.

One final example may illustrate this last point. The priest in T.L. 18 is priest for ever: 'there will be no one succeeding him for generations and generations for ever.'. This seems to be a reference to Ps. 110:4, a text quoted in Hebrews (cf. 5:6, 10; 6:20; ch. 7 passim) to prove that the priesthood of Jesus Christ (who is from the tribe of Judah) is of a totally different order than the levitical priesthood. Jesus Christ is called highpriest in 1 Clem. 36:1; 61:3; 64:1, Ignatius, Philad 9:1 and even 'eternal highpriest' in Polycarp, Phil. 13:2, Mart.Pol. 14:3 and Justin, *Dial.* 42:1[43]. The tendency to emphasize the differences between Jesus' priesthood and that belonging to the old dispensation did not encourage early Christian writers to look for possible connections between Jesus Christ and Levi. In fact, the explicit announcement: 'the Lord will raise up from Levi someone as a highpriest ...' would seem to be an unlikely statement to flow from the pen of a Christian author. Would not then at least T.S. 7:2 provide a clear proof of the existence of 'two Messiahs' in pre-Christian Testaments?

In a recent article[44] I have analyzed a number of places in the first Christian commentary on Genesis 49 and Deuteronomy 33, Hippolytus' 'Benedictions of Isaac, Jacob and Moses' which *does* connect Jesus Christ with Levi. In his commentary on Deut. 33:8-11 he quotes Ps. 110:4 and yet calls Christ a descendant of Aaron and Levi. In his commentary on Gen. 49:8-12 he admits

---

[43] Ps. 110:4 (probably also referred to in the ὃν εἶπε κύριος of T.R. 6:8) is often quoted in the *Dialogue*. Justin also uses the expression 'the eternal priest' (*Dial.* 19:4; 33:1; 34:2; 36:1; 42:1; 96:1; 118:2). See further the notes on T.L. 6:8 and 18:8 in H.W. Hollander - M. de Jonge, *Commentary*.

[44] 'Hippolytus' 'Benedictions of Isaac, Jacob and Moses' and the Testaments of the Twelve Patriarchs', *Bijdragen* 46 (1985), 245-260, section 4 'Jesus Christ, priest from the tribe of Levi'.

that Jesus, though clearly descendant of Judah, was from Judah *and* Levi as king and priest. For further details the study just mentioned may be consulted. Hippolytus (and others in the early church whose objections he answers in the second passage just mentioned) could connect Jesus as priest with Levi, notwithstanding the clear statements to the contrary in Hebrews T.S. 7:2 can be accounted for!

THE RELATION BETWEEN THE ANCIENT AND THE YOUNGER PESHIṬTA MSS IN JUDGES

by

P.B. Dirksen

The year 1972 saw the publication of the first volume of the Peshiṭta edition published by the Peshiṭta Institute of the University of Leiden under the auspices of the International Organisation for the Study of the Old Testament, six years after the appearance of the Sample Volume[1]. Both volumes included, among other books, Lebram's contribution to the Peshiṭta Project: the edition of the Syriac text of Tobit.

The critical apparatus in these volumes reflected earlier editorial policy: all textual evidence was included up to and including the 19th-century MSS. This policy was based on the sound consideration that the edition should make all evidence available so as to enable the user to make his own judgements. Yet, the work done in connection with the Peshiṭta Project made it more and more clear that the younger MSS did not contribute any valuable textual material. No reading peculiar to any of these MSS or to a group of related MSS has any claim to be preferable to the majority reading. It is true that in a limited number of cases younger MSS may preserve old readings, in which they differ from all or most other younger MSS, but this can only be ascertained if that reading is actually found in the old MSS. In general, no independent value for text criticism can be attributed to these MSS.

As early as 1960 M.H. Goshen-Gottstein had anticipated this judgement on the younger MSS in a plea not to include in the edition manuscripts later than the 10th century, except for 12a1, the well-known Buchanan Bible[2]. The

---

Abbreviations:

**List*: *List of Old Testament Peshiṭta Manuscripts* (Preliminary Issue), edited by the Peshiṭta Institute, Leiden, 1961.

*PIC: *Peshiṭta Institute Communication* (published in *Vetus Testamentum*)

* The writer is indebted to his colleague Mr. M. van Vliet for correcting the English text of this article in a number of cases.

[1] *The Old Testament in Syriac according to the Peshiṭta Version*, Part IV, fasc.6, Leiden, 1972; *The Old Testament in Syriac according to the Peshiṭta Version*, Sample Edition, Leiden, 1966.

[2] M.H. Goshen-Gottstein, 'Prolegomena to a Critical Edition of the Peshitta', in *Text and*

wealth of material collected and studied in connection with the Peshiṭta Project confirmed his findings and made it safe to actually execute this judgement in the following volumes. It is the merit of the sample and the first volume to give the user the material in full and in doing so to provide him with the means to check for himself.

The question remained where to draw the line between the MSS which should be disregarded and those which should be included as witnesses to the text of the Peshiṭta. In the second and following volumes this line was drawn between the 12th- and the 13th-century MSS. This new editorial policy had the merit of remaining on the safe side and of including the Buchanan Bible, which is the best witness to the text appearing in a number of later MSS[3].

This judgement on the younger MSS greatly reduced the number of the MSS to be considered for text-critical purposes. Yet, the question remained whether there was a possibility to further evaluate the remaining textual material and to discriminate between older and younger readings.

One of the most intriguing aspects of the text found in the MSS up to and including the 12th century is the fact that the early MSS up to and including some of the 9th century (to be referred to as 'ancient MSS') have a type of text of their own, with a number of readings found in some or all of them which are not found in the later MSS[4]. This was found to be true for Isaiah by Diettrich[5], for Lamentations by Albrektson[6], for Judges by the present writer[7] and for Exodus by Koster[8]. Further indications of it may be found in the Introductions to the volumes of the Peshiṭta edition already published. This raises the question as to whether the ancient MSS actually preserve an older text which through some cause or other all but disappeared[9], or whether the younger MSS together have a better text, in which case it must be assumed

---

Language in Bible and Qumran, Jerusalem/Tel Aviv, 1960, 163-204; also in *Scripta Hierosolymitana* 8 (1961), 26-67; 12a1 is MS Cambridge, Un. Libr. Oo.1.1,2; *List*, 4.

[3] See e.g. the Introductions to the volumes of *The Old Testament in Syriac* which have already appeared.

[4] For Judges the exceptions, already referred to in general, are 16g4, 18g4, 19g7. See the writer's *The Transmission of the Text in the Peshiṭta Manuscripts of the Book of Judges* (Monographs of the Peshiṭta Institute, Leiden, 1), Leiden, 1972; 5b1 (MS London Nat. Libr. Add. 14,425), containing Genesis and Exodus, stands apart with a deviating text. See M.D. Koster's study, mentioned below.

[5] G. Diettrich, *Ein Apparatus criticus zur Peshiṭta zum Propheten Jesaia* (BZAW viii), Giessen, 1905, xxvif.

[6] B. Albrektson, *Studies in the Text and Theology of the Book of Lamentations* (St.Th. Lundensia 21), Lund, 1963, 24.

[7] Dirksen, o.c., 40f.

[8] M.D. Koster, *The Peshiṭta of Exodus. The Development of its Text in the Course of Fifteen Centuries* (St. Sem. Neerlandica 19), Assen/Amsterdam, 1977, 143ff., 529ff.

[9] In his article 'East and West, Old and Young in the text tradition of the Old Testament Peshiṭta', PIC XIX, VT XXXV (1985), 468-84, the present writer has attempted to explain how it could come about that one MS provided the basic text for the later MSS, whereas the type of text found in the ancient MSS all but disappeared.

that their text goes back to one or more older MSS which have not been preserved, and that the present group of ancient MSS witness to a text deviating from it.

With respect to this question Koster made an important observation in his study on the Peshiṭta text of Exodus[10]. He found that in Exodus the early Nestorian MSS (9th- and 10th-century) differ little among themselves and together witness to a type of text which can be considered the basic text of all later MSS (his TR = Textus Receptus). This led him to the conclusion that one of the early Nestorian MSS actually had served as the source of this basic text. According to Koster this MS was 9b1[11], or a MS very close to it. This MS in its turn could well go back to 8a1[12].

It will be clear that Koster's view is of the utmost importance with respect to the question asked above. It would mean that the differences between the ancient and the younger MSS would have originated as deviations in the early Nestorian MS (9b1?) from the source MS. (8a1?). The consequence of it would be that all younger MSS can be disregarded for text-critical purposes, except for the early Nestorian MSS, or the one MS that was the source of the later readings, and even these MSS (this MS) could be disregarded if it could be ascertained that their (its) text goes back to 8a1. In that case it is in the ancient MSS (with or without the early Nestorian MS(S)) that we find the oldest form of the Peshiṭta text as far as MS evidence goes.

The aim of the following remarks is not to discuss Koster's conclusions as far as Exodus is concerned, but to take his lead and ask whether his conclusions are valid also for a book in another group of books, viz. Judges. If Koster's conclusions are correct we might expect that such an important development would have happened not just in one book, but before they can be applied to the Peshiṭta in general they have to be proven to be true with respect to other (groups of) books as well.

Three questions are to be asked:

1. Do the early Nestorian MSS together offer a text which is the basic text of the younger MSS?
2. If so, is then the early Nestorian MS to which the text of the younger MSS ultimately goes back one of the MSS known to us, and
3. how does this text relate to that of the known ancient MSS, especially to 8a1?

The early Nestorian MSS which need to be considered here are 9c1, 10c1, and 10c4[13]. The first two MSS have been dealt with in the present writer's

---

[10] Koster, o.c., 378, 531ff.

[11] 9b1: MS London, Nat. Libr., Add. 7145; *List*, 12.

[12] 8a1: MS Paris, Nat. Libr., Syr. 341; *List*, 37.

[13] 9c1: MS Paris, Nat. Libr., Syr. 372; *List*, 37f. 10c1: MS New Haven, Beinecke Rare Book Libr., B 47b; *List*, 32; 10c4: MS Cambridge, Mass., Houghton Libr. 137; M.H. Goshen-Gottstein,

study on Judges, the third became available only later on and its textual affinities have not yet been established. Therefore the text of 10c4 may be shortly described.

A part of Judges is missing, viz. 6:18-9:56. Folio 11 has been damaged, a triangular piece of it having disappeared. Moreover, on some folios the last few lines are illegible. The verses partly or wholly affected by these defects are 10:8-11:1; 11:9-18, 32-34; 12:9-12; 15:1-4; 15:19-16:2; 16:14-18; 18:3-5.

The MS has only one or two readings peculiar to it. In 11:24 it erroneously has *'allah* instead of *'allahan*, whereas in 19:9 it has *beṣafra* for *meḥar*, with, however, the latter reading in the margin, possibly from the copyist himself. In five other places the MS shares a reading with only one or two other MSS: in 2:20 it has *da'barw*, with final *waw*, together with 7a1 and five later MSS. In 5:5 it has *men* before *qedam* with 6h7 and 11c1, in 5:6 *pesaq* without final *waw* with 6h7, 8a1, 9a1 and three later MSS. In 21:8 (*seleq*) and 14 (*weyab*) it omits final *waw* together with 14/8a1. Everywhere else 10c4 agrees with 9c1 and 10c1 except for the places listed below, where one of these two MSS deviates from (almost) all other MSS.

When we now consider the three early Nestorian MSS together, it becomes clear that these MSS are closely related and that each one of them deviates from their common text only a few times. With the exclusion of orthographic details these deviations are the following:

9c1: There are six readings peculiar to this MS[14]. It omits a word in 18:9, and adds a word in 8:24 and 20:40. In 17:10 it has a clerical error. In the remaining two places, 9:49 and 19:7, the difference is over final *waw* in perfect forms.

10c1: This MS has seven unique readings[15]. A word is omitted in 5:9, 27; 16:27. In 6:18 the difference is over prefixed *waw*. In 21:3 the MS has *etpe'el* instead of *pe'al*, in 21:8 the preposition *be* instead of *le*. In 5:28 it reads *yetbat* instead of *yabbebat*. Moreover, in seven cases 10c1 stands apart together with one or only a few other *MSS*. This agreement seems to be purely accidental. The difference is over final *waw* in perfect forms in 1:33; 20:3; 21:24, over prefixed *waw* in 5:27, and between abs. and emph. state in 20:34. In 3:28 the preposition *le* is omitted and in 8:22 a word.

10c4: The readings which are peculiar to this MS or shared with one or only a few other MSS have been listed above.

Syriac Manuscripts in the Harvard College Library. A Catalogue (Harvard Sem. St. 23), Missoula, 1979, 23f.; cp. PIC XVII, VT XXXI (1981), 358.

[14] Dirksen, o.c., 20f. Judges 1:1-7:7 is missing. Approximately one quarter of each page is partly or wholly illegible.

[15] Dirksen, ibid.

Everywhere else the three MSS agree with each other. It is obvious that these MSS basically have the same text and that this common text is easily obtained when we simply disregard the deviations of each of these MSS mentioned above. There is, however, no reason to consider any of these MSS a copy of one of the other two in view of the readings peculiar to each of them. It would rather seem probable that all three MSS go back to a common source.

In passing it may be noted that from the small number of deviations it appears that these three MSS are the work of careful copyists, in contradistinction to most other MSS, both ancient and younger. In each of the three MSS their common text has been transmitted in almost a pure form.

It is now possible to deal with the three questions mentioned above.
The first is whether the three early Nestorian MSS share a type of text which can be considered the basic text of the younger MSS. The answer must be in the affirmative. When we disregard the deviating readings just listed, the three MSS (or where 9c1 or 10c4 is missing the other two) always support the younger MSS, when they differ from the ancient MSS and always agree with the majority of the younger MSS, or put otherwise: differences between the younger MSS are always caused by a deviation by a minority of these MSS (in most cases one MS or a group of related MSS) from the text found in these three Nestorian MSS. The conclusion to be drawn from this confirms that of Koster for Exodus: the common text of the early Nestorian MSS is the basic text of the younger MSS. This means that this basic text goes back either to one of these MSS or to another MS, no longer preserved, which either was derived from the same source, or was their common source itself. The text as it is now found in the various younger MSS and groups of related MSS is the result of a gradual branching out of this common root.

The second question, already implied in the above conclusion, is: has any of the known early Nestorian MSS actually been the common source of the later MSS? The consideration to be made with respect to this question is that one would expect at least the readings which are found in *all* younger MSS to occur also in their common source. The alternative would be that in different lines of text transmission all MSS would differ from this source MS in exactly the same way. This is very improbable. If we apply this consideration to the three early Nestorian MSS the answer must be that it is highly improbable that any of these was the source of the later MSS. Though the number of deviating readings is small, especially in 10c4, yet it would be hard to explain how all younger MSS would have happened to disagree with their ultimate ancestor in these places in the same way.

The alternatives were mentioned above. Do the younger MSS go back to another Nestorian MS, derived from the same source as 9c1, 10c1.4 and no longer extant? If this had been the case then we would expect readings in which this MS differed from the source MS to find their continuation in the later MSS. However, in no case do the younger MSS, together or in majority, differ from the common text of the three known early Nestorian MSS. This means that this unknown Nestorian MS would have been identical with the source MS. Since every MS is apt to differ from its *Vorlage* at least a few times, it would seem highly improbable that this MS ever existed. But there is no reason to dwell on this possibility anyway: instead of positing an intermediate MS identical with the source MS we may as well directly conclude that this source MS itself was the MS to which the younger MSS ultimately go back.

This leads us to the third question: can anything be said as to the relationship of this source MS to any of the ancient MSS?

For Judges there are five ancient MSS, apart from some fragments and a palimpsest: 6h7, 7a1, 7g1, 8a1, 9a1[16]. Four of these MSS need not be discussed here since the mere number of their unique readings precludes any possibility of any of them being the source of the later text tradition: 6h7 has 117 readings peculiar to itself, 7a1 106, 7g1 (with part of Judges missing) 36, 9a1 about 150 (including the readings shared with its direct descendant 17a8). There is no need to count the many readings where three or two of these MSS in various combinations differ from the early Nestorian MSS, the latter agreeing with the remaining one or two MSS.

The number of readings peculiar to 8a1, on the other hand, is much lower: seven.

> Twice the difference is over final *waw* in perfect forms (1:21; 19:9), once over the use of the suffix *he* (9:51), twice over prefixed *waw* (4:13; 10:14). In 19:17 a word is omitted and in 8:6 the MS has *le'abdayk* instead of *leḥaylak*.

In addition to these unique readings there are some thirty cases where 8a1 differs from the early Nestorian MSS with support of one or more of the ancient MSS, and in some cases with only one or a few younger MSS, whereas the Nestorian MSS agree with the remaining ancient MSS. It may suffice to give a few examples:

> In 1:33 8a1 and 6h7 have *baynat* instead of *bet*3°, found in 10c1.4 (9c1 is missing). In 3:19 8a1 and 6h7 omit a word whereas 10c1.4 have it with 9a1. In 11:5 *benay*2° is omitted, as in two younger MSS, whereas it is found in

[16] 6h7: MS London, Nat. Libr. Add. 14,438; *List*, 17; 7a1: MS Milan, Ambrosian Libr. B.21. Inf.; *List*, 28f.; 7g1: MS London, Nat. Libr. Add. 14,439; *List*, 17; 8a1: see note 12; 9a1: MS Florence, Bibl. Med. Laur., Orientali 58; *List*, 9. For a detailed survey of the unique readings in these MSS, see Dirksen, o.c., 1-7, 38.

the Nestorian MSS and the other ancient MSS. In 19:29 8a1 and 7a1 have *wašda*, whereas the three Nestorian MSS and 6h7, adding the feminine suffix, have *wašdah*.

Although the number of differences between 8a1 and the early Nestorian MSS is much smaller than is the case with the other ancient MSS, they still practically exclude the possibility that 8a1 served as *Vorlage* for the early Nestorian source MS. On the basis of textual evidence so far adduced, we can only say that the early Nestorian MSS stand much closer to 8a1 than to any of the ancient MSS.

We can, however, go yet a step further when we have a look at the corrections made in 8a1. 8a1 has been corrected in many places by a Nestorian hand. In Judges this has happened 46 times. Except for one or two cases the early Nestorian MSS agree with the corrected text.

The exceptions are 3:25 and possibly 6:18. In the first place 8a1^{c} reads *dela*, whereas the Nestorian MSS and almost all other MSS have *la*. In the second place 8a1^{c} has *w'esim*; 10c1 may have *'esim*, but the microfilm leaves some doubt. 10c4, unfortunately, breaks off just two words before.

In many of these 46 places 8a1^{c} is supported by one or more of the ancient MSS, but in twelve places 8a1^{c} disagrees with all other ancient MSS, to agree with the early Nestorian MSS (and the rest of the MSS). Some examples are the following:

In 1:15 8a1^{c} has *meṭul deb'ar'a* instead of *de'al 'ar'a*. In 1:26 *haw* is added and in 2:4 *kulhen* omitted. In 6:14 it has *meṭul d'at* instead of *w'at*. The other places are 3:28; 6:18; 9:26, 39; 12:3 (twice); 18:8; 20:12.

There can be no doubt that the corrected readings are related to the early Nestorian MSS some way or another. It could be assumed that 8a1 was corrected some time later on when the text of the early Nestorian MSS had established itself as the basic text of the later MSS, and that the new readings were taken from a later MS to adapt 8a1 to the current text[17]. Two observations, however, may make us pause before accepting this possibility. The first observation is that 8a1^{c} nowhere agrees exclusively with one particular MS or group of MSS, but always with the whole group of Nestorian + later MSS (in their common basic text). The other observation is that the corrector was quite serious about correcting 8a1, as appears from the number of corrections, including many which concern rather unimportant matters.

---

[17] So, e.g., Koster, o.c., 13.

Yet, he left many readings uncorrected in which 8a1 differs from any of the known MSS, or group of MSS, including more important textual deviations.

The best way to account for these observations is to assume that the MS from which the corrections in 8a1 were taken was also the *Vorlage* of the source MS of the early Nestorian MSS. It cannot have been this source MS itself, in view of the fact that 8a1 has not been corrected in a number of places where all three early Nestorian MSS go together. The suggested development would explain all differences between the ancient MSS and the younger ones, and the fact that 8a1^c stands halfway between them. These differences originated partly in this lost ancient MS as its unique readings, which subsequently were taken over in 8a1^c and in the Nestorian source MS, and partly in the latter MS when it was copied from the first. And so both sets of (originally) unique readings found their way into the early Nestorian MSS and the younger MSS. This development would also explain how the Nestorian MSS became relatively close to 8a1: if 8a1 was corrected on the basis of the lost ancient MS, then the two MSS must have been in Nestorian hands in the same place, which would make a direct relationship between these two MSS possible, even probable.

A final question remains yet to be answered. Through the whole of 8a1 a number of portions of text, which apparently had been missing, have been supplied by a later Nestorian hand, 14/8a1[18]. What is the relationship between the text of these portions and 8a1^c? Are they unrelated, from different hands and times or are they both from the same 14th-century hand? In the present writer's study on Judges it was said that the corrections and the later portions are 'probably' from the same 14th-century Nestorian hand[19]. Koster, in his study on Exodus is convinced that this is indeed the case[20]. If, however, as was argued above, the corrections of 8a1^c have been taken from a lost ancient MS, then it becomes dubious whether they were introduced by the 14th-century Nestorian hand. We would have to assume that this 14th-century reviser used this now lost ancient MS for the revision. This possibility is not to be excluded *a priori*, but there is a way to check this. It would be natural for this reviser to use the same MS from which he took the corrections, and which he apparently valued, for providing the missing portions in 8a1. These later portions then, should exhibit the same type of text as 8a1^c. This, however, is not the case. The text of this portion, beginning at 20:33, agrees in general with that of the younger MSS, as was to be expected. However, in no less than 31 cases does this portion have a reading which is either peculiar to itself or shared accidentally with only one or a few later MSS.

---

[18] *List*, 37.
[19] Dirksen, o.c., 6.
[20] Koster, o.c., 13.

In 21 cases the difference is over final *waw* in perfect forms (20:36, 42, 44, 48 (twice); 21:7, 8, 9, 10 (three times), 13 (twice), 14, 15, 16, 20 (twice), 23 (twice), 24), three times over prefixed *waw* (20:38; 21:4, 24), once over *seyame* (21:12). There are two additions (20:35; 21:12), and one omission (20:44). 14/8a1 has prefixed *dalath* instead of *lamadh* in 21:12. In 20:34 it has a feminine instead of a masculine suffix three times (twice the reading has been corrected by the addition of a *judh*; same hand?). In 21:12 it has *etpe'el* instead of *pe'al.*

If we realize that the corrector of 8a1 only once or twice introduced a small correction which is not found in the early Nestorian MSS, and that the later portion differs from these MSS 31 times, then it is clear that the corrections and the later addition do not come from the same source. We must assume that the corrections were introduced at an earlier stage and that later on the missing portion was supplied.

The above may be summarized in the following conclusions:
1. The basic text of the younger MSS is found in the early Nestorian MSS, 9c1, 10c1, 10c4.
2. The MS to which this basic text ultimately goes back is not any of these three MSS, but the same from which the latter derive.
3. That MS in its turn goes back to a MS related to 8a1.
4. The differences between the ancient and the younger MSS originated as two sets of unique readings, the first in the lost ancient MS, the second in the Nestorian source MS when it was copied from the former.
5. The corrections in 8a1 (8a1^{c}) were taken from that same lost ancient MS, and are unrelated to the portion added by a later Nestorian hand.

For text-critical studies the consequence of these conclusions is that the younger MSS can be disregarded. As the representative of their common text the best of the early Nestorian MSS (for Judges: 10c4), or possibly two of them, can be kept. Even this, however, is more than is strictly necessary. We may exclude the readings introduced by their source MS by going back to its *Vorlage*, to which we have a witness in 8a1^{c}.

KETMĀN

Zur Maxime der Verstellung in der antiken und frühislamischen Religionsgeschichte

von

Hans G. Kippenberg

Jürgen Lebram hat die Schranken, die zwischen jüdischen und heidnischen antiken Texten heruntergelassen waren, hochgeholt. Seine Studien haben die Verbindungen zwischen Jüdischem und Griechischem aufgezeigt. Die Gemeinsamkeiten, die dabei zutage traten, beruhten nicht zuletzt darauf, dass für sowohl Juden wie Griechen Religion eine öffentliche Sache war. Dem stimmten übrigens auch die Kirchenchristen zu. Daneben aber bildete sich vom 2.Jh.n.Chr. an eine andere Auffassung heraus: dass Religion vor der Öffentlichkeit verborgen gehalten werden darf und soll. Mein Beitrag zur Festschrift Lebram soll diese Auffassung dokumentieren und interpretieren. Ich möchte damit unterstreichen, dass das Prinzip von Öffentlichkeit die Religionsgeschichte nicht unbeeinflusst gelassen hat.

Untergang als Verschwinden aus der Öffentlichkeit.

Im Jahre 1896 erschien Max Webers Aufsatz: 'Die sozialen Gründe des Unterganges der antiken Kultur'. Was im Titel Untergang genannt wird, das ist allerdings in Webers Darstellung mehr eine allmähliche Umstrukturierung. Denn Weber zeichnet nach, wie die antiken Stadtgemeinden (im Westen) allmählich den feudalen Grundherrschaften weichen mussten und welches die Ursachen hierfür waren. Auch im Blick auf den Osten, wo die städtischen Bürgergemeinden dem Patrocinium erlagen, liefert Weber wertvolle Gesichtspunkte, wenn er feststellt: 'Die antike Kultur machte den Versuch, ihren Schauplatz zu wechseln, und verlagerte sich von der Stadt aufs Land.' Damit weicht Weber von einem organischen Verständnis vom Untergang ab und plädiert für ein soziologisches Modell. Einige dieser Strukturelemente dieses Modells sind detailliert studiert und diskutiert worden: etwa die Bürokratisierung des Römischen Reiches oder der Kolonat. Andere Elemente sind kaum oder gar nicht aufgegriffen worden. Eines davon führt auf religionshistorisches

Terrain. Ich möchte den Sachverhalt in der Form einer These mit Fragezeichen erläutern. M. Nilsson hatte beschrieben, wie die Kulte im antiken Griechenland anfänglich Eigentum von Geschlechtern waren, bevor sie zu öffentlichen Kulten der Stadtgemeinde geworden waren. Lässt sich nun am Ende der Antike gleichsam eine umgekehrte Entwicklung konstatieren: dass Kulte und Religion aus der städtischen Öffentlichkeit verschwanden und wiederum zum Eigentum naturwüchsiger Gruppen wurden?[1]

Wenn ich diese Möglichkeit untersuche, dann möchte ich dies nicht auf die naheliegendste Art tun. Ich möchte mich nicht in die Geschichte von Geheimkulten und staatlichen Religionsverboten vertiefen. Ich möchte vielmehr in der antiken und islamischen Religionsgeschichte Konzeptionen aufsuchen, die Religion als eine nicht-öffentliche Angelegenheit definieren. Wenn Anhänger einer Religion den öffentlichen Status ihres Bekenntnisses begründet und explizit fallenlassen, dann tragen bzw. trugen sie aktiv zu dem Untergang von Öffentlichkeit bei. Sie hätten ihn sozusagen selber zu verantworten. Ich finde es methodisch nebenbei notwendig, dem subjektiven Faktor bei dem Untergang der antiken Bürgergemeinde keine andere Rolle beizumessen, als bei ihrer Entstehung. Anders würde man mit zweierlei Mass messen.

Ich möchte das Thema noch ein wenig genauer einkreisen und daran erinnern, dass das öffentliche Eintreten für den Glauben sowohl im Judentum wie im Christentum hoch angesehen war. Das lässt sich recht klar an einem kleinen Detail zeigen. Es ist kein Zufall, dass der Begriff Ἰουδαϊσμός zum ersten Mal auftaucht als Juden sich unter Antiochus IV Epiphanes gegen den Ἑλληνισμός zur Wehr setzten (2 Makk. 2:21; 4:13; 8:1; 14:38), und dass auch der Begriff Χριστιανισμός bei einer der ersten Male in einem Märtyrerprozess fällt (Mar. Pol. 10,1). Juden und Christen teilten die Erwartung, dass der Glaube öffentlich, das heisst vor der Bürgergemeinde bzw. den Staatsbeamten, bekannt werden müsse. Man stösst hier auf eine gewisse Paradoxie, die in den christlichen Märtyrerakten offen zutageliegt: der Märtyrer bedarf amtlicher Institutionen. Christen fürchteten zutiefst eine reine Lynchjustiz. Nur die kaiserlichen Beamten garantierten ein ordentliches Verfahren, in dem der Angeklagte auch das Wort nehmen und sich bekennen konnte. Darum auch akzeptierten Christen die Prozessakte als Form ihrer Berichte über Martyrien. Weil das Martyrium auf eine bestehende Öffentlichkeit reflektiert, ist in Umkehrung dieses Sachverhaltes die Ablehnung des Martyriums ein ebenso sicherer Hinweis auf eine grundlegende Ablehnung der bestehenden Öffentlichkeit[2].

---

[1] M. Webers Artikel abgedruckt in *Soziologie * Weltgeschichtliche Analysen * Politik*, Stuttgart, 1968, 1-26; M.P. Nilsson in: Chantepie de la Saussaye, *Lehrbuch der Religionsgeschichte*, Band 2. 4.A, Tübingen, 1925, 387.

[2] Zum Begriff des Ἑλληνισμός: Chr. Habicht, '2. Makkabäerbuch'. In *Jüdische Schriften aus hellenistisch-römischer Zeit*. Band 1. Lieferung 3, Gütersloh, 1979.

Ehe ich diesem Phänomen weiter nachgehe, möchte ich mein Thema von anderen abgrenzen, die vage damit verbunden sind oder scheinen. Geheimhaltung esoterischer Traditionen, wie Juden und Christen sie praktizierten, hat evidenterweise nichts damit zu tun. Auch die Qumran-Essener hatten es ihren Mitgliedern zur Pflicht gemacht, den 'Männern des Frevels' auf Fragen nach Gesetz und Gebot (*torā wamišpat*) nicht zu antworten (1QS 5,15f) und 'den Rat des Gesetzes (*torā*) zu verbergen (*str*) inmitten der Männer des Frevels' (1 QS 9,17). Hier wird zwar die Wahrheit verborgen, nicht aber die Identität derer, die sie kennen. Diese Auffassung führt jedoch nahe an unser Thema heran. Erwähnen möchte ich auch noch, dass Bekennern zuweilen die Möglichkeit geboten wurde, scheinbar die geforderten rituellen Handlungen zu verrichten, während sie in Wirklichkeit ihrem Glauben treu bleiben konnten. Beispiel: dem jüdischen Märtyrer Eleasar wird geraten, 'er solle doch Fleisch bringen, das zu opfern ihm erlaubt sei, von ihm selbst zubereitet, sich aber so stellen, als ob er die vom König verordnete Portion vom Opferfleisch gegessen habe, damit er auf diese Weise dem Tode entgehe'. Eleasar lehnte solche Heuchelei (ὑπόκρισις) entschieden ab (2 Makk. 6:21-25). Diese Heuchelei ist vielleicht von vielen geübt worden, aber es ist darum lange noch nicht als Norm anerkannt worden. Dieser Punkt ist wichtig. Er zeigt nämlich, dass auch die schwerste Repression nicht dazu führen muss, das öffentliche Bekenntnis prinzipiell fallen zu lassen[3].

Es gab in der antiken und islamischen Religionsgeschichte Gruppen, die eine öffentliche Verstellung religiöser Identität erlaubten oder gar vorschrieben. Damit wurde die Religion der Öffentlichkeit entzogen. Religionsgeschichtlich gesehen betritt man hier unsicheren Boden. Wenn nämlich religiöse Identität nicht öffentlich verbindlich ist, dann fällt ein dringend benötigtes Instrument religionshistorischer Arbeit weg. Auch darum ist abzuraten, als verspäteter Ketzerverfolger auf die Suche nach untergetauchten Gruppen zu gehen, die sich dem Prinzip der Verstellung verschrieben haben. Es wäre dies eine aussichtslose Unternehmung, die auch in nichts als Fragwürdigkeiten enden würde. Ich wähle stattdessen eine andere Strategie. Ich suche und untersuche Konzepte, die die Praxis der Verstellung legitimiert haben. Dabei gehe ich davon aus, dass diese Konzepte Individuen dazu gedient haben, soziale Beziehungen zu bilden. Hypokrisis ist der entsprechende Begriff in griechischer Sprache. Ein wirklicher Schlüsselbegriff aber wurde erst das arabische taqīya bzw. das persische ketmān. Diese Begriffe wurden im schiitisierenden Islam ausgebildet. Zahllos sind die Beispiele dafür, dass sie subversives politisches Handeln legitimiert haben. Jedoch bedarf ein solches Konzept, soll es nicht blosse Anpassung beschönigen, einer verschworenen Gemeinschaft, wie viele

---

[3] G.A. Wevers, *Geheimnis und Geheimhaltung im rabbinischen Judentum*, Berlin, 1975.

gnostische Gruppen sie aus anderen Gründen bildeten. Nur wenn ein interner Diskurs der Wahrheit erhalten bleibt, gelingt ein Überleben.

Nicht alle Gruppen optierten von Anfang an für ketmān. Beispielsweise trieben Manichäer lange Zeit offene Mission. Erst spätere Zeugnisse von Augustinus (*Confessiones* IV,1) (4.Jh.n.Chr.) und von an-Nadīm (Fihrist tr. by B. Dodge 1970 S. 802) (10.Jh. abgefasst) zeigen eine hoffnungslose Lage, in der 'die Zurückgebliebenen ihre Religion verbargen' (an-Nadīm). Diesen Fällen möchte ich hier allerdings nicht nachgehen. Ich beschränke mich auf Konzepte, die es Gruppen gestattet haben, ihre Identität vor der Öffentlichkeit verborgen zu halten und die mittels der Verstellung eben diese Identität bewahrt haben[4].

'Sie geniessen das Götzenopferfleisch ohne irgendwelche Angst'.

Wir hören zum ersten Mal im Brief des Paulus an die Korinther (55 n.Chr.) von Christen, die 'im Götzenhause zu Tische liegen'. Sie können dies, weil sie stark sind (ἰσχυρός) und die γνῶσις haben (1 Kor. 8:10; 10:20-22). Der Verfasser der Apokalypse des Johannes (Ende des 1.Jh. in Kleinasien niedergeschrieben) wirft der Gemeinde von Pergamon vor, in ihren Reihen gäbe es Christen, die Götzenfleisch essen würden (Apok. 2:14f., 20). Mitte des 2. Jh. kommt Justin in seinem Dialog mit Tryphon auf dieses Thema erneut zu sprechen. Tryphon hält Justin vor, dass viele, die sich zu Jesus bekennen, 'Götzenfleisch essen und behaupten, keinen Schaden dadurch zu erleiden'. Justin muss tatsächlich bestätigen, dass es Lehrer im Namen Christi gibt, die den 'Macher des Ganzen' (ποιητὴς τῶν ὅλων) verleumden und an gesetzwidrigen (ἄνομος) und gottlosen (ἄθεος) Riten (τελετή) teilnehmen. Von denen heissen die einen Markianoi (sicher nicht die Markioniten HGK), andere Valentinianer, andere Basilidianer, andere Satornilianer und andere anders' (Dialogus 35,1.6.). Nich alles lässt sich mittels anderer Quellen überprüfen, aber doch einiges. Ich beginne mit Basilides, der unter den Kaisern Hadrian und Antoninus Pius (117-161 n.Chr.) in Alexandrien lehrte. 'Sie verachten aber auch das Götzenopferfleisch (*idolothyta*) und halten es für nichts, geniessen es vielmehr ohne irgendeine Angst (*trepidatio*)' (Irenaeus, *Adversus haereses* I 24,5).

Derselbe Gewährsmann Irenaeus, der sein Werk *Adversus haereses* um ca. 180 n.Chr. schrieb, weiss von den Vollkommensten unter den Valentinianern zu berichten: 'Sie essen das Opferfleisch bedenkenlos (ἀδιαφόρως) und meinen,

---

[4] Zur Struktur gnostischer Gruppenformung: H.G. Kippenberg, 'Gnostiker zweiten Ranges: Zur Institutionalisierung gnostischer Ideen als Anthropolatrie', *Numen* 30 (1983), 146-173; zum späten Manichäismus: G. Vayda, 'Die zindīqs im Gebiet des Islam am Beginn der 'Abbasidenzeit' (1938 erschienen). Abgedruckt in: G. Widengren (Hg.), *Der Manichäismus*, Darmstadt, 1977, 418-463.

dadurch nicht befleckt zu werden. Sie stellen sich zu jedem zu Ehren der Götzen veranstalteten Festvergnügen der Heiden als erste ein' (*Adversus haereses* I 6,3). Hier wird wiederum — wie dies auch die vorangegangenen Texte tun — vorausgesetzt, dass die Teilnahme am heidnischen Kult grosse Gefahren in sich birgt. Wer sich an den 'Tisch der Dämonen' (so anschaulich Paulus 1 Kor. 10:21) zu setzen wagte, der musste sich höherer Mächte versichert wissen. Auch die gnostischen Vollkommenen verwarfen den städtischen Kult als dämonisch, wie dies die Kirchenchristen taten. Für den normalen Christen bleibt es undenkbar, sich an ihm zu beteiligen. Nur 'die Vollkommensten von ihnen tun alles Untersagte ohne Scheu (ἀδεῶς)' (Irenaeus, *Adversus haereses* I 6,3). Es ist dies nebenbei eines der typischen Mittel, um aussergewöhnliches Ansehen zu erlangen: ein Held bricht mit einer geheiligten Tradition wie etwa dem Inzest-Verbot und demonstriert damit seine Überlegenheit über die bis dato geltenden Normen[5].

Wir hatten oben gesehen, dass die Christen, die sich heidnischer Opferhandlungen und Eidesleistungen verweigerten, brutal verfolgt wurden. Die Gnostiker blieben davon verschont, da sie zumindest äusserlich am städtischen Ritus teilnahmen. Es erstaunt darum nicht, dass Kirchenväter gelegentlich ihnen 'feige Täuschungen' (δειλίας σοφίσματα) vorwarfen (Clemens Alexandrinus, *Stromata* IV 16,3). Anfang des 3.Jh. klagte auch Tertullian in seiner Schrift *Scorpiace adversus Gnosticos* (in Karthago geschrieben): Wenn die Kirche Verfolgung erleidet, 'dann kommen die Gnostiker ans Licht, dann kriechen die Valentinianer hervor, dann sprudeln alle Gegner der Märtyrer hervor' (1,5). Jedoch wussten die Kirchenväter sehr wohl, dass viele Gnostiker dem Martyrium prinzipiell und nicht nur taktisch in Notzeiten jeden Wert absprachen. Schliesslich hatte ja der gnostische Christus selber nicht gelitten, sondern war von Jesus weggeflogen. Irenaeus bringt diese doketische Christologie in Zusammenhang mit der Ablehnung des Martyriums (*Adversus haereses* III 18,5). Das Martyrium ist eben einfach unnötig (IV 33,9). Doch dachten keineswegs alle Gnostiker so, wie K. Koschorke an Hand einiger Texte aus Nag Hammadi (*Apokryphon des Johannes* NHC I,2; weiter NHC VII 2,59 und VIII 2,138) zeigt und was auch die Fragmente des Herakleon, über die gleich zu sprechen sein wird, bestätigen[6].

Die Polemik der Kirchenväter hiergegen lässt zuweilen noch gnostische Reflektionen durchscheinen. Agrippa Castor, der eine 'Widerlegung des Basilides' geschrieben hatte, weiss zu berichten: Basilides 'habe gelehrt, es mache

---

[5] Zu *Korinth*: G. Theissen, 'Die Starken und Schwachen in Korinth'. In: *Studien zur Soziologie des Urchristentums*, Tübingen, 1983², 272-289; Heiligkeit durch *Normbruch*: L. de Heusch, 'Pour une dialectique de la sacralité du pouvoir'. In: derselbe (Hg.), *Le Pouvoir et le Sacré*, Brüssel, 1962, 15-47.

[6] Das patristische Material besprochen von W.H.C. Frend, 'The Gnostic Sects and the Roman Empire'. In *JEH* 5 (1954), 25-37 und von K. Koschorke, siehe Anm. 8.

nichts aus (ἀδιαφέρω) vom Götzenopferfleisch zu kosten und unbekümmert (ἀπαραφυλάκτως) in Zeiten von Verfolgung dem Glauben abzuschwören' (Eusebius, *Historia ecclesiae* IV 7,5-8). Man könnte dies so paraphrasieren: wer stark genug ist, um am Tisch der Dämonen zu liegen, der hat das Martyrium nicht nötig. Basilides hatte nämlich eine regelrechte Theorie der Märtyrer, die Clemens Alexandrinus bewahrt hat. Die Märtyrer leiden nicht etwa, weil eine Macht (δύναμις) ihnen nachstellt. Sie leiden, weil sie unbemerkt gesündigt haben, wobei Basilides auch mit Sünden in einem früheren Leben rechnet (Lehre von der Metempsychosis). Wer das Martyrium erleidet, reinigt sich mithin von dieser Sünde. Für ihn ist das Martyrium etwas Gutes (*Stromata* IV 81,1-83,2). Dass Basilides die Lehre von der Reinkarnation vertrat, bezeugt auch Origines *in Epistolam ad Romanos* V 1[7].

Nicht immer haben wir so ausführliche Begründungen. So notiert Origenes, dass Simon — um einen grösseren Anhang zu gewinnen — 'von seinen Jüngern (μαθητής) die Todesgefahr, die man die Christen zu wählen lehrte, wegnahm, indem er sie lehrte, dem Götzendienhst (εἰδωλολατρεία) gegenüber gleichgültig zu sein' (*Contra Celsum* VI 11). Dagegen sind wir über Argumentationen der Valentinianer wieder besser unterrichtet. Herakleon bestritt die Auffassung der Vielen, dass nur das Bekenntnis vor den Behörden (ὁμολογία ... ἐπὶ τῶν ἐξουσιῶν) wirklich zähle. Schliesslich könnten auch Heuchler das Bekenntnis mit dem Munde ablegen. Ausserdem hätten es nicht alle, die errettet wurden, abgelegt. 'Das Bekenntnis mit dem Munde ist nicht eine vollständige (καθολική), sondern eine partielle (μερική) Angelegenheit. Vollständiger aber ist das, von dem er jetzt sagt, es bestände in Werken und Taten entsprechend dem Glauben an ihn. Diesem (vollständigen) Bekenntnis folgt auch das partielle vor den Behörden, wenn es nötig ist und die Vernunft (λόγος) es rät' (Fragment 50 — Clemens Alexandrinus, *Stromata* IV 71f.). Diese Passage weist Berührungspunkte mit dem *Testimonium veritatis* auf, einem in Nag Hammadi gefundenen Traktat. Der Verfasser greift die in der Kirche zirkulierende Vorstellung auf: 'Wenn wir uns um des Namens willen dem Tod ausliefern, werden wir gerettet werden'. Doch fügt er hinzu: 'Aber so verhält es sich nicht' (NHC IX 34,1-7). Ein solches Zeugnis nur mit dem Wort und nicht mit Kraft beruht auf Unwissenheit (31,24). Auch eine andere Schrift der Bibliothek von Nag Hammadi, nämlich die *Apokalypse des Petrus*, sieht das so (NHC VII 79,11-21). Sie lehnt ebenfalls das Martyrium nicht rundweg ab, verwirft aber die Anschauung, es würde die Erlösung garantieren[8].

---

[7] H. Langerbeck, 'Die Anthropologie der alexandrinischen Gnosis'. In: *Aufsätze zur Gnosis*, Göttingen, 1967, 38-82.

[8] Zu dem Nag-Hammadi-Material liegen zwei vortreffliche Studien vor, die zugleich auch das patristische Material mitnehmen: K. Koschorke, *Die Polemik der Gnostiker gegen das kirchliche Christentum*, Leiden, 1978, 127-137 und E. Pagels, *Versuchung durch Erkenntnis*, Frankfurt, 1981, 120-156.

Die gnostische Verstellung, soweit sie aus diesen Texten deutlich wird, trägt die Züge eines bestimmten historischen Milieus. Sie reflektiert die Christenverfolgungen, in denen die Behörden die Christen zum paganen Opfer zwingen wollten. Und sie reflektiert weiter die Furcht, die Christen vor den paganen Kulten hatten. Der gnostische Vollkommene nämlich bewies seine Macht gerade darin, dass er diese Furcht nicht hatte. Er hat darum das Martyrium nicht nötig. Um es in den Begriffen unserer Eingangsüberlegung zu formulieren: die gnostische Position reflektiert noch die städtische Öffentlichkeit und deren Konflikte, entzieht ihr aber religiöse Relevanz.

'Verstellung in der Zeit der Verfolgung'.

Ich möchte zu zwei Fällen von Verstellung wechseln, die sich von diesem Typus entfernen und zugleich auf manche der schon besprochenen Texte noch ein anderes Licht werfen. In dem Buche *Elxai*, das Anfang des 2.Jh. geschrieben worden war, stand auch eine Aufforderung zur Verstellung. 'Er lehrt Verstellung (ὑπόκρισις) und sagt es sei keine Sünde, wenn jemand bei Gelegenheit in der Zeit einer drohenden Verfolgung Götzen verehrt, sofern er sie nicht aus Überzeugung verehrt und sofern er mit dem Munde und nicht mit dem Herzen bekennt... Ein Priester Pinehas aus dem Geschlechte Levis, Aarons und des alten Pinehas habe während der Gefangenschaft in Babylon die Artemis in Susa verehrt und sei so unter dem König Darius dem Todesverderben entronnen' (Epiphanius, *Panarion* XIX 1,8-2,1; 3,3 wird die Verstellung noch einmal kurz angeschnitten). Origenes bestätigt dies, wenn er von den Elkesaiten sagt, 'Er (Elxai?) lehrt, dass zu verleugnen gleichgültig ist und dass der, der dies versteht, unter Zwang zwar mit dem Mund, nicht aber mit dem Herzen verleugnet wird' (überliefert von Eusebius, *Historia ecclesiae* VI 38). Hier ist eine dualistische Anthropologie (Gegensatz Herz-Mund), die mit der Konzeption vom verborgenen Gott (von *'l* bzw. *ḥyl' ksy'*) zusammenhängt, mit einer Verstellung in der Verfolgungszeit verbunden worden. Legitimiert war dies durch ein ansonsten unbekanntes jüdisches Vorbild — das Gegenbild sollte man besser sagen zum Pinehas von 1 Makk. 2:26f. Damit verschiebt sich die Begründung der Verstellung. Begründeten die oben zitierten Gnostiker sie mit der Stärke der Vollkommenen, die vom Genuss des Götzenopferfleisches keinen Schaden davontragen, so Elxai mit der Abwendung von Todesgefahr. Bereits Origenes vermutet dies als Triebfeder der Simonianer. Ob auch der Bericht des Agrippa Castor über die Basilidianer so zu verstehen ist, wird man sich zumindest fragen müssen[9].

Der zweite Fall, den ich hier folgen lassen möchte, ist der der Paulikianer. Damit befinden wir uns bereits im 8./9. Jh.n.Chr., und zwar in Kleinasien. Die

[9] Zu den Elkesaiten: G. Luttikhuizen, *The Revelation of Elchesai*, Groningen, 1984.

Paulikianer waren heimlich in die orthodoxen Kirchen eingesickert und hielten ihre eigenen Lehren hinter einem 'rein verbalen Konformismus' (so die Beschreibung von P. Lemerle) verborgen. Petrus Siculus überliefert uns das Verhör eines Paulikianers durch den Patriarchen von Konstantinopel. Der Patriarch fragt ihn, warum er denn den orthodoxen Glauben geleugnet habe. Der Befragte aber bestreitet dies und verflucht die, die den orthodoxen Glauben geleugnet haben. 'Er nannte aber seine eigene Häresie orthodoxen Glauben'. Das Verhör geht in diesem Stile weiter und stets versteht der Paulikianer die offizielle Terminologie auf seine Weise. 'Wiederum über die heilige katholische und apostolische Kirche befragt, antwortet er ebenso, indem er die Versammlungen der Manichäer katholische Kirche nannte'. Der Angeklagte wurde daraufhin für unschuldig befunden (Petrus Siculus, *Historia Manichaeorum* 114-121). Die Paulikianer machten — wie Petrus Siculus erklärt — 'einen unstatthaften und ganz groben Gebrauch von der Allegorie' (*Historia* 14). Andere Berichterstatter bestätigen, dass die Paulikianer allegorisch zum Zweck der Verstellung sprachen und dass sie so der offiziellen Sprache paulikianische Bedeutung unterschoben (Petrus Higumenos 10f., 15; Photius 29 — beide Texte hg. von C. Astuc et alii)[10].

Die Paulikianer setzen den Untergang des Heidentums und den Sieg der Kirche voraus. Das Thema 'Götzenopferfleisch' war erledigt. An seine Stelle war das Thema 'Institution Kirche' getreten. War es notwendig, sich ihr anzupassen? Im berühmten Thomas-Evangelium findet sich eine pointierte Formulierung des Problems. 'Seine Jünger fragten ihn (Jesus) und sagten zu ihm: 'Willst du, dass wir fasten? Wie sollen wir beten? Sollen wir Almosen geben? Welche Speisevorschriften sollen wir beachten?' Jesus sagte: 'Lügt nicht, und das, was ihr hasst, tut nicht! Denn alles liegt vor dem Himmel bloss. Es gibt nämlich nichts Verborgenes, das nicht in Erscheinung treten wird, und nichts Verstecktes, das nicht enthüllt wird" (NHC II 2 Spruch 6). Die äusserlichen Handlungen sind für die Erlösung irrelevant, es zählt nur das Verborgene. Ich meine, dass man den Paulikianern eine ähnliche Auffassung zuschreiben kann, lehrten sie doch einen Dualismus zwischen dem bösen Gott dieser Welt und dem guten Gott der kommenden Welt (Petrus Siculus, *Historia* 36-38).

Etwas Anderes, Neues trat hinzu. Die Paulikianer waren streng organisiert. Die Allegorie auf ihren Lippen hatte auch mit militärisch-politischer Unterlegenheit zu tun. Wenn sie jedoch das Heft in der Hand hatten, dann liessen sie die Allegorie fallen. Verborgenheit hatte — zumindest implizit — die

[10] C. Astruc, W. Conus-Wolska, J. Gouillard, P. Lemerle, D. Papachryssanthou, J. Paramelle, 'Les sources grecques pour l'histoire des Pauliciens d'Asie Mineure. Texte critique et traduction'. In: *Travaux et Mémoires du Centre de Recherche d'Hist. et Civil. Byz.* 4 (1970), 1-227; P. Lemerle, 'L'histoire des Pauliciens d'Asie Mineure d'après les sources grecques'. In: *Travaux et Mémoires* ... 5 (1973), 1-144; N.G. Garsoïan, *The Paulician Heresy*, Paris/Den Haag, 1967.

Bedeutung von subversiv angenommen, der Gegenbegriff des In-Erscheinung-Tretens die Bedeutung von Aufstand. War bei den Elkesaiten die Verstellung ein Mittel, sich der Todesgefahr zu entziehen, so bei den Paulikianern, um unbemerkt Anhänger zu rekrutieren. Die Verstellung ist legitim, solange der böse Gott dieser Welt herrscht. Damit wird die Verstellung auf Dauer gestellt. Solange die Herrschaft des Falschen dauert, ist sie angebracht. Hier ist der Punkt erreicht, wo die wahre Religion definitiv der Öffentlichkeit entzogen und eine Angelegenheit verschworener Gemeinschaften wird. So wie oben die Gnostiker die Situation des Zerfalls der Bürgergemeinden voraussetzten und in ihre Konzeptionen einbezogen, so die Paulikianer den endgültigen Untergang der antiken Kultur.

'Wer keine taqīya *hat, hat keinen Glauben'.*

Es gibt keine Religion, die so auf Öffentlichkeit gespitzt war und ist, wie der Islām. Dennoch rechnen einige Suren des Qoran damit, dass der Gläubige in Notsituationen seinem Glauben öffentlich abschwört, um sein Leben zu erhalten. Sure 16,106 sagt allen Moslems, die frei und ungezwungen den Glauben verleugnen, Gottes Zorn an, 'ausser wenn einer (äusserlich zum Unglauben) gezwungen wird, während sein Herz im Glauben Ruhe gefunden hat'. Auf der gleichen Linie liegt auch Sure 3,28: die Gläubigen sollen nicht Ungläubige anstatt der Gläubigen zu Freunden nehmen. 'Anders ist es, wenn ihr euch vor ihnen fürchtet (von taqā)'. Sure 6,118 räumt ein, dass ein Moslem in einer Zwangslage Essensverbote verletzt. Taqīya hatte also ursprünglich die Bedeutung von Furcht, ehe es die Verstellung bezeichnete. Im Ḥadīṯ werden neben Fällen, in denen Anhänger Mohammeds sich für ihren Glauben töten liessen, auch solche erwähnt, in denen Mohammed billigte, dass ein Moslem in Gefahr von Not sein Bekenntnis verleugnete. 'Wenn der Machthaber zu jemand sagt: Du musst Allāh verleugnen, sonst töte ich dich, so steht es ihm frei' (Allāh zu verleugnen) heisst es bei Šaybanī.

In der frühen schiitischen Religionsgeschichte löste sich — ähnlich wie bei Paulikianern — die Verstellung von der Ausnahmesituation der Verfolgung und wurde eine umfassendere Maxime. Das ergab sich geradezu von selbst daraus, dass die Partei Alis und seiner Nachkommen permanent unterdrückt wurde. Der den Aliden wohlgesonnene Dichter Kumayt klagte darüber, dass er 'trotz seiner Liebe zu ihnen ... doch nur heimlich auf ihrer Bahn wandeln kann und eine andere Gesinnung vortäuschen muss'. Schliesslich scheint auch Ali selber seine Absichten verheimlicht zu haben, wenn man dem imamitischen Häresiographen al-Qummī glaubt[11].

[11] I. Goldziher, 'Das Prinzip der takijja im Islam' (1906 erschienen). In: *Gesammelte Schriften* Band 5, Hildesheim, 1970, 59-72; E. Kohlberg, 'Some Imāmī — Shīʿī Views on Taqiyya'. In: *JAOS* 95 (1975), 395-402.

Diese umfassendere Maxime ist in zweierlei Richtung weiter ausgearbeitet worden. Der imamitische Häresiograph an-Naubakhtī berichtet von einem Zweifel am husainidischen Imam Muhammad al-Bāqir (732 bzw. 735 n.Chr. gestorben). Ein gewisser ʿUmar b. Riyāḥ behauptete, er habe einst von al-Bāqir auf eine Frage eine bestimmte Antwort erhalten. Ein Jahr später habe er ihm dieselbe Frage noch einmal vorgelegt, nun aber eine entgegengesetzte Antwort bekommen. Er erhob gegen al-Bāqir Vorwürfe. Dieser aber antwortete: 'Unsere Antworten sind manchmal von taqīya diktiert'. Das aber akzeptierte er nicht, denn der Imam habe keinen Grund gehabt, ihn zu fürchten. Auch habe es keine weiteren Gesprächsteilnehmer gegeben. Es könne nicht jemand Imām sein, der widersprüchliche fatwās erteile (an-Naubakhtī 52f. übers. von M.J. Mashkur). Er trennte sich daher von der Gruppe um al-Bāqir und dessen Nachfolger Ǧaʿfar aṣ-Ṣadīq (gestorben 765), denn diese Gruppe hielt daran fest, dass ein Imam unter taqīya auch einander widersprechende Aussagen machen könne (an-Naubakhtī 56). Hier wird die taqīya zu einer Handlung innerhalb der schiitischen Gemeinschaft und ist nicht mehr nur eine Handlung gegenüber Anhängern der Umayyaden oder gegenüber Ungläubigen. Daraus folgte ein anderer Inhalt von taqīya: nämlich die Wortüberlieferung. Kann man den Ḥadīṯ denn noch glauben und sich ihnen anvertrauen, wenn Aussagen von Imamen auf Verstellung beruhen? Hierüber diskutierten und zerstritten sich sehr viel später im 18. Jh.n.Chr. die Akhbaris, die die Überlieferungen ('akhbār) zur allgemeinen Richtschnur schiitischer Urteilsfindung machen wollten, und die Usulis, die dem Konsensus ('iǧmā) und der Vernunft ('aql) der Muǧtahids vertrauen wollten. Letztere setzten sich durch, und zwar auch aus dem Grunde, weil die Überlieferungen der Imame zumindest teilweise aus taqīya entstanden waren. Doch war taqīya nicht ein Vorrecht der Imame, sondern wurde auch von Laien ausgeübt, ja sogar gefordert. 'Derjenige, der keine taqīya hat, hat keinen Glauben' (lā imān li-man lā taqīya lahu) (bei E. Kohlberg)[12].

Die Taqīya-Maxime wurde noch in anderer Weise ausgearbeitet und zwar im Zusammenhang mit dem Konzept der Verborgenheit (ghaybat) des Imam Mahdī. Als erste hatten Kaysāniten gelehrt, ihr Imam Muhammad b. al-Ḥanafīya sei im Berg Radwā verborgen und werde wiederkehren, um die Erde in Besitz zu nehmen. H. Halm zufolge fassten sie sein Verschwinden als Strafe auf. Doch wurde von den Imamiten später eine andere Begründung für die Verborgenheit des Imam gegeben: der Imam müsse sich vor den Feinden in Sicherheit bringen (aš-Šarīf al Murtaḍā (gest. 1045)). Es ist dies ein Vernunftbeweis dafür, dass der letzte Imam verborgen sein muss. Solange der Imam

[12] M.J. Mashkour, 'An=Nawbaḫti, Les sectes šiʿites'. In *RHR* 154 (1958), 90-95; zur Kontroverse zwischen Akhbaris und Usulis: A. Falaturi, 'Die Zwölfer-Schia aus der Sicht eines Schiiten: Probleme ihrer Untersuchung'. In: *Festschrift W. Caskel*, Leiden, 1968, 62-95; Zitat bei E. Kohlberg (s. Anm. 11) S. 396 mit Anm. 10.

verborgen ist, solange regiert auch taqīya das Handeln. Doch gilt auch das Umgekehrte: erwarten die Gläubigen die Rückkehr (rağʿa) des Imam Mahdī in allernächster Zukunft, dann steht auch das Ende der Verstellung bevor[13]. Hierfür noch ein Beispiel: Mehr als hundert Jahre nach dem unerwarteten Tod des für sie letzten Imams Ismaʿil, Sohn von Ğaʿfar aṣ-Ṣādiq (gest. 765), begannen ismailitische Missionare ihre Arbeit in verschiedenen Gebieten Irans (ca. 878 n.Chr.). Nizām al-Mulk, der sunnitische Wesir der Seldjuken, schildert in seinem Siyāsat-nāme, wie der Missionar Khalaf sich auf den Weg nach Ray machte. Er liess sich in dem Dorf Kulayn nieder und übte dort sein Handwerk der Stickerei aus. 'Er blieb dort, konnte aber mit niemandem über seine Geheimnisse reden, bis er nach tausendfachen Bemühungen einen auftrieb. Er lehrte ihn diese Religion (mazhab) und legte dar, dass sie die Religion der Leute des Hauses (ahl bayt) ist und verborgen (penhān) gehalten werden müsste, bis der Mahdī in Erscheinung träte. 'Sein Hervortreten ist nahe. Dann wird die Lehre öffentlich ('āškārā). Jetzt aber muss man sie lehren, damit ihr, wenn ihr ihn seht, nicht ohne Kenntnis der Religion seid" (ed. C. Schefer S. 185).

Taqīya bezeichnet das Handeln unter der Bedingung, dass der Mahdī noch nicht da ist. Selbst das treue Befolgen der islamischen Ritualgesetze konnte gegebenenfalls als Verstellung verstanden werden. Dafür ist das ismailitische Werk Haft Bab-i Baba ein Zeuge. Wenn der Qā'im erscheint, heisst es in ihm, wird 'der Schleier der taqīya, die die Tür der Šarīʿa ist', suspendiert (ed. W. Ivanow S. 21). Tatsächlich hat es einmal eine solche Suspendierung gegeben. Im Jahre 1164 n.Chr. rief sich einer der ismailitischen Herrscher über die Bergfestung Alamūt (Hasan II) als Qā'im aus und brach demonstrativ die islamischen Ritualgesetze[14].

Ich breche an dieser Stelle ab, obwohl auch noch Material aus späterer Zeit herangezogen werden könnte und sogar noch die Theologen und Ideologen der modernen Schia im Iran sich mit taqīya/ketmān (kritisch) auseinandergesetzt haben[15]. Ich hatte mir lediglich das Ziel gesteckt, zu zeigen, dass Religionen mit Überlegung und Absicht der Öffentlichkeit entzogen werden konnten. Ich möchte hier zwischen mehr objektiven Bedingungen, die die Handelnden vorfinden, auf der einen Seite und den Konzeptionen und Normen, die die Handelnden für richtig halten, auf der anderen Seite unterscheiden. Die Verstellung setzt sicherlich meistens voraus, dass Menschen wegen ihrer Überzeugungen bedroht werden. Doch zeigt der Blick auf jüdische

---

[13] H. Halm, *Die islamische Gnosis. Die extreme Schia und die ʿAlawiten*, Zürich/München, 1982, 55; A. Sachedina, 'A Treatise on the Occultation of the twelfth Imāmite Imam'. In: *StIsl* 48 (1978), 109-124.

[14] M.G.S. Hodgson, *The Order of the Assassins*, Den Haag, 1955.

[15] E. Meyer, 'Anlass und Anwendungsbereich der taqiyya'. In: *Der Islam* 57 (1980), 246-280.

oder christliche Märtyrerkonzeptionen, dass eine solche Bedrohung allein noch nicht zwangsläufig dazu führt, dass Verstellung eine religiös legitime Handlung wird. Die hier vorgelegten Textmaterialien bestätigen dies. In allen Fällen war Verstellung mehr als eine Notlüge: sie war Baustein in einem grösseren konzeptuellen Zusammenhang. Wenn Gnostiker sich am paganen Kult beteiligten, ohne ihre religiöse Identität zu verraten, dann spielte ein Konzept von 'Stärke' des Gnostikers mit. Elkesaiten und Paulikianer konzipierten Verstellung unter dualistischen Postulaten: die Welt des Mundes und die des Herzens gehören zu zwei einander feindlichen Reichen. Im Islam wurde die Verstellung anfangs als eine Art Notlüge in Verfolgungssituationen gestattet. Jedoch machten Schiiten (im weiten Sinne des Wortes: Anhänger Alis und seiner Nachkommen) daraus eine umfassendere Maxime. Verstellung herrscht, solange der Imām Mahdī noch verborgen ist. In allen diesen Fällen war Verstellung eine begründete Konzeption der Handelnden gewesen und konnte auch unabhängig von Verfolgungslagen Gültigkeit behalten. Das aber heisst: Untergang (als Verschwinden aus der Öffentlichkeit) kann eine begründete und überlegte Aktion sein.

Schlusshinweis: der polnische Verfasser Czeslaw Milosz, der 1980 den Nobelpreis für Literatur erhielt, geht in seinem 'Verführten Denken' auf ketmān ein als 'Kunst des inneren Vorbehalts'. Er sieht in ihm eine Chance der Intellektuellen in den 'Volksdemokratien', sich gegen die äusseren Umstände selber zu verwirklichen. Es ist dies eine einzigartige Verteidigung von ketmān.

DER AUFSTAND GEGEN GALLUS CAESAR

von

PETER SCHÄFER

Die Geschichte des spätantiken Judentums ist nicht sonderlich reich an herausragenden historischen Ereignissen. Dieser Mangel — zusammen mit einer ohnehin verbreiteten Tendenz, die jüdische Geschichte vorwiegend als Leidens- und Unterdrückungsgeschichte zu interpretieren[1] — hat die Historiker veranlasst, die wenigen vorhandenen Quellen nach allen, noch so versteckten, Hinweisen auf jüdische Aufstände gegen die verhasste römische Fremdherrschaft abzusuchen. Eine besondere Rolle spielt dabei der Aufstand gegen Gallus Caesar vom Jahre 351 n.Chr.[2].

Der Aufstand gehört in die Zeit der Nachfolgekämpfe der drei Söhne Konstantins I. — Konstantin II., Konstantius II. und Konstans — um das Erbe des grossen Vaters. Der Versuch einer gemeinsamen Herrschaft der drei Brüder als gleichberechtigte Augusti (ab 337), aber innerhalb der ihnen 335 von Konstantin I. zugewiesenen Verwaltungsbezirke[3], scheiterte bald. Konstantin II. versuchte, den jüngsten Bruder Konstans auszumanövrieren und Italien und Afrika seinem Herrschaftsgebiet einzugliedern, wurde von diesem aber im April 340 besiegt. Damit fiel Konstans die Alleinherrschaft über den gesamten Westen des Reiches zu, die er zunächst unangefochten ausübte, da sein Bruder Konstantius II. durch den 338 ausgebrochenen Krieg gegen die Perser im Orient gebunden war. Erst als Konstans seinerseits im Januar 350 durch den Usurpator Magnentius gestürzt wurde, musste Konstantius II. persönlich in den Kampf um den Westen des Reiches eingreifen. Im März 351 adoptierte er seinen Vetter Gallus und ernannte ihn zum Caesar des Ostens mit Sitz in Antiochia. Konstantius verliess den Orient und besiegte Magnentius — nachdem er ihm zunächst bei Atrans unterlegen war (Juni 351) — in der Schlacht bei Mursa in Pannonien im September 351. Obwohl die Kämpfe sich noch bis 353 hinzogen (im Sommer 353 beging Magnentius in Lugdunum Selbstmord), konnte Konstantius sich von da an als Alleinherrscher des gesamten Reiches betrachten. Die Herrschaft des Gallus als Caesar des Ostens

---

[1] Vgl. S.W. Baron, *History and Jewish Historians*, Philadelphia, 1964, 96: 'All my life I have been struggling against the hitherto dominant 'lachrymose conception of Jewish history''.

[2] Ich danke Herrn H. Blödhorn, Tübingen, und Herrn G. Reeg, Berlin, für wichtige Hinweise bei der Beschaffung der einschlägigen Literatur.

[3] Konstantin II: Gallien, Britannien, Spanien; Konstantius II: Orient; Konstans: Africa, Italien, Illyricum.

war nur von kurzer Dauer. Er scheint ein besonders grausames Regiment ausgeübt zu haben und wurde von Konstantius, der eine Erhebung befürchtete, Ende 354 unter dem Vorwurf des Hochverrats hingerichtet.

Die klassische Darstellung über den jüdischen Aufstand unter Gallus findet sich in dem Standardwerk von M. Avi-Yonah: *Geschichte der Juden im Zeitalter des Talmud*[4]. Da der Aufstand in einigen Quellen in das 15. Jahr des Konstantius datiert wird, das nach Avi-Yonah im Juni 351 begann[5], hält dieser den Herbst 351 für das wahrscheinlichste Datum des Aufstandes. Als unmittelbare Ursache vermutet er die Nachrichten über die Niederlage des Konstantius vom Juni 351 im Kampf gegen Magnentius, die Palästina im Herbst 351 erreicht haben könnten.

Der Aufstand brach nach Avi-Yonah in Sepphoris/Diocaesarea aus, verbreitete sich dann aber über ganz Galiläa und in der Küstenebene; verschiedene andere Städte, insbesondere Tiberias und Lod/Diospolis, schlossen sich an[6]. Der Aufstandsführer Patricius errichtete eine Regierung[7], wagte aber nicht, Jerusalem anzugreifen; immerhin schnitt die Besitznahme von Lod die Strasse von Alexandrien nach Antiochien, 'die Hauptverkehrsader des römischen Orients', ab. Da die Städte Sepphoris, Tiberias und Lod wichtige jüdische Industrieorte waren ('berühmt durch ihre Webereien'), berechtigt dies zu der Annahme, dass der Aufstand 'von Handwerkern und Industriellen begonnen (wurde), die durch die Edikte des Konstantius gegen das Halten nichtjüdischer Sklaven am schwersten in Mitleidenschaft gezogen wurden'[8].

Das römische Heer unter dem Feldherrn Ursicinus marschierte von Antiochia an der Küste entlang bis Akko/Ptolemais, in dessen Nähe es zu einer ersten grösseren militärischen Auseinandersetzung kam[9]. Danach wurden Sepphoris, Tiberias und Lod erobert und zerstört[10]. Insgesamt fielen neben den drei genannten Städten zahlreiche Dörfer und kleinere Ortschaften den Römern zum Opfer, darunter auch Beth-She'arim. Dennoch lagen die Städte, die als Mittelpunkt des Aufstandes erwähnt werden, nicht lange darnieder: Schon zur Zeit des Valens (375-378) 'wird Sepphoris wieder als eine rein jüdische Stadt beschrieben'[11], und 'Tiberias blieb nach wie vor die Hauptstadt

---

[4] Ursprünglich hebräisch *Bime Roma u-Bizantion*, Jerusalem, 1946 (^{2}1952, ^{3}1962), 153ff.; deutsche Ausgabe Berlin, 1962, 181ff.

[5] *Geschichte*, 182. Avi-Yonah rechnet wahrscheinlich vom Tod Konstantins des Grossen an (Pfingsten 337), obwohl Konstantius zusammen mit seinen Brüdern erst am 9. September 337 Augustus wurde; vgl. *Der Kleine Pauly* I, Sp. 1290, s.v. Constantius (2).

[6] Als Belege dafür dienen die unten analysierten griechisch-römischen Quellen.

[7] Die Quelle ist Aurelius Victor, s. unten 1.1.

[8] *Geschichte*, 183.

[9] Die Quelle ist Pesiqta Rabbati, s. unten 2.1.

[10] Quelle: Hieronymus, s. unten 1.2.

[11] Quelle: Theodoret, s. unten Anm. 36.

des jüdischen Palästina. Nur Lod scheint schwer gelitten zu haben, aber auch da blieb die jüdische Gemeinde bestehen'[12].

Auf den Aufstand folgte eine Zeit der römischen Okkupation mit 'Verfolgungen und Untersuchungen'[13]. Dennoch brachte der Aufstand den Juden Palästinas 'keinen dauernden Schaden und keine Minderung ihrer Rechte', zumal die 'offiziellen Spitzen des Volkes ... mit wenigen Ausnahmen' nicht am Aufstand teilnahmen[14]. Somit blieb der Aufstand eine zwar bemerkenswerte, aber insgesamt wenig folgenreiche Episode in der Geschichte des Judentums in Palästina.

Diese Sicht des Aufstandes dominiert — ungeachtet einiger Modifikationen[15] — bis heute in der Forschung. Im folgenden seien daher die einzelnen Quellen jeweils für sich analysiert, um zu einem methodisch abgesicherten Urteil zu gelangen.

1. *Griechisch-römische Quellen.*

1.1 *Sextus Aurelius Victor*[16].

> Aber schon vorher ... hatten Magnentius seinem Bruder Decentius ganz Gallien und Constantius dem Gallus, dessen Namen er in seinen geändert hatte, den Osten als Caesaren anvertraut. Sie selbst fochten während dreier Jahre die heftigsten Kämpfe aus; Constantius, der den Flüchtigen bis zum äussersten nach Gallien verfolgt hatte, brachte ihn, nach für beide vielfältiger Qual, dazu, sich selbst zu töten. Und inzwischen wurde der Aufstand der Juden, die ruchloserweise den Patricius in eine Art Königsherrschaft erhoben hatten, unterdrückt (*Et interea Judaeorum seditio, qui Patricium nefarie in regni speciem sustulerant, oppressa*). Nicht lange danach kam Gallus auf Befehl des Augustus wegen seiner Grausamkeit und seines wilden Übermutes ums Leben.

Da das Geschichtswerk des wichtigsten zeitgenössischen Historikers und Augenzeugen, Ammianus Marcellinus, für die Zeit vor 353 verlorengegangen

---

[12] *Geschichte*, 184.

[13] Als Quelle dienen die Ursicinus-Stellen in der rabbinischen Literatur, s. unten 2.3.ff.

[14] *Geschichte*, 186.

[15] Vgl. J. Geiger, 'The Last Jewish Revolt against Rome: A Reconsideration', *Scripta Classica Israelica* 5 (1979/80), 250-257; ders., 'Ha-mered bime Gallus ufarashat binyan ha-bayit bime Julianus', in: *Eretz-Israel from the Destruction of the Second Temple to the Moslem Conquest*, ed. Z. Baras, S. Safrai, M. Stern, Y. Tsafrir, vol. I: *Political, Social and Cultural History* (Hebr.), Jerusalem, 1982 (^{3}1984), 202-208; M. Stern, *Greek and Latin Authors on Jews and Judaism*, Vol. II: *From Tacitus to Simplicius*, Jerusalem, 1980, 500f.; G. Stemberger, *Die römische Herrschaft im Urteil der Juden*, Darmstadt, 1983, 100-103.

[16] *Liber de Caesaribus* 42,9-12, ed. F. Pichelmayr, Leipzig, 1911 (Nachdruck 1970), 128.

ist[17], ist S. Aurelius Victor unsere wichtigste Quelle für den Aufstand; seine *Caesares* wurden bald nach 360 abgeschlossen, stehen den Ereignissen des Jahres 351 also noch verhältnismässig nahe.

Aurelius Victor stellt den Aufstand in den historischen Rahmen der Kämpfe zwischen Konstantius II. und dem Usurpator Magnentius; darauf bezieht sich ohne Zweifel das 'inzwischen': Während Konstantius mit Magnentius beschäftigt war (und Gallus als seinen Caesar im Osten zurückgelassen hatte), wurde der jüdische Aufstand unterdrückt. Eine präzisere zeitliche Fixierung des 'inzwischen' wäre möglich, wenn dieses sich ausschliesslich auf den unmittelbar vorangehenden Satz bezöge (die Verfolgung des Magnentius bis nach Gallien), denn dann müsste der Aufstand nach dem Sommer 352 datiert werden, da Magnentius erst im Sommer 352 nach Gallien floh und Konstantius ihn dorthin verfolgte. Wahrscheinlich ist mit dem 'inzwischen' aber nur eine ganz allgemeine Zeitangabe gemeint und keine präzise Datierung.

Über den Aufstand selbst erfahren wir kaum mehr als die Tatsache selbst. Die einzige zusätzliche Information besteht nur darin, dass die Juden einen gewissen Patricius 'in eine Art Königsherrschaft' erhoben hätten. Über diesen Patricius ist viel spekuliert worden. Für Avi-Yonah steht es fest, dass Patricius ein Jude war. Er begründet dies damit, dass der Name Patricius im 4. Jahrhundert 'auch unter den Juden' durchaus üblich gewesen sei[18] und verweist als Beleg auf das *Corpus Inscriptionum Judaicarum* von J.-P. Frey[19]. Dies ist allerdings mehr als problematisch, denn Frey verzeichnet nur einen 'Pat...', den er zu 'Pat(rikios?)' rekonstruiert sowie eine 'Patrikia'[20].

Angesichts dieses überaus dürftigen Befundes ist es nicht erstaunlich, dass schon im Jahre 1946 von S. Lieberman die These vertreten wurde, dass wir es nicht mit einem *jüdischen* Aufstandsführer zu tun haben, sondern mit einem *heidnischen* römischen Offizier, der in Palästina als Gegenkaiser auftrat und dabei von den bzw. einigen Juden unterstützt wurde[21]. Dazu passen sehr gut die historischen Umstände, die wir aus Sextus Aurelius Victor sowie dem ab 353 erhaltenen Bericht des Ammianus Marcellinus (der zum Stab des Ursicinus gehörte) kennen. Die Abwesenheit des Konstantius in Gallien und dessen erste Misserfolge im Kampf gegen Magnentius ermutigten offensichtlich verschiedene Usurpatoren im Osten, die Herrschaft für sich zu reklamieren. 354 wurde Ursicinus von Gallus mit der Führung mehrerer Hochverratsprozesse in Antiochia beauftragt, unter denen Ammianus Marcellinus weder einen Aufstand der Juden noch eines gewissen Patricius erwähnt, aber am Ende hinzu-

[17] Vgl. dazu J. Geiger, 'Ammianus Marcellinus and the Jewish Revolt under Gallus. A Note', *Liverpool Classical Monthly* 4 (1979), 77.

[18] *Geschichte*, 181.

[19] Rome, 1936 (Neudruck New York, 1975).

[20] Nr. 350 und Nr. 266.

[21] 'Palestine in the Third and Fourth Centuries', *JQR* 36 (1946), 336ff.

fügt, dass 'Gallus ... viele (Fälle) dieser Art untersuchte, die im einzelnen zu berichten sich nicht lohnt ...'[22]. Es sprechen also gute Gründe für die Schlussfolgerung Liebermans, dass der 'jüdische' Aufstand unter Patricius nichts weiter als eine solcher (unbedeutender) Versuch eines römischen Usurpators war[23].

Gegen diese These werden im wesentlichen zwei Argumente vorgebracht: (1) Die Formulierung *in regni speciem* bei Aurelius Victor ist ungewöhnlich und passt schlecht zu einem 'Anwärter auf das Kaisertum; dessen Herrschaft ist nicht 'eine Art Königtum''[24].

Dieses Argument, das auch von M. Stern aufgegriffen wurde[25], ist gewiss ernstzunehmen; allerdings würde nur eine genauere Untersuchung des Sprachgebrauchs bei Aurelius Victor eine sichere Einschätzung seines Stellenwertes erlauben. Immerhin ist in einer Parallele, auf die J. Geiger hingewiesen hat[26], eine nahezu identische Wendung belegt. In *Liber de Caesaribus* 41,11 heisst es von Calocerus, dem 'Vorsteher der Kamelherdenverwaltung', dass er in seinem Wahnsinn 'die Insel Zypern plötzlich nach der Art des Königtums erobert hatte' (*repente Calocerus magister pecoris camelorum Cyprum insulam specie regni demens capessiverat*). Hier kann kein Zweifel daran bestehen, dass es sich um einen Usurpator handelte, der in die feingesponnene Haus- und Familienpolitik Konstantins des Grossen eingriff und auch sofort hingerichtet wurde (334 n.Chr.).
(2) Aurelius Victor spricht ausdrücklich von einem Aufstand der Juden (*Judaeorum seditio*).

Auch dieses Argument ist richtig, doch gilt hier ebenfalls der Einwand, dass die Formulierung nicht zwangsläufig auf einen jüdischen Aufstand mit jüdischen Zielen hindeutet; sie kann sich durchaus auch auf die überwiegend oder ausschliesslich jüdische Unterstützung eines lokalen römischen Usurpators beziehen[27].

Insgesamt ist der Quellenwert von Aurelius Victor im Blick auf die Frage eines jüdischen Aufstandes oder eines von jüdischer Seite unterstützten römischen Usurpators nicht mit letzter Sicherheit zu beurteilen. Der Name des Aufstandsführers Patricius[28] ist kein eindeutiges Indiz für einen römischen

---

[22] Ammianus Marcellinus, *Res Gestae* XIV,9,9 (ed. W. Seyfarth, Vol. I, Leipzig, 1978).

[23] Diese These vertritt auch J. Geiger (oben Anm. 15), ohne allerdings Lieberman zu erwähnen.

[24] Avi-Yonah, *Geschichte*, 182.

[25] Stern II, 501.

[26] *SCI* 5 (1979/80), 253; *Eretz-Israel* I, 207.

[27] Lieberman, *JQR* 36 (1946), 341; Geiger, *SCI* 5 (1979/80), 253f.; ders., *Eretz-Israel* I, 207.

[28] Schon 1867 hatte Z. Frankel ('Der Aufstand in Palästina zur Zeit des Gallus', *MGWJ* 16, 1867, 143-151) vorgeschlagen, in Patricius 'die Benennung für einen Edlen, Vornehmen, Patricier' zu sehen (S. 147). Diese These wurde wiederaufgegriffen von J. Cohen, 'Roman Imperial Policy Toward the Jews from Constantine Until the End of the Palestinian Patriarchate (ca. 429)', *Byzantine Studies* III,1 (1976), 22 Anm. 160: 'the term could also have denoted the noble title reinstituted by Constantine in the fourth century'. Cohen beruft sich dabei auf H.F. Jolowicz-B.

Usurpator, nicht zuletzt auch angesichts der Tatsache, dass die Namen der unzweifelhaft jüdischen Aufstandsführer in den Diaspora-Aufständen 115-117 n.Chr. mit Lukuas bzw. Andreas (Kyrenaika)[29] und Artemion (Zypern)[30] angegeben werden. Andererseits erlaubt die Formulierung bei Aurelius Victor[31] keineswegs den etwas apodiktischen Schluss von M. Stern, 'that Patricius was a Jew and that this Jewish revolt was of some importance'[32].

1.2 *Hieronymus*[33].

> Gallus, der Vetter des Constantius, wurde zum Caesar ernannt.
> Gallus unterdrückte die Juden, die, nachdem sie während der Nacht Soldaten getötet hatten, Waffen zum Rebellieren an sich gerissen hatten, indem er viele Tausende Menschen bis hin zum Kindesalter[34] tötete und übergab ihre Gemeinwesen (*civitates*) Diocaesarea, Tiberias und Diospolis sowie die meisten Städte dem Feuer.

Hieronymus eröffnet die lange Reihe der christlichen Autoren, die den Aufstand erwähnen. Er führte die um 303 n.Chr. veröffentlichte Chronik des Eusebius bis zum Jahre 378 fort, d.h. sein Bericht ist nicht viel später anzusetzen als der von Aurelius Victor.

Allerdings besteht inhaltlich zwischen Aurelius Victor und Hieronymus keinerlei Gemeinsamkeit; dass letzterer den ersteren gekannt und benutzt hat, ist mit Sicherheit auszuschliessen. Auf welche Quellen Hieronymus zurückgeht, ist völlig unbekannt. Folgende Informationen sind seinem Bericht zu entnehmen:

(1) Der Aufstand fiel in die 282. Olympiade und das 15. Regierungsjahr des Konstantius, d.h. je nach Zählung in das Jahr 351 oder 352 n.Chr.

(2) Die Juden überfielen (während der Nacht) ein römisches Lager und erbeuteten dabei Waffen. Über Ursachen, Verlauf und Ziele des Aufstandes wird nichts gesagt.

(3) Dafür erfahren wir etwas über die Unterdrückung des Aufstandes: Gallus

---

Nicholas, *Historical Introduction to the Study of Roman Law*, Cambridge, ³1972, 430: 'To Constantine is also due the revival of the word *patricius* in a totally different sense from that which it had previously had. It was at first simply a title, though conferred only on those who held the highest offices, but in the West after Theodosius it came to be appropriated to the great generals who, especially under weak emperors, exercised the real power ...'. Allerdings ist es vom Kontext her wenig wahrscheinlich, dass Aurelius Victor an einen Titel und nicht an einen Eigennamen dachte.

[29] Eusebius, *Historia Ecclesiastica* IV,2,4; Dio Cassius, *Historia Romana* LXVIII,32,1.

[30] Dio Cassius, *Historia Romana* LXVIII,32,2.

[31] Zusammen mit den anderen Quellen; dazu unten.

[32] Stern II, 501; affirmativ zitiert auch bei Stemberger, *Römische Herrschaft*, 100f. Anm. 195.

[33] *Chronicon*, ed. R. Helm, 1956 (*GCS* 47), 238.

[34] Wörtlich: 'unschuldigen Alter'.

Caesar ging brutal gegen die Rebellen vor und verschonte in seinem Wüten auch die kleinen Kinder nicht; die wichtigen jüdischen Städte Sepphoris/Diocaesarea, Tiberias und Lod/Diospolis sowie die meisten anderen jüdischen Ortschaften wurden dem Erdboden gleichgemacht.

Dieser Teil ist in verschiedener Hinsicht verdächtig. Die römische Grausamkeit gegenüber den Juden dürfte bei Hieronymus eher in die christlich-theologische Kategorie der 'verdienten Strafe' gehören denn unmittelbarer historischer Anschauung entstammen; insbesondere mag dies für den Kindermord gelten, der allzusehr an eine Umkehrung des Kindermordes zu Bethlehem erinnert.

Problematisch ist vor allem auch die angebliche Zerstörung der meisten jüdischen Ortschaften, die einen geographisch breit angelegten Aufstand insinuiert. Eine Zerstörung von Tiberias ist völlig ausgeschlossen. Die Stadt war bis zum Anfang des 5. Jahrhunderts ein so wichtiges Zentrum des rabbinischen Judentums, dass ihre Zerstörung mit Sicherheit auch in anderen Quellen erwähnt worden wäre. Auch von Lod hören wir nichts, das einen Aufstand und eine römische Strafexpedition vermuten liesse. Dasselbe gilt schliesslich für Sepphoris[35], von dem nicht nur keinerlei Nachrichten über eine Zerstörung vorliegen, sondern das in der Kirchengeschichte Theodorets im Jahre 373 als eine 'von den christusmörderischen Juden bewohnte' Stadt bezeichnet wird, in die rechtgläubige Christen von arianischen Häretikern in die Verbannung geschickt wurden[36]. Diese eher beiläufige Notiz passt sehr wohl zu den sonstigen Nachrichten über Sepphoris als einem der Zentren des galiläischen Judentums, aber schwerlich zu einer völligen Ausrottung seiner jüdischen Bevölkerung wenig mehr als 20 Jahre vorher[37].

Hieronymus erweist sich also kaum als ein unverdächtiger Kronzeuge des jüdischen Aufstandes gegen Gallus. Die meisten von ihm geschilderten Einzelheiten scheinen, wie dies schon Z. Frankel vermutet hat, auf seine 'lebhafte Phantasie', gepaart mit dem 'bei ihm häufig hervortretenden Glaubenshass'[38], zurückzugehen.

1.3 *Sokrates*[39].

Uber die Juden von Diocaesarea in Palästina. Zu den Geschehnissen kam noch ein anderer inländischer Krieg im Osten hinzu. Die Juden im palästi-

[35] Zu den rabbinischen und archäologischen Quellen s. unten.

[36] Theodoret, *Hist. eccl.* IV,22,35 (*GCS* 19, 260).

[37] Avi-Yonah, *Geschichte*, 184, interpretiert die Quellenlage dahingehend, dass die drei Städte eben 'nicht lange darnieder(lagen)' … 'Nur Lod scheint schwer gelitten zu haben, aber auch da blieb die jüdische Gemeinde bestehen'. Dies ist ein klassisches Beispiel für eine harmonistische Quellenzusammenschau auf der Basis von falschen oder zumindest ungeklärten Prämissen.

[38] *MGWJ* 16 (1867), 144.

[39] *Hist. eccl.* II,33 (*PG* 67, col. 295/296).

> nischen Diocaesarea erhoben nämlich die Waffen gegen die Römer und verheerten benachbarte Orte mit Streifzügen. Aber Konstantius Gallus, den der Kaiser, zum Caesar ernannt, in den Osten geschickt hatte, kämpfte sie, indem er eine Streitmacht (gegen sie) sandte, nieder und befahl, dass ihre Stadt Diocaesarea dem Erdboden gleichgemacht werde.

Sokrates Scholastikos (ca. 380-438) schrieb eine Kirchengeschichte, die von 305 bis 438 reicht und der die Verwendung zahlreicher Originalquellen sowie das Streben nach Objektivität bescheinigt wird[40]. Auf welche Quelle dieses kurze Stück zurückgeht, ist unbekannt; jedenfalls wird dies kaum Hieronymus gewesen sein. Seine Information reduziert sich darauf, dass die Juden Diocaesareas einen Aufstand gegen die Römer anzettelten und die Nachbarorte verunsicherten. Die Strafe der Römer richtet sich folgerichtig nur gegen diese Stadt, die völlig zerstört wird. Diese Fassung des Berichtes kann als die 'klassische' bezeichnet werden, da offensichtlich alle folgenden Berichte über den Aufstand direkt oder indirekt von ihr beeinflusst sind.

1.4 *Sozomenos*[41].

> Die Juden in Diocaesarea verwüsteten Palästina und die umliegenden Gebiete. Als sie Waffen erhoben hatten, konnten sie es nicht (mehr) ertragen, den Römern zu gehorchen. Als Gallus Caesar, der in Antiochia residierte, dies erfuhr, sandte er ein Heer (gegen sie), brachte sie in seine Hand (= überwältigte sie) und verwüstete Diocaesarea.

Die Kirchengeschichte des Sozomenos umfasst den Zeitraum von 324 bis 425 und wurde in der Zeit zwischen 439 und 450 verfasst. Ihre starke Abhängigkeit von der Kirchengeschichte des Sokrates[42] bestätigt sich auch in unserem kurzen Bericht, der in der Struktur mit Sokrates weitgehend identisch ist. Neu ist nur, dass die Juden von Diocaesarea 'Palästina und die umliegenden Gebiete' verwüsteten, doch ist diese Information zweifellos der Phantasie des Sozomenos oder einem Missverständnis des 'palästinischen Diocaesarea' bei Sokrates entsprungen.

1.5 *Paulus Diaconus*[43].

> Sodann verunsicherten die Juden, die im palästinischen Diocaesarea wohnten, die benachbarten Orte und versuchten, indem sie Waffen anlegten, den

[40] Vgl. B. Altaner-A. Stuiber, *Patrologie*, Freiburg, [8]1978, 226.
[41] *Hist. eccl.* IV,7 (*GCS* 50, 146).
[42] Altaner-Stuiber, *Patrologie*, 227.
[43] *PL* 95, col. 915.

Römern zu widerstehen. Danach vernichtete sie Gallus Caesar daher, als er in Antiochia weilte, indem er ein Heer (gegen sie) ausschickte und verwüstete die Stadt.

Der Langobarde Paulus Diaconus verfasste um 770 eine *Historia Romana*, die das *Breviarium* des Eutropius (reicht bis 364) bearbeitet und bis zum Jahre 553 erweitert[44]. Unser Bericht stimmt fast wörtlich mit Sokrates und Sozomenos überein und kann somit nicht als selbständige Quelle gewertet werden.

1.6 *Theophanes*[45].

In diesem Jahr erhoben sich die Juden in der Gegend von Palästina und töteten viele (Angehörige) von anderen Völkern, (nämlich) der Griechen und auch der Samaritaner. Sie selbst aber wurden gänzlich vom Heer der Römer getötet, und ihre Stadt Diocaesarea wurde zerstört.

Die *Chronographia* des Theophanes Homologetes, eine Fortsetzung der Chronik des Georgios Synkellos, umfasst den Zeitraum von 284 bis 813 und entstand in den Jahren 810 bis 814. Für die frühere Zeit kommt ihr kein eigener Quellenwert zu[46]. In unserem Abschnitt sind ganz offensichtlich aus dem 'palästinischen Diocaesarea' des Sokrates 'die Juden in der Gegend von Palästina' geworden; die Stadt Diocaesarea wird nun ganz unmotiviert erst am Schluss erwähnt. Desgleichen ist der erstmals hier auftauchende Mord an den Griechen und Samaritanern sehr wahrscheinlich aus der Verunsicherung der umliegenden Ortschaften herausgewachsen.

1.7 *Agapius*[47].

Im 18. Jahr des Konstantin und im dritten Jahre des Gallus erhoben sich die Juden Palästinas und überfielen verschiedene Ortschaften, eroberten sie und töteten viele Leute. Da schickte Konstantin den Gallus gegen sie, der sie vernichtete und ihre Ortschaften und Häuser zerstörte. Als Gallus diese Ortschaften erobert hatte, ergriffen ihn Überheblichkeit und Grössenwahn, und der Stolz überwältigte ihn.

Die einzige neue Information dieser um 942 abgefassten arabischen Chronik[48] besteht darin, dass der Aufstand drei Jahre später datiert wird als bei

[44] A. Kollautz, *LThK* VIII, 230f.; *Der Kleine Pauly* II, Sp. 469, s.v. Eutropius.

[45] *Chronographia*, ed. C. de Boor, Bd. I, Leipzig, 1883, 40.

[46] *Der Kleine Pauly* V, Sp. 718, s.v. Theophanes.

[47] *Patrologia Orientalis*, V/4: *Kitab al-'Unvan. Histoire Universelle*, écrite par Agapius (Mahboub) de Menbidj, éditée et traduite en Français par A. Vasiliev, I, Paris, 1947, 571f.

[48] Vgl. A. Baumstark, *Geschichte der syrischen Literatur*, Bonn, 1922, 6.

Hieronymus. Der Grund dafür könnte die unmittelbare zeitliche Verknüpfung des Aufstandes mit dem schmählichen Ende des Gallus sein (wie auch bei Michael Syrus)[49], die historisch wenig wahrscheinlich ist.

1.8 *Georgios Kedrenos*[50].

> Im 15. Jahr erhoben sich die Juden im Osten Palästinas und töteten viele der griechischen Völker und auch der Samaritaner. Sie selbst jedoch wurden gänzlich von den Römern getötet und ihre Stadt Diocaesarea wurde zerstört.

Die vom Ende des 11./Anfang des 12. Jahrhunderts stammende Weltchronik des Georgios Kedrenos zeichnet sich durch besondere Unselbständigkeit aus[51]. Unser Bericht ist ohne Zweifel von Theophanes abhängig, mit dem er nahezu wörtlich übereinstimmt[52].

1.9 *Michael Syrus*[53].

> In jener Zeit ermordeten die Juden von Diocaesarea in Palästina die Römer. Man schickte Armeen gegen sie, die sie vernichteten. Es steht geschrieben, dass Gallus, der Bruder Julians, die Juden vernichtete, überheblich wurde, rebellierte und auf der Insel Phlanon, wohin er sich geflüchtet hatte, getötet wurde.

Auch dieser Chronik aus dem 12. Jahrhundert[54] kommt für unsere Zeit kaum ein eigenständiger Quellenwert zu. Neu ist nur, dass die Juden die Römer ermordeten. Dies ist sinnvoller als die Tötung der Griechen und Samaritaner bei Theophanes und Georgios Kedrenos, bedeutet aber inhaltlich nichts weiter als eine andere Formulierung für den Aufstand gegen die Römer. Im übrigen ist Michael Syrus mehr an Gallus interessiert, dem persönlich er (wie Hieronymus) die Niederwerfung des Aufstandes zuschreibt. Der dem Gallus attestierte Hochmut geht vermutlich auf Sextus Aurelius Victor zurück. Unklar ist, woher der Tod des Gallus auf der Insel Phlanon stammt.

---

[49] S. unten 1.9.

[50] *Historiarum Compendium*, ed. I. Bekker, Bd. I, Bonn, 1838, 524 (*Corpus Scriptorum Historiae Byzantinae*).

[51] Vgl. K. Krumbacher, *Geschichte der byzantinischen Literatur von Justinian bis zum Ende des oströmischen Reiches (527-1453)*, Bd. I, München, ²1897 (Neudruck New York, o.J.), 268f.

[52] Geiger, *SCI* 5 (1979/80), 254 mit Anm. 20, hat die Quelle von Kedrenos vergeblich gesucht.

[53] *Chronique de Michel le Syrien*, ed. J.B. Chabot, Bd. I, Paris, 1899, 268.

[54] Vgl. Baumstark, *Geschichte der syrischen Literatur*, 298-300.

1.10 *Nikephoros Kallistos*[55].

Es erhoben sich nämlich auch die Juden von Diocaesarea gegen die Römer, ergriffen, indem sie das Joch der Knechtschaft abschüttelten, Waffen und verwüsteten Palästina sowie die umliegenden Gebiete. Gegen sie zog aus Antiochia, wo er sich aufhielt, Constantius Gallus, und errichtete, nachdem er sie besiegt hatte, ein gewaltiges Siegesdenkmal. Ihre Stadt zerstörte er bis auf das Fundament.

Die Kirchengeschichte des Nikephoros Kallistos (ca. 1256-1335) ist weniger an profanhistorischen als an dogmatischen Fragen interessiert[56]. Der Bericht über den Aufstand dürfte weitgehend von Sozomenos abhängig sein (die Verwüstung Palästinas und der umliegenden Gebiete). Die einzige über Sozomenos hinausgehende Information bezieht sich auf das Siegesdenkmal des Gallus, von dem wir nur hier hören und das sehr wahrscheinlich der Phantasie des Nikephoros entstammt.

2. *Rabbinische Literatur*.

2.1 *Pesiqta Rabbati 8,3*[57].

Israel sprach zu ihm (= Gott):
Herr der Welt, wann wirst du dies tun (nämlich Götzendienst und bösen Trieb ausrotten)?
Er antwortete ihnen:
Wenn ich tue (= erfülle), was oben geschrieben steht:
An jenem Tage, [Spruch des Herrn, wird sich ein grosses Geschrei erheben vom Fischertor usw.] (Zeph. 1:10).
Ein grosses Geschrei vom Fischertor: Das ist Akko, das nahe bei den Fischen gelegen ist.
Und ein Geheule von der Vorstadt (ebd.): Das ist Lod, das die Vorstadt Jerusalems war.
Und eine grosser Zusammenbruch von den Hügeln (ebd.): Das ist Sepphoris, das auf den Hügeln liegt.
Es heulen, die in der Senke wohnen (Zeph. 1:11): Das ist Tiberias, das tief wie eine Senke ist. …

Dieser Text ist eine der wichtigsten Quellen für Avi-Yonahs Rekonstruktion des Aufstandes. Er findet hier die Bestätigung für den Bericht des Hieronymus,

---

[55] *Eccl. Hist.* IX, 32 (*PG* CXLVI, col. 353/354).
[56] Vgl. V. Laurent, *LThK* X, Sp. 1284; Krumbacher, *Geschichte der byzantinischen Literatur* I, 291-293.
[57] Ed. Friedmann, 29af.

der ebenfalls Sepphoris, Tiberias und Lod erwähnt. Das Problem allerdings, dass Akko sonst nirgendwo mit dem Aufstand in Verbindung gebracht wird und dass es 'unwahrscheinlich sein (dürfte), dass es den Aufständischen gelungen wäre, sich der festen Küstenstadt Akko zu bemächtigen, deren Einwohner zum grössten Teil aus Nichtjuden bestanden'[58], wird durch einen 'Kunstgriff' gelöst: 'Eher handelt es sich wohl um eine Anspielung auf Kämpfe, die in der Nähe dieser Stadt ausgefochten wurden, als die römische Armee sich Galiläa näherte'[59]. Diese durch nichts begründete Hypothese wird nicht dadurch gesicherter, dass dies auch noch die einzige Niederlage der Rebellen gewesen sein soll, die die Entscheidung herbeiführte und den Römern den Weg nach Galiläa eröffnete. Der Versuch, den Midrash zu Zephania auf die Ereignisse um Gallus Caesar zu beziehen, entbehrt jeder Grundlage[60].

2.2 *Bereshit Rabba 31,11*[61] = *y Pesaḥim 1,1 fol. 27a.*

> R. Huna[62] sagte:
> Wir waren auf der Flucht vor den Gothen[63] in jenen Grotten von Tiberias[64] und hielten Lichter in unseren Händen:
> Wenn sie schwach leuchteten, wussten wir, dass es Tag war,
> und wenn sie hell leuchteten, wussten wir, dass es Nacht war.

Nach der Unterdrückung des Aufstandes durch die Truppen des Gallus kam, so Avi-Yonah, 'die militärische Besetzung'[65]. Unser Text (wie alle folgenden) sei repräsentativ für die 'Verfolgungen und Untersuchungen' in Tiberias; die in BerR erwähnten Gothen seien vielleicht die Leibwache des Patriarchen, 'die den Römern half«[66]. Auch dies ist reine Spekulation. Ob mit den Gothen hier einfach römische Truppen gemeint sind[67] oder konkret eine Leibwache[68], der Text enthält jedenfalls nicht den geringsten Hinweis auf einen Zusammenhang mit einem Aufstand. Sehr wahrscheinlich geht es um eine Polizei- oder Strafaktion der lokalen Behörden, deren Anlass nicht bekannt ist und von

---

58 *Geschichte*, 184.

59 Ebd.

60 So schon Frankel, *MGWJ* 16 (1867), 151 Anm. 5; Lieberman, *JQR* 36 (1946), 338 Anm. 72. Vorsichtig dagegen Geiger, *SCI* 5 (1979/80), 251; *Eretz-Israel* I, 204; Stern II, 501 (der den Text immerhin zu denen rechnet, die die Ereignisse widerspiegeln); Stemberger, *Römische Herrschaft*, 102.

61 Ed. Theodor-Albeck, 283.

62 y Pes: 'Rav Huna'.

63 'vor den Gothen' fehlt in y Pes.

64 y Pes: 'in jenen Grotten der grossen Säulenhalle'.

65 *Geschichte*, 184.

66 *Geschichte*, 186.

67 Stemberger, *Römische Herrschaft*, 102.

68 Jastrow I, 228.

denen es zu allen Zeiten und in allen Städten zahlreiche gegeben haben wird. Wenn zudem Rav Huna der Tradent des Stückes sein sollte, verbietet sich eine Datierung auf den Aufstand unter Gallus, da Rav Huna am Ende des 3. Jahrhunderts starb[69].

2.3 *y Yevamot 16,3 fol. 15c = y Sota 9,3 fol. 23c.*

> Rav Ḥiyya bar Ba sagte:
> Wer will, dass man (ihn) nicht erkennt, lege ein Pflaster auf seine Nase, und er wird nicht erkannt.
> Wie einst in den Tagen des Königs 'RSQYNS: Leute von Sepphoris wurden gesucht (= angeklagt). Da legten sie Pflaster auf ihre Nasen und wurden nicht erkannt. Aber schliesslich wurden sie denunziert und alle aufgrund dieser Aussage verhaftet.

Hier wird erstmals der römische General Ursicinus erwähnt, mit dessen Namen die meisten einschlägigen rabbinischen Texte verknüpft sind. Er war Feldherr Konstantius II. und erhielt 350 oder 351 den Oberbefehl im Perserkrieg[70]. Ohne Zweifel ist es genau diese Eigenschaft, in der er in Palästina und damit auch in den rabbinischen Quellen erscheint.

Was den konkreten Text betrifft, so handelt es sich offensichtlich wieder um eine lokale Strafaktion, diesmal in Sepphoris, zur Zeit des Ursicinus. Da der Aufenthalt des Ursicinus im Orient recht genau zu datieren ist (350/51-354 und 357-360)[71], müssen die Ereignisse in Sepphoris in diesen zeitlichen Rahmen gehören. Worum es konkret geht, wird nicht gesagt, doch fehlt wieder jeder Hinweis auf einen Aufstand.

2.4 *y Beṣa 1,6 fol. 60c.*

> Einst entschieden R. Liʿezer, R. Abba Mari und R. Matnaya für 'RSQYNS am Shabbat Brot (backen zu lassen), weil die Vielen (die Öffentlichkeit) seiner vielleicht bedürfen werden (könnten).

In diesem (und dem folgenden) Text geht es ganz offenkundig um die Versorgung der Truppen des Ursicinus: Die Rabbinen erlauben, was an sich strengstens verboten ist, am Shabbat für die römischen Soldaten Brot zu backen. Auch hier ist die zwangloseste Erklärung nicht eine Verfolgungssitua-

---

[69] Rav Huna II., vgl. H. Strack-G. Stemberger, *Einleitung in Talmud und Midrasch*, München, [7]1982, 93; Rav Huna I. war Zeitgenosse Rabbis.

[70] *Der Kleine Pauly* V, Sp. 1071, s.v. Ursicinus.

[71] Ebd.

tion (verschärfte römische Besatzung) nach dem Aufstand[72], sondern die Versorgung der *durchziehenden* Truppen des Ursicinus im Zusammenhang mit dem Perserkrieg.

2.5 *y Sanhedrin 3,6 fol. 21b = y Shevi'it 4,2 fol. 35a*[73].

R. Yonah und R. Yose entschieden, für 'RṬYQNS[74] am Shabbat (Brot) backen zu lassen.
... (Wiederspruch von R. Mani)
Er (= Ursicinus) beabsichtigte nicht, sie zu verfolgen[75],
sondern er wollte nur, dass (die Soldaten) warmes Brot zu essen bekämen.
...
R. Mani entschied, als PRWQL' nach Sepphoris kam, die Bäcker (am Shabbat) auf den Markt gehen zu lassen.
Die Rabbanin von Nayah (= Naweh)[76] entschieden, an Pesaḥ gesäuertes (Brot für die Soldaten) backen zu lassen.

Der historische Kontext dieses Textes ist derselbe wie in y Bẹsa (2.4.), nämlich der Perserfeldzug des Ursicinus. Inhaltlich wird die Erlaubnis der Rabbinen auf den Verkauf des Brotes am Shabbat und sogar auf das Backen von gesäuertem Brot an Pesaḥ (!) ausgedehnt.

Wenn mit Nayah das östlich von Gadara in der Dekapolis gelegene Naweh gemeint sein sollte, ist dies ein zusätzliches Argument für den Zusammenhang der Ursicinus-Texte mit dem Perserfeldzug (statt mit dem Aufstand gegen Gallus). Der sonst nicht bekannt PRWQL' = Proclus ist vermutlich ein römischer Offizier im Heere des Ursicinus.

2.6 *y Megillah 3,1 fol. 74a.*

Jener 'RSQYNS verbrannte die Torahrolle (der Synagoge) von Sennabris.
Man kam und fragte R. Yonah und R. Yose:
Darf man aus der Rolle[77] (noch) öffentlich vorlesen?
Er antwortete ihnen:
Es ist verboten.

---

[72] Avi-Yonah, *Geschichte*, 186f.; Stemberger, *Römische Herrschaft*, 101.

[73] In y Shevi nur die erste Hälfte.

[74] y Shevi: "'RSQYNS'.

[75] D.h., es handelte sich nicht um eine Verfolgung und somit um keine Bekenntnissituation. Die Entscheidung von R. Yonah und R. Yose ist demnach unbegründet.

[76] Jastrow II, 903 (und 884): 'east of Gadara in Galilee'; L.I. Levine, *Caesarea under Roman Rule*, Leiden, 1975, 97; G.A. Wewers, *Sanhedrin* (Übersetzung des Talmud Yerushalmi IV/4), Tübingen, 1981, 92: Nawe in Transjordanien.

[77] Wörtlich: 'aus dem Buch'.

Die Verbrennung einer Torahrolle in Sennabris an der Südwest-Seite des Sees Genezareth ist die einzige 'Schandtat' des Ursicinus, die Avi-Yonah im Zusammenhang mit dem Aufstand anführen kann[78]. Vom Kontext her ist ganz offenkundig, dass es sich nicht um eine absichtlich verbrannte Rolle handelt, sondern um eine — vermutlich versehentlich — beschädigte; anders ergibt die Frage nach der Weiterverwendung keinen Sinn. Schon Frankel[79] und Lieberman[80] haben erkannt, dass der Text sich daher wenig eignet, ihn zum Dokument der Religionsverfolgung unter Ursicinus hochzustilisieren[81]. Die einfachste Erklärung ist auch hier, dass der Vorfall nichts mit einem jüdischen Aufstand zu tun hat, sondern in den Umkreis des Perserkrieges (Durchzug römischer Truppen durch Galiläa) gehört.

2.7 *y Berakhot 5,1 fol. 9a.*

> R. Yonah und R. Yose begaben sich vor 'RSQYNS in Antiochia ('NṬWKY').
> Er sah sie und stand vor ihnen auf.
> Man sagte zu ihm:
> Vor jenen Juden stehst du auf?!
> Er antwortete ihnen:
> Ich sah ihre Gesichter (in einer Vision) im Kampf und siegte.

Der angebliche Besuch der Rabbinen Yonah und Yose bei Ursicinus im Hauptquartier des Gallus in Antiochien wird von Avi-Yonah damit begründet, dass sie Ursicinus bitten wollten, 'die Besetzung (sc. nach dem Aufstand) weniger schwer zu gestalten'[82]. Auch diese Interpretation ist reine Phantasie. Ein Kontakt der beiden Rabbinen — sie gelten als Häupter des Lehrhauses in Tiberias um 350[83] und werden nicht von ungefähr auch in den unter 2.6 und 2.5 zitierten Texten erwähnt — mit Ursicinus ist durchaus möglich, doch gibt es nicht den geringsten Hinweis auf einen Zusammenhang mit einem jüdischen Aufstand. Der Kern der Erzählung ist ohnehin eine klassische Wanderlegende[84], die nicht unbedingt für Historizität bürgt.

---

[78] *Geschichte*, 186.

[79] *MGWJ* 16 (1867), 150.

[80] *JQR* 36 (1946), 336f.

[81] So auch Stemberger, *Römische Herrschaft*, 102, der allerdings einen Zusammenhang mit den Kampfhandlungen des Aufstandes annimmt.

[82] *Geschichte*, 187.

[83] Strack-Stemberger, *Einleitung*, 100.

[84] Ant. XI, 331-335 (Alexander und der Hohepriester Jaddua); b Yom 69a (Alexander und Shimon der Gerechte). Avi-Yonah, *Geschichte*, 187, verweist noch auf die Vision Konstantins vor der Schlacht an der Milvischen Brücke; vgl. ferner den Kontext unseres Stückes in y Ber.

3. *Archäologische Evidenz.*

Von keiner der drei wichtigen jüdischen Städte, die nach Hieronymus im Verlaufe des Aufstandes unter Gallus zerstört sein sollen — Sepphoris, Tiberias und Lod —, liegen archäologische Erkenntnisse vor, die den Bericht des Hieronymus bestätigen[85]. So müssen andere Ortschaften herhalten, um die gravierenden Folgen des Aufstandes zu demonstrieren. Die Rolle des Kronzeugen fällt dabei Beth-She'arim zu, das für Avi-Yonah als Beispiel dafür dient (das einzige Beispiel freilich), dass 'bei dem römischen Durchmarsch ... einige am Wege liegende Städtchen hart mitgenommen (wurden)'[86]. Die Quelle für diese Erkenntnis ist der Ausgrabungsbericht von B. Mazar: 'Likewise, in the synagogue area and adjacent buildings, evidence was found proving that the city was laid waste and burnt in the middle of the fourth century C.E. Archaeological finds therefore serve as further testimony to the events which brought about the devastation and ruin of the Jewish settlements in Palestine, the great rebellion of the Jews in the days of Constantinus (sic) (337-361 C.E.) and its suppression by Gallus in 352 C.E.'[87].

Dieser Zusammenhang zwischen der Zerstörung von Beth-She'arim und dem Aufstand unter Gallus ist allerdings keineswegs so gesichert, wie Mazar und die von ihm abhängigen Arbeiten über den Aufstand[88] glauben machen wollen. In einer neuen umfassenden Untersuchung des Erdbebens vom Mai 363 (das zur Einstellung der Arbeiten am Neubau des Tempels in Jerusalem unter Julian führte) kommt Kenneth W. Russell[89] zu dem Ergebnis, dass sehr viel mehr Ortschaften in Palästina von diesem Erdbeben betroffen wurden als

---

[85] Wie schwer es den Forschern fällt, diesen Befund zu akzeptieren, zeigt zuletzt Stuart S. Miller in seiner Arbeit über Sepphoris (*Studies in the History and Traditions of Sepphoris*, Leiden, 1984, 59 Anm. 293): Nachdem er aufgezeigt hat, wie gut seine eigenen Ergebnisse zu den numismatischen Forschungen von Meshorer passen ('Meshorer draws on numismatic evidence to show that, for the most part, Sepphoris enjoyed unusually good relations with Rome. ... If Meshorer's assessment of the numismatic evidence is correct, the suggestion put forward here ... would seem even more cogent.'), kommt er zum Aufstand unter Gallus: 'The one difficulty with Meshorer's proposal is the turn of events during the fourth century. Why would Sepphoris, a city supposedly allied with Rome, become the center of the revolt (however limited) under Gallus?'. Es versteht sich von selbst, dass Miller sich dafür auf die üblichen literarischen Belege stützt. Die einzig logische Schlussfolgerung aus seinen eigenen Ergebnissen kommt ihm nicht in den Sinn, nämlich die angebliche Revolte unter Gallus mit ihrem Zentrum in Sepphoris in Frage zu stellen.

[86] *Geschichte*, 184.

[87] B. Mazar, *Beth She'arim: Report on the Excavations During 1936-1940*, Vol. I: *Catacombs 1-4*, New Brunswick, NJ, 1973 (englische Fassung der ursprünglich hebräischen Publikation von 1957), 6; vgl. auch 18f.

[88] Vgl. etwa Geiger, *SCI* 5 (1979/80), 251; Stern II, 501 und Stemberger, *Römische Herrschaft*, 101 Anm. 195, mit der charakteristischen Formulierung: 'Die Zerstörung der Synagoge von Bet Schearim knapp nach 350 erfolgte wohl im Aufstand gegen Gallus — vgl. B. Mazar ... —, was wohl einen gewissen Umfang der militärischen Aktionen vermuten lässt'.

[89] 'The Earthquake of May 19, A.D. 363', *BASOR* 238, 1980, 47-64.

bisher angenommen. Zu diesen Ortschaften rechnet er auch Beth-She'arim[90], das genau zwischen Caesarea und Sepphoris liegt, beides Orte, die nach dem von S.P. Brock edierten syrischen Dokument (Harvard Syriac 99, fol. 188b-190a)[91] ebenfalls durch das Erdbeben in Mitleidenschaft gezogen wurden.

Ähnliches dürfte auch für die Zerstörung von Chorazin[92] gelten, die J. Geiger (zusammen mit Beth-She'arim) als Bestätigung für 'Jerome's claim of a more widespread destruction' anführt[93]. Russell schlägt vor, die Zerstörung von Chorazin zu Beginn des 5. Jahrhunderts in Zusammenhang mit einem Erdbeben des Jahres 419 zu bringen[94].

Kann es somit keineswegs als erwiesen gelten, dass die Zerstörung von Beth-She'arim (und Chorazin) eine Folge des jüdischen Aufstandes unter Gallus war, drängt sich angesichts des Befundes über das Erdbeben des Jahres 363[95] eine andere Hypothese auf. Sepphoris, Tiberias und Lod gehören zur Liste der in Harvard Syriac 99 erwähnten Orte, die bei dem Erdbeben vom 19. Mai 363 ganz oder teilweise zerstört wurden[96]. Es ist also durchaus denkbar, dass der um 378 schreibende Hieronymus die Zerstörung der wichtigen jüdischen Zentren durch das Erdbeben des Jahres 363 mit dem jüdischen 'Aufstand' des Jahres 351/352 kontaminierte. Auf jeden Fall passt die Zerstörung aller drei Orte durch ein Erdbeben sehr viel besser zur oben analysierten Quellenlage als die Vernichtung durch militärische Strafaktionen der Römer, die sonst nicht bezeugt sind[97]. Dies gilt besonders auch für Sepphoris, das im Jahre 373 als überwiegend jüdische Stadt geschildert wird[98]: Die schnelle Wiederbesiedlung nach einem Erdbeben dürfte wahrscheinlicher sein als nach der Zerstörung und zwangsweisen Vertreibung der jüdischen Bevölkerung durch die römische Besatzungsmacht.

4. *Ergebnisse.*

1. Von den griechisch-römischen Texten ist Sextus Aurelius Victor die wichtigste Quelle. Seine sehr kurze Notiz ist allerdings keineswegs eindeutig,

---

90 Ebd., 56.

91 'A Letter Attributed to Cyril of Jerusalem on the Rebuilding of the Temple', *BSOAS* 40 (1977), 267-286.

92 Vgl. Z. Yeivin, 'Excavations at Khorazin in the Years 1962-1964' (Hebr.), *Eretz-Israel* 11, 1973, 144-157.

93 *SCI* 5 (1979/80), 251. Wobei Beth She'arim und Chorazin wohlgemerkt die einzigen archäologischen Belege sind. Für die von Hieronymus tatsächlich genannten Orte fehlt nach wie vor jedes archäologische Indiz.

94 *BASOR* 238 (1980), 61 Anm. 5.

95 Vgl. die Karte bei Russell, Fig. 5.

96 Vgl. Russell, *BASOR* 238 (1980), 51, Fig. 4.

97 Es fällt auf, dass der vermutlich *vor* dem Erdbeben von 363 schreibende Sextus Aurelius Victor nichts von einer Zerstörung jüdischer Städte erwähnt.

98 S. oben S. 190.

sondern erlaubt sowohl die Deutung auf einen von der jüdischen Bevölkerung unterstützten römischen Usurpator als auch auf eine lokale, ausschliesslich von Juden getragene, Erhebung gegen Gallus Caesar. In beiden Fällen wäre die Abwesenheit des Konstantius im Westen der unmittelbare Auslöser des Aufstandes gewesen. Irgendwelche Ziele des Aufstandes, die sich aus der besonderen Situation der Juden in Palästina ergeben, sind nicht zu erkennen.

2. Dem Bericht des Hieronymus kommt kein besonderer Quellenwert zu.
3. Die Schilderung des Sokrates Scholastikos deutet auf anti-römische Unruhen, die auf die Stadt Sepphoris und deren unmittelbare Umgebung begrenzt waren. Auch hier fehlt jeder Hinweis auf die innerjüdischen Ursachen und Ziele des Aufstandes.
4. Den übrigen Kirchenschriftstellern kommt kein selbständiger Quellenwert zu; sie sind weitgehend von Sokrates bzw. Sozomenos abhängig.
5. Die rabbinischen Texte belegen die Anwesenheit des Ursicinus in Palästina im Zusammenhang mit dessen Oberbefehl im Krieg gegen die Perser (350/51-354 und 357-360). Der Perserkrieg ist völlig ausreichend als Hintergrund für die in der rabbinischen Literatur geschilderten Ereignisse; für einen jüdischen Aufstand geben die Texte keinen Anhaltspunkt.
6. Die archäologischen Quellen haben bisher keinen Beweis für einen Aufstand im Jahre 351/52 erbracht. Der Befund deutet eher auf einen Zusammenhang mit dem Erdbeben im Jahre 363.
7. Für eine verschärfte römische Besatzungspolitik nach 351 oder gar für eine Verfolgung der jüdischen Religion fehlt jeder Hinweis.
8. Damit ist die Rekonstruktion des Aufstandsverlaufs und der Folgen durch Avi-Yonah weitgehend hinfällig.
9. Der Aufstand als solcher, d.h. als jüdischer Aufstand gegen die römische Fremdherrschaft, ist weiterhin ungesichert.

OROSIUS' *HISTORIAE ADVERSUS PAGANOS* IN ARABISCHER ÜBERLIEFERUNG

von

HANS DAIBER

Der in Praga/Nordportugal geborene spanische Priester Orosius schrieb 417/418 in Afrika auf Veranlassung von Augustinus und als Ergänzung zu dessen *De Civitate Dei* ein sieben Bücher umfassendes Geschichtswerk mit dem Titel *Historiae adversus paganos*[1]. Dieses will dem Nachweis dienen, dass die vorchristliche Welt mehr von Krieg und Elend (*miseriae bellorum*) heimgesucht wurde, als die jetzt lebende Menschheit; hierbei möchte Orosius beweisen, dass das Christentum an der Not der Zeit unschuldig sei. Dies geschieht in Form eines Abrisses der Weltgeschichte von Adam bis zum Jahre 417 n.Chr., welche nach Dan. 7 in vier Perioden eingeteilt wird. Dieses Schema von den vier Weltreichen dient gleichzeitig dem Nachweis der Existenz des einen Gottes und seines fortgesetzten Eingreifens in den Ablauf der Weltgeschichte[2].

Orosius' *Historiae adversus paganos* ist die erste christliche Universalgeschichte und wurde bis zur Renaissance viel gelesen[3]. Es ist daher kein Wunder, dass das Werk im Mittelalter in mehrere Sprachen übersetzt worden ist[4], nämlich in das Italienische (2. Hälfte des 13. Jh.s), in das Französische (1491) und ins Deutsche (1539). Die älteste, König Alfred zugeschriebene 'Übersetzung', ist die altenglische aus dem 9. Jahrhundert; sie ist mehr eine Paraphrase mit zahlreichen erklärenden Zusätzen[5]. Ein Jahrhundert später ist Oriosus' Werk unter dem Kalifen ʿAbdarraḥmān III von Cordoba (reg. von 300/912 bis 350/961)[6] von einem unbekannten Übersetzer in Spanien ins Arabische übertragen worden[7]. Diese Übersetzung ist nach der einzigen, im Jahre 712/1312 abgeschriebenen arabischen Handschrift Columbia University (New York) Nr. X, 893 von Giorgio Levi della Vida im Jahre 1951 bzw. 1954

---

[1] Vgl. Altaner/Stuiber, *Patrologie*, 231; Von den Brincken, 80-85 u. Goetz. Nicht zugänglich waren mir F. Fabbrini, *Paolo Orosio uno storico*, Roma, 1979, sowie die italienische Bearbeitung von Orosius' Geschichtswerk, welche 1976 in Mailand erschien: *Le storie contra i Pagani*, introduzione, testo e commentario a cura di A. Lippold, trad. di A. Bartalucci, G. Ciarini.

[2] Goetz, 1.

[3] Lippold, 438f.

[4] Goetz, 158.

[5] Vgl. unten zu Anm. 18.

[6] *EI*² I, 83f.

[7] Vielleicht in Zusammenarbeit mit einem Mozaraber; vgl. Levi della Vida, *La Traduzione*, 260ff.

untersucht worden[8]. Doch erst im Jahre 1982 ist der arabische Text in der Edition von ʿAbdarraḥmān Badawī zugänglich gemacht worden. Der Herausgeber informiert uns in der Einleitung über die Ausstrahlung dieser arabischen Version in der arabischen Literatur vom 9. bis zum 15. Jahrhundert n.Chr., nämlich bei Ibn Ǧulǧul (10. Jh.), Abū ʿUbaid al-Bakrī (gest. 487/1094), in einem anonymen Geschichtswerk, bei Muḥammad Ibn ʿAbdalmunʿim al-Ḥimyarī (gest. 727/1327), Ibn Ḫaldūn[9] (gest. 808/1406) und al-Maqrīzī (gest. 845/1441)[10]. Ferner hat der Herausgeber seiner sehr verdienstvollen Ausgabe eine kleine Liste von Wörtern beigefügt[11], welche vom üblichen Sprachgebrauch abweichen und spanisch-arabische Färbung verraten. Diese Liste lässt sich sicher im Rahmen eines sehr wünschenswerten lateinisch-arabischen Glossars und einer Untersuchung der lateinisch-arabischen Übersetzungstechnik erweitern. Eine solche Untersuchung wäre nicht nur reizvoll, weil Orosius' Geschichtswerk der einzige lateinische Text ist, der ins Arabische übersetzt wurde, sondern auch weil wir hier erstmals einen Einblick bekommen in die Arabischkenntnisse der Mozaraber; es ist denkbar, dass der muslimische Übersetzer — um einen solchen handelt es sich doch wohl[12] — von einem Mozaraber, der des Lateinischen mächtig war, in seiner Arbeit unterstützt wurde[13]. — Schliesslich erscheint es angesichts der zahlreichen Wiedergaben lateinischer Eigennamen in arabischer Umschrift der Mühe wert, der Frage nachzugehen, inwieweit hier nicht nur eine Transliteration vorliegt, sondern die damalige Schulaussprache des Lateinischen und die spezifische Aussprache des Spanisch-Arabischen die phonetische Transskription lateinischer Wörter geprägt haben[14]. Um solche sprachlichen Untersuchungen zu erleichtern, seien im Nachfolgenden alle die Texte zusammengestellt und — mit Ausnahme einiger noch zu nennender Texte — in Übersetzung vorgelegt, welche keine

---

[8] 'La traduzione araba delle storie di Orosio', in *al-Andalus* 19 (1954), 257-293. Der Aufsatz erschien zuerst in *Miscellanea G. Galbiati* III, Milano, 1951 (= Fontes Ambrosiani XXVII), 185-203.

[9] Vgl. auch W.J. Fischel in *Homenaje a Millas-Vallicrosa I*, Barcelona, 1954, 587ff.

[10] S. die Einleitung von Badawī, 4-38, u. Levi della Vida, *La traduzione*, 263-266. In einem Anhang hat Badawī die Oriosiusfragmente bei Ibn Ḫaldūn zusammengestellt; wie Badawī im einzelnen zeigt, lassen sich nicht alle in der arabischen Version des Orosius nachweisen.

[11] S. 498.

[12] Auf einen muslimisch-theologischen Hintergrund weist die Terminologie ed. Badawī, 415, wo der Übersetzer Orosius VII 1 zusammenfasst und dabei Fachausdrücke der islamischen Attributenlehre und Glaubenslehre benutzt; er benutzt den Gegensatz *qadīm/azalī/lam yazal* und *muḥdaṯ/ḫalq*, wozu man H. Daiber, *Das theologisch-philosophische System des Muʿammar Ibn ʿAbbād as-Sulamī* (gest. 830 n.Chr.), Beirut-Wiesbaden, 1975 (= Beiruter Texte und Studien 19), Index vergleiche. Oder ed. Badawī 449, 19 fügt der arab. Übersetzer dem Ausdruck *sabʿa ġilma* 'sieben Knaben' den koranischen Ausdruck *aṣḥāb al-kahf* zu (s. den Kommentar zu unserer Übersetzung). Vgl. ferner Levi della Vida, *La traduzione*, 285-287.

[13] Vgl. oben Anm. 7.

[14] Levi della Vida, *La traduzione*, 287, ist nur kurz darauf eingegangen. Eine ähnliche Untersuchung der Phonetik der lateinischen Eigennamen in der altenglischen Orosiusbearbeitung liegt vor in der Edition von J. Bately, Einl. CIX-CXVI.

Entsprechung im bekannten lateinischen Orosiustext haben. Damit werden wir in die Lage versetzt, die Quellen dieser Zusätze zu identifizieren und der Frage nachzugehen, inwieweit die sehr verschiedenartigen Zusätze und Abweichungen vom bekannten lateinischen Text einer einzigen Quelle entstammen oder mehreren. Hiermit soll einem Mangel der Ausgabe von Badawī abgeholfen werden, welche den Leser häufig im Unklaren darüber lässt, ob ein arabischer Passus eine Entsprechung im Lateinischen hat. Zuweilen wird — vielleicht infolge eines Missverständnisses des arabischen Übersetzers oder Kopisten oder gar vom lateinischen Redaktor beabsichtigt — ein Passus in der arabischen Version durch *qāla Hurūšiyūš* 'Orosius sagte' eingeleitet, ohne dass es sich um eine Passage aus dem bekannten lateinischen Text handelt[15]. Hier wird ein systematischer Vergleich mit den einschlägigen lateinischen Geschichtsquellen des 6. bis 10. Jahrhunderts n.Chr. weiterhelfen und viele Irrtümer in der arabischen Edition aufdecken. Gleichzeitig wird uns dieser eine Präzisierung der Angaben von G. Levi della Vida ermöglichen, der auf einige der nachfolgend genannten Quellen aufmerksam gemacht, aber hieraus teilweise falsche Schlüsse gezogen hatte[16].

Um die zukünftige Arbeit mit dem arabischen Orosius zu erleichtern, werden wir in diesem Artikel eine Stellenkonkordanz des lateinischen Orosius und der arabischen Entsprechungen vorlegen. Dann werden wir eine Übersicht aller Stellen geben, welche Zusätze zum Lateinischen enthalten. Mit Ausnahme des geographischen Zusatzes und der biblischen Geschichtszusätze werden sie hier in kommentierter Übersetzung vorgelegt.

Der Vergleich des Arabischen mit dem lateinischen Orosius ergibt zusammengefasst folgendes Resultat: Die arabische Version geht auf eine lateinische Bearbeitung des bekannten Orosiustextes zurück. Diese hat mehrere Quellen nebeneinander benutzt. Ein solches Resultat ist nicht überraschend. Wir wissen, dass die zwischen 889 und 899 angefertigte altenglische Version von Orosius' Geschichtswerk[17] gleichfalls Zusätze enthält, und zwar aus klassischen und patristischen Quellen; ferner zusätzliche geographische Informationen. Man nimmt hier an, dass diese Zusätze teilweise vom altenglischen Übersetzer stammen, welcher sich auf schriftliche oder mündliche Überlieferungen gestützt haben mag. Diese sollen teilweise bereits in der vom Übersetzer benutzten lateinischen Handschrift oder in einem Kommentar zu Orosius' Geschichtswerk gestanden haben. Ferner sei denkbar, dass der altenglische

[15] Vgl. ed. Badawī 83,1; 85,1; 86,1; 417 etc. (innerhalb von Zufügungen zum bekannten Orosiustext). Vgl. auch den Kommentar zu meiner Übersetzung von ed. Badawī 353,11 - 354,8.

[16] Er hatte z.B. fälschlicherweise noch angenommen, dass 'l'uso di Isidoro (sc. dessen *Chronica maiora*) non è diretto' (269f.); S. 279 behauptet Levi della Vida sogar, dass der lateinische Redaktor des vom arabischen Übersetzer benutzten Orosiustextes eine den *Chronica maiora* des Isidor verwandte, aber nicht mit ihr identische Chronik benutzt habe, um Lücken im Orosiustext zu füllen.

[17] Vgl. die Einleitung von Janet Bately zu ihrer Edition *The Old English Orosius*, LV ff.; LXI ff.

Bearbeiter ein lateinisch-lateinisch oder lateinisch-altenglisches Glossar mit erklärenden Zusätzen benutzt habe. — Nun sind die Zusätze zum altenglischen Orosius weniger tiefgreifend als im arabischen Orosius; es handelt sich um erklärende Details, ohne die Substanz des lateinischen Textes essentiell zu verändern, ohne zusätzliches Geschichtsmaterial einfügen und Textstücke des lateinischen Originals durch andere ersetzen zu wollen[18]. Im Unterschied hierzu hat der lateinische Bearbeiter des vom arabischen Übersetzer benutzten Orosiustextes systematisch eine Quelle eingearbeitet, welche nicht mit dem Gründungsjahr der Stadt Rom die Geschichte beginnen liess, sondern die Weltära einführte: gemeint ist Isidor von Sevillas (ca. 565-636)[19] *Chronica maiora*[20], deren chronologische, biographische und historische Angaben der lateinische Bearbeiter des Orosiustextes — teilweise mit Auslassungen und Umstellungen — in einer schildernden und teilweise erweiternden Paraphrase adaptiert hat. Ausserdem wurde den biblischen Nachrichten viel Aufmerksamkeit geschenkt und zahlreiche Kapitel eingefügt, welche — vermutlich über die *Vulgata* und die *Vetus latina* — auf das Alte Testament zurückgehen[21]. Ferner sind ganze Kapitel zugefügt worden, welche folgende Themen und Personen behandeln: die Sage vom trojanischen Pferd[22]; Octavianus[23]; die alexandrinischen Märtyrer (nach Eusebius' Kirchengeschichte)[24], der Tod von Diocletianus und Maximianus[25]; ferner Konstantin der Grosse (nach der Sylvesterlegende) und Constantius[26]. Und schliesslich ist in der geographischen Einleitung des Orosius ein zusätzliches geographisches Kapitel aufgenommen worden, welches auf Julius Honorius zurückgeht[27]. Darüber hinaus findet man erklärende Zusätze nach Isidors *Etymologien*[28] und zusätzliche Zitate und Hinweise auf römische Dichter; ferner zusätzliche genealogische Angaben zu einzelnen Personen und zusätzliche chronologische Angaben, welche schwerlich vom arabischen Übersetzer stammen, sondern in dessen lateinischer Vorlage gestanden haben.

Die arabische Version geht auf eine Redaktion des lateinischen Orosiustextes zurück, die — wie bereits Orosius selbst[29] — mehrere Quellen nebeneinan-

---

[18] Man vergleiche den Kommentar von Bately.
[19] Vgl. Von den Brincken, 91.
[20] Verfasst 615 n.Chr.; vgl. Von den Brincken, 1.
[21] Vgl. unten S. 218.
[22] S. meine Übersetzung v. ed. Badawī 124, 4-18.
[23] S. meine Übersetzung v. ed. Badawī 416, 5-417.
[24] S. meine Übersetzung v. ed. Badawī 449, 7-ult.
[25] S. meine Übersetzung v. ed. Badawī 456, 11-14.
[26] S. meine Übersetzung v. ed. Badawī 457-461,16.
[27] S. unten S. 217.
[28] Vgl. z.B. unten Anm. 109; 120; 121; 209 und 217, aber auch die Stellen aus Isidors *Chronica maiora*, die eine Parallele in Isidors *Etymologien* haben (s. den Kommentar zur deutschen Übersetzung); ferner Levi della Vida, *La traduzione*, 270.
[29] Vgl. Lippold, 443; Goetz, 25-29.

der benutzt und eingearbeitet hat. Dadurch ist die Substanz von Orosius' Geschichtswerk erweiter worden, ohne dass jedoch an der geschichtstheologischen Haltung von Orosius grundsätzliche Korrekturen angebracht worden wären. Lediglich an einer Stelle[30] bringt der lateinische Redaktor eine zusätzliche Nuance ins Spiel, die hier genannt zu werden verdient: Julius Caesars Ermordung wird auf unheilvolle Zustände wie Neid, Missgunst und Brudermord zurückgeführt. Und schliesslich erscheint der lateinische Redaktor nicht mehr nur ausschliesslich ein Stück apologetischer Geschichtsschreibung vorlegen zu wollen, sondern auch eine informierende Universalgeschichte, die die biblische Geschichte stärker berücksichtigt und somit offensichtlich nicht mehr ausschliesslich an den heidnischen Leser gerichtet ist.

Für die Datierung der Verfassungszeit der lateinischen Bearbeitung von Orosius' Geschichtswerk können wir zunächst von den Quellen ausgehen, welche der lateinische Redaktor herangezogen hat: Von ihnen liefert keine einen Anhaltspunkt für eine Datierung, die später ist, als die Generation nach Isidors Tod (gest. 636 n.Chr.), also 2. Hälfte des 7. Jahrhunderts. Eine einzige Ausnahme ist der arabische Titel von Teil VII: diesem zufolge[31] umfasst Teil VII 'die Nachrichten über die römischen Caesaren-Herrscher (*amlāk ar-Rūmāniyīn al-qayāṣira*) von der Zeit des Octavianus Caesar an, während dessen Regierung der Messias geboren wurde, bis hin zu der Abfassungszeit dieses Buches[32]; ausserdem was sich von den Dynastien der Gothen in Andalusien bis hin zur Invasion des *Ṭāriq* zufügen lässt[33]'. Leider ist von diesem vierzehn Kapitel umfassenden Schlussteil das letzte Kapitel nicht erhalten. Daher scheint es entgegen Levi della Vida[34] vorläufig nicht sicher beweisbar, dass dieses verlorene Kapitel tatsächlich einen Appendix enthalten hat, welcher die Geschichtsdarstellung des Orosius bis zur Eroberung Andalusiens durch *Ṭāriq Ibn Ziyād* (im Jahre 93/712)[35] weiterführt. Ausserdem müsste man in diesem Falle annehmen, dass die im arabischen Text fehlenden lateinischen Kapitel Orosius VII 34-43 (ed. Zangemeister 281, 18-301) erheblich zusammengekürzt und hauptsächlich durch diesen Appendix ersetzt gewesen sein müssen.

Doch setzen wir einmal entsprechend der arabischen Titelangabe die Existenz einer Geschichtsfortsetzung bis Ṭāriq voraus: In diesem Falle müsste man an eine Quelle des frühmittelalterlichen Spaniens denken, welche die Westgoten berücksichtigt hat. Wir kennen nun eine von einem nordspanischen Christen 883 n.Chr. verfasste Weltgeschichte, nämlich das *Chronicon Albel-*

---

[30] Vgl. meine Übersetzung von ed. Badawī 412,9-ult.
[31] Ed. Badawī 413.
[32] Sc. Orosius' Geschichtswerk.
[33] *wa-mā uḍīfa ilaihi min ba'din min duwal al-qūṭ bi-l-Andalus ilā duḫūl Ṭāriq 'alaihim.*
[34] *La traduzione*, 267f.
[35] S. *EI*[1] Art. '*Ṭārik*'.

dense seu Emilianense[36], welche tatsächlich einige Parallelen zur arabischen Orosiusversion aufweist:

1) Beide benutzen Isidors *Etymologien*[37] und Isidors Weltära und *aetates*;

2) entsprechend der arabischen Überschrift in Teil VII enthält das *Chronicon Albeldense* eine Fortsetzung, die über Isidor und seine Behandlung der Westgoten hinausgeht.

Dennoch scheinen die genannten Parallelen des arabischen Orosius zum *Chronicon Albeldense* nicht auf eine literarische Abhängigkeit zurückzugehen. Dagegen spricht die Tatsache, dass die Unterschiede zwischen beiden so gross sind, dass die Ähnlichkeiten nur auf die Benutzung von gemeinsamen Quellen zurückgeführt werden können[38]. Eine dieser gemeinsamen Quellen könnte nun die *Continuatio Hispana* gewesen sein, welche bis zum Jahre 754 n.Chr. reicht[39] und die Invasion der Sarazenen in Spanien beschreibt. Hierfür könnte der Hinweis in der genannten arabischen Titelüberschrift zu Teil VII sprechen. — Indessen macht auch hier das Fehlen des 14. Kapitels im arabischen Schlussteil den eindeutigen Nachweis einer literarischen Abhängigkeit von der *Continuatio Hispana* unmöglich. Somit bleiben vorläufig drei Datierungsmöglichkeiten für die lateinische Orosiusredaktion der arabischen Übersetzung übrig:

1) Sie ist in der zweiten Hälfte des 7. Jahrhunderts entstanden;

2) sie setzt die Kenntnis der *Continuatio Hispana* aus der Mitte des 8. Jahrhunderts voraus;

3) sie benutzt dieselbe Quelle wie die *Continuatio Hispana* zum *Chronicon Albeldense*, nämlich die Beschreibung des Westgotenreiches bis zur arabischen Invasion unter Ṭāriq im Jahre 712 n.Chr.

Mit der zuletzt genannten Möglichkeit kommen wir in die erste Hälfte des 8. Jahrhunderts. Diese Datierung ist vorläufig am wahrscheinlichsten, zumal keine literarische Abhängigkeit zwischen dem arabischen Orosius und der *Continuatio Hispana* nachweisbar ist. Ausserdem müsste das fehlende letzte (14.) Kapitel des arabischen Orosius einen unverhältnismässig langen Zeitraum umfasst haben, der den üblichen Textumfang der einzelnen arabischen Kapitel gesprengt hätte.

---

[36] Vgl. zu ihm Von den Brincken, 134-136.

[37] Z.B. Die Rückführung der Goten auf Magog (Isidor, *Etym.* IX 2.27) bringen das *Chronicon Albeldense*, PL 129, col. 1144 Par. 84 und der arabische Orosius ed. Badawī 88,15 = Ibn Ḫaldūn apud Badawī 469,1. Diese Überlieferung weicht von den übrigen, im Islam bekannten Gog-Magog-Traditionen ab: vgl. A.J. Wensinck, Art. '*Yādjūdj wa-mādjūdj*' in *EI*[1].

[38] Als Beispiel vgl. z.B. das Kapitel über Athanaricus in *Chronicon Albeldense*, PL 129, col. 1133 Par. 14 mit dem arabischen Orosius ed. Badawī 463, 4ff.

[39] Ed. Mommsen, *Chronica minora saec. IV.V.VI.VII*, vol. II (= Monumenta Germaniae historica. Auctores antiquissimi XI/2), Berolini[2], 1961, 323ff., zusammen mit der *Continuatio Byzantia-Arabica a. DCCXLI.* Beide Werke bilden die Anfänge der Geschichtsschreibung im christlichen Spanien nach der Maureninvasion; s. Von den Brincken, 135 (zu Anm. 255).

Nachfolgend sei nun eine Übersicht über all die arabischen Textstücke gegeben, die sich nicht im lateinischen Original des Orosius finden und von einem lateinischen Bearbeiter zugefügt worden sind. Wir sehen hierbei von den wohl vom Übersetzer stammenden Paraphrasen oder sinngemässen Zusammenfassungen des lateinischen Orosiustextes ab. Mit Ausnahme des geographischen sowie des bibelgeschichtlichen Zusatzes, von welchem wir lediglich die Chronologie der Weltjahre skizzieren, werden alle Ergänzungen des lateinischen Bearbeiters in leicht kommentierter deutscher Übersetzung vorgelegt. Wie man dem dortigen Quellennachweis entnehmen kann, liessen sich nicht alle Details auf eine bekannte lateinische Quelle zurückführen. Ausserdem hat sich die überragende und hier nicht erschöpfend behandelte Bedeutung der arabischen Orosiusüberlieferung für die frühmittelalterliche Legendenbildung gezeigt[40]; besondere Beachtung verdient hier das Kapitel über Konstantin den Grossen (arab. T. 457-460): der lateinische Redaktor des arabischen Orosiustextes beruft sich auf 'einen christlichen Gelehrten namens Silvester' (arab. T. 457, 13f.), aber auch auf eine von ihm selbst verfasste Konstantinbiographie, welche er in sein Werk 'Die Nachrichten der Zeit' (= Chronica) aufgenommen habe (arab. T. 459, paen.s.). Sicherlich wird die verwickelte Überlieferungsgeschichte der sog. Silvesterlegende (*Actus Silvestri*), welche vermutlich in der zweiten Hälfte des 5. Jahrhunderts in lateinischer Sprache konzipiert wurde und in verschiedenen — leider noch nicht in einer kritischen Edition herausgegebenen Redaktionen und Übersetzungen (in Griechisch, Syrisch, Armenisch, Deutsch und Französisch) vorliegt[41], von der vorliegenden arabischen Überlieferung profitieren können.

Bevor wir die Zufügungen der arabischen Version zusammenstellen, sei hier eine Stellensynopse des arabischen und lateinischen Textes vorausgeschickt. Sie soll eine Übersicht geben von den Abweichungen des Arabischen gegenüber dem Lateinischen. Ihr kann man entnehmen, an welchen Stellen das Arabische gegenüber dem Lateinischen eine Zufügung besitzt, aber auch umgekehrt, inwieweit der lateinische Redaktor das Orosiusoriginal geändert hat. Betrachtet man diese Änderungen, ergibt sich folgendes Bild: Der lateinische Redaktor hat nicht nur zugefügt, sondern auch an einigen Stellen seine Vorlage gekürzt, paraphrasiert und umgestellt. Redaktionelle Eingriffe des arabischen Übersetzers können wir hier mit grosser Wahrscheinlichkeit ausschliessen. Es handelt sich um Weglassungen geschichtstheologischer Einschübe, welche teilweise kurze historische Rückblenden enthielten[42]; um

[40] Vgl. oben S. 205.

[41] Vgl. Duchesne I CIX-CXX (wo eine Inhaltsangabe der Legende gegeben wird); Schrörs, 249ff.; Dölger, 394ff.; von Döllinger, 61-72; *RAC* III, 1957, Art. 'Constantinus der Grosse' (J. Vogt), Sp. 374-376; Speyer, 297f. und v.a. Levison, 'Konstantinische Schenkung', wo auch die nichtlateinische Überlieferung behandelt wird.

[42] Orosius I 2 Par. 106 - I 4 (ed. Zangemeister 16,6-17,ult.); I 6 (ed. Zangemeister 19,7-31); I 17 Par. 3 - I 18 (ed. Zangemeister 29,25-30,7); V 22 Par. 5-15 (ed. Zangemeister 178,30-180,2).

Weglassungen kurzer einleitender oder zusätzlicher historischer Skizzen[43]; um Weglassungen ganzer Kapitel über geschichtliche Ereignisse[44] oder des Restes eines Kapitels[45]; um Streichungen eines zusätzlich angefügten Paragraphen über L. Postumus und Gracchus sowie die Anzahl der von ihnen getöteten Feinde bzw. eroberten Städte[46] etc.— Ohne dass wir immer sagen können, nach welchen Kriterien der lateinische Redaktor seine Vorlage gekürzt und um andere Textstücke erweitert hat, ist das Bestreben deutlich, den Orosiustext gleichsam zu 'modernisieren' und zu Lasten vieler Details der heidnischen Geschichtsschreibung die biblische Heilsgeschichte mehr in den Vordergrund zu stellen.

Stellensynopse des arabischen und lateinischen Orosiustextes.

Lat. Text	Arab. Text	
1-16,6 (= I 1-2 Par. 105)	53-72	I 1-3
—	73-81	I 4
—	82-85	I 5
—	86-92,18	I 6
16,6-17,3 (= I 2 Schluss - 3)	—	
17,3-ult. (= I 4)	92,18-93,ult.	I 6
18,1-19,6 (= I 5)	94-95,16	I 7
—	95,17-97,ult.	I 7
19,7-31 (= I 6)	—	
19,32-20,7 (= I 7)	98,1-9	I 7
20,8-22,3 (= I 8)	98,10-100,2	I 7
—	100,3-101,14	I 7/8
22,4-19 (= I 9)	101,15-102,13	I 8
22,20-25,2 (= I 10)	102,14-105,3	I 8
—	105,4-106,12	I 8/
25,3-24 (= I 11)	115,3-116,5	I 9
25,25-26,26 (= I 12)	106,13-107,ult.	I 9
—	108,1-112,18	I 9
26,27-27,2 (= I 13)	112,19-113,10	I 9
—	113,11-115,2	I 9

[43] Orosius I 21 Par. 1-2 (ed. Zangemeister 32, 7-13); VI 3 Par. 1 (ed. Zangemeister 193, 26-28).

[44] II 4-5 ed. Zangemeister 38, 27-41, 33 (zur ältesten Geschichte Roms); II 13 Par. 1-7 ed. Zangemeister 50, 20-51, 12 (über Appius Claudius).

[45] IV 13 Par. 17-18 ed. Zangemeister 122, 28-34; VI 6 Par. 7 ed. Zangemeister 197,35-198,3; VI 12 Par. 2-8 ed. Zangemeister 209,2-210,4; VI 17 Par. 4-10 ed. Zangemeister 218,14-219,16.

[46] IV 20 Par. 33 ed. Zangemeister 135, 22-25.

25,3-24 (= I 11) (!)	115,3-116,5	I 9
—	116,10-117,7	I 9
27,3-29,15 (= I 14-16)	117,8-120,6	I 9
—	120,7-123,9	I 9
29,16-25 (= I 17 Par. 1-2)	123,10-124,4	I 9
29,25-30,7 (= I 17 Par. 3- I 18)	—	
—	124,4-154,16	I 9/10
30,8-21 (= I 19, Anf.)	154,17-155,6	I 10
—	155,7-157,2	I 10
30,21-31,16	157,3-158,6	I 10
31,17-32,6 (= I 20)	158,7-159,4	I 10
—	159,5-161,8	I 10
32,7-13 (= I 21 Par. 1-2)	161,9-17	I 10
—	161,18-162,9	I 10
32,14-34,19 (= I 21 Par. 3-21)	162,10-164,13 (Schluss kürzer)	I 10
35,1-36,5 (= II 1)	167,1-19	II 1
36,6-37,16 (= II 2)	167,20-169,1	II 1
37,17-38,26 (= II 3)	169,1-170,5	II 1
38,27-40,8 (= II 4)	—	
40,9-41,33 (= II 5)	—	
—	171,1-174,6	II 2
—	175,1-5	II 3
42,31-36 (aus II 6 Par. 10)	175,6-8	II 3
42,36-43,23 (= II 6 Par. 11-12)	175,9-176,22	II 3
43,24-44,11 (= II 7)	176,ult.-177,20 (i.d. 2. Hälfte abweichend, länger; Zusatz 177,21-ult.)	II 3
—	178,1-179,18	II 6(!)
44,12-45,22 (= II 8)	179,19-181,14	II 6(!)
—	182,1-7	II 7
45,23-46,34 (= II 9)	182,8-184,9	II 7
46,35-48,9 (= II 10)	184,10-185,14	II 7
48,10-49,21 (= II 11, ohne Schluss)	185,15-186,ult. (Lücke i.d. Hs.)	II 7
49,22-28 (= II 12 Par. 1)	187,3-5 (lückenhafte Hs.)	II 7
—	187,6-7	II 7
—	188,1-12	II 8
49,28-50,19 (= II 12)	188,13-189,17 (teilw. lückenhaft)	II 8
50,20-51,12 (= II 13 Par. 1-7)	—	

51,13-28 (= II 13 Par. 8-11)	189,18-190,14	II 8
—	190,15-16	II 8
—	191,1-5	II 9
51,29-54,5 (= II 14)	191,6-194,3	II 9
54,6-37 (= II 15)	194,4-195,2 (teilw. abweichend)	II 9
55,1-56,30 (= II 16)	195,3-197,3	II 9
56,30-59,9 (= II 17)	197,4-199,7	II 9
—	199,8-200,8	II 9/10
59,10-60,9 (= II 18, ohne letzten Satz)	200,9-201,11	II 10
60,11-62,9 (= II 19)	201,12-203,14	II 10
63-67,18 (III praef.; Par. 1-2)	207,1-211,5 (mit Auslassungen)	III 1
67,19-69,11 (= III 2)	211,6-212,ult.	III 1
69,12-35 (= II 3)	213,1-214,2	III 2
69,36-70,23 (= II 4)	214,3-10 (gekürzt)	III 2
70,24-34 (= II 5)	214,11-14	III 2
—	214,15-16	III 2
70,35-71,19 (= II 6)	214,17-215,16	III 2
71,20-35 (= II 7 Par. 1-5)	215,17-216,2	III 2
—	216,3-217,7	III 2/3
71,36-72,9 (= III 7 Par. 6-8)	217,8-11	III 3
72,10-73,18 (= III 8)	217,12-218,7	III 3
73,19-34 (= III 9)	218,8-15	III 3
73,35-74,10 (= III 10)	218,16-20	III 3
74,11-25 (= III 11)	218,21-219,9	III 3
74,26-78,10 (= III 12)	220,1-223,15 (teilw. abw.)	III 4
78,11-79,26 (= III 13)	223,16-225,3	III 4
79,27-80,36 (= III 14)	225,4-226,15	III 4
80,36-81,4 (= III 15 Par. 1)	226,16-18 (leicht gekürzt)	III 4
—	226,19-227,5	III 4/5
81,5-82,11 (= III 15 Par. 2-10)	227,6-228,12 (Ende kürzer)	III 5
—	228,13-229,6	III 5
82,12-84,7 (= III 16)	229,7-231,22	III 5/6
84,8-85,8 (= III 17)	231,23-233,5	III 6
85,9-25 (= III 18 Par. 1-4)	233,6-233,19	III 6
—	233,20-234,7	III 6/7
85,26-86,15 (= III 18 Par. 5-11)	234,8-235,15	III 7
86,16-87,28 (= III 19)	235,16-237,12	III 7

87,29-89,16 (= III 20)	237,13-239,9	III 7
—	239,10-240,10	III 7/8
89,17-90,11 (= III 21)	240,11-241,17	III 8
90,12-91,32 (= III 22)	241,18-243,13	III 8
91,33-92,11 (= III 23 Par. 1-5)	243,14-19 (kürzer)	III 8
92,12-95,21 (= III 23 Par. 6-37)	244,1-249,ult.	III 9
95,21-98,11 (= III 23 Par. 38-68)	250,1-253,10	III 10
—	253,11-12; 257,1-11	III 1/IV 1
99-100,25 (= IV praef.)	257,12-259,2 (lässt einl. Verweis auf Vergil, Aeneas weg.)	IV 1
100,26-103,7 (= IV 1)	259,3-261,paenult.	IV 1
103,8-104,3 (= IV 2)	261,ult.-262,3	IV 1
104,4-25 (= IV 3)	262,paenult.-263,15	IV 1
104,26-105,13 (= IV 4)	263,16-264,11	IV 1
105,14-106,32 (= IV 5)	264,12-265,18	IV 1
106,33-111,23 (= IV 6)	265,19-270,paenult.	IV 1
111,24-112,34 (= IV 7)	270,ult.-272,7	IV 1
112,35-114,33 (= IV 8)	272,8-274,7	IV 1
114,34-116,36 (= IV 9)	274,7-276,18	IV 1
116,37-118,5 (= IV 10)	276,19-278,6	IV 1
118,6-21 (= IV 11 Par. 1-4)	278,7-17	IV 1
—	278,18-279,6	IV 1/2
118,22-119,10 (= IV 11 Par. 5-10)	279,7-280,9	IV 2
119,10-120,ult. (= IV 12)	280,10-281,paenult. (leicht gekürzt)	IV 2
121,1-7 (= IV 13 Par. 1-2)	281,ult.-282,ult.	IV 2
121,8-122,28 (= IV 13 Par. 3-16)	283,1-285,13	IV 3
122,28-34 (= IV 13 Par. 17-18)	—	
—	285,14-286,6	IV 3/4
122,35-123,36 (= IV 14)	286,7-287,20	IV 4
123,37-124,ult. (= IV 15)	287,21-289,3	IV 4
125,1-127,12 (= IV 16)	289,4-291,14	IV 4
—	291,15-292,7	IV 4/5
127,13-128,24 (=IV 17 Par. 1-11)	292,8-293,ult.	IV 5
128,25-129,2 (= IV 17 Par. 12-14)	294,1-294,16	IV 6
129,3-30 (= IV 18 Par. 1-7)	294,17-296,7	IV 6
129,30-130,30 (= IV 18 Par. 8-16)	296,8-297,ult.	IV 6
130,30-131,17 (= IV 18 Par. 17-21)	298,1-299,2	IV 7
131,18-132,12 (= IV 19)	299,3-300,8	IV 7
132,13-133,9 (= IV 20 Par. 1-9)	300,9-301,ult.	IV 7
133,10-135,22 (= IV 20 Par. 10-32)	302,1-306,2	IV 8

135,22-25 (= IV 20 Par. 33)	—	
—	306,3-307,6	IV 8/9
135,26-136,28 (= IV 20 Par. 34-40)	307,7-308,ult.	IV 9
—	309,1-310,5	IV 9/10
136,29-138,5 (= IV 21)	310,6-312,15	IV 10
138,6-139,8 (= IV 22)	312,16-314,5	IV 10
139,9-140, ult. 8= IV 23)	314,6-315,ult. (kürzer)	IV 10/V 1
141-145,2 (= V 1-2)	319,1-15 (Zusammenfassung)	V 1
145,3-146,9 (= V 3)	319,16-321,12	V 1
146,10-149,11 (= V 4)	321,13-325,11	V 1
149,12-151,5 (= V 5)	325,12-328,15	V 1
151,6-34 (= V 6)	328,16-329,7	V 1
—	329,8-330,7	V 1/2
151,35-153,35 (= V 7)	330,8-332,8	V 2
153,36-154,1	—	
154,1-23 (= V 8)	332,9-333,6	V 2
154,24-155,19 (= V 9)	333,6-334,11	V 2
155,20-156,36 (= V 10 Par. 1-10)	334,12-335,ult.	V 2
156,37-157,7 (= V 10 Par. 11)	336,1-10	V 3
157,8-158,10 (= V 11)	336,10-337,ult.	V 3
158,11-159,23 (= V 12)	338,1-340,4	V 4
159,24-ult. (= V 13)	340,5-340,16	V 4
160,1-26 (= V 14)	340,17-341,11	V 4
—	341,12-342,6	V 4/5
160,27-164,9 (= V 15)	342,7-346,4	V 5
164,10-167,8 (= V 16)	346,5-350,15 (mit zusätzlichen Details 350,8-10/lat. T. V 16 Par. 23 S. 167,2-4)	V 5
167,9-168,33 (= V 17)	350,16-353,10	V 5
—	353,11-354,8	V 5/6
168,34-169,16 (= V 18 Par. 1-7)	354,9-355,ult.	V 6
169,17-170,10 (= V 18 Par. 8-14, Anf.)	356,1-357,ult.	V 7
170,10-26 (= V 18 Par. 14, Anf.-17, Anf.)	358,1-ult. (Zusatz 358,8-14)	V 8
170,26-171,11 (= V 18 Par. 17, Forts. -21)	359,1-ult.	V 9
171,12-172,21 (= V 18 Par. 22-30)	360,1-362,3	V 10
172,22-175,32 (= V 19)	362,4-365,paenult.	V 10
175,33-176,34 (= V 20)	365,ult.-367,16	V 10
176,35-178,14 (= V 21)	367,16-369,10	V 10

178,15-178,29 (= V 22 Par. 1-4)	369,11-370,3	V 10
178,30-180,2 (= V 22 Par. 5-15)	—	
180,3-15 (= V 22 Par. 16-18)	370,4-12	V 10
180,16-182,31 (= V 23)	370,13-373,8	V 10
182,32-185,ult. (= V 24)	373,9-376	V 10
—	379,1-2	VI 1
186-190,9 (= VI 1 Par. 1-27)	379,3-381,ult. (eine gekürzte u. teilw. bearbeitete Wiedergabe)	VI 1
190,10-19 (= VI 1 Par. 28-30)	382,1-6	VI 2
190,20-193,25 (= VI 2)	382,7-385,paenult.	VI 2
193,26-28 (= VI 3 Par. 1)	—	
193,29-194,17 (= VI 3 Par. 2-7)	385,ult.-386,16	VI 2
194,18-195,20 (= VI 4)	386,17-387,18	VI 2
195,21-197,8 (= VI 5)	387,18-389,2	VI 2
197,9-35 (=VI 6 Par. 1-6)	389,3-390,5	VI 2
197,35-198,3 (= VI 6 Par. 7)	—	
—	390,6-391,4	VI 2/3
198,4-35 (= VI 7)	391,5-392,16 (teilw. gekürzt)	VI 3
198,36-202,7 (= VI 8)	392,16-394,11	VI 3
202,8-203,8 (= VI 9)	394,12-395,12	VI 3
203,9-205,18 (= VI 10)	395,13-398,6	VI 3
205,19-208,ult. (= VI 11)	398,7-401,ult. (stark gekürzt, bes. ab lat. T.VI 11 Par. 20ff.)	VI 3
209,1-2 (= VI 12 Par. 1, Anf.)	vgl. 402,1-4	VI 3
209,2-210,4 (= VI 12 Par. 2-8)	—	
210,5-ult. (= VI 13)	413,1-404,10	VI 4
211,1-30 (= VI 14)	404,11-16	VI 4
211,31-215,ult. (= VI 15 Par. 1-29)	404,17-408,ult.	VI 4
216,1-28 (= VI 15 Par. 30-34)	409,1-410,4	VI 5
216,28-217,18 (= VI 16)	410,4-paenult.	VI 5
—	410,ult.-411,4	VI 5/6
217,18-218,2 (= VI 16 Par. 6-9)	411,5-ult.	VI 6
218,3-13 (= VI 17 Par. 1-3)	411,ult.-412,8	VI 6
218,14-219,16 (= VI 17 Par. 4-10)	—	
—	412,9-ult.-	VI 6
219,17-232 (siehe 416,5-417)		
233-235,10 (= VII 1)	415 (Zusf., vermutlich v. ar. Uebers., eingel. m. *ḥakā Hurūšyūš* 'Orosius erzählt')	VII 1

—	416,1-4	VII 2
219,17-232 (= VI 18-22)	vgl. 416,5-417 (abweichend, m. zusätzl. Ang.)	VII 2
235,11-239,7 (= VII 2-3)	418-419,11 (stark gekürzt)	VII 3
—	419,12-420,4	VII 3/4
239,8-241,13 (= VII 4)	420,4-422 (gekürzt m. Zus. 421,17-422,4)	VII 4
241,14-243,6 (= VII 5)	423-424,18 (kürzer)	VII 5
—	424,19-425,4	VII 5/6
243,7-245,29 (= VII 6)	425,4-426,9 (gekürzt, m. Zusätzen, z.B. 425,11-12)	VII 6
—	426,9-13	VII 6
245,30-247,20 (= VII 7)	426,14-428,16	VII 6
—	428,16-429,4	VII 6/7
247,21-249,3 (= VII 8)	429,5-430,14 (kürzer)	VII 7
249,4-250,37 (= VII 9 Par. 1-12)	430,15-432,17	VII 7
—	432,18-433,5	VII 7/8
251,1-12 (= VII 9 Par. 13-15)	433,6-12	VII 8
—	435,1-4	VII 9
251,13-252,12 (= VII 10)	434,1-2; 435,5-436,2	VII 8/9
—	436,3-6	VII 9
252,13-23 (= VII 11)	436,6-10	VII 9
—	436,11-14	VII 9
252,24-253,30 (= VII 12)	436,14-438,2	VII 9
—	438,3-7	VII 9
253,31-254,16 (= VII 13)	438,8-10	VII 9
—	438,11-15	VII 9
254,17-28 (= VII 14)	438,15-439,2	VII 9
—	439,3-440,4	VII 9/10
254,29-256,13 (= VII 15)	440,5-442,5	VII 10
—	442,5-443,5	VII 10/11
256,14-257,2 (= VII 16)	443,6-444,11	VII 11
—	444,12-15	VII 11
257,3-36 (= VII 17)	444,16-445,3	VII 11
—	445,2-6	VII 11
257,37-258,7 (= VII 18 Par. 1-2)	445,7-14	VII 11
258,8-11 (= VII 18 Par. 3)	445,15-16; 19-20	VII 11
—	445,16-19	VII 11
258,12-17 (= VII 18 Par. 4-5)	446,1-2; 447,6-7	VII 11/12
—	447,1-5	VII 12

—	447,7-11	VII 12
258,18-26 (= VII 18 Par. 6-8)	447,11-16 (gekürzt)	VII 12
—	447,17-20	VII 12
258,27-37 (= VII 19 Par. 1-2)	447,21-448,7	VII 12
—	448,8-12	VII 12
259,1-13 (= VII 19 Par. 3-5)	448,13-15 (gekürzt)	VII 12
—	448,16-20	VII 12
259,14-27 (= VII 20)	449,1-5 (gekürzt)	VII 12
—	449,6-9	VII 12
259,28-ult. (= VII 21 Par. 1-3)	vgl. 449,9-10; 450,1	VII 12
—	449,10-ult.	VII 12
—	450,1-5	VII 12
260,1-12 (= VII 21 Par. 4-6)	450,6-9	VII 12
—	450,9-13	VII 12
260,13-262,19 (= VII 22)	450,14-451,8 (gekürzt)	VII 12
—	451,9-13	VII 12
262,20-263,13 (= VII 23)	451,13-452,10	VII 12
—	452,11-13	VII 12
263,14-15 (= VII 24 Par. 1,Anf.)	452,13 (gekürzt)	VII 12
263,16-17 (= VII 24 Par. 1,Schl.)	—	
—	452,14-17	VII 12
263,18-27 (=VII 24 Par. 2-3)	452,17-24	VII 12
—	452,25-453,3	VII 12
263,28-35 (= VII 24 Par. 4)	453,3-7	VII 12
—	453,7-11	VII 12
263,36-266,16 (= VII 25)	453,12-456,10	VII 12
—	456,11-14	VII 12
266,17-274,17 (= VII 26-29 Par. 4)	457-461,10 (abweichend)	VII 13
274,17-20 (= VII 29 Par. 5)	461,11-14	VII 13
—	461,14-462,1	VII 13
274,22-275,36 (= VII 29 Par. 6-18)	—	
275,37-276,3 (= VII 30 Par. 1)	—	
276,3-26 (= VII 30 Par. 2-6)	462,1-12	VII 13
—	462,13-16	VII 13
276,27-277,4 (= VII 31)	462,17-463,3	VII 13
277,5-7 (= VII 32 Par. 1)	—	
—	463,4-14	VII 13
277,8-18 (= VII 32 Par. 2-4)	463,ult.-464,6	VII 13
—	464,6-7	VII 13
277,18-22 (= VII 32 Par. 5)	464,8-9	VII 13
277,22-32 (= VII 32 Par. 6-8,Anf.)	—	

277,32-278,25 (= VII 32 Par. 8, Schluss-Par. 14)	464,10-465,5	VII 13
278,26-29 (= VII 32 Par. 15)	—	
—	465,6-10	VII 13
278,30-281,17 (= VII 33)	465,11-466 (m. Auslassungen)	VII 13
281,18-301 (= VII 34-43)	—	

Abweichungen und Zusätze des arabischen Orosiustextes.

I

Im arabischen Orosius folgt auf den geographischen Teil von Orosius I 1-2[47] ein zusätzliches Kapitel[48] über die Meere, Inseln, Berge, Länder, Distrikte und Flüsse. Der arabischen Übersetzer lässt die einzelnen Namen aus und erwähnt nur ihre Anzahl, weil sie 'im Arabischen nicht bekannt seien'[49]. Nur die Flüsse werden namentlich genannt und im Einzelnen beschrieben[50]. — Der arabische Text beruft sich zu Beginn des Kapitels auf 'den Befund' (*mā wuğida*) in 'den Registern' (*ad-dawāwīn*) von Julius Caesar, welche von Nicodoxus <nqw-dẖst>[51], Didymus <dyḏmh> Theodotus (verschrieben zu <ṭwrftwr>[52]) und Polycrites <blqryṭh>[53] zusammengestellt worden seien. Dieses Kapitel entstammt, wie schon G. Levi della Vida[54] festgestellt hat, der *Cosmographia Iulii Honorii*[55]. Dieses Werk, welches in drei Rezensionen vorliegt — wovon die jüngste nicht später als in das 5. Jahrhundert zu datieren ist[56] — hat auch in das oben bereits genannte *Chronicon Albeldense*[57] sowie in die *Historia*

---

[47] Übersetzt von Yves Janvier, *La geographie d'Orose*, Paris, 1982, 35-57.

[48] Ed. Badawī, 73-81.

[49] Ed. Badawī, 73,12.

[50] Ed. Badawī, 74, 16-81.

[51] Das lateinische Original des Julius Honorius (s.u.) hat die Varianten Nicodomus, Nicodorus und Nicodoxus (s. *RE* 19, Sp. 626); der Auszug des *Chronicon Albeldense* (PL 129, col. 1125 A) hat die Lesart Nicodosus, welche am ehesten mit dem Arabischen übereinstimmt — ohne das natürlich aus diesem Detail auf eine literarische Abhängigkeit geschlossen werden kann (vgl. oben S. 207); weitere Varianten enthält die *Historia Ps.Isidoriana* (s. Anm. 58).

[52] Oder Theudotus. Levi della Vida, *La traduzione*, 269 las im Arabischen <ṭwdqtwr>.

[53] Levi della Vida, *La traduzione*, 269, falsch: Polyctitus. Der lateinische Text des Julius Honorius und das *Chronicon Albeldense* haben Polylitus.

[54] *La traduzione*, 269.

[55] Ed. A. Riese in *Geographi latini minores*, Heilbronnae, 1878 (Nachdr. Hildesheim, 1964), 21-55 (im Arabischen fehlt der Schluss von S. 53-55).

[56] Siehe Kubitschek, Art. 'Julius Honorius' in *RE* 19, 1917, 614-627, bes. 626,19ff.

[57] S. zu diesem Anm. 36.

Pseudoisidoriana Eingang gefunden[58]. Der dortige geographische Text gibt die *Cosmographia* des Iulius Honorius gekürzt wieder, so dass beide somit als Vorlage des arabischen Orosius ausscheiden[59]. Ferner ist somit deutlich, dass die *Cosmographia* in Spanien verbreitet war und gleichfalls dem wohl in Spanien ansässigen lateinischen Bearbeiter von Orosius' Geschichtswerk zugänglich war.

II

Auch das auf den geographischen Zusatz ziemlich abrupt folgende Stück biblischer Geschichte von der Schöpfung der Welt in sieben Tagen, von Adam bis Noah[60] und von Noah bis Abraham[61] finden wir nicht im Lateinischen, wo statt dessen ein geschichtstheologischer Teil mit einer Rückblende auf die Zeit nach Ninus, den ersten assyrischen König folgt[62]. Der arabische Orosius folgt hier in der Reihenfolge und im Aufbau seiner Zusätze Isidors *Chronica maiora*[63]. Diese hat auch das folgende Stück biblischer Geschichte[64] geprägt: Wir finden hier unter Einbeziehung der Chronologie des Isidor von Sevilla[65] und des biblischen Materials (vermutlich nach der Vulgata und Vetus Latina) folgende Geschichten des Alten Testamentes gestreift: Lot, Isaak und Jakob[66] (vgl. Gen. 13ff.); Josua[67]; Othniel[68] (vgl. Jud. 3); Ehud[69] (vgl. Jud. 3:15ff.); Debora[70] (vgl. Jud. 4); Gideon[71] (vgl. Jud. 6ff.); Abimelek[72] (vgl. Jud. 9); Thola und Jair[73] (vgl. Jud. 10); Jephtah[74] (vgl. Jud. 11); Ebzam[75] (vgl. Jud. 12:8-10); Abdon[76] (vgl. Jud. 12:13-15); Simson[77] (vgl. Jud. 13-16); Eli und die bösen Taten der Söhne Hophni und Pinehas sowie die Bundeslade bei den

---

[58] Vgl. Levi della Vida, *La traduzione*, 269.
[59] Vgl. noch oben S. 207.
[60] Ed. Badawī, 82-85.
[61] Ed. Badawī, 86-93.
[62] Orosius I 2 Par. 106, Schluss - I 4 ed. Zangemeister 16,6-17,ult.
[63] Ed. Mommsen, 426ff.
[64] Ed. Badawī, 95, 17-179.
[65] Vgl. unten S. 219f.
[66] Ed. Badawī, 95,17-97,ult.; im lateinischen Text nicht behandelt: vgl. I 6-8, wo I 6 lediglich Sodom und Gomorra erwähnt werden.
[67] Ed. Badawī, 105.
[68] Ed. Badawī, 106, 1-12.
[69] Ed. Badawī, 108, 3ff.
[70] Ed. Badawī, 109, 1-3.
[71] Ed. Badawī, 109,paenult.-112.
[72] Ed. Badawī, 113,11-114,1.
[73] Ed. Badawī, 114, 3-14.
[74] Ed. Badawī, 114,15; 116, 10-23.
[75] Ed. Badawī, 117, 1-7.
[76] Ed. Badawī, 120, 8-17.
[77] Ed. Badawī, 121,5-123,9.

Philistern[78] (vgl. 1. Sam. 1-5); Samuel und Saul (*Ṭālūt*)[79] (vgl 1. Sam. 8ff.); David[80] (vgl. 1. Sam. 16ff.); Salomon[81] (vgl. 1. Reg. 1ff.); Jerobeam[82] (vgl. 1. Reg. 11ff.); Abiam[83] (vgl. 1. Reg. 15:1-8); Asa[84] (vgl. 1. Reg. 15:9-24); Nadab[85] (vgl. 1. Reg. 15:25-32); Baesa, Jehu, Ela, Simri, Omri, Ahab, Elia, Elisa[86] (vgl. 1. Reg. 15:33ff.; 16ff.); Ahasja[87] (vgl. 2. Reg. 8:25ff.); Athalja[88] (vgl. 2. Reg. 11); Joas[89] (vgl. 2. Reg. 12f.); Amazja[90] (vgl. 2. Reg. 14); Usia, Menahem, Pekahja und Pekah[91] (vgl. 2. Reg. 15); Jotham[92] (vgl. 2. Reg. 15:32-38); Ahas[93] (2. Reg. 16); Hiskia[94] (vgl. 2. Reg. 18f.); Manasse[95] (vgl. 2. Reg. 21:1ff.); Amon[96] (vgl. 2. Reg 21:19-26); Josia[97] (vgl. 2. Reg 22); Joahas und Jojakim[98] (vgl. 2. Reg. 23:31ff.; 24); Zedekia[99] (vgl. 2. Reg. 24:18ff.); Haggai und Sacharja[100] (vgl. die entsprechenden prophetischen Bücher des Alten Testamentes). Zum Schluss wird[101] auf die Makkabäer verwiesen: 'Darnach ereignete sich, was im Buch der Makkabäer berichtet wird'.

III

Den oben aufgezählten Kapiteln aus dem Alten Testament hat der lateinische Redaktor des arabischen Orosiustextes an folgenden Stellen die Chronologie des Isidor von Sevilla (*Chronica maiora*) zugrundegelegt:

Arab.T. 97,9f.: Weltjahr 3434 — Geburt Josephs; Jakob 90 Jahre alt = Isidor Nr. 39.

97,paenult.s.: Weltjahr 3544 — Tod Josephs im Alter von 110 Jahren = Isidor Nr. 42.

---

[78] Ed. Badawī, 124,19-125.
[79] Ed. Badawī, 126-135,16.
[80] Ed. Badawī, 135,17-139,2.
[81] Ed. Badawī, 139,3-141,15.
[82] Ed. Badawī, 141,16-143,ult.
[83] Ed. Badawī, 144, 3-12.
[84] Ed. Badawī, 144, 13-19.
[85] Ed. Badawī, 144,20-145,2.
[86] Ed. Badawī, 145,3-148,2.
[87] Ed. Badawī, 148,16-150,2.
[88] Ed. Badawī, 150,4-151,2.
[89] Ed. Badawī, 151,3-152,4.
[90] Ed. Badawī, 152,5-153,8.
[91] Ed. Badawī, 153,9-154,16.
[92] Ed. Badawī, 155,7-156,3.
[93] Ed. Badawī, 156,4-157,2.
[94] Ed. Badawī, 159,5-161,5.
[95] Ed. Badawī, 161,18-162,9.
[96] Ed. Badawī, 171, 1-9.
[97] Ed. Badawī, 171,16-172,3.
[98] Ed. Badawī, 172,4-173,7.
[99] Ed. Badawī, 173,8-174,6.
[100] Ed. Badawī, 179, 1-13.
[101] Ed. Badawī, 179,14.

101,5: Weltjahr 3688 — Zeit des Moses; Ende des 144-jährigen Frondienstes der Israeliten in Ägypten = Isidor Nr. 44.
105,11f.: Weltjahr 3755 — Tod des Josua (regierte über Israel 27 Jahre) = Isidor Nr. 59.
106,5f.: Weltjahr 3765 — Tod des Othniel (regierte über Israel 40 Jahre) = Isidor Nr. 61 (abweichendes Weltjahr: 3795; vermutlich liegt im Arabischen ein Überlieferungsfehler vor).
108,4f.: Weltjahr 3875 — Tod des Ehud (regierte über Israel 80 Jahre) = Isidor Nr. 65.
109,3f.: Weltjahr 3915 — Tod der Debora (regierte über Israel 40 Jahre) = Isidor Nr. 73.
110,3f.: Weltjahr 3955 — Tod des Gideon (regierte über Israel 40 Jahre) = Isidor Nr. 77.
113,15f.: Weltjahr 3959 — Tod des Abimelek (regierte über Israel 3 Jahre) = Isidor Nr. 81.
114,5f.:Weltjahr 3981 — Tod des Thola (regierte über Israel 23 Jahre) = Isidor Nr. 83.
114,13f.: Weltjahr 4003 — Tod des Jair (regierte über Israel 22 Jahre) = Isidor Nr. 86.
116,12f.: Weltjahr 4009 — Tod des Jephtah (regierte über Israel 6 Jahre) = Isidor Nr. 89.
117,4f.: Weltjahr 4016 — Tod des Ebzam (regierte über Israel 7 Jahre) = Isidor Nr. 92.
120,10f.: Weltjahr 4024 — Tod des Abdon (regierte über Israel 8 Jahre) = Isidor Nr. 94.
121,7f.: Weltjahr 4044 — Tod des Simson (regierte über Israel 20 Jahre) = Isidor Nr. 98.
126,5f.: Weltjahr 4129 oder 4127 — Tod des Samuel (regierte über Israel 40 Jahre) = Isidor Nr. 104.
135,19.: Weltjahr 4164 — Tod des David = Isidor Nr. 107.
139,4f.: Weltjahr 4204 — Tod des Salomon (regierte über Israel 40 Jahre) = Isidor Nr. 111.
141,17f.: Weltjahr 4221 — Tod des Jerobeam (regierte über Israel 17 Jahre) = Isidor Nr. 113.
144,6f.: Weltjahr 4224 — Tod des Abiam (regierte über Israel 3 Jahre) = Isidor Nr. 117.
144,15f.: Weltjahr 4265 — Tod des Asa (regierte über Israel 41 Jahre) = Isidor Nr. 119.
146,9f.: Weltjahr 4290 — Tod des Jehu (Yahūšafāṭ) (regierte über Israel 25 Jahre) = Isidor Nr. 121 (Josaphat).
148,17: Weltjahr 4299[102] — Tod des Ahasja = Isidor Nr. 125.

[102] Im Druck steht falsch *arba'ata ālāf wa-iṯnataini wa-tis'a wa-tis'īna sanatan.*

150,10f.: Weltjahr 4306 — Tod des Athalja (regierte über Israel 7 Jahre) = Isidor Nr. 127.
151,5f.: Weltjahr 4346 — Tod des Joas (regierte über Israel 40 Jahre) = Isidor Nr. 130.
152,11.: Weltjahr 4375 — Tod des Amazja (regierte 29 Jahre) = Isidor Nr. 134.
153,13-15: Weltjahr 4427 — Tod des Usia (regierte über Israel 52 Jahre) = Isidor Nr. 135.
155,11-13: Weltjahr 4443 — Tod des Jotham (regierte über Israel 16 Jahre) = Isidor Nr. 142.
156,10f.: Weltjahr 4459 — Tod des Ahas (regierte über Israel 16 Jahre) = Isidor Nr. 145.
159,9-11: Weltjahr 4488 — Tod des Hiskia (regierte über Israel 29 Jahre) = Isidor Nr. 148.
161,21-23: Weltjahr 4543 — Tod des Manasse (regierte über Israel 55 Jahre) = Isidor Nr. 151.
171,5f.: Weltjahr 4555 — Tod des Amon (regierte über Israel 12 Jahre) = Isidor Nr. 155.
173,10: Weltjahr 4609 — Tod des Zedekia (regierte über Israel 11 Jahre) = Isidor Nr. 163.

IV

Auch im nachfolgenden, nichtbiblischen Teil hat der lateinische Redaktor den Orosiustext mit Isidor von Sevillas *Chronica maiora* kombiniert und hierbei dessen Zählung nach Weltjahren übernommen. Er hat dabei weitere Quellen mit herangezogen. Um einen konkreten Eindruck zu bekommen, seien sie hier in Übersetzung vorgelegt.

Arab.T. 101,7-14: 'In dieser Zeit[103] lebte Prometheus, dem man in den Büchern die Erfindung der Wunder zuschreibt[104]. Die Erinnerung an seine Herkunft und an seinen Namen hörte auf zu bestehen, da sie für (unser) astrologisches Wissen nicht (mehr) deutlich ist[105]. Sein Enkel Mercurius zeichnete sich in verschiedenen Wissenschaften aus. Nachdem er gestorben war, brachte man ihn mit den Götzen (*al-auṯān*) in Verbindung[105]. — [106]In jener Zeit war der erste, welcher Wein anbaute, ein mann namens Heracles <yrğl> [106]. — [107]In jener Zeit erbaute <ğbrs> (= Cecrops), der König der Griechen (ar-Rūm al-Ġirīqiyīn) die Stadt Athen, zu welcher die Athener (al-

[103] Sc. während des 144jährigen Frondienstes der Israeliten in Ägypten.
[104] Isidor, *Chron. mai.* Nr. 45.
[105] Isidor, *Chron. mai.* Nr. 47.
[106] Vgl. Isidor, *Chron. mai.* Nr. 58: Vitis in Graecia invenitur.
[107] Isidor, *Chron. mai.* Nr. 49 (der arabische Übersetzer gibt den Schluss nicht genau wieder).

Aṯānasiyūn) gehören[107]. [108]Er (war) der erste, der dem Götzen Jupiter einen Stier opferte. Er verpflichtete die ihm Gehorsamen dazu, ihn zu verehren[108]. — Jupiter ist ein Götze mit dem Namen 'glänzender (Planet) Jupiter'[109]. [110]Damals erfanden <brmfws> (= Coretes) und <frwnyṭs> (= Corybantes) verschiedene Musikarten für das Komponieren von Liedern und Regeln für verschiedene Arten von Musikinstrumenten und Blasinstrumenten[110]'.

109,14-21: '[111]In jener Zeit lebte der Arzt Apollo. Er war der erste Arzt. Auf ihn wird die Wissenschaft der Medizin zurückgeführt[111]. Er gehörte zu den Nachkommen der <šǧsnyh> (= Sicinii?[112]), welche zu den Griechen gehörten. — [113]In jener Zeit wurde die Überlieferung ersonnen, welche beschreibt, wie der Leiter der Schmiede in Rom, genannt Daedalus und sein Sohn Icarus Flügel aus Federn machten und damit tatsächlich geflogen sind[113]. — [114]In jener Zeit war der erste König der Römer (ar-Rūm al-Laṭīniyīn) in Italien ein Mann namens <bnqš> (= Picus), der Sohn des Saturnus šṭrnš, eines Sohnes von <bwb> [114]. Der (genannte) Vater von ihm ist derjenige, von dem die Römer behaupten, dass er der Götze Saturn ist, welchen die Römer während der Heidenzeit eine Zeitlang unter dem Namen 'leuchtender (Stern) Mars' verehrt haben'.

112,14-18: '[115]In jener Zeit wurde die Stadt Tarsus erbaut[115]. [116]Während dieser) ereignete sich die bekannte Geschichte (*šanuʿa ḫabaru*[117]) von dem berühmten (*al-failasūf*) Orpheus <'rf'ws> [118]; ausserdem die Geschichte von dem in der Musikwissenschaft, nämlich im Ordnen der Melodien und Komponieren der Lieder berühmten <*ṯḫšlš*> [116]. [119]In jener Zeit erfand der berühmte (*al-failasūf*) Mercurius <mrkwrs> die Laute für (das Vortragen) eines Liedes[119]'.

114,18-115,2: 'Während seiner (sc. des Richters Jephtah) Zeit hat Cadmus <kdms>, der Sohn des <msrsyh>, des Sohnes von ... <sbʿʾn>, eines Sohnes von Saturnus šṭrnš, des Sohnes von Noah, das Alphabet der lateinischen (!)[120] Sprache zusammengestellt und festgelegt. Es existierte vor ihm

---

[108] Isidor, *Chron. mai.* Nr. 50.

[109] Vgl. Isidor, *Etym.* V 30,7: quintum ab stella jovis, quam Phaethontem (= φαέθοντα 'leuchtend') aiunt.

[110] Isidor, *Chron. mai.* Nr. 51.

[111] Isidor, *Chron. mai.* Nr. 74; vgl. Isidor, *Etym.* V 39,10 (Hs.B) und IV 3,1.

[112] Vgl. Isidor, *Chron. mai.* Nr. 103: regnum(que) Siciniorum.

[113] Isidor, *Chron. mai.* Nr. 75.

[114] Isidor, *Chron. mai.* Nr. 76: Hac aetate primus regnat Latinis Picus, qui fertur fuisse Saturni filius.

[115] Isidor, *Chron. mai.* Nr. 78.

[116] Vgl. (nicht in allen Details identisch) Isidor, *Chron. mai.* Nr. 79: Orfeus Thrax Linusque magister Herculis artis musicae inventores clari habentur.

[117] Vgl. den Parallelausdruck *kāna ḫabaru*... ed. Badawī 120,18.

[118] In der arabischen Textausgabe steht <'rq'ws>.

[119] Vgl. Isidor, *Chron. mai.* Nr. 77a; *Etym.* III 22,6.

[120] *al-lisān al-laṭīnī*; vgl. aber Isidor, *Etym.* I 3,6: Cadmus Agenoris Filius Graecas litteras a Phoenice in Graeciam decem et septem primus attulit ...; ferner Isidor, *Chron. mai.* Nr. 62.

noch nicht. — In jener Zeit lebte im Lande der Griechen der bekannte Catmus <ktmws>. Er lehrte die Griechen das griechische Alphabet; es wird auf ihn zurückgeführt[121]. /115/ In jener Zeit waren in ihrem Land <brsqls> (= Clinus) und <’swn> (= Antion) berühmt, zwei Männer, auf die die Musikwissenschaft zurückgeführt wird, nämlich das Verfassen von Melodien und das Komponieren von Liedern[122]’.

120,18-121,4:‘(Während der Regierung des Richters Abdon) ereignete sich die Geschichte von Aeneas <’n’s>, des lateinischen Königs, der ganz Italien in Aufruhr brachte; sie (ist) in den Büchern (erwähnt). Gemeint sind die Kriege, worüber sich Vergilius[123] <frqlys> in seinen allgemein bekannten Gedichten äusserte ... [124]. Unter der Leitung dieses Aeneas ereigneten sich während eines Zeitraumes von drei Jahren all die Angriffe, Morde und qualvollen Kriege, die so bekannt und so viel beschrieben worden sind, dass sie nicht mehr beschrieben zu werden brauchen. /121/ Wir haben (auch) eine Beschreibung der qualvollen Kriege des Philippus, des makedonischen (? aš-<šğyny>) Königs der Griechen unterlassen, d.h. der Kriege, die ganz Asien und Griechenland umfassten’.

124,4-18:[125] ‘Denn die Griechen verfertigten, als sie während ihrer 10-jährigen Belagerung (Troja) nicht (erobern) konnten, eine grosse Pferdefigur von Holz, welche hohl war und sich auf Rädern bewegen liess. In ihr brachten sie 500 Krieger unter. Darauf gab ihnen ihr Vorgesetzter[126] den Auftrag, ihn (selbst) mit schmerzhaften Peitschenschlägen zu züchtigen. Da schlugen sie ihn, liessen ihn mit der (Pferde-)Figur zurück, und gingen weg, um ihre Schiffe zu betreten und ihre Regimenter darauf vorzubereiten, die Rückkehr in ihr Land vorzutäuschen. Als nun die Einwohner der Stadt (Troja) herauskamen,

---

[121] Isidor, *Etym.* V 39,10: Catmus litteras Graecis dedit.

[122] Isidor, *Chron. mai.* Nr. 63.

[123] Vgl. Vergil, *Aeneis.*

[124] Lücke in der arab. Hs.

[125] Hier wird ausführlich die Geschichte vom trojanischen Pferd erzählt. Zu den klassischen Quellen hierüber vgl. Margaret R. Scherer, *The Legends of Troy in Art and Literature*, New York, London, 1963, 110ff. Der arabische Orosius folgt (mit einigen Modifikationen) der Version des Vergil, *Aeneis* II 59ff. Die bei ihm beschriebene Geschichte vom Fall Trojas wird im lateinischen Orosius nur gestreift (vgl. Cohen, 58ff.); sie ist in Details verschieden von Dictys Cretensis (250 n.Chr.; vgl. Cohen, 65), s. die engl. Übersetzung von R.M. Frazer, *The Trojan War. The Chronicles of Crete and Dares the Phrygian*, Bloomington and London, 1966, Buch V, 9ff. Sie fehlt bei Dares Phrygius (6. Jh., vgl. Cohen, 66ff.) und in dessen mittellateinischen Bearbeitungen: vgl. Jürgen Stohlmann, *Anonymi Historia Trogana Daretis Frigii. Untersuchungen und kritische Ausgabe*, Ratingen, Düsseldorf, 1968.

[126] Bei Vergil ist es Sinon, der sich selbst verstümmelt. Die Varianten des arabischen Orosius lassen sich nicht in der nachhomerischen Überlieferung über Trojas Fall (vgl. *RE*, Art. ‘Sinon’; Rich. Heinze, *Vergils epische Technik*, Darmstadt, 1957, 7ff.; 63ff.; 79ff.) nachweisen. In der arabischen Version erscheint die antike Sinon-Figur als Priester des Pferdegötzenbildes; dieser sei seinem Lügenbericht an die Trojaner zufolge als Strafe für seine Voraussage, dass Troja uneinnehmbar sei, von seinen eigenen Landsleuten zusammengeschlagen worden.

fanden sie die (Pferde-)Figur und vor ihr den zusammengeschlagenen Mann. (Dieser) antwortete ihnen auf ihre Frage: 'Diese Figur ist ihr Götzenbild, welches sie verehren' — zuvor hatten (die Griechen) in listiger Weise den Anschein gegeben, es zu verehren — 'und ich bin sein Diener und Priester. Nachdem sie mich dazu genötigt hatten, sie über seine (des Götzenbildes) Aussage zur Lage der Stadt aufzuklären, informierte ich sie über seine (Aussage), dass (Troja) uneinnehmbar und unbezwingbar sei. Darauf wurden sie deswegen wütend über mich und schlugen mich, wie ihr sehen könnt' — während er (doch) bei ihnen angesehen und bekannt war. Er fuhr fort: 'Daraufhin fürchteten sie den Zorn ihres Gottes, da sie mich zusammengeschlagen zurückgelassen[127] hatten, dann es (das Götzenbild) und mich aufgegeben hatten und in ihr Land zurückgekehrt waren. Ich kann euch darüber informieren, dass (das Götzenbild) eine wahrhaftiger Gott ist. Wenn ihr es ehrt, hilft es euch gegen (die Griechen) und bestimmt ihren Untergang'. — Da freuten sich (die Trojaner) hierüber, nahmen hierauf die (Pferde-)Figur und zogen sie auf ihren Rädern, bis sie die Stadt erreichten. Da das (Stadt-)Tor nicht geräumig genug hierfür war, schlugen sie hierfür eine Bresche in die Mauer. Als es nun Nacht geworden war, näherten sich diejenigen (wieder), welche ihre Rückkehr in ihre Heimat vorgetäuscht hatten'.

135,19-24: '(Die Anzahl) der Jahre bis zum Ende der Zeit Davids beläuft sich auf 4164 Jahre[128]. [129]Zu seiner Zeit gab es unter den Israeliten Propheten, nämlich Gad <ġ'ṯ> [130], Nathan[131] und <ḥ'ḍ'f> (= Asaph[132]). [129]— [133]In jener Zeit erbaute Dido Karthago in Afrika[133]. [134]Damals lebte der italienische (!) Dichter <myrš>, der Sohn des Marcion <mrǧywn> und damals begann die Herrschaft der griechischen Lakedämonier (ar-Rūm al-<lsḏmwnyyn>), welche zu den Griechen gehörten[134]'.

144,1f.: 'Zu seiner (sc. Jerobeams) Zeit lebte die weise Sybille, welche in den Büchern der Gelehrten (*al-falāsifa*) beschrieben wird. Von ihr stammen Gedichte und (verschiedene) Arten von Weissagungen und Wissenschaften[135]'.

161,6: 'Zu seiner (des Hiskia) Zeit lebte in Italien der berühmte <šn'tš> (= Senatus!)[136]'.

---

[127] *irtaddū minnī*. Badawī rekonstruiert das ihm zufolge in der Hs. zerstörte Wort als *rakasū*, wozu jedoch die nachfolgende Präposition *min* nicht passt.

[128] Isidor, *Chron. mai.* Nr. 107.

[129] Isidor, *Chron. mai.* Nr. 110; vgl. *Etym.* V 39,13 (Hss. BC).

[130] 2. Sam. 24:11ff.

[131] 2. Sam. 7:12; 1. Chron. 17.

[132] Vgl. 1. Chron. 16.

[133] Isidor, *Chron. mai.* Nr. 109; vgl. *Etym.* V 39,13.

[134] Vgl. Isidor, *Chron. mai.* Nr. 105-106: Lacedaemoniorum regnum Exoritur atque (in Graecia) Homerus (poeta primus) fuisse putatur.

[135] Vgl. Isidor, *Chron. mai.* Nr. 116: Sybilla Eritria inlustris habetur.

[136] Vgl. Isidor, *Chron. mai.* Nr. 150.

171,12-15: '(Zu jener Zeit war König) der Lateiner (ein Mann) namens Tarquinius Priscus <ṭrqwynwš> bršqwš. Er war es, der die Königsherrschaft in Rom festigte und ausschliesslich die Könige mit dem purpurnen Gewand auszeichnete. Sein Verhalten ...[137] war gerecht. Er hob die Zersplitterung der Lateiner auf und sorgte für Einmütigkeit unter ihnen. Seine Herrschaft dauerte 30 Jahre[138]'.

172,4-5: 'Zu seiner (des Josia) Zeit gab es unter den Propheten den Propheten Jeremia <yrmy'>, den Sohn des Hilkia <'lğy'> aus <h'rwn>[139]'.

172,17-19: 'Zu seiner (des Jojakim) Zeit lebten die Propheten Daniel, der Sohn des ʿAbd eines Sohnes des Amon <'mwn>, des Sohnes von Manasse <mnš'>; <ġrry'> (= Azarias) und <myšyl> (= Misahel) <bnwlw'š>, der Sohn des <brmy'>, eines Sohnes von Jojakim, des Sohnes von Hizkia. Die mit ihnen[140] zusammenhängenden bekannten Geschichten ereigneten sich in der Stadt Babel[141]'.

175,1-5: 'Die Erbauung Roms fand — entsprechend der Äusserung des Orosius[142] — vor jener Zeit und zu einem geringen Teil in der Zeit des Hizkia, des Königs von Juda statt[143]. Aber wir haben jenes auf diese Stelle verschoben, weil die Nachrichten über die Könige Judas (hierzu) in Beziehung stehen'.

177,21-ult.: 'Darauf wendet sich der Bericht den Israeliten zu: sie befanden sich 70 Jahre in babylonischer Gefangenschaft[144] und kehrten aus ihr (in ihre Heimat) zurück im zweiten Jahre der Regierung des Darius <d'ry>[145], welcher nach Cyrus <ğyrš> die Herrschaft über die Perser übernommen hatte. Seine Herrschaft dauerte 23 Jahre[146]'.

178: 'Darius herrschte über das Reich der Perser 23 Jahre. (Die Anzahl) der Weltjahre bis zum Ende seiner Zeit beläuft sich auf 4710 Jahre[147]. [148]Im (ersten) Jahr seiner Herrschaft verwirklichte sich die Rückkehr der Juden nach Jerusalem. Denn sie beendeten (ihren) 70-jährigen (Aufenthalt), welche der

---

[137] Eine Lücke in der arab. Hs.

[138] Vgl. Isidor, *Chron. mai.* Nr. 156 (kürzer u. teilweise abweichend).

[139] Vgl. Isidor, *Chron. mai.* Nr. 159.

[140] *allaḏīna*: ed. Badawī 172,-6 hat *allaḏī*.

[141] Vgl. Isidor, *Chron. mai.* Nr. 162: Tunc Danihel, Ananias, Azarias et Misahel in Babylone claruerunt.

[142] Vgl. Orosius II 4 Par. 1.ed. Zangemeister 38,30f. II 4 steht nicht in der arabischen Übersetzung (s. oben die Synopse).

[143] Sc. vor der Zeit des Zedekia; vgl. Isidor, *Chron. mai.* Nr. 146: Zeit des Ahas, dessen Tod in das Weltjahr 4459 verlegt wird, während Hiskias Tod in Nr. 148 auf das Weltjahr 4488 verlegt wird.

[144] Vgl. Isidor, *Chron. mai.* Nr. 167.

[145] Isidor, *Chron. mai.* Nr. 171.

[146] Isidor, *Chron. mai.* Nr. 170 (abweichend: 33 Jahre).

[147] Isidor, *Chron. mai.* Nr. 170 nennt als Weltjahr 4713 und als Regierungszeit des Darius 23 Jahre.

[148] Vgl. Esra 1:1-11.

Prophet Jeremia[149] ihnen verkündigt hatte als (Dauer ihrer Gefangenschaft) bis zu ihrem Abschluss mit dem Auszug aus der Gefangenschaft bei Nebukadnezar. Unter Darius verwirklichte sich ihre Rückkehr. — Dem Cyrus, dem König der Perser vor ihm, hatte Gott im ersten Jahr seiner Herrschaft zu grossem Ansehen verholfen[150], worauf er aus eigenen Stücken an alle Bewohner seines Reiches folgendes Schreiben richtete: Cyrus, der König der Perser, berichtet folgendes: 'Der Herr, der Gott des Himmels, hat mir die Herrschaft über die Welt übertragen. Er hat mir befohlen, sein Haus (= Tempel) in der Stadt Jerusalem, im Lande Juda, aufzubauen. Wer unter euch zu ihren Einwohnern gehört, soll zu ihr zurückkehren und das Haus des Herrn, des Gottes von Israel, aufbauen. Sein Gott ist mit ihm; denn es ist Gott, der in Jerusalem ist'. Darauf verpflichtete er seine Untertanen, ihnen mit Geld, Nahrung und allem für sie Gutem zu helfen. Er überliess ihnen die goldenen und silbernen Geräte, welche sich Nebukadnezar in Jerusalem angeeignet hatte. Dann kehrten sie nach Syrien zurück und begannen mit dem Bau des (Gottes-)Hauses[148]. — [151]Da wandten sich gegen sie einige ihrer Feinde, machten sie bei dem König der Perser verhasst[152] und versetzten ihn in Furcht vor denen, die in jener Stadt sich ihm widersetzten; sie erinnerten ihn an etwas, was durch ihre Vorfahren geschehen war und verzögerten daher die Fortsetzung des Baues bis zum 2. Jahr der Herrschaft des Darius. (Doch) sollte sich das durch die Prophetenzeugen ausgesprochene[153]. Wort Gottes verwirklichen[151]'.

182,3-7: 'Xerxes <šẖš'r> regierte 20 Jahre[153]. (Die Anzahl) der Weltjahre bis zum Ende der Zeit des Xerxes, des Sohnes von Darius, beläuft sich auf 4722 Jahre[154]. [155]Während seiner Zeit lebten in Athen die berühmten Persönlichkeiten Aeschylus <'šylyws, bty'rwš> (= Pindarus) und Sophocles, von welchen die Trauergedichte stammen[155]. [156]Zu seiner Zeit lebte Herodot <hrwdts>, der Verfasser der Geschichten[156]'.

187,6-188,12: '(Wir wollen uns) dem Herrscher der Perser nach Xerxes (zuwenden), nämlich seinem Sohn Artaxerxes <'rtšẖš'r>: Er regierte 40 Jahre. — Das achte Kapitel aus Teil II: Artaxerxes, der Sohn des Xerxes regierte 40 Jahre. (Die Anzahl) der Weltjahre bis zum Ende seiner Zeit beläuft sich auf 4762 Jahre[157]. [158]Zu seiner Zeit erneuerte der Prophet Esdra <ʿzyr>

[149] Vgl. Anm. 144 u. 145 und Jerem. 25:12; 29:10.

[150] *aʿazzahū*; oder ist hier entsprechend Esra 1:1 *aġarrahū* 'dazu angespornt, (dass er aus eigenen Stücken ...)' zu verbessern?

[151] Vgl. Esra 4.

[152] *wa-baġġaḍūhum*; ed. Badawī 178,-3 hat nicht passendes *wa-baġauhum*.

[153] Isidor, *Chron. mai.* Nr. 173. Vgl. auch Anm. 147.

[154] S. die Liste der Weltjahre. Allerdings hat Isidor, *Chron. mai.* Nr. 173 '4733'.

[155] Isidor, *Chron. mai.* Nr. 174.

[156] Isidor, *Chron. mai.* Nr. 175.

[157] Isidor, *Chron. mai.* Nr. 176 (allerdings wird als Weltjahr 4773 genannt).

[158] Isidor, *Chron. mai.* Nr. 177; vgl. *Etym.* VI 3,2.

das Buch der Thora[158]. [159]Zu seiner Zeit vollendete Nehemias <nhymy'š>, der Anführer der Juden, den Bau der Stadtmauern von Jerusalem[159]. [160]Zu seiner Zeit lebte Aristarchus <'rštrqš> und der berühmte Aristophanes <'rštfwns>, von welchem Trauergedichte stammen[160]. [161]In jener Zeit lebte der berühmte Arzt Hippocrates (Abuqrāṭ) und der berühmte Socrates[161]. Damals war die Erinnerung an sie und die Nachricht über sie sehr verbreitet; ihre Wissenschaften standen in Athen in hohem Ansehen. Sie waren alle Athener (Aṯīnāšiyūn)'.

190,15-191,6: 'Dann wendet sich der Bericht dem Herrscher der Perser nach Artaxerxes zu, nämlich seinem Sohn Darius Nothus <d'ry nwṭw>. Er regierte 19 Jahre. — Das neunte Kapitel aus Teil II: Darius Nothus: Er regierte 19 Jahre. Die Anzahl der Weltjahre bis zum Ende seiner Zeit beläuft sich auf 4781 Jahre[162]. Zu seiner Zeit wurde der berühmte Plato geboren[163]'.

199,8-200,8: 'Darauf wendet sich der Bericht dem Herrscher der Perser nach Darius Nothus zu, nämlich seinem Sohn Artaxerxes. Er regierte 40 Jahre. — Das zehnte Kapitel aus Teil II: Artaxerxes, der Sohn des Darius, des Sohnes von Xerxes, einer Sohnes von Darius: er regierte 40 Jahre. 'Die Anzahl' der Weltjahre bis zum Ende seiner Zeit beläuft sich auf 4821 Jahre[164]. Zu seiner Zeit wurde das in der Sammlung der Prophetenbücher Esther zugeschriebene Buch verfasst[165]. Damals verbreitete sich der Ruhm des bekannten Platon und Xenophon <zyqwn> [165]. Beide sind Athener[166]'.

216,3-217,7: 'Zu jener Zeit (sc. die Zeit der Geburt Alexanders des Grossen) übernahm die Herrschaft über die Perser Artaxerxes mit dem Beinamen Ochus. Seine Herrschaft dauerte 26 Jahre. — Das dritte Kapitel aus Teil III: Artaxerxes Ochus: Er regierte 26 Jahre. (Die Anzahl) der Weltjahre bis zum Ende seiner Zeit beläuft sich auf 4846 Jahre[167]. Zu seiner Zeit lebten der Redner (*al-mutakallim*) Demosthenes <dmst'n> aus Macedonien <al-mǧdwny> [168] und der berühmte Aristoteles, der Sohn des Nicomachus aus Macedonien[169]. Damals starb der berühmte Plato in Athen[170]'.

226,19-227,5: 'Darauf wendet sich der Bericht dem Herrscher der Perser nach Artaxerxes Ochus zu, nämlich seinem Sohn Xerxes. (Er regierte) vier

---

[159] Isidor, *Chron. mai.* Nr. 178.

[160] Isidor, *Chron. mai.* Nr. 179.

[161] Isidor, *Chron. mai.* Nr. 180; die arabische Version lässt wie die lat. Hs. V Democritus aus.

[162] Isidor, *Chron. mai.* Nr. 181 (nennt abweichend 4792 als Weltjahr).

[163] Isidor, *Chron. mai.* Nr. 182; vgl. *Etym.* V 39,20.

[164] Isidor, *Chron. mai.* Nr. 183 (abweichendes Weltjahr: 4832).

[165] Isidor, *Chron. mai.* Nr. 184.

[166] *Aṯīnāšiyān*: wohl verschrieben für Socratici Isidor, *Chron. mai.* Nr. 185 (ist in der arabischen Schrift leicht möglich).

[167] Isidor, *Chron. mai.* Nr. 186 (Weltjahr abweichend 4858).

[168] Isidor, *Chron. mai.* Nr. 187.

[169] Isidor, *Chron. mai.* Nr. 188; vgl. (auch zu Demosthenes) *Etym.* V 39,21.

[170] Isidor, *Chron. mai.* Nr. 189.

Jahre. — Das fünfte Kapitel aus Teil III: Xerxes regierte vier Jahre. (Die Anzahl) der Weltjahre bis zum Ende seiner Zeit beläuft sich auf 4851 Jahre[171]. Zu jener Zeit verbreitete sich die Kunde von dem berühmten Athener (al-aṯīnāšī) Socrates (= Xenocrates)[172]'.

228,13-229,6: 'Darauf wendet sich der Bericht dem Herrscher der Perser nach Xerxes zu, nämlich dem, welcher von Alexander (dem Grossen) besiegt wurde. Er regierte sechs Jahre. — Das sechste Kapitel aus Teil III: Darius, der Sohn des Xerxes, König der Perser: Er regierte sechs Jahre. (Die Anzahl) der Weltjahre bis zum Ende seiner Zeit beläuft sich auf 4857 Jahre[173]. [174]Zu Beginn seiner Dynastie siegte Alexander (der Grosse) über das Land der Illyrer <'yryqw> und Thraker <ṭw'dyš>, sowie über die Stadt Jerusalem[175], nämlich Bait al-maqdis[176]. Er betrat den Tempel und brachte darin Gott ein Opfer dar[174]'.

233,20-234,7: 'Darauf wendet sich der Bericht dem König Alexander dem Grossen, dem Sohne des Philippus zu, nämlich (der Zeit) nach der Beendigung der Herrschaft der Perser. (Alexander der Grosse) regierte sieben Jahre. — Das siebte Kapitel aus Teil III: Alexander der Grosse: Er regierte sieben Jahre. (Die Anzahl) der Weltjahre bis zum Ende der Zeit des Makedoniers Alexander, Philippus' Sohn, welcher Darius, den König der Perser tötete, beläuft sich auf 4864 Jahre. Wir rechnen ihm sieben Jahre seit der Ermordung des Darius zu. Tatsächlich hat er bereits davor fünf Jahre an der Stelle seines Vaters über die griechischen Stämme geherrscht[177]'.

239,10-240,10: 'Darauf wendet sich der Bericht seinem (Alexander des Grossen) Nachfolger zu, der die Herrschaft in Alexandrien übernahm, nämlich Ptolemaeus, dem Sohn des <l'wy> (= Lagus). Seine Herrschaft dauerte 40 Jahre. — Das achte Kapitel aus Teil III: Ptolemaeus: Er regierte 40 Jahre. — (Die Anzahl) der Weltjahre bis zum Ende seiner Zeit beläuft sich auf 4904 Jahre. Er war ein Makedonier[178]. [179]Er war es, der die Juden ausplünderte. Viele von ihnen begaben sich (damals) nach Ägypten[179]. Zu seiner Zeit lebten in Rom der berühmte Zenon <znwn> und der berühmte <'wqr'ṭys> (=

[171] Isidor, *Chron. mai.* Nr. 190 (Weltjahr abweichend 4862).

[172] Isidor, *Chron. mai.* Nr. 191; vgl. *Etym.* V 39,21.

[173] Vgl. Isidor, *Chron. mai.* Nr. 192 (Weltjahr abweichend 4868).

[174] Isidor, *Chron. mai.* Nr. 193.

[175] Vgl. auch Isidor, *Etym.* V 39,21.

[176] Der übliche arabische Name für Jerusalem.

[177] Isidor, *Chron. mai.* Nr. 195 (Weltjahr abweichend 4873).

[178] Isidor, *Chron. mai.* Nr. 196 (Weltjahr abweichend 4913). Übrigens tauchen die Angaben über die Herrscher nach Alexander dem Grossen und ihre Regierungszeiten bei Ḥamza al-Iṣfahānī, *Ta'rīḫ sinī mulūk al-arḍ wa-l-anbiyā'* (verfasst 350/961), Beirut 1961 (auf der Grundlage der Edition v. J.M.P. Gottwaldt, Leipzig, 1844), 58ff. auf; al-Iṣfahānī hat vermutlich eine Quelle benutzt, die ihrerseits auf Isidors *Chronica maiora* zurückgegriffen hat.

[179] Isidor, *Chron. mai.* Nr. 197.

Theophrastus)[180]. (Auch) dieser[181] war berühmt. Zu seiner Zeit wurde das erste der 'Makkabäer' <mkb'wrm> genannten Bücher geschrieben[182]; sie gehören zu den Chroniken der Juden nach ihrer Rückkehr aus Babel, welche zusammen mit den Prophetenbüchern schriftlich niedergelegt wurden'.

253,11-12; 257,1-11: 'Darauf wendet sich der Bericht dem zu, der nach Ptolemaeus, dem Sohn des <l'wy> (= Lagus) die Herrschaft Alexandriens[183] übernahm, nämlich seinem Sohn Ptolemaeus Philadelphus <'dlfš>. — Das erste Kapitel aus Teil IV: Ptolemaeus Philadelphus: Er regierte 38 Jahre. (Die Anzahl) der Weltjahre bis zum Ende seiner Zeit beläuft sich auf 4942 Jahre[184]. [185]Er war es, der die in Ägypten gefangen gehaltenen Juden freiliess und die heiligen Geräte an den Propheten <ʿzyr> (= Eleazar) zurückgab. Er war es, der unter den jüdischen Gelehrten die siebzig Übersetzer auswählte, welche die Bücher der Thora und der Propheten aus dem Hebräischen in das Griechische und das Lateinische übersetzten[185]. Er war berühmt als Astronom. Zu seiner Zeit lebte der Astronom <'r'ṭṯyns> (= Aratus), auf welchen die Astronomie zurückgeht[186]. In jener Zeit führte man in der Stadt Rom das Silber als Zahlungsmittel ein[187]'.

278,18-279,6: 'Darauf wendet sich der Bericht dem zu, der nach Ptolemaeus Philadelphus die Herrschaft Alexandriens[188] übernahm, nämlich seinem Sohn Euergetes <'lṭrlṭš>. Er regierte 26 Jahre. — Das zweite Kapitel aus Teil IV: Ptolemaeus Euergetes <'ywrǧts>: Er regierte 26 Jahre. (Die Anzahl) der Weltjahre bis zum Ende seiner Zeit beläuft sich auf 4968 Jahre [189]. Zu seiner Zeit schrieb Jesus, der Sohn des Sirach <šr'q>, des Sohnes von Jesus, einem Sohn des <yzwd'q> al-Hārūnī das Buch der Schrift (*al-qalam*), welches im Buch der Thora ihm beigelegt wird[190]'.

285,14-286,6: 'Darauf wendet sich der Bericht dem zu, der nach Ptolemaeus Euergetes <'yryṭws> die Herrschaft Alexandriens übernahm, nämlich seinem Bruder Ptolemaeus Philopater <flb'ṭr>. (Er regierte) 17 Jahre. — Das vierte Kapitel aus Teil IV: Ptolemaeus, der Sohn des Philopater: Er regierte 17 Jahre[191]. (Die Anzahl) der Weltjahre bis zum Ende seiner Zeit beläuft sich auf

---

[180] Isidor, *Chron. mai.* Nr. 198.

[181] Wohl Ptolemaeus.

[182] Isidor, *Chron. mai.* Nr. 199.

[183] Badawī hat falsch al-Iskandar; vgl. aber z.B. ed. Badawī 285,14.

[184] Isidor, *Chron. mai.* Nr. 200 (wie in *Etym.* V 39,22 abweichendes Weltjahr 4951).

[185] Isidor, *Chron. mai.* Nr. 201. Die im Arabischen zugefügte Bemerkung, dass Thora und Prophetenbücher von den jüdischen Gelehrten ins Lateinische übersetzt wurden, ist natürlich nicht richtig; Hieronymus kann schwerlich als jüdischer Gelehrter klassifiziert werden.

[186] Isidor, *Chron. mai.* Nr. 202.

[187] Isidor, *Chron. mai.* Nr. 203.

[188] Ed. Badawī hat falsch al-Iskandar; vgl. aber z.B. ed. Badawī 285,14.

[189] Isidor, *Chron. mai.* Nr. 204 (Weltjahr abweichend 4977).

[190] Isidor, *Chron. mai.* Nr. 205 u. *Etym.* V 39,22 (kürzer und ohne die Zusätze, die das Arabische zum Namen bringt).

[191] Ed. Badawī 286,3 falsch *tisʿa ʿašrata* '19'.

4975 Jahre[192]. Er war es, der von den Juden ungefähr 60 000 tötete und besiegte[193]. Zu seiner Zeit siegte Marcellus <mrğ'lš>, der Sohn des <sfrwnyh> (= Sophronius?), der Führer der Römer, über Sizilien[194]'.

291,15-292,7: 'Darauf wendet sich der Bericht dem zu, der nach Ptolemaeus Philopater die Herrschaft Alexandriens übernahm, nämlich seinem Sohn Ptolemaeus Epiphanes <'bf'ns>. Er regierte 24 Jahre. — Das fünfte Kapitel aus Teil IV: Ptolemaeus Epiphanes: Er regierte 24 Jahre. (Die Anzahl) der Weltjahre bis zum Ende seiner Zeit beläuft sich auf 5009 Jahre[195]. Zu seiner Zeit wurde über die Geschichten und Kriege der Juden, welche zusammen mit den Prophetenbüchern aufgezeichnet wurden, das zweite, den Makkabäern <mkb'wrm> zugeschriebene Buch verfasst[196]. Damals lebte der bekannte Dichter <'myrs> (= Ennius)[197]'.

305,3-307,6: 'Darauf wendet sich der Bericht dem Herrscher Alexandriens nach Ptolemaeus Epiphanes zu, nämlich seinem Sohn Ptolemaeus Philometor. Er regierte 35 Jahre. — Das neunte Kapitel aus Teil IV: Ptolemaeus Philometor: Er regierte 35 Jahre. — (Die Anzahl) der Weltjahre bis zum Ende seiner Zeit beläuft sich auf 5039 Jahre[198]. [199]Er war es, der Antiochus, den Befehlshaber Syriens besiegte. Damals wurden den Juden verschiedene Arten von Heimsuchungen und Bestrafungen auferlegt[199]'.

309,1-310,5: '— Darauf wendet sich der Bericht dem Herrscher Alexandriens nach Alexander Philometor zu, nämlich seinem Sohn Euergetes <'yry'ṭs>; er regierte 29 Jahre. — Das zehnte Kapitel aus Teil IV: Ptolemaeus Euergetes: Er regierte 29 Jahre. (Die Anzahl) der Weltjahre bis zum Ende seiner Zeit beläuft sich auf 5068 Jahre[200]. Zu seiner Zeit siegten die Römer über Andalus[201]'.

329,8-330,7: '— Darauf wendet sich der Bericht dem zu, der nach Ptolemaeus Euergetes die Herrschaft über Alexandrien übernahm, nämlich seinem Sohn Soter <šwṭ'r>. Er regierte 17 Jahre. — Das zweite Kapitel aus Teil V: Ptolemaeus Soter: Er regierte 17 Jahre. — (Die Anzahl) der Weltjahre bis zum Ende seiner Zeit beläuft sich auf 5085 Jahre[202]. Zu seiner Zeit wurden in Rom

---

[192] Isidor, *Chron. mai.* Nr. 206 (Weltjahr abweichend 4994).

[193] Isidor, *Chron. mai.* Nr. 207.

[194] Isidor, *Chron. mai.* Nr. 208 (nennt nicht den Vater von Marcellus).

[195] Isidor, *Chron. mai.* Nr. 209 (nennt wie *Etym.* V 39,23 abweichend das Weltjahr 5018).

[196] Isidor, *Chron. mai.* Nr. 210.

[197] Isidor, *Chron. mai.* Nr. 211. Es ist nicht nötig, mit Badawī (welcher diesen Namen mit Homer identifiziert!) hier einen Überlieferungsfehler anzunehmen und im Arabischen zu ergänzen 'damals (kümmerte man sich nicht um die Veröffentlichung der Gedichte) des bekannten Dichters Homer'.

[198] Isidor, *Chron. mai.* Nr. 212 (Weltjahr abweichend 5053).

[199] Isidor, *Chron. mai.* Nr. 213.

[200] Isidor, *Chron. mai.* Nr. 215 (Weltjahr abweichend 5082).

[201] Isidor, *Chron. mai.* Nr. 216.

[202] Isidor, *Chron. mai.* Nr. 217 (abweichendes Weltjahr 5099).

der berühmte Cicero <ǧyǧrwn>, der Sohn des <štrnyn> und der bekannte Varro <b'rw>, der Sohn des <bqštr'ṭ> geboren[203]. Damals siegten die Römer über den Herrscher der Thrazier <aṭ-ṭr'ǧyyn>[204]'.

341,12-342,6: 'Darauf wendet sich der Bericht dem zu, der nach Ptolemaeus Soter die Herrschaft Alexandriens übernahm, nämlich seinem Bruder Ptolemaeus Alexander. (Er regierte) zehn Jahre. — Das fünfte Kapitel aus Teil V: Alexander: Er regierte zehn Jahre. (Die Anzahl) der Weltjahre bis zum Ende seiner Zeit beläuft sich auf 5095 Jahre[205]. Damals lebte der römische Dichter <'wr'šys> (Lucretius?[206]), welcher sich selbst aus Liebes(leidenschaft) tötete[207]. Von ihm gibt es eine Geschichte, um die wir unser Buch nicht verlängern wollen'.

350,8-10 (vgl. Orosius V 16 Par. 23 S.167,2-4): '— Darauf wurde ihm (sc. Publicius Malleolus, der seine Mutter umgebracht hatte) hierfür eine Strafe auferlegt, welche ihrem (der Römer) Gesetz zufolge dem[208] drohte, der seine Mutter oder seinen Vater tötete: Er wurde nämlich zusammen mit einem Hahn, einem Affen und einer Schlange in einen Behälter gesteckt, der von Stierleder gemacht war oder von Ḥalfā'-Gras, das mit Pech und Teer zusammengefügt worden ist; darauf wurde er in ihm in das tiefe Meer geworfen[209].

353,11-354,8: 'Zu jener Zeit, (nämlich) 646 Jahre nach der Gründung Roms, führten die Römer heftig miteinander Krieg und waren in Kriege verwickelt, die man innere (Wirren) nennt. Orosius sagte: Wegen ihrer Vielzahl können wir nicht über sie berichten, sondern wir beschreiben nur (einige) Punkte hiervon[210]. — Darauf wendet sich der Bericht dem zu, der nach Ptolemaeus Alexander die Herrschaft Alexandriens übernahm, nämlich seinem Sohn Ptolemaeus Dionysius <dywnsys>. (Er regierte) 38 Jahre. — Das sechste Kapitel aus Teil V: Ptolemaeus Dionysius: Er regierte 38 Jahre. (Die Anzahl) der Weltjahre bis zum Ende seiner Zeit beläuft sich auf 5133 Jahre[211]. Zu

[203] Isidor, *Chron. mai.* Nr. 218 (ohne die zusätzlichen Namensangaben).

[204] Isidor, *Chron. mai.* Nr. 219.

[205] Isidor, *Chron. mai.* Nr. 220; vgl. *Etym.* V 39,24 (jeweils mit dem abweichenden Weltjahr 5109).

[206] So Isidor. Oder hatte der arabische Übersetzer 'Horatius' in seiner Vorlage? Das arabische Schriftbild kann sowohl 'Horatius' gelesen werden als auch als Verschreibung <lw[q]r'šyš> = Lucretius interpretiert werden.

[207] Isidor, *Chron. mai.* Nr. 222: Poeta quoque Lucretius nascitur, qui postea sese furore amatorio interfecit.

[208] *li-man*: Badawī 350,8 hat *ʿamman*; vgl. aber Levi della Vida, 'La traduzione', 283, Anm.

[209] Isidor, *Etym.* V 27,36 (hierauf verwies bereits Levi della Vida, 'La traduzione', 283).

[210] Vgl. im vorangehenden lateinischen Orosiustext V 17 Par. 2-3 (arab. T. 351,2-4): evolvere ac percurrere mihi discordiarum ambages et inextricabiles seditionum causas incommodum simul ac longum videtur; sane breviter strinxisse sufficiat, ... Demnach liegt im oben übersetzten Zusatz zum lat. Text Orosius V 17 (ed. Zangemeister 167,9-168,33 = arab. T. ed. Badawī 350,16-353,10) eine Wiederholung von Orosius V 17 Par. 2-3 (ed. Zangemeister 167, 14-16) = arab. T. 351, 1-4 vor.

[211] Isidor, *Chron. mai.* Nr. 226, mit einer abweichenden Regierungszeit (30 Jahre) und mit einem abweichenden Weltjahr (5147).

seiner Zeit lebte der berühmte Cato <q'ṭwn>[212], der Dichter Vergilius[213], der berühmte Apollodorus <'blwdrys>[214] und der Dichter Cicero[215]. Damals siegte Pompeius <bmb'yš>, der Führer der Römer, über Jerusalem und veranlasste die Juden, ihm Tribut zu entrichten[216]'.

358,8-14: 'Julius wurde aber Caesar <qyṣr> genannt, weil er mit vollständigem (Kopf)Haar geboren wurde, welches bis zu seinen Augen reichte. Der Name des Haares lautet im literarischen Latein (*al-ʿağamīya l-faṣīḥa*) 'caesarius' <ğ'šryh>. Daher wird er 'Caesar' <ğ'šr> genannt, und das ist auf Arabisch 'Qaiṣar'. Seine Mutter war bereits gestorben, bevor sie ihn zur Welt gebracht hatte. Daher wurde für ihn ihr Bauch gespalten und er aus ihm herausgeholt. Darauf blieb er am leben und erlangte schliesslich die Königsherrschaft. Dann sagte man zu ihm daher 'Caesar' <ğyšr> (nämlich) wegen des Aufschneidens, wodurch er herausgeholt wurde. Denn zu dem Gespaltenen sagt man im Lateinischen (*al-ʿağamīya*) 'caesus' <ğ'šyš>. Die Könige nach ihm in Rom nahmen diesen Namen zusätzlich zu ihren (anderen) Namen, um sich damit zu erhöhen und zu ehren[217]'.

379,1-2: 'Die Herrschaft Alexandriens, nämlich die makedonische (sic), dauerte bis zum Beginn der Herrschaft des Gaius <ğ'yh> Caesar, welcher der erste Herrscher der Römer war, (nämlich) 281 Jahre'.

390,6-391,4: '— Darauf wendet sich der Bericht dem Herrscher Alexandriens nach Ptolemaeus Dionysius zu, nämlich Cleopatra <klwbṭrh>. (Sie regierte) zwei Jahre. — Das dritte Kapitel aus Teil VI: Cleopatra: Sie regierte 2 Jahre. (Die Anzahl) der Weltjahre bis zum Ende seiner Zeit beläuft sich auf 5135 Jahre[218]'.

410,ult.-411,4: 'Darauf wendet sich der Bericht der Herrschaft über Ägypten zu, nämlich dem ersten römischen Herrscher. Er regierte fünf Jahre. — Das sechste Kapitel aus Teil VI: Julius Caesar: Er regierte fünf Jahre. (Die Anzahl) der Weltjahre bis zum Ende seiner Zeit — er war der erste Caesarenherrscher — beläuft sich auf 5140 Jahre[219]'.

412,9-ult. (eingeschoben nach der Wiedergabe von Orosius, lat. T. VI 17 Par. 1-3 S.218,3-13): 'Hätten die Einwohner Roms daran gedacht, was sie sich damals gegenseitig antaten, wären sie davon abgelenkt gewesen, das für wichtig zu halten, was ihnen heute von anderen widerfährt. Dann hätten sie ihre Feinde daran gehindert, Caesar zu ermorden, nachdem er ihr Reich gefestigt hatte, für sie die Völkerschaften unterworfen und all die zu Unterta-

---

[212] Isidor, *Chron. mai.* Nr. 228.
[213] Isidor, *Chron. mai.* Nr. 229 (fügt noch Horatius zu).
[214] Isidor, *Chron. mai.* Nr. 230.
[215] Isidor, *Chron. mai.* Nr. 231.
[216] Isidor, *Chron. mai.* Nr. 227; vgl. *Etym.* V 39,25.
[217] Vgl. zu diesem etymologischen Exkurs Isidor, *Etym.* IX 3,12.
[218] Isidor, *Chron. mai.* Nr. 232; vgl. *Etym.* V 39,25 (jeweils mit abweichendem Weltjahr 5149).
[219] Isidor, *Chron. mai.* Nr. 233; vgl. *Etym.* V 39,25 (jeweils mit abweichendem Weltjahr 5154).

nen gemacht hatte, welche sich ihnen widersetzten — hätten sie ihnen hier in richtiger Weise den Rücken zugekehrt. Doch wie sollte es auch anders sein, wo sie doch so sehr enttäuscht und erfolglos waren, dass sie ihn (Caesar) mit ihren (eigenen) Händen töteten — weil sie ihm neidisch und missgünstig waren. Ferner führte jenes zu den fünf Kriegen, welche Octavianus Caesar veranlasste (vgl. ed. Zangemeister, 219, 13), weil er sich an Julius (Caesar), seinem Onkel rächen wollte. Er vergoss das Blut der Römer, tötete ihren Adel und gab ihr Heer in einem Umfang preis, der nicht (mehr nur) ein Ausgleich für alle früheren Mörder unter ihnen war. All diese Schicksalsschläge, die wie erwähnt ihretwegen ihnen selbst und den Völkern widerfahren sind, haben keine andere Ursache als ihren Hochmut, ihre Bosheit, ihre masslose Unwissenheit und ihre Grausamkeit gegenüber ihren Opponenten (*ʿalā ḫilāfihim*; Badawī, 416,5 falsch *ʿalā aḫlāqihim*). Dies sind Eigenschaften, deren Besitzer man nicht als glücklich bezeichnen kann und deren Eigentümer man einem gerechten Urteil zufolge nicht mit der Tugend in Beziehung bringen kann. Hieraus wird im Vergleich der Unterschied zwischen ihrer Zeit damals und ihrer Zeit heute deutlich'.

416,1-4 (vgl. 412,21-22): 'Das zweite Kapitel aus Teil VII: Caesar Octavianus <'ktby'n>: Er regierte 56 Jahre. (Die Anzahl) der Weltjahre bis zum Ende seiner Zeit beläuft sich auf 5196 Jahre[220]'.

416,5-417: '720 Jahre nach der Gründung Roms[221] übernahm Octavianus die Herrschaft in Rom. Sein Onkel war Julius Caesar. Ihm war anvertraut worden, was unter seiner (des Julius Caesar) Obhut gestanden hatte und er war sein Erbe. Damals kam nun Octavianus Caesar aus Andalusien nach Rom, wie er noch ein junger Mann, 28 Jahre alt war. Er war von dem Wunsch beseelt, Caesar zu rächen. Durch ihn entstanden qualvolle Kriege, mächtige Kämpfe und zahlreiche Schlachten. Er führte gegen die Mörder des Julius Caesar auf verschiedene Arten Krieg; ohne Anlass war er mit ihnen in viele Schlachten verwickelt, sodass er viele von ihnen tötete und den Rest unterwarf. Ferner führte er darnach Krieg gegen die Nationen in Ost und West, in der Gegend von Persien, Ägypten, Konstantinopel, Andalusien, Afrika und anderen Ländern, bis die ganze Welt ihm untertan war, ihre Könige sich vor ihm beugten und ihre Fürsten ihm Gehorsam erwiesen. Darauf machte er sie tributpflichtig.

[222]Im vierten Jahr seiner Herrschaft legte er den Weltbewohnern eine Steuer

---

[220] Isidor, *Chron. mai.* Nr. 235; vgl. *Etym.* V 39,26 (jeweils mit abweichendem Weltjahr 5210).

[221] Orosius VI 18 Par. 1 ed. Zangemeister 219,17 nennt das Jahr 710. Man beachte, dass einige der nachfolgenden Angaben des lat. Textes zu Beginn des vorliegenden arabischen Textes eingearbeitet worden sind.

[222] Levi della Vida, 'La traduzione', 289 weist auf eine Parallele in der *Historia Pseudoisidoriana* (11. Jh.?), gemeint ist ed. Mommsen, S. 380, Par. 5. Bei aller Ähnlichkeit im Inhalt sind die Unterschiede zum arabischen Orosius gross — wie auch Levi della Vida (l.c.) feststellt; dieser hat weitere Parallelen zwischen beiden Texten nachgewiesen; dennoch könne man nicht von einer Abhängigkeit der *Historia Pseudoisidoriana* vom bekannten arabischen Orosiustext sprechen. Nun

in Form von Bronze[223] auf. So empfing er in der Steuer den Wert dessen, was er jedem Fürsten in der gesamten Welt als Zahlungsverpflichtung in Form von Gold aufzuerlegen pflegte. Überdies liess er in den entfernten Ländern um jeden Preis nach Bronze suchen, bis dass es (sogar) den Wert des Goldes überstieg. So versammelte er davon viel und liess davon schwere Platten und Pflöcke schlagen, womit das Tal von Rom und seine Hänge über eine Länge von 40 Meilen bedeckt wurde; seine Breite war unglaublich. Jenes machte auf die Leute einen solchen Eindruck, dass sie es als Datum (für die Zeitrechnung) nahmen. Es ist die Zeitrechnung der Lateiner (*al-ʿağam*) bis heute[224].

---

enthält, wie Levi della Vida bereits festgestellt hat, die *Historia Pseudoisidoriana* einige Besonderheiten, die nur aus einer arabischen Vorlage abgeleitet werden können; hinzugefügt sei die aus der Kosmographie des Julius Honorius (S. 21; vgl. oben S. 14) übernommene Namensliste Nochodoxus, Ridimus, Pelagius und Todora, deren Verschreibungen leicht auf eine arabische Vorlage zurückgeführt werden können. Wie kann nun die *Historia Pseudoisidoriana* einerseits inhaltlich ähnliche Passagen, wie der arabische Orosius, ja selbst Besonderheiten haben, die auf eine arabische Vorlage weisen — andererseits aber dennoch von dem bekannten arabischen Orosiustext so sehr abweichen, dass 'tuttavia nemmeno qui puo parlarsi di dipendenza' (Levi della Vida 289)? Levi della Vida stellt die Möglichkeit zur Diskussion, ob nicht im islamischen Spanien eine weitere arabische Version des Orosius im Umlauf gewesen sei, welche besser war als die Version, welche in der von Badawī herausgegebenen arabischen Hs. erhalten ist; er hält es nicht für unmöglich, dass es im 10. Jh. in Spanien zwei voneinander unabhängige arabische Übersetzungen des Orosius gab, wovon die eine Interpolation eines spanischen Interpolators enthalte (Levi della Vida 290; 293). Indessen scheint mir vorläufig nur sicher, dass die *Historia Pseudoisidoriana* sowohl arabische Vorlagen benutzt hat, als auch lateinische. Bevor wir nicht neues Textmaterial haben, ist es wohl besser, anzunehmen, dass die lateinische, vom arabischen Übersetzer des Orosius benutzte Redaktion z.T. dieselben lateinischen Quellen benutzte, wie die *Historia Pseudoisidoriana*; verwirrend ist der Vergleich beider Texte vielleicht deswegen geworden, weil darüber hinaus der Kompilator der *Historia Pseudoisidoriana* (oder seine Quelle) auf den arabischen Orosiustext zurückgegriffen haben könnte (z.B. in den Zitaten aus Julius Honorius' Kosmographie oder in der Passage ed. Mommsen, 381, Par. 6 Schluss, welche wohl auf den arabischen Orosius zurückgeht: s. Levi della Vida 289f.). Man sollte daher vorläufig nicht von einer zweiten arabischen Orosiusübersetzung ausgehen, sondern mit der Möglichkeit rechnen, dass der lateinische Kompilator der *Historia Pseudoisidoriana* seine arabischen Vorlagen nach den lateinischen Quellen ergänzen konnte. Er kann somit nicht nur arabische und lateinische Quellen kombiniert oder dieselben lateinischen Quellen benutzt haben, die der lateinische Redaktor der arabischen Orosiusversion heranzog; es ist schliesslich auch denkbar, dass er seine Wiedergaben arabischer Quellen auf Grund seiner Kenntnis lateinischer Quellen revidiert haben könnte. Levi della Vidas These von einer zweiten arabischen Orosiusübersetzung steht daher noch auf schwachen Füssen. Vielleicht kann uns eine Analyse der von Levi della Vida ('La traduzione', 290; vgl. *Bronze Era*, 189) genannten hebräischen Romchronik weiterhelfen (vgl. zu ihr auch M. Alonso in al-Andalus 26 (1961), 19-21), welche Abraham Ibn David Ha-Levi aus Cordoba (gest. 1170 o. 1180 n.Chr.) vermutlich nach arabischen Quellen (darunter vielleicht auch eine arabische Version des Orosius) angefertigt hat. Allerdings beweist die leichtgekürzte Wiedergabe der Geschichte von der Einführung der sog. span. Zeitrechnung in Abraham Ibn Davids *Sefer Ha-Qabbala* nicht auf eine Abhängigkeit vom bekannten arabischen Orosius: vgl. die Übersetzung von Gerson D. Cohen, *The Book of Tradition (Sefer Ha-Qabbalah) by Abraham ibn Daud*, Philadelphia, 1967, S. 38 (Text 120ff.). Cohen (S. 162) stellt vermutlich zu Recht fest, dass Ibn David den Orosius und die *Chronica maioria* des Isidor von Sevilla 'by way of intermediate channels' benutzt habe.

[223] *aṣ-ṣufr*.

[224] I. Levi della Vida ('La traduzione', 272, Anm. 1 und ausführlich *The 'Bronze Era'*, ges. 186ff.) zeigt, handelt es sich um die sog. spanische Zeitrechnung, welche in Spanien zumindest seit

/417/ [225]Er (Octavianus) war der erste, der Anspruch auf alleinige Herrschaft in Rom erhob; durch ihn liessen die Kriege in der gesamten Welt nach; die Herrscher aller Nationen liessen ihn in ihrem Gehorsam ihm gegenüber und in ihrer Angst vor ihm die Stelle des Mazedoniers Alexander des Grossen, des Sohnes von Philippus, einnehmen. Bei ihm haben sich in der Stadt Tarraco <ṭrkwh> in Andalusien die Fürsten des Ostens, aus Hind (Indien) und Sind (westliches Indien), aus China, Asien und allen bekannten Ländern des Ostens, des Südens, des Nordens und des Westens eingefunden, um ihn um Versöhnung zu bitten und sich ihm im Frieden zu unterwerfen. Sie wollten ihm gehorsam sein und gestanden ihm den Vorrang und die Herrschaft zu[225].

Orosius sagte: Die Gesandten der Herrscher im äussersten Westen bezeugten ihm in derselben Weise den Gehorsam wie Alexander (dem Grossen) im äussersten Osten.

Orosius sagte: [226]Zu seiner (sc. des Octavianus) Zeit wurde der Messias geboren[227]. Die vierzig Wochen erfüllten sich, welche der Prophet Daniel verkündigt hatte[228]. Bei den Juden hörte das Königreich und der geweihte Zustand auf zu bestehen[226].

Er (Orosius) sagte: Jene Zeichen sind ein Vorbote für den Messias und die Offenbarung des Glaubens. Als nämlich Octavianus Caesar zu Beginn seiner Herrschaft in die Stadt Rom kam, erschien am heiteren Himmel um die Sonne ein wunderbar leuchtender und strahlender Kreis, wie ihn die Leute noch nie gesehen haben[229]. Ferner sprudelte darnach, als das Reich durch ihn wohlgeordnet war, Öl aus einer Quelle in der Gegend von Rom, so dass vom Anfang bis zu Ende des Tages von ihm die Gräben überströmt waren[230].

Orosius sagte: — [231]Gott möge sich seiner erbarmen[231] —: Dies alles gehört zu den Zeichen des Messias, des Herrn, ebenso wie (die Tatsache,) dass Octavianus Caesar die Herrschaft erhielt, gleichfalls zu den Segnungen seiner (Christi) Geburt gehörte. Durch ihn (Christus) umfasste der Glaube (*ad-dīn*) alle Weltbewohner und (durch ihn) wurde der Glaube (*al-īmān*) zum Allgemeingut[232]. Die Nationen gaben ihre Götzen auf; die Ungläubigen gaben ihre Götter auf und wandten sich der Verehrung des Messias zu — und was

---

dem 5. Jh. n.Chr. bis zum 14. u. 15. Jh. in Kraft war und mit der auch im arabischen Orosius wiedergegebenen Legende erklärt wurde.

[225] Vgl. Orosius VI 21 Par. 19-20 ed. Zangemeister 230, 3-14.

[226] Vgl. Isidor, *Chron. mai.* Nr. 237.

[227] Vgl. Orosius VI 22 Par. 5 ed. Zangemeister 231, 28-30.

[228] Dies steht nicht im lat. Orosius; vgl. Isidor, *Chron. mai.* Nr. 236 und Dan. 9:20ff.

[229] Vgl. Orosius VI 20 Par. 5 ed. Zangemeister 226, 27-29.

[230] Vgl. Orosius VI 20 Par. 6 ed. Zangemeister 227, 3-5; VI 18 Par. 34 ed. Zangemeister 223, 13-15; VI 20 Par. 7 ed. Zangemeister 227, 20f.

[231] Ein Zusatz des arab. Übersetzers.

[232] Vgl. *Chronicon Albeldense* (geschr. 883 n.Chr.), PL 129, col. 1129B: Octavianus reg. an. LVI. Huius anno XII Christus natus est. Iste solus omnem mundum imperavit.

Orosius weiter berichtete. Wir haben seine Übersetzung unterlassen, weil wir kurz sein wollen und übermässige Ausführlichkeit nicht mögen'.

419,12-420,4: 'Dann regierte nach ihm an seiner (sc. des Octavianus) Stelle sein Sohn Tiberius <ṭyb'ryš> Caesar. Er regierte 23 Jahre. Das vierte Kapitel aus Teil VII: Tiberius Caesar: Er regierte 23 Jahre. (Die Anzahl) der Weltjahre bis zum Ende seiner Zeit beläuft sich auf 5219 Jahre[233]'.

421,17-422,4: 'Hierüber[234] sagte der römische Dichter <mrks> (= Marcus? Marcius?), welcher ein Heide war: 'Als die Leute die Sonnenfinsternis als etwas betrachteten, das von der (ihnen vertrauten) Art und Weise abweicht, hielten sie sie für ewige Nacht. Deswegen wird die Welt in Schrecken versetzt und meint, dass über sie etwas hereingebrochen sei, das unaufhörlich und ewig bleibe[235]'.

(Ferner) hat (der Dichter) darüber[236] gesagt: 'Die Söhne Jakobs haben eines Tages ihren Herrn, ihren Jesus gekreuzigt, ihren (viel) gerühmten Erlöser; sie glaubten, so ihn verhehlen zu können. Aber ER wollte doch nur (ihre) Rechtleitung'.

Darauf erwähnte er die Apostel und sagte: 'Es ist, als ob ich eine Zeitlang im Lichte Seiner Zeichen stand, welches sich zu (allen) Zeiten gestärkt erhebt und aufsteigt'[237].

Es ist eine lange Äusserung.

424,19-425,4: 'Dann regierte nach ihm Claudius <qlwdys> Caesar, der Sohn des Tiberius, eines Sohnes von Octavianus. Das sechste Kapitel aus Teil VII: Claudius Caesar: Er regierte 14 Jahre. (Die Anzahl) der Weltjahre bis zum Ende seiner Zeit beläuft sich auf 5237 Jahre[238]'.

425,11-12: 'Zu Beginn seiner (des Claudius Caesar) Dynastie schrieb der Apostel Matthaeus <mt'ws> in Syrien sein Evangelium in hebräischer Sprache auf[239]'.

426,9-13: 'Nach ihm regierte sein Sohn Nero <nyrwn> Caesar. (Er regierte) 14 Jahre. Nero, der Sohn des Claudius, eines Sohnes von Tiberius, des Sohnes von Octavianus Caesar: (Er regierte) 14 Jahre. Er ist der sechste

---

[233] Isidor, *Chron. mai.* Nr. 238 (abweichendes Weltjahr 5233).

[234] Sc. über die zuvor nach Orosius lat. T. VII 4 Par. 13-14 geschilderten Zeichen, welche die Kreuzigung Christi begleiteten, wie Erdbeben und Sonnenfinsternis.

[235] Dies ist eine umschreibende Wiedergabe des auch im lateinischen Orosius (VII 4 Par. 14 ed. Zangemeister 240, 32) genannten Verses 'Impiaque aeternam timuerunt saecula noctem'. Orosius nennt nicht seine Quelle, vgl. aber Vergil, *Georgica* I 468. Auf die Stelle verweist Levi della Vida, 'La traduzione', 275, ohne allerdings den Zusammenhang mit dem Arabischen zu erkennen.

[236] D.h. die Kreuzigung Christi und ihre Zeichen. Levi della Vida ('La traduzione', 276) jedoch bezieht *fīhā* auf die Gedichte und übersetzt 'nella stessa poesia'.

[237] Vgl. Apostelgeschichte 13:47.

[238] Isidor, *Chron. mai.* Nr. 243 (abweichendes Weltjahr 5751).

[239] Isidor, *Chron. mai.* Nr. 245; vgl. *Etym.* V 39, 26 (allerdings nicht unter Claudius Caesar, sondern unter Gaius Caligula) und VI 2, 35.

der Caesaren. (Die Anzahl) der Weltjahre bis zum Ende seiner Zeit beläuft sich auf 5261 Jahre[240]'.

428,16-429,4: 'Er (sc. Nero) ist der letzte Herrscher aus der Familie des Julius. Ihre Herrschaft dauerte 116 Jahre. [241]Darauf übernahm nach ihm die Herrschaft Vespasianus <bšbšy'n>, der Sohn des <lwǧyh>: (Er regierte) neun Jahre und nachdem Rom zerrüttet war, (noch) ein Jahr. Das siebte Kapitel aus Teil VII: Vespasianus Caesar: Er regierte neun Jahre. (Die Anzahl) der Weltjahre bis zum Ende seiner Zeit beläuft sich auf 5261 Jahre[241]'.

432,18-433,5: 'Vespasianus starb nach neun Jahren Herrschaft. An seine Stelle trat sein Sohn Titus ṭyṭwš. (Er regierte) zweieinhalb Jahre. Das achte Kapitel aus Teil VII: Titus Caesar, der Sohn des Vespasianus: Er regierte zwei Jahre und sechs Monate. Das ist von der Gründung Roms an gerechnet im Jahre 820[242]. (Die Anzahl) der Weltjahre bis zum Ende seiner Zeit beläuft sich auf 5263 Jahre[243]'.

433,12-18: 'Darauf starb Titus in demselben Haus, in dem sein Vater Vespasianus gestorben war — nachdem er das Alter[244] von 41 Jahren erreicht hatte. (Das Volk) vermisste ihn überaus und die Leute trauerten sehr um ihn. Titus war der mildeste Herrscher der Römer[245]. [246]Er beherrschte am besten unter ihnen die griechische und die lateinische Sprache und verstand sich am meisten auf alle Wissenschaftszweige[246]. [247]Er hatte sich zu den guten und edlen Eigenschaften verpflichtet und strebte nach allem, was vorzüglich und ruhmvoll ist[247]. [248]Er pflegte zu sagen: 'Jeden Tag unseres Lebens, an dem wir nicht einem Beklagenswerten helfen, einen Armen unterstützen, einem Unterdrückten gegenüber seinem Unterdrücker beistehen oder einem Menschen helfen — haben wir aus unserem Leben verloren und es ist, als ob wir an ihm nicht gelebt haben[248]. [249]Von ihm gibt es in lateinischer und griechischer Sprache Schriften und Gedichte; (ferner gibt es) Wissenschaften, die auf ihn zurückgehen[249]'.

---

[240] Isidor, *Chron. mai.* Nr. 246 (abweichendes Weltjahr 5765). Es fehlt dort die Angabe, dass Nero der sechste Caesar sei. Zu einem weiteren Zusatz in der nachfolgenden Wiedergabe von Orosius VII 7 (nämlich zu Par. 3) s. Levi della Vida, 'La traduzione', 289; Levi della Vida weist auf eine Parallele in der *Historia Pseudoisidoriana* ed. Mommsen, S. 381 Par. 6 (vgl. dazu oben Anm. 222).

[241] Isidor, *Chron. mai.* Nr. 250 (abweichendes Weltjahr 5775): Vespasianus regnavit ann. X.

[242] Vgl. den lat. Orosius VII 9 Par. 13 (wo man statt dessen das Jahr 828 findet).

[243] Isidor, *Chron. mai.* Nr. 252 (abweichendes Weltjahr 5777 und kürzer): Titus regnavit ann. II.

[244] *'umr*; ed. Badawī hat falsch <'nr>

[245] Vgl. Anm. 247.

[246] Vgl. Isidor, *Chron. mai.* Nr. 253.

[247] Eine sinngemässe Wiedergabe von Isidor, *Chron. mai.* Nr. 255.

[248] Vgl. Isidor, *Chron. mai.* Nr. 256.

[249] Vgl. zu ihm Anm. 246.

435,1-4: 'Das neunte Kapitel aus Teil VII: Domitianus <dwmyṭ'n> Caesar, der Sohn des Vespasianus: Er regierte 15 Jahre[250]. (Die Anzahl) der Weltjahre bis zum Ende seiner Zeit beläuft sich auf 5278 Jahre[251]'.

436,3-6: 'An seiner (sc. des Domitianus) Stelle regierte Nerva <nrb'>, der Sohn des Titus. Seine Herrschaft dauerte zwei Jahre. — Nerva, der Sohn des Titus, eines Sohnes von Vespasianus Caesar: Er regierte eineinhalb Jahre. — (Die Anzahl) der Weltjahre bis zum Ende seiner Zeit beläuft sich auf 5280 Jahre[252]'.

436,11-14: 'Dann regierte nach ihm (sc. Nerva) Traianus <ṭry'n>. — Seine Herrschaft dauerte 19 Jahre. — Traianus, der Sohn des Antoninus Caesar: Er regierte 19 Jahre. — (Die Anzahl) der Weltjahre bis zum Ende seiner Zeit beläuft sich auf 5299 Jahre[253]'.

438,3-7: 'Nach ihm (sc. Traianus) übernahm sein Bruder Hadrianus <'dry'n> Caesar die Herrschaft. — Seine Herrschaft dauerte 21 Jahre. — (Die Anzahl) der Weltjahre bis zum Ende seiner Zeit beläuft sich auf 5320 Jahre[254]'.

438,11-15: 'Als er (Hadrianus) nun dem Tode nahe war, ordnete er seinen Sohn Antoninus <'ntwnynš> als Nachfolger an. — (Dieser) regierte nach ihm 22 Jahre. — Antoninus, der Sohn des Hadrianus Caesar: Er regierte 22 Jahre. — (Die Anzahl) der Weltjahre bis zum Ende seiner Zeit beläuft sich auf 5342 Jahre[255]'.

439,3-440,4: 'Nach ihm (sc. Antoninus) regierte Marcus <mrks> Aurelius <'wr'lyš>, genannt Antoninus der Kleine. (Er regierte) 18 Jahre. — Das zehnte Kapitel aus Teil VII: Marcus regierte zusammen mit seinem Bruder Aurelius 19 Jahre. — (Die Anzahl) der Weltjahre bis zum Ende seiner Zeit beläuft sich auf 5360 Jahre[256]'.

442,5-443,5: 'Nach ihm (sc. Marcus Aurelius) regierte sein Sohn Commodus <kmdt> 13 Jahre. — Das elfte Kapitel aus Teil VII: Commodus Caesar: Er regierte 13 Jahre. — (Die Anzahl) der Weltjahre bis zum Ende seiner Zeit beläuft sich auf 5373 Jahre[257]'.

444,12-15: 'Nach beiden (sc. Pertinax und Iulianus) regierte Severus sb'rs 18

---

[250] Vgl. die identische Angabe im lat. T. VII 10 Par. 1. Isidor, *Chron. mai.* Nr. 257 jedoch '16 Jahre'.

[251] Isidor, *Chron. mai.* Nr. 257 nennt 5293 als Weltjahr.

[252] Isidor, *Chron. mai.* Nr. 262 (abweichendes Weltjahr 5794 und Regierungszeit von einem Jahr).

[253] Isidor, *Chron. mai.* Nr. 264 (abweichendes Weltjahr 5313). Die Regierungszeit (21 Jahre) stimmt mit der Angabe Orosius VII 13 Par. 1 überein.

[254] Isidor, *Chron. mai.* Nr. 268 (abweichendes Weltjahr 5334).

[255] Isidor, *Chron. mai.* Nr. 272 (abweichendes Weltjahr 5356).

[256] Vgl. Isidor, *Chron. mai.* Nr. 276 mit der abweichenden Regierungsdauer von 18 Jahren und mit dem abweichenden Weltjahr 5375. Eine Regierungszeit von 19 Jahren bietet aber Orosius lat. T. VII 15 Par. 1.

[257] Isidor, *Chron. mai.* Nr. 278 (abweichendes Weltjahr 5388). Die Regierungsdauer von 13 Jahren nennt auch Orosius, lat. T. VII 16 Par. 1.

Jahre. — Severus, der Sohn des <'rtṯ>, eines Sohnes von Antoninus Caesar[258]. — (Die Anzahl) der Weltjahre bis zum Ende seiner Zeit beläuft sich auf 5392 Jahre[259]'.

445,2-6: 'Bassianus <bsy'nws> übernahm nach ihm (sc. Severus) die Herrschaft für den Zeitraum von sieben Jahren. — Antoninus Bassianus Caesar: Er regierte sieben Jahre. — (Die Anzahl) der Weltjahre bis zum Ende seiner Zeit beläuft sich auf 5399 Jahre[260]'.

445,16-19: 'Er (sc. Ophilus Macrinus) übernahm (die Herrschaft der Römer). — Seine Herrschaft dauerte ein Jahr. — Macrinus, der Sohn des Marcus Caesar: Er regierte ein Jahr. — (Die Anzahl) der Weltjahre bis zum Ende seiner Zeit beläuft sich auf 5400 Jahre[261]'.

447,1-5: 'Das 12. Kapitel aus Teil VII: Antoninus, der Sohn des Aurelius: Er regierte vier Jahre. — (Die Anzahl) der Weltjahre bis zum Ende seiner Zeit beläuft sich auf 5404 Jahre[262]'.

447,7-11: 'Nach ihm (sc. Antoninus) übernahm die Herrschaft Alexander, der Sohn des Marcus. (Er regierte) 13 Jahre. — Alexander, der Sohn des Marcus: Er regierte 13 Jahre. — (Die Anzahl) der Weltjahre bis zum Ende seiner Zeit beläuft sich auf 5417 Jahre[263]'.

447,17-20: 'Nach ihm (sc. Alexander, der Sohn des Marcus) übernahm Maximianus <mğšmy'n>[264] die Herrschaft. (Er regierte) drei Jahre. — Maximianus, der Sohn der Lucia <lwğyh>: Er regierte drei Jahre. — (Die Anzahl) der Weltjahre bis zum Ende seiner Zeit beläuft sich auf 5420 Jahre[265]'.

448,8-12: 'Nach der Ermordung des Maximianus übernahm die Herrschaft Gordianus <ġrdy'n> Caesar. Seine Herrschaft dauerte sieben Jahre. — Gordianus, der Sohn des Valentianus Caesar: Er regierte sieben Jahre. — (Die Anzahl) der Weltjahre bis zum Ende seiner Zeit beläuft sich auf 5427 Jahre[266]'.

[258] Die Angabe der Regierungsdauer fehlt im Arabischen und ist vermutlich ausgefallen.

[259] Isidor, *Chron. mai.* Nr. 283 (abweichendes Weltjahr 5407). Die Regierungsdauer von 18 Jahren nennt auch der lat. Orosius VII 17 Par. 1.

[260] Isidor, *Chron. mai.* Nr. 288, mit abweichender Namensform: Antoninus Caracalla Severi filius regnavit ann. VII (Weltjahr 5414).

[261] Isidor, *Chron. mai.* Nr. 290 (abweichendes Weltjahr 5415); zur Regierungszeit vgl. auch den lat. Orosius VII 18 Par. 3.

[262] Isidor, *Chron. mai.* Nr. 291 (abweichendes Weltjahr 5418 und abweichende Regierungszeit von drei Jahren). Die im Arabischen genannte Regierungsdauer stimmt mit dem lat. Orosius VII 18 Par. 4 (Schluss) überein.

[263] Isidor, *Chron. mai.* Nr. 294 (abweichendes Weltjahr 5531). Die genannte Regierungsdauer geht auf den lat. Orosius VII 18 Par. 6 zurück.

[264] Zu erwarten ist eigentlich Maximinus (s. lat. Orosius VII 19 Par. 1); hier liegt wohl eine Verwechslung mit dem VII 25 genannten Maximianus vor. Die Hss. BCEL in Isidor, *Chron. mai.* lesen Maximianus.

[265] Isidor, *Chron. mai.* Nr. 297 (abweichendes Weltjahr 5434). Zur Regierungsdauer s. lat. Orosius VII 19 Par. 2.

[266] Isidor, *Chron. mai.* Nr. 300 (abweichendes Weltjahr 5441). Zur Regierungszeit s. lat. Orosius VII 20 Par. 1 (Schluss).

448,16-20: 'Nach ihm (sc. Gordianus) übernahm Philippus <flbs>, der Sohn des Aurelianus die Herrschaft. — Seine Herrschaft dauerte sieben Jahre. — Philippus, der Sohn des Aurelianus Caesar: Er regierte sieben Jahre. — (Die Anzahl) der Weltjahre bis zum Ende seiner Zeit beläuft sich auf 5434 Jahre[267]'.

449,7-ult. (Einschub in Orosius, lat. T. VII 27): '[268]Decius, der Sohn des <mğšmt> (= Maximus?) Caesar: Er regierte ein Jahr. — (Die Anzahl) der Weltjahre bis zum Ende seiner Zeit beläuft sich auf 5435 Jahre[268]. [269]Er hat seinen Sohn an die Spitze gestellt und blieb selbst noch Führer. Durch ihn erlitten die Christen überaus grosse[270] Drangsal und (von ihm) wurden die Gläubigen verfolgt[269]. Eine Gruppe Märtyrer wurde für ihren Glauben ermordet.

[271]Zu seiner Zeit erlitten Christophorus <h̲rštwfrš> und zusammen mit ihm eine Schar von Märtyrern im Gebiet von Antiochien das Martyrium. Zu seiner Zeit erlitten das Martyrium (ferner) ein Mann namens <ts>[272], eine Frau namens Quinta <qw'nṭt>[273]; eine weitere Frau namens Apollonia[274] wurde ins Feuer geworfen. Quinta aber banden sie, als sie sich weigerte, die Götzen anzubeten, mit Fesseln und schleiften sie über die Strassen der Stadt[275], so dass ihr Körper in Stücke zerrissen wurde[276]..

Durch ihn erlitt ein Mann namens Serapion <šr'fywn> das Martyrium; er wurde schrecklich gefoltert[277]. (Ferner) erlitt eine Schar Gläubiger das Martyrium für ihren Glauben; Fabianus, der 'Patriarch' <bṭryrk> von Rom, wurde (für seinen Glauben) getötet[278].

Zu seiner Zeit gab es die Siebenschläfer[279], die Bewohner der Höhle[280]; er

---

[267] Isidor, *Chron. mai.* Nr. 302 (abweichendes Weltjahr 5448). Orosius VII 19 Par. 3 nennt als Dauer der Herrschaft abweichend 'annis sex'.

[268] Isidor, *Chron. mai.* Nr. 305 (abweichendes Weltjahr 5449).

[269] Vgl. Orosius VII 21 Par. 2-3.

[270] *sābiġa*; Badawī 449,10 hat nicht passendes *sābiʿa*.

[271] Das nachfolgende Stück ist bereits von Levi della Vida ('La traduzione', 277) mit italienischer Übersetzung vorgelegt worden. Er hat auf Eusebius' *Historia ecclesiastica* als indirekte Quelle verwiesen. Doch vorläufig gibt es keine Anhaltspunkte, die gegen eine Benutzung des Eusebius in der lateinischen Übersetzung des Rufinus sprechen.

[272] Vgl. Metras bei Eusebius, *Hist. eccles.* (hier und im nachfolgenden nach der lat. Übers. v. Rufinus) VI 41 Par. 3.

[273] Ed. Badawī 449,13 <qw'bṭt>; aber vgl. Eusebius, *Hist. eccles.* VI 41 Par. 3.

[274] Ed. Badawī 449,14 hat <'llwyn>, was leicht aus <'blwnyt> verschrieben sein kann.

[275] Gemeint ist Alexandrien: s. Eusebius, *Hist. eccles.* VI 41 Par. 1.

[276] S. Eusebius, *Hist. eccles.* VI 41 Par. 4.

[277] Vgl. Eusebius, *Hist. eccles.* VI 41 Par. 8.

[278] Vgl. Eusebius, *Hist. eccles.* VI 39 Par. 1.

[279] Wörtlich 'die sieben Knaben' (*as-sabʿa ġilma* (!)).

[280] *asḥāb al-kahf*: vgl. zu dem koranischen Terminus (s. Sure 18,9/8) die gleichlautenden Artikel v. A.J. Wensinck in *EI*^{1} u. R. Paret in *EI*^{2}. Es scheint nicht ausgeschlossen, dass der lateinische Bearbeiter des vom arabischen Übersetzer benutzten Orosiustextes die vorliegende Notiz über die Siebenschläfer Gregor von Tours' (lebte 538-594) *Passio septem dormientium apud Ephesum*

(Decius) errichtete vor ihnen (eine Mauer)[281]. Gott — erhaben ist er[282] — weckte sie nach langer Zeit auf.

450,1-5: 'Die Herrschaft übernahm Gallus <ġ'lš> Hostilianus <'wstly'ns>. (Er regierte) zwei Jahre. — Gallus Hostilianus Caesar: Er regierte zwei Jahre. — (Die Anzahl) der Weltjahre bis zum Ende seiner Zeit beläuft sich auf 5437 Jahre[283].

450,9-13: 'Die Herrschaft übernahm nach ihn (sc. Gallus) sein Bruder Gallienus ġlynwš Valerianus <blry'n>[284]. — Seine Herrschaft dauerte 15 Jahre. — Gallienus Valerianus Caesar: Er regierte 15 Jahre. — (Die Anzahl) der Weltjahre bis zum Ende seiner Zeit beläuft sich auf 5452 Jahre[285].

451,9-13: 'Nach ihm (Gallienus Valerianus Caesar) übernahm die Herrschaft Claudius <qlwdys>, der Sohn des Valerianus, eines Sohnes von Marcella (oder: Marcellus: <mrglh>). — Seine Herrschaft dauerte zwei Jahre. — Claudius, der Sohn des Valerianus Caesar: Er regierte zwei Jahre. — (Die Anzahl) der Weltjahre bis zum Ende seiner Zeit beläuft sich auf 5454 Jahre[286].

452,11-13: 'An seiner (sc. des Aurelianus) Stelle regierte Tacitus ṭ'ġtš, der Sohn des <'lyš>, für ein Jahr. — Tacitus, der Sohn des <'lyš> Caesar: Er regierte ein Jahr. — (Die Anzahl) der Weltjahre bis zum Ende seiner Zeit beläuft sich auf 5460 Jahre[287].

452,14-17: 'Nach ihm regierte Probus <brwbs>, der Sohn des Claudius sechs Jahre. — Probus, der Sohn des Claudius Caesar: Er regierte sechs Jahre. — (Die Anzahl) der Weltjahre bis zum Ende seiner Zeit beläuft sich auf 5466 Jahre[288].

452,25-453,3: 'Nach ihm (sc. Probus) übernahm die Herrschaft Carus <q'rws> zusammen mit seinen beiden Söhnen Carinus <mqryn>[289] und Numerianus <nwm'ry'n>[290]. — Seine Herrschaft dauerte zwei Jahre. —

---

entnommen hat, der ältesten abendländischen Darstellung der Legende (vgl. Altaner/Stuiber, 477; O. Bardenhewer, *Geschichte der altchristlichen Literatur V*, Freiburg/Br., 1932, 361f.).

[281] Gemeint ist am Eingang der Höhle, in der die Siebenschläfer sich aufhielten.

[282] Zusatz des arabischen Übersetzers.

[283] Isidor, *Chron. mai.* Nr. 307 (abweichendes Weltjahr 5451) anders: Gallus et Volusianus filius regnaverunt ann. II. Vgl. aber Orosius VII 21 Par. 4.

[284] Der Übersetzer identifiziert fälschlicherweise die beiden Personen (genannt Orosius VII 22 Par. 1).

[285] Isidor, *Chron. mai.* Nr. 309 (abweichendes Weltjahr 5466). Die Angabe der Regierungsdauer im arabischen Orosius geht auf Orosius VII 22 Par. 1 zurück.

[286] Isidor, *Chron. mai.* Nr. 313 (abweichendes Weltjahr 5468). Die Angabe über die Regierungsdauer ist exakter in Orosius VII 23 Par. 1, Schluss.

[287] Isidor, *Chron. mai.* Nr. 318 (abweichendes Weltjahr 5474). Über die Dauer der Herrschaft ist Orosius VII 24 Par. 1 exakter: sexto ménse occisus in Ponto est. Hierauf nimmt das Arabische ed. Badawī 452,13 Bezug mit der Angabe 'er wurde getötet, bevor sein (Regierungs-)Jahr abgelaufen war'.

[288] Isidor, *Chron. mai.* Nr. 320 (abweichendes Weltjahr 5480). Die Angabe über die Regierungsdauer ist bei Orosius VII 24 Par. 2 genauer: annis sex et mensibus quattuor.

[289] So die arab. Hs., wohl für <qryn>.

[290] Arab. Hs. <nwmn'ry'n>.

Carus Caesar, der Narbonenser: Er regierte zwei Jahre. — (Die Anzahl) der Weltjahre bis zum Ende seiner Zeit beläuft sich auf 5468 Jahre[291]'.

453,7-11: 'Nach ihm (sc. Carus) übernahm Diocletianus <dywqlz'n> die Herrschaft. — Seine Herrschaft dauerte 20 Jahre. — Diocletianus, der Sohn des Marcus (?<mrkh>) Caesar: Er regierte 20 Jahre. — (Die Anzahl) der Weltjahre bis zum Ende seiner Zeit beläuft sich auf 5488 Jahre[292]'.

456,11-14: 'Diocletianus (und Maximianus) hörten während ihrer (Regierungs-)Zeit nicht auf, die Christen zu verfolgen[293], bis sie beide umkamen — nachdem Gott sich an ihnen in der Welt gerächt hatte. Denn Gott sandte über ihn (Diocletianus) verschiedene Krankheiten, so dass sein Körper von Würmern zerfressen war und seine Zähne mitsamt seinem Unterkiefer ausfielen. Darauf starb er[294]. — Den Maximianus befiel eine Krankheit, durch die sein Körper verbrannte; er starb in Tarsus, von Gott verflucht und von seinen Engeln verabscheut'.

457-461,16: 'Das 13. Kapitel aus Teil VII: Constantinus <qsṭnṭyn>, der Sohn des Constantius <qsṭnš>, des Sohnes von <w'sṭnyws>, eines Sohnes von <'ršmyws>, des Sohnes von <dqywn>, eines Sohnes von <ġ'lys>, des Sohnes von Octavianus, der grosse Augustus <'ġšt>: Er regierte 31 Jahre. — (Die Anzahl) der Weltjahre bis zum Ende seiner Zeit beläuft sich auf 5519 Jahre[295]. Er war der erste, der den Glauben an den Messias propagierte sowie die Zerstörung der Götzenbilder, das Niederreissen der Tempel, den Bau von Kirchen und das Missionieren[296] befahl. Seine Mutter war Helena <hl'nt> aus der Stadt Edessa. In ihr wuchs er auf und erlernte alle Wissenschaften. Er hatte stets ausserordentlichen Erfolg und war ausserordentlich siegreich durch die ihm widerfahrene Unterstützung und (göttliche) Hilfe gegen die ihn Bekämpfenden ... und Teilung ..., zehn von allen Provinzen ..., wer in seiner Stadt ... von den Bezirken der Griechen über ...[297] was an Irrtümer ersonnen wurde.

Dieser Constantinus hatte sich anfänglich dem Heidentum (*maǧūsīya*) verschrieben, war gegen die Christen gewalttätig und verfolgte sie. Aber er hat sich dem (christlichen) Glauben wegen eines Grundes zugewandt, den einer der

---

[291] Isidor, *Chron. mai.* Nr. 322 (abweichendes Weltjahr 5482). Die Angabe über die Regierungsdauer ist identisch mit Orosius VII 24 Par. 4.

[292] Isidor, *Chron. mai.* Nr. 324 (abweichendes Weltjahr 5502): Diocletianus et Maximianus regnaverunt ann. XX. Die Angabe über die Regierungsdauer ist identisch mit Orosius VII 25 Par. 1.

[293] Vgl. Isidor, *Chron. mai.* Nr. 325: Diocletianus divinis libris adustis Christianos tote orbe persequitur.

[294] Man vergleiche die ähnliche Krankheit, mit der Eusebius' *Vita Constantini* I 57 zufolge Maximinianus für seine Christenverfolgung bestraft wird. Weniger ausführlich ist Eusebius, *Hist. eccles.* VIII 13,11 u. Append. 3 in seiner Beschreibung der Krankheiten des Diocletianus und Maximinianus.

[295] Isidor, *Chron. mai.* Nr. 329 (abweichendes Weltjahr 5534 und abweichende Regierungsdauer von 30 Jahren).

[296] Wörtlich 'das Ermutigen (*taqwiya*) zum Glauben'.

[297] Die arab. Hs. ist teilweise unleserlich.

christlichen Gelehrten namens Silvester <šlbštr>[298] schriftlich über ihn niedergelegt hat. Er war zu seiner (Constantinus') Zeit 'Patriarch' <btryrk> in Rom. Er (Constantinus) hörte dann auf, die Christen zu verfolgen und zu bedrängen[299]. Dieser (genannte) Gelehrte (sc. Silvester) berichtete[300], dass König Constantinus an Aussatz[301] litt, welcher (ganz) über ihn die Oberhand gewonnen hatte. Daher war er in grosser Sorge. Er versammelte die in der Medizin bewanderten Leute, welche Einsicht in die Krankheitsursachen hatten und sich auf die Heilung verstanden und fragte sie nach ihrer Ansicht über seine Krankheit sowie nach einem Heilmittel für seine Krankheit. Sie waren sich eins über (passende) Heilmittel, die sie ihm nannten. Sie legten ihm die Verpflichtung auf, nach Einnahme (der Heilmittel) eine Stunde in einem Brunnen zu baden[302], der voll von Säuglingsblut ist, welches aus ihnen (den Säuglingen) fliesst. Da befahl er, eine grosse Schar von Säuglingen aus der Masse und Menschenmenge zu versammeln. (Dann) gab er den Auftrag, sie am Brunnen an einem Tag zu schlachten, da er selbst anwesend ist, um in jenem Blut zu baden, solange es frisch ist. Darauf ging er an die Stelle, auf welcher er (seinen Leuten) befohlen hatte, sich für ihn mit den Säuglingen bereit zu halten. Als er nun aus seinem Palast erschien, hörte er das Schreien, /458/ Kreischen und Heulen der Frauen, welchen ihre Kinder weggenommen waren. Da prüfte er ihre Angelegenheit. Und als Constantinus berichtet wurde, dass sie die Mütter der Säuglinge waren, welche zum Vergiessen ihres Blutes versammelt worden waren, da erbarmte er sich ihrer, hatte Mitleid mit ihnen und ihren Säuglingen und sprach: 'Wir befehlen nicht das Töten solcher Nachkommen unserer Feinde, wenn wir sie überwunden und besiegt haben; vielmehr geben wir den Auftrag, sie zu schonen und von ihnen abzulassen. Wie können wir es erlauben, die Nachkommen unserer Untertanen und der uns Folgsamen zu töten?! Das Ertragen der über mich gekommenen Krankheit[303] ist für mich würdiger und notwendiger, als das Umbringen dieser Schar von Menschen und das Sterben von deren Mütter aus Kummer über ihren Tod'. Darauf befahl er, sie mit ihren Kindern freizulassen und von ihnen allen abzulassen.

Nachdem er sich nun jene darauffolgende Nacht in sein Bett begeben hatte, sah er in seinem Traum einen alten Mann, der zu ihm sagte: 'Du hast dich der

---

[298] Vgl. Anm. 41.

[299] Dieser Satz steht hier an verkehrter Stelle und gehört oben vor der Erwähnung Silvesters eingefügt.

[300] Vgl. zum nachfolgenden den (nicht vollständigen) lateinischen Text der Silvesterlegende ed. Mombritius, *Sanctuarium* II 510,34ff. und zur Bekehrungslegende Levison, 458f.; Schrörs, 246. Der lateinische Orosius berichtet nichts über die Bekehrung Konstantin des Grossen.

[301] *Dā' al-ǧuḏām* (ed. Badawī hat falsch *al-ǧuzām*).

[302] *yastanqi'u*: das Wort ist zweimal belegt und in seiner Bedeutung identisch mit dem von R.P.A. Dozy, *Supplément aux dictionnaires arabes* ([3]Leyde-Paris, 1967) s.v. verzeichneten 8. Stamm.

[303] Lies <*al*>-*'illata l-ḥādiṯata*

Säuglinge und ihrer Mütter erbarmt; du hast beschlossen, deine Krankheit zu erdulden und (die Säuglinge) freizugeben. Daher hat Gott sich deiner erbarmt, dich von deiner Krankheit geheilt und dich von deiner Erkrankung genesen lassen. Schicke nun unter den Gläubigen nach einem Mann namens Silvester, der sich aus Furcht vor dir entfernt hatte, achte auf seine Anordnung und folge seinem Ansporn, so dass deine Gesundheit in deinem Körper und in deinem Geist wiederkehrt!' — Da erwachte Constantinus, voller Schrecken über das, was er gesehen hatte. Er schickte nach dem Bischof Silvester eine Schar von seinen Dienern, um ihn zu sich kommen zu lassen. (Jener Silvester) war (nun) der Meinung, dass (Constantinus) ihn umbringen lassen wollte. Aber da nahm ihn Constantinus in Güte und Ehrerbietung auf, informierte ihn über seinen Traum, (worauf jener) ihn in einem langen Bericht über die (christliche) Religion aufklärte. Wir haben diesen Abschnitt hierüber abgekürzt; (ferner) lasse ich seinen Bericht über das Streitgespräch des Silvester mit den Juden[304] und weitere Nachrichten aus, weil ich kurz sein will.

Darauf schickte er nach allen ...[305] wie das, was sie unter ihnen Philippus <flbs> erwiesen hatten, der vor ihm erfolgreich war (?). Darauf begab er sich aus Rom weg und erbaute Konstantinopel <qsṭnṭynyt>. Die Christen wurden seit der Zeit des ungläubigen Nero <nyrwn>, welcher die Apostel Petrus <byṭr>, Paulus <bwls> umbringen liess und (seit der Zeit) eines heidnischen über Rom regierenden Herrschers verfolgt und ermordet; die einen wurden gefangengesetzt, die anderen deportiert. Aber die Heiden pflegten sich trotzdem jeden Tag zum Glauben zu bekehren, während sie Zeichen sahen und ihnen erstaunliche Wunder vor Augen kamen, welche Gott durch die heiligen Märtyrer offenbarte.

[306]Dieser Constantinus setzte die Heiden davon in Kenntnis, dass er eine Stadt bauen wolle, um sie als Wohnsitz im Lande der Byzantiner (ar-Rum al-

---

[304] Vgl. zu den Streitgesprächen des Silvester mit den Juden auch unten zu Anm. 309. Dazu die *Acta Silvestri* ed. Mombritius, *Sanctuarium* II, 516ff.; Levison, 397 sowie zum hier angedeuteten antijüdischen Dialog Levison, 414ff. und dort gegebene Verweise; ferner Lipsius, 82ff. Den *Acta Silvestri* folgt hier auch die Sächsische Weltchronik (s. unten Anm. 306), 119-121 Par. 81.

[305] Die arabische Hs. ist hier beschädigt.

[306] Die nachfolgende Legende von der Gründung Konstantinopels entstammt der Silvesterlegende (s. Levison, 403). Auf die Ähnlichkeit des arabischen Orosius zu dieser hatte bereits Levi della Vida ('La traduzione', 278, Anm. 2) hingewiesen, und zwar — weil das Stück in der Ausgabe von Mombritius fehlt — nach der lateinischen Hs. der Silvesterlegende in cod.lat. 206f., 163v-176r in Brussel (s. Catalogus codicum hagiographicorum Bibliothecae Regiae Bruxellensis 1, 1886, S. 119,65). Von dieser Rezension hänge auch Aldhelmus (gest. 709 n.Chr.) in seiner Schrift *De virginitate* Kp. XXV ab: s. Monumenta Germaniae historica, auctores antiquissimi XV ed R. Ehwald, Berlin 1919 (^{2}1961), 258f. Ferner können wir eine gekürzte Wiedergabe in der aus dem 13. Jh. stammenden Sächsischen Weltchronik finden: s. *Deutsche Chroniken und andere Geschichtsbücher des Mittelalters* II, Dublin/Zürich, 1971 (= Monumenta Germaniae Historica. Scriptorum qui vernacula lingua usi sunt II), 119 Par. 79. Der Nachweis im arabischen Orosius zeigt, dass die Legende über die Gründung von Konstantinopel schon früh fester Bestandteil der Silvesterlegende gewesen ist.

Ġirīqiyīn) zu nehmen. Er (wollte damit) dem Lande der Perser und anderer Nationen des Ostens nahe sein, weil sie sich häufig von den Caesaren trennten und lossagten. Die Mehrzahl der Byzantiner hatte sich /459/ zur Religion des Messias bekehrt und folgte seiner Religion. — so plante er (Constantinus) diese Sache, fügte die Dinge zu seinen Gunsten (?) und dachte darüber nach, was er davon versuchen könnte. (Dann) zog er tatsächlich mit seinen Truppen und Heeren in jene Richtung aus. Da erschien ihm während jener Reise im Traum eine alte und schwerfällige Frau mit hässlichem Gesicht, blassem Aussehen und hässlichem Anblick. Da wunderte er sich hierüber und ihr Aussehen erschreckte ihn. Hierauf verwandelte sie sich vor ihm in ein schönes Mädchen von vollkommener Gestalt, schönem Aussehen, geschmückt mit dem schönsten Schmuck und in einer äusserst vornehmen Kleidung. Darauf überreichte sie ihm eine Krone und setzte sie ihm auf sein Haupt. Da erwachte er voller Schrecken, war eine Zeitlang voller Unruhe, dachte über das Geschehene nach, schlummerte dann wieder ein und schlief (weiter). Darauf sah er, wie jemand zu ihm kam und zu ihm sagte: 'Constantinus, wisse, dass diese alte und betagte Frau, die du gesehen hast, die Stadt Byzanz <bznṭt> ist; du wirst sie zerstören, ihre ausgelöschte Schönheit widerherstellen, ihr ihre Schönheit zurückgeben, deine Herrschaft in ihr festigen und sie nach dir bis zum Ende der Zeit als Erbe weitergeben'.

Als er dann aus seinem Schlaf erwachte, wurde ihm sein Vorhaben noch deutlicher, die Stadt zu gründen und er beschloss, Byzanz zu bauen. Daher mobilisierte er seine Leute für ihren Bau und ordnete an, sie zum Wohnplatz und Wohnsitz zu machen. Dann begab er sich zu ihr mit all seinen Dienern, Leuten, Heerscharen und Besitztümern. Er baute sie auf vortreffliche Weise und vollendete sie auf vollkommene Weise. Sie formt das Zentrum des Landes der Byzantiner; daher sagt man zu ihnen 'Byzantiner' (al-Bizanṭ). Nachdem er sie also vollendet hatte, bezeichnete er sie mit dem Namen 'Qusṭanṭīnīya' (= Konstantinopel). Er weilte dauernd in ihr und versammelte in ihr um sich die Anhänger des Messiasglaubens und die christlichen Leiter, machte die hervorragenden Personen unter ihnen zu Führern und unterwarf die Heiden und die Götzendiener. Hierbei leisteten ihm die Heiden Roms Widerstand, wandten sich gegen ihn, kündigten ihm den Gehorsam auf und setzten über sich einen heidnischen Herrscher. Hierüber machte sich Constantinus Sorgen. Zwischen ihm und (den Heiden Roms) hat sich eine lange Geschichte abgespielt, deren Anführung zu lange dauern würde. Z.B. bat er Gott, ihn zu unterstützen und ihm den Sieg zu verleihen oder ihm Frieden zu schenken... [307] aus Furcht vor ihm und reuig zu ihm umkehrend. Da vergab er ihnen und akzeptierte ihre Reue. Er betrat mit ihnen die Stadt Rom und herrschte über sie im Zeichen des Messiasglaubens. Von ihm gibt es über die Jahre, die er lebte, über die von

[307] Die arab. Hs. ist hier unleserlich.

ihm abgeschlossenen Verträge und über die von ihm festgelegten Gesetze ein Bericht, der in unserem 'Die Nachrichten der Zeit' genannten Buch vorkommt.

/460/ Darauf zog er zum Kampf gegen die Perser aus, besiegte und unterwarf sie. Der überwiegende Teil der Welt war ihm untertan, mehr als den Caesaren vor ihm. Während einer Zeitspanne von 20 Jahren seiner Regierung griff eine gothische Gruppe eines seiner Länder an, machte einen feindlichen Einfall und richtete Unheil an. Darauf organisierte er gegen sie einen Kriegszug und bekämpfte sie, bis er sie besiegt und aus seinem Land vertrieben hatte. Er liess sie den grossen 'Donaus' <dnwbyh> genannten Fluss überschreiten.

In seinem Traum erschienen (ihm) Leinenstücke und Standarten in der Form eines Kreuzes und jemand sprach zu ihm: 'Wenn Du Deinen Widersacher besiegen willst, dann benutze dieses Zeichen in all Deinen Kleidern und Trachten'[308]. Darauf schickte er damals seine Mutter Helena <hl'nt> nach Jerusalem mit der Bitte, in ihr nach den Spuren des Messias suchen zu lassen, Kirchen erbauen und die Bestimmungen des (christlichen) Glaubens verwirklichen zu lassen. Von ihr gibt es hierüber Nachrichten. Ferner (gibt es Nachrichten über) Streitgespräche mit den Juden[309]; sie sind über die Länder der Welt weit verbreitet und bekannt und in dem Buch des Eusebius <'ws'byws> niedergelegt worden[310], das die Schilderung der Kirche und ihrer Leiter umfasst. — Darauf liess sie (Helena) dort die grossen Kirchen erbauen und machte grosse Schenkungen[311]. Darnach kehrte sie zu ihrem Sohn Constantinus zurück.

Ferner: Als König Constantinus (alters-)schwach wurde[312], übertrug er die Herrschaft an seinen Sohn Constantius <qnsṭntys>. Dessen Herrschaft dauerte 24 Jahre.

Constantius, der Sohn des Constantinus Caesar. Er regierte 24 Jahre. (Die Anzahl) der Weltjahre bis zum Ende seiner Zeit beläuft sich auf 5543 Jahre[313]. Er war ein Sympathisant des Arius <'ryš>[314], welcher während der Zeit seines Vaters Constantinus wegen seines Unglaubens verstossen worden war. Denn Arius stand während der Regierungszeit seines Vaters in Beziehung zu

---

[308] *šaklika*: Hier liegt spanisch-arabischer Sprachgebrauch vor; vgl. Dozy (s. Anm. 302) s.n.

[309] Vgl. dazu oben Anm. 304.

[310] Tatsächlich findet man in der hier genannten Kirchengeschichte des Eusebius nichts hierüber. Es ist von der ausgehenden Antike her bekannt, dass Eusebius' Name als Autorität fälschlicherweise z.B. in Schilderungen über Märtyrer begegnet (s. Speyer, 40f.). Der unbekannte Verfasser der Silvesterlegende behauptet, hier Eusebius' umfangreiches Werk über die Bischöfe der Kirche benutzt zu haben (vgl. Levison, 406f.; Speyer, 71 u. 298).

[311] Vgl. Eusebius, *Vita Constantini* III, 41ff.

[312] *tadannā*: dieser Stamm ist nicht in den Wörterbüchern verzeichnet; er erscheint identisch mit dem 1. Stamm *danā* 'he was or became weak' (s. E.W. Lane, *Arabic-English Lexicon* I, 1-8, New York, 1955-6, s.v.).

[313] Isidor, *Chron. mai.* Nr. 335 (abweichendes Weltjahr 5558).

[314] Vgl. G. Gentz, Art. 'Arianer' in *RAC*.

Constantius und zu seiner Tante, der Schwester des Constantius. Er liess nicht nach, /461/ ihnen beiden gegenüber zuvorkommend zu sein, sie oft zu besuchen und sich ständig mit ihnen zu unterhalten, bis dass seine Listen bei ihnen Erfolg hatten und sie beide von seiner schmählichen Lehre überzeugt waren. Nachdem nun die Herrschaft auf Constantius übergegangen war, versetzte (dieser) ihn (Arius) in seine Hauptstadt und übernahm dessen Glauben an sein hässliches Bekenntnis. (Arius) lehrte (die Existenz) von drei Göttern und verwarf die Einheit (Gottes)[315].

Zu seiner Zeit lebte Athanasius <'ṯn'šywš> [316], der oberste Bischof[317] in Alexandrien. Zwischen ihm und Arius entspann sich ein langer Disput[318] über das Bekenntnis. Der Herrscher Constantius liess von den römischen Heiden einen scharfsinnigen und gelehrten Philosophen namens Probus <brwbs> zugegen sein. So liess (Constantius) sich in einem langen Bericht des (Probus) über beide und über das Streitgespräch informieren, das einige Tage dauerte, bis es für den Schiedsrichter Probus klar war, dass Bischof Athanasius, der die Einheit Gottes lehrte[319], im Recht und Arius, der die Existenz von drei Gottheiten behauptete, im Unrecht war. Darauf ordnete er an ... [320] und ging dazu über, ihm zu helfen ... [320]. Damals ereignete sich das <'nṭrw-brqṭ'yt> [321] genannte Schisma, nämlich das Schisma der <lsbryqy>-Leute'.

Dann folgt 461,11-14 eine Übersetzung von Orosius, lat. T. 274,17-20, der sich diese geschichtstheologische Bemerkung anschliesst:

'Da vergalt ihm Gott seine böse Lehre damit, dass nach ihm der Bösewicht Julianus <yly'n> die Herrschaft übernahm, der Sohn seines Onkels Constantius[322]. Seine Herrschaft dauerte ein Jahr. Julianus, der Sohn des Constantius Caesar: Er regierte ein Jahr. (Die Anzahl) der Weltjahre bis zum Ende seiner Zeit beläuft sich auf 5544 Jahre[323]'.

Dann folgt Orosius, lat. T. VII 30 Par. 2-6 S. 276,3-26 = arab. Übers. 462,1-12.

462,13-16: 'Nach ihm (Julianus) übernahm die Herrschaft Jovianus <'by'n>, der Sohn des Constantinus <qsṭnṭyn> Caesar. Er regierte ein

[315] *at-tauḥīd.*

[316] Seit 328 n.Chr. Metropolit von Alexandrien: s. G.Gentz, Art. 'Athanasius' in *RAC* I, 859-866.

[317] *al-usquf al-ʿāmm.*

[318] *munāẓara.*

[319] Gemeint ist die Lehre vom ὁμοούσιος-Sein Gottes.

[320] Die arab. Hs. ist hier lückenhaft.

[321] Schwerlich ἀνθρωποπάθεια (so Badawī 461,10 u. Anm. 2). Gemeint ist Arius' Lehre von der Unbeschreibbarkeit Gottes, mit welchem im Gegensatz zu Athanasius' ὁμοούσιος nichts ἴδιον oder ὅμοιον ist.

[322] Die arab. Hs. hat <mğšnṭnš>; vgl. aber Orosius VII 29 Par. 14f.

[323] Isidor, *Chron. mai.* Nr. 343 hat abweichend eine zweijährige Regierungszeit und das Weltjahr 5560; Orosius VII 30 Par. 1 ed. Zangemeister 276,2 liest: anno uno et mensibus octo. Vielleicht liegt im Arabischen eine Verwechslung mit dem nachfolgenden Abschnitt über Jovianus vor: die arabische Schreibung von Julianus und Jovianus ist leicht verwechselbar.

Jahr. — (Die Anzahl) der Weltjahre bis zum Ende seiner Zeit beläuft sich auf 5544 Jahre[324]'.

463,4-14: 'Dann regierte nach ihm 14 Jahre Valentianus <flnsy'n>, der Sohn des Constantius <qsṭnš>. — Valentianus, der Sohn des Constantius Caesar: Er regierte 14 Jahre. — (Die Anzahl) der Weltjahre bis zum Ende seiner Zeit beläuft sich auf 5559 Jahre[325].

[326]Damals hatten sich die Gothen <al-qūṭ> in zwei Gruppen gespalten: der Führer der einen Gruppe war <qrwbld> (= Fridigernus?) und der Führer der anderen wurde Athanaricus <'ṭnrq> genannt, welcher vom Führer der Römer unterstützt wurde. Damals folgten Christen der Lehre des verfluchten Arius[326] und [327]damals erfand[328] Ulfilas <ġlflt> das gothische Alphabet und übersetzte die Offenbarungen[329] ins Gothische[327]. [330]Damals lebten Photinus <fwṭyn>, Eunomius <'rnwbys> und Apollinaris <'bln'rs>, welche Abhandlungen über den Glauben schrieben[330]'.

Dann folgt 463,ult.-464,6 = lat. T. VII 32 Par. 2-4 S. 277,8-18.

464,6-7: 'Zu seiner (Procopius') Zeit regierte der Patriarch (<al-baṭriyark>) Damasus <d'm's> über Rom[331]. Zu seiner Zeit starb der Gottesdiener Martin, der im Frankenland bekannte Bischof[332]'.

Dann folgt 464,8-9 = lat. T. VII 32 Par. 5 S. 277,18-22; darauf folgt 464,10-11 = lat. T. VII 32 Par. 8 S. 277,32-33; darauf 464,12-465,5 = lat. T. VII 32 Par. 9-14 S. 277,34-278,25.

465,6-10: 'Dann übernahm sein (sc. Valentianus) Bruder Valens <w'lns> die Herrschaft. Seine Herrschaft dauerte vier Jahre. — Valens: Er regierte vier Jahre[333]. — (Die Anzahl) der Weltjahre bis zum Ende seiner Zeit beläuft sich auf 5563 Jahre[334]. Er glaubte an die Lehre des verfluchten Arius'.

---

[324] Isidor, *Chron. mai.* Nr. 346 (abweichendes Weltjahr 5561).

[325] Isidor, *Chron. mai.* Nr. 348 (Weltjahr 5575): Valentinianus et Valens frater eius regnaverunt ann. XIIII.

[326] Vgl. Isidor, *Chron. mai.* Nr. 349. Die lateinische Isidorhs. y teilt mit dem Arabischen die Namensvariante Athanaricus (statt Ataricus).

[327] Isidor, *Chron. mai.* Nr. 350.

[328] *ṣanaʿa*: wörtlich 'verfertigte'.

[329] *al-kutub al-munzala* 'die offenbarten Schriften'.

[330] Isidor, *Chron. mai.* Nr. 351.

[331] Zu Damasus I (366-384 n.Chr.) vgl. Altaner/Stuiber, 354.

[332] Gemeint ist Martin von Tours (gest. 397), über den zahlreiche Legenden entstanden: Sulpicius Severus (gest. um 420) verfasste eine *Vita Martini* sowie als Ergänzung dazu drei *Briefe* und die *Dialoge*, welche Martin als Apostel Galliens und als ersten abendländischen Mönchsvater zeigen (s. Altaner/Stuiber, 231); im 6. Jh. verfasste Gregor von Tours (538-594) sein *De virtutibus S. Martini* (4 Bücher über Wunder am Grab des hl. Martin von Tours: s. Altaner/Stuiber, 477). Auch Isidor von Sevilla, *De viris illustribus* Par. XXII hat ihm einen Artikel gewidmet (s. ed. Carmen Codoner Merino, *El 'de viris illustribus' de Isidoro de Sevilla*, Salamanca, 1964, 145f.). Vgl. schliesslich Isidor, *Chron. mai.* Nr. 355.

[333] Vgl. Orosius VII 32 Par. 15 u. 33 Par. 1.

[334] Vgl. Isidor, *Chron. mai.* Nr. 348 (nennt als Weltjahr für Valentianus und Valens 5575 und als Regierungsdauer 14 Jahre).

Häufiger zitierte Literatur und Abkürzungen

- Altaner, Bertold/Stuiber, Alfred: *Patrologie.* 8.A. Freiburg-Basel-Wien, 1978. *Chronicon Albeldense.* In: *PL* 129, Paris, 1853, col. 1123-1146.
- Cohen, A.E.: *De versie op Troje van de westerse middeleeuwse geschiedsschrijvers tot 1160,* Diss. Assen, 1941.
- Dölger, Franz Josef: *Die Taufe Konstantins und ihre Probleme,* in: Konstantin der Grosse und seine Zeit. Gesammelte Studien, Freiburg, 1913 (= XIX Suppl.h. d. Römischen Quartalschrift), 377-447.
- Duchesne, L.: *Le liber pontificalis.* I Paris, 1955.
- EI^1 = *Enzyklopaedie des Islam.* I-IV u. Ergänz.bd., Leiden; Leipzig, 1913-1938.
- EI^2 = *Encyclopaedia of Islam.* 1 ff. Leiden/London, 1960 ff.
- Eusebius Caesarensis: (*Historia ecclesiastica,*, dt.). *Kirchengeschichte.* Hrsg. u. eingel. v. Heinrich Kraft. Die Übers. v. Philipp Haeuser (Kempten, 1932) wurde neu durchges. v. Hans Armin Gärtner, München, 1967.
- id.: (*Vita Constantini,* dt. in:) *Ausgewählte Schriften, nach dem Urtext übersetzt.* II, Kempten, 1880, 5-233.
- Goetz, Hans-Werner: *Die Geschichtstheologie des Orosius,* Darmstadt, 1980. = Impulse der Forschung 32.
- *Historia Pseudoisidoriana.* In: *Chronica minora saec.IV.V.VI.VII.* Ed. Th. Mommsen, Vol. II, Berolini, ^{2}1961 (= Monumenta Germaniae historica. Auctores antiquissimi XI/2), 377-388.
- Isidor von Sevilla: *Chronica maiora.* In: *Chronica minora saec. IV.V.VI.VII.* Ed. Th. Mommsen, Vol. II, Berolini, ^{2}1961 (= Monumenta Germaniae historica. Auctores antiquissimi XI/2), 391-481.
- id. *Etymologiarum sive originum libri XX.* Recogn. W.M. Lindsay. I-II, Oxonii, 1911 (repr. 1971).
- Levi della Vida, Giorgio: 'The 'Bronze Era' in Moslem Spain'. In: *Journal of the American Oriental Society* 63 (1943), 183-191.
- id.: 'La traduzione araba delle storie di Orosio'. In: *al-Andalus* 19 (1954), 257-293.
- Levison, Wilhelm: 'Konstantinische Schenkung und Silvesterlegende'. In: id., *Aus rheinischer und fränkischer Frühzeit.* Ausgewählte Aufsätze. Düsseldorf, 1948, 390-465.
- Lippold, Adolf: 'Griechisch-makedonische Geschichte bei Orosius'. In: *Chiron* 1 (1971), 437-455.
- Lipsius, Richard Adalbert: *Die Edessenische Abgar-Sage.* Braunschweig, 1880.
- Mombritius, Boninus: *Sanctuarium seu vitae sanctorum* (Neudr. besorgt v. H. Quentin u. A. Brunet). II. Paris, 1910.
- Orosius: *Historiae adversus paganos.* Ed. C. Zangemeister, Lipsiae, 1889.
- id.: (*Historiae adversus paganos,* altengl. Bearb.) *The Old English Orosius.* Ed. by Janet M. Bately, London-New York-Toronto, 1980.
- id.: (*Historiae adversus paganos,* anon. arab. Bearb. aus d. 1. Hälfte des 10. Jh. n.Chr.) *Ta'rīḫ al-'ālam* (Hrsg. v.) 'Abdarraḥmān Badawī, Beirut, 1982.
- *PL* = *Patrologia latina.*
- *RAC* = *Reallexikon für Antike und Christentum.* Hrsg. v. Theodor Klauser, Stuttgart, 1950ff.
- *RE* = *Paulys Real-Encyklopädie der classischen Altertumswissenschaft.* Neue Bearbeitung begonnen v. G. Wissowa, fortgeführt v. W. Kroll u. K. Mittelhaus, Stuttgart, 1894ff.
- Schrörs, Heinrich: 'Die Bekehrung Konstantins des Grossen in der Überlieferung'. In: *Zeitschrift für katholische Theologie* 40 (1916), 238-257.
- Speyer, Wolfgang: *Die literarische Fälschung im heidnischen und christlichen Altertum,* München, 1971. = Handbuch der Altertumswissenschaft. 1. Abt., 2. t.
- Von den Brincken, Anna-Dorothee: *Studien zur lateinischen Weltchronistik bis in das Zeitalter Ottos von Freising,* Düsseldorf, 1957.
- Von Döllinger, Joh. Jos. Ign.: *Die Papst-Fabeln des Mittelalters,* Stuttgart, ^{2}1890.

ETHICAL TERMINOLOGY IN HEYKHALOT-TEXTS

by

N.A. van Uchelen

It is not far-fetched to state that in the multi-coloured world picture of Merkavah-mysticism[1] its vertical orientation is one of the most conspicuous features. To the first aspirations of the mystic believer belonged a journey through the heavenly palaces to the heavenly throne. His cosmological space-scheme is compressed in the image of the ladder. According to several texts[2], the man who had a ladder in his house apparently was a good mystic.

Halakhic features.

This vertical orientation, however, did not keep the *yored merkavah* off his earthly life. His striving for the heavenly throne did not absolve him from his earthly obligations. It is the merit of Scholem and Lieberman to have paid attention to this more horizontal orientation of Merkavah-mysticism[3]. Both scholars investigated the passage concerning the story of Nechunya's recall from his mystic journey. His pupils made him break off his mystic enterprise by means of a piece of unclean cloth, which had been touched by a menstruating woman. We do not have to enter into the details of the story here[4]. The closing sentence of the article of Lieberman is significant: 'This passage of the Heikhaloth demonstrates that the Jewish mystics were not *rabbanan deagga-*

---

[1] With Merkavah-mysticism in this article is meant a configuration of descriptions and concepts to be found in the traditional corpus of Heykhalot- and Merkavah-texts. The broad outline of these texts has been drawn by I. Gruenwald, *Apocalyptic and Merkavah Mysticism*, Leiden/Köln, 1980. For a more strict outline, see the writer's *Joodse Mystiek. Merkawa, tempel en troon*, Amstelveen, 1983. The most important manuscripts are edited by P. Schäfer, *Synopse zur Hekhalot-Literatur*, Tübingen, 1981. In the article this edition is cited as: Schäfer, followed by the number of the paragraph.

[2] See e.g. *Pirqey Heykhalot Rabbati*, ed. S.A. Wertheimer and A.J. Wertheimer, in: *Batei Midrashot* I, Jerusalem, 1968², chapter XV,2 (= Schäfer, 263); XVI,1 (= Schäfer, 258); XXII,3 (= Schäfer, 237).

[3] G. Scholem, *Jewish Gnosticism, Merkabah Mysticism and Talmudic Tradition*, New York, 1965, 9-13; S. Lieberman, 'The Knowledge of Halakha by the Author (or Authors) of the Heikhaloth', in: I. Gruenwald, *o.c.*, 241-244.

[4] The story is to be found in *Pirqey Heykhalot Rabbati* XX,1, 2, 3 (= Schäfer, 225, 226, 227). See also L.H. Schiffman, 'The Recall of Rabbi Neḥuniah ben Ha-Qaanah from Ecstasy in the Hekhalot Rabbati', *A.J.S. Review* 1 (1976), 269-281; M Schlüter, 'Die Erzählung von der Rückholung des R. Nehunya ben Haqana aus der Merkava-Schau in ihrem redaktionellen Rahmen', *Frankfurter Judaistische Beiträge* 10 (1982), 65-109.

data (rabbis who dealt with aggadah only), but were scholars also at home in the subtle intricacies of the Halakha' (p.224). In the story of Nechunya's recall these intricacies are halakhic rules concerning 'clean' and 'unclean', in connection with the halakhic technical terms *niddah* (the menstruant) and *ṭevilah* (the ritual immersion)[5].

Beside this halakhic subject another halakhic trait evidently can be traced in the Heykhalot-texts. It is true, this second halakhic trait is not mentioned explicitly, but in many texts it is present as a presupposition. For, wherever in the Heykhalot-texts mention is made of the daily fulfilling of the prayers[6], we can be sure the halakhic obligation to say the *shema'* ('Hear, Israel') and to recite the benedictions is implied. To vary the text of Mishnah Avot we appear to be allowed to say: 'The rules about menstruation, immersion and reading the *shema'*, (these) are essentials of the halakha in the Heykhalot- and Merkavah-texts'[7]. Several instances in the Heykhalot-texts show that the *yoredey merkavah* in this respect present themselves as, so to say, *rabbanan dehalakhwata* (rabbis who know to deal with halakha). The Heykhalot-texts give evidence of the saying of the prayers three times a day. To adhere to this daily earthly obligation had its far-reaching consequences for the course of things in heaven.

So far I argued on the assumption that following the halakha belongs to the so-called earthly obligations. From this point of view one might say that complying with the halakhic requirements goes with the more horizontal aspect of Merkavah-mysticism. Though it is as difficult to give a clear-cut definition of halakha as to define mysticism, the following circumscription of halakha can be helpful: 'Its world is one of down-to-earth practicalities in which decisions are required that shall be simultaneously feasible socially, defensible jurisprudentially and maintainable ethically'[8].

Ethical concomitants.

Within the 'world of down-to-earth practicalities', however, not all requirements and decisions belong to the centre of the halakha. Even the Sages

---

[5] For the halakhic problem concerning *niddah* and *ṭevilah*, see e.g. *Mishnah Miqwa'ot* I,8, VIII,2; *Mishnah Niddah* X,7; *Mishnah Zavim* I,4. The duty of *ṭevilah* is also one of the prescriptions during the fasting-preparations of the mystics, see e.g. *Pirqey Heykhalot Rabbati* XL,3 (= Schäfer, 299); *Ma'aseh Merkabah*, ed. G. Scholem, *o.c.*, par. 11 (= Schäfer, 560), par. 19 (= Schäfer, 573); *Merkabah shelemah*, ed. S. Musajow, Jerusalem, 1921, fol.Va (= Schäfer, 683).

[6] See e.g. *Pirqey Heykhalot Rabbati* X,5 (=Schäfer, 163) XIII,2, 3, 4 (= Schäfer, 172, 173, 189); compare also Gruenwald, *o.c.*, 154.

[7] See *Mishnah Avot* III,18.

[8] R. Loewe, 'Potentialities and Limitations of Universalism in the Halakha', in: *Studies in Rationalism, Judaism and Universalism. In Memory of Leon Roth*, ed. R. Loewe, London, 1966, 115-150, esp. 117.

themselves already differentiated between halakhot and other normative elements[9]. To put it in the words of Lichtenstein: 'traditional halakhic Judaism demands of the Jew both adherence to Halakha and commitment to an ethical moment that — though different from halakha — is nevertheless of a piece with it and in its own way fully imperative'[10].

If thus 'the Halakha is open ended' (Rabinovitch, 91), one can state it in this way: the wide world of halakha forms a system of interlocking circles. The circles, having their own partial areas, are the ethical or moral concomitants of the halakha as the centre. In their mutual connection these circles interact with each other and with the centre. To the concomitants of the halakha, as interdependent and interconnected ethical systems, in any case the following can be reckoned:

1) The ethical system of *derekh eretz* ('the way of the world'). The system includes a set of rules concerning natural and normal human conduct. This circle contains all those practicalities which belong to the natural order of social intercourse. This generally accepted standard of interhuman relations relies on 'recommendations rather than commandments'[11]. The circle interacts with the centre; though not being the same as halakha, it never functions without halakha[12].

2) The ethical system of *mitzwot beney Noach* ('the commandments of the sons of Noach'). According to rabbinic traditions this system consists of a framework of seven[13] commandments, describing the minimal moral duties. The circle of these practicalities traditionally dates from the time before the Lawgiving on the Sinai (see *Jubilees* VII, 20 ssq.). As a consequence every non-Jew is supposed to accept these commandments, whereas the Jews are

---

[9] Compare *Midrash Mekhilta*, Beshallaḥ, Massekhta deWayassa' (ed. Horowitz-Rabin), 157-158 on Ex. 15:26: 'If thou wilt diligently hearken to the voice of the Lord, thy God, and wilt do that which is right in his eyes, — these are *aggadot*; and wilt give ear to his commandments, — these are *gezerot*; and keep all his statutes, — these are *halakhot*.

[10] A. Lichtenstein, 'Does Jewish Tradition recognize an Ethic Independent of Halakha?', in: *Modern Jewish Ethics*. Theory and Practice, ed. by M. Fox, Ohio State University Press, 1975, 62-88, esp. 83. See for the same problem in the same book: N.L. Rabinovitch, 'Halakha and Other Systems of Ethics. Attitudes and Interactions', 89-102; this scholar, too, does not conceive halakha as a system with a complete ordering: 'This leaves the field open for constructing partial and schematic conjectural ethical theories to serve as a background for the given moral code that is the Halakha', p. 90.

[11] See Simon S. Schlesinger/Ed. Staff, 'Derek Erez', *E.J.* V, 115.

[12] The interdependency in a general sense is mutual, compare e.g. *Mishnah Avot* III,17 ('If there is no study of the law, there is no accepted human behaviour; if there is no accepted human behaviour, there is no study of the law'); the interdependency, however, is restricted: halakha includes *derekh eretz*, but *derekh eretz* does not include halakha; compare e.g. *Midrash Mekhilta, o.c.*, on Ex. 13:22 ('The passage comes and learnes you *derekh eretz* (is) from *torah*'); for more instances, see W. Bacher, *Die exegetische Terminologie der jüdischen Traditionsliteratur*, Darmstadt, 1965, Erster Teil, 25, s.v. *derekh eretz*.

[13] For an enumeration see *Mishnah Avodah Zarah* VIII,14; for other lists with more commandments, see e.g. *Bavli Sanhedrin* 57b; *Midrash Tehillim* on Ps. 21; also *Acts* 15:20.

obliged to observe the whole Torah. This circle also has its interaction with the centre: having validity with reference to the non-Jews, many if not all of these commandments bear upon the Jews as well.

3) The third and last concomitant to be mentioned in relation with halakha, is the ethical system of actions or attitudes which fall *lifnim mishurat hadin* ('beyond the line of the law')[14]. These actions go beyond the strict letter of the law, thus belonging to the domain of 'supra-legal conduct' (Lichtenstein, 83)[15].

The practicalities of this third circle are carried out by a man who even fulfils an obligation and observes commandments, where and when it is no longer his duty. Such a man is called a *tzaddiq* or a *chasid*[16]. Within this circle the observation of commandments is more than halakha, though never without halakha.

Ethical terminology.

Considering the title of this article: 'Ethical terminology in Heykhalot-texts', I assume the adjective 'ethical' to be an aspect of halakha. For, first we came upon much 'halakha' in the Heykhalot-texts and next 'ethics' is found to be a dimension of halakha[17].

Ethics in this framework I conceive as a set of norms or an area of normative motifs, which forms an interlocking circle with halakha, having its inherent connections with it[18]. Hereafter two instances will be given of ethical terminology, denotating an area of normative motifs within the Heykhalot-texts.

---

[14] See E.E. Urbach, *Chazal, 'emunot wede'ot*, Jerusalem, 1971, Chapter XIII, 290-294.

[15] Compare e.g. *Mishnah Avot* V,10 ('There are four types among men: he that says, 'What is mine is mine and what is thine is thine' — he is the common type; 'What is mine is thine and what is thine is mine' — he is the ignorant man; 'What is mine is thine and what is thine is thine' — he is the saintly man (*chasid*); 'What is thine is mine and what is mine is mine own' — he is a wicked man'). See also R. Mach, *Der Zaddik im Talmud und Midrasch*, Leiden, 1957, .6 ('Sich *lifnim mishoerath hadin* befinden, ... kann ... bedeuten ..., dass man sich selber in Bezug auf religiöse Vorschriften Erschwerungen auflegt und mehr tut als das Gesetz verlangt').

[16] See J. Dan, *Sifrut hamusar wehaderush*, Jerusalem, 1975, Chapter VII, 140; also G. Scholem, 'Der Gerechte', in: *Von der mystischen Gestalt der Gottheit.* Studien zu Grundbegriffen der Kabbala (Suhrkamp Taschenbuch, Wissenschaft 209), Zürich, 1977, 83-134 ('Der Zaddik und der Chassid stellen Idealtypen dar, die nicht aus ihrem Verhältnis zum Verständnis der Tora, sondern aus ihrem Verhältnis zu deren Vollzug definiert werden', 84).

[17] See title and subject of R. Gordis' article 'The Ethical Dimension of the Halakha', *Conservative Judaism* 26 (1972), 70-74; this article serves as an answer to S. Siegel, 'Ethics and Halakha', *id.* 25 (1971), 33-34.

[18] See J. Neusner, 'What is normative in Jewish Ethics', *Judaism* 16 (1967), 3-20; following an explanation of Fackenheim, Neusner states that a 'three-term relationship between man, his neighbour and God' ('moral commandments'; v.U.: ethics) functions within a 'two-term relation between man and God' ('Torah'; v.U.: halakha).

The first passage, taken from the collection traditionally known as *Heykhalot Rabbati*, concerns the profile of the mystic[19]. His qualities of character are summed up by Nechunya. This teacher and leader experienced the wicked role of Rome in the case of the ten martyrs[20]. Therefore, as it is written, he stands up and reveals to his pupils 'the secret of the world', namely 'the quality (or qualified attitude, *middah*), which fits in with the man who is eligible to have a mystic vision' (*ra'uy lehistakkel*).

By way of a sketch we first come, in our text, upon a series of heavenly attributes, being the potential objects of the mystic vision. The objects, in connection with the verb *lehistakkel*, are among others (for the complete list, see note 25): the king, his beauty, his glory and several classes of angels, such as Chayyot, Ofannim and Keruvim. The enumeration of this series, however, postpones the direct filling in of the quality or qualified attitude, Nechunya was about to reveal. This quality seems to be a necessary condition for the vision of the mystic objects. That is the reason why this topic is introduced once again by a following question: 'What is that quality like?'.

The answer to this question is given now, at first sight seeming to be threefold. That quality fits in

1. with a man who has a ladder (*sullam*) in his house;
2. with every man who goes up and down to the Merkavah, with nobody interfering;
3. with everyone who is 'pure' (*naqi*) and 'free' (*meno'ar*).

The second part of the answer may be derived from another passage in the *Heykhalot Rabbati* (see Schäfer, 237). In our passage (Schäfer, 199), we only find it in four manuscripts. In the other passage (Schäfer, 237) however, it is present in the same wording in the seven manuscripts.

So the answer appears to be twofold; the meaning of it, however, is unambiguous: the man who has a ladder in his house is the one who is 'pure' and 'free' (from). Wherein his purety lies and what he is free from, now follows in a series of earthly vices. The enumeration of these vices is the same in all manuscripts. Thus the mystic has to be free from: *'avodah zarah* (idolatry); *we-gilluy 'arayot* (incest-relations); *u-shefikhut damim* (murder); *we-lashon hara'* (slander); *u-shevu'at shaw'* (perjury); *we-chillul hashem* (desecration of the Name); *wa-'azzut panim* (brazenness) and *we-eyvat chinnam* (jealousy). After these eight vices, explicitly enumerated, we find a final more implicit circumscription: *wekhol 'aśeh welo' ta'aśeh shomer* ('and everyone who observes the positive and the negative commandments')[21]. With these

[19] See *Pirqey Heykhalot Rabbati*, *o.c.*, V,1, 2 (= Schäfer, 198, 199).

[20] See J. Dan, 'Pirqey Heykhalot Rabbati uma'aśeh 'aśeret harugey hamalkhut', *Eshel Beer Sheba* (1980), 63-80; M. Oron, 'Nusaḥim maqbilim shel sippur 'aśeret harugey hamalkhut weshel sefer heykhalot rabbati', *Eshel Beer Sheba* (1981), 81-95.

[21] The manuscripts only show very slight variations as to the wording of the enumeration. In

closing circumscription the 613 *mitzwot* are meant[22]. We cannot be sure, however, whether this series forms a unit. So much is clear: the first eight vices depend on the words 'pure' (*naqi*) and 'free' (*meno'ar*). Moreover, these vices are knit together, for we find the copulative *waw*'s seven times after the opening preposition 'from' (*min*).

From a literary and thematic point of view the closing circumscription does not fit in the series: the rule of the 'everyone who observes ...' has a positive formulation in the appearance of a sentence. Preceding it we only find a series of negative concepts, being the eight vices. The problem is, do we have to look upon the closing rule as an addition: supplying what the series does not contain? Or, has the circumscriptive rule to be taken as a kind of recapitulation of the above-mentioned vices? Some of the vices in any case are to be reckoned to the list of negative commandments.

A more exact look at the series of vices itself makes it clear, that four of them traditionally belong to the 'commandments of the sons of Noach'. They are: idolatry, incest-relations, murder and desecration of the Name. The first three of these form a recurring scheme. In rabbinic literature they function as representatives of the 'commandments of the sons of Noach' as a whole[23]. From the point of view of the interlocking circles the 'commandments of the sons of Noach' belong to one of the concomitants of halakha.

Considered as ante-halakhic, they represent universal ethics and as such do not belong to the essentials of halakha. The other four of the series are: slander, perjury, brazenness and jealousy. As the others do, they have their place in the field of human relations in general. For, to be pure and free from slander or jealousy does not particularly seem to be a matter of halakhic duty. In this field of general relations the well known rule of 'to go free from his duty' after the fulfilment of a halakhic requirement does not count. Formally it seems to be possible to fulfil the requirements of e.g. *ṭevilah* ('immersion' or *qeri'ah* ('reading'), even if one is known as a person of brazenness or jealousy.

The latter four vices, from which a true *yored* has to be free, are set off from halakha in objective and scope. Their concern is the development of human

---

stead of *shaw'*, N 8128 reads *sheqer* ('lie') and V 228 has *shem* ('name'); instead of *chinnam*, M 40 reads *chakham* ('scholar'); instead of *wekhol* and *lo'*, M 40 reads *we'al* and *we'al lo'*; instead of *wekhol*, D 436 has *we'al*.

[22] See S. Schechter, *Aspects of Rabbinic Theology. Major Concepts of the Talmud*, New York, 1969[3], Chapter X ('The Torah and its Aspect of Law'); also B. de Vries, *Hoofdlijnen en motieven in de ontwikkeling der Halachah*, Haarlem 1959, 10 (with references).

[23] See M. Kadushin, 'Introduction to Rabbinic Ethics', in: *Jehezkel Kaufmann Jubilee Volume* (Studies on the Occasion of his Seventieth Birthday), Jerusalem, 1968, 88-114, esp. 96; also his *Worship and Ethics. A Study in Rabbinic Judaism*, North Western University Press, 1964, esp. 25 and 228. The 'three cardinal sins' are typified by Kadushin as 'the strongest negative drives'; this characterisation is based on Maimonides: 'The Sages said: On three transgressions man will be punished in this world and he will not have a share in the world to come: idolatry, incest-relations and murder — and slander counterbalances them all'; compare *Yad*, De'ot, VII, 3.

character: 'hence men's feelings, thoughts and motivations are subject to its scrutiny'[24]. This domain of human relations and this level of internal qualities do not belong to the centre of halakha. Without doubt it has its internal connections with it. The positive or negative qualities in this field surely have to do with a man who tries to observe his halakhic duties (*chovot*). To have certain ethical qualities or to be free from bad qualities is a matter of the duties of the heart.

So much is clear, in the passage of *Heykhalot Rabbati* we have to do with an official profile of the mystic. The text makes the impression of having a fixed form with a formal set of data. On the one hand the data consist of a series of heavenly attributes, on the other hand we find a series of norms. The first series points out what in heaven can be seen in mystic trance and vision. The second series denotes what has to be done, or better, what must not be done on earth by the mystic believer. He has to be free from a series of vices in order to obtain a vision of a series of heavenly objects. In mutual relation the two series are measured out: there is a balance of numbers in each of them. The heavenly objects in a way seem to correspond with the earthly vices. That means: the true mystic, the *yored*, will be able to have a mystic vision of eight objects[25], when he is free from eight vices or mischiefs. To be free from these vices forms the condition for having a mystic vision of the heavenly objects.

Apart from other conditions regularly mentioned in the Heykhalot-texts, such as the times of fasting, the regularity of study, the training of mnemonic technics, the theurgical skill with formulas and the perfect knowledge of halakhic intricacies, there is also a set of normative elements or ethical norms which has its relevance.

The catalogue of norms is set off by a succession of mystic goals. We might say that we find here a balance of interdependent possibilities. The active or practical character of this type of mysticism is in this text brought to the fore in the interaction, which is a mutuality between ethical norms on earth and mystic goals in heaven.

In the collection of texts known as *Ma'aśeh Merkavah* we come upon a fine illustration of such a train of thought. This collection mainly consists of a dialogue between Yishmael and Aqiva. At a given moment[26] Yishmael asks: 'What is the measure (or: distance) from bridge to bridge?' Aqiva gives as an

[24] Boaz Cohen, *Law and Ethics in the Light of Jewish Tradition*, New York, 1957, 12.

[25] It is striking to find how four manuscripts (V 228; M 22; B 238 and N 8182) contain exactly the same eight objects, actually in the same sequence. The other three manuscripts show some more objects as a result of another literary division. Of course only those objects are to be counted which form the beginning of a new unit, indicated by the preposition *be*. The series runs as follows: (eligible to have a mystic vision) of the king; of his glory; of the keruvim; of the lightning; of the glitter; of the ardent stream; of the bridges and of the burning clouds.

[26] See G. Scholem, *Jewish Gnosticism*, o.c., Appendix C, p. 107, par. 9 (= Schäfer 558).

answer: 'Sincerity and piety in your heart (*yashrut wechasidut bilevaveka*) and you will know, what is the measure in heaven'. The text goes on: 'He said to me:
when I went up
to the first palace, I was a pious man (*chasid*);
in the second palace, I was a clean man (*ṭahor*);
in the third palace, I was a sincere man (*yashar*);
in the fourth palace, I was a perfect man (*tamim*);
in the fifth palace, I attained to holiness (*qedushah*);
in the seventh palace, I said: You are God, the living and everlasting'.
The tradition of this enumerative series is well anchored from a textcritical point of view. We find the same sequence and the same wording in the five available manuscripts[27]. Here we have a terse reproduction of the close-fitting connection between two series: on the one hand the successive heavenly palaces as mystic goals; on the other hand the corresponding succession of ethical norms.

What we have come upon in both texts, the *Heykhalot Rabbati* as well as the *Ma'aśeh Merkavah*, is a design of thought, which expresses a reciprocity between two parallel lists. The lists, however, are not identical. But both of them do contain a set of norms or normative elements, whether they are negative ethical concepts which a man has to be free from, or positive ethical features. For as such we have to understand indications as: pious, clean, sincere, perfect and holiness[28]. These positive ethical figures fit in with men who are not content 'with minimum standards of conduct' and who try to go 'beyond the letter of the law'[29]. It is their aim to live in accordance whith the rule of saintliness, the so-called *mishnat chasidut*[30].

What we tried to do so far, is to trace ethical terminology in Heykhalot-texts[31]. As a matter of fact we found some ethical terminology, stored up in

---

27 In three of them only one word is missing. D 436 and M 40 do not have *qedushah* at the level of the fifth palace; in M 22 the word *yashar* does not appear at the level of the third palace.

28 See R. Mach, *Der Zaddik*, o.c., 3 ('Verwandte Begriffe ... zu einer mehr oder weniger allgemeinen Bezeichnung der sittlich-religiösen Beschaffenheit der Menschen'.); also L. Jacobs, 'The Concept of Ḥasid in Biblical and Rabbinic Literatures', *JSS* 8 (1957), 143-154.

29 L. Jacobs, 'o.c.', 150.

30 Compare *Bavli Shabbat* 120a; *Bavli Bava Metzi'a* 52b; *Bavli Ḥullin* 130b. See also L. Jacobs, 'o.c.', 150; B. de Vries, *Hoofdlijnen en motieven*, *o.c.*, 31, 32 (III,5: Wet en Moraal (*Liphenim mishurat haddin*)); Zeev Falk, 'Mi-Mishnat Ḥasidim', in *Sefer Zikkaron leBenyamin de Vries*, Jerusalem, 1969, 62-69.

31 One surely has to bear in mind the character of the lists. As literary patterns they are of a stereotyped character, functioning as an ethical stock-phrase. They nevertheless are tightly interwoven with texts or units of a mystic character. Literary criticism has to find out if this ethical stock-phrase is original (forming an integral part of the mystic text and originating from authentic mystic circles) or additional (added by later copyists who for instance belonged to the more ethical movement of the Chasidey Ashkenaz).

literary patterns. These patterns have to be compared with each other, because their form is fixed in the same way. What we did not try to do, is to suggest that the compared literary forms indicate an identical overall design of thought, which would be characteristic of Merkavah-mysticism as a whole. For it cannot be denied that the patterns occur in different collections. As fixed forms they are located in different contexts; they probably have a different 'Sitz im Leben' and may stem from different times and areas.

Nevertheless, this does not make so much difference. Both instances show a terminology which expresses negative ethical concepts and positive ethical figures. Within the framework of Heykhalot-texts they are to be considered as conditional for the mystic vision, as are regularity in fasting and studying and as are mnemonic and theurgical skills.

DE APOKRIEFEN VAN HET OUDE TESTAMENT IN NEDERLANDSE BIJBELOVERZETTINGEN TOT 1637

(with a summary in English)

door

C.C. DE BRUIN

Dat in de ontwikkelingsgang van de nederlandse bijbeloverzetting zich de geschiedenis van de Kerk afspiegelt, is ook af te lezen uit de lotgevallen der oudtestamentische apokriefen in onze taal. Gedurende de Middeleeuwen diende als basistekst de Vulgata, de bijbel van de toenmalige Kerk. De eerste pogingen om gedeelten van deze apokriefen in onze landstaal over te brengen dateren uit de eerste eeuwen van het christendom in de lage landen bij de zee. Er zijn van deze proeven geen schriftelijke getuigenissen bewaard om de eenvoudige reden dat de predikers in de eredienst de liturgische Schriftles van de dag na voorlezing in het Latijn onmiddellijk lieten volgen door een mondelinge *ad-hoc*-weergave in de moedertaal. Naderhand is men ertoe overgegaan de bijbelperikopen van het misboek schriftelijk in de volkstaal over te brengen. We kunnen slechts gissen in welke tijd daarmee een begin gemaakt is. Het enige middel om die leemte in onze kennis op te vullen, is op zoek te gaan naar een handschrift dat voorzover we weten de oudste redactie van het *epistolarium* in de moedertaal bevat. Dat handschrift is weliswaar een betrekkelijk late westvlaamse kopie uit de tijd rondom het jaar 1350, maar vast staat dat de tekst teruggaat op een oud origineel. Ik kan de lezer ter kennisneming een fragment uit het *Epistolarium* van Leningrad — want hierom gaat het — aanbieden, enige verzen uit Jesus Sirach 36:

> Ontfarme di onzer alre, God, ende sich ons ende toech ons dat licht dire ontfarmichede ende zende dine vrese up die lieden die di niet ne zouken, dat si bekennen dat ne gheen Here es dan du, ende dat si vertrecken dine grootheit. Hef up dine hant over die vreimde lieden, dat si zien dine moghentheid.

In het midden van de 14de eeuw werden de oudtestamentische apokriefen in hun geheel vertaald en opgenomen in de zgn. Eerste Historiebijbel die van circa 1359 tot 1388 door een onbekende kartuizer monnik van het klooster Herne in Zuid-Brabant is vervaardigd. Deze monnik volgde de traditionele plaatsing van deze boeken zoals hij die aantrof in zijn exemplaar van de Vulgata. Zijn overzetting diende als kopij voor het eerste in de nederlandse taal gedrukte boek, de Delftse Bijbel van 1477. Uit deze wiegedruk citeer ik het hierboven genoemde fragment uit Sirach 36.

> Ontferme ons, God alre dinghen, ende ansie ons ende thoen ons dat licht dijnre ontfermherticheit ende sende die vrese op die heydene die di niet en sochten, soe dat si bekennen dat gheen God en is sonder dij, dat si dine grote dinghen vertellen. Heffe op dine handen optie vreemde heyden, op dat si dijn macht sien mogen. Want ghelijck dattu geheilicht biste in ons in haren anscouwen, also sultstu verheven worden in hem in onsen aenscouwen dat si dij bekennen, want ten is gheen god sonder dij. Vernyewe die teykenen ende verwandele die wonderen. Glorificeer dijn hant ende den rechten arm. Verwecke den toren ende stort neder die gramscap. Verhefft den wedersake ende quelle den viant. Haeste tijt ende ghedencke teynde dat si dine wonderen vertellen.

De aandachtige lezer kan constateren dat er weinig verschillen te bespeuren zijn tussen de oudste versie en de inkunabel, hetgeen leidt tot de conclusie dat er een vaste lijn loopt door de tekstoverlevering van die tijd.

In het begin van de Hervormingstijd was de duitse reformator Andreas Karlstadt (c. 1480-1541) een der eersten die de canoniciteit van enige bijbelboeken, in het bijzonder van de apokriefen van het Oude Testament, aan de orde stelde. In zijn geschrift *De Canonicis Scripturis* beriep hij zich op Hieronymus. De kerkvader had een duidelijk onderscheid gemaakt tussen die boeken in de Septuagint die teruggingen op een Hebreeuwse oertekst, en andere die grotendeels gebaseerd waren op een Grieks origineel. Hij had bedenkingen geopperd tegen de inhoud van sommige verhalen, zonder echter de door de Septuagint kerkelijk gewaarborgde authenticiteit *expressis verbis* discutabel te stellen. Luther formuleerde zijn standpunt kernachtig met zijn definitie: 'Apocrypha, das sind Bücher so der heiligen Schrift nicht gleich gehalten und doch nützlich und gut zu lesen sind'. Ten behoeve van zijn in 1534 verschenen komplete bijbel zonderde hij de apokriefe boeken dan ook af van het geheel van kanonieke boeken waarin ze tot dan toe waren ingelijfd. Hij voegde ze als een appendix toe aan de boeken van het Oude Testament waarvan de canoniciteit onbetwistbaar was, daarmee te kennen gevend dat naar zijn mening de schrijvers niet door de heilige Geest waren geïnspireerd. Hiermee luidde hij een controverse tussen Rome en de Reformatie in die gedurende de 16de en 17de eeuw de gedachtenwisseling over deze kwestie zou beheersen.

Een eerste symptoom van dit meningsverschil kan men ontmoeten in de proloog van de 'correctuers' van de in 1528 voltooide Bijbel van de Antwerpse uitgever Willem Vorsterman. Hoewel zij Hieronymus' zienswijze delen, poneren zij met nadruk de stelling dat alle boeken van de H. Schrift, de oudtestamentische apokriefen inbegrepen, 'als van Godt ons gegeven' zijn 'voor zijn schaepkens daer in te weyden'. De correctoren van Vorsterman brachten krachtens hun grondhouding dan ook geen wijziging aan in de plaatsing van de apokriefen; zij namen de volgorde in acht die in de Vulgata gebruikelijk was. Als voorbeeld van hun vertaling leg ik de lezer de perikoop uit Sirach 36 voor.

> Ontfermt onser, God alre dinghen, ende aensiet ons ende toont ons dat licht uwer ontfermherticheden ende seyndt uwe vreese over die heydenen die u niet en hebben gesocht, op datsi bekennen datter gheen God en si dan ghi, op dat si u grootdadicheden vertellen. Heft op uwe hant over dye vremde lieden, dat si u macht sien. Want ghelijc ghi in haer aenscouwen geheylicht zijt in ons, also sult ghi in onsen aenschouwen groot ghemaect worden in hen, op dat si u ooc bekennen, ghelijc wi u bekent hebben. Vernieut die teekenen ende verandert die wonderlicheden. Maect heerlic u hant ende uwen rechteren arme. Verwect die verborgentheyt ende stort wt die gramscap. Verheft de wederpartie ende quest den viant. Haeste tijt ende gedenct eynde, op datsi uwe wonderen vertellen.

Lijnrecht tegenover deze handelwijze stond de reformatorische praktijk van de Antwerpse drukker Jacob van Liesvelt die in zijn tal van malen herdrukte bijbeledities zonder enig commentaar, op voorgang van Luther, de apokriefe boeken als een aanhangsel bij het Oude Testament opnam. De perikoop Sirach 36: 1-10 luidt in de Liesveltbijbel van 1542 als volgt:

> Ontfermt onser, o du Here God alre dingen, ende aensiet ons ende toont ons dat licht uwer ontfermherticheden ende inseyndt uwe vreese over die heydenen die u niet en hebben versocht, op dat si bekennen datter geen God en sy dan ghi, op dat si u grootdadicheden vertellen. Heft op uwe hant over die vreemde lieden dat si u macht sien. Want gelijc ghi in haren aenscouwen gheheylicht sijt in ons, also sult ghi onsen aenscouwen groot gemaect werden in hem, op dat si u ooc bekennen gelijc wi u bekent hebben, want noyt en was eenich God dan ghi alleene. O Here, vernieut die teekenen ende verandert die wonderlicheden. Maect heerlic u hant ende uwen rechten arme. Verwect die verbolgentheyt ende wtstort die gramscap. Verdrijft den wedersaker ende quelt den viant. Laet die ure haestelic comen, gedenct des eedts op dat si uwe wonderen vertellen.

Het reformatorisch beginsel spreekt onloochenbaar uit het voorwoord dat Jan Gheylliaert schreef bij zijn *Bibel in Duyts* die hij in 1556 samen met Steven Mierdman in het Oostfriese Emden uitgaf. Hij parafraseert daarin de boven geciteerde karakterisering van Luther en neemt, naar het voorbeeld van de zwitserse Bijbel van Zürich (1531) die hij goeddeels volgde, de apokriefen als toevoegsel bij de kanon van het Oude Testament op.

Gaandeweg manifesteerde zich in het standpunt van de hervormingsgezinden ten aanzien van de oudtestamentische apokriefen, in het bijzonder bij de Calvinisten, een scherper omlijnde mening. In 1562 verschenen te Emden twee boeken die nauw met elkaar verbonden zijn. In de eerste plaats de editio princeps van de *Belydenisse des gheloofs*, waarschijnlijk door Godfried van Wingen bewerkt naar de franse *Confession de Foy* van Guido de Brès, en ter perse gelegd door de calvinistische drukker Gillis van der Erven. Artikel V van deze geloofsbelijdenis die op basis van de Schrift als *norma fidei* groot gezag kreeg, zegt dat wij de boeken van de Heilige Schrift aanvaarden als heilig en kanoniek 'om ons gheloove na de selve te reguleren, daer op te gronden ende daer mede te bevestigen. Ende gelooven sonder eenige twijffelinge al wat in deselve begrepen is, ende dat niet so seere om datse de Kercke aen neemt ende voor sodanighe houdt, maer in sonderheydt om dat ons de H. Geest getuygenisse geeft in onse herten, dat se van God zijn, dewijl se ooc het bewijs van dien by haer selven hebben'. Met onmiskenbare duidelijkheid stipuleert de opsteller van de geloofsbelijdenis zijn beginsel: de bijbelboeken accepteren wij als kanoniek, niet allereerst omdat de Kerk dat voorschrijft maar in het bijzonder om het *testimonium internum Spiritus Sancti*. Hieraan ligt dezelfde overtuiging ten grondslag als aan Luther's zienswijze: voor hem tellen alleen die boeken waarin hij Christus herkent en ervaart. Vandaar dat Guido de Brès in artikel VI de autoriteit van de niet-kanonieke boeken ontkent, al acht hij ze, mét Luther, wel nuttig voorzover hun inhoud niet in strijd is met de kanonieke boeken.

De zo juist geciteerde passage die te vinden is in de calvinistische geloofsbelijdenis van De Brès, stelt buiten twijfel dat de auteur zich hier richt tegen het decreet over de kanon van de H. Schrift waarvan de bewoordingen zijn geformuleerd in de vierde zitting, d.d. 6 april 1546, van het Concilie van Trente. Hierin werd gedecreteerd dat 'de boeken (van de H. Schrift) met al hun delen, zoals ze gewoonlijk in de Katholieke Kerk worden gelezen en in de oude, algemeen verspreide uitgave [= de Vulgata] voorkomen, als heilig en tot de kanon behorend moeten worden aangenomen'. Door dit besluit rekende Trente de apokriefen tot de kanonieke boeken, met dien verstande dat de toenmalige concilievaders, wetende dat de apokriefen (grotendeels) niet overgeleverd waren in een Hebreeuwse maar in een Griekse tekstvorm, deze boeken bij voorkeur de term 'deutero-kanonieke' boeken meegaven.

Het tweede boek dat in bovengenoemd jaar 1562 te Emden het licht zag en de houding van de gereformeerden van die tijd illustreert, is de *Biblia, dat is De gantsche H. Schrift*. Zoals gezegd waren de auteur en de drukker dezelfde personen als degenen die de *Belijdenisse des geloofs* bezorgd hebben. Wat ons in de gegeven samenhang het meest interesseert, is de nadrukkelijke 'Waerschouwinghe tot den Leser' waarmee de 'Apocryphi' — die hier nog als een aparte bundel boeken aan het einde van het Oude Testament voorkomen — worden ingeleid. Wat de hedendaagse lezer van deze bijbel zou kunnen intrigeren, is het antwoord op de vraag hoe het mogelijk is dat men een verzameling heilige boeken kan laten volgen door een 'set' van boeken waarvan de heiligheid twijfelachtig, zelfs ongeloofwaardig is. Op dit probleem kom ik aan het einde van mijn bijdrage terug.

In zijn *Waerschouwinghe tot den Leser* zet Godfried van Wingen uiteen welke betekenis aan de term Apokriefen toe te kennen is. De 'oude vaders' hebben hiermee te kennen willen geven, aldus zegt hij, 'dat men ze moeste houden voor private ende eyghen gheschriften, ende niet voor Autentijck, ghelijck ghemeyne verseghelde ende gheapprobeerde brieven. Daeromme is tusschen dese Boecken ende de andere sulck onderscheyt als tusschen eenen brief die voor eenen Notaris ghepasseert is ende gheseghelt om van allen menschen aenghenomen te worden, ende tusschen eenen brief van eenen sonderlijcken mensche geschreven'. Het heeft er alle schijn van dat hij hiermee, in een scherpzinnig bedachte metafoor, een verklaring wil geven van het feit dat hij, ondanks de Waerschouwinghe die hij vooraf liet gaan — klinkt dit woord niet als een 'bijsluiter' bij een medicijn? — de apokriefen in zijn bijbel de plaats geeft die hun naar zijn mening toekomt.

Om de lezer te gerieven die Van Wingen's vertaling van de perikoop Sirach 36: 1-10 met die van vorige bijbels wil vergelijken, bied ik haar hier nu aan.

> Here almachtighe God, ontferme u onser ende siet daer in ende verschrickt alle volcken. Heft uwe handt op over de vreemden dat sy uwe macht sien. Ghelijck als ghy voor haren ooghen waert by ons, alsoo verthoont u heerlicken aen hen voor onsen ooghen, op dat sy bekennen, ghelijck als wy bekennen dat daer geen ander Godt en zy dan ghy Heere alleen. Doet nieuwe teeckenen ende nieuwe wonderen. Bewijst uwe hant ende uwen rechten arm heerlicken. Verweckt de grimmicheydt ende ghiet den toorne uut. Ruckt den tegenpartijder wech ende vernielt den vyandt. Ende haest u daermede ende denckt aen uwen eedt, op dat men uwe wonderdaedt prijse.

Het is in deze samenhang dienstig, kennis te nemen van de toelichting die Godfried van Wingen verstrekt bij de inhoud van deze apokriefen. Hij beroept zich voor het feit dat hij deze boeken toch opneemt op de 'sonderlijcke geleerde man Theodorus Bibliander' die in een boek *De optimo genere explicandi Hebraica* (1535) zijn licht had laten schijnen over de positie der oudtestamentische apokriefen te midden van de kanonieke en niet-kanonieke boeken. De zwitserse theoloog uit de school van Zwingli (hij leefde van c. 1504 tot

1564) — hij was eerder een bijbelse humanist dan een rasechte Calvinist — had betoogd dat zij een tussenperiode innamen tussen enerzijds de onvervalste op de Hebreeuwse grondtekst berustende bijbelboeken en anderzijds de groep pseudo-epigrafische geschriften met hun soms wilde verdichtselen. Maar er is nog een andere reden waarom Buchmann — zo luidde zijn niet-vergriekste naam — hier even onze aandacht verdient. Hij behoorde tot de humanistische geleerden van die tijd die zich bezig hielden met de oorsprong van de taal. Grondig kenner van het Hebreeuws als hij was, was hij met anderen op grond van een toenmalige — uiteraard onhoudbare maar voor die tijd kenmerkende — theorie met betrekking tot de Babylonische spraakverwarring tot de slotsom gekomen dat het Hebreeuws de oertaal van de mensheid was. Het wil mij voorkomen dat de belangstelling voor en kennis van het Hebreeuws onder sommige nederlandse predikanten van die tijd, behalve door een gedegen opleiding waar en hoe dan ook opgedaan, mede gestimuleerd is door een opvatting als de hier gesignaleerde; zij was weliswaar een misvatting maar versterkte bij hen het besef dat de in het Hebreeuws overgeleverde boeken van het joodse Oude Testament 'authentieker' waren dan de in het Grieks geboekstaafde apokriefen in de Septuagint. Godfried van Wingen mag dan het Hebreeuws niet zo grondig gekend hebben dat hij in staat was zelfstandig de basistekst in het Nederlands over te zetten — voor het Oude Testament richtte hij zich in hoofdzaak o.a. naar een duitse Lutherbijbel — toch had hij wel zoveel respect voor de drie heilige talen dat hij als rechtgeaard calvinist een onversneden, op de Hebreeuwse grondtekst van het Oude Testament berustende overzetting van de kanonieke boeken de voorkeur zou hebben gegeven.

Overigens is het niet raadzaam de kennis van het Hebreeuws bij de meeste theologen uit het einde van de 16de eeuw te overschatten. Maar al te vaak kwam het voor dat de studiosi onder hen voor het rechte begrip van het Hebreeuws teruggrepen op de calvinistische latijnse vertaling van het Oude Testament van de hand van Tremellius die van 1575 tot 1579 in 5 delen verschenen is. Het vijfde stuk, dat de overzetting van de Apokriefen behelst, is vervaardigd door diens medewerker Franciscus Junius Senior. Laatstgenoemde, als bijbelkenner en filoloog ook in de Nederlanden bekend — hij werd hoogleraar te Leiden — nam de taak op zich de overzetting van de apokriefe boeken uit het Grieks in het Latijn te verzorgen. Het valt ons op dat meer dan een nederlandse theoloog — zelfs Marnix van St. Aldegonde! — voorgaf de Hebreeuwse grondtekst te volgen terwijl hij in feite de Latijnse vertaling van Tremellius-Junius zorgvuldig raadpleegde, een verschijnsel dat zich niet alleen hier te lande voordeed maar alom in West-Europa.

Het voor ons hedendaags besef opmerkelijke in deze calvinistische latijnse bijbel is het gemak waarmee Junius, na in de proloog tot zijn bewerking van de apokriefen uit het Grieks in het Latijn de staf gebroken te hebben over hun geringe geloofwaardigheid en betrouwbaarheid, overgaat tot de vervulling van de opdracht die hem door Tremellius was verleend: de vertaling van de apokriefen uit het Grieks in het Latijn. Gezien vanuit onze optiek had hij, ook krachtens zijn beginsel, kunnen weigeren deze taak te aanvaarden en Tremellius het voorstel kunnen doen een collectie boeken die, als het erop aankwam, niet thuishoorden in de kanon, achterwege te laten. Het antwoord op de gestelde vraag stel ik uit tot het slot van mijn overzicht.

Met de voortgang der jaren begon in de kring van de gereformeerde predikanten de overtuiging veld te winnen dat de algemeen gebruikte gereformeerde Emder Bijbel van 1562 — onder een 'nick-name' bekend geworden als de Bijbel van Deux aes — dringend herziening behoefde. In de eerste plaats om de naar hun smaak al te vrije, soms parafraserend-verklarende vertaaltrant die naar hun overtuiging in onvoldoende mate recht deed aan de gewijde oertekst. Een nieuwe overzetting rechtstreeks uit de grondtekst, die met meer getrouwheid het Hebreeuws op de voet zou volgen, moest de oude vervangen. In deze samenhang spraken zij ook over de plaats die de oudtestamentische apokriefen in dit geheel dienden in te nemen. Moesten zij gehandhaafd blijven of was het gewenst de apokriefen achterwege te laten? Geen wonder dat in de beraadslagingen van de plaatselijke kerkvergaderingen, de bijeenkomsten van de classes en de provinciale synodes de zaak van de apokriefe boeken, in één adem met de nog belangrijker kwestie van de bijbeloverzetting in het algemeen, herhaaldelijk te berde gebracht is. Het zou overdreven zijn te stellen dat toenmaals in de zo juist genoemde colleges beide zaken in welhaast elke bijeenkomst aan de orde zijn geweest. Desalniettemin mogen we op goede gronden aannemen dat de drang naar vernieuwing in kracht begon toe te nemen. In het bijzonder de predikanten die hun ambtswerk ernstig opvatten en het Oude Testament plachten te bestuderen aan de hand van de grondtaal, wensten een nieuwe bijbel. Kon aan dit verlangen geen gevolg gegeven worden, dan waren sommigen van hen desnoods bereid genoegen te nemen met een bewerking van de duitse vertaling van de calvinist Johannes Piscator (1546-1625). De predikant Abraham Costerus (c. 1575-1658) wierp zich op als tolk van deze verlangens. In 1614 publiceerde hij een boek onder de titel *Verdedinghe der H. Schriftuere* waarin hij zijn mening omtrent de 'onvasticheyt der Apocryphe Boecken' op niet-mis-te-verstane wijze kenbaar maakt. Hij noemt vier redenen waarom de apokriefen, anders dan de 'Roomsche Kercke' leert, uit de kanon geweerd dienen te worden. Deze boeken zijn niet in het Hebreeuws gesteld. Christus heeft, evenmin als de apostelen, ooit op deze geschriften een beroep gedaan. Ze behelzen hooguit enige aanwijzingen voor de levenswandel van de christen.

De Nationale Synode die in 1618-19 te Dordrecht gehouden is, kreeg de opdracht deze kwesties te regelen. Uit het verslag van haar beraadslagingen hieromtrent blijkt dat ook enige buitenlandse afgevaardigden deelnamen aan het overleg. Het engelse synodelid Samuel Ward bepleitte handhaving van de apokriefe boeken in de nieuwe overzetting. Bij de vervaardiging van de Engelse Authorized Version, ook wel bekend als de *King James Bible*, die in 1607 het licht had gezien, was hij als medewerker nauw betrokken geweest, speciaal bij de overzetting van de apokriefen. Het lag voor de hand dat de aanhangige zaak hem na aan het hart lag en dat hij de traditie in ere wilde houden. Hiertegenover betoogde de reformatorische godgeleerde Giovanni Diodati (1576-1649) die als afgevaardigde van het ministerie van predikanten te Genève de zittingen van de Dordtse Synode bijwoonde, dat de apokriefen niet opgenomen moesten worden; zij waren immers een *corpus alienum* dat in de kanon van de Schrift niet paste. In zijn zienswijze werd hij krachtig gesteund door Gomarus. Merkwaardig lijkt het dat Diodati zelf in zijn voortreffelijke in 1603 uitgekomen bijbelvertaling in het Italiaans, zijn moedertaal, de apokriefe boeken wèl had opgenomen. Het kan niet anders of sinds 1603 was hij gekomen tot een andere waardeschatting van de niet-kanonieke boeken.

Na langdurige deliberatiën nam de Synode eindelijk het besluit de apokriefe boeken in een nieuwe vertaling op te doen nemen, met dien verstande dat zij in de druk zouden verschijnen met een apart titelblad, een prefatie waarin gewaarschuwd zou worden tegen mogelijke misvattingen, een kleiner lettertype, zonder kanttekeningen. Kortom, alle middelen moesten worden aangewend om duidelijk het niet-kanonieke karakter van de apokriefen uit te laten komen. En wat nog het meest radicale element in het besluit was, was de eis dat de apokriefen met een afzonderlijke bladzijdennummering *achter* het Nieuwe Testament geplaatst zouden worden en zouden fungeren als een aanhangsel van de H. Schrift. Beide partijen hebben enige concessies gedaan, al overheerst de indruk dat de synode terwille van de consensus met andere calvinistische kerken tenslotte met enige tegenzin gezwicht is voor de druk die vooral door de engelse gedelegeerden, in overleg met hun lastgever Koning Jacobus I, is uitgeoefend. Trouwens, in hun prefatie zeggen de vertalers van de Statenbijbel onomwonden dat zij ook om deze reden de apokriefen hadden opgenomen.

De vertaling van de apokriefen is tenslotte tijdens de voorbereidende werkzaamheden voor de totstandkoming van de in 1637 verschenen Statenvertaling, ter hand genomen door Antonius Walaeus en Festus Hommius. Ik deel hier hun vertaling van Sirach 36: 1-10 mee.

> Ontfermt u over ons Heere, ghy Godt aller dingen, ende siet ons aen. Ende sendt uwe vreese over alle de volckeren die u niet en soecken. Verheft uwe hande over de vremde volckeren, laetse uwe vermogentheyt sien. Gelijck ghy voor hare oogen gheheiligt zijt gheweest in ons, dat ghy oock also voor ons groot gemaeckt mooght worden in haer. Ende datse u moghen kennen

ghelijckerwijs oock wy u kennen, want daer en is geen Godt behalven ghy, o Heere. Vernieuwt uwe teeckenen, ende verandert uwe wonderen. Verheerlickt uwe handt ende rechten arm, opdat sy uwe wonderen mogen vertellen. Verweckt uwe gramschap, ende giet uwen toorn uyt. Neemt den teghenpartijder wech, ende verbrijselt den vyant. Maeckt dat de tijdt haest kome, ende ghedenckt aen den toorne, ende laet uwe wonderen vertelt worden.

De 'lay-out' van de druk is geschied conform de wensen die de Synode kenbaar had gemaakt. Niet altijd is echter een kleinere drukletter gebezigd; er zijn tal van latere uitgaven die typografisch uniform zijn uitgevoerd.

Het besluit van de Dordtse vaders de apokriefen als een afzonderlijk aanhangsel helemaal achter in de gedrukte bijbel te doen plaatsen, hield een duidelijke wenk in. Zonder enige moeite konden de boekbinders de losse vellen — boeken werden toentertijd veelal in die vorm verkocht — die de apokriefen bevatten, terzijde laten, en zo op wens van de bestellers uitsluitend het kanonieke deel van de H. Schrift aanbieden. Het behoeft nauwelijks toelichting dat deze handelwijze, die neerkwam op een geruisloze verwijdering van een appendix, niet indruiste tegen de principiële bedoelingen van de Synode. Reeds korte tijd na 1637 is er een begin gemaakt met de uitgave van bijbels zonder apokriefen.

Ik ben nog een verklaring schuldig van het feit dat vertalers eeuwen lang in weerwil van de bezwaren die zij tegen de inhoud van de apokriefen hadden, deze boeken toch een plaats gaven in hun bijbels. Hun gedrag is herhaaldelijk als inconsequent en in strijd met de logica gekenschetst. Men bedenke evenwel dat hun eerbied voor een traditie, daterend uit de tijd van de Septuagint en ten onzent doorgaand tot de Statenvertaling, bij mogelijke twijfel toch de doorslag gaf. Ik hoop aangetoond te hebben dat in de loop der jaren bij ons de positieve waardering voor de apokriefen begon te tanen, in het bijzonder onder calvinisten. Het spreekt dan ook vanzelf dat hier te lande eerder nog dan elders bijbeluitgaven werden bezorgd zonder de oudtestamentische apokriefen.

Summary.

In Dutch versions of the Bible from c. 1350 to c. 1650 the apocrypha of the Old Testament do not always appear in the same place, and sometimes they are lacking altogether. In the first *Historiebijbel* (1359-1388) and in the earliest printed Bible in Dutch, the Delft Bible of 1477, the apocrypha figure in the same place as in the Vulgate. The same applies to the Bible of Vorsterman, Antwerp 1528. However, Jacob van Liesvelt of Antwerp, whose first complete Bible appeared in 1526, relegated the apocrypha to the end of the Old Testament, as an appendix. In this he followed Luther.

From 1562 onward, Dutch Calvinists became more and more explicit in limiting and dismissing the authority of the apocrypha. In their Bible printed at Emden in 1562, the Calvinists Godfried van Wingen and Gillis van der Erven thought it necessary to preface the apocrypha with a 'Warning to the Reader', in which the apocrypha were characterized as 'private' and 'unauthentic' writings, in contradistinction to the 'authentic' books based on Hebrew texts. In spite of the low esteem in which the apocrypha were held by Calvinists, these books were still included in the Emden Bible of 1562 (known as the 'Deux Aes Version') as well as in the Dutch Authorized Version (known as the 'States' Version', 1637).

The Synod of Dordrecht, however, decided that in the latter the apocrypha had to be printed separately, in smaller type, and placed after the New Testament, i.e., at the end of the Bible as a whole. Moreover, the apocrypha had to be distinguished from the canonical books by the insertion of a title-page and a warning against possible misconceptions, and by a separate pagination. The obvious intention of all this was to enable buyers of the States' Version to purchase a Bible without the apocrypha. No wonder that soon after 1637 there appeared editions of the States' Version without the apocrypha. The same thing happened to protestant versions in other countries of Europe, but later than in the Netherlands.

That the apocrypha were repeatedly included in protestant Bibles despite the serious objections raised by reformed translators, printers and publishers, can be attributed to the influence of the canon of the Septuagint and its long tradition in the history of the Bible.

THE APOCALYPSE WITHIN: SOME INWARD INTERPRETATIONS OF THE BOOK OF REVELATION FROM THE SIXTEENTH TO THE EIGHTEENTH CENTURY*

by

ALASTAIR HAMILTON

The sixteenth- and seventeenth-century interpretations of the Book of Revelation which have received the largest amount of scholarly attention have been political[1]. And indeed, whether historicist, preterist or futurist, the majority of the commentaries published in the period identified at least some of the visions in the Book with particular historical events. In this article I propose to deal with an entirely different type of interpretation — an inward interpretation which implicitly rejected any political allusion and which took the visions to emblematize forces conflicting within the soul of man. I make no claim to providing an exhaustive study of such commentaries, but I shall limit myself to examining the two best known specimens composed in the late sixteenth century and will then give some indication of further developments, especially in England, in the seventeenth and eighteenth centuries.

In an introductory passage to his commentary on Revelation which appeared in 1627 the Flemish Jesuit Cornelius a Lapide mentioned the only inward interpretation he seems to have known of — that of the Spanish Biblical scholar Benito Arias Montano — and, although he acknowledged slight differences, he placed it in the medieval tradition of spiritual commentaries[2]. Certainly the patristic and medieval exegetes quoted by a Lapide — Ticonius, Primasius, Bede, Anselm, Haymo, the Victorines, Rupert of Deutz and Denys the Carthusian — have something in common with the inward commentators. They either rejected a historical-political significance outright or added a spiritual interpretation to persons and places existing in history. For Primasius

* I would like to thank Dr Eamon Duffy, Professor Alfonso Ingegno and Dr Geoffrey Nuttall for their advice on the subject of this article.

[1] For a recent survey see C.A. Patrides & Joseph Wittreich (eds.), *The Apocalypse in English Renaissance thought and literature*, Manchester, 1984. The bibliography, compiled by J. Wittreich, (pp.369-440), includes both commentaries and secondary sources.

[2] Cornelius a Lapide, *Commentaria in Apocalypsin S.Iohannis*, Antwerp, 1717, 8: 'Quod sit argumentum, quae materia Apocalypseos? Mire hic variant Interpretes. Primo, aliqui Apocalypsin generatim accipiunt, putantque in ea generaliter tantum describi dissidia et bella inter probos et improbos, ac utrorumque finem et exitum. Ita Ticonius, et ex eo Primasius et Beda, quos fere sequuntur Ansbertus, Anselmus, Rupertus, Haymo, Richardus, Hugo, Thomas et Dionysius. Huc accedit Arias Montanus, qui censet in Apocalypsi describi pugnam carnis et spiritus in quolibet homine. Verum prius nimis generale, posterius hoc mysticum est et tropologicum.'

and Bede Asia is thus equated with pride; Babylon is commonly interpreted as the sum of all evil, the beast as the devil and the whore as the rejection of God. At the same time, however, the Book was invariably regarded as prophesying the triumph of the Church of Christ. Chapters 4 and 5 were seen as a description of this Church, and the last chapters as an account of its victory. In the inward interpretations which I shall be discussing the Church of Christ disappears and is replaced by the human soul.

Benito Arias Montano was the first to admit that his interpretation of the Book of Revelation in his *Elucidationes in omnia S. Apostolorum scripta* of 1588, original though it might seem, was not of his own devising[3]. He had taken it from the Dutch spiritual writer Hendrik Jansen van Barrefelt who wrote under the pseudonym of Hiël, 'the uniform life of God', and Hiël, in his turn, leads us to a particular attitude towards the Scriptures which had developed in Northern Europe in reaction to Luther's ideas. This attitude, fostered by Thomas Müntzer and shared by Sebastian Franck, Sébastien Castellion, Valentin Weigel and others, was based on the belief that the Spirit was of far greater importance than the Letter and that the Scriptures could only be understood by the man enlightened by that same Spirit with which they had been written[4]. To this must be added a further conviction, held by such men as David Joris and Hendrik Niclaes: the world had entered the last of the three ages of time, the age of the Spirit corresponding to the theological virtue of Charity, in which the seventh seal on the Scriptures would be removed for the spiritual man[5].

Hiël, a native of Gelderland, had been a weaver, and he prided himself on his ignorance of any language except Dutch[6]. He had once been an Anabaptist and had then joined the Family of Love shortly after its foundation by Hendrik Niclaes in Emden in 1540. Despite his professed ignorance of languages and an apparent lack of education Hiël was profoundly imbued with the spiritual ideas circulating in the Low Countries and Germany, and above all he venerated the medieval tract which all the spiritual writers in Northern Europe claimed as one of their main sources, the *Theologia Germanica.* In 1573 Hiël, who by this time resided chiefly in Cologne, broke away from Hendrik Niclaes and, in the years following, he devoted himself to writing his own books. These included his commentary on the Book of

[3] Benedictus Arias Montanus, *Elucidationes in Omnia Sanctorum Apostolorum Scripta. Eiusdem in S.Ioannis Apostoli Et Evangelistae Apocalypsin Significationes*, Antwerp, 1588, 429. (Hereafter *Elucidationes.*)

[4] Cf. Steven E. Ozment, *Mysticism and Dissent. Religious Ideology and Social Protest in the Sixteenth Century*, New Haven, 1973.

[5] Cf. Alastair Hamilton, *The Family of Love*, Cambridge, 1981, 17-23, 34-39.

[6] On Hiël see Alastair Hamilton, 'Hiël and the Hiëlists: The Doctrine and Followers of Hendrik Jansen van Barrefelt', *Quaerendo* 7 (1977), 243-286.

Revelation, the *Verklaring der Openbaringe Johannis In het ware Wesen Jesu Christi.*

Refusing to commit himself to any visible church but displaying a certain preference for Catholicism rather than for Protestantism, Hiël carried to its extreme conclusion the attitude of the 'spirituals' towards the Letter. Rather than attempting any philological interpretation of the Bible he used the Bible as a text illustrating his own doctrine. To it he applied a single scheme of interpretation: throughout the Scriptures, he maintained, there could be detected a figurative indication of the eternal struggle in the soul of man between the sinful earthly being or nature, dominated by earthly wisdom, and the divine nature of God. Only by killing earthly wisdom and the lusts and properties in his soul would man enable Christ to be reborn within himself and be united with God, thereby restoring that 'oneness' referred to at the beginning of the *Theologia Germanica.*

In his foreword to his commentary on Revelation Hiël says that the divine mysteries and prophecies which have so long remained sealed have at last been opened 'in the heart of the obedient man'[7] and he dismisses any literal or historical interpretation of this or any other Book as a delusion of sinful earthly wisdom[8]. John of Patmos becomes the grace of God, Patmos the death of sin, Asia a muddy place in the human heart or nature to which sins and earthly desires cleave, and the message to the seven churches, each of which is regarded as a particular point in the human heart, is interpreted as the revelation of the divine nature of Christ and the cleansing of sin in the heart of man. To the visions of judgement on the enemies of God and the victory of the faithful which occupy the greater part of the Book Hiël applies his scheme with considerable ingenuity. In Chapter 4 the throne on which Christ is seated is interpreted as divine repose and the four living creatures signify four kinds of knowledge in human nature: the knowledge of prophecy under the Law, the knowledge of Sin, the knowledge of mercy and the knowledge of obedience to God. Taken together they represent fallen humanity or earthly postlapsarian nature, restless because of its earthly senses and lusts, and in perpetual search of repose in the divine being.

---

[7] Hiël, *Verklaring der Openbaringe Johannis*, Haarlem, 1703, (hereafter *Verklaring*), 3: 'Want de verborgen Goddelijcke Gesichten en Prophetien, die lang geslooten zijn geweest, worden nu, door den wesentlijcken Geest Christi, in het Herte van de gehoorsame Menschheyt open gedaen ...'; 19: 'Want in dese Openbaringe is een sonderlinge verborgentheyt begrepen, daar de beeldische Sin des vleesches, door het aartsche Vernuft, niet aan mag, noch de voorige Wet of Propheten, noch de bekentenisse Christi na den vleesche, konnen dese verborgen Openbaring niet in de wesentlijckheyt Godts begrijpen. Daarom is't een Openbaring, die in den laatsten deel des tijts door het wesentlijck Licht Christi bekent en verklaart sal worden ...'

[8] Ibid., 7: 'Daar na soo hebben wy oock gesien, wat al onrechte Oordelen en Sententien, dat het aartsche Vernuft uyt de getuygenis van de Openbaring Johannis geeft; waar door dat wy noch beweegt en gedreven zijn, deselve na het Wesen, daar se de Gratie en Genade Godts uyt betuygt heeft, te verklaren.'

The seven seals are the laws of the hidden nature of God which can only be satisfied by the humble obedience of Christ (the Lamb). The opening of the seventh seal (Chapter 8) is the removal of the law of sin and death by the goodness of God. The opening is followed by knowledge of the uniform life in the divine being (the silence in heaven). The seven angels which then appear represent the strength of God distributing punishment and death among the earthly lusts. The two witnesses (Chapter 11) are the Law and the Prophets who will prophesy until man recognises the heavenly nature in his soul and sin is overcome by the death of Christ. They will be killed for a while by the beast, envious evil in the heart of unregenerate man, but will subsequently be revived and called up to heaven. Finally, when the heart of man (God's temple) is opened in heaven and the hidden bond of God (the ark) is seen and felt in the soul the earthly nature will tremble as if stricken by an earthquake and a tempest will destroy all earthly senses, lusts and thoughts.

The woman clothed with the sun with the moon under her feet in Chapter 12 is the love of God, the 'great red dragon' the poison of earthly wisdom dressed in deceitful earthly holiness. For a time the love of God lies hidden in the depraved heart of man (the woman in the wilderness), but it is lighted by the hope of faith (the one thousand two hundred and sixty days) until it reaches the heavenly sun of God's righteousness. In the meantime a battle takes place in the depraved human heart (the war in heaven between Michael and the dragon): God's righteousness (Michael) slays earthly wisdom (the dragon and his angels). Earthly wisdom can thus no longer appear to be heavenly but must fall to earth and suffer death. On earth it combats the simple love of God or the woman with the venom of the earthly senses (the serpent), but nature's love (the earth) comes to her assistance.

In Chapter 13 the beast from the sea is depraved evil come to kill all virtues in the human heart. It derives its strength from the dragon, the poison of earthly wisdom, while the beast with two horns like a lamb and speaking like a dragon is hypocritical earthly holiness in the flesh which prevents the simple soul from praying to God (the mark on the right hand or the forehead). The number of the beast is the whole of humanity.

Babylon is interpreted as the confusion of earthly senses; the whore is false earthly wisdom, her golden jewels hypocritical holiness and the cup full of abominations the carnal appetites. The beast with seven heads is the evil caused by earthly wisdom and its rule on earth; its seven heads are the doctrines of earthly wisdom and the seven kings are personal vindictiveness under the guise of holiness. The succession of the kings is taken to signify the disappearance and subsequent return of evil, as is the capture and the return of the dragon at the beginning of Chapter 20. The fall of Babylon and the lamentations of the merchants in Chapter 18 are interpreted as the downfall of earthly wisdom and desires and the realisation in the human soul that the sanctity of earthly wisdom can no longer be trusted. The marriage of the Lamb is the union of the human soul with the divine being; the 'new heaven and new earth' in the last two chapters are the new life in the divine being and the new life in the natural being following the ultimate defeat of evil.

As Hiël presents it the Book of Revelation is the description of a number of mystical progressions, some taking place concurrently, others successively, towards union with God. There is no question of any reference to a church, visible or invisible. The temple is always interpreted as the human heart or soul, and the visions are of states within each one of us: to see them we must look within our souls. The Book must be read with a spirit of love, Hiël adds in his epilogue, and with a readiness to yield to God. Only thus will its true contents be understood and appreciated[9].

We do not know when Hiël finished his commentary. It seems to have been printed in Dutch for the first time by Augustijn van Hasselt in Cologne in 1592[10], but a French translation has recently come to light[11] which is almost certainly far earlier and which Arias Montano probably knew about by September 1583[12]. Arias Montano himself seems to have received a manuscript version soon after.

After spending the best part of seven years abroad, first supervising, and then contriving to obtain Papal approval of, the great Polyglot Bible printed by Christophe Plantin in Antwerp under the aegis of Philip II, Arias Montano[13] had returned to Spain and had been appointed royal chaplain and librarian of the Escorial early in 1577. In Antwerp he had become a close friend of Plantin and there encountered a group of men, mainly the printer's relatives and agents, who were former followers of Hendrik Niclaes but had

---

[9] Ibid., 144-145: 'Daar door dat een verstandig Mensch de waarschouwinge niet kleyn achten sal; want sy treft nu alle Vleesch in sijne tegenwoordigheyt: Alsoo dat men de Straffe niet langer op eenen anderen kan leggen, die buyten hem is. Maar een iegelijck, die Godes Waarheyt in haar heylige Wesen lief heeft, die gaa nu tot in't binnenste Herte sijns Gemoets, namentlijck in't Herte sijns Levens; en bespreeke of berade sig daar met God, soo veel als hy hem kent en in der Zielen gevoelt; en vragen de Kennisse Godes, hoe hy de wesentlijcke Waarheyt in der Zielen genaken sal? om met het godloose wesen niet te vergaan. Ende als hy den Mont Gods te recht gevraagt heeft, soo sal Hy hem Antwoort geven, ende sal seggen: Wilt gy met het godloose wesen niet vergaan, soo wend uwen lust des levens van het aartsche Adamsche wesen, ende brengt uwe uytterste Liefde des Herten tot in mijn heylig Wesen, ende laat u geen ding liever en waarder zijn, dan te vereenigen met mijn heylig Wesen. Ende als de liefde tot mijn heylig Wesen in der Zielen soo krachtig is, datse het aartsche Leven tot eenen Doot baart, soo zijt gy seecker (segt de Goetheyt Gods tot de Mensheyt) dat gy met mijn heylig Wesen vereenigen en leven sult.'

[10] Cf. Hiël's letters to Jan Moretus about this edition. Alastair Hamilton, 'Seventeen Letters from Hendrik Jansen van Barrefelt (Hiël) to Jan Moretus', *De Gulden Passer*, 57 (1979), 105-112.

[11] This important discovery was made at the Bibliothèque de l'Arsenal in Paris by Jean-François Maillard. Cf. his 'Christophe Plantin et la Famille de la Charité en France: Documents et Hypothèses' in: *Mélanges sur la littérature de la Renaissance à la mémoire de V.-L. Saulnier*, Genève, 1984, 240-241.

[12] Cf. B. Rekers, *Benito Arias Montano (1527-1598)*, London-Leiden, 1972, 86.

[13] Ibid., 1-12.

quarreled with the founder of the Family of Love in 1573. Preferring the spirituality of Hiël to that of Hendrik Niclaes, Plantin and his circle did their utmost to promote Hiël's ideas. The caution with which Plantin published his writings makes it difficult to tell exactly what he printed and when. Hiël's two main works, *Het Boeck Der Ghetuygenissen vanden verborghen Acker-schat* and the first volume of his epistles or *Sendt-Brieven*, appeared in about 1581; some three years later Plantin, then in Leiden, produced the first edition of *Imagines et Figurae Bibliorum* containing scenes from the Bible engraved by Pieter van der Borcht and accompanied by Hiël's commentaries; and either shortly before or shortly after, in Antwerp, there appeared the French translation of Hiël's commentary on the Book of Revelation.

There is no evidence that Arias Montano knew of Plantin's dealings with Hendrik Niclaes or that he actually met Hiël when he was staying in Antwerp. All we can say for sure is that he received a number of writings by Hiël, in French or Latin manuscript translations, between 1583 and 1586, that he admired them all, and that none seems to have gratified him as much as the commentary on the Book of Revelation[14]. Hiël's commentary arrived as Arias Montano was completing his scholia to the second half of the New Testament. He had, he admitted, read many interpretations of the last Book, but the only one which had revealed to him its true significance was Hiël's[15]. In February 1586 he asked Plantin whether Hiël would allow him to base his scholia on it, saying that he would add nothing of his own[16], and when his *Elucidationes in omnia S. Apostolorum scripta* appeared, printed by Plantin in Antwerp in 1588 and bearing a privilege and approval dated June 1587, the section on Revelation was preceded by a foreword acknowledging his debt.

The first question raised by Arias Montano's adoption of Hiël's commentary is the extent of his fidelity to the original text. Maurits Sabbe, who published Bruno Becker's conclusions about the relations between the two men in 1926[17], stated that Arias Montano took nine tenths of his commentary from Hiël, and this is indeed true. Sabbe printed seventeen examples of scholia taken from Chapter 9 and one could do as much for the rest of the commentary. Nevertheless there are certain differences between the surviving Dutch text and Arias Montano's scholia. Some are due to the particular forms of the two commentaries. While Hiël wrote an actual commentary, reproducing or paraphrasing the original text and providing his own interpretation either between brackets or worked into the text itself, Arias Montano gave marginal scholia. He omitted Hiël's foreword and his epilogue, as well as

[14] Ibid., 86-93.
[15] Arias Montanus, *Elucidationes*, 429.
[16] B. Rekers, op.cit., 89.
[17] Maurice Sabbe, 'Les rapports entre B. Arias Montanus et H. Jansen Barrefelt (Hiël)', *De Gulden Passer* 4 (1926), 19-43.

certain admonitions to the reader. On occasion he added a scholium of his own in the spirit of Hiël to passages on which Hiël had not commented[18], and, in the first chapter (in which he deviates more from Hiël than in any other) he gives an explanation of the term 'Apocalypse' not to be found in the Dutch[19]. In his foreword and epilogue Hiël justified his own understanding of the Book of Revelation by making two claims: he was living in the 'last age of time' and he was living 'within' the spirit of God. He was thus a divine mouthpiece with privileges not necessarily conferred on his neighbour. Arias Montano made no reference to the 'last age of time' and this alone gives his interpretation a slightly different bias to the original.

At the end of his commentary Arias Montano elucidated his terminology with a division of man into three conditions[20]. The first, 'essentia Dei, sive divina', is that part of God's nature which He started to communicate to man and which is referred to in Psalm 82 (Vulg.81):6: 'Ego dixi: Dii estis, Et filii Excelsi omnes'. The second, 'Natura humana, sive naturalis essentia', is the human nature which God gave to man before the Fall, and the third, 'improba essentia, sive decepta, vel prolapsa humanitas' is what man became after the Fall. This third condition is again divided into two parts: 'feritas', which Arias Montano describes as the moral corruption of the pagans and Barbarians, and 'industria', or wisdom of men which deceives us and leads us into error. Each of these conditions is to be found in Hiël. The 'essentia Dei' is the 'goddelijcke Wesen'; 'natura humana' the 'natuurlijcke' or 'menschelijcke Wesen'; 'improba essentia' is the 'aertsche Wesen', 'feritas' 'verwoestheit' and 'industria' 'aertsche vernuft'. But Hiël appears to have been less consistent in observing this division than Arias Montano. He frequently uses 'aertsche Wesen' and 'aertsche vernuft' interchangeably, and although the division may clarify certain passages in Hiël he did not necessarily attach to it the same importance that Arias Montano did.

For Arias Montano the scheme had implications which extended far beyond his familiarity with the works of Hiël. He had planned his New Testament commentaries in about 1565, well before he ever left Spain for the Low Countries, and in the preface he then wrote and which was later included in his *Elucidationes in omnia S. Apostolorum scripta*, 'De Christi Iesu Veritate

---

[18] E.g. his scholium to Rev. 17:6, 'the blood of the saints', *Elucidationes*, 467: 'Innocentis simplicis essentiae Dei, cuius necem sensus humanae naturae non reformatae, omnes in terrestris humanitatis corde adiuverunt.'

[19] Ibid., 430: 'Materiam scripti indicat esse, visionem et revelationem, id est, doctrinam per imagines traditam, cuius vera significatio divino dono continget Dei et Christi servis; idque non verbis tantum, sed magis rebus ipsis, quas veritas cito consecutura probaturaque sit. Atque revelatio haec Iesu Christi esse dicitur, utpote cuius virtutem efficientiamque docet, et veritatis testimonio confirmat.'

[20] Ibid., 482.

Disputatio'[21], there could be perceived a tendency which was to alarm the inquisitors in the early seventeenth century and lead to the expurgation of a part of Arias Montano's work: the tendency to suggest that, through the grace of the New Dispensation, the elect were free of the 'touchwood' of sin. This potential antinomianism, expressed with more or less caution, appears throughout Arias Montano's Biblical commentaries, and was detected by the inquisitors in the threefold division of man[22]. When he drew up his scheme Arias Montano may have had Erasmus' *Enchiridion* in mind, but Erasmus[23], who gives as his own source Origen's commentary on Romans, used the division in his arguments for the freedom of will, something Arias Montano did not do. Erasmus, however, points to the other, Pauline, source — 1 Thess. 5:23: 'may your spirit, soul and body be kept sound and blameless at the coming of our Lord Jesus Christ' — and this passage also interested Arias Montano. In his scholium to it Arias Montano wrote of 'the extinction of that human war in which the flesh strives against the spirit and the spirit against the flesh[24], an interpretation to which the inquisitors objected[25] and which can be taken to confirm their suspicion that the war seen by Arias Montano in the Book of Revelation led to the complete suppression of sin in the souls of the elect and the predominance of a divine nature which man already carried in his heart.

Arias Montano's admiration for Hiël must be considered in connection with his own religious convictions, and perhaps the best definition of his views is in one of the caustic *bons mots* attributed to Joseph Justus Scaliger. 'Montanus estoit bon Papiste, et a fait de bonnes choses, mais aussi de pietres: il avoit une Religion particuliere, ainsi que Raphelenge le Pere a dit à Scaliger'[26]. 'Bon Papiste' Arias Montano was in some respects, but not perhaps in all. There can be little doubt that he considered himself a good Catholic and, especially where the doctrine of solfidianism was concerned, that he was decidedly anti-Lutheran. His determination to combat the Reformer's ideas on justification

---

[21] Ibid., 12-30.

[22] The manuscript note in the expurgated Spanish editions is based on the 1640 Index of Sotomayor: 'Cum omnia huius libri misteria Arias referat ad triplicem hominis naturam, seu conditionem divinam, humanam integram, et humanam lapsam, quae sapiunt illam suam extinctionem fomitis, in sancti novi testamenti prae antiquis, quem saepe repetit, caute legendum est.'

[23] Erasmus, *Enchiridion Militis Christiani*, Darmstadt, 1968, 138-140. For the consequences which Erasmus draws from this tripartite division see André Godin, *Erasme lecteur d'Origène*, Genève, 1982, 36-43.

[24] *Elucidationes*, 264-265: 'Salom perfectionem et pacem significat. non qualem mundus dat precatur his Apostolus, verum quam solus dat Deus per Unctum suum, Spiritus sancti essentia et virtute, humanum illud extinguens bellum, quo caro concupiscit adversus spiritum, et spiritus adversus carnem; atque divisionem, dissidium et pugnantiam illam singulari dono ac beneficio componens, ita ut ima summis concordent. Atque integer spiritus et anima et corpus in adventu Domini nostri Salutaris Uncti servetur.'

[25] 'Caute accipe quod dixit de extinctioni concupiscentiae etc.'

[26] *Scaligerana*, Cologne, 1695, 270.

by faith appears throughout his New Testament commentaries[27] and his *Dictatum Christianum*[28]. It appears in all that he wrote before, during and after his stay in the Low Countries. Faith, he insisted, had to be live faith which produced works. To this he returned repeatedly, commenting at length on the passages Luther had used for his own purposes and at still greater length on those passages and Books (like the Epistles of St. James) which Luther had neglected because they did not suit his purposes. On this subject Arias Montano spoke the language of the Council of Trent, and here we find all the orthodoxy we might expect from a man who had formed part of the Spanish delegation at Trent, who was sent to the Low Countries as his sovereign's emissary, and who was responsible for drawing up an expurgatory index.

In spite of the pious dedications of the two parts of his New Testament commentaries to the Church of Rome Arias Montano was never an altogether conventional Catholic commentator of the Scriptures. Contempt for scholasticism and neglect of the Church Fathers are constant features of his writings. In his *Elucidationes in Quatuor Evangelia*, printed by Plantin in 1575, Arias Montano does interpret certain parables, like those of the mustard seed (Mt. 13:31) and the net (Mt. 13:47), as referring to the Church, 'Ecclesia', but this approach changes markedly in his later works. For this, and for his increasing reluctance to contribute to the Spanish plan of formulating a reply to the Centuriators of Magdeburg[29], there may have been personal reasons — his difficulties in obtaining approval of the Polyglot Bible, the spectacle of fellow Hebrew scholars in Spain being tried by the Inquisition and the suspicions which he too aroused in more orthodox and conservative circles, and, finally, his direct experience of Spanish policy in the Low Countries where he became an ever more convinced advocate of moderation[30]. Certainly one of the more striking aspects of his commentaries to the last part of the New Testament, written between 1575 and 1587, is his refusal to see any prophetic allusion to the triumph of the Roman Catholic Church.

Hiël's aconfessional treatises were designed to appeal to a man increasingly disenchanted by many sides of Roman Catholicism. Arias Montano received them at a time when he had interrupted his commentaries to the Epistles. He had finished his scholia to Philippians in 1580, but only wrote his commentary to Colossians in 1585. By 1585 he had read some of Hiël's writings and he

---

[27] Cf., in his *Elucidationes in Quatuor Evangelia*, Antwerp, 1575, his scholia to Mt. 7:26; 8:11, 13; 9:21; 25:7, 24; Mk. 1:2; 2:17; 5:30, 35; 9:23; Lk. 5:13; 7:50; 17:20; Jn. 7:38. And in *Elucidationes* his scholia to Tit. 3:7; Heb. 11:39; Jas. 2:14-16.

[28] *Dictatum Christianum*, Antwerp, 1575, 100-104.

[29] Cf. José L. de Orella y Unzue, *Respuestas católicas a las Centurias de Magdeburgo (1559-1588)*, Madrid, 1976, 369-386.

[30] Cf.B. Rekers, op.cit., 13-69.

appears to have been particularly struck by Hiël's interpretation, in the commentary to Revelation and elsewhere, of Scriptural references to 'the temple of God' as the human heart or soul. Arias Montano had taken no notice of the more obvious New Testament references to the temple in those Epistles he had commented before 1580 — 1 Cor. 3:16; 1 Cor. 6:19; 2 Cor. 6:16; Eph. 2:21. In 1585, however, he developed a sudden interest in the image, commenting on it in 2 Thess. 2:4. A year later he completed his scholia to Hebrews and here, too, the tabernacle (8:2) was interpreted as the heart and soul of man in what seems a deliberate contrast to more orthodox Catholic interpreters like Alfonso Salmeron who saw in it a clear allusion to the Church.

If what Raphelengius described to Scaliger as Arias Montano's 'Religion particuliere'[31] can explain his reception of Hiël it should also underline his independence of mind rather than allow us to classify him as a member of any particular sect, and the question remains why Arias Montano, a Biblical scholar who was far from rejecting a philological and historical approach to the Scriptures in his other Biblical commentaries, should have applied Hiël's deliberately unphilological commentary to the Book of Revelation. His admiration for Hiël may account for certain expressions in his letters to Plantin; it may even have affected him deeply on personal level; but it hardly explains his insertion of Hiël's commentary in a work in which it was manifestly out of place. To this question I can only give a conjectural answer. In his foreword to Revelation Arias Montano stressed the difficulty he had had in understanding the Book and thanked Hiël for revealing its mysteries. He realised, he wrote, that the Book could only be understood by those to whom God had imparted the meaning of its allegories, by the 'pious and the simple who profess the truth, do not place too much trust in their human intelligence and their judgement, and who know the true path to Christ ...'. He also expressed his disappointment in other commentaries which were probably in some way political or historical[32]. Arias Montano's treatment of Revelation would be

---

[31] The conservative bishop of Rurmond, Wilhelmus Lindanus, regarded Arias Montano as a Pelagian. On 19 November 1586 he wrote to Baronius that: 'nos absolvendo illi operi contra Pelagianismum per D.Ariam Montanum pertinaciter renovatum impendemus ...' and repeated the charge in May of the following year. Baronius, *Epistolae* III, Rome, 1770, 144, 147.

[32] *Elucidationes*, 429: 'Fateor me, quamvis Domini viam ante annos triginta divino beneficio in sacris libris edoctum, tamen ex Ioannis Apocalypsi omnia fere praeter unum et alterum ad summumque tria capita, eademque non secundum seriem constituta, post multa etiam commentatorum expositorumque scripta consulta ignoravisse: Dicere autem solitum saepe, mihi melius quam commentatoribus, quos legere contigerat, Apocalypsis lectionem intelligi, utpote not intellectam confitenti, cum illi tanquam perceptam et declaratu facilem suis commentariis exponere pergerent. quorum variae expositiones obscuriorem difficilioremque quam antea mihi lectionem reddiderunt. Atque in hoc sensu desiderioque perpetuo persistenti, Dei providentia effectum est, ut cuiusdam Christianae veritatis viventis testis, cui nomen ipsa Christi virtus et veritas Hiël indidit, opera ac

understandable if he shared the scepticism of so many humanists and reformers about the Book's canonicity. Since it was in the canon of the Vulgate he had to write a commentary to it, but by writing a mystical commentary of the type provided by Hiël he could avoid all the historical and philological problems which the Book posed. He did not have to deal with the problem of authorship; he did not have to elucidate any of the veiled references to political circumstances, transparent though they were; above all he did not have to interpret the Book as prophesying the triumph of the Church of Rome.

Arias Montano's New Testament commentaries remained popular well into the eighteenth century both amongst Catholics and Protestants. After being prohibited from 1607 to 1612 the many copies circulating in Spain were indeed expurgated[33], but of all the commentaries the least expurgated remained the scholia to Revelation, accompanied merely by a general recommendation of caution referred mainly to the tripartite division of man. Arias Montano thus took his place amongst the standard commentators on the Book and was quoted by other exegetes even if they pursued a different line of interpretation. Almost ten years before Cornelius a Lapide's commentary another Jesuit, the Spaniard Luis de Alcazar, had given Arias Montano considerable publicity in his own commentary published in 1618. Although he did not share Arias Montano's view of the Book he agreed that his interpretation was ingenious and 'not to be dismissed'[34].

---

subsidio, aliqua praetensa fuerit lucis pars, qua huius libri mysteria omnia, diaboli operum accusationem, eorumdemque per Christum damnationem, dissolutionem, et interitum, abolitionemque spectare cognoscerem, nec posse plene atque abunde percipi, nisi ab iis quibus idem qui sermonis huius author est Deus, rem ipsam de qua agitur, efficienter communicet. posse autem a piis atque simplicibus veri amatoribus, nihilque proprio humano ingenio ac iudicio indulgentibus, Christique sincerae viae non ignaris, transfigurationis huius specimen ut tribus in monte sancto discipulis ostendi ...'

[33] On Arias Montano and the Index see B. Rekers, op.cit., 68-69; F.H. Reusch, *Der Index der verbotenen Bücher*, Bonn, 1883, I, 575-575.

[34] Ludovicus ab Alcasar, *Vestigatio arcani sensus in Apocalypsi*, Lyons, 1618, 19: 'Arias vero in sua illa spirituali accommodatione, dum Apocalypseos bella vult intra unius hominis pectus includere; non video, qua ratione possit in bello illo spiritali, quod intra unius hominis pectus geritur, distinguere duo veluti bella, quorum primum respondeat bello Ierosolymitano, et alterum bello Gentilicio: et alterius exitus sit, decimam partem Ierosolymae corruere; alterius vero, universam Babylonem conflagrare: atque his succedere mille annorum pacem; ac demum Antichristi bellum. Etenim, licet mysticum duarum urbium praelium in hominis pectore pie meditari, subtile sit inventum, nec improbandum; ceterum ille trium bellorum ordo ad mysticum hoc bellum transferri non potest. Nec contendit Arias omnia per ordinem ad subtilissimam illam normam redigere. Posse vero multa non ordinatim, sed promiscue, et absque filo accommodari, non inficior. Quin imo existimo, si Arias suam illam applicatione in litterali sensu stabiliret, multa praeterea illum ingeniose pro votis aptare potuisse. Nam in perfidae Ierosolymae bello adversus Dei Ecclesiam poterat contemplari, quam acriter Deo conentur obsistere ii, *qui semel fuerant illuminati, et gustaverant donum caeleste, et verbum Dei, et prolapsi sunt*, ad Hebraeos 6.4. Quorum ex numero vix decima tandem pars, id est, perpauci sese illi submittent. In bello etiam Romae ethnicae adversus Ecclesiam gesto, idoneus sese dabat sermo de eorum repugnantia; qui cum Deum non

Hiël's commentary on its own had a far more restricted circulation. No surviving copy is known of the first Dutch edition of 1592. The work was reprinted in Dutch in Amsterdam in 1639 and in Haarlem in 1703 but the rarity of the surviving copies suggests that editions were limited. The same almost certainly applies to the sixteenth-century French translation. In England the commentary was still less fortunate. The only known translation is in manuscript and was done anonymously in 1657. By 1704 it was in the library of Henry Hoare and remained at Stourhead until it was purchased by the Cambridge University Library in 1887[35]. The language in which the work was most successful was German. It was translated together with the rest of Hiël's writings and printed in Amsterdam in 1687, and it acquired a considerable popularity in Pietist circles. There was, however, a further channel through which Hiël's ideas on the Book of Revelation and on the Scriptures in general were divulged: the second (and third) series of his commentaries to Biblical illustrations engraved by Pieter van der Borcht IV. From 1592, when they were printed for the first time by Raphelengius in Leiden, to the early eighteenth century when they were printed for the last time by Izaak Enschedé in Haarlem, they were launched on the Dutch market by a succession of Amsterdam printers and were sold both inside and outside the Netherlands[36].

By the time Hiël was being read and recommended by the German Pietists inward interpretations of passages of Revelation were relatively common, especially in England. Here they coincided with a sudden interest in Northern European mysticism and the translation of certain spiritual writers who had previously been unknown. Although the works of Hendrik Niclaes had been translated in the 1570s and a Latin version of the *Theologia Germanica* had appeared in England in 1632, the years in which Northern European spirituality really entered the country were the late 1640s. A single work by Sebastian Franck was translated in 1640, but after 1645 the entire works of Jacob Boehme began to appear and inward commentaries of the Book of Revelation probably owed more to him than to anyone else.

Unlike Hiël Boehme never wrote a systematic commentary to Revelation but simply took passages to illustrate points in his theosophical system[37]. Nor was he consistent in applying an exclusively inward interpretation. He did, on occasion, treat the Book of Revelation as a book of prophecy in which the

antea cognoverint, ab eo clementer ad gratiam invitantur; ex quibus quantumvis reluctentur, multo tamen plures Christi luce solent illustrari, et eius amore incendi; dummodo divini verbi concionatores suum strenue munus obeant.'

[35] Cambridge University Library, Ms.Add.2806.

[36] Cf. Alastair Hamilton, 'From Familism to Pietism. The fortunes of Pieter van der Borcht's Biblical illustrations and Hiël's commentaries from 1584 to 1717', *Quaerendo* 11 (1981), 271-301.

[37] See, for example, Chapter 36 of his *Mysterium Magnum* on the whore of Babylon. Jacob Boehme, *Theosophia Revelata. Das ist: Alle Göttlichen Schriften*, 1715, cols. 3018-3033.

downfall of the religious authorities of his day was clearly predicted[38]. The ambiguity of Boehme's attitude stood him in good stead when his works were translated into English after 1645, for it assured him a success in those Independent circles where the barriers between inward and outward interpretations were blurred and where a belief in inward regeneration went hand in hand with the conviction that the Saints were about to triumph on earth[39]. The coexistence of such beliefs, particularly prevalent in the years immediately following the Civil War, is exemplified in the sermons and writings of William Erbery[40] and is later perceptible in Quaker circles. The passages of Revelation which proved most susceptible to double interpretations were the verses on the whore, the dragon and the fall of Babylon, and we thus find Isaac Penington reminding his readers in 1659: 'if ever ye espy the Dragon, the beast, Antichrist, the whore, the false Prophet, ye must look at home, and read within: and there having found the thing, and seen it in the true light, ye will be able to read it certainly abroad also'[41].

Some twenty-five years later Mrs Jane Leade, the pious head of the Philadelphian Society who venerated Boehme, commented more extensively on the Book of Revelation. Like Boehme Mrs Leade believed in the progressive opening of the seven seals in her own soul, 'in my own particular, through my Soul's waiting with the Lamb's rising Power, in a particular experience of my own in the divine Mystery'[42]. Her interpretation of the opening of the seals is sometimes strongly reminiscent of Hiël's. Take the interpretation of the rider in Rev. 6:4: 'I rejoyc'd in nothing more than to see him who sate upon the Red Horse, slaying with his Sword the Beasts and creeping things of the Earth; that is, all the moving stirring Essences, springing from the original source of Evil, and to find him taking away Peace from the earthly Life, so that the earthly Mind is bereft of all Peace, Rest, Content and Satisfaction in all its goings out, whether in Thought, Word or Action'. The sword in the

[38] In Chapter 3 of *De Triplici Vita Hominis*. Ibid., col. 863: 'Und deutet uns die Offenbarung klar, wie der Geist Mercurius habe ein Sigel nach dem andern aufgetahn, und alle Plagen und Greuel un uns ausgeschüttet, und nur eitel Krieg, Zank und Bosheit, eitel List und Falschheit, mit Wunder und Kräften in uns eröfnet: Wie er uns dan fein abmahlet mit einem greulichen Thiere, gleich einem Drachen mit sieben Häuptern und zehen Hörnern, und auf seinen Häuptern sieben Kronen; und sitzet unsere fromme Geistlichkeit oben auf den Drachen, fein wol geschmückt und gekrönet.'

[39] Cf. Geoffrey F. Nuttall, *The Holy Spirit in Puritan Faith and Experience*, Oxford, 1946, 118-133.

[40] Cf. *The Testimony of William Erbery*, London, 1658, 16, 19, 40-41, 64-66, 164. For a discussion of Erbery as an 'inward' interpreter see David Brady, *The Contribution of British Writers between 1560 and 1830 to the Interpretation of Revelation 13.16-18*, Tübingen, 1983, 137-139.

[41] Isaac Penington, *Babylon the Great Described*, London, 1659, 9.

[42] Jane Leade, *The Revelation of Revelations*, London, 1683, 12.

same verse 'is Christ's rising Life in his Saints enabling them to conquer the Essences of the earthly Life (which is the Beast) in themselves[43].

As Mrs Leade's interpretation progresses, however, we see that, like so many Independents earlier in the century, she applied both an outward and an inward significance to the last chapters of the Book. 'It was given me to observe', she wrote, 'that there are six Engagements, to which six Overcomings do answer, mentioned in the Revelation, and to every Conquest a most high and wonderful Reward promised; all which is to encourage to follow him cheerfully, who is our Leader, who hath sworn that time shall be no longer than till he hath gotten the Victory over the Beast and the Whore, and hath destroyed the Dragon's Kingdom in every Property within us, who are elected to reign in his Life with him in his Throne, with a train of new created Powers, in the Properties of the redeemed Earth in the Souls Essence; and then we shall know how unconfined the Lordly Dominion over all outward things is, even over all the Beasts of this visible Earth, who must be subjected to the Lamb who hath taken his Victorious Crown, and put it on the Heads of the holy Warriors, that have passed through all, and are come to the last Overcoming, that gives entrance into the seventh Seal'. She reminded her readers that the heavenly kingdom 'shall not only be inward, in the Properties of the Soul, but shall also exercise its dominion over this visible Principle'[44]. 'But if we will know how near the time is', she continued, 'we must not look without us, but in the unsealed Book of Life within us; there you will find the fore-going Signs, which are first to be accomplished in your own Heavens and Earth'[45].

Jacob Boehme is most unlikely ever to have read Arias Montano or Hiël, yet Boehme's spirituality had roots very similar to that of Hiël. Both writers use the language of the *Theologia Germanica*, and what little success Hiël had in England in the eighteenth century was closely connected with the success of Boehme. The last example of an inward interpretation of a passage in the Book of Revelation which I shall advance is by a man not quite as enthusiastic as Mrs Leade, but nevertheless a devout admirer of Boehme and a commender of Hiël[46] (whom he read in the late seventeenth-century German translation). This is the nonjuror William Law who had once had a deep influence on John Wesley and who, despite the latter's rejection of the mysticism which Law favoured, remained a revered figure in nonconformist circles throughout the eighteenth and early nineteenth century. In the second part of his *Spirit of*

---

[43] Ibid., 12-13.

[44] Ibid., 17.

[45] Ibid., 28.

[46] Dr William's Library, London. Ms (W) I.1.43, p.33. On 30 November 1782 Thomas Langcake wrote to Henry Brooke: 'William Law said to me that Jacob Behmen was the first in Excellency, Hiel the next, and in the third place the Quakers.'.

Prayer which appeared in 1750 he wrote: 'Much learned pain has been often taken to prove Rome, or Constantinople, to be the Seat of the Beast, the Antichrist, the Scarlet Whore, &c. But alas! they are not at such a Distance from us, they are the Properties of fallen human Nature, and are all of them alive in our own Selves, till we are dead or dying to all the Spirit and Tempers of this World. They are everywhere, in every Soul, where the heavenly Nature, and Spirit of the Holy Jesus is not. But when the human Soul turns from itself, and turns to God, dies to itself and lives to God in the Spirit, Tempers, and Inclinations of the Holy Jesus, loving, pitying, suffering, and praying for all its Enemies, and overcoming all Evil with Good, as this Christ of God did; then, but not till then, are these Monsters separate from it. For Covetousness and Sensuality of all kinds, are the very devouring Beast; Religion governed by a worldly, trading Spirit, and gratifying the partial Interest of Flesh and Blood, is nothing else but the Scarlet Whore; Guile, and Craft, and Cunning, are the very Essence of the old Serpent; Self-Interest and Self-Exaltation are the whole Nature of Antichrist. Pride, Persecution, Hatred and Envy, are the very Essence of the fiery Dragon'[47].

When writing this passage Law may well have had Boehme or even Penington (for whom he also professed his esteem) in mind, but it is just possible that he was thinking of a passage in Hiël's commentary not included by Arias Montano: 'Och, gy Wijsen en Simpelen in't Wesen Gods; merckt doch, en leert dit Wijf in haar valsche Hoerdery in u kennen: Het is (gelijck boven gesegt is) het valsche aartsche Vernuft, dat buyten het Wesen Gods met de Memorie in alle eygenschappen des vleesches sijn bedrijf heeft; en verciert hem selven met sijne geveynsde heyligheyt en andere kloecke valsche listigheden, dat 'tselfs meent, en de slechte eenvoudige Mensheyt wijs-maakt, dat 't God selfs zy. En met dit Wijf hebben alle Sinnen der overwesender Mensheyt Onkuysheyt en Hoerery bedreven; en zijn van haren Wijn droncken geworden; en in hare Dronkenschap hebben sy het Bloet der Heyligen, het onnosele eenvoudige Wesen Gods, in't Herte van de aartsche Mensheyt helpen dooden. Och, let hier wel op.'[48].

---

[47] William Law, *The Spirit of Prayer. The Spirit of Love*, Cambridge, 1969, 74.
[48] Hiël, *Verklaring*, 110-111.

THE IDEA OF THE PRE-EXISTENCE OF THE SOUL OF CHRIST: AN ARGUMENT IN THE CONTROVERSY BETWEEN ARIAN AND ORTHODOX IN THE EIGHTEENTH CENTURY*

by

J. van den Berg

In his *Briefe betreffende den allerneuesten Zustand der Religion und der Wissenschaften in Gross-Brittanien* (1752) the German theologian Georg Wilhelm Alberti wrote (in a postscript to a letter on the Trinitarian controversies):

> Ich habe vergessen, von einer andern Meynung, betreffende die Lere von der h. Dreyeinigkeit, etwas zu sagen, welche doch manchen angesehenen Gönner gehabt hat, auch noch hat: ich meyne die Praeexistenz der Seele Christi ... Der neueste Verteidiger der Lere von der Praeexistenz der Seele Christi, welcher zu den Gründen seiner Vorgänger vor diese Meynung noch mehrere hinzu gethan, ist D. Isaac Watts, von welchem man dergleichen nicht vermuten sollte. Er hat schon lange diese Meynung geheget, wie er meldet, und sie zu der Zeit, da seine Gemüts- und Leibeskräfte am stärkesten gewesen, untersuchet, und höchst wahrscheinlich gefunden; doch seinen Aufsatz davon bey dreissig Jahre liegen lassen, ob sich vielleicht das Wahrscheinliche dieser Meynung verlieren mögte; weil dis aber nicht geschehen, so hat er ihn endlich A. 1746 drucken lassen[1].

In 1746 a work by Watts on Christology did indeed appear, under the title *The Glory of Christ as God-Man display'd*; first anonymously, then (in a reissue of the same year) with the author's name on the title-page[2]. If Alberti is right as regards the time which elapsed between the writing and the publishing of the work, *The Glory of Christ* was written before 1720[3]. As we shall see, in the years after 1720 Watts published a number of works on christological subjects. In spite of what Alberti mentions, the reasons for the delay in publishing *The*

---

* I thank Dr. Norma E. Emerton, Cambridge, for her correction of the English text.

[1] G.W. Alberti, *Briefe* ... (III), Hannover, 1752, 742, 745.

[2] 'The title is a cancel': *British Museum Gen. Cat. of Printed Books* 253, c. 993. I used the edition of this work in *The Works of ... Isaac Watts*, ed. by D. Jennings and the late P. Doddridge VI, London, 1753, 762-861.

[3] Alberti's information is confirmed by, or perhaps borrowed from, a passage in *The Glory of Christ*, where Watts remarks that Henry More's *The Great Mystery of Godliness*, which appeared in 1660, was published 'near threescore years ago': *Works* VI, 853.

Glory of Christ remain somewhat mysterious; the more so, as before 1746 he had already touched on the doctrine of the pre-existence of the human soul of Christ in more than one work. However this may be, *The Glory of Christ* distinguished itself from earlier works by the fact that here this doctrine was fully and explicitly discussed, as appears from the title of the third discourse: 'The Glories of Christ as God-Man displayed, by tracing out the early existence of his human nature as the first-born of GOD, or as the first of all creatures, before the formation of this world'.

The Independent minister Isaac Watts (1674-1748) was one of the most prominent English Dissenters[4]. He was a voluminous author; in his own times his works enjoyed a large degree of popularity abroad as well as in England[5]. The hymns he wrote (some of which have become classics) are a mirror of his evangelical spirituality. While essentially orthodox[6] and a defender of the Trinitarian tradition, he was a man of a mild and irenic attitude. In 1720, at a time when 'the Arian controversy'[7] began to divide the Dissenting community, he still thought 'a happy medium might be found out to secure liberty and the gospel together'[8]. His theological approach and his stand amidst the conflicts of his day may be characterized as a Dissenting *via media.*

The Arian controversy started right at the beginning of the eighteenth century, in 1702, with the publication of a work by a Presbyterian minister in Dublin, Thomas Emlyn (1663-1741): *An Humble Inquiry into the Scripture Account of Jesus Christ*[9]. For his arianizing ideas, Emlyn was imprisoned, but this could not stop the spread of his views; one of the historians of Dissent, Michael R. Watts, remarks that it was Emlyn's Arianism which became the prevailing heresy of the early eighteenth century[10]. Arianizing tendencies not only spread within the Dissenting circle, but also within the Church of England. When in 1712 Samuel Clarke, rector of St. James's, Westminster, well known for his support of Newton and his controversy with Leibniz, published his *The Scripture-Doctrine of the Trinity,* in which he taught the subordination of the Son to the Father, he was accused of Arianism, though

---

[4] His main biographies are: T. Milner, *The Life, Times and Correspondence of the Rev. Isaac Watts, D.D.*, London, 1834; A.P. Davies, *Isaac Watts. His Life and Work* (1943), London, 1948.

[5] For his popularity in the Netherlands, see: J. van den Berg and G.F. Nuttall, *Philip Doddridge (1702-1751) and the Netherlands*, ch. II (forthcoming).

[6] For this, see T. Milner, 724-729; A.P. Davies, 109-126.

[7] For 'the Arian controversy', see J.H. Colligan, *The Arian Movement in England*, Manchester, 1913; E.M. Wilbur, *A History of Unitarianism* (II), Cambridge (Mass.), 1952, 236-270; R. Thomas, 'Presbyterians in transition', in C.G. Bolam and others, *The English Presbyterians*, London, 1968, 113-218; M.R. Watts, *The Dissenters* I, Oxford, 1978, 371-382.

[8] Quoted from R. Thomas in *The English Presbyterians*, 170.

[9] For Emlyn, see esp. E.M. Wilbur, *Unitarianism*, 244ff. Emlyn gave an account of the proceedings against him in 'A true Narrative of the Proceedings ... against Mr. Thomas Emlyn', *The Works of Mr. Thomas Emlyn* I, London, 1746, 1-79.

[10] *The Dissenters* I, 373.

(like, to a certain extent, Emlyn) he did not consider himself an Arian[11]. He could only escape ecclesiastical prosecution by promising to keep silent on the subject, but of course his ideas as laid down in his work could not be silenced; they exercised a not inconsiderable influence, especially in the Dissenting community. All this resulted in a mounting tension within the circle of the Dissenters which came to a head in 1719, when at a conference of the London Dissenting ministers, held at Salters' Hall, a narrow majority opted for liberty with regard to the interpretation of the doctrine of the Trinity[12].

It should be added, that among this majority only a few were indeed Arians; furthermore, that most of those who objected against the orthodox Trinitarian creed were not Socinians: they saw Christ as a pre-existent being, which even might be called God, subordinate to the Father but far exalted above all human beings, and thus able to act as Mediator in the work of atonement. This form of Arianism left much of the traditional theological concepts intact. The theology of the eighteenth-century Arians was a mixture of biblicism and rationalism. Influenced as the arianizing theologians were by the rationalist method of John Locke, they were protagonists of a free and open inquiry into the Scriptures, and they refused to submit to the authority of credal formulas for which they found no warrant in the Bible. This does not imply that they were radicals who wanted to turn upside down the whole structure of traditional theology; their Arianism could, however, easily drift into an explicitly anti-trinitarian form of Unitarianism, as indeed happened in many cases in the second half of the eighteenth century[13].

Isaac Watts had not taken part in the Salters' Hall conference, nor did he want to be identified with one of the two conflicting parties as to the question of subscription or non-subscription to certain credal formulas[14]. But he was deeply concerned about the Trinitarian controversy as such, as appears from a dissertation he published in 1724 under the title 'The *Arian* invited to the orthodox faith: or, A plain and easy method to lead such as deny the proper

---

[11] For Clarke's attitude towards traditional Arian doctrine, see J.H. Colligan, *The Arian Movement in England*, 37. Clarke explicitly declined to be called an Arian, while Emlyn, who sympathized with Clarke, declared he did not agree wholly with Arius (nor with Socinus): 'A true Narrative', *Works* I, 16. Still, from some passages in Emlyn's 'A Vindication of the Worship of the Lord Jesus Christ, On Unitarian Principles' (1706; *Works* I, esp. 276f.) and in his 'A Vindication of the Bishop of Gloucester's Discourse' (1707; *Works* I, esp. 377f.), we may deduce that ultimately, in spite of his reservations, he sympathized with Arius.

[12] For 'Salters' Hall', see R. Thomas, 'The Non-Subscription Controversy amongst Dissenters in 1719: the Salters' Hall Debate', *Journal of Ecclesiastical History* 4 (1953), 162-186.

[13] For the transition from Arianism to Unitarianism, see E.M. Wilbur, *Unitarianism*, ch. XV and XVI, and H.L. Short, 'From Presbyterian to Unitarian', in *The English Presbyterians*, 219-235. Emlyn already used the term 'Unitarian', but his Arian 'Unitarianism' should not be identified with the more radical Unitarianism of a later generation.

[14] For Watts and 'Salters' Hall', see T. Milner, *Life*, 322ff.

deity of *Christ*, into the belief of that great article'[15]. Watts's irenical spirit is revealed in the preface to the three *Dissertations* of which 'The *Arian* ...' formed part:

> I would not willingly call every man an enemy to *Christ*, who lives under some doubts of supreme godhead. My charity inclines me to believe that some of them, both read their bibles carefully, and pray daily for divine instruction to lead them into all truth: That they honour and adore that glorious person whom they believe to be the brightness of his Father's glory, and by whom he created the worlds, who condescended to take a human body, and to die for sinners ...[16].

Furthermore, in 'The *Arian* ...' Watts distinguished between 'the ancient Arians' who believed the Son and the Holy Spirit to be 'mere creatures', and 'the modern refiners of the *Arian* scheme', who have granted that there is 'a peculiar, strict and perfect union and communion, between the Father and the Son'; for this, he referred to Clarke's *Scripture-Doctrine of the Trinity*[17]. 'Where is', Watts asked, 'the inconvenience, or difficulty, of allowing this to be called a personal union, whereby what is proper to God may be attributed to *Christ*, and what is proper to the man *Christ* may be attributed to God ...?'[18]

It is interesting that it was precisely in the context of an 'invitation to Arians' that Watts mentioned for the first time in his works the doctrine of the pre-existence of Christ's human soul

> which seems to be the most obvious and natural sense of many scriptures, if we can believe that it was formed the first of creatures before the foundation of the world, and was present with God in the beginning of all things, which is no hard matter for an *arian* to grant. Then we also justly believe this union between God and man to have begun before the world was, in some unknown moment of God's eternity: For when the human soul of *Christ* was first brought into existence, it might be united in that moment to the divine nature[19].

Here, the idea of the pre-existence of the soul of Christ is used by Watts as a bridge to span the gap between the Arian and the orthodox. Watts realized that in doing this he was in danger of being himself accused of Arianism. In

---

[15] The first of three *Dissertations relating to the Christian doctrine of the Trinity*, *Works* VI, 493-544.

[16] *Works* VI, 499.

[17] The reference is to Part 1, nos. 594 and 600 of Clarke's work.

[18] *Works* VI, 505.

[19] *Works* VI, 507.

the preface to four *Dissertations relating to the Christian doctrine of the Trinity* of 1725 he wrote that if a man 'explain the trinity according to the ancient *Athanasians* ... he is censured perhaps as a downright tritheist. If he follow the scholastic scheme ... which has been called modern orthodoxy, he incurs the charge of *sabellianism*. If he dare propose the doctrine of the pre-existent soul of *Christ* ... he is accused of favouring the *arian* and *nestorian* errors, even though all this time he strongly maintains the proper deity of *Christ* ...'[20]. He knew quite well, that even 'the nicest care' could not exempt a man from 'these inconveniences'. It was perhaps his awareness of the possibility of such inconveniences which made him hesitate to publish his broader and more fundamental exposition of the doctrine of the pre-existence of Christ, which (as we saw) did not appear before 1746.

Just like the other works on the Trinity and on Christology, this work, too, was defined by the context of the Arian controversy. Watts thought the Socinian doctrines had been effectively refuted by many learned authors; now, the point at issue was whether or not Christ in his 'complex person' included the godhead: 'This is the great and important question of the age'[21]. In the attempts to solve this question, the doctrine of the pre-existence of Christ's soul could play an important part:

> ... if, by a more careful inspection of the word of God, we shall find it revealed there with unexpected evidence, that the 'human soul of our Lord *Jesus Christ* had an existence, and was personally united to the divine nature, long before it came to dwell in flesh and blood' ... will not such thoughts as these spread a new lustre over all our former ideas of the glory of *Christ* ...?[22]

Watts was indeed convinced that Scripture offered plentiful evidence for the doctrine he advocated. Many texts, especially in the New Testament, affirm the pre-existence of Christ. Some of them directly refer to his divine nature. Other texts 'carry not with them such a full and convincing evidence of his godhead as utterly to exclude all other interpretations'. Lastly, there are also texts which 'in their most natural, obvious and evident sense seem to refer to some intelligent being belonging to our Lord *Jesus Christ*, which is inferior to godhead'; these texts 'most naturally lead us to the belief of the pre-existence of his human soul'. In a note, Watts explains that if in this connection he speaks of the soul of Christ as being an angel or an angelic spirit, he means that the soul of Christ was without a body, or was a messenger of God the Father; and if he speaks of him as a super-angelic spirit, he intends to express

[20] *Works* VI, 547.
[21] *Works* VI, 731.
[22] *Works* VI, 803.

that Christ's soul had 'both natural and deputed powers far superior to angels'[23]. Of course he wanted to prevent possible misunderstandings with regard to expressions which, taken out of their context, somehow smacked of Arianism.

One of his main proof-texts was Phil. 2:5, 6, 7. According to Watts, the Arians raise a plausible objection against the 'vulgar explanation of the trinity and the divinity of Christ', because 'that scheme allows no real self emptying, no literal and proper abasement and suffering of the Son of God', but only a 'nominal suffering'. The Son of God himself 'really suffered nothing ... but was all the while possessed of the highest glory, and of the same unchangeable blessedness': the godhead himself is 'impassible', and thus cannot really suffer pain or loss, nor undergo 'proper sensible humiliation, shame or sorrow'. All objections of the Arians are solved, however, if we apply the notion of self-emptying to the pre-existent soul of Christ. This doctrine of the pre-existence of Christ's soul

> sets the whole scheme of the self-denial and sufferings of *Christ*, in as glorious and advantageous a light as their doctrine can pretend to do; and yet at the same time secures the divinity of *Christ*, together with all the honours of it's condescending grace, by supposing this pre-existent soul always personally united to his divine nature. Thus all this sort of pretences for the support of the *arian* error is destroyed at once, by admitting this doctrine.

The same doctrine also helps us in defending the doctrine of Christ's deity against other 'cavils' of the Arians. They consider a number of things mentioned in the Old Testament, such as the eating and drinking with Abraham, the wrestling with Jacob etc. 'too mean and low condescensions for the great God of heaven and earth to practice'. But again, all difficulties are solved if we see these events as appearances of 'this glorious spirit'[24] — a human soul, which was 'like a glass through which the godhead shone with inimitable splendor ...'[25].

Watts found corroborative evidence for the doctrine he defended in the testimony of the ancient Jews, among whom 'there was a tradition of the pre-existence of the soul of the *Messiah*'. In this connexion he referred to Philo's exegesis of Ex. 23:20 and to the Septuagint translation of Is. 9:6. Furthermore, he quoted the *Pesikta*[26]: 'After God had created the world, he put his hand under the throne of his glory, and brought out the soul of the *Messiah*, with

[23] *Works* VI, 805f.
[24] *Works* VI, 841f.
[25] *Works* VI, 825.
[26] The quotation is borrowed from Bishop Fowler's *A Discourse of the Descent of the Man-Christ Jesus from Heaven* (see below). In Oxford, where Bishop Fowler had studied, three mss. of

all his attendants, and said unto him, Wilt thou heal and redeem my sons after six thousand years? He answered, I am willing to do so ...'. Also in cabbalistic literature the pre-existence of the Messiah's soul is mentioned, and though, according to Watts, 'we allow no more credit to these traditions than to other *jewish* tales, yet it discovers their ancient notion of the pre-existence of the soul of the *Messiah* ...'[27]. And in ancient christian tradition the doctrine was also to be found: '*Origen* seems to be a believer of the pre-existent soul of *Christ*'[28].

Furthermore, Watts could refer to a number of modern authorities, who shared his opinions on this point. Just as the doctrine of the millennium was long obscured,

> and yet now it has arisen into further evidence, and has obtained almost universal assent, so this doctrine of *Christ's* pre-existent soul, though it might have lain dormant several ages, yet since that excellent man doctor *Henry More* has published it near threescore years ago in his 'great mystery of godliness', it has been embraced, as bishop *Fowler* asserts, 'by many of our greatest divines, as valuable men as our church can boast of; though most of them have been too sparing in owning it, for fear, I suppose, of having their orthodoxy called in question'[29].

On one important point, however, Watts differed from More: he rejected the idea (held, as we shall see, by More and Origen) that not only the soul of Christ, but all souls were pre-existent, 'for which opinion I think there is neither in scripture nor in reason any just foundation ...'[30].

Next to More, Watts mentioned a number of other authors who also held the doctrine of the pre-existence of Christ's soul. Among them was Robert Fleming (1660?-1716), a Presbyterian minister to whose *Christology* (3 vls., 1705-1708) Watts more than once refers[31], and Edward Fowler (1632-1714), Bishop of Gloucester, who formed a link between the Cambridge Platonists and the eighteenth-century authors on the subject and to whom because of this we shall return below[32]. Alberti remarks: 'Es ist diese Meynung auch ausser

the *Pesikta de Rav-Kahana* (one of the oldest homiletical midrashim) have been preserved: *Encyclopaedia Judaica* XIII, c. 333ff.

[27] *Works* VI, 821f.

[28] *Works* VI, 853. For Origen and the doctrine of the pre-existence of the soul of Christ, see M.E. Wiles, 'The Nature of the Early Debate about Christ's Human Soul', *Journal of Ecclesiastical History* 16 (1965), 142f.; R. Lorenz, 'Die Christusseele im Arianischen Streit', *Zeitschrift für Kirchengeschichte* 94 (1983), 37.

[29] *Works* VI, 853.

[30] *Works* VI, 823.

[31] 'His 'Christology' ... shows that while himself orthodox on the person of Christ, he was resolutely opposed to any form of subscription': *Dictionary of National Biography*, s.v. Fleming.

[32] For adherents of the doctrine of the pre-existence of the soul of Christ, see also J.A.B. Jongeneel, *Het redelijke geloof in Jezus Christus* (diss. Leiden), Wageningen, 1971, 75.

England von einigen angenommen worden, wobey ich mich aber nicht aufhalte'[33]. Of this, I have only been able to find one instance[34]: a French work, anonymously published in London in 1739 under the title *Dissertation Théologique et Critique, Dans laquelle on tâche de prouver, par divers passages des Saintes Ecritures, que l'Ame de Jésus-Christ étoit dans le Ciel une Intelligence pure et glorieuse, avant que d'être unie à un corps humain dans le sein de la Bienheureuse Vierge Marie.* In his preface, the author gives the impression that his views are new, and that his work is purely the result of his own studies.

> Il ne nous paroît pas qu'aucun motif humain nous ait induit le moins du monde a prendre le sentiment que nous avons adopté. Nous avons suspendu notre jugement pendant bien des années, nous avons lu et relu, surtout le Nouveau Testament ...[35].

One of his critics, Armand de la Chapelle, minister of the Walloon church at The Hague[36], wrote in a review of the *Dissertation* in the *Bibliothèque Raisonnée*: 'Il n'est *nouveau* par rapport à l'Angleterre'; yet he remarked that one should not doubt the author's solemn declarations as regards this point[37]. According to the *Dictionnaire* of J.B. Ladvocat[38], the author was Pierre Roques (1685-1745), minister of the French church at Basle, whose theology in general was of the same type as that of Watts[39]. It is peculiar, though of course not impossible, that a French author should have developed spontaneously a doctrine which for quite a number of years had already been defended by English authors, one of whom (Henry More) he could even have read in Latin[40]. However this may be, the author of the *Dissertation* brought

---

[33] G.W. Alberti, *Briefe*, 746.

[34] Apart, perhaps, from the rather eccentric Dutch Cartesian layman Willem Deurhoff (1650-1717), who according to some of his opponents taught the pre-existence of Christ's soul: B. de Moor, *Commentarius perpetuus in Johannis Marckii Compendium* III, Lugd. Bat., 1765, 695.

[35] *Dissertation*, f. [*3ro].

[36] According to *Nieuw Nederlandsch Biografisch Woordenboek* VII, s.v., he wrote the theological reviews in the *Bibl. Raisonnée*; cf. [J.B.] Ladvocat, *Dictionnaire Historique Portatif* II, La Haye, 1754, s.v. Roques.

[37] *Biobliothèque Raisonnée des ouvrages des savans de l'Europe* XXIV (1740), 135. La Chapelle referred to the Cambridge Platonists Henry More, Joseph Glanville and George Rust, whose opinions he knew from a work, entitled *Two choice and useful Treatises*, London, 1682. His astonishment would have been still greater, had he known that a number of other authors had defended the idea of the pre-existence of Christ's soul more emphatically than the authors he mentioned had done.

[38] *Dictionnaire, loc. cit.*

[39] For Roques and his theology, see J. van den Berg, 'Le Vray Piétisme: Die aufgeklärte Frömmigkeit des Basler Pfarrers Pierre Roques', *Zwingliana* 16 (1983), 35-53.

[40] A Latin edition of More's *Opera Omnia* appeared in London in 3 vls. between 1675 and 1679; a reprint of the theological vol. in 1700. See the bibliography in F.I. Mackinnon (ed.), *Philosophical Writings of Henry More*, New York, 1925, 240f.

forward the doctrine of the pre-existence of Christ's soul with no less vigour than Watts did. Like Watts, he rejected the idea that all souls were pre-existent:

> Il y a peu de gens qui croient que les ames soient éternelles, et il est facile de réfuter cette hypothèse. Nous disons la même chose de l'opinion de ces Docteurs Juifs qui croient la pré-existence des ames, et qui ont enseigné qu'elles avoient été toutes créées au commencement du monde.

This he knew from John Lightfoot's *Horae Hebraicae et Talmudicae*, from which he quoted: 'Repositorium est, ait R. Salom., et nomen ejus est Goph: atque a Creatione formatae sunt omnes animae quae erant nascendae, atque ibi repositae'[41].

Another parallel with Watts is that the author of the *Dissertation* also hoped the doctrine of the pre-existence of Christ's soul would be a means to bring the Arians and the orthodox together. His tone is even more conciliatory than that of Watts:

> ... on pourroit peut-être par ce moïen rapprocher les sentimens des Ariens et des Orthodoxes au sujet de la divinité du Sauveur. Les Ariens ont cru qu'il y avoit en J.C. quelque nature excellente qui avoit existé dans le ciel, et qui étoit inférieure au Dieu souverain ... En cela ils avoient raison ... Les Orthodoxes au contraire suivent l'Ecriture, lorsqu'ils enseignent que la Parole, qui est le Dieu Créateur des cieux et de la terre, a habité réellement et purement en J.C. ... Toute la vérité ne paroît pas se trouver toute entière, ni dans l'un, ni dans l'autre de ces deux systèmes; mais en réunissant ces deux opinions ... on a un système complet et lié de tout ce que l'Ecriture nous enseigne de la personne de notre grand Médiateur ...[42].

Yet, however irenic he was, at the same time the author strongly maintained he was essentially orthodox: 'Nous le déclarons donc hautement encore, nous sommes fort éloignés du sentiment des Ariens et des Sociniens'[43]. While La Chapelle had no difficulty in admitting this, he strongly criticized the idea of the pre-existence of the soul of Christ and the arguments used by the author in support of his thesis. The doctrine of a pre-existent soul of Christ, destined to animate a human body for the work of redemption implied that this work

---

[41] *Dissertation*, 4. Lightfoot refers to 'R. Solomon' (Rashi) and other Jewish authors in his notes on John 9:2; he has, however, his reservations with regard to the general acceptance of the idea of the pre-existence of souls among the Jews: 'Horae Hebraicae et Talmudicae impensae in Evangelium Sancti Joannis' (1671) in J. Lightfoot, *Opera Omnia* II, Roterodami, 1686, 638.

[42] *Dissertation*, 113.

[43] *Dissertation*, f. [*3ro].

preceded the work of creation — an idea, acceptable only to supralapsarians! Furthermore, the created pure Intelligence which was identified with the soul of Christ differed only in terminological respect from the Second Person of the Arian Trinity. In the context of this doctrine, the divine nature of Christ would be completely useless ('inutile'). Besides, would not this doctrine lead to a recognition of three natures in one person? And lastly, why should only one soul be pre-existent; would it not be easier to believe in the pre-existence of all souls[44]? Another critic, the Genevan pastor François de Roches, was prepared to concede that the doctrine proposed in the *Dissertation* could help to explain some obscure passages in Scripture, but would it not be better to leave these in obscurity than to risk 'd'ébranler des Véritez très consolantes pour l'Homme pécheur'[45]?

Leaving aside other authors, I mention as a third representative of the doctrine of the pre-existence of the soul of Christ Bishop Fowler, because he forms a link between later authors on the subject and the Cambridge Platonists. Edward Fowler (1632-1714) was a friend and protégé of Henry More, whom he admired and from whom he borrowed some of his ideas[46], but Principal Tulloch cautions us not to consider him a Cambridge Platonist: 'He had but slight hold of the principles of the Cambridge theology, and has sketched them ... from a superficial and somewhat confused point of view'[47]. In 1706 Fowler — then Bishop of Gloucester — published *A Discourse of the Descent of the Man-Christ Jesus from Heaven; together with His Ascension to Heaven again* ... Fowler thought the doctrine of the pre-existence of the soul of Christ could be used as an argument in the struggle with the Socinians 'for its depriving them of the Advantages they have for the Retorting of the Charge against them of wresting Scripture'[48]. 'For further Satisfaction' Fowler referred the reader to Henry More's *An Explanation of the Grand Mystery of Godliness* (1660). It sounds improbable, when he adds: 'Which I never happen'd to look into, till after I had penned what I thought sufficient upon that Part ...'[49], but perhaps Fowler only wanted to say that, though acquainted with More's ideas, he had compared his own work *a posteriori* with that of More. Still, there is a difference between More and Fowler. Like More, Fowler appeals to the fact that this doctrine was 'a Doctrine of the ancient *Jewish* Church'[50]. More was primarily interested in the doctrine of the pre-existence

---

[44] *Bibliothèque Raisonnée* XXIV, 135-138.

[45] F. de Roches, *Défense du Christianisme* II, Lausanne et Genève, 1740, 246.

[46] *D.N.B.*, s.v.; cf. F.J. Powicke, *The Cambridge Platonists. A study* (1926), Hamden (Conn.), 1971, 151, 197.

[47] J. Tulloch, *Rational Theology and Christian Philosophy in England in the Seventeenth Century* II, Edinburgh, ²1874, 439.

[48] *Discourse*, 44.

[49] *Discourse*, 66.

[50] *Discourse*, 25.

of all souls, which he also met with in Jewish tradition[51]; a subject about which Fowler wrote in an almost sceptical tone, when he remarked that 'the Fanciful Rabbins' grafted upon the pre-existence of 'their *Messias*' the pre-existence of all souls. At any rate, in Fowler's view the doctrine of the pre-existence of the soul of Jesus was not dependent on that of the existence of all human souls before the creation of the body[52]. With the followers and successors of the Cambridge Platonists, the accent indeed had shifted from a full-fledged Platonist position to a more rationalist attitude.

Fowler was attacked by the Dean of St. Paul's, William Sherlock (1641-1707), who elaborately excused himself for attacking 'a Venerable Prelate, for whom I have had an old Friendship, and a very particular Respect and Honour'. He thought it, however, unavoidable to devote a chapter of his *The Scripture Proofs of our Saviour's Divinity Explained and Vindicated* (1706) to a refutation of Fowler's *Discourse*, because 'it nearly affects the Cause of Christianity, in its most vital and fundamental Parts: which I hope his Lordship was not aware of ...'[53]. According to Sherlock, the Bishop, by assuming a union between the soul of Christ and the Second Person in the Trinity, jumbled Arianism and Nestorianism together, 'an *Arian* Soul, and a *Nestorian* Union'[54].

To this accusation, Fowler indignantly replied in a new work, which appeared in the same year[55]. In his turn, Fowler indirectly accused Sherlock of heresy by referring to the fact that the latter had been indicted of Socinianism or tritheism because of his *A Discourse concerning the Knowledge of Jesus Christ* (1674)[56]. In the context of our subject it is interesting to note that Sherlock's supposed 'tritheism' had made Emlyn turn away from trinitarian doctrine[57]. Again, Fowler appealed to More; furthermore, as Watts (probably following Fowler) would do some decades later, he mentioned the fact that just as the doctrine of the millennium, which he connected with the name of Joseph Mede, had lain in obscurity for some time, his doctrine had lain in obscurity since Origen[58].

More than once we have mentioned the name of Henry More (1614-1687), one of the leading Cambridge Platonists, with whom the doctrine of the pre-existence of the soul of Christ in its new form originated. As we have already

[51] See J. van den Berg, 'Menasseh ben Israel, Henry More and Johannes Hoornbeeck on the pre-existence of the soul' (forthcoming).

[52] *Discourse*, 41, 33.

[53] *Scripture Proofs*, 219.

[54] *Scripture Proofs*, 248.

[55] *Reflections upon the Late Examination of the Discourse of the Descent of the Man-Christ Jesus from Heaven* ..., London, 1706.

[56] *Reflections*, 10.

[57] With regard to Sherlock and his sympathizers, Emlyn even used the term 'polytheism': 'A Narrative ...', *Works* I, 15.

[58] *Reflections*, 115.

seen, More, as a Platonist, was most of all concerned with the idea of the pre-existence of all souls. In the context of an exposition of this doctrine he teaches the pre-existence of the soul of Christ, which according to him is implied in many places of the Old and the New Testament. With regard to the Old Testament, he refers to the fact that in the '*Apparitions* of *Angels* to the ancient *Patriarchs*, it was *Christ* himself that appeared'[59]; in this context he quotes Calvin's commentary on Daniel: 'In eo nihil est absurdi, quod Christus aliquam speciem humanae naturae exhiberet antequam manifestatus esset in carne'[60]. From the New Testament, More mentions a number of texts from the gospel of St. John (3:13, 31; 6:26, 38; 17:4, 5); furthermore, Phil. 2:6, 7, 8 and 1 John 4:2. In connection with the last text, he remarks: 'Here St. *John* seems to cabbalize ... that is, to speak in the Language of the Learned of the Jews: For the genuine Sense is: *He that confesses that Jesus is the Messiah come into the Flesh*, or *into a Terrestrial Body, is of God*: Which implies that he was, before he came into it'[61].

There is a line running from More to Watts, though in the eighteenth century the idea of the pre-existence of Christ's soul received a different function as a mediating doctrine in the struggle between the Arians and the orthodox. As such, however, it had no results whatever. The Arians could not accept it because of its Trinitarian background. *A fortiori* it was unacceptable to the successors of the Arians, the Unitarians, to whom such metaphysical speculations as the doctrine of a pre-existent angelic being which at the same time was the Second Person in the Trinity were utterly alien. And the orthodox thought it a dangerous doctrine, which weakened rather than strengthened the orthodox position because of its supposed concessions to Arianism. After Watts, the doctrine simply fades away; even Watts's friend and admirer Philip Doddridge (1702-1751) only mentions it in passing, without any sign of agreement[62]. If Goethe had been aware of all this, it would have confirmed him in his opinion, expressed in the well-known lines:

Zwei Gegner sind es, die sich boxen,
Die Arianer und Orthodoxen,
Durch viele Säcla dasselbe geschicht,
Es dauert bis an das jüngste Gericht[63].

---

[59] *An Explanation of the Grand Mystery of Godliness* (1660) in *The Theological Works of ... Henry More*, London, 1708, 16.

[60] More refers to an *obiter dictum* in Calvin's commentary on Dan. 10:16-18: J. Calvinus, 'Praelectiones in Danielem Prophetam', *Corpus Reformatorum* LXIX (*Opera Calvini* XLI), c. 210 (here, 'exhibueret').

[61] *Loc. cit.*

[62] P. Doddridge, *A Course of Lectures on the Principal Subjects in Pneumatology, Ethics and Divinity*, Lecture CXXIII, Solution 6.

[63] From the 'Zahme Xenien', *Werke* 5 (1. Abt.), Weimar, 1893, 130.

DER MEHRWERT DES WORTES

Hermeneutische Erwägungen

von

H.J. Heering

Doch dürfte diese Haltung, die alle Zukunft von Gott erwartet und die Verwirrung der irdischen Welt als tiefe Not begreift, auch heute noch viele Christen erfüllen. Immerhin kann das apokalyptische Denken, das es ja vor allem mit der Geschichte zu tun hat, dem Christen zum Verstehen und Beurteilen politischer Fragen und Stellungnahmen helfen.

J.C.H. Lebram, *Das Buch Daniel*, Schluss der Einleitung.

Mit diesen Sätzen beschliesst Lebram die Einleitung seines wissenschaftlichen Daniel-Kommentars. Sie stehen ganz unschuldig da; Lebram hat dabei wahrscheinlich an das breite, nicht nur an das sachverständige Publikum gedacht, für das er seine Arbeit bestimmt hat und das doch etwas vom Lesen 'haben' möchte. Aber natürlich: eigentlich gehört solch eine in unsere Zeit hineinspringende Äusserung nicht in eine exegetische Arbeit. Oder doch? Wann ist der Exeget 'fertig'?

Was unser Autor so kurz gefasst ausspricht, hat er inhaltlich in seiner Einleitung dargelegt und im Kommentar aus dem Buch Daniel herausanalysiert: dass das Buch zur apokalyptischen Literatur gehört und dass diese Literatur mit der Weisheitstradition des Altertums verwandt ist — eine Weisheitstradition, die nicht spezifisch jüdisch, sondern vielmehr allgemein-hellenistisch ist. Damit hat die Apokalyptik ihre universale Bedeutung — und hat sie im Judentum eine Spaltung zuwegegebracht. Das apokalyptische Warten auf Gott, bis Er die böse Welt erlösen wird (bald?), steht im Widerspruch zum Prophetismus, der von der Umkehr und Gerechtigkeit des Volkes den Anbruch des Gottesreiches erwartet. Als es dann wirklich zur Spaltung kam, folgte die Christengemeinde der Apokalyptik, das Judentum dem Prophetismus (so hat es auch Buber gesagt). Trotzdem beriefen sich auch die Makkabäer auf Daniel: die Erlösung durch Gott sollte und konnte von den Menschen beschleunigt werden! Die Botschaft Daniels sei jedoch: Hoffen und helfen, ohne dass die Welt sich ändern lässt. Unser Kommentator meint, diese Botschaft sei nützlich für unsere Zeit.

In seinem Buch betreibt Lebram keine Hermeneutik. Aber mit seiner kurzen Bemerkung überschreitet er die Grenzen der Exegese: es ist die Hermeneutik, die nicht nur historisch-philologisch die alten Texte zu erklären und auszulegen versucht, sondern ihre Bedeutung in die eigene Epoche überbringen möchte. Es hat immer Gläubige und Wissenschaftler gegeben, die eine solche Hermeneutik als überflüssig betrachteten: der Schriftsinn ist ohnehin klar, *Scriptura suus interpres*. Lebram scheint nicht ohne weiteres dieser Meinung zu sein. Aber wenn wir uns seine zitierte Bemerkung anschauen, können wir uns fragen, ob das genügt: im Buch Daniel wird die Erlösung mit ihren kosmischen Dimensionen in naher Zukunft erwartet, das Hoffen hat also da einen kürzer gemessenen Sinn, als es für den heutigen Menschen möglich ist. Die eigentliche Hermeneutik soll erst anfangen? Wie aber macht man die Bedeutung eines Textes für das Heute klar, wenn der Text auf Fragen antwortet, die wir nicht gestellt haben, und wenn wir Fragen haben, die der Text nicht beantwortet?

1.

Man verteidigt heute keine eigen-artig biblische Exegese und Hermeneutik mehr. Wohl haben Karl Barth und seine Mitkämpfer für die 'dialektische Theologie' sich in den zwanziger Jahren gegen die Alleinherrschaft der historisch-kritischen Methode gewehrt, die die Bibel als ein wichtiges, aber kurioses Buch zu verstehen gab, über zweitausend Jahre alt und geographisch mehr als zweitausend Kilometer von uns entfernt. Das spezifisch Biblische könnte nur vom Heiligen Geist verständlich gemacht werden. Man hat Barths Römerbrief-Kommentar deshalb 'pneumatische Exegese' vorgeworfen. Sehr schnell hat Barth diese Qualifizierung abgelehnt und gemeint, man sollte mit der Bibel nicht anders verfahren als bei der Erklärung irgendeines anderen säkularen Textes — man sollte nur sachgemäss exegetisieren und dem Gehalt des Textes Recht tun, Poesie sei als Poesie erklärt, Geschäftsbriefe als geschäftlich, religiöse Literatur als den Umgang zwischen Gott und Menschen betreffende Schriften. Hat die theologische Enzyklopädie 'Religion in Geschichte und Gegenwart' in ihrer zweiten Auflage von 1927 noch ausführlich über 'pneumatische Exegese' berichtet, in der dritten Auflage von 1965 kommt das Stichwort im Register nicht mehr vor. Auch die Hermeneutik hat für die Bibel keine spezifische Behandlung beansprucht.

Für die Theologie heisst das, dass die historisch-kritische, philologische Exegese noch immer die feste Grundlage für jede Hermeneutik bildet. Gerade deshalb hat man sich in den letzten Jahrzehnten mehr denn je um den jüdischen Ursprung und das jüdische Verständnis des Alten und des Neuen Testaments bemüht. Diese Bemühung hing zusammen mit dem jüdischen Réveil nach 1900 und, in seinem Gefolge, mit der erneuten Konfrontation zwischen Judentum und Christentum (nach 1930). Die Dramatik dieser Konfrontation, nach und während der Kulmination der Entfremdung und Verfolgung des jüdischen Volkes, braucht nicht erwähnt zu werden. Man hört wieder auf die Denker der jüdischen Orthodoxie und Aufklärung (der Haskala), wie Hermann Cohen, Leo Baeck, Franz Rosenzweig, Martin Buber, Emmanuel Levinas, Abraham Heschel, Emil Fackenheim, Flusser, Lapide und andere. Nach Rosenzweig und Buber machte vor allem Levinas sich die Mühe, die Prinzipien der Schriftauslegung anhand seiner Talmudstudien ans Licht zu bringen. Wir werden ihn darüber fragen, damit 'unsere' Exegese sich daran spiegeln kann.

2.

Für das Judentum, schreibt *Levinas*, hat der Talmud die gleiche Autorität wie die Schrift selber, und die mündliche Tradition, vom Lernen getragen, kontinuiert bloss den Talmud in dieser Autorität. Die Schrift fängt an mit der Tora, und schon die Tora beginnt mit der Aufklärung und Aktualisierung und Ausbreitung des am Sinai gegebenen Gotteswortes über die sich ständig ändernde Lebenswelt. Der heutige Jude kann die Schrift also nur in der Weise verstehen, wie der Talmud es macht (AV 95, 109). Seine Autorität ist jedoch nicht autoritär — er berichtet die Diskussionen der Rabbiner der ersten fünf Jahrhunderte n.Chr.; es wird nicht ein für allemal dekretiert, was Wahrheit ist und was getan werden soll, sondern der Leser soll die dialogische Suche nach der Wahrheit mitmachen und sie sich überlegen, wenn es auch oft bei kontrastierenden Meinungen bleibt.

Bei dieser Suche wird eine Vielheit von Methoden angewandt: die buchstäbliche und historische Erklärung, überdies die allegorische, analogische, symbolische, assoziative; der Zahlenwert der Buchstaben wird benutzt, der Sinn des Textes wird intuitiv oder mystisch erfasst usw., so sehr, dass die historisch-buchstäbliche Interpretation in den Hintergrund gerät. Levinas: 'Der buchstäbliche Sinn, der ganz und gar bedeutsam ist, ist noch nicht das Gedeutete' (le signifié, QLT 19). Die anderen Deutungen haben auch ihr Recht, denn sie holen nur zum Vorschein, was der Mehrwert oder die Vollheit (plénitude) des Wortes schon umfasst (cf. DL 93ff.) Wie willkürlich die allegorische, symbolische Deutung auch scheint, 'die Worte der Rabbiner legen intellektuelle Strukturen und Kategorien fest, die im Absoluten des Gedankens gelegen sind' (DL 96). Es gilt diese vernünftige Bedeutung aufzusuchen, die in den oft skurril scheinenden Argumenten angedeutet wird. In dieser Hinsicht, so sagt Levinas, argumentiert der Talmud zwar nicht philosophisch, aber er bietet das Material zum Philosophieren (QLT 12, DL 121). Um so mehr als in der Schrift 'alles schon gedacht ist' (QLT 16, AV 9), jede Zeit kann daraus holen, was sie braucht. Nur muss man wissen, wie man das macht! Der Text offenbart seine Geheimnisse nicht leichtfertig, nicht ohne menschliches Studium, nicht ohne ernsthaftes Fragen, nicht ohne Bewerbung (sollicitation AV 136, siehe auch Goud, 540). In diesem Sinn kann von kontinuierender Offenbarung gesprochen werden (AV 109, 95, 136).

Es ist das *Leben* selbst in seinem Fortgang und seinen Fragen, das diesen Druck auf den Text ausübt. Oder doch: es ist der *Glaube*, der den Text recht zu befragen weiss. Zudem: es ist die *Tradition*, in die sich der Frager hineinstellt. Auch: er fragt als Angehöriger seines *Volkes* nach seiner Tradition. So dass der Goi Schrift und Talmud nie verstehen kann? Auch der Nichtjude kann aus dem Leben heraus fragen, auch er kann sich sagen lassen, dass dem alten Volk der Lebensweg nicht nur für sich selbst, sondern für die ganze Menschheit offenbart ist. Wobei nachdrücklich betont wird, dass es nicht sosehr darauf ankommt, wie man denkt, sondern wie man lebt. — In dieser umfassenden Weise sei die rabbinische Exegese paradigmatisch für alle richtige Exegese, heisst es bei Levinas (SS 170).

Versuchen wir die Voraussetzungen dieser Methode zu explizieren, dann finden wir
— die kontinuierte *Identität des Judentums* in den Jahrtausenden und in der ganzen Welt (QLT 16);
— das wesentliche *Unverändertsein des Menschen* während seiner ganzen Geschichte;
— also die fundamentale *Unwichtigkeit der Geschichte*: die Umstände wechseln, der Mensch nicht, und mit ihm auch das Ethische nicht;
— in der Exegese gibt es keine Anachronismen (DL 95);
— deshalb ist es möglich zu sagen, 'tout a été pensé', wir brauchen es uns bloss anzueignen und es anzuwenden;
— die alten Worte haben also ihren *Surplus*, ihren Mehrwert über die damalige Bedeutung, auch über unser anfängliches Verständnis, über unsere divergierenden Meinungen, selbst (transzendent) über das in Worten Festlegbare hinaus (AV 7, 135).

Aber Aktualisierung ist nötig und deshalb Rationalisierung: 'le signifié' soll auf's Neue herausgeholt werden, d.h. Levinas zufolge soll der religiöse oder ethische Sinn wieder zum Sprechen gebracht werden (AV 3).

In all' dem ist die vielfältige rabbinische Methode paradigmatisch für die Exegese der heiligen Bücher.

3.

Die Geschichte der Bibelexegese muss meines Wissens noch geschrieben werden. Sie fing im hellenistischen Zeitalter an — als Hellenisierung, in stärkerem oder schwächerem Masse. Zum Beispiel wurde das prophetische, irdische, zukünftige Reich Gottes zum transzendenten Himmelreich platonisiert. Diese Hellenisierung, in der auch babylonische, parsische und ägyptische Einflüsse wirkten, hat als Apokalyptik und Chokma zum Teil schon im Neuen Testament und sogar im Alten Testament angefangen. Die Exegese unterschied eine literarische und (gleichwertige) mystisch-symbolische Deutung. Von der letzten hat die kirchliche Kunst reichlich profitiert. Langsam gewann die buchstäblich-historische Exegese die Oberhand, bis sie nach der Aufklärung im 19. Jahrhundert das Prädikat der Wissenschaftlichkeit monopolisierte. Dieses Monopol konnte erst erworben werden, als Zeit und Geschichte nicht mehr als *mē on* erlebt wurden, sondern als ontologische Kategorien zur Geltung gelangt waren, also nach Lessing und Herder. Es war dieser Historismus, in dem die Hermeneutik sich als selbständige Disziplin neben die Exegese stellte. Wahrheit und Sinn haben einen historischen Charakter — also: wie kann ein zeitgebundener Text Wahrheit und Sinn in einem anderen Zeitalter vermitteln? Dazu kam der kulturelle Pluralismus der modernen Welt, in seiner Gefolgschaft der Relativismus und Skeptizismus, wenn nicht sogar der Nihilismus. Wie kann in einer pluralistischen Gesellschaft ein Text noch universalen Sinn haben? Allegorische, analogische, symbolische, mystische und mythologische Deutungen wurden als nichtwissenschaftlich abgelehnt, konnten also nicht helfen.

Oder doch? Noch immer spielen Ausdrücke wie 'das rechte Leben' ('la vraie vie est absente' — Rimbaud), 'Leib und Seele', 'die Zeichen der Zeit', Befreiung und Erlösung, das irdische und das himmlische Jerusalem, spielen auch Gebote und Verbote wie 'Du sollst nicht töten' ihre Rolle, wiewohl man sich meistens bewusst ist, dass sie nicht genau dasselbe bezeichnen wie damals. Sogar der Mythos hat, nach aller Entmythologisierung durch Bultmann, wieder an Ansehen gewonnen (Kolakowski u.a.). Wittgenstein kam zur rechten Zeit, den Anspruch auf Sinn und Bedeutsamkeit der nicht-nur-rationalen Sprachspiele zu verteidigen. Rehabilitierung der verurteilten Methoden? Aber wie rechtfertigen solche Sprachspiele sich? Und wie wird, wenn die Exegese sie gebraucht, dem Unfug gewehrt?

4.

Levinas wendete die rabbinischen Methoden nie an. Er benutzte nur ihre Ergebnisse. Als seine philosophische Aufgabe sieht er, diese Ergebnisse womöglich zu rationalisieren, um sie für den heutigen Gebrauch geeignet zu machen. Er respektiert die seines Erachtens oft abstrusen Methoden ihrer Ergebnisse wegen und behauptet, dass diese befremdlichen Wege also doch ihre Ratio haben. Wir nannten die impliziten Voraussetzungen seiner Arbeit. Im Vergleich dazu müssten die formalen Voraussetzungen der *heutigen nichtjüdischen Hermeneutik und Exegese* folgendermassen aussehen:

Man geht nicht sosehr von der Identität aus, als vielmehr von der *Kontinui-*

tät des Menschseins. Tempora mutantur *et nos mutamur in illis* — und dennoch bleibt es bei dem *nos*. J.H. van den Berg schrieb sein berühmtes Buch *Metabletica* über die Änderungen des Menschseins im Laufe der Geschichte und Thomas S. Kuhn und Michel Foucault haben die Wesensfremdheit der alternierenden Geschichtsperioden beschrieben: Der Historismus ist nicht überwunden. Wenn dennoch ein Verständnis alter Texte möglich ist, dann geschieht das nicht durch Identifizierung, sondern eben durch Verständnis, durch Dialog, durch Horizontverschmelzung (Gadamer), wobei das heutige Vorverständnis nicht eliminiert, sondern gerade eingeschaltet wird. Der hermeneutische *Circulus vitiosus* kann nur dann als überwindbar bezeichnet werden, wenn man den Mehrwert des Wortes annimmt: dasselbe alte Wort hat unserer Generation bei aller Kontinuität eben etwas anderes zu sagen als seiner eigenen Zeit.

Kann man trotzdem von der Identität des Christentums sprechen? Auch diese soll man nicht statisch auffassen. Schon die Bibel, mit ihrer tausendjährigen Geschichte, zeigt Entwicklungen, Neufassungen, Neuanfänge. Wenn Levinas sich von diesen Verschiebungen Rechenschaft gibt, beruft er sich auf die kontinuierende Identität des *Geistes des* jüdischen *Volkes*, wie er sich auch im Talmud und im daran anschliessenden Lernen manifestiert. Das Christentum würde dasselbe umgekehrt sagen: die Kontinuität wird nicht getragen vom Geist des Volkes, sondern vom *Volk des Geistes*, von dem das Volk Christi inspirierenden heiligen Geist. Nicht das Volk, in seinem ganzen Umfang, ist Träger und Garant des Geistes, sondern der heilige Geist ist Träger und Massstab des Gottesvolkes. — Es ist auch die Rede davon gewesen, die Kontinuität sei von der Kongenialität abhängig; daran ist sicherlich etwas Wahres. Aber J.N. Sevenster hat gezeigt, dass Kongenialität nicht nur unzulänglich ist, sondern bisweilen ein richtiges Verständnis verhindert, indem sie den Sinn des Textes übereilt mit der eigenen Einsicht vereinbart. Die Theologie hat sich immer auf das *Testimonium Spiritus Sancti* berufen. Voraussetzung der Hermeneutik bleibt jedoch, dass *Geschichte und Geschichtlichkeit ernst genommen werden.* Ob sie Fortschritt oder Niedergang oder nur Weitergang bedeuten, sei hier übergangen. Wie auch ausser acht gelassen wird, dass die Geschichte in der Theologie auf sehr verschiedene Weise gewertet ist. In dieser Hinsicht steht die römisch-katholische Exegese der jüdischen am nächsten. Die einmalige Wahrheit der Schrift wird in der Tradition fortgesetzt und autoritativ ausgelegt. Nur ist diese Tradition autoritär und unfehlbar der Kirchenführung, Papst und Konzil mit ihrer Lehre, anvertraut, während die jüdische Tradition wohl befolgt werden will, aber eine solche absolute Autorität nicht kennt, sicher nicht in Glaubenssachen. — In der Reformation hat man die Autorität der Tradition immer abgelehnt, ihr jedoch in der Anerkennung des Kanons, der Dogmen und Sitten implizit stets zugestimmt, wie sie auch hat zugeben müssen, dass schon die Bibel die Schriftwerdung einer langen Tradition ist. — Der Freiprotestantismus hat sich seit der Aufklärung bemüht, den wesentlichen, überzeitlichen Gehalt aus den unterschiedlichen Büchern der Schrift und aus den späteren Glaubensschriften herauszuholen und im ständigen Wechsel der datierten Formen und Formulierungen zu aktualisieren. Unter den Voraussetzungen der Hermeneutik Levinas' war: *Tout a été pensé*, nämlich in der Schrift —, auch für die moderne, technokratische, industrielle Gesellschaft, wie er nachdrücklich hinzufügte. Auf christlicher Seite hat die Reformation das am stärksten betont, womit sie allerdings meinte, das Alte Testament erfülle sich im Neuen Testament. Seit den Aposteln also nichts Neues, nur Auslegung und Anwendung des schon Gesagten. Zwar hat auch Rom seine Tradition damit gerechtfertigt, aber eine rom-artige, autoritative, autoritäre Instanz der Auslegung und Anwendung wurde im Protestantismus, wenigstens im Prinzip, abgelehnt. Der Freiprotestantismus hat viel Wert darauf gelegt zu zeigen, dass sich an alten Texten — nicht an allen! — *neue* Einsichten anknüpfen lassen; das Schriftwort sei in seinen Hauptgestalten (wenn sie auch nie aus ihrem Kontext herausgelöst werden können) *normativ*, nicht definitiv, und reformatorische Theologen wie Berkhof, sowie eine wachsende Zahl der neu-katholischen Theologen, stimmen dem gegenwärtig bei.

Also alles ist in den Schriften noch nicht explizit gesagt, und es wäre noch die Frage, ob alle Wörter einen Sinn für das heutige Leben haben. Das Wort sagt zunächst, was es buchstäblich, grammatikalisch und historisch zu sagen hat. Eine ganze mythologische Welt ist für uns passé, unverständlich geworden. Aber wir können, sagt Bultmann, die Texte entmythologisieren, wir können aufhören, auch selbst mythologisch zu sprechen. Das will nicht sagen, so meint er, dass wir auch den Mythos missen können. Es gibt Wahrheit, die sich nur erzählen, kaum argumentieren lässt; die im Transzendenten, nicht im Immanenten fusst; die uns zugesagt, wiewohl nie auf Erden realisiert wird. So weit wie Bultmann werden wenige Theologen und Gläubige gehen. Aber dass Texte auch als Mythen für die moderne Welt verständlich sind, hat vieler Zustimmung gewonnen. Man sagt jetzt, die Bibel argumentiere nicht rational, sie erzähle; sie soll deshalb durch die Zeiten und Länder 'weiter-erzählt' werden (Berkhof); es wird gefragt nach einer erzählenden Theologie und einer erzählenden Predigt und Katechese. Und da der Urtext seine assoziativen, allegorischen, symbolischen, bildenden, mythischen und mystischen Elemente hat, darf die Exegese bzw. die Hermeneutik davon in ihrer Methode Gebrauch machen. Auch der Mensch hat für sein Leben nicht nur ein rationales, sondern ein vielfältiges Verständnis der Wirklichkeit nötig!

Die Hermeneutik findet also ihre Ratio und ihre Rechtfertigung im *Mehrwert des Wortes*. Erstens, weil jede Aussprache in jede andere Sprache übersetzt werden kann; selbst in derselben Sprache soll dasselbe Wort jedesmal 'mit anderen Worten' gesagt werden, wie es der Gesprächscharakter und die Situation erfordern. Das stellt die zeitgemässe Hermeneutik in eine ungeheure Spannung: lebten das Judentum und das Christentum bis vor kurzem 'aus dem einen Buche', in geschlossenen Kulturen, wo auch der sonstigen Bücher wenige waren, heute ist, weit mehr als in Predigers Zeit, 'viel Büchermachens kein Ende'. Eine solche Konzentration ist uns nicht mehr gestattet — aber wie kann der Glaube leben ohne Konzentration? Hermeneutik in einer vielförmigen, vielnormigen Welt verlangt eine intensive Konzentration und Sensitivität, Sensitivität für den Nächsten und für die Situation und auch für die Sprache und ihre Möglichkeiten, ihre Nuancen und Töne. — Zweitens will Mehrwert sagen, dass das Glaubenswort die Qualität des Neuen hat, des Novums, des noch Unerfüllten. Person und Welt werden auf dieses Neue bezogen. — Drittens: In alledem hat das Glaubenswort den Mehrwert der Transzendenz, es verweist auf das, was 'kein Auge gesehen hat und kein Ohr gehört hat und in keines Menschen Herz gekommen ist', es offenbart den Gott, der sich verbirgt, seine Aussage verweist auf das Unsagbare. Die Theologie muss das in den Texten Gesagte *rationalisieren* — da würde die Theologie Levinas von Herzen beistimmen. Aber was ist damit gemeint? Lässt der Sinn jedes Textes sich in den logischen Strukturen der Ratio fassen? Wir haben schon gesehen, dass dem nicht so ist. Levinas meint mit Rationalisierung Verständlichmachung für die Menschen, die es angeht, und da werden alle Verständnismöglichkeiten des Menschen eingeschaltet. Nebenbei sollen die Grenzen der Allgemeinverständlichkeit und *a fortiori* die der Beweisbarkeit aufgezeigt werden. Für Levinas zeigt die Rationalisierung sich als Ethisierung der (biblischen) Wahrheit. Hat auch die Johanneische *alētheia* nicht noch den praktischen Gehalt des hebräischen *emet*? Ein Gehalt, der im Laufe der Kirchengeschichte fast verlorenging zugunsten der Wahrheit als Doktrin und Glaubenstheorie. Jetzt ist man wieder mehr auf der Suche nach dem Glauben als Praxis, nach der Wahrheit des Ethischen, nach der Nachfolge Christi, und man möchte bei den Juden lernen. Wenn auch im Evangelium — und zwar in Gefolgschaft des Alten Testaments — die Beziehung zwischen Gott und Mensch und Welt mehr ist (niemals weniger!) als Moral; das Ethische wird vom Glauben umfasst und getrieben. Selbst Glaubenskategorien wie Reich Gottes, Gnade, Schöpfung, Demut lassen sich politisch 'rationalisieren'.

Spiegelt sich auch die jüdische Voraussetzung vom *Judentum als Paradigma des Humanum* in der christlichen Hermeneutik? Das Christentum hat die Erwählung des jüdischen Volkes stets bejaht. Leider hat es beansprucht, die Erwählung des jüdischen Volkes sei historisch auf die Kirche übergegangen; besser wäre es, man sagte: Juden und Christen gehörten zusammen in der Erwählung. Und wie das faktische Leben der Christen und ihrer Gesellschaft den Gedanken einer begrenzten Erwählung aufkommen liess, so wird durch die Absage einer Mehrheit der Juden an die jüdische Lebensführung die Überzeugung der Erwählung und des Paradigmas des (ganzen) jüdischen Volkes unglaubwürdig. Nicht das Volk sei Paradigma des Menschlichen, sondern das ihm anvertraute *Wort*, das richtige Judentum. So wären das heutige Judentum und Christentum zusammen die Erben und Verwalter des Gotteswortes.

Und die rabbinischen, talmudischen Methoden als Paradigma der Exegese? Ihre Ergebnisse zeigen ihren Sinn; Methoden wie das Errechnen der Zahlenwerte oder die Berücksichtigung der Klangverwandtschaft der Worte bleiben uns fremd, weil wir Zahl und Klang nicht mit Sinn in Verbindung bringen können. Anders steht es mit der allegorischen, analogischen, symbolischen, mystischen Deutung, und zwar weil der Mensch von jeher immer schon allegorisch, symbolisch usw. gedacht und gedichtet hat. Sein Weltverständnis hat immer die Symbolik, die Analogie und 'Einfühlung' zu Hilfe gerufen. Ist das unbeschränkt erlaubt und wahrheitsgetreu? Führt so die Auslegung des Textes nicht häufig dazu, dass etwas in ihn hineininterpretiert wird? Hat der Dichter des Hohen Liedes wirklich die Liebe zwischen Israel und seinem Herrn oder zwischen der Seele und Christus, ihrem Bräutigam, (Bach, Revius) besungen? Ist es andererseits verboten, das aus den Liedern herauszuhören? Ist man unbedingt nur dem ersten Sinn, dem lexikalischen und historischen, dem vom Autor gemeinten, verpflichtet? Der Geist wehet, wo er will ... Für Levinas ist Exegese kein Stillestehen bei den Texten, sondern ein Weitergehen innerhalb der Tradition, Arbeit am neuen Sinn des alten Wortes, und, wie wir sahen, viele nichtjüdische Theologen stimmen ihm im wesentlichen darin bei. Nur soll man sich verantworten: man soll wissen und auch sagen, was man tut und wie man es tut.

5.

Wir wollen nicht bei den formalen Methoden der Exegese und Hermeneutik bleiben: suchen wir ein inhaltliches *Beispiel.* Lebrams zitierter Satz deutet auf das Kommen des Gottesreiches und die menschliche Beteiligung daran. Ohne Zweifel lebte der (lebten die?) Verfasser des Danielbuches in der Erwartung des bald eintretenden Endes der Geschichte. Zwar wird dieses Eintreten nicht bewirkt durch menschliche Tat, selbst nicht durch die Umkehr Israels, sondern ausschliesslich durch das unerforschliche Handeln Gottes. Lebram jedoch schreibt: 'Doch dürfte die Haltung, die alle Zukunft von Gott erwartet ... auch heute noch viele Christen erfüllen'. Zukunft, nicht das nahe apokalyptische Ende: mit seiner hermeneutischen Äusserung hat Lebram einiges aus dem Text herausgelassen und die Haltung des Glaubens betont. U.a. gab die von ihm aufgespürte Verbindung zwischen Apokalyptik und Weisheitsliteratur, zwischen biblischem Judentum und hellenistischer Umwelt, ihm dazu ein Recht. Aber selber erzählt er, wie die Makkabäer und Zeloten die Danieltexte ganz anders gelesen und interpretiert haben! — Im grossen und ganzen geht Levinas' Hermeneutik mit der Lebrams parallel. Ihm sagt die Eschatologie nichts, der Messianismus jedoch alles. In der Geschichte ist uns das Dienen und Warten der messianischen Existenz aufgegeben, dazu ist der Jude, ja jeder Mensch erwählt: zur Disponibilität für den Einbruch der Transzendenz im Antlitz des leidenden Nächsten, zum erlösenden Dienst am Mitmenschen. Doch auch die südamerikanischen Christen-für-den-Sozialismus, die zwar nicht das Gottesreich errichten, aber doch die sozialen Verhältnisse in die Richtung des Reiches umstrukturieren möchten, berufen sich auf Levinas und sein Bibelverständnis!

Genug, um zu zeigen, dass ein Text wie der des Danielbuches sehr unterschiedlich interpretiert werden kann, dass aber der Text innerhalb seines Kontextes, im Rahmen der Bibel als Ganzes, den Interpretationen Grenzen setzt, so dass die polare Beziehung der Interpretationen, wie sehr sie sich auch voneinander unterscheiden mögen, erhalten bleibt. Davidische Messiasgestalt, apokalyptischer Menschensohn, Danielsches Martyrium, dazu das Kreuztragen Christi: steht im Brennpunkt dieser Polaritäten nicht die Gestalt des leidenden Knechtes, der das Heil auf Erden bringt?

6.

Lebram machte mit seiner kurzen Bemerkung einen kleinen Sprung von der Exegese in die Hermeneutik. Richtiger, eines Sprunges bedurfte es nicht, Exegese und Hermeneutik fliessen ineinander über. In einer richtigen Übersetzung aus der Ursprache in die der heutigen Umwelt fängt die hermeneutische Arbeit schon an. Umgekehrt ruht jede Verständlichmachung auf einem historischen Verständnis des zugrunde liegenden Textes. Und vielleicht sollte man sagen, dass die eigentliche Hermeneutik nicht nur auf Verständnis zielt, sondern auf Anerkennung der Relevanz, auf Ich-Bezogenheit und Lebenshaltung. Aber dann soll erst recht in Betracht gezogen werden, dass ein Text, der offensichtlich seiner Relevanz für das Menschenleben *coram Deo* wegen notiert und tradiert ist, nicht recht erklärt wird, wenn dieser Aspekt nicht das volle icht empfängt.

So verstanden, bildet die Hermeneutik das offene Ende der Exegese: der Mehrwert des Wortes evoziert einen Plural der Übersetzungen und Deutungen, jedesmal mit Perspektiven in die Transzendenz. 'Unified language', wie sie im Wiener Kreis angestrebt wurde, wäre der Tod der Sprache, wie doktrinäre Festlegung den Tod des Glaubens bedeutet. Die Offenheit der Hermeneutik ist jedoch nicht unbegrenzt, der Mehrwert liegt jedesmal in dem einen bestimmten Wort oder Text, in der einen Erzählung oder dem einen Diskurs, deren ursprüngliche Bedeutung durch die Exegese dargelegt wird.

Abkurzungen

AV E. Levinas, *L'au-delà du verset. Lectures et discours talmudiques* (1982).
DL E. Levinas, *Difficile liberté. Essais sur le judaïsme* (1963).
Goud J.F. Goud, *Levinas en Barth. Een Godsdienstwijsgerige en ethische vergelijking*, dissertatie, Leiden, 1984.
QLT E. Levinas, *Quatre lectures talmudiques* (1968).
SS E. Levinas, *Du sacré au saint. Cinq nouvelles lectures talmudiques* (1977).

BIBLIOGRAPHY OF THE WRITINGS OF J.C.H. LEBRAM 1943-1984

by

JOHANNES VAN DER KLAAUW

LIST OF ABBREVIATIONS USED IN THIS BIBLIOGRAPHY

BiOr	*Bibliotheca Orientalis* (Leiden)
JSJ	*Journal for the Study of Judaism*
NAKG	*Nederlands Archief voor Kerkgeschiedenis*
NTT	*Nederlands Theologisch Tijdschrift*
OTS	*Oudtestamentische Studiën*
TRE	*Theologische Realenzyklopädie*
TvG	*Tijdschrift voor Geschiedenis*
VC	*Vigiliae Christianae*
VT	*Vetus Testamentum*
ZAW	*Zeitschrift für die alttestamentliche Wissenschaft*
ZNW	*Zeitschrift für die neutestamentliche Wissenschaft*

EDITORIAL WORK.

Editor of *Studia Post-Biblica*, Leiden, vols. 16 (1970) - 34 (1983) ...

Member of the 'Apokryphenkommission der Deutschen Evangelischen Kirche'; 'Vorwort' (anonymous) to *Die Apokryphen nach der deutschen Übersetzung Martin Luthers. Revidierter Text 1970*, Stuttgart, 1971, 5-6.

Editor of 'Theology, Religious Studies and Judaic Studies', in: *Tuta sub aegide Pallas. E.J. Brill and the World of Learning*, Leiden, 1983, 1-16.

BOOKS AND ARTICLES.

Das hebräische Priestertum nach J und E, Diss. Heidelberg, 1943, (Masch.).

'Die Peschitta zu Tobit 7.11-14.5', *ZAW* 69 (1957), 185-211.

'ΜΥΣΤΗΡΙΟΝ ΒΑΣΙΛΕΩϚ', in: *Abraham unser Vater. Juden und Christen im Gespräch über die Bibel.* FS Otto Michel zum 60. Geburtstag. Hrsg. Otto Betz, Martin Hengel, Peter Schmidt (Arbeiten zur Geschichte des Spätjudentums und Urchristentums 5), Leiden/Köln, 1963, 320-324.

'Der Aufbau der Areopagrede', *ZNW* 55 (1964), 221-243.

'Die Weltreiche in der jüdischen Apokalyptik. Bemerkungen zu Tobit 14, 4-7', *ZAW* 76 (1964), 328-331.

'Nachbiblische Weisheitstraditionen', *VT* 15 (1965), 167-237.

'Zwei Bemerkungen zu katechetischen Traditionen in der Apostelgeschichte', *ZNW* 56 (1965), 202-213.

'Die Theologie der späten Chokma und häretisches Judentum', *ZAW* 77 (1965), 202-211.

The Old Testament in Syriac according to the Peshiṭta Version. Sample Edition: *Tobit*, Leiden, 1966.

'Aspekte der alttestamentlichen Kanonbildung', *VT* 18 (1968), 173-189.

'Jakob segnet Josephs Söhne. Darstellungen von Genesis XLVIII in der Überlieferung und bei Rembrandt', *OTS* 15 (1969), 145-169.

'Zur Chronologie in den Makkabäerbüchern', in: *Das Institutum Judaicum der Universität Tübingen* in den Jahren 1968-1970, Tübingen, o.J., 71-74 (Masch.).

'Apokalyptik und Hellenismus im Buche Daniel. Bemerkungen und Gedanken zu Martin Hengels Buch über *Judentum und Hellenismus*, *VT* 20 (1970), 503-524.

'Eine stoische Auslegung von Ex 3,2 bei Philo', in: *Das Institutum Judaicum der Universität Tübingen* 1971-1972, Tübingen, o.J., 30-34 (Masch.).

'Purimfest und Estherbuch', *VT* 22 (1972), 208-222.

The Old Testament in Syriac according to the Peshiṭta Version. IV, 6, *Tobit*, Leiden, 1972 (slightly revised re-edition of the 1966 sample edition).

The Old Testament in Syriac according to the Peshiṭta Version. IV, 6, *1 (3) Esdras*, in co-operation with W. Baars, Leiden, 1972.

'Der Idealstaat der Juden', in: *Josephus-Studien. Untersuchungen zu Josephus, dem antiken Judentum und dem Neuen Testament*. Otto Michel zum 70. Geburtstag gewidmet. Hrsg. Otto Betz, Klaus Haacker, Martin Hengel, Göttingen, 1974, 233-253.

'Perspektiven der gegenwärtigen Danielforschung', *JSJ* 5 (1974), 1-33.

'Die literarische Form des vierten Makkabäerbuches', *VC* 29 (1974), 81-96.

'Hebräische Studien zwischen Ideal und Wirklichkeit an der Universität Leiden in den Jahren 1575-1619', *NAKG* 56 (1975), 317-357. Also in: *In Navolging*. Een bundel studies aangeboden aan C.C. de Bruin, edd. M.J.M. de Haan e.a., Leiden, 1975, 317-357.

'König Antiochus im Buch Daniel', *VT* 25 (1975), 737-772.

'Ein Streit um die hebräische Bibel und die Septuaginta', in: *Leiden University in the*

Seventeenth Century. An Exchange of Learning, edd. Th.H. Lunsingh Scheurleer and G.H.M. Posthumus Meyjes, Leiden, 1975, 21-63.

'Die älteste Übersetzung des Alten Testaments', in: *Der Bestseller ohne Leser. Überlegungen zur sinnvollen Weitergabe der Bibel*, Hrsg. Siegfried Meurer, Stuttgart, 1976, 22-32.

'Apokalyptiek als keerpunt in het joodse denken', *NTT* 30 (1976), 271-281.

Lijden en redding in het antieke Jodendom. Voordracht gehouden voor het Oosters Genootschap in Nederland op 28 april 1978, Leiden, 1978 (Oosters Genootschap in Nederland; 8).

'Apokalyptik/Apokalypsen II. Altes Testament', in: *TRE* 3 (1978), 192-202.

'Jerusalem, Wohnsitz der Weisheit', in: *Studies in Hellenistic Religions*, ed. M.J. Vermaseren (Etudes préliminaires aux religions orientales dans l'empire romain, 78), Leiden, 1979, 103-128.

'Eerste ontmoetingen tussen Rome en de Joden', *Phoenix* 26 (1979), 94-106.

Legitimiteit en charisma. Over de herleving van de contemporaine geschiedschrijving in het jodendom tijdens de 2e eeuw v.Chr., Inaugural address, Leiden, 1980.

'Daniel/Danielbuch', in: *TRE* 8 (1981), 325-349.

'De Hasidaeis. Over Joodse studiën in het oude Leiden', *Voordrachten Faculteitendag 1980. Rijksuniversiteit te Leiden*, Introduction by A.A.H. Kassenaar, Leiden, 1981, 21-31.

'Esther (Buch)' (in co-operation with Johannes van der Klaauw), in: *TRE* 10 (1982), 391-395.

'Zwei Danielprobleme' [zu Klaus Koch, unter Mitarbeit von Till Niewisch und Jürgen Tubach, *Das Buch Daniel*, Darmstadt, 1980], *BiOr* 39 (1982), 510-517.

'Mozes als ideale koning en schenker van hemelse openbaring. Een Joods-hellenistische tekst uit de 1e eeuw n. Chr. (*De Vita Mosis* I, 148-162)', in: *Schrijvend verleden. Documenten uit het Oude Nabije Oosten vertaald en toegelicht.* Uitgegeven door K.R. Veenhof, Leiden/Zutphen, 1983, 392-398.

'The Piety of the Jewish Apocalyptists', in: *Apocalypticism in the Mediterranean World and the Near East.* Proceedings of the International Colloquium on Apocalypticism. Uppsala, August 12-17, 1979, ed. David Hellholm, Tübingen, 1983, 171-210.

'Judaic Studies', in: 'Theology, Religious Studies and Judaic Studies', in: *Tuta sub aegide Pallas. E.J. Brill and the World of Learning*, Leiden, 1983, 11-16.

Das Buch Daniel (Zürcher Bibelkommentare), Zürich, 1984.

Reviews.

D. Daube, *Collaboration with Tyranny in Rabbinic Law*, London, 1965.
NTT 20 (1966), 459-460.

U. Kellermann, *Nehemia: Quellen, Überlieferung und Geschichte*, Berlin, 1967.
VT 18 (1968), 564-570.

A. Meeks, *The Prophet-King. Moses Traditions and the Johannine Christology*, Leiden, 1967.
NTT 22 (1968), 440-442.

J.D. Purvis, *The Samaritan Pentateuch and the Origin of the Samaritan Sect*, Cambridge (Mass.), 1968.
BiOr 26 (1969), 382-383.

B.J. Malina, *The Palestinian Manna Tradition. The Manna Tradition in the Palestinian Targums and its Relationship to the New Testament Writings*, Leiden, 1968.
VT 20 (1970), 124-128.

J. Bowker, *The Targums and Rabbinic Literature. An Introduction to Jewish Interpretations of Scripture*, Cambridge, 1969.
NTT 24 (1970), 448-449.

W. Klatt, *Hermann Gunkel. Zu seiner Theologie der Religionsgeschichte und zur Entstehung der formgeschichtlichen Methode*, Göttingen, 1969.
NTT 24 (1970), 298-299.

R. Brunner (Hrsgb.), *Gesetz und Gnade im Alten Testament und im jüdischen Denken*, Zürich, 1969.
NTT 25 (1971), 202-203.

J. Macdonald, *The Samaritan Chronicle, No. II (or: Sepher ha-Yamim). From Joshua to Nebuchadnezzar*, Berlin, 1969.
NTT 25 (1971), 204-205.

P. Richardson, *Israel in the Apostolic Church*, Cambridge, 1969.
VC 26 (1972), 148-152.

R. Abraham b. Isaac ha-Levi TaMaKh, *Commentary on the Song of Songs. Based on Mss and Early Printings with an Introduction, Notes, Variants and Comments* by Leon A. Feldman, Assen, 1970.
NTT 26 (1972), 84-85.

J. Le Moyne, *Les Sadducéens*, Paris, 1972.
JSJ 3 (1972), 185-187.

H.P. Rüger, *Text und Textform im hebräischen Sirach. Untersuchungen zur Textgeschichte und Textkritik der hebräischen Sirachfragmente aus der Kairoer Geniza*, Berlin, 1970.
NTT 26 (1972), 397-398.

H.W. Hoehner, *Herod Antipas*, Cambridge, 1972.
VC 27 (1973), 232-235.

Ch. Albeck, *Einführung in die Mischna*, Berlin, 1971.
NTT 27 (1973), 362-364.

J. Hadot, *Penchant mauvais et volonté libre dans la sagesse de Ben Sira (L'Ecclésiastique)*, Bruxelles, 1970.
VC 27 (1973), 301-302.

L. Finkelstein, *Pharisaism in the Making. Selected Essays*, New York, 1972.
JSJ 4 (1973), 77-79.

G. Maier, *Mensch und freier Wille nach den jüdischen Religionsparteien zwischen Ben Sira und Paulus*, Tübingen, 1971.
NTT 27 (1973), 256-257.

W. Bunte, *Texte zur Religion des Judentums aus Talmud und Midrasch*, Neukirchen, 1972.
JSJ 4 (1973), 7.

A.F. Verheule, *Wilhelm Bousset. Leben und Werk*, Amsterdam, 1973.
NTT 28 (1974), 168-169.

M. Gilbert, *La critique des dieux dans le livre de la Sagesse (Sg 13-15)*, Rome, 1973.
JSJ 5 (1974), 72-74.

J.N. Sevenster, *The Roots of Pagan Anti-Semitism in the Ancient World*, Leiden, 1975.
JSJ 7 (1976), 75-77.

M. Hengel, *Eigentum und Reichtum in der frühen Kirche, Aspekte einer frühchristlichen Sozialgeschichte*, Stuttgart, 1973.
BiOr 34 (1977), 257.

W.C. van Unnik, *Het Godspredikaat 'Het Begin en het Einde' bij Flavius Josephus en in de Openbaring van Johannes*, Amsterdam, 1976.
NTT 31 (1977), 164-166.

G.A. Wevers, *Geheimnis und Geheimhaltung im rabbinischen Judentum*, Berlin/New York, 1975.
JSJ 8 (1977), 105-107.

J.J. Collins, *The Apocalyptic Vision of the Book of Daniel*, Missoula, 1977.
JSJ 9 (1978), 214-215.

L. Monloubou (réd.), *Apocalypses et théologie de l'espérance* (Congrès de Toulouse 1975), Paris, 1977.
BiOr 36 (1979), 111-115.

J. Baumgarten, *Paulus und die Apokalyptik. Die Auslegung apokalyptischer Überlieferungen in den echten Paulusbriefen*, Neukirchen, 1975.
NTT 33 (1979), 309-311.

J.-D. Gauger, *Beiträge zur jüdischen Apologetik: Untersuchungen zur Authentizität von Urkunden bei Flavius Josephus und im I. Makkabäerbuch*, Köln/Bonn, 1977.
JSJ 10 (1979), 97-99.
BiOr 37 (1980), 82-83.

S.J.D. Cohen, *Josephus in Galilee and Rome. His Vita and Development as a Historian*, Leiden, 1979.
BiOr 37 (1980), 354-355.

D.M Rhoads, *Israel in Revolution 6-74 C.E. A Political History Based on the Writings of Josephus*, Philadelphia, 1976.
BiOr 37 (1980), 352-353.

H. Jagersma, *Geschiedenis van Israel in het oudtestamentische tijdvak*, Kampen, 1979.
NTT 35 (1981), 154-155.

H. Mulder, *Proselieten tussen Ja en Neen. Missionaire en anti-missionaire activiteiten in het Jodendom*, Kampen, 1980.
NTT 35 (1981), 343-345.

S. Applebaum, *Jews and Greeks in Ancient Cyrene*, Leiden, 1979.
BiOr 38 (1981), 679-682.

E. von Nordheim, *Die Lehre der Alten. I. Das Testament als Literaturgattung im Judentum der hellenistisch-römischen Zeit*, Leiden, 1980.
BiOr 38 (1981), 413-416.

P. Schäfer, *Studien zur Geschichte und Theologie des rabbinischen Judentums*, Leiden, 1978.
BiOr 39 (1982), 654-659.

R. Braun, *Kohelet und die frühhellenistische Popularphilosophie*, Berlin, 1973.
BiOr 39 (1982), 647-651.

Chr. Münchow, *Ethik und Eschatologie. Ein Beitrag zum Verständnis der frühjüdischen Apokalyptik mit einem Ausblick auf das Neue Testament*, Göttingen, 1981.
NTT 36 (1982), 335-337.
JSJ 13 (1982), 208-211.
BiOr 40 (1983), 175-178.

R. Melnick, *From Polemics to Apologetics. Jewish-Christian Rapprochement in 17th century Amsterdam, Assen, 1981.*
TvG 96 (1983), 246-247.

H. Conzelmann, *Heiden - Juden - Christen. Auseinandersetzungen in der Literatur der hellenistisch-römischen Zeit*, Tübingen, 1981.
NAKG 63 (1983), 219-221.

T. Penar, *Northwest Semitic Philology and the Hebrew Fragments of Ben Sira*, Rome, 1975.
BiOr 41 (1984), 180.

Popularizing Publications.

'Sinn der Weltgeschichte. Daniel und die Offenbarung an Johannes', *Stuttgarter Erklärungsbibel*, Stuttgart, 1971, 13-70.

'De TeNaCH als reducerende kanon', *In de Waagschaal* 1 (1972), 9-12.

'Varianten van Hemelvaart', *Schrift* 20 (1972), 50-55.